A HISTORY OF INDIAN PHILOSOPHY

A History of Indian Philosophy

SURENDRANATH DASGUPTA

VOLUME III

Principal Dualistic and Pluralistic Systems

MOTILAL BANARSIDASS PUBLISHERS
PRIVATE LIMITED • DELHI

6th Reprint : Delhi, 2015
First Indian Edition : Delhi, 1975
First Edition : Cambridge, 1922

ISBN : 978-81-208-0414-2 (Vol.III)
ISBN : 978-81-208-0408-1 (Set)

MOTILAL BANARSIDASS
41 U.A. Bungalow Road, Jawahar Nagar, Delhi 110 007
8 Mahalaxmi Chamber, 22 Bhulabhai Desai Road, Mumbai 400 026
203 Royapettah High Road, Mylapore, Chennai 600 004
236, 9th Main III Block, Jayanagar, Bengaluru 560 011
8 Camac Street, Kolkata 700 017
Ashok Rajpath, Patna 800 004
Chowk, Varanasi 221 001

Printed in India

by RP Jain at NAB Printing Unit,
A-44, Naraina Industrial Area, Phase I, New Delhi-110028
and published by JP Jain for Motilal Banarsidass Publishers (P) Ltd,
41 U.A. Bungalow Road, Jawahar Nagar, Delhi-110007

To the

HON. SRI JAWAHARLAL NEHRU

who went through great sufferings and hardships all his life in the cause of the liberation of his countrymen, and who is still labouring with almost superhuman effort for the unification of the subcontinent of India, and who is working with steady devotion and faith for the establishment of peace at home and among the nations of the world, the foremost Indian who is piloting the progress of the country through troubled waters in the most hazardous period of India's history, this work is most respectfully dedicated as a tribute of personal gratefulness

PREFACE

The second volume of this work was published as long ago as 1932. Among the many reasons which delayed the publication of this volume, one must count the excessive administrative and teaching work with which the writer is saddled; his continued illness; the regrettable failure of one eye through strenuous work, which often makes him depend on the assistance of others; and the long distance between the place of publication and Calcutta. The manuscript of the fourth volume is happily ready.

In writing the present volume the author has taken great trouble to secure manuscripts which would present a connected account of the development of theistic philosophy in the South. The texts that have been published are but few in number and the entire story cannot be told without constant reference to rare manuscripts from which alone the data can be collected. So far, no work has been written which could throw any light on the discovery and interpretation of a connected history of Vaiṣṇava thought. It would have been well if the Tamil and Telegu works could have been fruitfully utilized in tracing the history of Vaiṣṇavism, not only as it appeared in Sanskrit but also as it appeared in the vernaculars of the South. But the author limited himself as far as possible to Sanskrit data. This limitation was necessary for three reasons: first, the author was not master of the various vernaculars of South India; secondly, the inclusion and utilization of such data would have made the present book greatly exceed its intended scope; and thirdly, the inclusion of the data from the vernacular literature would not have contributed materially to the philosophical problems underlying the theistic speculations dealt with in this work. Looked at from the strictly philosophical point of view, some of the materials of the present book may be regarded as somewhat out of place. But, both in the present volume and the volume that will follow it, it will be impossible to ignore the religious pathology that is associated with the devotional philosophy which is so predominant in the South and which so much influenced the minds of the people not only in the Middle Ages but also in the recent past and is even now the most important element of Indian religions.

Philosophy in India includes not only morality but religion also. The most characteristic feature of religion is emotion or sentiment associated with a system of beliefs, and as such in the treatment of the dominant schools of philosophy that originated in South India one cannot help emphasizing the important pathological developments of the sentiment of devotion. The writer hopes, therefore, that he may be excused both by those who would not look for any emphasis on the aspect of *bhakti* or religious sentiment and also by those who demand an over-emphasis on the emotional aspect which forms the essence of the Vaiṣṇava religion. He has tried to steer a middle course in the interest of philosophy, which, however, in the schools of thought treated herein is so intimately interwoven with religious sentiment.

The writer has probably exceeded the scope of his treatment in dealing with the Āṟvārs, whose writings are in Tamil, but there also he felt that without referring to the nature of the devotional philosophy of the Āṟvārs the treatment of the philosophy of Rāmānuja and his followers would be historically defective. But though the original materials for a study of the Āṟvārs are in Tamil, yet fortunately Sanskrit translations of these writings either in manuscript or in published form are available, on which are almost wholly based the accounts given here of these Tamil writers.

The treatment of the Pañcarātra literature offered some difficulty, as most of these works are still unpublished; but fortunately a large volume of this literature was secured by the present writer in manuscript. Excepting Schrader's work, nothing of any importance has been written on the Pañcarātra School. Though there are translations of the *bhāṣya* of Rāmānuja, there has been no treatment of his philosophy as a whole in relation to other great philosophers of his School. Practically nothing has appeared regarding the philosophy of the great thinkers of the Rāmānuja School, such as Veṅkaṭa, Meghanādāri and others, most of whose works are still unpublished. Nothing has also been written regarding Vijñānabhikṣu's philosophy, and though Nimbārka's *bhāṣya* has been translated, no systematic account has yet appeared of Nimbārka in relation to his followers. The writer had thus to depend almost wholly on a very large mass of published and unpublished manuscript literature in his interpretation and chronological investigations, which are largely based upon internal evidence;

though, of course, he has always tried to utilize whatever articles and papers appeared on the subject. The subjects treated are vast and it is for the scholarly reader to judge whether any success has been attained in spite of the imperfections which may have crept in.

Though the monotheistic speculations and the importance of the doctrine of devotion can be traced even to some of the Ṛg-veda hymns and the earlier religious literature such as the *Gītā* and the *Mahābhārata* and the *Viṣṇupurāṇa*, yet it is in the traditional songs of the Āṛvārs and the later South Indian philosophical writers, beginning from Yāmuna and Rāmānuja, that we find a special emphasis on our emotional relation with God. This emotional relation of devotion or *bhakti* differentiated itself in many forms in the experiences and the writings of various Vaiṣṇava authors and saints. It is mainly to the study of these forms as associated with their philosophical perspectives that the present and the succeeding volumes have been devoted. From this point of view, the present and the fourth volumes may be regarded as the philosophy of theism in India, and this will be partly continued in the treatment of Śaiva and Śākta theism of various forms. The fourth volume will deal with the philosophy of Madhva and his followers in their bitter relation with the monistic thought of Śaṅkara and his followers. It will also deal with the theistic philosophy of the *Bhāgavatapurāṇa* and the theistic philosophy of Vallabha and the followers of Śrī Caitanya. Among the theistic philosophers the followers of Madhva, Jayatīrtha and Vyāsatīrtha occupied a great place as subtle thinkers and dialecticians. In the fifth volume, apart from the different schools of Śaiva and Śākta thinkers, the Tantras, the philosophy, of grammar, of Hindu Aesthetics, and of Hindu Law will be dealt with. It is thus expected that with the completion of the fifth volume the writer will have completed his survey of Hindu thought so far as it appeared in the Sanskrit language and thus finish what was begun more than twenty years ago.

A chapter on the *Cārvāka* materialists has been added as an appendix, since their treatment in the first volume was practically neglected.

The writer has a deep debt of gratitude to discharge to Dr F. W. Thomas—the late Boden Professor of Sanskrit at Oxford, and a highly esteemed friend of his who, in spite of his various activities, pressure of work and old age, has been a true *jñānabandhu* to the author, helping him with the manuscript and the proofs, and offering him valuable suggestions as regards orthography, punctuation and idiomatic usage. Without this continued assistance the imperfections of the present work would have been much more numerous. The author is specially grateful to his wife, Dr Mrs Surama Dasgupta, Śāstrī, M.A., Ph.D. (Cal. et Cantab.) for the continued assistance that he received from her in the writing of this book and also in reading a large mass of manuscripts for the preparation of the work. Considering the author's great handicap in having only one sound eye it would have been impossible for him to complete the book without this assistance. He is also grateful to Dr Saṭindra Kumar Mukherjee, M.A., Ph.D., for the help that he received from him from time to time.

SURENDRANATH DASGUPTA

June 1939

CONTENTS

CHAPTER XV

THE BHĀSKARA SCHOOL OF PHILOSOPHY

PAGE

1 Date of Bhāskara 1
2 Bhāskara and Śaṅkara 3
3 The Philosophy of Bhāskara's *Bhāṣya* 6

CHAPTER XVI

THE PAÑCARĀTRA

1 Antiquity of the Pañcarātra 12
2 The Position of the Pañcarātra Literature 14
3 The Pañcarātra Literature 21
4 Philosophy of the *Jayākhya* and other *Saṃhitās* 24
5 Philosophy of the *Ahirbudhnya-saṃhitā* 34

CHAPTER XVII

THE ĀṚVĀRS

1 The Chronology of the Āṛvārs 63
2 The Philosophy of the Āṛvārs 69
3 Āṛvārs and Śrī-vaiṣṇavas on certain points of controversy in religious dogmas 85

CHAPTER XVIII

AN HISTORICAL AND LITERARY SURVEY OF THE VIŚIṢṬĀDVAITA SCHOOL OF THOUGHT

1 The Aṛagiyas from Nāthamuni to Rāmānuja 94
2 Rāmānuja 100
3 The Precursors of the Viśiṣṭādvaita Philosophy and the contemporaries and pupils of Rāmānuja 105
4 Rāmānuja Literature 114
5 The Influence of the Āṛvārs on the followers of Rāmānuja . . . 134

CHAPTER XIX

THE PHILOSOPHY OF YĀMUNĀCĀRYA

1 Yāmuna's doctrine of Soul contrasted with those of others . . . 139
2 God and the World 152
3 God according to Rāmānuja, Veṅkaṭanātha and Lokācārya . . . 155
4 Viśiṣṭādvaita doctrine of Soul according to Rāmānuja and Veṅkaṭanātha 159
5 *Acit* or Primeval Matter: the *Prakṛti* and its modifications . . 162

CHAPTER XX

PHILOSOPHY OF THE RĀMĀNUJA SCHOOL OF THOUGHT

PAGE

1 Śaṅkara and Rāmānuja on the nature of Reality as qualified or unqualified 165
2 Refutation of Śaṅkara's *avidyā* 175
3 Rāmānuja's theory of Illusion—All knowledge is Real . 179
4 Failure of theistic proofs 189
5 Bhāskara and Rāmānuja 192
6 Ontological position of Rāmānuja's Philosophy 195
7 Veṅkaṭanātha's treatment of *Pramāṇa* 201
8 Veṅkaṭanātha's treatment of Doubt 207
9 Error and Doubt according to Veṅkaṭanātha 210
10 Perception in the light of elucidation by the later members of the Rāmānuja School 220
11 Veṅkaṭanātha's treatment of Inference 225
12 Epistemology of the Rāmānuja School according to Meghanādāri and others 235
13 The Doctrine of Self-validity of Knowledge 247
14 The Ontological categories of the Rāmānuja School according to Veṅkaṭanātha 251
(*a*) Substance 251
(*b*) Criticism of the Sāṃkhya Inference for Establishing the Existence of *Prakṛti* 256
(*c*) Refutation of the Atomic Theory of *Nyāya* in relation to Whole and Part 262
(*d*) Criticism of the Sāṃkhya Theory of *Sat-kārya-vāda* . . . 265
(*e*) Refutation of the Buddhist Doctrine of Momentariness . 268
(*f*) Refutation of the Cārvāka criticism against the Doctrine of Causality 276
(*g*) The Nature of the Senses according to Veṅkaṭanātha . . 280
(*h*) The Nature of *ākāśa* according to Veṅkaṭanātha . 282
(*i*) Nature of Time according to Veṅkaṭanātha . . . 284
(*j*) The Nature of Soul according to Veṅkaṭanātha . . 286
(*k*) The Nature of Emancipation according to Veṅkaṭanātha . 292
15 God in the Rāmānuja School 296
16 Dialectical criticism against the Śaṅkara School . . . 304
17 Meghanādāri 346
18 Vātsya Varada 349
19 Rāmānujācārya II alias Vādi-Haṃsa-Navāmvuda 352
20 Rāmānujadāsa alias Mahācārya 361
21 *Prapatti* Doctrine as expounded in *Śrīvacana-bhūṣaṇa* of Lokācārya and Saumya Jāmātṛ Muni's Commentary on it 374
22 Kastūrī-Raṅgācārya 381
23 Śaila Śrīnivāsa 384
24 Raṅgācārya 395

CHAPTER XXI

THE NIMBĀRKA SCHOOL OF PHILOSOPHY

PAGE

1 Teachers and Pupils of the Nimbārka School 399
2 A General Idea of Nimbārka's Philosophy 404
3 Controversy with the Monists by Mādhava Mukunda . . . 416
(a) The Main Thesis and the Ultimate End in *Advaita Vedānta* are untenable 416
(b) Refutation of the Śaṅkara Theory of Illusion in its various Aspects 422
(c) Refutation of the Śaṅkarite View of *Ajñāna* 424
4 The *Pramāṇas* according to Mādhava Mukunda 426
5 Criticism of the views of Rāmānuja and Bhāskara 429
6 The Reality of the World 435
7 Vanamālī Miśra 440

CHAPTER XXII

THE PHILOSOPHY OF VIJÑĀNA BHIKṢU

1 A General Idea of Vijñāna Bhikṣu's Philosophy. 445
2 The Brahman and the World according to Vijñānā-mṛta-bhāṣya . 454
3 The Individual 460
4 Brahma-Experience and Experience 465
5 Self-Luminosity and Ignorance 468
6 Relation of Sāṃkhya and Vedānta according to Bhikṣu . . . 471
7 Māyā and Pradhāna 476
8 Bhikṣu's criticism of the Sāṃkhya and Yoga 479
9 *Īśvara-gītā*, its Philosophy as expounded by Vijñāna Bhikṣu . . 482

CHAPTER XXIII

PHILOSOPHICAL SPECULATIONS OF SOME OF THE SELECTED PURĀṆAS

1 *Viṣṇu Purāṇa* 497
2 *Vāyu Purāṇa* 502
3 *Mārkaṇḍeya Purāṇa* 506
4 *Nāradīya Purāṇa* 507
5 *Kūrma Purāṇa* 509

APPENDIX TO VOLUME I

The *Lokāyata*, *Nāstika* and *Cārvāka* 512–550

INDEX 551

CHAPTER XV

THE BHĀSKARA SCHOOL OF PHILOSOPHY

Date of Bhāskara.

UDAYANA, in his *Nyāya-kusumāñjali*, speaks of Bhāskara as a commentator on the Vedānta in accordance with the traditions of the *tridaṇḍa* school of Vedānta and as holding the view that Brahman suffers evolutionary changes[1]. Bhaṭṭojī Dīkṣita also, in his *Tattva-viveka-ṭīkā-vivaraṇa*, speaks of Bhaṭṭa Bhāskara as holding the doctrine of difference and non-difference (*bhedābheda*)[2]. It is certain, however, that he flourished after Śaṅkara, for, though he does not mention him by name, yet the way in which he refers to him makes it almost certain that he wrote his commentary with the express purpose of refuting some of the cardinal doctrines of Śaṅkara's commentary on the *Brahma-sūtra*. Thus, at the very beginning of his commentary, he says that it aims at refuting those who, hiding the real sense of the *sūtra*, have only expressed their own opinions, and in other places also he speaks in very strong terms against the commentator who holds the *māyā* doctrine and is a Buddhist in his views[3]. But, though he was opposed to Śaṅkara, it was only so far as Śaṅkara had introduced the *māyā* doctrine, and only so far as he thought the world had sprung forth not as a real modification of Brahman, but only through *māyā*. For

1 *Tridaṇḍa* means "three sticks." According to Manu it was customary among some Brahmins to use one stick, and among others, three sticks.

Paṇḍita Vindhyeśvarī Prasāda Dvivedin, in his Sanskrit introduction to Bhāskara's commentary on the *Brahma-sūtra*, says that the Vaiṣṇava commentators on the *Brahma-sūtra* prior to Rāmānuja, Taṅka, Guhadeva, Bhāruci and Yāmunācarya, the teacher of Rāmānuja, were all *tridaṇḍins*. Such a statement is indeed very interesting, but unfortunately he does not give us the authority from which he drew this information.

2 "*Bhaṭṭabhāskaras tu bhedā-bheda-vedānta-siddhānta-vādī*"; Bhaṭṭojī Dīkṣita's *Vedānta-tattva-ṭīkā-vivaraṇa*, as quoted by Paṇḍita Vindhyeśvarī Prasāda in his Introduction to Bhāskara's commentary.

3 *sūtrā-bhiprāya-saṃvṛtyā svābhiprāyā-prakāśanāt*
vyākhyātaṃ yair idaṃ śāstraṃ vyākhyeyaṃ tan-nivṛttaye.
Bhāskara's Commentary, p. 1.

Also "*ye tu bauddha-matāvalambino māyā-vādinas te' pi anena nyāyena sūtra-kāreṇai' va nirastāḥ.*" *Ibid.* II. 2. 29.

In another place Śaṅkara is referred to as explaining views which were really propounded by the Mahāyāna Buddhists—*vigītaṃ vicchinna-mūlaṃ māhāyānika-bauddha-gāthitaṃ māyā-vādaṃ vyāvarṇayanto lokān vyāmohayanti. Ibid.* I. 4. 25.

both Śaṅkara and Bhāskara would agree in holding that the Brahman was both the material cause and the instrumental cause (*upādāna* and *nimitta*). Śaṅkara would maintain that this was so only because there was no other real category which existed; but he would strongly urge, as has been explained before, that *māyā*, the category of the indefinite and the unreal, was associated with Brahman in such a transformation, and that, though the Brahman was substantially the same identical entity as the world, yet the world as it appears was a *māyā* transformation with Brahman inside as the kernel of truth. But Bhāskara maintained that there was no *māyā*, and that it was the Brahman which, by its own powers, underwent a real modification; and, as the Pañcarātras also held the same doctrine in so far as they believed that Vāsudeva was both the material and the instrumental cause of the world, he was in agreement with the Bhāgavatas, and he says that he does not find anything to be refuted in the Pañcarātra doctrine[1]. But he differs from them in regard to their doctrine of the individual souls having been produced from Brahman[2].

Again, though one cannot assert anything very positively, it is possible that Bhāskara himself belonged to that particular sect of Brahmins who used three sticks as their Brahminic insignia in preference to one stick, used more generally by other Brahmins; and so his explanation of the *Vedānta-sūtra* may rightly be taken as the view of the *tridaṇḍī* Brahmins. For in discussing the point that fitness for Brahma-knowledge does not mean the giving up of the religious stages of life (*āśrama*), with their customs and rituals, he speaks of the maintenance of three sticks as being enjoined by the Vedas[3].

Mādhavācārya, in his *Śaṅkara-vijaya*, speaks of a meeting of Śaṅkara with Bhaṭṭa Bhāskara, but it is difficult to say how far this statement is reliable[4]. From the fact that Bhāskara refuted Śaṅkara and was himself referred to by Udayana, it is certain that he flourished some time between the eighth and the tenth centuries. Paṇḍita Vindhyeśvarī Prasāda refers to a copper-plate found by the

[1] *Vāsudeva eva upādāna-kāraṇaṃ jagato nimitta-kāraṇaṃ ceti te manyante... tad etat sarvaṃ śruti-prasiddham eva tasmān nātra nirākaraṇīyaṃ paśyāmaḥ. Bhāskara-bhāṣya*, II. 2. 41.

[2] *Ibid.*

[3] *Ibid.* III. 4. 26, p. 208; see also Paṇḍita Vindhyeśvarī's Introduction.

[4] *Śaṅkara-vijaya*, XV. 80.

late Dr Bhāwdājī in the Mārāṭhā country, near Nasik, in which it is stated that one Bhāskara Bhaṭṭa of the lineage (*gotra*) of Śāṇḍilya, son of Kavicakravartī Trivikrama, who was given the title of Vidyāpati, was the sixth ancestor of Bhāskarācārya of Śāṇḍilya lineage, the astronomer and writer of the Siddhānta-śiromaṇi; and he maintains that this senior Vidyāpati Bhāskara Bhaṭṭa was the commentator on the *Brahma-sūtra*[1]. But, though this may be possible, yet we have no evidence that it is certain; for, apart from the similarity of names[2], it is not definitely known whether this Vidyāpati Bhāskara Bhaṭṭa ever wrote any commentary on the *Brahma-sūtra*. All that we can say, therefore, with any degree of definiteness, is that Bhāskara flourished at some period between the middle of the eighth century and the middle of the tenth century, and most probably in the ninth century, since he does not know Rāmānuja[3].

Bhāskara and Śaṅkara.

There is a text of the *Chāndogya Upaniṣad*, VI. I. I, which is treated from two different points of view by Śaṅkara and Bhāskara in connection with the interpretation of *Brahma-sūtra*, II. I. 14[4]. Śaṅkara's interpretation of this, as Vācaspati explains it, is that, when clay is known, all clay-materials are known, not because the clay-materials are really clay, for they are indeed different. But, if so, how can we, by knowing one, know the other? Because the clay-materials do not really exist; they are all, and so indeed are all that pass as modifications (*vikāra*), but mere expressions of speech (*vācārambhaṇam*), mere names (*nāmdheyam*) having no real

[1] Paṇḍita Vindhyeśvarī Prasāda's Introduction.

[2] We hear of several Bhāskaras in Sanskrit literature, such as Lokabhāskara, Śrāntabhāskara, Haribhāskara, Bhadantabhāskara, Bhāskaramiśra, Bhāskara-śāstrī, Bhāskaradīkṣita, Bhaṭṭabhāskara, Paṇḍita Bhāskarācārya, Bhaṭṭabhāskaramiśra, Trikāṇḍamaṇḍana, Laugākṣibhāskara, Śāṇḍilyabhāskara, Vatsabhāskara, Bhāskaradeva, Bhāskaranṛsiṃha, Bhāskarāraṇya, Bhāskarānandanātha, Bhāskarasena.

[3] He makes very scanty references to other writers. He speaks of Śāṇḍilya as a great author of the Bhāgavata school. He refers to the four classes of Māheśvaras, Pāśupata, Śaiva, Kāpālika and Kāṭhaka-siddhāntin, and their principal work *Pañcādhyāyi-śāstra*; he also refers to the *Pāñcarātrikas*, with whom he is often largely in agreement.

[4] *tad-ananyatvam ārambhaṇa-śabdādibhyaḥ. Brahma-sūtra*, II. I. 14. *yathā saumya ekena mṛt-piṇḍen asarvaṃ mṛṇmayaṃ vijñātaṃ syādvācārambhaṇaṃ vikāro nāmadheyaṃ mṛttike'ty'eva satyaṃ* (Ch. VI. I. I).

entities or objects to which they refer, having in fact no existence at all[1].

Bhāskara says that the passage means that clay alone is real, and the purport of speech depends on two things, the objects and the facts implied and the names which imply them. The effects (*kārya*) are indeed the basis of all our practical behaviour and conduct, involving the objects and facts implied and the expressions and names which imply them. How can the cause and effect be identical? The answer to this is that it is true that it is to the effects that our speech applies and that these make all practical behaviour possible, but the effects are in reality but stages of manifestation, modification and existence of the cause itself. So, from the point of view that the effects come and go, appear and disappear, whereas the cause remains permanently the same, as the ground of all its real manifestations, it is said that the cause alone is true—the clay alone is true. The effect, therefore, is only a state of the cause, and is hence both identical with it and different from it[2]. The effect, the name (*nāmadheya*), is real, and the scriptures also assert this[3].

Bhāskara argues against Śaṅkara as follows: the arguments that the upholder of *māyā* (*māyāvādin*) could adduce against those who believed in the reality of the many, the world, might be adduced against him also, in so far as he believes in monism (*advaita*). A person who hears the scriptures and philosophizes is at first under the veil of ignorance (*avidyā*); and, if on account of this ignorance his knowledge of duality was false, his knowledge of monism might equally for the same reason be considered as false. All Brahma-knowledge is false, because it is knowledge, like the knowledge of the world. It is argued that, just as from the false knowledge of a dream and of letters there can be true acquisition

[1] *Bhāmatī, Brahma-sūtra*, II. I. 14. Rāhu is a demon which is merely a living head with no body, its sole body being its head; but still we use, for convenience of language, the expression "Rāhu's head" (*Rāhoḥ śiraḥ*); similarly clay alone is real, and what we call clay-materials, jugs, plates, etc., are mere expressions of speech having no real objects or entities to which they can apply—they simply do not exist at all—but are mere *vikalpa; vācā kevalaṃ ārabhyate vikāra-jātaṃ na tu tattvato'sti yato nāmadheya-mātram etat;...yathā rāhoḥ śiraḥ...śabda-jñānā'-nupātī vastu-śūnyo vikalpa iti; tathā cā'vastutayā anṛtam vikāra-jātaṃ.*

[2] *vāg-indriyasya ubhayam ārambhaṇam vikāro nāmadheyam...ubhayam ālambya vāg-vyavahāraḥ pravartate ghaṭena udakam āhare' ti mṛṇmayam ity asya idaṃ vyākhyānam...kāraṇam eva kāryā-tmanā ghaṭavad avatiṣthate...kāraṇa-syā'vasthā-mātraṃ kāryaṃ vyatiriktā'vyatiriktaṃ śukti-rajatavad āgamāpāya-dharmitvāc ca anṛtam anityam iti ca vyapadiśyate. Bhāskara-bhāṣya*, II. I. 14.

[3] *atha nāma-dheyaṃ satyasya satyamiti, etc. Ibid.*

of good and evil or of certain meanings, so from the false knowledge of words and their meanings, as involved in the knowledge of monistic texts of the Upaniṣads, there may arise right knowledge. But such an argument is based on false analogy. When from certain kinds of dreams someone judges that good or evil will come to him, it is not from nothing that he judges, since he judges from particular dream experiences; and these dream experiences are facts having particular characters and features; they are not mere nothing, like the hare's horn; no one can judge of anything from the hare's horn. The letters also have certain shapes and forms and are definitely by common consent and agreement associated with particular sounds; it is well known that different letters in different countries may be used to denote one kind of sound. Again, if from a mistake someone experiences fear and dies, it is not from nothing or from something false that he dies; for he had a real fear, and the fear was the cause of death and was roused by the memory of a real thing, and the only unreality about it was that the thing was not present there at that time. So no example could be given to show that from false knowledge, or falsehood as such, there could come right knowledge or the truth. Again, how can the scriptures demonstrate the falsehood of the world? If all auditory knowledge were false, all language would be false, and even the scriptural texts would be non-existent.

Further, what is this "*avidyā*," if it cannot be described? How can one make anyone understand it? What nonsense it is to say that that which manifests itself as all the visible and tangible world of practical conduct and behaviour cannot itself be described[1]. If it is beginningless, it must be eternal, and there can be no liberation. It cannot be both existent and non-existent; for that would be contradictory. It cannot be mere negation; for, being non-existent, it could not bring bondage. If it brings bondage, it must be an entity, and that means a dual existence with Brahman. So the proposition of the upholder of *māyā* is false.

What is true, however, is that, just as milk gets curdled, so it is God Himself who by His own will and knowledge and omnipotence transforms Himself into this world. There is no inconsistency in God's transforming Himself into the world, though He is partless;

1 *yasyāḥ kāryam idaṃ kṛtsraṃ vyavahārāya kalpate*
nirvaktuṃ sā na śakye' ti vacanaṃ vacanār-thakaṃ. *Bhāskara-bhāṣya.*

for He can do so by various kinds of powers, modifying them according to His own will. He possesses two powers; by one He has become the world of enjoyables (*bhogya-śakti*), and by the other the individual souls, the enjoyers (*bhoktṛ*); but in spite of this modification of Himself He remains unchanged in His own purity; for it is by the manifestation and modification of His powers that the modification of the world as the enjoyable and the enjoyer takes place. It is just as the sun sends out his rays and collects them back into himself, but yet remains in himself the same[1].

The Philosophy of Bhāskara's Bhāṣya.

From what has been said above it is clear that according to Bhāskara the world of matter and the selves consists only in real modifications or transformations (*pariṇāma*) of Brahman's own nature through His diverse powers. This naturally brings in the question whether the world and the souls are different from Brahman or identical with him. Bhāskara's answer to such a question is that "difference" (*bheda*) has in it the characteristic of identity (*abheda-dharmaś ca*)—the waves are different from the sea, but are also identical with it. The waves are manifestations of the sea's own powers, and so the same identical sea appears to be different when viewed with reference to the manifestations of its powers, though it is in reality identical with its powers. So the same identical fire is different in its powers as it burns or illuminates. So all that is one is also many, and the one is neither absolute identity nor absolute difference[2].

The individual souls are in reality not different from God; they are but His parts, as the sparks of fire are the parts of fire; but it is the peculiarity of these parts of God, the souls, that though one with Him, they have been under the influence of ignorance, desires and deeds from beginningless time[3]. Just as the *ākāśa*, which is all the same everywhere; and yet the *ākāśa* inside a vessel or a house is not just the same *ākāśa* as the boundless space, but may in some

[1] *Bhāskara-bhāṣya*, II. I. 27, also I. 4. 25.

[2] *abheda-dharmaś ca bhedo yathā mahodadher abhedaḥ sa eva taraṅgādy-ātmanā vartamāno bheda ity ucyate, na hi taraṅgā-dayaḥ pāṣāṇā-diṣu dṛśyante tasyaiva tāḥ śaktayaḥ śakti-śaktimatoś ca ananyatvaṃ anyatvaṃ co-palakṣyate yathā'gner dahana-prakāśanā-di-śaktayaḥ. . . . tasmāt sarvam ekā-nekā-tmakaṃ nā'tyantam abhinnaṃ bhinnaṃ vā. Ibid.* II. I. 18.

[3] *Ibid.* I. 4. 21.

sense be regarded as a part of it; or just as the same air is seen to serve different life-functions, as the five *prāṇas*, so the individual souls also may in some sense be regarded as parts of God. It is just and proper that the scriptures should command the individual souls to seek knowledge so as to attain liberation; for it is the desire for the highest soul (*paramātman*) or God or Brahman that is the cause of liberation, and it is the desire for objects of the world that is the cause of bondage[1]. This soul, in so far as it exists in association with ignorance, desires and deeds, is atomic in nature; and, just as a drop of sandal paste may perfume all the place about it, so does the atomic soul, remaining in one place, animate the whole body. It is by nature endowed with consciousness, and it is only with reference to the knowledge of other objects that it has to depend on the presence of those objects[2]. Its seat is in the heart, and through the skin of the heart it is in touch with the whole body. But, though in a state of bondage, under the influence of ignorance, etc., it is atomic, yet it is not ultimately atomic in nature; for it is one with Brahman. Under the influence of *buddhi*, *ahaṃkāra*, the five senses and the five *vāyus* it undergoes the cycle of rebirths. But though this atomic form and the association with the *buddhi*, etc., is not essential to the nature of the soul, yet so long as such a relation exists, the agency of the soul is in every sense real; but the ultimate source of this agency is God Himself; for it is God who makes us perform all actions, and He makes us perform good actions, and it is He who, remaining within us, controls all our actions.

In all stages of life a man must perform the deeds enjoined by the scriptures, and he cannot rise at any stage so high that he is beyond the sphere of the duties of work imposed on him by the scriptures[3]. It is not true, as Śaṅkara says, that those who are fit to

[1] *rāgo hi paramātma-viṣayo yaḥ sa mukti-hetuḥ viṣaya-viṣayo yaḥ sa bandha-hetuḥ. Bhāskara-bhāṣya.*

[2] *Ibid.* II. 3. 18, 22, 23.

[3] *Bhāskara-bhāṣya*, I. I. I. In holding the view that the *Brahma-sūtra* is in a sense continuous with the *Mīmāṃsā-sūtra*, which the former must follow—for it is after the performance of the ritualistic duties that the knowledge of Brahman can arise, and the latter therefore cannot in any stage dispense with the need for the former—and that the *Brahma-sūtras* are not intended for any superior and different class of persons, Bhāskara seems to have followed Upavarṣa or Upavarṣācārya, to whose commentary on the *Mīmāṃsā-sūtra* he refers and whom he calls the founder of the school (*śāstra-sampradāya-pravartaka*). *Ibid.* I. I. I, and II. 2. 27. See also I. I. 4: *ātma-jñānā-dhikṛtasya karmabhir vinā apavargā-nupapatter jñānena karma samuccīyate.*

have the highest knowledge are beyond the duties of life and courses of ritualistic and other actions enjoined by the scriptures, or that those for whom these are intended are not fit to have the highest knowledge; in other words, the statement of Śaṅkara that there cannot be any combination (*samuccaya*) of knowledge (*jñāna*) and necessary ritualistic duties of life (*karma*) is false. Bhāskara admits that pure *karma* (ritualistic duties) cannot lead us to the highest perception of the truth, the Brahman; yet knowledge (*jñāna*) combined with the regular duties, i.e. *jñāna-samuccita-karma*, can lead us to our highest good, the realization of Brahman. That it is our duty to attain the knowledge of Brahman is also to be accepted, by reason of the injunction of the scriptures; for that also is one of the imperative duties imposed on us by the scriptures—a *vidhi*—the self is to be known (*ātmā vā are draṣṭavyaḥ*, etc.). It is therefore not true, as Śaṅkara asserted, that what the ritualistic and other duties imposed on us by the scriptures can do for us is only to make us fit for the study of Vedānta by purifying us and making us as far as possible sinless; Bhāskara urges that performance of the duties imposed on us by the scriptures is as necessary as the attainment of knowledge for our final liberation.

Bhāskara draws a distinction between cognition (*jñāna*) and consciousness (*caitanya*), more particularly, self-consciousness (*ātma-caitanya*). Cognition with him means the knowledge of objective things, and this is a direct experience (*anubhava*) arising out of the contact of the sense organ, *manas*, and the object, the presence of light and the internal action of the memory and the sub-conscious impressions (*saṃskāra*). Cognition is not an active operation by itself, but is rather the result of the active operation of the senses in association with other accessories, such that whenever there is a collocation of those accessories involving the operation of the senses there is cognition[1]. Bhāskara is therefore positively against the contention of Kumārila that knowledge is an entity which is not directly perceived but only inferred as the agent which induces the intellectual operation, but which is not directly known by itself. If an unperceived entity is to be inferred to explain the cause of the per-

[1] *jñāna-kriyā-kalpanāyāṃ pramāṇā-bhāvāt.... ālokendriya-manaḥ-saṃskāreṣu hi satsu saṃvedanam utpadyate iti tad-abhāve notpadyate, yadi punar aparaṃ jñānaṃ kalpyate tasyāpy anyat tasyāpy anyad ity anavasthā; na ca jñāna-kriyānumāne liṅgam asti, samvedanam iti cen na, agṛhīta-sambandhatvāt. Bhāskara-bhāsva*, I. I I.

ceived intellectual operation, then another entity might be inferred as the cause of that unperceived entity, and another to explain that and so on, and we have a vicious infinite (*anavasthā*). Moreover, no unperceived entity can be inferred as the cause of the perceived intellectual operation; for, if it is unperceived, then its relation with intellectual operation is also unperceived, and how can there be any inference at all? Thus, cognition is what we directly experience (*anubhava*) and there is no unperceived entity which causes it, but it is the direct result of the joint operation of many accessories. This objective cognition is entirely different from the subjective consciousness or self-consciousness; for the latter is eternal and always present, whereas the former is only occasioned by the collocating circumstances. It is easy to see that Bhāskara has a very distinct epistemological position, which, though similar to Nyāya so far as the objective cognition is concerned, is yet different therefrom on account of his admission of the ever-present self-consciousness of the soul. It is at the same time different from the Śaṅkarite epistemology, for objective cognition is considered by him not as mere limitation of self-consciousness, but as entirely different therefrom[1]. It may also be noted that, unlike Dharmarājādhvarīndra, the writer of the Sanskrit epistemological work, *Vedānta-paribhāṣā*, Bhāskara considers *manas* as a sense-organ[2]. On the subject of the self-validity of knowledge Bhāskara thinks that the knowledge of truth is always self-valid (*svataḥ-pramāṇa*), whereas the knowledge of the false is always attested from outside (*parataḥ pramāṇa*)[3].

As has already been said, Bhāskara does not think that liberation can be attained through knowledge alone; the duties imposed by the scriptures must always be done along with our attempts to know Brahman; for there is no contradiction or opposition between knowledge and performance of the duties enjoined by the scriptures. There will be no liberation if the duties are forsaken[4]. The state of salvation is one in which there is a continuous and unbroken consciousness of happiness[5]. A liberated soul may associate or not associate itself with any body or sense as it likes[6]. It is as omniscient,

[1] *kecid āhuḥ ātmā pramāyām indriya-dvāropādhi-nirgama-viṣayeṣu vartate... tad idam asamyag darśanam;...ālokendriyādibhyo jñānam utpadyamānaṃ... cānyad iti yuktam. Bhāskara-bhāṣya.*

[2] *Ibid.* II. 4. 17.

[3] *Ibid.* I. 4. 21.

[4] *Ibid.* III. 4. 26.

[5] *Ibid.* IV. 4. 8.

[6] *Ibid.* IV. 4. 12.

omnipotent and as one with all souls as God Himself[1]. The attachment (*rāga*) to Brahman, which is said to be an essential condition for attaining liberation, is further defined to be worship (*samārādhana*) or devotion (*bhakti*), while *bhakti* is said to be attendance on God by meditation (*dhyānādinā paricaryā*). *Bhakti* is conceived, not as any feeling, affection or love of God, as in later Vaiṣṇava literature, but as *dhyāna* or meditation[2]. A question may arise as to what, if Brahman has transformed Himself into the world, is meant by meditation on Brahman? Does it mean that we are to meditate on the world? To this Bhāskara's answer is that Brahman is not exhausted by His transformation into the world, and that what is really meant by Brahman's being transformed into the world is that the nature of the world is spiritual. The world is a spiritual manifestation and a spiritual transformation, and what passes as matter is in reality spiritual. Apart from Brahman as manifested in the world, the Brahman with diverse forms, there is also the formless Brahman (*niṣprapañca brahman*), the Brahman which is transcendent and beyond its own immanent forms, and it is this Brahman which is to be worshipped. The world with its diverse forms also will, in the end, return to its spiritual source, the formless Brahman, and nothing of it will be left as the remainder. The material world is dissolved in the spirit and lost therein, just as a lump of salt is lost in water[3]. This transcendent Brahman that is to be worshipped is of the nature of pure being and intelligence (*sal-lakṣaṇa* and *bodha-lakṣaṇa*)[4]. He is also infinite and unlimited. But, though He is thus characterized as being, intelligence, and infinite, yet these terms do not refer to three distinct entities; they are the qualities of Brahman, the substance, and, like all qualities, they cannot remain different from their substance; for neither can any substance remain without its qualities, nor can any qualities remain without their substance. A substance does not become different by virtue of its qualities[5].

Bhāskara denies the possibility of liberation during lifetime (*jīvan-mukti*); for so long as the body remains as a result of the

[1] *muktaḥ kāraṇā-tmānaṃ prāptaḥ tadvad eva sarva-jñaḥ sarva-śaktiḥ. Bhāskara-bhāṣya*, IV. 4. 7.

[2] *Ibid.* III. 2. 24.

[3] *Ibid.* II. 2. 11, 13, 17.

[4] *Ibid.* III. 2. 23.

[5] *na dharma-dharmi-bhedena svarūpa-bheda iti; na hi guṇa-rahitaṃ dravyam asti na dravya-rahito guṇaḥ. Ibid.* III. 2. 23.

previous *karmas*, the duties assigned to the particular stage of life (*āśrama*) to which the man belongs have to be performed; but his difference from the ordinary man is that, while the ordinary man thinks himself to be the agent or the doer of all actions, the wise man never thinks himself to be so. If a man could attain liberation during lifetime, then he might even know the minds of other people. Whether in *mukti* one becomes absolutely relationless (*niḥsambandhaḥ*), or whether one becomes omniscient and omnipotent (as Bhāskara himself urges), it is not possible for one to attain *mukti* during one's lifetime, so it is certain that so long as a man lives he must perform his duties and try to comprehend the nature of God and attend on Him through meditation, since these only can lead to liberation after death[1].

[1] *Bhāskara-bhāṣya*, III. 4. 26.

CHAPTER XVI

THE PAÑCARĀTRA.

Antiquity of the Pañcarātra.

THE Pañcarātra doctrines are indeed very old and are associated with the *puruṣa-sūkta* of the Ṛg-veda, which is, as it were, the foundation stone of all future Vaiṣṇava philosophy. It is said in the *Śata-patha Brāhmaṇa* that Nārāyaṇa, the great being, wishing to transcend all other beings and becoming one with them all, saw the form of sacrifice known as pañcarātra, and by performing that sacrifice attained his purpose[1]. It is probable that the epithets "*puruṣo ha nārāyaṇaḥ*" became transformed in later times into the two ṛṣis Nara and Nārāyaṇa. The passage also implies that Nārāyaṇa was probably a human being who became a transcending divinity by performing the Pañcarātra sacrifice. In the later literature *Nārāyaṇa* became the highest divinity. Thus Veṅkaṭa Sudhī wrote a *Siddhānta-ratnāvalī* in about 19,000 lines to prove by a reference to scriptural texts that Nārāyaṇa is the highest god and that all other gods, Śiva, Brahmā, Viṣṇu, etc., are subordinate to him[2]. The word *Brahman* in the Upaniṣads is also supposed in the fourth or the last chapter of the *Siddhānta-ratnāvalī* to refer to Nārāyaṇa. In the *Mahābhārata* (*Śānti-parvan*, 334th chapter) we hear of Nara and Nārāyaṇa themselves worshipping the unchanging Brahman which is the self in all beings; and yet Nārāyaṇa is there spoken of as being the greatest of all. In the succeeding chapter it is said that there was a king who was entirely devoted to Nārāyaṇa, and who worshipped him according to the *sātvata* rites[3]. He was so devoted to Nārāyaṇa that he considered all that belonged to him, riches, kingdom, etc., as belonging to Nārāyaṇa. He harboured in his house great saints versed in the Pañcarātra system. When under the patronage of this king great saints performed sacrifices, they were unable to have a vision of the great Lord Nārāyaṇa, and Bṛhaspati became angry.

[1] *Śata-patha Brāhmaṇa* XIII. 6. 1.

[2] The *Siddhānta-ratnāvalī* exists only as a MS. which has not yet been published.

[3] We have an old *Pañcarātra-saṃhitā* called the *Sātvata-saṃhitā*, the contents of which will presently be described.

Other sages then related the story that, though after long penance they could not perceive God, there was a message from Heaven that the great Nārāyaṇa was visible only to the inhabitants of Śveta-dvīpa, who were devoid of sense-organs, did not require any food, and were infused with a monotheistic devotion. The saints were dazzled by the radiant beauty of these beings, and could not see them. They then began to practise asceticism and, as a result, these holy beings became perceivable to them. These beings adored the ultimate deity by mental *japa* (muttering God's name in mind) and made offerings to God. Then there was again a message from Heaven that, since the saints had perceived the beings of Śveta-dvīpa, they should feel satisfied with that and return home because the great God could not be perceived except through all-absorbing devotion. Nārada also is said to have seen from a great distance Śveta-dvīpa and its extraordinary inhabitants. Nārada then went to Śveta-dvīpa and had a vision of Nārāyaṇa, whom he adored. Nārāyaṇa said to him that Vāsudeva was the highest changeless God, from whom came out Saṅkarṣaṇa, the lord of all life; from him came Pradyumna, called *manas*, and from Pradyumna came Aniruddha, the Ego. From Aniruddha came Brahmā, who created the universe. After the *pralaya*, Saṅkarṣaṇa, Pradyumna and Aniruddha are successively created from Vāsudeva.

There are some Upaniṣads which are generally known as Vaiṣṇava Upaniṣads, and of much later origin than the older Pañcarātra texts. To this group of Upaniṣads belong the *Avyakto-paniṣad* or *Avyakta-nṛsiṃhopaniṣad*, with a commentary of Upaniṣad-brahmayogin, the pupil of Vāsudevendra, *Kali-santaraṇopaniṣad*, *Kṛṣṇopaniṣad*, *Garuḍopaniṣad*, *Gopālatāpainī Upaniṣad*, *Gopālottara-tāpanī Upaniṣad*, *Tārāsāropaniṣad*, *Tripād-vibhūti-mahānārāyaṇa Upaniṣad*, *Dattātreyopaniṣad*, *Nārāyaṇopaniṣad*, *Nṛsiṃha-tāpinī Upaniṣad*, *Nṛsiṃhottara-tāpinī Upaniṣad*, *Rāmatāpinī Upaniṣad*, *Rāmottarottara-tāpinī Upaniṣad*, *Rāma-rahasya Upaniṣad*, *Vāsudevo-panisad*, with the commentaries of Upaniṣad-brahmayogin. But these Upaniṣads are mostly full of inessential descriptions, ritualistic practices and the muttering of particular *mantras*. They have very little connection with the Pañcarātra texts and their contents. Some of them—like the *Nṛsiṃha-tāpinī*, *Gopālatāpanī*, etc.—have been utilized in the Gauḍīya school of Vaiṣṇavism.

The Position of the Pañcarātra Literature.

Yāmuna, in his *Āgama-prāmāṇya*, discusses the position of the Pañcarātras as follows. It is said that any instruction conveyed through language can be valid either by itself or through the strength of the validity of some other proofs. No instruction of any ordinary person can be valid by itself. The special ritualistic processes associated with the Pañcarātra cannot be known by perception or by inference. Only God, whose powers of perception extend to all objects of the world and which are without any limitation, can instil the special injunctions of the Pañcarātra. The opponents, however, hold that a perception which has all things within its sphere can hardly be called perception. Moreover, the fact that some things may be bigger than other things does not prove that anything which is liable to be greater and less could necessarily be conceived to extend to a limitless extent[1]. Even if it be conceived that there is a person whose perception is limitless, there is nothing to suggest that he should be able to instruct infallibly about the rituals, such as those enjoined in the Pañcarātra. There are also no *āgamas* which prescribe the Pañcarātra rites. It cannot be ascertained whether the authors of the Pañcarātra works based them on the teachings of the Vedas or gave their own views and passed them on as being founded on the Vedas. If it is argued that the fact that the Pañcarātra, like other texts of *Smṛti* of Manu, etc., exist proves that they must have a common origin in the Vedas, that is contradicted by the fact that the Pañcarātra doctrines are repudiated in the *smṛti* texts founded on the Vedas. If it is said that those who follow the Pañcarātra rites are as good Brahmins as other Brahmins, and follow the Vedic rites, the opponents assert that this is not so, since the Pañcarātrins may have all the external marks and appearance of Brahmins, but yet they are not so regarded in society. At a social dinner the Brahmins do not sit in the same line with the *Bhāgavatas* or the followers of the Pañcarātra.

[1] *atha ekasmin sātiśaye kenāpyanyena niratiśayena bhavitavyam iti āhosvit samāna-jātīyenā'nyena nir-atiśaya-daśām adhirūḍhena bhavitavyam iti:*

na tāvad agrimaḥ kalpaḥ kalpyate'nupalambhataḥ
na hi dṛṣṭaṃ śarāvādi vyomeva prāpta-vaibhavam.

Āgama-prāmāṇya, p. 3.

The very word *sātvata* indicates a lower caste[1], and the words *bhāgavata* and *sātvata* are interchangeable. It is said that a *sātvata* of the *pañcama* caste who by the king's order worships in temples is called a *bhāgavata*. As a means of livelihood the sātvatas worship images and live upon offerings for initiation and those made to temple gods; they do not perform the Vedic duties, and have no relationship with the Brahmins, and so they cannot be regarded as Brahmins. It is also said that even by the sight of a man who takes to worship as a means of livelihood one is polluted and should be purified by proper purificatory ceremonies. The Pañcarātra texts are adopted by the degraded sātvatas or the bhāgavatas, and these must therefore be regarded as invalid and non-Vedic. Moreover, if this literature were founded on the Vedas, there would be no meaning in their recommendation of special kinds of rituals. It is for this reason that Bādarāyaṇa also refutes the philosophical theory of the Pañcarātra in the *Brahma-sūtra*.

It may, however, be urged that, though the Pañcarātra injunctions may not tally with the injunctions of Brahminic *Smṛti* literature, yet such contradictions are not important, as both are based upon the Vedic texts. Since the validity of the Brahminic *Smṛti* also is based upon the Vedas, the Pañcarātra has no more necessity to reconcile its injunctions with that than they have to reconcile themselves with the Pañcarātra.

The question arises as to whether the Vedas are the utterances of a person or not. The argument in favour of production by a person is that, since the Vedas are a piece of literary composition, they must have been uttered by a person. The divine person who directly perceives the sources of merit or demerit enjoins the same through his grace by composing the Vedas for the benefit of human beings. It is admitted, even by the Mīmāṃsakas, that all worldly affairs are consequent upon the influence of merit and demerit. So the divine being who has created the world knows directly the sources of merit and demerit. The world cannot be produced directly through the effects of our deeds, and it has to be admitted that there must be some being who utilizes the effects of our deeds, producing the world in consonance with them. All the scriptural

[1] Thus Manu says:

vais'yāt tu jāyate vrātyāt sudhanvācārya eva ca
bhāruṣaś ca nijaṅghaś ca maitra-sātvata eva ca.

Āgama-prāmāṇya, p. 8.

texts also support the admission of such an omnipotent and omniscient God. It is this God who, on the one hand, created the Vedas, directing the people to the performance of such actions as lead them to mundane and heavenly happiness, and on the other hand created the Pañcarātra literature for the attainment of the highest bliss by the worship of God and the realization of His nature. There are some who deny the legitimate inference of a creator from the creation, and regard the Vedas as an eternally existent composition, uncreated by any divine being. Even in such a view the reason why the Vedas and the consonant *Smṛtis* are regarded as valid attests also the validity of the Pañcarātra literature. But, as a matter of fact, from the Vedas themselves we can know the supreme being as their composer. The supreme God referred to in the Upaniṣads is none other than *Vāsudeva*, and it is He who is the composer of the Pañcarātra. Further, arguments are adduced to show that the object of the Vedas is not only to command us to do certain actions or to prohibit us from doing certain other actions, but also to describe the nature of the ultimate reality as the divine person. The validity of the Pañcarātra has therefore to be admitted, as it claims for its source the divine person Nārāyaṇa or Vāsudeva. Yāmuna then refers to many texts from the *Varāha*, *Liṅga* and *Matsya Purāṇas* and from the *Manu-saṃhitā* and other *smṛti* texts. In his *Puruṣa-ninṇaya* also, Yāmuna elaborately discusses the scriptural arguments by which he tries to show that the highest divine person referred to in the Upaniṣads and the Purāṇas is Nārāyaṇa. This divine being cannot be the Śiva of the Śaivas, because the three classes of the Śaivas, the Kāpālikas, Kālamukhas and Pāśupatas, all prescribe courses of conduct contradictory to one another, and it is impossible that they should be recommended by the scriptural texts. Their ritualistic rites also are manifestly non-Vedic. The view that they are all derived from Rudra does not prove that it is the same Rudra who is referred to in the Vedic texts. The Rudra referred to by them may be an entirely different person. He refers also to the various Purāṇas which decry the Śaivas. Against the argument that, if the Pañcarātra doctrines were in consonance with the Vedas, then one would certainly have discovered the relevant Vedic texts from which they were derived, Yāmuna says that the Pañcarātra texts were produced by God for the benefit of devotees who were impatient of following elaborate details described in the

Vedic literature. It is therefore quite intelligible that the relevant Vedic texts supporting the Pañcarātra texts should not be discovered. Again, when it is said that Śāṇḍilya turned to the doctrine of *bhakti* because he found nothing in the four Vedas suitable for the attainment of his desired end, this should not be interpreted as implying a lowering of the Vedas; for it simply means that the desired end as recommended in the Pañcarātras is different from that prescribed in the Vedas. The fact that Pañcarātras recommend special ritual ceremonies in addition to the Vedic ones does not imply that they are non-Vedic; for, unless it is proved that the Pañcarātras are non-Vedic, it cannot be proved that the additional ceremonies are non-Vedic without implying argument in a circle. It is also wrong to suppose that the Pañcarātra ceremonies are really antagonistic to all Vedic ceremonies. It is also wrong to suppose that Bādarāyaṇa refuted the Pañcarātra doctrines; for, had he done so, he would not have recommended them in the *Mahābhārata*. The view of the Pañcarātras admitting the four *vyūhas* should not be interpreted as the admission of many gods; for these are manifestations of Vāsudeva, the one divine person. A proper interpretation of Bādarāyaṇa's *Brahma-sūtras* would also show that they are in support of the Pañcarātras and not against them.

Even the most respected persons of society follow all the Pañcarātra instructions in connection with all rituals relating to image-worship. The arguments of the opponents that the Bhāgavatas are not Brahmins are all fallacious, since the Bhāgavatas have the same marks of Brahmahood as all Brahmins. The fact that Manu describes the *pañcama* caste as *sātvata* does not prove that all *sātvatas* are *pañcamas*. Moreover, the interpretation of the word *sātvata* as *pañcama* by the opponents would be contradictory to many scriptural texts, where *sātvatas* are praised. That some *sātvatas* live by image-building or temple-building and such other works relating to the temple does not imply that this is the duty of all the Bhāgavatas. Thus Yāmuna, in his *Āgama-prāmāṇya* and *Kāśmīrāgama-prāmāṇya*, tried to prove that the Pañcarātras are as valid as the Vedas, since they are derived from the same source, viz. the divine Person, *Nārāyaṇa*[1].

[1] The *Kāśmīrāgama* is referred to in the *Āgama-prāmāṇya*, p. 85, as another work of Yāmuna dealing more or less with the same subject as the *Āgama-prāmāṇya*, of which no MS. has been available to the present writer.

From the tenth to the seventeenth century the Śaivas and the Śrīvaiṣṇavas lived together in the south, where kings professing Śaivism harassed the Śrīvaiṣṇavas and maltreated their temple-gods, and kings professing Śrīvaiṣṇavism did the same to the Śaivas and their temple-gods. It is therefore easy to imagine how the sectarian authors of the two schools were often anxious to repudiate one another. One of the most important and comprehensive of such works is the *Siddhānta-ratnāvalī*, written by Veṅkaṭa Sudhī. Veṅkaṭa Sudhī was the disciple of Veṅkaṭanātha. He was the son of Śrīśaila Tātayārya, and was the brother of Śrī Śaila Śrīnivāsa. The *Siddhānta-ratnāvalī* is a work of four chapters, containing over 300,000 letters. He lived in the fourteenth and the fifteenth centuries, and wrote at least two other works, *Rahasya traya-sāra* and *Siddhānta-vaijayantī*.

Many treatises were written in which the Pañcarātra doctrines were summarized. Of these Gopālasūri's *Pañcarātra-rakṣā-saṃgraha* seems to be the most important. Gopālasūri was the son of Kṛṣṇadeśika and pupil of Vedāntarāmānuja, who was himself the pupil of Kṛṣṇadeśika. His *Pañcarātra-rakṣā* deals with the various kinds of rituals described in some of the most important Pañcarātra works.

It thus seems that the Pañcarātra literature was by many writers not actually regarded as of Vedic origin, though among the Śrīvaiṣṇavas it was regarded as being as authoritative as the Vedas. It was regarded, along with the Sāṃkhya and Yoga, as an accessory literature to the Vedas[1]. Yāmuna also speaks of it as containing a brief summary of the teachings of the Vedas for the easy and immediate use of those devotees who cannot afford to study the vast Vedic literature. The main subjects of the Pañcarātra literature are directions regarding the constructions of temples and images,

[1] Thus Veṅkaṭanātha, quoting Vyāsa, says:

idaṃmaho-paniṣadaṃ catur-veda-sam-anvitaṃ
sāṃkhya-yoga-kṛtāntena pañca-rātrā-nu-śabditam.

Seśvara-Mīmāṃsā, p. 19.

Sometimes the Pañcarātra is regarded as the root of the Vedas, and sometimes the Vedas are regarded as the root of the Pañcarātras. Thus Veṅkaṭanātha in the above context quotes a passage from Vyāsa in which Pañcarātra is regarded as the root of the Vedas—"*mahato veda-vṛkṣasya mūla-bhūto mahān ayam.*" He quotes also another passage in which the Vedas are regarded as the root of the Pañcarātras—"*śrutimūlam idaṃ tantraṃ pramāṇa-kalpa-sūtravat.*" In another passage he speaks of the Pañcarātras as the alternative to the Vedas—"*alābhe veda-mantrāṇāṃ pañca-rātro-ditena vā.*"

descriptions of the various rituals associated with image-worship, and the rituals, dealing elaborately with the duties of the Śrī-vaiṣṇavas and their religious practices, such as initiation, baptism, and the holding of religious marks. The practice of image-worship is manifestly non-Vedic, though there is ample evidence to show that it was current even in the sixth century B.C. It is difficult for us to say how this practice originated and which section of Indians was responsible for it. The conflict between the Vedic people and the image-worshippers seems to have been a long one; yet we know that even in the second century B.C. the Bhāgavata cult was in a very living state, not only in South India, but also in Upper India. The testimony of the Besnagar Column shows how even Greeks were converted to the Bhāgavata religion. The *Mahābhārata* also speaks of the *sātvata* rites, according to which Viṣṇu was worshipped, and it also makes references to the *Vyūha* doctrine of the Pañcarātras. In the *Nārāyaṇīya* section it is suggested that the home of the Pañcarātra worship is Śveta-dvīpa, from which it may have migrated to India; but efforts of scholars to determine the geographical position of Śveta-dvīpa have so far failed.

In the *Purāṇas* and the *smṛti* literature also the conflict with the various Brahminic authorities is manifest. Thus, in the *Kūrma purāṇa*, chapter fifteen, it is said that the great sinners, the Pañcarātrins, were produced as a result of killing cows in some other birth, that they are absolutely non-Vedic, and that the literatures of the Śāktas, Śaivas and the Pañcarātras are for the delusion of mankind[1]. That Pañcarātrins were a cursed people is also noticed in the *Parāśara purāṇa*[2]. They are also strongly denounced in the *Vaśiṣṭha-saṃhitā*, the *Śāmba-purāṇa* and the *Sūta-saṃhitā* as great sinners and as absolutely non-Vedic. Another cause of denouncement was that the Pañcarātrins initiated and admitted within their

[1] *kāpālaṃ gāruḍaṃ śāktaṃ, bhairavaṃ pūrva-paścimaṃ,*
pañca-rātraṃ, pāśupataṃ tathānyāni sahasraśaḥ.
Kūrma-purāṇa, Ch. 15.

(As quoted in the *Tattva-kaustubha* of Dīkṣita but in the printed edition of the B.J. series it occurs in the sixteenth chapter with slight variations.)

The *Skanda-purāṇa* also says:

pañcarātre ca kāpāle, tathā kālamukeh'pi ca.
śākte ca dīkṣitā yūyaṃ bhaveta brāhmaṇādhamāḥ.

[2] *dvitīyaṃ pāñcarātre ca tantre bhāgavate tathā*
dīkṣitāś ca dvijā nityaṃ bhaveyur garhitā hareḥ.

(As quoted by Bhaṭṭojī Dīkṣita in his *Tattva-kaustubha*, MS. p. 4.)

sect even women and Śūdras. According to the *Aśvalāyana-smṛti*, no one but an outcast would therefore accept the marks recommended by the Pañcarātras. In the fourth chapter of the *Vṛhan-nāradīya-purāṇa* it is said that even for conversing with the Pañcarātrins one would have to go to the Raurava hell. The same prohibition of conversing with the Pañcarātrins is found in the Kūrma-purāṇa, and it is there held that they should not be invited on occasions of funeral ceremonies. Hemādri, quoting from the *Vāyu purāṇa*, says that, if a Brahman is converted into the Pañcarātra religion, he thereby loses all his Vedic rites. The *Liṅga-purāṇa* also regards them as being excommunicated from all religion (*sarva-dharma-vahiṣkṛta*). The *Āditya* and the *Agni-purāṇas* are also extremely strong against those who associate themselves in any way with the Pañcarātrins. The *Viṣṇu*, *Śātātapa*, *Hārīta*, *Bodhāyana* and the *Yama saṃhitās* also are equally strong against the Pañcarātrins and those who associate with them in any way. The Pañcarātrins, however, seem to be more conciliatory to the members of the orthodox Vedic sects. They therefore appear to be a minority sect, which had always to be on the defensive and did not dare revile the orthodox Vedic people. There are some Purāṇas, however, like the *Mahābhārata*, *Bhāgavata* and the *Viṣṇu-purāṇa*, which are strongly in favour of the Pañcarātrins. It is curious, however, to notice that, while some sections of the Purāṇas approve of them, others are fanatically against them. The Purāṇas that are specially favourable to the Pañcarātrins are the *Viṣṇu*, *Nāradīya*, *Bhāgavata*, *Gāruḍa*, *Padma* and *Varāha*, which are called the *Sāttvika purāṇas*[1]. So among the *smṛtis*, the *Vāśiṣṭha*, *Hārīta*, *Vyāsa*, *Pārāśara* and *Kāśyapa* are regarded as the best[2]. The *Pramāṇa-saṃgraha* takes up some of the most important doctrines of the Pañcarātrins and tries to prove their authoritativeness by a reference to the above *Purāṇas* and *smṛtis*, and also to the *Mahābhārata*, the *Gītā*, *Viṣṇudharmottara*, *Prājāpatya-smṛti*, *Itihāsasamuccaya*, *Harivaṃśa*, *Vṛddha-manu*, *Śāṇḍilya-smṛti*, and the *Brahmāṇḍa-purāṇa*.

[1] Thus the *Pramāṇa-saṃgraha* says:

> *vaiṣṇavaṃ nāradīyaṃ ca tathā bhāgavataṃ śubhaṃ*
> *gāruḍaṃ ca tathā pādmaṃ vārāhaṃ śubha-darśane*
> *sāttvikāni purāṇāni vijñeyāni ca ṣaṭpṛthak.*

[2] *Ibid.* p. 14. *Tattva-kaustubha*, MS. p. 13.

The Pañcarātra Literature.

The Pañcarātra literature is somewhat large and only a few works have been printed. The present writer, however, had the opportunity of collecting a large number of manuscripts, and an attempt will here be made to give a brief account of this literature, which, however, has no philosophical importance. One of the most important of these *saṃhitās* is the *Sātvata-saṃhitā*. The *Sātvata* is referred to in the *Mahābhārata*, the *Ahirbudhnya-saṃhitā*, the *Īśvara-saṃhitā* and other *saṃhitās*. In the *Sātvata-saṃhitā* we find that the Lord (*Bhagavān*) promulgates the *Pañcarātra-Śāstra* at the request of Saṃkarṣaṇa on behalf of the sages[1]. It consists of twenty-five chapters which describe the forms of worshipping Nārāyaṇa in all His four *Vyūha* manifestations (*vibhava-devatā*), dress and ornaments, other special kinds of worship, the installation of images and the like. The *Īśvara-saṃhitā* says that the *Ekāyana Veda*, the source of all Vedas, originated with *Vāsudeva* and existed in the earliest age as the root of all the other Vedas, which were introduced at a later age and are therefore called the *Vikāra-veda*. When these *Vikāra-vedas* sprang up and people became more and more worldly-minded, Vāsudeva withdrew the *Ekāyana Veda* and revealed it only to some selected persons, such as Sana, Sanatsujāti, Sanaka, Sanandana, Sanatkumāra, Kapila and Sanātana, who were all called *ekāntins*. Other sages, Marīci, Atri, Āṅgirasa, Pulastya, Pulaha, Kratu, Vasiṣṭha and Svayambhuva, learnt this *Ekāyana* from Nārāyaṇa, and on the basis of it the Pañcarātra literature on the one hand was written, in verse, and the various *Dharma-śāstras* on the other hand were written by Manu and other *ṛṣis*. The Pañcarātra works, such as *Sātvata*, *Pauṣkara*, and *Jayākhya* and other similar texts, were written at the instance of Saṃkarṣaṇa in accordance with the fundamental tenets of the *Ekāyana Veda*, which was almost lost in the later stage. Śāṇḍilya also learnt the principles of the *Ekāyana Veda* from Saṃkarṣaṇa and taught them to the *ṛṣis*. The contents of the *Ekāyana Veda*, as taught by Nārāyaṇa, are called the *Sātvika-śāstra*; those *Śaṣtras* which are partly based on the *Ekāyana Veda* and partly due to the contribution of the sages themselves are called the *Rājasa-Śāstra*; those which are merely the contribution of

[1] Published at Conjeeveram, 1902.

human beings are called the *Tāmasa Śāstra*. The *Rājasa Śāstra* is of two kinds, the *Pañcarātra* and the *Vaikhānasa*. *Sātvata*, *Pauṣkara* and *Jayākhya* were probably the earliest Pañcarātra works written by the sages, and of these again the *Sātvata* is considered the best, as it consists of a dialogue between the Lord and Saṃkarṣaṇa.

The *Īśvara-saṃhitā* consists of twenty-four chapters, of which sixteen are devoted to ritualistic worship, one to the description of images, one to initiation, one to meditation, one to *mantras*, one to expiation, one to methods of self-control, and one to a description of the holiness of the Yādava hill[1]. The chapter on worship is interspersed with philosophical doctrines which form the basis of the Śrīvaiṣnava philosophy and religion.

The *Hayaśīrṣa-saṃhitā* consists of four parts; the first part, called the *Pratiṣṭhā-kāṇḍa*, consists of forty-two chapters; the second, the Saṃkarṣaṇa, of thirty-seven chapters; the third, the *Liṅga*, of twenty chapters; and the fourth, the *Saura-kāṇḍa*, of forty-five chapters[2]. All the chapters deal with rituals concerning the installation of images of various minor gods, the methods of making images and various other kinds of rituals. The *Viṣṇu-tattva-saṃhitā* consists of thirty-nine chapters, and deals entirely with rituals of image-worship, ablutions, the holding of Vaiṣṇava marks, purificatory rites, etc.[2] The *Parama-saṃhitā* consists of thirty-one chapters, dealing mainly with a description of the process of creation, rituals of initiation, and other kinds of worship[3]. In the tenth chapter, however, it deals with *yoga*. In this chapter we hear of *jñāna-yoga* and *karma-yoga*. *Jñāna-yoga* is regarded as superior to *karma-yoga*, though it may co-exist therewith. *Jñāna-yoga* means partly practical philosophy and the effort to control all sense-inclinations by that means. It also includes *samādhi*, or deep concentration, and the practice of *prāṇāyāma*. The word *yoga* is here used in the sense of "joining or attaching oneself to." The man who practises *yoga* fixes his mind on God and by deep meditation detaches himself from all worldly bonds. The idea of *karma-yoga* does not appear to be very clear; but in all probability it means worship of Viṣṇu. The *Parāśara saṃhitā*, which was also available

[1] Published at Conjeeveram, 1921.
[2] It has been available to the present writer only in MS.
[3] This *saṃhitā* has also been available to the present writer only in MS.

only in manuscript, consists of eight chapters dealing with the methods of muttering the name of God.

The *Padma-saṃhitā*, consisting of thirty-one chapters, deals with various kinds of rituals and the chanting of *mantras*, offerings, religious festivities and the like[1]. The *Parameśvara-saṃhitā*, consisting of fifteen chapters, deals with the meditation on *mantras*, sacrifices and methods of ritual and expiation[2]. The *Pauṣkara-saṃhitā*, which is one of the earliest, consists of forty-three chapters, and deals with various kinds of image-worship, funeral sacrifices and also with some philosophical topics[2]. It contains also a special chapter called *Tattva-saṃkhyāna*, in which certain philosophical views are discussed. These, however, are not of any special importance and may well be passed over. The *Prakāśa-saṃhitā* consists of two parts. The first part is called *Parama-tattva-nirṇaya*, and consists of fifteen chapters; the second, called *Para-tattva-prakāśa*, consists of twelve chapters only[2]. The *Mahā-sanatkumāra-saṃhitā*, consisting of four chapters and forty sections in all, deals entirely with rituals of worship[2]. It is a big work, containing ten thousand verses. Its four chapters are called *Brahma-rātra*, *Śiva-rātra*, *Indra-rātra* and *Ṛṣi-rātra*. The *Aniruddha-saṃhitā-mahopaniṣad* contains thirty-four chapters and deals entirely with descriptions of various rituals, methods of initiation, expiation, installation of images, the rules regarding the construction of images, etc.[2] The *Kāśyapa-saṃhitā*, consisting of twelve chapters, deals mainly with poisons and methods of remedy by incantations[2]. The *Vihagendra-saṃhitā* deals largely with meditation on *mantras* and sacrificial oblations and consists of twenty-four chapters. In the twelfth chapter it deals extensively with *prāṇāyāma*, or breath-control, as a part of the process of worship[2]. The *Sudarśana-saṃhitā* consists of forty-one chapters and deals with meditation on *mantras* and expiation of sins. *Agastya-saṃhitā* consists of thirty-two chapters. The *Vasiṣṭha* contains twenty-four chapters, the *Viśvāmitra* twenty-six chapters and the *Viṣṇu-saṃhitā* thirty chapters. They are all in manuscripts and deal more or less with the same subject, namely, ritualistic worship. The *Viṣṇu-saṃhitā* is, however, very much under the influence of Sāṃkhya and holds *Puruṣa* to be all-pervasive. It also invests Puruṣa with dynamic

[1] It has been available to the present writer only in MS.
[2] These works also were available to the present writer only in MS.

activity by reason of which the *prakṛti* passes through evolutionary changes. The five powers of the five senses are regarded as the power of Viṣṇu. The power of Viṣṇu has both a gross and a transcendental form. In its transcendental form it is power as consciousness, power as world-force, power as cause, power by which consciousness grasps its objects and power as omniscience and omnipotence. These five powers in their transcendental forms constitute the subtle body of God. In the thirtieth chapter the *Viṣṇu-saṃhitā* deals with *yoga* and its six accessories (*ṣaḍ-aṅga-yoga*), and shows how the *yoga* method can be applied for the attainment of devotion, and calls it *Bhāgavata-yoga*. It may be noticed that the description of human souls as all-pervasive is against the Śrīvaiṣṇava position. The *aṣṭāṅga yoga* (*yoga* with eight accessories) is often recommended and was often practised by the early adherents of the Śrīvaiṣṇava faith, as has already been explained. The *Mārkaṇḍeya-saṃhitā* consists of thirty-two chapters, speaks of 108 *saṃhitās*, and gives a list of ninety-one *saṃhitās*[1]. The *Viṣvaksena-saṃhitā* consists of thirty-one chapters. It is a very old work and has often been utilized by Rāmānuja, Saumya Jāmātṛ muni and others. The *Hiraṇya-garbha-saṃhitā* consists of four chapters.

Philosophy of the Jayākhya and other Saṃhitās.

The Pañcarātra literature is, indeed, vast, but it has been shown that most of this literature is full of ritualistic details and that there is very little of philosophy in it. The only *saṃhitās* (so far as they are available to us) which have some philosophical elements in them are the *Jayākhya-saṃhitā*, *Ahirbudhnya-saṃhitā*, *Viṣṇu-saṃhitā*, *Vihagendra-saṃhitā*, *Parama-saṃhitā* and *Pauṣkara-saṃhitā*; of these the *Ahirbudhnya* and the *Jayākhya* are the most important.

The *Jaya* starts with the view that merely by performance of the sacrifices, making of gifts, study of the Vedas, and expiatory penances, one cannot attain eternal Heaven or liberation from bondage. Until we can know the ultimate reality (*para-tattva*) which is all-pervasive, eternal, self-realized, pure consciousness, but which through its own will can take forms, there is no hope of salvation. This ultimate reality resides in our hearts and is in itself

[1] These are also in MS. Schrader enumerates them in his *Introduction to Pañcarātra*.

devoid of any qualities (*nir-guṇa*), though it lies hidden by the qualities (*guṇa-guhya*) and is without any name (*a-nāmaka*).

A number of sages approached Śāṇḍilya in the mountain of Gandhamādana with inquiry concerning the manner in which this ultimate reality may be known. Śāṇḍilya in reply said that this science was very secret and very ancient, and that it could be given only to true believers who were ardently devoted to their preceptors. It was originally given to Nārada by Viṣṇu. The Lord Viṣṇu is the object of our approach, but He can be approached only through the scriptures (*Śāstra*); the *Śāstra* can be taught only by a teacher. The teacher therefore is the first and primary means to the attainment of the ultimate reality through the instructions of the scriptures.

The *Jayākhya-saṃhitā* then describes the three kinds of creation, of which the first is called *Brahma-sarga*, which is of a mythological character; it is stated that in the beginning Brahmā was created by Viṣṇu and that he, by his own egoism, polluted the creation which he made and that two demons, Madhu and Kaiṭabha, produced from two drops of sweat, stole away the Vedas and thus created great confusion. Viṣṇu fought with them by His physical energies, but was unsuccessful. He then fought with them by His "*mantra*" energy and thus ultimately destroyed them.

The second creation is that of the evolution of the Sāṃkhya categories. It is said in the *Jayākhya-saṃhitā* that in the *pradhāna* the three *guṇas* exist together in mutual unity. Just as in a lamp the wick, the oil and the fire act together to form the unity of the lamp, so the three *guṇas* also exist together and form the *pradhāna*. Though these *guṇas* are separate, yet in the *pradhāna* they form an inseparable unity (*bhinnam ekātma-lakṣaṇam*). These *guṇas*, however, are separated out from this state of union, and in this order of separation *sattva* comes first, then *rajas* and then *tamas*. From the threefold unity of the *guṇas* the *buddhi-tattva* is evolved, and from this are produced the three kinds of *ahaṃkāra*, *prakāśātmā*, *vikṛtyātmā* and *bhūtātmā*. From the first kind of *ahaṃkāra*, as *taijasa* or as *prakāśātmā*, the five cognitive senses and the *manas* are produced. From the second kind of *ahaṃkāra* the five conative senses are evolved. From the *ahaṃkāra* as *bhūtātmā* the five *bhūta-yoni* or sources of elements (otherwise called the five *tanmātra*) are produced, and from these are derived the five gross elements. The *prakṛti* is unintelligent and material in nature, and so, as may well be expected, the evolution from *prakṛti* is also material in nature. The natural question in this connection is: how can matter begin to produce other material entities? The answer given to this question is that, though both a paddy seed and a piece of rice are material by nature, yet there is productivity in the former, but not in the latter; so, though the *prakṛti* and its evolutes are both material in nature, yet one is produced out of the other. The products of the unintelligent *prakṛti*, being suffused with the glow of the self as pure consciousness, one with Brahman, appear as being endowed with consciousness[1]. Just as a piece of iron becomes endowed with magnetic powers, so the *prakṛti* also becomes endowed with intelligence through its association with the intelligent self in unity with Brahman. The question, however, arises how, since matter and intelligence are as different from each other as light from darkness, there can be any association between the unconscious *prakṛti* and the pure intelligence. To this the reply is that the individual soul (*jīva*) is a product of a beginningless association of *vāsanā* with pure consciousness. For the removal of this *vāsanā* a certain power emanates from Brahman and, impelled by His will, so works within the inner microcosm of man that the pure consciousness in the *jīva* is ultimately freed from the *vāsanā* through the destruction of his *karma*, and he becomes ultimately one with Brahman. The *karma* can bear fruits only when they are associated with their receptacle, the *vāsanā*. The self, or the soul, is brought into association with the *guṇas* by the energy of God, and it can thereby come to know its own *vāsanā*, which are non-intelligent by nature and a product of the *guṇa*[2]. So long as the self is in association with the covering of *māyā* it experiences good and evil. The association of consciousness with matter is thus effected through the manifestation of a special energy of God by which the self is made to undergo the various experiences through its association with *māyā*. As soon as the bond is broken, the self as pure consciousness becomes one with Brahman.

1 *cid-rūpam ātma-tattvaṃ yad abhinnaṃ brahmaṇi sthitaṃ*
tenaitac churitaṃ bhāti acic cinmayavad dvija.
Jayākhya-saṃhitā (MS.), III. 14.

When this section was written the *Jayākhya-saṃhitā* was not published. It has since been published in the Gaekwad's oriental series.

2 *māyāmaye dvijā-dhāre guṇā-dhāre tato jaḍe*
śaktyā saṃyojito hy ātmā vetty ātmīyāś ca vāsanāḥ. *Ibid.* III. 24.

The third creation is the pure creation (*śuddha-sarga*), in which God, otherwise called Vāsudeva, evolved from out of Himself three subsidiary agents, Acyuta, Satya and Puruṣa, which are in reality but one with Him and have no different existence. In His form as Puruṣa God behaves as the inner controller of all ordinary gods, whom He goads and leads to work. And it is in this form that God works in all human beings bound with the ties of *vāsanā*, and directs them to such courses as may ultimately lead them to the cessation of their bondage.

God is pure bliss and self-conscious in Himself. He is the highest and the ultimate reality beyond all, which is, however, self-existent and the support of all other things. He is beginningless and infinite and cannot be designated either as existent or as non-existent (*na sat tan nāsad ucyate*). He is devoid of all *guṇas*, but enjoys the various products of the *guṇas*, and exists both inside and outside us. He is omniscient, all-perceiving, the Lord of all and all are in Him. He combines in Him all energies, and is spontaneous in Himself with all His activities. He pervades all things, but is yet called non-existent because He cannot be perceived by the senses. But, just as the fragrance of flowers can be intuited directly, so God also can be intuited directly[1]. All things are included in His existence and He is not limited either in time or in space. Just as fire exists in a red-hot iron-ball as if it were one therewith, so does God pervade the whole world. Just as things that are imaged on a mirror may in one sense be said to be in it and in another sense to be outside it, so God is in one sense associated with all sensible qualities and in another sense is unassociated therewith. God pervades all the conscious and the unconscious entities, just as the watery juice pervades the whole of the plant[2]. God cannot be known by arguments or proof. His all-pervading existence is as unspeakable and undemonstrable as the existence of fire in wood and butter in milk. He is perceivable only through direct intuition. Just as logs of wood enter into the fire and are lost in it, just as rivers lose themselves in the ocean, so do the Yogins enter into the essence of God. In such circumstances there is difference between the rivers and the ocean into which they fall, yet the dif-

[1] *sva-saṃvedyaṃ tu tad viddhi gandhaḥ puṣpādiko yathā.*
Jayākhya-saṃhitā, IV. 76.

[2] *cetanā-cetanāḥ sarve bhūtāḥ sthāvara-jaṅgamāḥ*
pūritāḥ parameśena rasenauṣadhayo yathā. *Ibid.* IV. 93.

ference cannot be perceived[1]. There is thus both a difference between the waters of the rivers and the ocean and an absence of difference, even as between the devotees of God and God. The doctrine here preached is thus a theory of *bhedābheda* or unity-in-difference.

Brahman is here described as being identical with consciousness, and all objects of knowledge (*jñeya*) are regarded as existing inside the mind[2]. The true knowledge is unassociated with any qualifications, and it can rise only through the process of Yogic practice by those who have learnt to be in union with God[3].

When through the grace of God one begins to realize that all the fruits of actions and all that one does are of the nature of the *guṇas* of *prakṛti*, there dawns the spiritual inquiry within one, as to one's own nature, and as to the nature of the essence of sorrow, and one approaches the true preceptor. When the devotee continues to think of the never-ending cycle of rebirths and the consequent miseries of such transitoriness and other afflictions associated with it, and also undergoes the various bodily disciplines as dictated by his Gurus, and is initiated into the "*mantras*," his mind becomes disinclined to worldly joys and pure like the water in the autumn, or the sea without any ripple, or like a steady lamp unfluttered by the wind. When the pure consciousness dawns in the mind, all possible objects of knowledge, including the ultimate object of knowledge, arise in the mind, and the thought and the object become held together as one, and gradually the Supreme knowledge and cessation that brings "*Nirvāṇa*" are secured. All that is known is in reality one with the thought itself, though it may appear different therefrom. This ultimate state is indescribable through language. It can only be felt and realized intuitively without the application of logical faculty or of the sense-organs. It can be referred to only by means of images. It is transcendental by nature, ultimate and absolutely without any support. It is the mere being which reveals itself in the joy of the soul. Of the two ways of

[1] *sarit-saṃghād yathā toyam saṃpraviṣṭam maho-dadhau*
alakṣyaś co' dake bhedaḥ parasmin yogināṃ tathā.
Jayākhya-saṃhitā, IV. 123.

[2] *brahmā-bhinnaṃ vibhor jñānaṃ śrotum icchāmi tattvataḥ*
yena saṃprāpyate jñeyam antaḥ-karaṇa-saṃsthitam. *Ibid.* IV. 1.

[3] *sarvo'-pādhi-vinirmuktaṃ jñānam ekānta-nirmalam*
utpadyate hi yuktasya yogābhyāsāt krameṇa tat. *Ibid.* V. 2.

Samādhi which proceed through absorptive emotions (*bhāva-jā*) and the way of the practice of *mantras* it is the latter that is the more efficacious. The practice of *mantras* removes all obstacles to self-realization produced by *māyā* and its products.

In describing the emanation of Acyuta, Satya and Puruṣa from Vāsudeva, the *Jayākhya-saṃhitā* holds that such an emanation occurs only naturally and not as a result of a purposive will; and the three entities, Acyuta, Satya and Puruṣa, which evolve out of Vāsudeva, behave as one through mutual reflections, and in this subtle form they exist in the heart of men as the operative energy of God, gradually leading them to their ultimate destination of emancipation and also to the enjoyment of experiences.

The *Jayākhya-saṃhitā* describes knowledge as two-fold, as *sattākhya* (static) and as *kriyākhya* (dynamic). The *kriyākhya-jñāna* involves the moral disciplines of *yama* and *niyama*, and it is by the continual habit and practice of the *kriyākhya-jñāna* of *yama* and *niyama* that the *sattākhya-jñāna*, or wisdom, may attain its final fulfilment. The *yama* and the *niyama* here consist of the following virtues: purity, sacrifice, penance, study of the Vedas, absence of cruelty, and ever-present forgiveness, truthfulness, doing good to all creatures including one's enemies, respect for the property of others, control of mind, disinclination of mind to all things of sensual enjoyment, bestowing gifts upon others according to one's own power, speaking true and kind words, constancy of mind to friends and enemies, straightforwardness, sincerity and mercifulness to all creatures. The equilibrium of the three *guṇas* is called *Avidyā*, which may be regarded as the cause of attachment, antipathy and other defects. *Ātman* is the term used to denote the pure consciousness, as tinged with *guṇas*, *avidyā* and *māyā*.

The position described above leads to the view that God emanates from Himself as His tripartite energy, which forms the inner microcosm of man. It is by virtue of this energy that the pure consciousness in man comes into association with his root-instincts and psychosis in general, by virtue of which the psychical elements, which are themselves unconscious and material, begin to behave as intelligent. It is by virtue of such an association that experience becomes possible. Ultimately, however, the same indwelling energy separates the conscious principle from the unconscious elements and thereby produces emancipation, in which the conscious element of the individual becomes merged in Brahman. The association of the conscious element with the unconscious psychosis, which has evolved from *prakṛti*, is not due to a false imaging of the one or the other, or to an illusion, but to the operative power of the indwelling energy of God, which exists in us. The individual, called also the *Ātman*, is the product of this forced association. When the complex element is disassociated from the psychosis and the root-instincts, it becomes merged in Brahman, of which it is a part and with which it exists in a state of unity-in-difference. The difference between this view and that of the *Sāṃkhya* is that, though it admits in general the Sāṃkhya view of evolution of the categories from *prakṛti*, yet it does not admit the theory of *Puruṣa* and the transcendental illusion of *Puruṣa* and *prakṛti*, which is to be found in the classical Sāṃkhya of Īśvara kṛṣṇa. There is no reference here to the teleology in *prakṛti* which causes its evolution, or to the view that the *prakṛti* is roused to activity by God or by *Puruṣa*. *Prakṛti* is supposed here to possess a natural productive power of evolving the categories from out of itself.

The *Jayākhya-saṃhitā* speaks of the devotee as a *yogin* and holds that there are two ways of arriving at the ultimate goal, one through absorptive trance, and the other through the practice of concentration on the *mantras*. In describing the process of *Yoga*, it holds that the *yogin* must be a man who has his senses within his absolute control and who is devoid of antipathy to all beings. Full of humility, he should take his seat in a lonely place and continue the practice of *prāṇāyāma* for the control of mind. The three processes of *prāṇāyāma*, viz. *pratyāhāra*, *dhyāna*, and *dhāraṇā*, are described. Then, Yoga is stated to be of three kinds, *prākṛta*, *pauruṣa* and *aiśvarya*, the meaning of which is not very clear. It may, however, be the meditation on *prakṛti*'s ultimate principle, or on *Puruṣa*, or the Yoga, which is intended for the attainment of miraculous power. Four kinds of *āsanas* are described, namely, that of *Paryaṃka*, *Kamala*, *Bhadra* and *Svastika*. The Yogic posture is also described. The control of the mind, which again is regarded as the chief aim of yoga, may be of two kinds, namely, of those tendencies of mind which are due to environments and of those that are constitutional to the mind. It is by increasing the *sattva* quality of the mind that it can be made to fix itself upon an object. In another classification we hear of three kinds of *yoga*, *sakala niṣkala* and *Viṣṇu*, or *sabda*, *vyoma* and *sa-vigraha*. In the *sakala* or the *sa-vigraha* type of *yoga* the *yogin* concentrates his mind on the gross idol of the deity; and then gradually, as he becomes habituated, he concentrates his mind on the notion of a glowing circular disc; then on the dimension of a pea; then on the dimension of a horse-hair; then on a human hair of the head; then on the human hair of the body; and as a consequence of the perfection of this practice the path of the *brahma-randhra* opens up for him. In the *niṣkala* type of *yoga* the *yogin* meditates upon the ultimate reality, with the result that his own essence as Brahman is revealed to him. The third form consists in the meditation on the *mantras*, by which course also the ultimate reality is revealed to the *yogin*. Through the process of the *yoga* the *yogin* ultimately passes out by the channel of his *brahma-randhra* and leaves his body, after which he attains unity with the ultimate reality, Vāsudeva[1].

In the fourth chapter of the *Viṣṇu-Saṃhitā* (Manuscript) the three *guṇas* are supposed to belong to *Prakṛti*, which, with its evolutes, is called *Kṣetra*, God being called *Kṣetrajña*[2]. The *prakṛti* and God exist together as it were in union[3]. The *prakṛti* produces all existences and withdraws them within it in accordance with the direction or the superintendence of the *Puruṣa*[4], though it seems to behave as an independent agent. *Puruṣa* is described as an all-pervading conscious principle.

The *Viṣṇu-saṃhitā*, after describing the three kinds of egoism as *sāttvika*, *rājasa* and *tāmasa*, speaks of the *rājasa ahaṃkāra* not only as evolving the conative senses but also as being the active principle directing all our cognitive and conative energies. As the cognitive energy, it behaves both as attention directed to sense-perception and also to reflection involving synthetic and analytic activities. The *Viṣṇu-saṃhitā* speaks further of the five powers of God, by which the Lord, though absolutely qualityless in Himself, reveals Himself through all the sensible qualities. It is probably in this way that all the powers of *prakṛti* exist in God, and it is in this

[1] *Jayākhya-saṃhitā*, Ch. 33. In Ch. 34 the process of *yoga* by which the *yogin* gradually approaches the stage of the final destruction of his body is described.

[2] *kṣetrākhyā prakṛtir jñeyā tad-vit kṣetra-jña īśvaraḥ.*
Viṣṇu-saṃhitā, IV.

[3] *ubhayaṃ cedam atyantam abhinnam iva tiṣṭhati.* *Ibid.*

[4] *tan-niyogāt svatantreva sūte bhāvān haraty api.* *Ibid.*

sense that the *kṣetra* or the *prakṛti* is supposed to be *abhinna*, or one with God. These powers are (1) *cic-chakti*[1], that is, power of consciousness, which is the unchangeable ground of all works. Second is His power as the enjoyer, or *puruṣa*. The third power is the causal power, manifested as the manifold universe. The fourth power is the power by which sense-objects are grasped and comprehended in knowledge. The fifth power is that which resolves knowledge into action. The sixth power is the power that reveals itself as the activity of thought and action[2]. It seems, therefore, that what has been described above as *puruṣa*, or enjoyer, is not a separate principle, but the power of God; just as *prakṛti* itself is not a separate principle, but a manifestation of the power of God.

The process of *Bhāgavata-yoga* described in *Viṣṇu-saṃhitā* consists primarily of a system of bodily and moral control, involving control of the passions of greed, anger, etc., the habit of meditation in solitary places, the development of a spirit of dependence on God, and self-criticism. When, as a result of this, the mind becomes pure and disinclined to worldly things, there arises an intellectual and moral apprehension of the distinction of what is bad and impure from what is good and pure, whence attachment, or *bhakti*, is produced. Through this attachment one becomes self-contented and loyal to one's highest goal and ultimately attains true knowledge. The process of *prāṇāyāma*, in which various kinds of meditations are prescribed, is also recommended for attainment of the ultimate union with God, which is a state of emancipation. The view here taken of *bhakti*, or devotion, shows that *bhakti* is used here in the simple sense of inclination to worship, and the means to the fruition of this worship is *yoga*. The so-called *bhakti*-school of the Bhāgavatas was so much under the influence of the *yoga*-system that a *bhakta* was required to be a *yogin*, since *bhakti* by itself was not regarded as a sufficient means to the attainment of salvation. In the tenth chapter of the *Parama-saṃhitā* the process of *yoga* is described in a conversation between Brahmā and Parama. It is said there that the knowledge attained by *yoga* is better than any other

1 *cic-chaktiḥ sarva-kāryābdiḥ kūṭasthaḥ parameṣṭhy asau*
dvitīyā tasya yā śaktiḥ puruṣākhyādi-vikriyā
viśvā'-khyā vividhā-bhāsā tṛtīyā karuṇā'-tmikā
caturthī viṣayaṃ prāpya nivṛtty-ākhyā tathā punaḥ. *Viṣṇu-saṃhitā.*

2 *pūrvā-jñāna-kriyā-śaktiḥ sarvākhyā tasya pañcamī.* *Ibid.*

3 *tasmāt sarva-prayatnena bhākto yogī bhavet sadā.* *Ibid.* Ch. 30.

kind of knowledge. When deeds are performed without *yoga* wisdom, they can hardly bring about the desired fruition. *Yoga* means the peaceful union of the mind with any particular object[1]. When the mind is firmly fixed on the performance of the deed, it is called *karma-yoga*[2]. When the mind is unflinchingly fixed on knowledge, it is called *jñāna-yoga*[3]. He, however, who clings to the Lord Viṣṇu in both these ways attains ultimately supreme union with the highest Lord. Both the *jñāna-yoga* and the *karma-yoga*, as the moral discipline of *yama* and *niyama* on the one hand and *vairāgya* (disinclination) and *samādhi* on the other, are ultimately supported in Brahman. It may be remembered that in the *Gītā*, *karma-yoga* means the performance of the scriptural caste-duties without any desire for their fruits. Here, however, the *karma-yoga* means *yama* and *niyama*, involving *vrata*, fasting (*upavāsa*) and gifts (*dāna*), and probably also some of the virtues of diverse kinds of self-control. The term *vairāgya* means the wisdom by which the senses are made to desist from their respective objects; and the term *samādhi* means the wisdom by which the mind stays unflinchingly in the Supreme Lord. When the senses are through *vairāgya* restrained from their respective objects, the mind has to be fixed firmly on the Supreme Lord, and this is called *yoga*. Through continual practice, as the *vairāgya* grows firm, the *vāsanās*, or the root-instincts and desires, gradually fall off. It is advised that the *yogin* should not make any violent attempt at self-control, but should proceed slowly and gently, so that he may, through a long course of time, be able to bring his mind under complete control. He should take proper hygienic care of himself as regards food and other necessities for keeping the body sound and should choose a lonely place, free from all kinds of distractions, for his *yoga* practice. He should not on any account indulge in any kind of practice which may be painful to his body. He should further continue to think that he is dependent on God and that birth, existence and destruction are things which do not belong to him. In this way the pure *bhakti* will rise in his mind,

1 *yat karoti samādhānaṃ cittasya viṣaye kvacit*
anukūlam a-saṃkṣobhaṃ saṃyoga iti kīrtyate.
Parama-saṃhitā, Ch. 10 (MS.).

2 *yadi karmāṇi badhnanti cittam askhalitaṃ naram*
karma-yogo bhavaty eṣaḥ sarva-pāpa-praṇāśanaḥ. *Ibid.*

3 *yadi tu jnāna evārthe cittaṃ badhnāti nirvyathaḥ*
jñāna-yogaḥ sa vijñeyaḥ sarva-siddhi-karaḥ śubhaḥ. *Ibid.*

through which he will gradually be able to extract the root of attachment. He should also train himself to think of the evils of alluring experiences which have not yet been enjoyed, and he should thus desist from attaching himself to such experiences.

As regards the preference of *karma-yoga* to *jñāna-yoga* and *vice versa*, the view maintained here is that there can be no rule as regards the preference. There are some who are temperamentally fitted for *karma-yoga* and others for *jñāna-yoga*. Those who are of a special calibre should unite both courses, *karma-yoga* and *jñāna-yoga*.

Philosophy of the Ahirbudhnya-saṃhitā.

In the *Ahirbudhnya-saṃhitā* Ahirbudhnya says that after undergoing a long course of penance he received from Saṃkarṣaṇa true knowledge and that this true knowledge was the science of Sudarśana, which is the support of all things in the world[1]. The ultimate reality is the beginningless, endless and eternal reality, which is devoid of all names and forms, beyond all speech and mind, the omnipotent whole which is absolutely changeless. From this eternal and unchangeable reality there springs a spontaneous idea or desire (*saṃkalpa*). This Idea is not limited by time, space or substance. Brahman is of the nature of intuition, of pure and infinite bliss (*niḥsīma-sukhānubhava-lakṣaṇa*), and He resides everywhere and in all beings. He is like the waveless sea. He has none of the worldly qualities which we find in mundane things. He is absolutely self-realized and complete in Himself, and cannot be defined by any expressions such as "this" or "such." He is devoid of all that is evil or bad and the abode of all that is blissful and good. The Brahman is known by many names, such as "*paramātman*," "*ātman*," "*bhagavān*," "*vāsudeva*," "*avyakta*," "*prakṛti*," "*pradhāna*," etc. When by true knowledge the virtues and sins accumulated during many lives are destroyed, when the root-instincts or tendencies called *vāsanā* are torn asunder and the three *guṇas* and their products cease to bind a person, he directly realizes the nature of Brahman or the absolute reality, which can neither be described

[1] *sudarśana-svarūpaṃ tat procyamānaṃ mayā śṛṇu*
śrute yatrā' khilādhāre saṃśayās te na santi vai.
Ahirbudhnya-saṃhitā, III. 2. 5.

nor defined by language as "this" or as "such." The Brahman intuitively perceives all things and is the soul of all, and therefore, the past, present and the future have all vanished away from Him. Brahman does not exist therefore in time, as He is beyond time. Similarly He is beyond all primary and secondary qualities, and yet he possesses the six qualities. Of the qualities knowledge is regarded as the first and the foremost. It is spiritual and self-illuminating; it enters into all things and reflects them, and is eternal. The essence of Brahman is pure consciousness, and yet He is regarded as possessing knowledge as a quality[1]. The power (*śakti*) of Brahman is regarded as that by which He has originated the world[2]. The spontaneous agency (*kartṛtva*) of God is called His majesty (*aiśvarya*). His strength (*bala*) is that by virtue of which He is never fatigued in His untiring exertion. His energy (*vīrya*) is that by virtue of which, being the material cause of the world, He yet remains unchanged in Himself. His self-sufficiency (*tejas*) is that by virtue of which He creates the world by His own unaided efforts. These five qualities are, however, all regarded as qualities of knowledge, and knowledge alone is regarded as the essence of God. When such a Brahman, which is of the nature of knowledge and is endowed with all qualities, resolves Himself into the idea of splitting Himself into the many, it is called Sudarśana.

The powers of all things are in themselves of an unspeakable nature and cannot exist separately (*a-pṛthak-sthita*) from the substances in which they inhere. They are the potential or subtle states of the substance itself, which are not perceived separately in themselves and cannot be defined as "this" or "not this" in any way, but can only be known from their effects[3]. So God has in Him the power (*śakti*) which exists as undifferentiated from Him, as the moonbeam from the moon. It is spontaneous, and the universe is but a manifestation of this power. It is called bliss (*ānanda*), be-

1 *ajaḍaṃ svā-tma-saṃbodhi nityaṃ sarvā-vagāhanaṃ*
jñānaṃ nāma guṇaṃ prāhuh prathamaṃ guṇa-cintakāḥ
svarūpaṃ brahmaṇas tac ca guṇaś ca parigīyate.
Ahirbudhnya-saṃhitā, III. 2. 53.

2 *jagat-prakṛti-bhāvo yaḥ sā śaktiḥ parikīrtitā* *Ibid.* 2. 57.

3 *śaktayaḥ sarva-bhāvānām acintyā a-pṛthak-sthitāḥ*
svarūpe naiva dṛśyante dṛśyante kāryatas tu tāḥ
sūkṣmāvasthā hi sā teṣāṃ sarva-bhāvā-nugāminī
idantayā vidhātuṃ sā na niṣeddhuṃ ca śakyate. *Ibid.* 2, 3.

cause it does not depend on anything (*nirapekṣatayānanda*); it is eternal (*nitya*), because it is not limited in time; it is complete (*pūrṇa*), because it is not limited by any form; it manifests itself as the world and is therefore called *Lakṣmī*[1]. It contracts itself into the form of the world and is therefore called *Kuṇḍalinī*; and it is called *Viṣṇu-śakti* because it is the supreme power of God. The power is in reality different from Brahman; but yet it appears as one therewith. With this power He is always engaged in an eternal act of creation, untired, unfatigued, and unaided by any other agent (*satataṃ kurvato jagat*)[2]. The power of God manifests itself in two ways, as static entities such as *avyakta*, *kāla* and *puruṣa* and as activity. *Śakti*, or power of God as activity (*kriyā*), is spontaneous and of the nature of will and thought resulting in action[3]. This is also called *saṃkalpa*, or the Idea, which is irresistible in its movement whereby it produces all material objects and spiritual entities, such as *avyakta*, *kāla* and *puruṣa*[4]. It is this power, which is otherwise designated as *lakṣmī* or *viṣṇu-śakti*, that impels the *avyakta* into the course of evolution, and the *puruṣa* to confront the products of *prakṛti* and run through the experiences. When it withdraws these functions from these entities, there is *pralaya* or dissolution. It is by the force of this power that at the time of creation the *prakṛti* as the composite of the three *guṇas* is urged into creative evolution. The association of the *puruṣa* with the *prakṛti* also is brought about by the same power. This Idea is vibratory by nature and assumes diverse forms, and thus by its various transformations produces various categories[5].

In the original state all the manifold world of creation was asleep, as it were, in an equilibrium in which all the qualities of God were completely suspended, like the sea when there are no waves ruffling its breast. This power, which exists in an absolutely static or suspended state, is pure vacuity or nothingness (*śūnyatva-rūpiṇī*); for it has no manifestation of any kind. It is self-dependent

[1] *jagattayā lakṣyamāṇā sā lakṣmīr iti gīyate.* *Ahirbudhnya-saṃhitā*, III. 9.

[2] *Ibid.* II. 59.

[3] *svātantrya-mūla icchā-tmā prekṣā-rūpaḥ kriyā-phalaḥ.*
Ibid. III. 30.

[4] *unmeṣo yaḥ susaṃkalpaḥ sarvatrāvyāhataḥ kṛtau*
avyakta-kāla-puṃ-rūpāṃ cetanācetanātmikām. *Ibid.* III. 30, 31.

[5] *so'yaṃ sudarśanaṃ nāma saṃkalpaḥ spandanā-tmakaḥ*
vibhajya bahudhā rūpaṃ bhāve bhāve'vatiṣṭhate. *Ibid.* III. 39.

and no reason can be assigned as to why it suddenly changes itself from a potential to an actual state[1]. It is one and exists in identity with the Brahman, or the ultimate reality. It is this power which creates as its own transformation all categories pure and impure and all material forms as emanations from out of itself. It manifests itself as the *kriyā*, the *vīrya*, *tejas* and the *bala* of God, mere forms of its own expression and in all forms of duality as subject and object, as matter and consciousness, pure and impure, the enjoyer and the enjoyed, the experiencer and the experienced, and so on. When it moves in the progressive order, there is the evolutionary creation; and, when it moves in the inverse order, there is involution.

From a pair of two different functions of this power the different forms of pure creation come into being. Thus from knowledge (*jñāna*) and the capacity for unceasing work of never-ending creation (*bala*) we have the spiritual form of Saṃkarṣaṇa. From the function of spontaneous agency (*aiśvarya*) and the unaffectedness in spite of change (*vīrya*) is generated the spiritual form of Pradyumna; and from the power that transforms itself into the world-forms (*śakti*) and the non-dependence on accessories (*tejas*) is produced the form as Aniruddha. These three spiritual forms are called *vyūha* (conglomeration) because each of them is the resultant of the conglomeration of a pair of *guṇas*. Though the two *guṇas* predominate in each *vyūha*, yet each *vyūha* possesses the six qualities (*ṣaḍ-guṇa*) of the Lord; for these are all but manifestations of Viṣṇu[2]. Each of these forms existed for 1600 years before the next form emanated from it, and at the time of the involution also it took 1600 years for each lower form to pass into the higher form. Schrader, alluding to the *Mahā-Sanatkumāra-Saṃhitā*, says: "Vāsudeva creates from His mind the white goddess Śānti and together with her Saṃkarṣaṇa or Śiva; then from the left side of the latter is born the red goddess Śrī, whose son is Pradyumna or Brahman; the latter, again, creates the yellow Sarasvatī and to-

1 *tasya staimitya-rūpā yā śaktiḥ śūnyatva-rūpinī*
svātantryād eva kasmāc cit kvacit sonmeṣam ṛcchati
ātma-bhūtā hi yā śaktiḥ parasya brahmaṇo hareḥ.
Ahirbudhnya-saṃhitā, v. 3 and 4.

2 *vyāpti-mātraṃ guṇo' nmeṣo mūrtti-kāra iti tridhā*
cātur-ātmya-sthitir viṣṇor guṇa-vyatikaro-dbhavā. *Ibid.* v. 21.

gether with her Aniruddha or Puruṣottama, whose Śakti becomes the black Rati, who is the threefold *Māyā-kośa*."[1] Schrader further draws attention to the fact that these couples are all outside the *brahmāṇḍa* and are therefore different in nature from the mundane gods, such as Śiva, etc. The *vyūhas* are regarded as fulfilling three different functions, (1) the creation, maintenance and destruction of the world; (2) the protection of the mundane beings; and (3) lending assistance to those devotees who seek to attain the ultimate emancipation. Saṃkarṣaṇa exists as the deity superintending all the individual souls and separates them from the *prakṛti*[2]. The second spiritual form superintends the minds (*manas*) of all beings and gives specific instruction regarding all kinds of religious performances. He is also responsible for the creation of all human beings and from among them such beings as have from the beginning dedicated their all to God and become absolutely attached to Him[3]. As Aniruddha, he protects the world and leads men to the ultimate attainment of wisdom. He is also responsible for the creation of the world, which is an admixture of good and evil (*miśra-varga-sṛṣṭiṃ ca karoti*)[4]. These three forms are in reality but one with Vāsudeva. These *avatāras* are thus the pure *avatāras* of Viṣṇu.

In addition to these there are two other forms of manifestation, called *āveśāvatāra* and *sākṣād-avatāra*. The former is of two kinds, *svarūpāveśa* (as in the case of *avatāras* like Paraśurāma, Rāma, etc.) and *śakty-āveśa* (as the influx of certain special functions or powers of God, e.g. in the case of Brahmā or Śiva, who are on special occasions endowed with certain special powers of God). These secondary *āveśāvatāras* are by the will of God produced in the form of human beings, as Rāma, Kṛṣṇa, in the form of animals, as the Boar, the Fish and the Man-lion, or even as a tree (the crooked mango tree in the Daṇḍaka forest). These forms are not the original transcendental forms of God, but manifest divine functions

[1] Introduction to the *Pañcarātra* by Schrader, p. 36.

[2] *so'yaṃ samasta-jīvānām adhiṣṭhātṛtayā sthitaḥ*
saṃkarṣaṇas tu deveśo jagat sṛṣṭi-manās tataḥ
jīva-tattvam adhiṣṭhāya prakṛtes tu vivicya tat.

Quoted from *Viṣvaksena-saṃhitā* from Varavara's commentary on Lokācārya's *Tattva-traya*, p. 125.

[3] See quotations from *Viṣvaksena-saṃhitā* in *Tattva-traya*, pp. 126, 127.

[4] *Ibid.* p. 128.

through the will of God[1]. The primary forms (*ṣākṣād-avatāra*) of incarnation are derived directly from the part of the Lord just as a lamp is lighted from another, and they are thus of a transcendent and non-mundane nature. Those who seek to attain liberation should worship these transcendent forms, but not the others[2]. The *Viṣvaksena-saṃhitā* quoted in the *Tattva-traya* considers Brahman, Śiva, Buddha, Vyāsa, Arjuna, Pāvaka and Kuvera as inspired persons or *āveśāvatāras* who should not be worshipped by those who seek liberation. Another *saṃhitā* quoted there includes Rāma, Ātreya and Kapila in the list.

Again, from each *vyūha* three subsidiary *vyūhas* are said to appear. Thus from Vāsudeva we have, Keśava, Nārāyaṇa, and Mādhava; from Saṃkarṣaṇa arise Govinda, Viṣṇu and Madhusūdana; from Pradyumna arise Trivikrama, Vāmana and Śrīdhara, and from Aniruddha arise Hṛṣīkeśa, Padmanābha and Dāmodara. These are regarded as the deities superintending each month, representing the twelve suns in each of the *rāśis*. These gods are conceived for purposes of meditation. In addition to these, thirty-nine *vibhava* (manifesting) *avatāras* (incarnations) also are counted in the *Ahirbudhnya-saṃhitā*[3]. The objects for which these incarnations are made are described by Varavara as, firstly, for giving com-

[1] *mad-icchayā hi gauṇatvaṃ manuṣyatvam ive'cchayā...a-prākṛta-svā-sādhāraṇa-vigraheṇa saha nāgatam...gauṇasya manuṣyatvā-divad aprākṛta-divya-saṃsthānam itara-jātīyaṃ kṛtvā avatāra-rūpatvā-bhāvāt sva-rūpeṇa nā' gatam iti siddham.* Tattva-traya, p. 130.

[2] *prādurbhāvās tu mukhyā ye mad-aṃśatvād viśeṣataḥ*
ajahat-svabhāvā vibhavā divyā-prākṛta-vigrahāḥ
dīpād dīpā ivotpannā jagato rakṣaṇāya te
arcyā eva hi seneśa saṃsṛty-uttaraṇāya te
mukhyā upāsyāḥ seneśa anarcyān itarān viduḥ.

Ibid. p. 131.

[3] *Ahirbudhnya-saṃhitā*, p. 46. According to the *Viṣvaksena-saṃhitā* all the *avatāras* have come straight from Aniruddha or through other *avatāras*. Thus Brahman comes from Aniruddha and from him Maheśvara; Hayaśīrṣa comes from Matsya, a manifestation of Kṛṣṇa. According to the *Padma-tantra*, Matsya, Kūrma and Varāha come from Vāsudeva, Nṛsiṃha, Vāmana, Śrīrāma, and Paraśurāma from Saṃkarṣaṇa, Balarāma from Pradyumna and Kṛṣṇa and Kalki from Aniruddha (*Padma-tantra*, I. 2. 31, etc.). But according to the *Lakṣmī-tantra* (II. 55) all the *vibhavas* come from Aniruddha. There is another kind of *avatāra*, called *arcāvatāra*. The image of Kṛṣṇa, Nṛsiṃha, etc., when duly consecrated according to the *Vaiṣṇava* rites, becomes possessed with the power of Viṣṇu and attains powers and influences which can be experienced by the devotee (*Viṣvaksena-saṃhitā*, quoted in *Tattva-traya*). In the aspect in which Aniruddha controls all beings as their inner controller, he is regarded as the *antaryāmy-avatāra*. There are thus four kinds of *avatāras*, *vibhava*, *āveśa*, *arcā* and *antaryāmin*. The thirty-nine *vibhava avatāras* are Padmanābha, Dhruva, Ananta,

panionship in mundane forms to those saints who cannot live without it, and this is the interpretation of the word *paritrāṇa* (protection) in the *Gītā*; secondly, for destroying those who are opposed to the saints; thirdly, for establishing the Vedic religion, the essence of which is devotion to God[1].

In the form as *antaryāmin*, or the inner controller, the Lord resides in us as the inner controller of the self, and it is through His impulsion that we commit evil deeds and go to Hell or perform good deeds and go to Heaven. Thus we cannot in any way escape

Śaktyātman, Madhusūdana, Vidyādhideva, Kapila, Viśvarūpa, Vihaṅgama, Kroḍātman, Vaḍavāvaktra, Dharma, Vāgīśvara, Ekārṇavaśāyin, Kamaṭheśvara, Varāha, Narasiṃha, Pīyūṣaharaṇa, Śrīpati, Kāntātman, Rāhujit, Kālanemighna, Pārijātahara, Lokanātha, Śāntātman, Dattātreya, Nyagrodhaśāyin, Ekaśṛṅgatanu, Vāmanadeva, Trivikrama, Nara, Nārāyaṇa, Hari, Kṛṣṇa, Paraśurāma, Rāma, Vedavid, Kalkin, Pātālaśayana. They are of the nature of *tejas* and are objects of worship and meditation in their specific forms, as described in the *Sātvata-saṃhitā* (XII), or in the *Ahirbudhya-saṃhitā* (LXVI). In the Nārāyaṇīya section of the *Mahābhārata* Vihaṅgama or Haṃsa, Kamaṭheśvara or Kūrma, Ekaśṛṅgatanu or Matsya, Varāha, Nṛsiṃha, Vāmana, Paraśurāma, Rāma, Vedavid and Kalkin are mentioned as the ten *avatāras*. The *avatāra* Kroḍātman, Lokanātha and Kāntātman are sometimes spoken of as Yajña Varāha, Manu Vaivasvata and Kāma respectively. The latter is sometimes spoken of probably as Dhanvantari (see Schrader's Pañcarātra, p. 45). The twenty-three *avatāras* spoken of in the *Bhāgavata-purāṇa* (I. 3) are all included in the above list. It is, however, doubtful whether Vāgīśvara is the same as Hayaśīrṣa, and Śāntātman as Sanaka or Nārada, as Schrader says. The *vibhava-avatāras* mentioned in Rūpa's *Laghu-bhāgavatāmṛta* are mostly included in the above list, though some names appear in slightly different form. Following the *Brahma-saṃhitā*, Rūpa, however, regards Kṛṣṇa as the real form (*svayaṃ-rūpa*) of God. According to him, being one with God, He may have His manifestations in diverse forms. This is called *avatāra* as *ekātma-rūpa*. This *ekātma-rūpa-avatāra* may again be of two kinds, *sva-vilāsa* and *svā-ṃśa*. When the *avatāra* is of the same nature as the Lord in powers and other qualities, He is called a *svāṃśā-vatāra*. Thus, Vāsudeva is called a *sva-vilāsa-avatāra*. But when the *avatāra* has inferior powers, He is called a *śvā-ṃśa-avatāra*. Saṃkarṣaṇa, Pradyumna, Aniruddha, Matsya, Kūrma, etc., are thus called *svā-ṃśa-avatāra*. When God, however, infuses one only with parts of His qualities, he is called an *āveśa-avatāra*. Nārada, Sanaka, etc., are called *āveśa-avatāras*. The manifestation of the Lord in the above forms for the good of the world is called *avatāra*.

pūrvo-kta-viśva-kāryā-rthām a-pūrvā iva cet svayam
dvārā-ntareṇa vā' viḥ-syur avatārās tadā smṛtāḥ
Laghu-bhāgavatāmṛta, p. 22.

The *aṃśāvatāra* is sometimes called *puruṣāvatāra*, while the manifestation of special qualities as in Brahmā, Viṣṇu, Śiva, etc., is called *guṇāvatāras*. The *vibhavāvatāras* are generally regarded as *līlāvatāras*; *vide* also *Sātvata-saṃhitā*, Ch. IX (77–84) and Ch. XII.

[1] *Tattva-traya*, p. 138. The word *sādhu* is here defined as "*nirmatsarāḥ mat-samāśrayaṇe pravṛttāḥ man-nāma-karma-svarūpāṇāṃ vāṅ-manasā-gocaratayā mad-darśanena vinā ātma-dhāraṇa-poṣaṇādikam alabhamānāḥ kṣaṇa-mātra-kālaṃ kalpa-sahasraṃ manvānāḥ praśithila-sarva-gātrā bhaveyuḥ.*"

from this inner controller. In another of His forms He stays within our heart as the object of our meditation[1]. Again, when certain images are made of earth, stone, or metals, and they are properly installed with proper ceremonials, these are inspired with the presence of God and with His special powers. These are called *arcāvatāras*, or image-incarnations, for purposes of worship by which all desirable ends may be achieved. There are thus five kinds of existence for the Lord: firstly as his absolute state (*para*), secondly as *vyūha*, thirdly as *vibhavāvatāra* (primary and secondary), fourthly as *antaryāmin*, and fifthly as *arcāvatāra*[2].

In the *Ahirbudhnya-saṃhitā* we hear also that by the power of *sudarśana*, or the divine Idea (by the activity of which the *vyūha* forms are produced), a divine location is produced which is of the nature of knowledge and bliss radiant with its (*sudarśana's*) glow. All the experiences that are enjoyed here are blissful in their nature, and the denizens of this transcendent spiritual world who experience them are also blissful in their nature, and their bodies are constituted of knowledge and bliss[3]. The denizens of this world are souls emancipated in the last cycle. They remain attached, however, to the form of the deity to which they were attached in the mundane life[4].

The Lord in the highest form is always associated with His power (*Śakti*) Lakṣmī or Śrī[5]. In the *Tattva-traya* and its commentary by Varavara we hear of three consort deities, Lakṣmī, Bhūmi and Nīlā. Schrader points out that these deities are identified (in the *Vihagendra-saṃhitā* and in the *Sītā-upaniṣad*) with will (*icchā*), action (*Kriyā*), and the direct manifesting power (*sākṣāt-śakti*). In the *Sītā-upaniṣad*, to which Schrader refers, *Sītā* is described as the Mahālakṣmī which exists in the three forms, *icchā*, *jñāna* and *kriyā*. Sītā is there regarded as the power which exists different from, and as one with, the supreme Lord, constituting within herself all the conscious and unconscious entities of the universe. It exists also in three forms as Lakṣmī, Bhūmi and

[1] *Tattva-traya*, 139, 140.

[2] See quotation from *Viṣvaksena-saṃhitā* quoted in *Tattva-traya*, p. 122.

[3] *śuddhā pūrvoditā sṛṣṭir yā sā vyūhā-di-bhedinī*
sudarśanā-khyāt saṃkalpāt tasya eva prabho-jjvalā.
jñānānandamayī styānā deśa-bhāvaṃ vrajaty' uta
sa deśaḥ paramaṃ vyoma nirmalaṃ puruṣāt param, etc.
Ahirbudhnya-saṃhitā, VI. 21–22.

[4] *Ibid.* VI. 29.

[5] *Ibid.* VI. 25.

Nīlā, as benediction, power, and as the Sun, the Moon and Fire. The third form is responsible for the development of all kinds of vegetation and all temporal determinations[1].

In the sixth chapter of the *Ahirbudhnya-saṃhitā* the intermediate creation is described. It is said there that the power of God as the supreme ego is at once one and different from Him. The Lord cannot exist without His power nor can the power exist without Him. These two are regarded as the ultimate cause of the world. The manifestations that are revealed as the *vyūhas* and the *vibhavas* are regarded as pure, for through their meditations the *yogins* attain their desired end[2]. From the *vyūha* and the *vibhava* proceed the impure creation (*śuddhetarā-sṛṣṭi*)[3]. Power is of two kinds, i.e. power as activity, and power as determinants of being or existence (*bhūti-śakti*). This *bhūti-śakti* may be regarded as a moving Idea (*saṃkalpamayī mūrti*). The process of activity inherent in it may be regarded as manifesting itself in the form of ideas or concepts actualizing themselves as modes of reality. The impure creation is of a threefold nature as *puruṣa*, *guṇa* and *kāla* (time). *Puruṣa* is regarded as a unity or colony of pairs of males and females of the four castes, and these four pairs emanate from the mouth, breast, thighs and legs of Pradyumna. From the forehead, eyebrows, and ears of Pradyumna also emanate the subtle causal state of time and the *guṇas* (*sūkṣma-kāla-guṇā-vasthā*). After the emanation of these entities the work of their growth and development was left to Aniruddha, who by the fervour of his Yoga evolved the original element of time in its twofold form as *kāla* and *niyati*. He also evolved the original energy as *guṇa* into the three forms of *sattva*,

[1] Certain peculiar interpretations of the *icchā-śakti*, *kriyā-śakti* and *sākṣāt-śakti* are to be found in the *Sītā-upaniṣad*. The *Sātvata-saṃhitā* (IX. 85) describes twelve other energies such as

lakṣmīḥ, puṣṭir, dayā nidrā, kṣamā, kāntis sarasvatī,
dhṛtir maitrī ratis tuṣṭir matir dvādaśāmī smṛtā.

See also Schrader's Introduction to Pañcarātra, p. 55. The theory of these energies is associated with the *avatāra* theory.

[2] Schrader, on the evidence of *Padma-tantra*, says that god as *para* or ultimate is sometimes identified with and sometimes distinguished from the *vyūha* Vāsudeva. The *para* Vāsudeva becomes *vyūha* Vāsudeva with His one half and remains as Nārāyaṇa, the creator of the primeval water (*māyā*). Pañcarātra, p. 53.

[3] *bhūtiḥ śuddhetarā viṣṇoḥ puruṣo dvi-caturmayaḥ*
sa manūnāṃ samāhāro brahma-kṣattrādi-bhedinām.
Ahirbudhnya-saṃhitā, VI. 8–9.

rajas and *tamas* in succession, i.e. the original primeval energy as *guṇa* (called sometimes *prakṛti* in cognate literature) was first evolved into *sattva guṇa*; from it evolved the *rajas*, and from the *rajas* evolved the *tamas*. This original undeveloped *guṇa* produced from Pradyumna (which, in other words, may be termed *prakṛti*) receives impregnation from the fervour of Aniruddha, and thereby evolves itself first into *sattva*, then into *rajas*, and then into *tamas*. This doctrine can therefore be regarded as *sat-kārya-vāda* only in a limited sense; for without this further impregnation from the fervour of Aniruddha, it could not by itself have produced the different *guṇas* of *sattva*, *rajas* and *tamas*[1].

Aniruddha, however, was directed by Pradyumna not only to develop the unconscious power (*śakti*) but also the *puruṣa* which exists as it were inside that power, which shows itself as *niyati* (destiny) and *kāla* (time). From the unconscious power as destiny and time evolves first the *sattva* and from it the *rajas* and from the *rajas* the *tamas*. According to the *Viṣvaksena-saṃhitā*, Aniruddha created Brahmā and Brahmā created all the men and women of the four castes[2].

Buddhi evolves from *tamas* and from that *ahaṃkāra* and from that evolve the five *tan-mātras*, and also the eleven senses. From the five *tan-mātras* the five gross elements are produced, and from these, all things, which are the modifications of the gross elements.

The word *puruṣa* is used here in a special sense, and not in the ordinary Sāṃkhya sense. *Puruṣa* here signifies a colony of selves, like cells in a honeycomb[3]. These selves are associated with the beginningless *vāsanās* or root-impressions. They are but the special

[1] *antaḥstha-puruṣāṃ śaktiṃ tām ādāya sva-mūrti-gāṃ*
saṃvardhayati yogena hy anirudhaḥ sva-tejasā.
Ahirbudhnya-saṃhitā, VI. 14.

[2] The *Viṣvaksena-saṃhitā* criticizes in this connection the Vedic people, who did not believe in the monotheistic God but depended on the Vedic sacrificial rituals and work for the attainment of Heaven and ultimately fell down to the course of mundane life (*saṃsāra*):

trayī-mārgeṣu niṣṇātāḥ phala-vāde ramanti te
devādīn eva manvānā na ca mām menire param
tamaḥ-prāyās tv ime kecin mama nindāṃ prakurvate
saṃlāpaṃ kurvate vyagraṃ veda-vādeṣu niṣṭhitāḥ
māṃ na jānanti mohena mayi bhakti-parāṅmukhāḥ
svargā-diṣu ramanty ete avasāne patanti te.
Tattva-traya, p. 128.

[3] *sarvātmanāṃ samaṣṭir yā kośo madhu-kṛtām iva.*
Ahirbudhnya-saṃhitā, VI. 33.

manifestations (*bhūti-bhedāḥ*) of God and are in themselves omniscient; but they are permeated by *avidyā* (ignorance) and the afflictions which are involved in its very nature, through the power of God acting in consonance with His thought-movement[1]. These selves thus rendered impure and finite are called *jīvas*, and it is they who thus suffer bondage and strive for salvation, which they afterwards attain. The *puruṣa*, being made up of these selves (*jīvas*), which are impure, is also partly impure, and is therefore regarded as both pure and impure (*śuddhy-aśuddhimaya*, VI. 34). This *puruṣa* contains within it the germs of all human beings, which are called *manus*. They are in themselves untouched by afflictions (*kleśa*) and the root-impression (*āśaya*), and are omniscient and impregnated through and through by God. Their association with *avidyā* through the will of God is therefore external. The germ of the caste-distinction and distinction as male and female is regarded as primordial and transcendent (compare *puruṣa-sūkta*), and the distinction is said to exist even in these *manus* which are said to be divided in four pairs. The *avidyā* imitates the spiritual movement of thought, and through it the individual selves, though pure in themselves, are besmeared with the impurities of root-impressions. These selves remain in the stage of conglomeration or association through the desire of Viṣṇu, the Lord, and this stage is called *puruṣa* (*puruṣa-pada*)[2]. They are made to appear and disappear from the nature of God. Being a manifestation of His own nature, they are uncreated, eternally existing, entities which are the parts of the very existence (*bhūty-aṃśaḥ*) of God.

Through the impulse or motivation of the thought-activity of God, an energy (*śakti*) is generated from Aniruddha. Moved again by the desire of God, the aforesaid *manus* descend into this energy and remain there as a developing foetus (*tiṣṭhanti kalalībhūtāḥ*, VI. 45). The energy of Viṣṇu is of a twofold nature, as dynamic activity (*kriyākhya*) and as determining being (*bhūti*), the latter being the result of the former[3]. This dynamic activity is different

1 *ātmano bhūti-bhedās te sarva-jñāḥ sarvato-mukhāḥ*
bhagavac-chakti-mayaivaṃ manda-tīvrādi-bhāvayā
tat-tat-sudarśano-nmeṣa-nimeṣā-nukṛtā-tmanā
sarvato'vidyayā viddhāḥ kleśamayā vaśīkṛtāḥ.
Ahirbudhnya-saṃhitā, VI. 35, 36.

2 *viṣṇoḥ saṃkalpa-rūpeṇa sthitvāsmin pauruṣe pade. Ibid.* VI. 41.

3 *kriyākhyo yo'yam unmeṣaḥ sa bhūti-parivartakaḥ. Ibid.* VI. 29.

from God, the possessor of this energy. It is designated variously *Lakṣmī* and desire (*saṃkalpa*) or free will (*svātantrya-mūla icchātmā*). This will operates as an intellectual visualization (*prekṣā-rūpaḥ kriyā-phalaḥ*), which again produces the other manifestations of God as *avyakta*, *kāla* and *puruṣa*. At the time of each creation He associates the *avyakta* with the evolutionary tendencies, the *kāla* with its operative movement (*kalana*) and the *puruṣa* with all kinds of experiences. At the time of dissolution these powers are withdrawn.

In the foetus-like condition of the *manus* in the energy (*śakti*) of God there exist the entities of *guṇa* and *kāla*. Through the operation of the supreme energy or will of God (*Viṣṇu-saṃkalpa-coditaḥ*) there springs up from time-energy (*kāla-śakti*) the subtle Destiny (*niyati*), which represents the universal ordering element (*sarva-niyāmakaḥ*). The time and *guṇa* exist in the womb of the *śakti*. The conception of this *śakti* is thus different from that of *prakṛti* of the Sāṃkhya-Pātañjala in that the *guṇas* are the only root-elements, and time is conceived as somehow included in the operation of the *guṇas*. As the *niyati* is produced from the time-energy, the *manus* descend into this category. Later on there springs from *niyati*, time (*kāla*) through the will of God, and then the *manus* descend again into this category[1]. It has already been said that the *kāla* energy and *guṇa* are co-existing elements in the primordial *śakti* of God. Now this *guṇa*-potential manifests itself in a course of gradual emergence through time. As the *sattva-guṇa* first manifests itself through time, the *manus* descend into that category and later on, with the emergence of *rajas* from *sattva* and of *tamas* from *rajas*, they descend into the *rajas* and the *tamas*. The emergence of *rajas* from *sattva* and of *tamas* from *rajas* is due to the operation of the will-activity of God (*viṣṇu-saṃkalpa-coditāt*). Though the will-dynamic of Viṣṇu is both immanent and transcendent throughout the process of succeeding emergents, yet Viṣṇu is regarded as specially presiding over *sattva*, Brahmā over *rajas*, and Rudra over *tamas*. *Tamas* is regarded as heavy (*guru*), agglutinative (*viṣṭam-*

[1] In describing the process of dissolution it is said that at one stage the universe exists only as time (*kāla*). The energy manifested in time (*kāla-gata-śaktiḥ*) is called *kāla*, and it is this energy that moves all things or behaves as the transformer of all things (*aśeṣa-prakālinī*). *Ahirbudhnya-saṃhitā*, IV. 48. Time is described also as the agent that breaks up all things, just as the violence of a river breaks its banks: *Kalayaty akhilaṃ kālyaṃ nadī-kūlaṃ yathā rayaḥ*. *Ibid.* VI. 51.

bhana), delusive (*mohana*) and statical (*apravṛttimat*); *rajas* is always moving and sorrowful; *sattva* is described as light, transparent and devoid of impurities or defects and pleasurable[1]. With the development of the three *guṇas* through the will of God, a part of these *guṇas* attains sameness of character, and this part is the unity of the three *guṇas* (*traiguṇya*), the equilibrium of *guṇas* (*guṇa-sāmya*), ignorance (*avidyā*), nature (*svabhāva*), cause (*yoni*), the unchangeable (*akṣara*), the causeless (*ayoni*), and the cause as *guṇa* (*guṇa-yoni*)[2].

This participation in equal proportions (*anyūnānatirikta*) of the *guṇas* in a state of equilibrium (*guṇa-sāmya*), which is essentially of the nature of *tamas* (*tamomaya*), is called the root (*mūla*) and the *prakṛti* by the Sāṃkhyists, and the *manus* descending into that category by gradual stages are known by the names conglomeration (*samaṣṭi*), *puruṣa*, the cause (*yoni*), and the unchangeable (*kūṭastha*). The category of time, which is the transforming activity of the world (*jagataḥ saṃprakalanam*), associates and dissociates the *puruṣa* and the *prakṛti* for the production of the effects. The thought power of God, however, works through the tripartite union of time, *prakṛti* and the *manus*, behaving as the material cause, like a lump of clay, and produces all the categories beginning with *mahat* to the gross elements of earth, water, etc. Like water or clay, the *prakṛti* is the evolutionary or material cause, the *puruṣa* is the unchangeable category that contributes to the causal operation merely by its contiguity[3]. The category of time is the internal dynamic pervading the *prakṛti* and the *puruṣa*. The trinity of *prakṛti*, *puruṣa* and *kāla* is the basis for the development of all the succeeding categories. In this

[1] *sattvaṃ tatra laghu svacchaṃ guṇa-rūpam anāmayam. Ahirbudhnya-saṃhitā*, VI. 52; *tad etat pracalaṃ duḥkhaṃ rajaḥ śaśvat pravṛttimat. Ibid.* VI. 57; *guru viṣṭambhanaṃ śaśvan mohanaṃ cāpravṛttimat. Ibid.* VI. 60.

[2] *sudarśanamayenai'va saṃkalpenā'tra vai hareḥ*
codyamāne'pi sṛṣṭy-arthaṃ pūrṇaṃ guṇa-yugaṃ tadā
aṃśataḥ sāmyam āyāti viṣṇu-saṃkalpa-coditam. Ibid. VI. 61–62.

The passage is somewhat obscure, in so far as it is difficult to understand how the *guṇas* become partially (*aṃśataḥ*) similar. The idea probably is that, when the *guṇas* are moved forward for creative purposes, *some parts* of these *guṇas* fail to show their distinctive features, and show themselves as similar to one another. In this stage the specific characters of only these evolving *guṇas* are annulled, and they appear as one with *tamas*. The proportion of *sattva* that appears to be similar to *tamas* is also the proportion in which *tamas* becomes similar to *rajas*.

[3] *payo-mṛd-ādivat tatra prakṛtiḥ pariṇāminī*
pumān apariṇāmī san sannidhānena kāraṇam
kālaḥ pacati tattve dve prakṛtiṃ puruṣaṃ ca ha. Ibid. VII. 5, 6.

trinity *prakṛti* is the evolutionary cause that undergoes the transformation, *puruṣa*, though unmoved in itself, is that which by its very presence gives the occasion for the transformation, and time is the inner dynamic that behaves as the inner synthetic or structural cause. But these causes in themselves are not sufficient to produce the development of the trinity. The trinity is moved to develop on the evolutionary line by the spiritual activity of God. *Puruṣa* is regarded as the *adhiṣṭhāna-kāraṇa*, *kāla* as the principle of inner activity, and the spiritual activity of God as the transcendent and immanent agent in which the causal trinity finds its fundamental active principle. As the first stage of such a development there emerges the category of *mahat*, which is called by different names, e.g. *vidyā*, *gauḥ*, *yavanī*, *brāhmī*, *vadhū*, *vṛddhi*, *mati*, *madhu*, *akhyāti*, *īśvara*, and *prajñā*. According to the prominence of *tamas*, *sattva* and *rajas*, the category of *mahat* is known by three different names, *kāla*, *buddhi* and *prāṇa*, in accordance with the moments in which there are special manifestations of *tamas*, *sattva* and *rajas*[1]. Gross time as moments, instants or the like, the intelligizing activity of thought (*buddhi*) and the volitional activity (*prāṇa*) may also be regarded as the tripartite distinction of *mahat*[2]. There seems to be a tacit implication here that the activity implied in both thought and volition is schematized, as it were, through time. The unity of thought and volition is effected through the element of time; for time has been regarded as the *kalana-kāraṇa*, or the structural cause. The *sattva* side of the *mahat* manifests itself as virtue (*dharma*), knowledge (*jñāna*), disinclination (*vairāgya*), and all mental powers (*aiśvarya*). The opposite of these is associated with that moment of *mahat* which is associated with the manifestation of *tamas*.

With the evolution of the *mahat* the *manus* descend into it. From the *mahat* and in the *mahat* there spring the senses by which the objects are perceived as existent or non-existent[3]. Again, from and in the *mahat* there springs the *ahaṃkāra* through the influence

[1] *kālo buddhis tathā prāṇa iti tredhā sa gīyate*
tamaḥ-sattva-rajo-bhedāt tat-tad-unmeṣa-sañjñayā.
Ahirbudhnya-saṃhitā, VII. 9.

[2] *kālas truṭi-lavādy ātmā buddhir adhyavasāyinī*
prāṇaḥ prayatanākāra ity' etā mahato bhidāḥ. *Ibid.* VII. 11.

[3] *bodhanaṃ nāma vaidyaṃ tadindriyaṃ teṣu jāyate*
yenārthān adhyavasyeyuḥ sad-asat-pravibhāginaḥ. *Ibid.* VII. 14.

of the spiritual energy of God[1]. This *ahaṃkāra* is also called by the names of *abhimāna*, *prajāpati*, *abhimantā* and *boddhā*. The *ahaṃkāra* is of three kinds, *vaikārika*, *taijasa* and *bhūtādi*, in accordance with the predominance of *sattva*, *rajas* or *tamas*. The *ahaṃkāra* manifests itself as will, anger, greed, mind (*manas*), and desire (*tṛṣā*). When the *ahaṃkāra* is produced, the *manus* descend into it. From *ahaṃkāra* there is then produced the organ of thinking (*cintanātmakam indriyam*) of the *manus* called *manas*. It is at this stage that the *manus* first become thinking entities. From the *tamas* side of *ahaṃkāra* as *bhūtādi* there is produced the *śabda-tan-mātra*, from which the *ākāśa* is produced. *Ākāśa* is associated with the quality of *śabda* and gives room for all things. *Ākāśa* is thus to be regarded as unoccupied space, which is supposed to be associated with the quality of sound[2]. With the emergence of *ākāśa* the *manus* descend into that category. From the *vaikārika ahaṃkāra* there spring the organs of hearing and of speech[3]. The *manus* at this stage become associated with these senses. Then from the *bhūtādi*, by the spiritual desire of God, the touch-potential is produced, and from this is produced the air (*vāyu*). By the spiritual desire of God the sense-organ of touch and the active organ of the hand are produced from the *vaikārika ahaṃkāra*. At this stage the *manus* become associated with these two receptive and active senses. From the *bhūtādi* there is then produced the light-heat potential from which is produced the gross light-heat. Again, from the *vaikārika ahaṃkāra* the visual organ and the active organ of the feet are produced, and the *manus* are associated with them. From the *bhūtādi* the taste-potential is produced, and from it is produced water. Further, from the *vaikārika ahaṃkāra* there is produced the taste-organ and the sex-organ, and the *manus* are associated with them. From the *bhūtādi* there is produced the odour-potential and from it the earth. Also, from the *vaikārika ahaṃkāra* there arises the cognitive sense of smelling and the active sense of secretion. The *manus* at this stage descend into this category through the spiritual creative desire of God[4].

[1] *vidyayā udare tatrāhaṃkṛtir nāma jāyate. Ahirbudhnya-saṃhitā*, VII. 15.

[2] *śabdai'-ka-guṇam ākāśam avakāśapradāyi ca. Ibid.* VII. 22.

[3] *tadā vaikārikāt punaḥ śrotraṃ vāg iti vijñāna-karme-ndriya-yugaṃ mune. Ibid.* VII. 23–24.

[4] *Ibid.* VII. 39, 40.

The process of development herein sketched shows that one active sense and one cognitive sense arise together with the development of each category of matter, and with the final development of all the categories of matter there develop all the ten senses (cognitive and conative) in pairs. In the chapter on the gradual dissolution of the categories we see that with the dissolution of each category of matter a pair of senses also is dissolved. The implication of this seems to be that there is at each stage a co-operation of the material categories and the cognitive and conative senses. The selves descend into the different categories as they develop in the progressive order of evolution, and the implication of this probability is that the selves, having been associated from the beginning with the evolution of the categories, may easily associate themselves with the senses and the object of the senses. When all the categories of matter and the ten senses are developed, there are produced the function of imagination, energy of will (*saṃrambha*), and the five *prāṇas* from *manas*, *ahaṃkāra* and *buddhi*; and through their development are produced all the elements that may co-operate together to form the concrete personality[1]. The order followed in the process of development in evolution was maintained in an inverse manner at the time of dissolution.

The above-mentioned *manus* produce in their wives many children, who are called *mānavas*. They in their turn produce many other children who are called the new *mānavas*, or the new men, in all the four castes. Those among them who perform their work for a hundred years with true discriminative knowledge enter into the supreme person of Hari. Those, however, who perform their *karmas* with motives of reaping their effects pass through rebirths in consonance with their actions. As has been said before, the *manus* may be regarded as the individuated forms of the original *kūṭastha puruṣa*. All the *jīvas* are thus but parts of Viṣṇu's own self-realizing being (*bhūty-aṃśa*). Now the *prakṛti*, which is also called *vidyā*,

[1] *saṃkalpaś caiva saṃrambhaḥ prāṇāḥ pañcavidhās tathā*
manaso'haṃkṛter buddher jāyante pūrvam eva tu
evaṃ saṃpūrna-sarvaṅgāḥ prāṇāpānādi-saṃyutāḥ
sarve-ndriya-yutās tatra dehino manavo mune.
Ahirbudhnya-saṃhitā, VII. 42, 43.

Thus from *bhūtādi*, acting in association with *taijasa ahaṃkāra*, are produced successively the five *tan-mātras* of *śabda*, *sparśa*, *rūpa*, *rasa* and *gandha*, from each of which in the same order are produced the five *bhūtas* of *ākāśa*, *vāyu*, *tejas*, *ap* and *pṛthivī*. Again, from the associated work of *taijasa* and *vaikārika ahaṃkāra* there are produced the five cognitive and conative senses.

and which at the time of the creative process showers itself as rain and produces the food-grains, and which at the beginning of the dissolution shows itself as a drying force, begins to manifest itself as showering clouds and produces the food-grains. By consuming the food thus produced by nature men fall from their original state of perfect knowledge (*jñāna-bhraṃśaṃ prapadyante*). At such a stage the original *manus* produce the scriptures for the guidance of those men who have fallen from their original omniscience. Thence men can only attain their highest goal by following the guidance of the scriptures[1]. It thus appears that the power of Viṣṇu as consciousness, bliss and action splits itself into twofold form as the realizing activity and the object, called respectively the *bhāvaka* and the *bhāvya*. The former is the thought-activity of the Lord and the latter is that part of Him which manifests itself as the object of this activity. This leads to the pure and the impure creation. The *kūṭastha puruṣa* of the four *manus* stands intermediate between the pure and the impure creation[2]. There is nothing whatsoever outside the sphere of the *Sudarśana śakti* of the Lord.

On the central question of the relation of God with the *jīvas* the general view of the Pañcarātra, as well as that of the *Ahirbudhnya*, seems to be that at the time of dissolution they return to God and remain in a potential form in Him, but again separate out at the time of the new creation. At the time of emancipation, however, they enter into God, never to come out of Him. But though they enter into Him, they do not become one with Him, but have an independent existence in Him or enter into the abode of Viṣṇu, the *Vaikuṇṭha*, which is often regarded as identical with Him. This is probably a state of what is found in many places described as the *sālokya-mukti*. In the fourteenth chapter of the *Ahirbudhnya-saṃhitā mukti* is described as the attainment of Godhood (*bhagavattā-mayī mukti*, or *vaiṣṇavaṃ tad viśet padam*)[3]. The means by

[1] *tat tu vaidyaṃ payaḥ prāśya sarve mānava-manavāḥ*
jñāna-bhraṃśaṃ prapadyante sarva-jñāḥ svata eva te.
Ahirbudhnya-saṃhitā, VII. 61, 62.

Compare this with the Jewish Christian doctrine of the fall of man, as suggested by Schrader's introduction to the Pañcarātra, p. 78.

[2] *aṃśayoḥ puruṣo madhye yaḥ sthitaḥ sa catur-yugaḥ*
śuddhe-tara-mayaṃ viddhi kūṭasthaṃ taṃ mahā-mune. *Ibid.* VII. 70.

Compare the view of the Gauḍīya school, which regards the *jīva* as the *taṭasthā śakti* of God, which is between the *antaraṅgā* and the *vahiraṅgā śakti*.

[3] *Ibid.* XIV. 3, 4 and 41.

which *mukti* can be attained is said to be a virtuous course of action without seeking any selfish ends[1]. The *jīvas* are described as beginningless, infinite, and as pure consciousness and bliss, and as being largely of the nature of God (*bhagavanmaya*); but still they are described as owing their existence to the spiritual energy of God (*bhagavad-bhāvitāḥ sadā*)[2]. This idea is further clarified when it is said that side by side with the *bhāvya* and the *bhāvaka* powers of God we have a third power called the *puṃ-śakti*, of which we hear in the *Gītā* as *Kṣetrajña-śakti* and in the Gauḍīya school as *taṭastha śakti*[3]. Apart from the three powers of God as creation, maintenance and destruction, He has a fourth and a fifth power called favour (*anugraha*) and disfavour (*nigraha*). The Lord is, of course, self-realized and has no unachieved end, and has absolutely unimpeachable independence; but still in His playful activity He acts like a king just as He wishes[4]. This idea of *krīḍā* is repeated in the *Gauḍīya* school as *līlā*. All these activities of His are but the different manifestations of His thought-activity called *sudarśana*. In His own playful activity as disfavour He covers up the natural condition of the *jīva*, so that in place of His infinitude, he appears as atomic, in place of His omnipotence, he can do but little, in place of His omniscience, He becomes largely ignorant and possesses but little knowledge. These are the three impurities and the three types of bondage. Through this covering activity the *jīva* is afflicted with ignorance, egoism, attachment, antipathy, etc. Being afflicted by ignorance and the passions, and being goaded by the tendency towards achieving the desirable and avoiding the undesirable, He performs actions leading to beneficial and harmful results. He thus undergoes the cycle of birth and rebirth, and is infested with different kinds of root-instincts (*vāsanā*). It is through the power of this bondage and its requirements that the powers of creation, maintenance and destruction are roused and made active to arrange for rewards and punishments in accordance with the *karmas* of the *jīvas*. As proceeding from the very playful nature of God, which precedes time (*kāla*), and is beginningless, the bondage also is said to be beginningless. The above description of bondage as happening

[1] *sādhanaṃ tasya ca prokto dharmo nirabhisandhikaḥ.*
Ahirbudhnya-saṃhitā, XIV, 4.

[2] *Ibid.* [3] *puṃ-śaktiḥ kālamayy anyā pumān so'yam udīritaḥ. Ibid.* XIV. 10.

[4] *sarvair an-anuyojyaṃ tat svātantryaṃ divyam īśituḥ*
avāpta-viśva-kāmo'pi krīḍate rājavad vaśī. Ibid. XIV. 13.

at some time through a process of fall from original nature is by way of analysis of the situation. Through the power of God as *anugraha*, or grace, God stops the course of *karma* for a *jīva* on whose condition of sorrow and suffering He happens to take pity. With the cessation of the good and bad deeds and their beneficent and harmful results through the grace of God the *jīva* looks forward to emancipation and is moved by a feeling of disinclination and begins to have discriminative knowledge. He then turns to scriptures and to teachers, follows the course of action dictated by Sāṃkhya and Yoga, and attains the Vedāntic knowledge, finally to enter the ultimate abode of Viṣṇu.

Lakṣmī is regarded as the ultimate eternal power of Viṣṇu, and she is also called by the names Gaurī, Sarasvatī and Dhenu. It is this supreme power that manifests itself as Saṃkarṣaṇa, Pradyumna and Aniruddha. Thus, these separate powers are observable only when they manifest themselves, but even when they do not manifest themselves they exist in God as His great supreme power Lakṣmī. It is this Lakṣmī that is called Brahmā, Viṣṇu, or Śiva. The *vyakti*, *avyakti*, *puruṣa* and *kāla* or *sāṃkhya* and *yoga* are all represented in the Lakṣmī. Lakṣmī is the ultimate supreme power into which all the others resolve themselves. As distinct from the other manifested powers it is often called the fifth power. The emancipated person enters into this Lakṣmī, which is regarded as the highest abode of Viṣṇu (*paraṃ dhāma* or *paramaṃ padam*), or the highest Brahman. This power (*śakti*) is also regarded as having an inner feeling of bliss; and yet it is of the nature of bliss, and is designated as the *bhāva* form of Viṣṇu and also as the *ujjvala* (shining). This *śakti* is also regarded as discharging the five functions (*pañca-kṛtya-karī*) of creation, maintenance, destruction, grace and disfavour mentioned above. Brahman, as associated with this *śakti*, is called the highest Viṣṇu as distinguished from the lower Viṣṇu, the god of maintenance. This *śakti* is always in a state of internal agitation though it may not be observed as such from outward appearance. This internal agitation and movement are so subtle that they may appear to be in a state of absolute calmness like that of the ocean[1]. Thus *śakti* is also called the *māyā* of Viṣṇu[2].

[1] *sadā pratāyamānā'pi sūkṣmair bhāvairalakṣaṇaiḥ.*
nirvyāpāreva sā bhāti staimityam iva co'dadheḥ.
tayai vo'pahitaṃ Brahma nirvikalpaṃ nirañjanaṃ.
Ahirbudhnya-saṃhitā, LI. 49.

[2] *māyā'ścarya-karatvena pañca-kṛtya-karī sadā. Ibid.* LI. 58.

It is a part of this power that transforms itself as the *bhāvya* and the *bhāvaka śakti*, of which the latter is also known by the name *sudarśana*. The *bhāvya* shows itself as the world, and its objective import is the world.

The thought-activity by which the concept shows itself in the ideal and in the objective world as thought and its significance, the object, is the epitome of the power of Sudarśana. When all the external movement of the objective is ideally grasped in the word, we have also in it the manifestation of the power of Sudarśana, or the supreme thought-activity of God. All the causality of the objective world is but a mode of the manifestation of the Sudarśana power. Thus not only all the movements of the external world of nature and the movement implied in speech, but the subjective-objective movement by which the world is held together in thought and in speech are the manifestation of the Sudarśana power. All expressions or manifestations are either in the way of qualities or actions, and both are manifestations of the Sudarśana power of God. Our words can signify only these two ways of being. For this reason they refer only to the Sudarśana, which is attributive to God, but cannot express the nature of God. Words, therefore, cannot reveal the nature of God. The word may hold the universe within it as its mystic symbol and may represent within it all its energies, but, in any case, though it may engulf within it the whole universe and secure the merging of the universe in itself and can identify itself with God, such identification can only be with the Sudarśana power of God, and the entrance into God, or the realization of Him through the word or thought, can only be through the Sudarśana power, which is a part of Lakṣmī. Thus unity with God can only mean union with Sudarśana, or entrance into Lakṣmī[1].

Adoration (*namaḥ*) means the spontaneous acceptance of the highest Lord as the master on the part of a man who has achieved it through a wise enlightenment[2]. Superiority (*jyāyān*) consists of greatness of qualities and existence in earlier time[3]. God alone is superior, and everything else is inferior. The relation between the latter and the former is that the latter exists for the former or is dependent on the former. This relation is called (*śeṣa-śeṣitā*). The

[1] *Ahirbudhnya-saṃhitā*, LI. 69–78.

[2] *prekṣāvataḥ pravṛttir yā prahvī-bhāvā-tmikā svataḥ*
utkṛṣṭaṃ param uddiśya tan namaḥ parigīyate. *Ibid.* LII. 2.

[3] *kālato guṇataś caiva prakarṣo yatra tiṣṭhati*
śabdas taṃ mukhyayā vṛttyā jyāyān ity avalambate. *Ibid.* LII. 4.

relation between the two is that one should be the adorer and the other the adored (*nantṛ-nantavya-bhāva*). True adoration is when such an adoration proceeds naturally as a result of such a relation, without any other motive or end of any kind—the only idea being that God is supremely superior to me and I am absolutely inferior to Him[1]. This process of adoration not only takes the adorer to God, but also brings God to him. The presence of any motive of any kind spoils the effectuation of the adoration. This adoration is the first part of the process of *prapatti*, or seeking the protection of God[2]. Now on account of the presence of beginningless root-impressions (*vāsanā*), and of natural insignificance of power and association with impurity, man's power of knowledge or wisdom becomes obstructed; and when a man becomes fully conscious of such weakness, he acquires the quality of *kārpaṇya* or lowliness. A feeling or consciousness of one's independence obstructs this quality of lowliness. The great faith that the supreme God is always merciful is called the quality of *mahā-viśvāsa*. The idea that God is neutral and bestows His gifts only in proportion to one's deeds obstructs this quality. The idea that, since He is all-merciful and all-powerful, He would certainly protect us, produces the quality of faith in God's protective power. The notion that God, being qualityless, is indifferent to any appeal for protection obstructs this quality. Acceptance of the Lord as the supreme master whose commands should on no account be disobeyed produces the quality of docility (*prātikūlya-vivarjana*). Service of God in a manner not prescribed in the scriptures obstructs this quality. The strong resolve of the mind to work in accordance with God's wishes, with the full conviction that the sentient and the non-sentient of the world are but parts of His nature, produces the quality of submission. An inimical disposition towards the beings of the world obstructs this quality. A true adoration (*namaḥ*) to God must be associated with all the aforesaid qualities. True adoration must carry with it the conviction that the sense of possession that we have in all things, due to beginningless instinctive passions and desires, is all false, and the adorer should feel that he has neither independence nor anything that he may call his own. "My body, my

[1] *upādhi-rahitenā' yaṃ yena bhāvena cetanaḥ*
namati jyāyase tasmai tad vā namanam ucyate.
Ahirbudhnya-saṃhitā, LII. 9.

[2] *phalepsā tad-virodhinī. Ibid.* LII. 15.

riches, my relations do not belong to me, they all belong to God"; such is the conviction that should generate the spirit with which the adoration should be offered. The adorer should feel that the process of adoration is the only way through which he can obtain his highest realization, by offering himself to God and by drawing God to himself at the same time. The purpose of adoration is thus the supreme self-abnegation and self-offering to God, leaving nothing for oneself. The world comes out of God and yet exists in a relation of inherence, so that He is both the agent and the material cause of the world, and the adorer must always be fully conscious of the greatness of God in all its aspects.

The above doctrine of *prapatti*, or *nyāsa*, or *śaraṇā-gati*, as the means of winning God's grace, has also been described in Chapter XXVII and it virtually means the qualities just described[1]. *śaraṇā-gati* is here defined as prayer for God's help in association with the conviction of one's being merged in sin and guilt, together with a belief in one's absolute helplessness and a sense of being totally lost without the protecting grace of God[2]. The person who takes to the path of this *prapatti* achieves the fruits of all *tapas*, sacrifices, pilgrimages and gifts, and attains salvation easily without resorting to any other methods[3]. It is further said that on the part of the devotee following the path of *prapatti* all that is necessary is to stick firmly to the attitude of absolute dependence on God, associated with a sense of absolute helplessness. He has no efforts to make other than to keep himself in the prayerful spirit; all the rest is done by God. *Prapatti* is thus a *upāya-jñāna* and not a *upāya*; for it is a mental attitude and does not presuppose any action. It is like a boat on which the passenger merely sits, while it is the business of the boatman to do the rest[4].

1 *ṣoḍhā hi veda-viduṣo vadanty enaṃ mahā-mune*
ānukūlyasya saṃkalpaḥ prātikūlyasya varjanaṃ
rakṣiṣyatī ti viśvāso goptṛva-varaṇaṃ tathā.
ātma-nikṣepa-kārpaṇye ṣaḍ-vidhā śaraṇā-gatiḥ.
Ahirbudhnya-saṃhitā, XXXVII. 27, 28.

2 *aham asmy aparādhānām ālayo'kiñcano' gatiḥ*
tvam evo 'pāyabhūto me bhave'ti prārthanā-matiḥ.
śaraṇāgatir ity-uktā sā deve'smin prayujyatāṃ.
Ibid. XXXVII. 30, 31.

3 *Ibid.* XXXVII. 34 and 35.

4 *atra nāvi' ti dṛṣṭāntād upāya-jñānam eva tu*
nareṇa kṛtyam anyat tu nāvikasye'va taddhareḥ.
Ahirbudhnya-saṃhitā.

Describing the process of pure creation, it is said that at the time of *pralaya* all effects are reduced to a dormant state, and there is no movement of any kind. All the six qualities of the Lord, namely *jñāna*, *śakti*, *bala*, *aiśvarya*, *vīrya* and *tejas* described above, are in a state of absolute calmness like the sky without a puff of air in it[1]. This assemblage of powers in a state of calmness is Lakṣmī, which exists as it were like the very void. From its own spontaneity it seems to wish to burst forth and turn itself into active operations. This power of God, though differentiated from Him, may be regarded as being His very nature. It is only when it thus comes out in active forms that it can be recognized as power, or *śakti*. When embedded in the potential form, it is indistinguishable from the Lord Himself. These *guṇas* of God should not, however, be confused with the *guṇas* of *prakṛti*, which evolve at a much lower stage in the course of the process of impure creation.

As regards the *vyūhas*, it is said that Saṃkarṣaṇa carries in him the whole universe, as if it were a spot at the parting of the hairs (*tilakālaka*). The universe as it exists in Saṃkarṣaṇa is still in an unmanifested form. He is the support of the universe (*aśeṣa-bhuvana-dhara*)[2]. The *manus*, time and *prakṛti* came out of Pradyumna[3]. It is through the influence of Pradyumna that men are actuated to perform their work in accordance with the *śāstras*[4]. Aniruddha, also called Mahā-viṣṇu, is the god of power and energy, and it is through his efforts that the creation and the maintenance of the world are possible. It is he who makes the world grow[5]. It is through him that the world lives without fear and ultimate salvation is possible. According to Śaṅkara's account Saṃkarṣaṇa stands for the individual soul, Pradyumna for *manas* and Aniruddha for the Ego (*ahaṃkāra*)[6]. Such a view is rather rare in the existing Pañcarātra literature. In the *Viṣvaksena-saṃhitā*, as quoted in the *Tattva-traya*, it is said that Saṃkarṣaṇa acts as the superintendent

1 *pūrṇa-stimita-ṣāḍ-guṇyam asamīrā-mvaro-pamam.*
Ahirbudhnya-saṃhitā, V. 3.

2 All the *śāstras* are said to have been produced by Saṃkarṣaṇa, and it is in him that they disappear at the time of *pralaya*. *Ahirbudhnya*, LV. 16.

3 *Ibid.* VI. 9–12.

4 *Ibid.* LV. 18. Pradyumna is also called Vīra.

5 There are, however, many conflicting views about these functions of the different *vyūhas*. See *Lakṣmī-tantra*, IV. 11–20, also *Viṣvaksena-saṃhitā*, as quoted in the *Tattva-traya*.

6 *Vedānta-sūtra*, II. 2. 42, Śaṅkara's commentary.

of the souls, and Pradyumna is described as *manomaya* or the mind, but nothing is said about Aniruddha. In the *Lakṣmī-tantra*, VI. 9–14, it is said that Saṃkarṣaṇa was like the soul, *buddhi* and *manas* and Vāsudeva, the playful creative activity. In the *Viṣvaksena-saṃhitā* Aniruddha is regarded as the creator of the *miśra-varga* (pure-impure creation, such as *niyati*), etc., and Saṃkarṣaṇa is regarded as the being who separated the principle of life from nature and became Pradyumna. But in the *Ahirbudhnya* the difference between the *puruṣa* and *prakṛti* starts in the Pradyumna stage, and not in the Saṃkarṣaṇa stage, and Aniruddha is regarded in the *Ahirbudhnya* as the superintendent of the *sattva* and therethrough of all that come from it and the *manus*[1]. According to the *Ahirbudhnya* Lakṣmī is described as the power of God, but according to *Uttara-nārāyana* we have Lakṣmī and Bhūmi, and according to the *Tattva-traya* Lakṣmī, Bhūmi and Nīlā. In the *Vihagendra-saṃhitā*, II. 8, these three are regarded as *icchā*, *kriyā* and *sākṣāt-śakti* of the Devī. In the *Sītā-upaniṣad* also we have the same interpretation, and this is also associated there with *Vaikhānasa* tradition. The *Vihagendra* speaks of the eight śaktis of Sudarśana, *kīrti*, *śrī*, *vijayā*, *śraddhā*, *smṛti*, *medhā*, *dhṛti* and *kṣamā*, and in the *Sātrata-saṃhitā* (IX. 85) we hear of the twelve śaktis emanating from the Śrīvatsa of Viṣṇu: these are *lakṣmī*, *puṣṭi*, *dayā*, *nidrā*, *kṣamā*, *kānti*, *sarasvatī*, *dhṛti*, *maitrī*, *rati*, *tuṣṭi* and *mati*.

The Pañcarātra is based partly on the Vedic and partly on the Tāntric system[2]. It therefore believes in the esoteric nature of the *mantras*. It has already been said that the world has come into being from the Sudarśana power; so all the natural, physical and other kinds of energies and powers of all things in the world are but manifestation of the Sudarśana. The power of the Sudarśana also manifests itself in the form of all living beings and of all that is inanimate, of the course of bondage and also of emancipation. Whatever is able to produce is to be regarded as the manifestation of Sudarśana[3]. The *mantras* are also regarded as the energy of

[1] *Ahirbudhnya-saṃhitā*, VI. 57.

[2] *veda-tantramayo-dbhūta-nānā-prasavaśālinī. Ibid.* VI. 9.

[3] *sudarśanāhvayā devī sarva-kṛtya-karī vibhoḥ*
tan-mayaṃ viddhi sāmarthyaṃ sarvaṃ sarva-padārthajaṃ
dharmasyārthasya kāmasya mukter bandha-trayasya ca
yad yat sva-kārya-sāmarthyaṃ tat-tat-saudarśanaṃ vapuḥ.
Ibid. XVI. 4 and 6.

Viṣṇu as pure consciousness[1]. The first manifestation of this power, like a long-drawn sound of a bell, is called *nāda*, and it can only be perceived by the great *yogins*. The next stage, like a bubble on the ocean, is called *bindu*, which is the identity of a name and the objective power denoted by it. The next stage is the evolution of the objective power (*nāmy-udaya*), which is also called *Śabda-brahman*. Thus, with the evolution of every alphabetic sound there is also the evolution of the objective power of which it is the counterpart. *Ahirbudhnya* then goes on to explain the evolution of the different vowel and consonant sounds from the *bindu*-power. By fourteen efforts there come the fourteen vowels emanating through the dancing of the serpent power (*Kuṇḍalī-śakti*) of Viṣṇu[2]. By its twofold subtle power it behaves as the cause of creation and destruction. This power rises in the original locus (*mūlā-dhāra*) and, when it comes to the stage of the navel, it is called *paśyantī* and is perceived by the *yogins*. It then proceeds to the lotus of the heart and then passes through the throat as the audible sound. The energy of the vowel sounds passes through the *suṣumnā nāḍī*. In this way the different consonant sounds are regarded as the prototypes of different manifestations of world-energy, and these again are regarded as the symbols of different kinds of gods or superintendents of energy[3]. An assemblage of some of these alphabets in different orders and groups, called also the lotus or the wheel (*cakra*), would stand for the assemblage of different types of complex powers. The meditation and worship of these *cakras* would thus be expected to bring the objective powers typified by them under control. The different gods are thus associated with the different *cakras* of *mantras*; and by far the largest portion of the Pañcarātra literature is dedicated to the description of the rituals associated with these, the building of corresponding images, and the temples for these subsidiary deities. The meditation of these *mantras* is also regarded as playing diverse protective functions.

In consonance with the ordinary method of the Tāntric works

[1] *sākṣād viṣṇoḥ kriyā-śaktiḥ śuddha-saṃvinmyī parā.*
Ahirbudhnya-saṃhitā, XVI. 10.

This *kriyā-śakti* is also called *sāmarthya* or *yoga* or *pārameṣṭhya* or *mahātejas* or *māyā-yoga*. *Ibid.* XVI. 32.

[2] *naṭī'va kuṇḍalī-śaktir ādyā viṣṇor vijṛmbhate.* *Ibid.* XVI. 55.

[3] *viṣṇu-śaktimayā varṇā viṣṇu-saṃkalpa-jṛmbhitāḥ*
adhiṣṭhitā yathā bhāvais tathā tan me niśāmaya. *Ibid.* XVII. 3.

the *Ahirbudhnya* describes the nervous system of the body. The root (*kāṇḍa*) of all the nerves is said to be at about nine inches above the penis. It is an egg-shaped place four inches in length and breadth and made up of fat, flesh, bone and blood. Just two inches below the penis and about two inches from the anus we have a place which is called the middle of the body (*śarīra-madhya*), or simply the middle (*madhya*). It is like a quadrilateral figure, which is also called the *āgneya-maṇḍala*. The place of the root of the *nāḍīs* is also called the navel-wheel (*nābhi-cakra*), which has twelve spokes. Round the *nābhi-cakra* there exists the serpent (*kuṇḍalī*) with eight mouths, stopping the aperture called *brahma-randhra* of the *suṣumnā* by its body[1]. In the centre of the *cakra* there are the two *nāḍīs* called the *alambuṣa* and *suṣumṇā*. On the different sides of the *suṣumnā* there are the following *nāḍīs*: *Kuhu*, *Varuṇa*, *Yaśasvinī*, *Piṅgalā*, *Pūṣā*, *Payasvinī*, *Sarasvatī*, *Śaṅkhinī*, *Gāndhārī*, *Iḍā*, *Hasti-jihvā*, *Viśvodarā*. But there are on the whole 72,000 *nāḍīs* in the body. Of these, *Iḍā*, *Piṅgalā* and *suṣumṇā* are the most important. Of these, again, *suṣumṇā*, which goes to the centre of the brain, is the most important. As a spider remains inside the meshes of its thread, so the soul, as associated with *prāṇa* or life-force, exists inside this navel-wheel. The *suṣumṇā* has five openings, of which four carry blood, while the central aperture is closed by the body of the *Kuṇḍalī*. Other *nāḍīs* are shorter in size and are connected with the different parts of the body. The *Iḍā* and the *Piṅgalā* are regarded as being like the sun and the moon of the body.

There are ten *vāyus*, or bio-motor forces of the body, called *prāṇa*, *apāna*, *samāna*, *udāna*, *vyāna*, *nāga*, *kūrma*, *kṛkara*, *devadatta* and *dhanañjaya*. The *prāṇa vāyu* remains in the navel-wheel, but it manifests itself in the regions of the heart, mouth and the nose. The *apāna vāyu* works in the anus, penis, thighs, the legs, the belly, the testes, the lumbar region, the intestines, and in fact performs the functions of all the lower region. The *vyāna* exists between the eyes and the ears, the toes, nose, throat and the spine. The *udāna* works in the hands and the *samāna* through the body as a whole, probably discharging the general circulation[2]. The func-

[1] *Ahirbudhnya-saṃhitā*, XXXII. 11. This is indeed different from the description found in the *Śākta Tantras*, according to which the *Kuṇḍalī* exists in the place down below described as the *śarīra-madhya*.

[2] *Ibid.* XXXII. 33–37. These locations and functions are different from what we find in the *Āyur-Veda* or the *Śākta Tantras*.

tion of the *prāṇa* is to discharge the work of respiration; that of the *vyāna*, to discharge the work of turning about towards a thing or away from it. The function of the *udāna* is to raise or lower the body, that of the *samāna*, to feed and develop it. The function of eructation or vomiting is performed by the *nāga vāyu*, and *devadatta* produces sleep and so on. These *nāḍīs* are to be purified by inhaling air by the *iḍā* for as long as is required to count from 1 to 16. This breath is to be held long enough to count from 1 to 32, and in the interval some forms of meditation are to be carried on. Then the yogin should inhale air in the same manner through the *piṅgalā* and hold that also in the same way. He should then exhale the breath through the *Iḍā*. He should practise this for three months thrice a day, three times on each occasion, and thus his *nāḍīs* will be purified and he will be able to concentrate his mind on the *vāyus* all over his body. In the process of the *prāṇāyāma* he should inhale air through the *Iḍā* long enough to count from 1 to 16. Then the breath is to be retained as long as possible, and the specific *mantra* is to be meditated upon; and then the breath is to be exhaled out by the *piṅgalā* for the time necessary to count from 1 to 16. Again, he has to inhale through the *Piṅgalā*, retain the breath and exhale through the *Iḍā*. Gradually the period of retention of the breath called *kumbhaka* is to be increased. He has to practise the *prāṇāyāma* sixteen times in course of the day. This is called the process of *prāṇāyāma*. As a result of this, he may enter the stage of *samādhi*, by which he may attain all sorts of miraculous powers, just as one may by the meditation of the wheel of *mantras*.

But before one begins the purification of the *nāḍīs* described above one should practise the various postures (*āsanas*) of which *cakra*, *padma*, *kūrma*, *mayūra*, *kukkuṭa*, *vīra*, *svastika*, *bhadra*, *siṃha*, *mukta* and *gomukha* are described the *Ahirbudhnya*. The practice of these postures contributes to the good health of the *yogins*. But these physical practices are of no avail unless one turns to the spiritual side of *yoga*. *Yoga* is defined as the union of the lower and the higher soul[1]. Two ways for the attainment of the highest reality are described in the *Ahirbudhnya*—one is that of self-offering or self-abnegation (*ātma-samarpaṇa* or *hṛd-yāga*) through the meditation on the highest in the form of some of His powers, as this

1 *saṃyogo yoga ity ukto jīvātm-paramā-tmanoḥ.*
Ahirbudhnya-saṃhitā, XXXI. 15.

and that specific deity, by the practice of the *mantras*; and the other is that of the *yoga*[1]. *Ahirbudhnya*, however, concentrates its teachings on the former, and mentions the latter in only one of its chapters. There are two types of soul, one within the influence of the *prakṛti* and the other beyond it. The union with the highest is possible through *karma* and *yoga*. *Karma* is again of two kinds, that which is prompted by desires (*pravartaka*) and that which is prompted by cessation of desires (*nivartaka*). Of these only the latter can lead to emancipation, while the former leads to the attainment of the fruits of desires. The highest soul is described as the subtle (*sūkṣma*), all-pervading (*sarva-ga*), maintaining all (*sarva-bhṛt*), pure consciousness (*jñāna-rūpa*), without beginning and end (*anādy-ananta*), changeless (*a-vikārin*), devoid of all cognitive or conative senses, devoid of names and class-notions, without colour and quality, yet knowing all and pervading all, self-luminous and yet approachable through intuitive wisdom, and the protector of all[2]. The *yoga* by which a union of our lower souls with this highest reality can be effected has the well-known eight accessories, *yama*, *niyama*, *āsana*, *prāṇāyāma*, *pratyāhāra*, *dhāraṇa*, *dhyāna* and *samādhi*.

Of these, *yama* is said to consist of beneficial and yet truthful utterance (*satya*), suffering at the sufferings of all beings (*dayā*), remaining fixed in one's path of duty even in the face of dangers (*dhṛti*), inclination of all the senses to adhere to the path of right conduct (*śauca*), absence of lust (*brahma-carya*), remaining unruffled even when there is a real cause of anger or excitement (*kṣamā*), uniformity of thoughts, deeds and words (*ārjava*), taking of unprohibited food (*mitāhāra*), absence of greed for the property of others (*asteya*), cessation from doing injury to others by word, deed or thought (*ahiṃsā*)[3]. *Niyama* is described as listening to Vedāntic texts (*siddhānta-śravaṇa*), gifts of things duly earned to proper persons (*dāna*), faith in scriptural duties (*mati*), worship of Viṣṇu through devotion (*īśvara-pūjana*), natural contentment with

[1] *yad vā bhagavate tasmai svakiyātma-samarpaṇam*
viśiṣṭa-daivatāyā' smai cakra-rūpāya mantrataḥ
viyuktaṃ prakṛteḥ śuddhaṃ dadyād ātma-haviḥ svayam.
Ahirbudhnya-saṃhitā, XXX. 4, 5.

[2] *Ibid.* XXXI. 7–10.

[3] *Ibid.* 18–23. The list here given is different from that of Patañjali, who counts *ahiṃsā, satya, asteya, brahma-carya* and *aparigraha* as *yamas*. See *Yoga-sūtra*, II. 30.

whatever one may have (*santoṣa*), asceticism (*tapaḥ*), faith in the ultimate truth being attainable only through the Vedas (*āstikya*), shame in committing prohibited actions (*hrī*), muttering of *mantras* (*japa*), acceptance of the path dictated by the good teacher (*vrata*)[1]. Though the *Yoga* is here described as the union of the lower and the higher soul, the author of the *Ahirbudhnya* was aware of the *yogānuśāsana* of Patañjali and his doctrine of *Yoga* as the repression of mental states (*citta-vṛtti-nirodha*)[2].

The *Ahirbudhnya* defines *pramā* as the definite knowledge of a thing as it really exists (*yathārthā-vadhāraṇam*), and the means by which it is attained is called *pramāṇa*. That which is sought to be discovered by the *pramāṇas* as being beneficial to man is called *pramāṇārtha*. This is of two kinds, that which is supremely and absolutely beneficial, and that which indirectly leads thereto, and as such is called *hita* and *sādhana*. Oneness with God, which is supremely blissful, is what is called supremely beneficial (*hita*). Two ways that lead to it are those of *dharma* and *jñāna*. This knowledge is of two kinds, as direct intuition (*sākṣātkāra*) and as indirect or inferential (*parokṣa*). *Dharma* is the cause of knowledge, and is of two kinds, one which leads directly, and the other indirectly, to worship of God. Self-offering or self-abnegation with reference to God is called indirect *dharma*, while the way in which the *Yogin* directly realizes God is called the direct *dharma*, such as is taught in the Pañcarātra literature, called the *sātvata-śāsana*. By the Sāṃkhya path one can have only the indirect knowledge of God, but through Yoga and Vedānta one can have a direct intuition of God. Emancipation (*mokṣa*) is as much an object of attainment through efforts (*sādhya*) as *dharma*, *artha* and *kāma*, though the last three are also mutually helpful to one another[3].

[1] *Ahirbudhnya-saṃhitā*, pp. 23–30. This list is also different from that of Patañjali, who counts *śauca*, *santoṣa*, *tapaḥ*, *svādhyāya* and *īśvara-praṇidhāna* only as *niyamas*. See *Yoga-sūtra*, II. 32.

[2] *Ibid.* XIII. 27, 28.

[3] *Ibid.* XIII.

CHAPTER XVII

THE ĀṚVĀRS.

The Chronology of the Āṛvārs.

In the *Bhāgavata-purāṇa*, xi. 5. 38–40, it is said that the great devotees of Viṣṇu will appear in the south on the banks of Tāmraparṇī, Kṛtamālā (Vaigai), Payasvinī (Palar), Kāverī and Mahānadī (Periyar)[1]. It is interesting to note that the Āṛvārs, Nāmm'-āṛvār and Madhura-kaviy-āṛvār, were born in the Tāmraparṇī country, Periy-āṛvār and his adopted daughter Āṇḍāḷ in the Kṛtamāla, Poygaiy-āṛvār, Bhūtatt'-āṛvar, Pēy-āṛvār and Tiru-maṛiṣai Pirān in the Payasvinī, Toṇḍar-aḍi-poḍiy-āṛvār, Tiru-pāṇ-āṛvār and Tiru-maṅgaiy-āṛvār in the Kāverī, and Periy-āṛvār and Kula-śēkhara Perumāl in the Mahāṇada countries. In the *Bhāgavata-māhātmya* we find a parable in which Bhakti is described as a distressed woman who was born in the Drāviḍa country, had attained her womanhood in the Carnatik and Mahārāṣṭra, and had travelled in great misery through Guzerat and North India with her two sons *Jñāna* and *Vairāgya* to Brindaban, and that owing to the hard conditions through which she had to pass her two sons had died. This shows that at least according to the traditions of the *Bhāgavata-purāṇa* Southern India was regarded as a great stronghold of the *Bhakti* cult.

The Āṛvārs are the most ancient Vaiṣṇava saints of the south, of whom Saroyogin or Poygaiy-āṛvār, Pūtayogin or Bhūtatt'-āṛvār, Mahadyogin or Pēy-āṛvār, and Bhaktisāra or Tiru-maṛiṣai Pirān are the earliest; Nāmm'-āṛvār or Śaṭhakopa, Madhura-kaviy-āṛvār, Kula-śēkhara Perumāl, Viṣṇucittan (or Periy-āṛvār) and Goḍa (Āṇḍāḷ) came after them and Bhaktāṅghrireṇu (Toṇḍar-aḍi-poḍiy-āṛvār), Yogivāha (Tiru-pān-āṛvār) and Parakāla (Tiru-maṅgaiy-

[1] This implies that the *Bhāgavata-purāṇa* in its present form was probably written after the Āṛvārs had flourished. The verse here referred to has been quoted by Veṅkaṭanātha in his *Rahasya-traya-sāra*. The *Prapannā-mṛta* (Ch. 77) however refers to three other Vaiṣṇava saints who preceded the Āṛvārs. They were (i) Kāsārayogin, born in Kāñcī, (ii) Bhūtayogīndra, born in Mallipura, (iii) Bhrānta-yogīndra called also Mahat and Mahārya who was the incarnation of Viṣvaksena. It was these sages who advised the five *saṃskāras* of Vaiṣṇavism (*tāpaḥ pauṇḍras tathā nāma mantro yāgaś ca pañcamaḥ*). They preached the emotional Vaiṣṇavism in which *Bhakti* is realized as maddening intoxication associated with tears, etc. They described their feelings of ecstasy in three works, comprising three hundred verses written in Tamil. They were also known by the names of Mādhava, Dāsārya and Saroyogin.

āṟvār) were the last to come. The traditional date ascribed to the earliest Āṟvār is 4203 B.C., and the date of the latest Āṟvār is 2706 B.C.[1], though modern researches on the subject bring down their dates to a period not earlier than the seventh or the eighth century A.D. Traditional information about the Āṟvārs can be had from the different "*Guru-paramparā*" works. According to the *Guru-paramparā*, Bhūtatt-, Poygaiy- and Pēy-āṟvārs were incarnations of Viṣṇu's *Gadā*, *Śaṇkha* and *Nandaka*, and so also Kadanmallai and Mayilai, while Tiru-maṟiṣai Pirān was regarded as the incarnation of the *cakra* (wheel) of Viṣṇu. Nāmm'-āṟvār was incarnation of Viṣvaksena and Kula-śēkhara Peru-māl of the *Kaustubha* of Viṣṇu. So Periy-āṟvār, Toṇḍar-aḍi-poḍiy-āṟvār and Tiru-maṅgaiy-āṟvār were respectively incarnations of *Garuḍa*, *Vanamālā* and *Śārṅga* of Viṣṇu. The last Āṟvār was Tiru-pāṇ-āṟvār. Āṇḍāḷ, the adopted daughter of Periy-āṟvār, and Madhura-kaviy-āṟvār, the disciple of Nāmm'-āṟvār, were also regarded as Āṟvārs. They came from all parts of the Madras Presidency. Of these seven were Brahmins, one was a *Kṣattriya*, two were *śūdras* and one was of the low Panar caste. The *Guru-paramparās* give incidents of the lives of the Āṟvārs and also fanciful dates B.C. when they are said to have flourished. Apart from the *Guru-paramparās* there are also monographs on individual Aṟvārs, of which the following are the most important: (1) *Divya-sūri-carita* by Garuḍa-vāhana Paṇḍita, who was a contemporary of Rāmānuja; (2) *Guru-paramparā-prabhāvam* of Pinb'-aṟagiya Peru-māl Jīyar, based on the *Divya-sūri-carita* and written in *maṇi-pravāḷa* style, i.e. a mixture of Sanskrit and Tamil; (3) *Periya-tiru-muḍiy-aḍaivu* of Āṇbillai Kaṇḍāḍai-yappan, written in Tamil; (4) *Upadeśa-ratna-mālai* of Maṇavāḷa Mā-muni, written in Tamil, contains the list of Āṟvārs; (5) *Yatīndra-pravaṇa-prabhāvam* of Pillai Lokācāryar. The other source of information regarding the Āṟvārs is the well-known collection of the works of Āṟvārs known as *Nāl-āyira-divya-prabandham*. Among these are the commentaries on the *Divya-prabandham* and the *Tiru-vāy-moṟi* of Nāmm'-āṟvār. In addition to these we have the epigraphical evidence in inscriptions scattered over the Madras Presidency[2].

[1] *Early History of Vaiṣṇavism in South India*, by S. K. Aiyangar, pp. 4–13; also Sir R. G. Bhandarkar's *Vaiṣṇavism, Śaivism and Minor Religious Sects*, pp. 68, 69.

[2] Sir Subrahmanya Ayyar Lectures, by the late T. A. Gopi-nātha Rāu, 1923.

Maṇavāḷa Mā-muni, in his *Yatīndra-pravaṇa-prabhāvam*, says that the earliest of the Ārvārs, Pēy-ārvār, Bhūtatt'-ārvār, Poygaiy-ārvār, and Tiru-maṛiṣai Pirān, flourished at the time of the Pallavas, who came to Kāñcī about the fourth century A.D. Again, Professor Dubreuil says that Mamallai, the native town of Bhūtatt'-ārvār, did not exist before Narasiṃhavarman I, who founded the city by the middle of the seventh century. Further, Tiru-maṅgaiy-ārvār praised the Vaiṣṇava temple of Kāñcī built by Parameśvarvarman II. It seems, therefore, that the Ārvārs flourished in the eighth century A.D., which was the period of a great Vaiṣṇava movement in the Cola and the Pāṇḍya countries, and also of the Advaitic movement of Śaṅkara[1].

According to the traditional accounts, Nāmm'-ārvār was the son of Kāṛi, holding a high post under the Pāṇḍyas, and himself bore the names of Kāṛimāṛan, Parāṅkuśa and Śaṭhakopa, that his disciple was Madhura-kaviy-ārvār, and that he was born at Tirukkurgur. Two stone inscriptions have been found in Madura of which one is dated at Kali 3871, in the reign of King Parāntaka, whose *uttara-mantrin* was the son of Māṛa, who was also known as Madhura-kaviy-ārvār. The other is dated in the reign of Māṛañ-jadaiyan. The Kali year 3871 corresponds to A.D. 770. This was about the year when Parāntaka Pāṇḍya ascended the throne. His father Parāṅkuśa died about the year A.D. 770. Māṛaṅkāri continued as *uttara-mantrin*. Nāmm'-ārvār's name Kāṛimāṛan shows that Kāṛi the *uttara-mantrin* was his father. This is quite in accordance with the accounts found in *Guru-paramparā*. These and many other evidences collected by Gopi-nātha Rāu show that Nāmm'-ārvār and Madhura-kaviy-ārvār flourished at the end of the eighth century A.D. or in the first half of the ninth century. Kula-śēkhara Peru-māl also flourished probably about the first half of the ninth century. Periy-ārvār and his adopted daughter Āṇḍāḷ were probably contemporaries of Śrīvallabhadeva, who flourished about the middle of the ninth century A.D. Toṇḍar-adi-poḍiy-ārvār was a contemporary of Tiru-maṅgaiy-ārvār and Tiru-pān-ārvār. Tiru-maṅgaiy-ārvār referred to the war drum of Pallavamalla, who reigned between A.D. 717 and A.D. 779, and these Ārvārs could not have flourished before that time. But Tiru-maṅgaiy-ārvār, in his praise

---

[1] Sir Subrahmanya Ayyar Lectures, by the late T. A. Gopi-nātha Rāu, 1923, p. 17.

of Viṣṇu at Kāñcī, refers to Vairamegha Pallava, who probably flourished in the ninth century. It may therefore be supposed that Tiru-maṅgaiy lived about that time. According to Mr S. K. Aiyangar the last of the Āṛvārs flourished in the earlier half of the eighth century A.D.[1] Sir R. G. Bhandarkar holds that Kula-śēkhara Peru-māl flourished about the middle of the twelfth century. He was a king of Travancore and in his *Mukunda-mālā* he quotes a verse from the *Bhāgavata-purāṇa* (XI. 2. 36). On the basis of the inscriptional evidence that Permāḍi of the Seṇḍa dynasty, who flourished between 1138–1150, conquered Kula-śekharāṅka, and identifying Kula-śēkhara Peru-māl with Kula-śekharāṅka, Bhandarkar comes to the conclusion that Kula-śēkhara Peru-māḷ lived in the middle of the twelfth century A.D., though, as we have already seen, Mr Rāu attempts to place him in the first half of the ninth century. He, however, does not take any notice of the views of Sir R. G. Bhandarkar, who further thinks that the earliest Āṛvārs flourished about the fifth or the sixth century A.D. and that the order of the priority of the Āṛvārs as found in the *Guru-paramparā* lists is not reliable. One of the main points of criticism used by Aiyangar against Bhandarkar is the latter's identification of Kula-śēkhara Peru-māl with Kula-śekharāṅka. The works of the Āṛvārs were written in Tamil, and those that survive were collected in their present form in Rāmānuja's time or in the time of Nātha-muni; this collection, containing 4000 hymns, is called *Nāl-āyira-divya-prabandham*. But at least one part of it was composed by Kuruttalvan or Kuruttama, who was a prominent disciple of Rāmānuja, and in a passage thereof a reference is made to Rāmānuja also[2]. The order of the Āṛvārs given in this work is somewhat different from that given in the *Guru-paramparā* referred to above, and it does not contain the name of Nāmm'-āṛvār, who is treated separately. Again, Pillān, the disciple and apostolic successor of Rāmānuja, who commented on the *Tiru-vāy-moṛi* of Nāmm'-āṛvār, gives in a verse all the names of the Āṛvārs, omitting only

[1] *Indian Antiquary*, Vol. XXXV, pp. 228, etc.

[2] This part is called *Rāmānuja-nurrundādi*. The order of the Āṛvārs given here is as follows: Poygaiy-āṛvār, Bhūtatt'-āṛvār, Pēy-āṛvār, Tiru-pāṇ-āṛvār, Tiru-maṛiṣai Pirān, Toṇḍar-aḍi-poḍiy-āṛvār, Kula-śēkhara, Periy-āṛvār, Āṇḍāḷ, Tiru-maṅgaiy-āṛvār. Veṅkaṭanātha, however, in his *Prabandha-sāram* records the Āṛvārs in the following order: Poygaiy-āṛvār, Bhūtatt'-āṛvār, Pēy-āṛvār, Tiru-maṛiṣai Pirān, Nāmm'-āṛvār, Madhura-kaviy-āṛvār, Kula-śēkhara, Periy-āṛvār, Āṇḍāḷ, Toṇḍar-aḍi-poḍiy-āṛvār, Tiru-pān-āṛvār, Tiru-maṅgaiy-āṛvār.

Āṇḍāḷ[1]. Thus it appears that Kula-śēkhara was accepted as an Ārvār in Rāmānuja's time. In Veṅkaṭanātha's (fourteenth-century) list, contained in one of his Tamil *Prabandhams*, all the Ārvārs excepting Āṇḍāḷ and Madhura-kaviy-ārvār are mentioned. The *Prabandham* contains also a succession list of teachers according to the Vaḍakalai sect, beginning with Rāmānuja[2].

Kula-śēkhara, in his *Mukunda-mālā*, says that he was the ruler of Kolli (Uraiyūr, the Cola capital), Kudal (Madurā) and Koṅgu. Being a native of Travancore (Vañjikulam), he became the ruler of the Pāṇḍya and Cola capitals, Madurā and Uraiyūr. After A.D. 900, when the Cola king Parāntaka became supreme and the Cola capital was at Tanjore instead of at Uraiyūr, the ascendency of the Travancore country (Kerala) over the Cola and the Pāṇḍya kingdoms would have been impossible. It could only have happened either before the rise of the great Pallava dynasty with Narasiṃhavarman I (A.D. 600) or after the fall of that dynasty with Nandivarman (A.D. 800). If Tiru-maṅgaiy-ārvār, the contemporary of Vairamegha, be accepted as the last Ārvār, then Kula-śēkhara must be placed in the sixth century A.D. But Gopi-nātha Rāu interprets a passage of Kula-śēkhara as alluding to the defeat and death of a Pallava king at his hands. He identifies this king with the Pallava king Dantivarman, about A.D. 825, and is of the opinion that he flourished in the first half of the ninth century A.D. In any case Bhandarkar's identification of Kula-śēkhara with Kula-śekharāṅka (A.D. 1150) is very improbable, as an inscription dated A.D. 1088 makes a provision for the recital of Kula-śēkhara's "*Tettarumtiral.*"[3] Aiyangar further states that in several editions of the *Mukunda-mālā* the quotation from the *Bhāgavata-purāṇa* referred to by Bhandarkar cannot be traced. We may thus definitely reject the view of Bhandarkar that Kula-śēkhara flourished in the middle of the twelfth century A.D.

There is a great controversy among the South Indian historians and epigraphists not only about the chronological order of the

[1] *Bhūtaṃ Saraś ca Mahad-anvaya-Bhaṭṭanātha-*
Śrī-Bhaktisāra-Kulaśekhara-Yogivāhān
Bhaktāṅghrireṇu-Parakāla-Yatīndramiśrān
Śrī-mat-Parāṅkuśa-muniṃ praṇato'smi nityam.
Verse quoted from Aiyangar's *Early History of Vaiṣṇavism.*

[2] Rāmānuja's preceptor was Periya Nambi, then come Alavandar, Manakkal Nambi, Uyyakkondar, Nāthamuni, Śaṭhakopa, Viṣvaksena (Senai Nathan), Mahālakṣmī and Viṣṇu. Aiyangar, *Early History of Vaiṣṇavism*, p. 21.

[3] *Ibid.* p. 33.

different Āṟvārs, but also regarding the dates of the first and the last, and of those who came between them. Thus, while Aiyangar wished to place the first four Āṟvārs about the second century A.D., Gopi-nātha Rāu regards them as having flourished in the middle of the seventh century A.D.[1] Again, Nāmm'-āṟvār is placed by Aiyangar in the middle of the sixth century, while Gopi-nātha Rāu would place him during the first half of the ninth century. While Aiyangar would close the history of the Āṟvārs by the middle of the seventh century, Gopi-nātha Rāu would place Kula-śēkhara in A.D. 825, Periy-āṟvār in about the same date or a few years later, and Toṇḍar-aḍi-poḍiy-āṟvār, Tiru-maṅgaiy-āṟvār and Tiru-pān-āṟvār (contemporaries) about A.D. 830. From comparing the various matters of controversy, the details of which cannot well be described here, I feel it wise to follow Gopi-nātha Rāu, and am inclined to think that the order of the Āṟvārs, except so far as the first group of four is concerned, is not a chronological one, as many of them were close contemporaries, and their history is within a period of only 200 years, from the middle of the seventh century to the middle of the ninth century.

The word Āṟvār means one who has a deep intuitive knowledge of God and one who is immersed in the contemplation of Him. The works of the Āṟvārs are full of intense and devoted love for Viṣṇu. This love is the foundation of the later systematic doctrine of *prapatti*. The difference between the Āṟvārs and the Aragiyas, of whom we shall speak later on, is that, while the former had realized Brahman and had personal enjoyment of His grace, the latter were learned propounders who elaborated the philosophy contained in the works of the Āṟvārs. Poygaiy, Bhūtatt' and Pēy composed the three sections of one hundred stanzas each of *Tiru-vantādi*[2]. Tiru-maṟiṣai Pirān spent much of his life in Triplicane, Conjeevaram and Kumbakonaṁ. His hymns are the *Nan-mukham Tiru-vantādi*, containing ninety-six stanzas, and *Tiru-chaṇḍa-vṛuttam*. Nāmm'-āṟvār was born of a Śūdra family at Kurukur, now Āḻvārtirunagari in the Tinnevelly district. He was the most voluminous writer

[1] These are Pēy-āṟvār, Bhūtatt'-āṟvār, Poygaiy-āṟvār and Tiru-maṟiṣai Pirān, the first three being known as Mudal-āṟvārs among the Śrīvaiṣṇavas.

[2] As a specimen of *Tiru-vantādi* one may quote the following passage: "With love as lamp-bowl, desire as oil, mind melting with bliss as wick, with melting soul I have kindled the bright light of wisdom in the learned Tāmil which I have wrought for Nārāyaṇa."—Bhūtam, quotation from Hooper's *Hymns of the Āḻvāṟs*, p. 12, n.

among the Āṟvārs and a great mass of his poetry is preserved in the *Nāl-āyira-divya-prabandham*. His works are the *Tiru-vṛuttam*, containing one hundred stanzas, *Tiru-vāṣiriyam*, containing seven stanzas, the *Periya tiru-vantādi* of eighty-seven staṇzas, and the *Tiru-vāy-moṟi*, containing 1102 stanzas. Nāmm'-āṟvār's whole life was given to meditation. His disciple Madhura-kavi considers him an incarnation of Viṣṇu. Kula-śēkhara was a great devotee of Rāma. His chief work is the *Peru-māl-tiru-moṟi*. Periy-āṟvār, known as Viṣṇucitta, was born at Śrībittiputtūr. His chief works are *Tiru-pall'-āṇḍu* and *Tiru-moṟi*. Āṇḍāḷ, adopted daughter of Periy-āṟvār, was passionately devoted to Kṛṣṇa and considered herself as one of the Gopīs, seeking for union with Kṛṣṇa. She was married to the God Raṅganātha of Śrīraṅgam. Her chief works are *Tiru-pāvai* and *Nacchiyār*. Tirumoṟi Toṇḍar-aḍi-poḍiy-āṟvār was born at Mandaṇgudi. He was once under the seduction of a courtesan called Devādevī, but was saved by the grace of Raṅganātha. His chief works are *Tiru-mālai*, and the *Tiru-paḷḷiy-eṟuchi*. Tiru-pāṇ-āṟvār was brought up by a low-caste childless *panar*. His chief work was *Amalan-ādibirān* in ten stanzas. Tiru-maṅgaiy was born in the thief-caste. His chief works are *Periya-tiru-moṟi*, *Tiru-kuṟun-dāṇḍakam*, *Tiru-neḍun-dāṇḍakam*, *Tiru-veṟugūtt-irukkai*, *Ṣiṟiya-tiru-maḍal* and *Periya-tiru-maḍal*. Tiru-maṅgaiy was driven to brigandage, and gained his divine wisdom through the grace of Raṅganātha. The *Nāl-āyira-divya-prabandham*, which contains the works of the Āṟvārs, is regarded in the Tamil country as the most sacred book and is placed side by side with the Vedas. It is carried in procession into the temple, when verses from it are recited and they are recited also on special occasions of marriage, death, etc. Verses from it are also sung and recited in the hall in front of the temple, and it is used in the rituals along with Vedic *mantras*.

The Philosophy of the Āṟvārs.

As the hymns of the Āṟvārs have only a literary and devotional form, it is difficult to utilize them for philosophical purposes. As an illustration of the general subject-matter of their works, I shall try to give a brief summary of the main contents of Nāmm'-āṟvār's (Śaṭhakopa) work, following Abhirāmavarācārya's *Dramiḍopaniṣat-tātparya*[1]. The feeling of devotion to God felt by Śaṭhakopa

[1] MS. from Government Oriental Manuscript Library, Madras.

could not be contained within him, and, thus overflowing, was expressed in verses which soothed all sufferers; this shows that his affection for suffering humanity was even greater than that of their own parents. Śaṭhakopa's main ideal was to subdue our so-called manhood by reference to God (*puruṣottama*), the greatest of all beings, and to regard all beings as but women dependent on Him; and so it was that Śaṭhakopa conceived himself as a woman longing for her lover and entirely dependent on him. In the first of his four works he prayed for the cessation of rebirth; in the second he described his experiences of God's great and noble qualities; in the third he expressed his longings to enjoy God; and in the fourth he described how all his experiences of God's communion with him fell far short of his great longings. In the first ten stanzas of his first centum he is infused with a spirit of service (*dāsya*) to God and describes his experiences of God's essential qualities. In the next ten stanzas he describes the mercy of God and recommends every one to give up attachment to all other things, which are of a trifling and temporary nature. Then he prays to God for his incarnation on earth with Lakṣmī, His consort, and pays adoration to Him. He continues with a description of his mental agonies in not attaining communion with God, confessing his own guilt to Him. He then embraces God and realizes that all his failings are his own fault. He explains that the spirit of service (*dāsya*) does not depend for its manifestation and realization on any elaborate rituals involving articles of worship, but on one's own zeal. What is necessary is true devotion (*bhakti*). Such a devotion, he says, must proceed through an intense enjoyment of the nature of the noble qualities of God, so that the devotee may feel that there is nothing in anything else that is greater than them. With a yielding heart he says that God accepts the service of those who, instead of employing all the various means of subduing a crooked enemy, adopt only the means of friendliness to them[1]. God is pleased with those who are disposed to realize the sincerity of their own spirit, and it is through this that they can realize God in themselves. God's favour does not depend on anything but His own grace, manifesting itself in an all-embracing devotion. He says, in the second *śataka*, that the devotee, having,

[1] *kauṭilyavatsu karaṇa-tritaye'pi jantuṣv*
ātmīyam eva karaṇa-tritayaika-rūpyam
sandarśya tānapi hariḥ sva-vaśīkarotīty
ācaṣṭa sāndra-karuṇo munir aṣṭamena.

Dramiḍopaniṣat-tātparya. MS.

on the one hand, felt the great and noble qualities of God, and yet being attached to other things, is pierced through with pangs of sorrow in not realizing God in communion, and feels a bond of sympathy with all humanity sharing the same grief. Through the stories of God related in the Purāṇas, e.g. in the *Bhāgavata*, Śaṭhakopa feels the association of God which removes his sorrow and so increases his contact with God. He then describes how the great saints of the past had within their heart of hearts enjoyed an immersion in the ocean of God's bliss, which is the depository of all blissful emotion; and he goes on to express his longings for the enjoyment of that bliss. Through his longings for Him there arose in Śaṭhakopa great grief of separation, devoid of any interest in furthering unworthy ends; he communicated to Him his great sorrow at his incapacity to realize Him, and in so doing he lost consciousness through intensity of grief. As a result God Kṛṣṇa appeared before him, and he describes accordingly the joy of the vision of God. But he fears to lose God, who is too mighty for him, and takes refuge in his great attachment to Him. Next he says that they only realize God who have a sense of possession in Him. He describes God's noble qualities, and shows that the realization of the proximity of God is much more desirable than the attainment of emancipation. He says that the true definition of *mokṣa* is to attain the position of God's servant[1].

In the beginning of the third centum he describes the beauty of God. Then he bemoans the fact that, on account of the limitations of his senses and his mind, he is unable to enjoy the fullness of His beauty. Next he describes the infinitude of God's glory and his own spirit of service to Him. Then he envisages the whole world and the words that denot the things of the world as being the body of God[2]. Then he expres es the pleasure and bliss he feels in the service of God, and says that even those who cannot come into contact with God in His own essence can find solace in directing their minds to His image and to the stories of Kṛṣṇa related in the

1 *mokṣādaraṃ sphuṭam avekṣya munir mukunde*
mokṣaṃ pradātuṃ sadṛkṣa-phalaṃ pravṛtte
ātme-ṣṭam asya pada-kiṅkarataika-rūpaṃ
mokṣā-khya-vastu navame niraṇāyi tena.
Dramiḍopaniṣat-tātparya. MS.

2 *sarvaṃ jagat samavalokya vibhoś śarīraṃ*
tad-vācinaś ca sakalān api śabda-rāśīn
taṃ bhūta-bhautika-mukhān kathayan padārthān
dāsyaṃ cakāra vacasaiva muniś caturthe. Ibid.

Purāṇas. He then absorbs himself in the grief of his separation from God and hopes that by arresting all the inner senses he may see God with his own eyes. He also regrets the condition of other men who are wasting their time in devotion to gods other than Kṛṣṇa. He goes on to describe the vision of God and his great joy therein.

In the fourth centum he describes the transitoriness of all things considered as enjoyable, and the absolute superiority of the bliss of pleasing God. He goes on to explain how, through cessation of all inclination to other things and the increase of longing for God in a timeless and spaceless manner, and through the pangs of separation in not realizing Him constantly, he considers himself as a woman, and through the pangs of love loses his consciousness[1]. Then he describes how Hari is pleased with his amour and satisfies his longings by making Him enjoyable through the actions of mind, words and body by His blissful embraces[2]. Next he shows how, when he attempted to realize Kṛṣṇa by his spiritual zeal, Kṛṣṇa vanished from his sight and he was then once more filled with the grief of separation. Again he receives a vision of God and feels with joy His overwhelming superiority. He further describes how his vision of God was like a dream, and how, when the dream ceased, he lost consciousness. To fill up the emptiness of these occasional separations, he sorrowfully chanted the name of God, and earnestly prayed to Him. He wept for Him and felt that without Him everything was nothing. Yet at intervals he could not help feeling deep sympathy for erring humanity which had turned its mind away from God. According to him the real bondage consists in the preference man gives to things other than God. When one can feel God as all-in-all, every bond is loosened.

In the fifth centum he feels that God's grace alone can save man. He again describes himself as the wife of God, constantly longing for His embrace. In his grief and lamentation and his anxiety to meet God, he was overcome by a swoon which, like the night, dimmed all his senses. At the end of this state he saw the orna-

1 *taṃ puruṣā-rtham itarā-rtha-rucer nivṛttyā*
sāndra-spṛhaḥ samaya-deśa-vidūragaṃ ca
ipsuḥ śucā tad-an-avāpti-bhuvā dvitīye
strī-bhāvanāṃ samadhigamya munir mumoha.
Dramiḍopaniṣat-tātparya. MS.

2 *prītāḥ paraṃ harir amuṣya tadā svabhāvād*
etan-mano-vacana-deha-kṛta-kriyābhiḥ
srak-candana-pramukha-sarva-vidha-svabhogyaḥ
saṃśliṣṭavān idam uvāca munis tṛtīye. *Ibid.*

ments of God, but could not see Him directly, and was thus filled both with grief and happiness. As a relief from the pangs of separation he found enjoyment in identifying himself in his mind with God and in imitating His ways, thinking that the world was created by him[1]. In a number of verses (seventy or eighty) he describes how he was attached to the image of the God Kṛṣṇa at Kumbhakonam and how he suffered through God's apathy towards him in not satisfying him, His lover, with embraces and other tokens of love, and how he became angry with His indifference to his amorous approaches and was ultimately appeased by God, who satisfied him with loving embraces and the like. Thus God, who was divine lord of the universe, felt sympathy and love for him and appeased his sorrows in the fashion of a human lover[2]. He describes his great bliss in receiving the embrace of God. Through this rapturous divine love and divine embrace he lost all mundane interest in life.

In the ninth centum the sage, finding he could not look at the ordinary things of life, nor easily gain satisfaction in the divine presence of God in the whole world, fixed his mind on His transcendental form (*aprākṛta-vapuḥ*) and became full of wailing and lamentation as a means of direct access to it. A great part of this centum is devoted to laments due to his feeling of separation from God. He describes how through constant lamentation and brooding he received the vision of God, but was unhappy because he could not touch Him; and how later on God took human form in response to his prayers and made him forget his sufferings[3]. In many other verses he again describes the emotions of his distress at his separation and temporary union with God; how he sent messages to God through birds; how he felt miserable because He delayed to meet him; how he expected to meet Him at appointed times, and how his future actions in Heaven should be repeated in

1 *śokaṃ ca taṃ pari-jihīrṣur ivākhilānāṃ*
sargā-di-kartur anukāra-rasena śaureḥ
tasya pravṛttir akhilā racitā maye' ti
tad-bhāva-bhāvita-manā munir āha ṣaṣṭhe.
Dramiḍopaniṣat-tātparya. MS.

2 *kopaṃ mama praṇaya-jaṃ praśamayya kṛṣṇa*
svā-dhīnatām ātanute' ti sa-vismayaḥ saḥ
svyīāṃ viruddha-jagad-ākṛtitāṃ ca tena
sandarśitām anubabhūva munis tṛtīye. *Ibid.*

3 *saṅgaṃ nivarttya mama saṃsṛti-maṇḍale māṃ*
saṃsthāpayan katham asī' ty anucoditena
āścaryya-loka-tanutām api darśayitvā
vismāritaḥ kila śucaṃ hariṇā' ṣṭame' sau. *Ibid.*

earth and how his behaviour to God was like that of the Gopīs, full of ardent love and eagerness. In the concluding verses, however, he says that the real vision of God can come only to a deeply devoted mind and not to external eyes.

Hooper gives some interesting translations from the *Tiru-vṛuttam* of Nāmm'-ārvār, a few of which may be quoted here to illustrate the nature of his songs of love for God[1]:

> Long may she love, this girl with luring locks,
> Who loves the feet that heavenly ones adore,
> The feet of Kaṇṇan, dark as rainy clouds:
> Her red eyes all abrim with tears of grief,
> Like darting *Kayal* fish in a deep pool[2].
> Hot in this village now doth blow the breeze
> Whose nature coolness is. Hath he, this once,
> The rain-cloud hued, his sceptre turned aside
> To steal the love-glow from my lady, lorn
> For tuḷasī, with wide eyes raining tears?[3]

In separation from the lord the Ārvār finds delight in looking at darkness, which resembles Kṛṣṇa's colour:

> Thou, fair as Kaṇṇan's heaven, when he's away
> What ages long it is! He here, a span!
> Whether friends stay for many days, or go,
> We grieve. Yet, be this spreading darkness blest
> In spite of many a cunning trick it has[4].
> What will befall my girl with bracelets fair,
> With tearful eyes like gleaming *Kayal* big,
> Who wanders with a secret pain at heart
> For blooms of tuḷasī fresh from the Bird's Lord
> Who with that hill protected flocks in storm?[5]

The Ārvār then laments and pleads with swans and herons to take his message:

> The flying swans and herons I did beg,
> Cringing: "Forget not, ye, who first arrive,
> If ye behold my heart with Kaṇṇan there
> Oh, speak of me and ask it 'Sir not yet
> Hast thou returned to her? And is it right?'"

[1] *Hymns of the Āḷvars*, by J. S. M. Hooper, pp. 61–88.

[2] The maid who is represented as speaking here stands for Ārvār's disciple, and the lady in love is the mistress, and Kaṇṇan is Kṛṣṇa, the Lord.

[3] This is also a speech from the maid, and *tuḷasī* stands for Kṛṣṇa.

[4] The time of separation is felt to be too long, and the time of union is felt to be too short.

[5] Lamentation of the mother for the girl, the Ārvār.

The Āṛvār then laments that the clouds will not take his message. He speaks of the resemblance between the clouds and the Lord:

> Tell me, ye clouds, how have ye won the means
> That we are thus like Tirumāl's blest form?
> Bearing good water for protecting life,
> Ye range through all the sky. Such penance, sure,
> As makes your bodies ache, has won this grace!

The friend speaks of the callousness of the lord:

> E'en in this age-long time of so-called night
> When men must grope, he pities not that she
> Stands in her deep immitigable grief....
> The jungle traversed by the fawn-eyed girl
> With fragile waist, whom sinful I brought forth
> After long praise of Kaṇṇan's lotus feet....

The Āṛvār sees a likeness of his lord in the blue water-lily, and sees the lord's form everywhere:

> All places, shining like great lotus pools
> On a blue mountain broad, to me are but
> The beauties of his eye—the lord of earth
> Girt by the roaring sea, heaven's lord, the lord
> Of other good souls, black-hued lord—and mine!

The Āṛvār speaks of the greatness of the lord:

> Sages with wisdom won by virtuous toil
> Assert "His colour, glorious beauty, name,
> His form—are such and such." But all their toil
> Has measured not the greatness of my lord:
> Their wisdom's light is but a wretched lamp.

The foster-mother pities the mistress unable to endure the length of the night:

> This child of sinful me, with well-formed teeth,
> Round breasts and rosy mouth, keeps saying, "These
> Fair nights eternal are as my desire
> For tuḷasī!"...

Again the foster-mother pities the girl as too young for such ardent love:

> Breasts not yet full, and short her tresses soft;
> Skirt loose about the waist; with prattling tongue
> And innocent eyes....

Again the lord replies to a friend's criticism of his infatuation for his mistress:

Those lilies red, which are the life of me—
The eyes of her who's like the heaven of him....

The mistress is unable to endure the darkness and is yet further vexed by the appearance of the moon:

Oh, let the crescent moon which cleaves the dark
Encompassing of night, cleave me as well!
Ah, does it issue forth in brightness now,
That happy bloom may come to desolate me
Who only long for flowers of tuḷasī?

The mistress's friend despairs at the sight of her languishing:

...Ah! as she sobs and lisps
The cloud-hued's names, I know not if she'll live
Or if her frame and spirit mild must pass!

Again in Kula-śēkhara's *Tirumal-Tiru-moṛi*, C. 5:

Though red fire comes itself and makes fierce heat,
The lotus red blooms not
Save for the fierce-rayed one
Who in the lofty heavens has his seat.
Vitruvakōḍu's Lord, Thou wilt not remove
My woe, my heart melts not save at Thy boundless love....

With gathered waters all the streams ashine
Must spread abroad and run
And enter the deep sea
And cannot stand outside. So refuge mine,
Save in the shining bliss of entering Thee, is none,
Vitruvakōḍu's Lord, thick cloud-hued, virtuous one![1]

Again from the same book[2]:

No kinship with the world have I
Which takes for true the life that is not true.
"For thee alone my passion burns," I cry,
"Raṅgan, my Lord!"
No kinship with this world have I—
With throngs of maidens slim of waist:
With joy and love I rise for one alone, and cry
"Raṅgan, my Lord!"

[1] Hooper, *op. cit.* p. 48. [2] *Ibid.* p. 44.

Again in the *Tiru-pāvai*, a well-known section of the *Nāl-āyira-divya-prabandham*, the poetess Āṇḍāḷ conceives herself as a Gopī, requesting her friends to go with her to wake the sleeping Kṛṣṇa,

After the cows we to the jungle go
And eat there—cowherds knowing nought are we,
And yet how great the boon we have, that thou
Wast born among us! Thou who lackest nought,
Gōvinda, kinship that we have with thee
Here in this place can never cease!—If through
Our love we call thee baby names, in grace
Do not be wroth, for we—like children—we
Know nought—O Lord, wilt thou not grant to us
The drum we ask? Ah, Ēlōrembāvāy![1]

Again Periy-āṛvār conceives himself as Yaśodā and describes the infant Kṛṣṇa as lying in the dust and calling for the moon!

(1) He rolls round in the dust, so that the jewel on his brow keeps swinging, and his waist-bells tinkle! Oh, look at my son Gōvinda's play, big Moon, if thou hast eyes in thy face—and then, be gone!

(2) My little one, precious to me as nectar, my blessing, is calling thee, pointing, pointing, with his little hands! O big Moon, if thou wishest to play with this little black one, hide not thyself in the clouds, but come rejoicing![2]

Again, Tiru-maṅgaiy says:

Or ever age creep on us, and we need
The staff's support; ere we are double bent
With eyes fix'd on the ground in front, and feet
That totter, sitting down to rest, all spent:
We would worship Vadari
Home of him who mightily
Suck'd his feignéd mother's breast
Till she died, ogress confest.

Again Āṇḍāḷ says:

Daughter of Nandagōpāl, who is like
A lusty elephant, who fleeth not,
With shoulders strong: Nappinnāi, thou with hair
Diffusing fragrance, open thou the door!
Come see how everywhere the cocks are crowing,
And in the *māthavi* bower the Kuyil sweet
Repeats its song.—Thou with a ball in hand,
Come, gaily open, with thy lotus hands
And tinkling bangles fair, that we may sing
Thy cousin's name! Ah, Ēlōrembāvāy!

[1] Hooper, *op. cit.* p. 57. [2] *Ibid.* p. 37.

Thou who art strong to make them brave in fight,
Going before the three and thirty gods,
Awake from out thy sleep! Thou who art just,
Thou who art mighty, thou, O faultless one,
Who burnest up thy foes, awake from sleep!
O Lady Nappinnāi, with tender breasts
Like unto little cups, with lips of red
And slender waist, Lakshmi, awake from sleep!
Proffer thy bridegroom fans and mirrors now,
And let us bathe! Ah, Elōrembāvāy![1]

In describing the essential feature of the devotion of an Ārvār like Namm'-ārvār, called also Parāṅkuśa or Śaṭhakopa, Gōvindāchāryar, the author of *The Divine Wisdom of the Drâviḍa Saints* and *The Holy Lives of the Âzhvârs*, says that according to Nāmm'-ārvār, when one is overcome by *bhakti*-exultation and self-surrendering devotion to God he easily attains truth[2]. Nāmm'-ārvār said that God's grace is the only means of securing our salvation, and no effort is required on our part but to surrender ourselves to Him. In the following words Nāmm'-ārvār says that God is constantly trying to woo us to love Him:

Blissful Lord, heard I; anon my eyes in floods did run,
Oh what is this? I asked. What marvel this? the Perfect one,
Through friendly days and nights, elects with me to e'er remain,
To union wooing me, His own to make; nor let me "lone."

Nāmm'-ārvār again writes that God's freedom is fettered by His mercy. Thus he says: "O mercy, thou hast deprived God of the freedom of His just will. Safe under the winds of mercy, no more can God Himself even of His will tear Himself away from me; for, if He can do so, I shall still exclaim, I am Victor, for He must purchase the freedom of His will by denying to Himself mercy." Illustrating the position, he refers to the case of a devout lady who clasped the feet of the Lord in Varadarāja's shrine at Kāñcī and said: "God I have now clasped thy feet firmly; try if thou canst, spurn me and shake thyself off from me."

Nāmm'-ārvār used the term *Tuvaḷil* or *Ninṛu kumiṛume*, a Tamil expression of love, which has been interpreted as signifying a continuous whirling emotion of love boring deeper and deeper, but never scattering and passing away. This circling and boring of

[1] Hooper, *op. cit.* p. 55.
[2] *Bhagavad-vishayam*, Bk. I, p. 571, as quoted in Gōvindāchāryar's *Divine Wisdom of the Drâviḍa Saints*.

love in the heart is mute, silent and incapable of expression; like the cow, whose teats filled with milk tingle, cannot withal express by mouth her painful longing to reach her calf who is tethered away from her. Thus, true love of God is perpetual and ever growing[1]. The difference between the love of Nāmm'-āṟvār and of Tiru-mańgaiy-āṟvār is said to have been described by Yāmuna, as reported in the *Bhagavad-vishayam*, as of two different kinds. Tiru-mańgaiy-āṟvār's love expresses the experience of a constant companionship with God in a state of delirious, rapturous reciprocation of ravishing love. He was immersed in the fathomless depth of love, and was in the greatest danger of becoming unconscious and falling into a stupor like one under the influence of a narcotic. Nāmm'-āṟvār, however, was in a state of urgent pursuit after God. He was thus overcome with a sense of loneliness and unconscious of his individual self. He was not utterly intoxicated. The energy flowing from a mind full and strong with the ardent expectation of meeting his bridegroom and beloved companion still sustained him and kept him alive[2]. This state is described in *Tiru-vāy-moṟi* in the following manner:

Day and night she knows not sleep,
In floods of tears her eyes do swim.
Lotus-like eyes! She weeps and reels,
Ah! how without thee can I bear;
She pants and feels all earth for Him.

This love of God is often described as having three stages: recollection, trance and rallying. The first means the reminiscence of all the past ravishment of soul vouchsafed by God. The second means fainting and desolation at such reminiscences and a consciousness of the present absence of such ravishing enjoyments. The third is a sudden lucidity whilst in the state of trance, which being of a delirious nature may often lead to death through the rapid introduction of death-coma[3].

The Āṟvārs were not given to any philosophical speculation but only to ecstatic experiences of the emotion of love for God; yet we sometimes find passages in Nāmm'-āṟvār's works wherein he reveals his experience of the nature of soul. Thus he says: "It is not possible to give a description of that wonderful entity, the soul

[1] *Divine Wisdom of the Drâviḍa Saints*, pp. 127–128.

[2] See the *Bhagavad-vishayam*, Bk. VI, p. 2865; also *Divine Wisdom*, pp. 130, 131.

[3] *Bhagavad-vishayam*, Bk. VII, p. 3194; also *Divine Wisdom*, p. 151.

(*ātmā*)—the soul which is eternal, and is essentially characterized by intelligence (*jñāna*)—the soul which the Lord has condescended to exhibit to me as His mode, or I related to Him as the predicate is to the subject, or attribute is to substance (or consonants to the vowel A)—the soul, the nature of which is beyond the comprehension of even the enlightened—the soul, which cannot be classed under any category as this or that—the soul whose apperception by the strenuous mental effort called *yoga* (psychic meditation) is even then not comparable to such perception or direct proof as arises from the senses conveying knowledge of the external world—the soul (as revealed to me by my Lord) transcending all other categories of things, which could be grouped as 'body' or as 'the senses,' or as 'the vital spirit' (*prāṇa*), or as 'the mind' (*manas*), or as 'the will' (*buddhi*), being destitute of the modifications and corruptions to which all these are subject;—the soul, which is very subtle and distinct from any of these;—neither coming under the description 'good,' nor 'bad.' The soul is, briefly, an entity which does not fall under the cognizance of sense-knowledge[1]."

Soul is here described as a pure subtle essence unassociated with impurities of any kind and not knowable in the manner in which all ordinary things are known. Such philosophical descriptions or discussions concerning the nature of reality, or an investigation into the logical or epistemological position of the religion preached by them, are not within the scope and province of the Āṟvārs. They sang songs in an inspired manner and often believed that they themselves had no hand in their composition, but that it was God who spoke through them. These songs were often sung to the accompaniment of cymbals, and the intoxicating melody of the music was peculiar to the Āṟvārs and entirely different from the traditional music then current in South India. A study of the works of the Āṟvārs, which were collected together by the disciples of Rāmānuja at his special request, and from which Rāmānuja himself drew much inspiration and food for his system of thought, reveals an intimate knowledge of the Purāṇic legends of Kṛṣṇa, as found in the *Viṣṇu-purāṇa* and the *Bhāgavata*[2]. There is at least one passage, already referred to, which may well be interpreted as

[1] *Divine Wisdom*, p. 169; also *Tiru-vāy-moṟi*, VIII. 5–8.

[2] Sir R. G. Bhandarkar notes that the Āṟvār Kula-śekhara, in his work *Mukunda-mālā*, quotes a passage from the *Bhāgavata-purāṇa* (XI. 2. 36) (*The

alluding to Rādhā (Nappinnāi), who is described as the consort of Kṛṣṇa. The Āṛvārs refer to the legends of Kṛṣṇa's early life in Brindavan and many of them play the role either of Yośodā, the friends of Kṛṣṇa, or of the Gopīs. The spiritual love which finds expression in their songs is sometimes an earnest appeal of direct longing for union with Kṛṣṇa, or an expression of the pangs of separation, or a feeling of satisfaction, and enjoyment from union with Kṛṣṇa in a direct manner or sometimes through an emotional identification with the legendary personages associated with Kṛṣṇa's life. Even in the *Bhāgavata-purāṇa* (XI, XII) we hear of devotional intoxication through intense emotion, but we do not hear of any devotees identifying themselves with the legendary personages associated with the life of Kṛṣṇa and expressing their sentiment of love as proceeding out of such imaginary identification. We hear of the Gopī's love for Kṛṣṇa, but we do not hear of any person identifying himself with Gopī and expressing his sorrow of separation. In the *Viṣṇu-purāṇa*, *Bhāgavata-purāṇa* and the *Harivaṃśa*, the legendary love tales are only episodes in the life of Kṛṣṇa. But they do not make their devotees who identified themselves with the legendary lovers of Kṛṣṇa realize their devotion through such an imaginary identification. All that is therein expressed is that the legendary life of Kṛṣṇa would intensify the devotion of those who were already attached to Him. But the idea that the legend of Kṛṣṇa should have so much influence on the devotees as to infuse them with the characteristic spirits of the legendary personages in such a manner as to transform their lives after their pattern is probably a new thing in the history of devotional development in any religion. It is also probably absent in the cults of other devotional faiths of India. With the Āṛvārs we notice for the first time the coming into prominence of an idea which achieved its culmination in the lives and literature of the devotees of the Gauḍīya school of Bengal, and particularly in the life of Caitanya, which will be dealt with in the fourth volume of the present work. The trans-

Vaiṣṇavism, Śaivism and Minor Religious Systems, p. 70). This has been challenged by S. K. Aiyangar, in his *Early History of Vaiṣṇavism in South India*, who says that this passage is absent from all the three editions (a Kannaḍa, a Grantha, and a Devanāgarī Edition) which were accessible to him (p. 28). It is further suggested there that the allusion in the passage is doubtful, because it generally occurs at the end of most South Indian books by way of an apology for the faults committed at the time of the recitation of holy verses or the performance of religious observances.

fusion of the spirits of the legendary personages in the life-history of Kṛṣṇa naturally involved the transfusion of their special emotional attitudes towards Kṛṣṇa into the devotees, who were thus led to imagine themselves as being one with those legendary personalities and to pass through the emotional history of those persons as conceived through imagination. It is for this reason that we find that, when this spirit was emphasized in the Gauḍīya school and the analysis of erotic emotions made by the rhetorical school of thinkers from the tenth to the fourteenth century received recognition, the Gauḍīya Vaiṣṇavas accepted the emotional analysis of the advancing stages of love and regarded them as indicating the stages in the development of the sentiment of devotion. As is well illustrated in Rūpa Gosvāmī's *Ujjvala-nīla-maṇi*, the transition from ordinary devotion to deep amorous sentiment, as represented in the legendary lives of Gopīs and Rādhā, was secured by sympathetic imitation akin to the sympathetic interest displayed in the appreciation of dramatic actions. The thinkers of the rhetorical school declare that a spectator of a dramatic action has his emotions aroused in such a manner that in their excess the individual limitations of time and space and the history of individual experiences which constitute his ordinary personality vanish for the time being. The disappearance of the ordinary individual personality and the overflow of emotion in one direction identify the person in an imaginary manner not only with the actors who display the emotion of the stage, but also with the actual personalities of those dramatic figures whose emotions are represented or imitated on the stage. A devotee, may, by over-brooding, rouse himself through auto-intoxication to such an emotional stage that upon the slightest suggestion he may transport himself to the imaginary sphere of a Gopī or Rādhā, and may continue to feel all the earnest affections that the most excited and passionate lover may ever feel.

It seems fairly certain that the Āṟvārs were the earliest devotees who moved forward in the direction of such emotional transformation. Thus King Kula-śēkhara, who was an Āṟvār and devotee of Rāma, used to listen rapturously to the *Rāmāyaṇa* being recited to him. As he listened he became so excited that, when he heard of Rāma's venturing forth against Rāvaṇa, his demon opponent, he used to give orders to mobilize his whole army to march forward towards Laṅkā as an ally of Rāma.

The devotional songs of the Āṛvārs show an intense familiarity with the various parts of the legendary life of Kṛṣṇa. The emotions that stirred them were primarily of the types of parental affection (as of a mother to her son), of friends and companions, servants to their masters, sons to their father and creator, as also that of a female lover to her beloved. In the case of some Āṛvārs, as that of Nāmm'-āṛvār and Tiru-maṇgaiy-āṛvār, the last-mentioned type assumes an overwhelming importance. In the spiritual experiences of these Āṛvārs we find a passionate yearning after God, the Lord and Lover; and in the expressions of their love we may trace most of the pathological symptoms of amorous longings which have been so intensely emphasized in the writings of the Vaiṣṇavas of the Gauḍīya school. In the case of the latter, the human analogy involving description of the bodily charms of the female lover is often carried too far. In the case of the Āṛvārs, however, the emphasis is mostly on the transcendant beauty and charm of God, and on the ardent longings of the devotee who plays the part of a female lover, for Kṛṣṇa, the God. The ardent longing is sometimes expressed in terms of the pitiable pathological symptoms due to love-sickness, sometimes by sending messengers, spending the whole night in expectation of the Lord, and sometimes in the expressions of ravishing joy felt by the seemingly actual embrace of the Lord. We hear also of the reciprocation of love on the part of the Lord, who is described as being infatuated with the beauty and charms of the beloved, the Āṛvār. In the course of these expressions, the personages in the legendary account of Kṛṣṇa's life are freely introduced, and references are made to the glorious episodes of His life, as showing points that heighten the love of the lady-lover, the Āṛvār. The rapturous passions are like a whirlpool that eddies through the very eternity of the individual soul, and expresses itself sometimes in the pangs of separation and sometimes in the exhilaration of union. The Āṛvār, in his ecstatic delight, visualizes God everywhere, and in the very profundity of his attainment pines for more. He also experiences states of supreme intoxication, when he becomes semi-conscious, or unconscious with occasional breaks into the consciousness of a yearning. But, though yearning after God is often delineated on the analogy of sex-love, this analogy is seldom carried to excess by studied attempts at following all the pathological symptoms of erotic love. It therefore represents a very chaste form of the expressions of divine love in terms of human love. The Āṛvārs were probably the pioneers in showing how love for God may be on terms of tender equality, softening down to the rapturous emotion of conjugal love. The Śaivism of South India flourished more or less at the same time. The hymns of the Śaivas are full of deep and noble sentiments of devotion which can hardly be excelled in any literature; but their main emphasis is on the majesty and the greatness of God and the feeling of submission, self-abnegation and self-surrender to God. The spirit of self-surrender and a feeling of clinging to God as one's all is equally dominant among the Āṛvārs; but among them it melts down into the sweetness of passionate love. The Śaiva hymns are indeed pregnant with the divine fire of devotion, but more in the spirit of submissive service. Thus, Māṇikka-vāchakar, in his *Tiru-vācha kam*, speaking of Śiva, says[1]:

And am I not Thy *slave*? and did'st Thou not make me Thine own,
I pray?
All those Thy servants have approached Thy Foot; this body full of sin
I may not quit, and see Thy face—Thou Lord of Çiva-world!—I fear,
And *see not how to gain the sight!*

All *false* am I; *false* is my heart; and *false* my love; yet, if he weep,
May not Thy sinful servant Thee, Thou Soul's Ambrosial sweetness,
gain?
Lord of all honied gladness pure, in grace unto Thy servant teach
The way that he may come to Thee!

. . . . . .

There was no love in me towards Thy Foot,
O Half of Her with beauteous fragrant locks!
By magic power that stones to mellow fruit
converts, Thou mad'st me lover of Thy Feet.
Our Lord, Thy tender love no limit knows.
Whatever sways me now, whate'er my deed,
Thou can'st even yet Thy Foot again to me
display and save, O Spotless Heavenly One!

The devotee also felt the sweetness of God's love and the fact that it is through Divine Grace that one can be attracted towards Him and can love Him:

[1] Pope's translation of the *Tiru vācha-kam*, p. 77.

Honey from any flower sip not, though small
as tiniest grain of millet seed!
Whene'er we think of Him, whene'er we see,
whene'er of Him our lips converse,
Then sweetest rapture's honey ever flows,
till all our frame in bliss dissolves!
To Him alone, the mystic Dancer, go;
and breathe His praise, thou humming-bee!

Āṟvārs and Śrī-vaiṣṇavas on certain points of controversy in religious dogmas.

The Aṟagiyas Nāthamuni, Yāmuna, Rāmānuja and their adherents largely followed the inspirational teachings of the Āṟvārs, yet there were some differences of opinion among them regarding some of the cardinal points of religious faith. These have been collected in separate treatises, of which two may be regarded as most important. One of them is called *Aṣṭādaśa-rahasyārtha-vivaraṇa*, by Rāmānuja himself, and the other is called *Aṣṭādaśa-bheda-nirṇaya*[1]. Veṅkaṭanātha and others also wrote important treatises on the subject. Some of these points of difference may be enumerated below.

The first point is regarding the grace of God (*svāmi-kṛpā*). It is suggested by the Āṟvārs that the grace of God is spontaneous and does not depend on any effort or merit on the part of the devotee. If God had to depend on anything else for the exercise of His divine prerogative grace, it would be limited to that extent. Others, however, say that God's grace depends on the virtuous actions of the devotees. If that were not so, all people would in time be emancipated, and there would be no need of any effort on their part. If it was supposed that God in His own spontaneity extended His grace to some in preference to others, He would have to be regarded as partial. It is therefore to be admitted that, though God is free in extending His mercy, yet in practice He extends it only as a reward to the virtuous or meritorious actions of the devotee. God, though all-merciful and free to extend His mercy to all without effort on their part, does not actually do so except on the occasion of the meritorious actions of His devotees. The extension of God's mercy is thus both without cause (*nirhetuka*) and with cause (*sahetuka*)[2].

[1] Both these are MSS.

[2] *kṛpā-sva-rūpato nir-hetukaḥ, rakṣaṇa-samaye cetanā-kṛta-sukṛtena sa-hetuko bhūtvā rakṣati.* (*Aṣṭādaśa-bheda-nirṇaya*, MS. p. 2.)

Here the latter view is that of Rāmānuja and his followers. It must, however, be pointed out in this connection that the so-called differences between the Āṛvārs and the Rāmānujists on the cardinal points of religious faith are a discovery of later research, when the writings of the Āṛvārs had developed a huge commentary literature and Rāmānuja's own writings had inspired many scholars to make commentaries on his works or to write independent treatises elucidating his doctrines. The later scholars who compared the results of the Āṛvār and the Rāmānuja literatures came to the conclusion that there are some differences of view between the two regarding the cardinal faith of religion. This marks a sharp antithesis between the Āṛvāric Teṅgalai school and the Vaḍagalai school, of which latter Veṅkaṭa was the leader. These differences are briefly narrated in the *Aṣṭādaśa-bheda-nirṇaya*. The cardinal faith of religion according to Rāmānuja has been narrated in the *Aṣṭādaśa-rahasyārtha-vivaraṇa*. The main principle of religious approach to God is self-surrender or *prapatti*. *Prapatti* is defined as a state of prayerfulness of mind to God, associated with the deep conviction that He alone is the saviour, and that there is no way of attaining His grace except by such self-surrender[1]. The devotee is extremely loyal to Nārāyaṇa and prays to Him and no one else, and all his prayers are actuated by deep affection and no other motive. The virtue of *prapatti* involves within it universal charity, sympathy and friendliness even to the most determined enemy[2]. Such a devotee feels that the Lord (*svāmī*), being the very nature of his own self, is to be depended on under all circumstances. This is called the state of supreme resignation (*nirbharatva*) in all one's affairs[3]. The feeling of the devotee that none of the assigned scriptural duties can be helpful to him in attaining the highest goal

[1] *an-anya-sādhye svābhīṣṭe mahā-viśvāsa-pūrvakam*
tad-eko' pāyatā yācñā prapattiḥ śaraṇā-gatiḥ.
Aṣṭādaśa-rahasyārtha-vivaraṇa, p. 3.

Rāmānuja, in his *Gadya-trayam*, says that such a state of prayerfulness of mind is also associated with confessions of one's sins and shortcomings and derelictions, and with a feeling that the devotee is a helpless servant of God extremely anxious to get himself saved by the grace of the Saviour. See the *Gadya-trayam*, *Śaraṇā-gati-gadyam*, pp. 52–54.

[2] This is technically known as *Prapatti-naiṣṭhikam* (*Aṣṭādaśa-rahasyārtha-vivaraṇa*, pp. 3–7). Cf. the parables of the pigeon and the monkey in the above section.

[3] The interpretation is forced out of the conception of the word "svāmin," which etymologically involves the word "*svam*" meaning "one's own."

is technically called "*upāya-śūnyatā*," i.e. the realization of the uselessness of all other means. The devotee always smiles at all the calamities that may befall him. Considering himself to be a servant of God, he cheerfully bears all the miseries that may be inflicted on him by God's own people. This is technically called "*pāratantrya*," or supreme subordination. The devotee conceives his soul as a spiritual essence which has no independence by itself and is in every respect dependent on God and exists for God[1]. The Vaiṣṇavas are often called *ekāntins*, and have sometimes been wrongly considered as monotheists; but the quality of *ekāntitva* is the definite characteristic of self-surrender and clinging to God in an unshaken manner—the fullest trustfulness in Him under all adverse circumstances. The devotee's mind is always exhilarated with the divine presence of the Lord who animates all his senses—his inclinations, emotions and experiences. The fullness with which he realizes God in all his own activities and thoughts, and in everything else in the universe, naturally transports him to a sphere of being in which all mundane passions—antipathy, greed, jealousy, hatred—become impossible. With the divine presence of God he becomes infused with the spirit of friendship and charity towards all beings on earth[2]. The devotee has to take proper initiation from the preceptor, to whom he must confess all that is in his mind, and by abnegating all that is in him to his preceptor, he finds an easy way to conceive himself as the servant of Viṣṇu[3]. He must also have a philosophical conception of the entirely dependent relation of the human soul and all the universe to God[4]. Such a conception naturally involves realization of the presence of God in all our sense activities, which

[1] *jñāna-mayo hi ātmā śeṣo hi paramā-tmanaḥ iti jñānā-nandamayo jñānā-nanda-guṇakaḥ san sva-rūpaṃ bhagavad-adhīnaṃ sa tad-artham eva tiṣṭhatī' ti jñātvā' vatiṣṭhate iti yad etat tad-a-prākṛtatvam.*

Aṣṭādaśa-rahasyārtha-vivaraṇam, p. 11.

[2] This virtue is technically called *nitya-raṅgitva*.

[3] The five *saṃskāras* that a *paramaikāntin* must pass through are as follows:

tāpaḥ pauṇḍras tathā nāma mantro yāgaś ca pañcamaḥ
amī te pañca saṃskārāḥ paramaikānti-hetavaḥ. *Ibid.* p. 15.

[4] This is technically called *sambandha-jñānitvam*. The conception that everything exists for God is technically called *śeṣa-bhūtatvam*. *Ibid.* p. 18.

This naturally implies that the devotee must work and feel himself a servant of God and of His chosen men. The service to humanity and to God then naturally follow from the philosophical conception of the dependence of the human souls, and of the universe, on God as a part of Him and to be controlled by Him in every way. This is again technically called *śesa-vṛtti-paratva*. *Ibid.* pp. 19–20.

presence in its fullness must easily lead to the complete control of all our senses. Through the realization of God's presence in them, the devotees play the part of moral heroes, far above the influences of the temptation of the senses[1]. The normal religious duties, as prescribed in the Vedas and the *smṛtis*, are only for the lower order of the people; those who are given entirely to God with the right spirit of devotion need not follow the ordinary code of duties which is generally binding for all. Such a person is released by the spontaneous grace of God, and without performing any of the scriptural duties enjoys the fruits of all[2]. He is always conscious of his own faults, but takes no notice of the faults of others, to which he behaves almost as a blind man; he is always infused with the consciousness that all his actions are under the complete sway of the Lord. He has no enjoyment for himself, for he always feels that it is the Lord who would enjoy Himself through all his senses[3].

In the *Aṣṭādaśa-bheda-nirṇaya* it is said that according to the Āṛvārs, since emancipation means the discovery of a lost soul to God or the unlimited servitude of God, emancipation is for the interest of God and not of the devotee. The service of the servant is for the servitude of God alone. It has therefore no personal interest for the devotee[4]. According to the Aṛagiyas, however, emancipation, though primarily for the interest of the Lord, is also

[1] This is technically called the *nitya-śūratva*.

[2] *jñāna-niṣṭho virakto vā mad-bhakto hy a-napekṣakaḥ*
sa liṅgān āśramān tyaktvā cared a-vidhi-gocaraḥ

ity evam iṣaṇa-traya-vinirmuktas san bhagavan-nir-hetuka-kaṭākṣa eva mokṣo-pāyaḥ iti tiṣṭhati khalu so'dhikārī sakala-dharmāṇām avaśyo bhavati. Aṣṭādaśa-rahasyārtha-vivaraṇa, p. 23

This spirit of following God, leaving all other scriptural duties, is technically called *a-vidhi-gocaratva*. In another section of this work Rāmānuja describes *mokṣa* or salvation as the conviction that the nature of God transcends, in bliss, power and knowledge, all other conceivable things of this or any other universe. A desire to cling to God as a true means of salvation is technically called *mumukṣutva*. The doctrine of *a-vidhi-gocaratva* herein described seems to be in conflict with Rāmānuja's view on the subject explained in the *bhāṣya* as interpreted by his many followers. This may indicate that his views underwent some change, and these are probably his earlier views when he was under the influence of the Āṛvārs.

[3] This is technically called *parā-kāśatva* (*Ibid.* pp. 23–24). The attitude of worshipping the image as the visible manifestation of God is technically called *upāya-svarūpa-jñāna*. The cessation of attachment to all mundane things and the flowing superabundance of love towards God, and the feeling that God is the supreme abode of life, is technically called *ātmā-rāmatva*.

[4] *phalaṃ mokṣa-rūpam, tad bhagavata eva na svārthaṃ yathā pranaṣṭa-dṛṣṭa-dravya-lābho dravyavata eva na dravyasya; tathā mokṣa-phalaṃ ca svāmina eva*

at the same time for the interest of the devotee, because of the intense delight he enjoys by being a servant of God. The illustration of lost objects discovered by the master does not hold good, because human beings are conscious entities who suffer immeasurable sorrow which is removed by realizing themselves as servants of God. Though the devotee abnegates all the fruits of his actions in a self-surrender, yet he enjoys his position in the servitude of God and also the bliss of the realization of Brahman. Thus, those who take the path of knowledge (*upāsaka*) attain Brahma knowledge and the servitude of God, and those who take the path of self-surrender (*prapatti*) also attain Brahma knowledge and the servitude of God. In the state of salvation (*mukti*) there is no difference of realization corresponding to the variation of paths which the seekers after God may take[1]. Again, in the Āṛvār school of thought, besides the four ways of scriptural duties, philosophic wisdom, devotion to God and devotion to teachers, there was a fifth way, viz. that of intense self-surrender to God, i.e. *prapatti*. But the Aṛagiyas thought that apart from *prapatti* there was only one other way of approaching God, namely devotion, *bhakti-yoga*. Rāmānuja and his followers maintain that *karma-yoga* and *jñāna-yoga* only help to purify the mind, as a preparation for *bhakti-yoga*. The devotion to the preceptor is regarded only as a form of *prapatti*; so there are only two ways of approach to God, viz. *bhakti-yoga* and *prapatti*[2].

Further, *Śrī* occupies an important position in Śrī-vaiṣṇavism. But as there are only three categories in the Śrī-vaiṣṇava system, a question may naturally arise regarding the position of *Śrī* in the threefold categories of *cit*, *acit* and *parameśvara*. On this point the view of the older school, as described in Ramya-jāmātṛ muni's *Tattva-dīpa*, is that *Śrī* is to be identified with human souls and is therefore to be regarded as atomic in nature[3]. Others, however, think that *Śrī* is as all-pervasive as Viṣṇu. Filial affection (*vātsalya*)

na muktasya; yad vā phalaṃ kaiṅkaryaṃ tat parā-rtham eva na svā-rtham; para-tantra-daśā-kṛtaṃ kaiṅkaryaṃ sva-tantra-svāmy-artham eva. Aṣṭādaśa-bheda-nirṇaya, p. 2.

[1] *Ibid.* p. 3.

[2] *ataḥ prapatti-vyatirikto bhakti-yoga eka eve' ti. Ibid.* p. 4.

[3] *Ibid.* In the next section it is urged that, according to some, *Nārāyaṇa* and not *Śrī* is the only agent who removes our sins, but others hold that sins may be removed also by *Śrī* in a remote manner, or, because *Śrī* is identical with *Nārāyaṇa*; as the fragrance is with the flower, she has also a hand in removing the sins. *Ibid.* p. 5.

lakṣmyā upāyatvaṃ bhagavata iva sākṣāt abhyupagantavyam. Ibid.

for God is interpreted by the older schools as involving an attitude in which the faults of the beloved devotee are points of endearment to Him[1]. In the later view, however, filial affection is supposed to involve an indifference or a positive blindness towards the faults of the devotee. God's mercy is interpreted by the older school as meaning God's affliction or suffering in noticing that of others. Later schools, however, interpret it as an active sympathy on His part, as manifested in His desire to remove the sufferings of others on account of His inability to bear such miseries[2].

Prapatti, otherwise called *nyāsa*, is defined by the older school as a mere passivity on the part of the Lord in accepting those who seek Him or as a mental state on the part of the seeker in which he is conscious of himself only as a spirit; but such a consciousness is unassociated with any other complex feeling, of egoism and the like, which invests one with so-called individuality. It may also mean the mental state in which the seeker conceives himself as a subsidiary accessory to God as his ultimate end, to Whom he must cling unburdened by any idea of scriptural duties[3]; or he may concentrate himself absolutely on the supreme interest and delight that he feels in the idea that God is the sole end of his being. Such a person naturally cannot be entitled without self-contradiction to any scriptural duty. Just as a guilty wife may return to her husband, and may passively lie in a state of surrender to him and resign herself, so the seeker may be conscious of his own true position with reference to God leading to a passive state of surrender[4]. Others think that it involves five elements: (i) that God is the only saviour;

[1] *yathā kāmukaḥ kāminyā mālinyaṃ bhogyatayā svīkaroti tathā bhagavān āśrita-doṣaṃ svīkaroti itare tu vātsalyaṃ nāma doṣādarśitvam. Aṣṭādaśa-bheda-nirṇaya*, p. 6.

It is further suggested that, if a devotee takes the path of *prapatti*, he has not to suffer for his faults as much as others would have to suffer.

[2] The first alternative is defined as *para-duḥkha-duḥkhitvaṃ dayā*. The second alternative is *svārtha-nirapekṣa-para-duḥkha-sahiṣṇutā dayā; sa ca tan nirākaraṇecchā*. In the first alternative *dayā* is a painful emotion; in the second it is a state of desire, stirred up by a feeling of repugnance, which is midway between feeling and volition. *Ibid.* p. 6.

[3] *prapattir nāma a-nivāraṇa-mātram a-cid-vyāvṛtti-mātraṃ vā a-vidheyaṃ śeṣatva-jñāna-mātram vā para-śeṣatai-ka-rati-rūpa-pariśuddha-yāthātmya-jñāna-mātraṃ vā. Ibid.* p. 6.

According to some, any of these conditions would define *prapatti* "*ato'prati-ṣedhādy-anyatamai' va iti kecit kathayanti.*" *Ibid.*

[4] *atyanta-para-tantrasya virodhatvena anuṣṭhānā-nupapatteḥ, pratyuta anuṣṭatur ānarthakyamuktam Śrīvacana-bhūṣaṇa, ciram anya-parayā bhāryayā kadācid bhartṛ-sakāśam āgatayā mām aṅgīkuru iti vākyavat cetana-kṛta-prapattir iti. Ibid.* p. 6.

(ii) that He is the only end to be attained; (iii) that He alone is the supreme object of our desires; (iv) that we absolutely surrender and resign ourselves to Him[1]; and (v) supreme prayerfulness—all associated with absolute trustfulness in Him.

There are some who define the *prapanna*, or seeker of God, as one who has read the Āṛvār literature of *prabandhas* (*adhīta-prabandhaḥ prapannaḥ*). Others, however, think that the mere study of the *prabandhas* cannot invest a man with the qualities of *prapatti*. They think that he alone is entitled to the path of *prapatti* who cannot afford to adopt the dilatory courses of *karma-yoga*, *jñāna-yoga* and *bhakti-yoga*, and therefore does not think much of these courses. Again, the older school thinks that the person who adopts the path of *prapatti* should give up all scriptural duties and duties assigned to the different stages of life (*āśrama*); for it is well evidenced in the *Gītā* text that one should give up all one's religious duties and surrender oneself to God. Others, again, think that the scriptural duties are to be performed even by those who have taken the path of *prapatti*. Further, the older school thinks that the path of knowledge is naturally against the path of *prapatti*; for *prapatti* implies the negation of all knowledge, excepting one's self-surrendering association with God. The paths of duties and of knowledge assume an egoism which contradicts *prapatti*. Others, however, think that even active self-surrender to God implies an element of egoism, and it is therefore wrong to suppose that the paths of duties and of knowledge are reconcilable with *prapatti* on account of its association with an element of egoism. The so-called egoism is but a reference to our own nature as self, and not to *ahaṅkāra*, an evolute[2]. Again, some think that even a man who has

[1] In the second alternative it is defined as follows:

an-anya-sādhye svā-bhīṣṭe mahā-viśvāsa-pūrvakam
tad-eko'-pāyatā yācñā prapattiś śaraṇā-gatiḥ.

These are the five *aṅgas* of *prapatti*, otherwise called *nikṣepa*, *tyāga*, *nyāsa* or *śaraṇā-gati* (*Aṣṭādaśa-bheda-nirṇaya*, pp. 6, 7). The difference between the first and second alternative is that, according to the former, *prapatti* is a state of mind limited to the consciousness of its true nature in relation to God; on the part of God also it indicates merely a passive toleration of the seekers flocking unto Him (*a-nivāraṇa-mātram*). In the second alternative, however, *prapatti* is defined as positive self-surrendering activity on the part of the seekers and unconditional protection to them all on the part of God. It is, therefore, that on the first alternative the consciousness of one's own true nature is defined in three ways, any one of which would be regarded on that alternative as a sufficient definition of *prapatti*. The first one is merely in the cognitive state, while the second involves an additional element of voluntary effort.

[2] *Ibid.* pp. 8, 9.

adopted the path of *prapatti* may perform the current scriptural duties only with a view to not lending any support to a reference to their cases as pretexts for neglect of normal duties by the unenlightened and the ignorant, i.e. those that have adopted the path of *prapatti* should also perform their duties for the purpose of *loka-saṃgraha.* Others, however, think that the scriptural duties, being the commandments of God, should be performed for the satisfaction of God (*bhagavat-prīty-artham*), even by those who have taken the path of *prapatti.* Otherwise they would have to suffer punishment for that.

The accessories of *prapatti* are counted as follows: (i) A positive mental attitude to keep oneself always in consonance with the Lord's will (*ānukūlyasya saṃkalpaḥ*); (ii) a negative mental attitude (*prātikūlyasya varjanam*), as opposing anything that may be conceived as against His will; (iii) a supreme trustfulness that the Lord will protect the devotee (*rakṣiṣyatīti viśvāsaḥ*); (iv) prayer to Him as a protector (*goptṛtva-varaṇam*); (v) complete self-surrender (*ātma-nikṣepaḥ*); (vi) a sense of complete poverty and helplessness (*kārpaṇyam*). The older school thinks that the man who adopts the path of *prapatti* has no desires to fulfil, and thus he may adopt any of these accessories which may be possible for him according to the conditions and inclinations of his mind. Others, however, think that even those who follow the path of *prapatti* are not absolutely free from any desire, since they wish to feel themselves the eternal servants of God. Though they do not crave for the fulfilment of any other kind of need, it is obligatory upon them to perform all the six accessories of *prapatti* described above.

The older school thinks that God is the only cause of emancipation and that the adoption of the path of *prapatti* is not so; the later school, however, thinks that *prapatti* is also recognized as the cause of salvation in a secondary manner, since it is only through *prapatti* that God extends His grace to His devotees[1]. Again, the older schools think that there is no necessity for expiation (*prāyaścitta*) for those who adopt the path of *prapatti*; for with them God's grace is sufficient to remove all sins. The later schools, however, think that, if the follower of the path of *prapatti* is physically fit to perform the courses of expiation, then it is obligatory on him. According to the older school a man possessing the eight kinds of devo-

[1] *Aṣṭādaśa-bheda-nirṇaya*, p. 10.

tion (*bhakti*), even if he be a *mleccha*, is preferred to a Brahman and may be revered as such. According to the later schools, however, a devotee of a lower caste may be shown proper respect, but he cannot be revered as a Brahman. Again, on the subject of the possibility of pervasion of the atomic individual souls by God, the older schools are of opinion that God by His infinite power may enter into the atomic individuals; the later schools, however, think that such a pervasion must be of an external nature, i.e. from outside. It is not possible for God to penetrate into individual souls[1]. As regards *Kaivalya* the older schools say that it means only self-apperception. He who attains this state attains the highest stage of eternity or immortality. The later school, however, thinks that he who has merely this self-apperception cannot attain immortality through that means only; for this self-apperception may not necessarily mean a true revelation of his nature with reference to God. He can realize that only as he passes through higher spheres and ultimately reaches Vaikuṇṭha—the abode of God, where he is accepted as the servant of the Lord. It is such a state that can be regarded as eternal[2].

[1] *Aṣṭādaśa-bheda-nirṇaya*, p. 12. The view is supported by a reference to Varadācārya's *Adhikaraṇa-cintāmaṇi*.

[2] The eighteen points of dispute as herein explained have been collected in the *Aṣṭādaśa-bheda-nirṇaya*, according to the ancients in a verse quoted from them as follows:

> *bhedaḥ svāmi-kṛpā-phalā-nya-gatiṣu śrī-vyāpty-upāyatvayos*
> *tad-vātsalya-dayā-nirukti-vacasornyāse ca tat kartari*
> *dharma-tyāga-virodhayos sva-vihite nyāsā-ṅga-hetutvayoḥ*
> *prāyaścitta-vidhau tadīya-bhajane' nuvyāpti-kaivalyayoḥ.* *Ibid.* p. 1.

CHAPTER XVIII

AN HISTORICAL AND LITERARY SURVEY OF THE VIŚIṢṬĀ-DVAITA SCHOOL OF THOUGHT

The Aṛagiyas from Nāthamuni to Rāmānuja.

A. GŌVINDĀCHĀRYAR has written a book, *The Holy Lives of the Âzhvârs*, based upon a number of old works[1]. The writings of the Āṛvārs may be sub-divided generally into three *rahasyas* (or mystical accounts) called *Tiru-mantra-churukku*, *Dvaya-churukku*, *Carama-śloka-churukku*. These three *rahasyas* have also been dealt with in later times by very prominent persons, such as Veṅkaṭanātha, Rāghavācārya and others. Some account of these, in the manner of these later writers, will be briefly given in the proper place, since the scope of this work does not permit us to go into the details of the lives of the Āṛvārs. The hagiologists make a distinction between the Āṛvārs and the Aṛagiyas in this, that, while the former were only inspired men, the latter had their inspirations modified by learning and scholarship. The list of Aṛagiyas begins with Nāthamuni. There is some difficulty in fixing his age. The *Guru-paramparā*, the *Divya-sūri-carita* and the *Prapannāmṛta*, are of opinion that he was in direct contact with Nāmm'-āṛvār, otherwise called Śaṭhakopa, or Kaṛimāṛan, or rather with his disciple Madhura-kaviy-āṛvār. Thus, the *Prapannāmṛta* says that Nāthamuni was born in the village called Vīranārāyaṇa, near the Cola country. His father's name was Īśvara Bhaṭṭa, and his son was Īśvaramuni[2]. He went on a long pilgrimage, in the course of which he visited the northern countries, including Mathurā, Vṛndāvana and Haridvāra, and also Bengal and Purī. After returning to his own place he found that some of the

[1] (1) *Divya-sūri-carita* (an earlier work than the *Prapannāmṛta*, which often alludes to it) by Garuḍa-vāhana Paṇḍita, contemporary and disciple of Rāmānuja; (2) *Prapannāmṛta*, by Ananta-sūri, disciple of Śaila-raṅgeśa guru; (3) *Prabandha-sāra*, by Veṅkaṭanātha; (4) *Upadeśa-ratna-mālai* by Ramyajāmātṛ-mahā-muni, otherwise called Varavara-muni or Periya-jīyar or Maṇavāla Māmuni; (5) Guru-paramparā-prabhāvam by Pinb'-aṛagiya Peru-māl Jīyar; and (6) Pazhanadai-vilakkan.

[2] It is said that he belonged to the lineage of Śaṭhakopa or Śaṭha-marṣaṇa. His other name was Śrī-raṅga-nātha. (See introduction to *Catuḥ-ślokī*, Ananda Press, Madras, p. 3.)

Śrīvaiṣṇavas, who came from the Western countries to the temple of Rājagopāla, recited there ten verses by Kaṛimāṛa. Nāthamuni, who heard those hymns, realized that they were parts of a much bigger work and decided to collect them. He went to Kumbhakoṇa, and under the inspiration of God proceeded to the city of Kurakā, on the banks of Tāmraparṇī, and there met Madhura-kaviy-āṛvār, the disciple of Nāmm'-āṛvār, and asked him if the hymns of Nāmm'-āṛvār were available. Madhura-kaviy-āṛvār told him that after composing a big book of hymns in Tamil and instructing Madhura-kaviy-āṛvār the same, Nāmm'-āṛvār had attained salvation. The work could not, therefore, obtain currency among the people. The people of the locality had the misconception that the study of the work would be detrimental to the Vedic religion. So they threw it into the river Tāmraparṇī. Only one page of the book, containing ten verses, was picked up by a man who appreciated the verses and recited them. Thus only these ten verses have been saved. Nāthamuni recited twelve thousand times a verse composed by Madhura-kaviy-āṛvār in adoration of Nāmm'-āṛvār, and, as a result of that, Nāmm'-āṛvār revealed the purport of the whole work to him. But when Nāthamuni wanted to know all the verses in detail he was advised to approach an artisan of the place who was inspired by Nāmm'-āṛvār to reveal all the verses to him. So Nāthamuni received the entire work of Nāmm'-āṛvār from the artisan. He then gave it to his pupil Puṇḍarīkākṣa, and Puṇḍarīkākṣa gave it to his disciple Rāma Miśra, and Rāma Miśra gave it to Yāmuna, and Yāmuna gave it to Goṣṭhīpūrṇa, and Goṣṭhīpūrṇa gave it to his daughter Devakī Śrī. Nāthamuni brought the hymns together, and, through his two nephews, Meḷaiyagaṭṭāṛvār and Kiḷaiyagaṭṭāṛvār, set them to music in the Vedic manner; from that time forward these hymns were sung in the temples and were regarded as the Tamil Veda[1]. The oldest *Guru-paramparā* and *Divya-sūri-carita*, however, say that Nāthamuni obtained the works of Nāmm'-āṛvār directly from him. The later Śrīvaiṣṇavas found that the above statements did not very well suit the traditional antiquity of the Āṛvārs, and held that Madhura-kaviy-āṛvār was not the direct disciple of Nāmm'-āṛvār and that Nāthamuni attained the high age of three hundred years. But, if, as we found before, Nāmm'-āṛvār's date be fixed in the ninth century, no such supposition

[1] *Prapannāmṛta*, Chs. 106 and 107.

becomes necessary. Gopīnātha Rāu refers also to a Sanskrit inscription in the middle of the tenth century, in which it is stated that the author of the verses was a disciple of Śrīnātha. If this Śrīnātha is the same as Nāthamuni, then the computation of Nāthamuni's date as falling in the tenth century is quite correct. He had eleven disciples, of whom Puṇḍarīkākṣa, Karukānātha and Śrīkṛṣṇa Lakṣmīnātha were the most prominent. He wrote three works, *Nyāya-tattva*, *Puruṣa-ninṇaya* and *Yoga-rahasya*[1]. Nāthamuni is also described as a great yogin who practised the *yoga* of eight accessories (*aṣṭāṅga-yoga*)[2]. The *Prapannāmṛta* says that he died by entering into *yoga* in the city of Āgaṅgā (probably Gaṅgaikoṇḍaṣoḍapuram). Gopī-nātha, however, thinks that he could not have died in that city, for it was not founded by Rajendracola, otherwise called Gaṅgaikoṇḍasola, before 1024, which must be later than the date of Nāthamuni. Nāthamuni lived probably in the reign of Parāntaka Cola I, and died before or in the reign of Parāntaka Cola II, i.e. he lived eighty or ninety years in the middle of the tenth century. He had made an extensive tour in Northern India as far as Mathurā and Badarī-nātha and also to Dvārakā and Purī. Śrīkṛṣṇa Lakṣmīnātha, disciple of Nāthamuni, wrote an extensive work on the doctrine of *prapatti*. He was born at a place called Kṛṣṇamaṅgala. He was well-versed in the Vedas, and was a specialist in Vedānta and also a great devotee, who constantly employed himself in chanting the name of Viṣṇu (*nāma-saṅkīrtana-rataḥ*). He used often to go about naked and live on food that was thrown to him. The hagiologists say that he entered into the image of the temple and became one with God. Puṇḍa-

[1] The *Nyāya-tattva* is referred to by Veṅkaṭanātha in his *Nyāya-pariśuddhi* (p. 13) as a work in which Gautama's *Nyāya-sūtras* were criticized and refuted:

bhagavan-nātha-munibhir nyāya-tattva-samāhvayā
avadhīryā' kṣapādādīn nyabandhi nyāya-paddhatiḥ
Nyāya-pariśuddhi, p. 13.

[2] The practice of *aṣṭāṅga-yoga* was not a new thing with Nāthamuni. In giving an account of Tiru-maṛiṣai Pirān, also called Bhaktisāra, the *Prapannāmṛta* says that he first became attached to the god Śiva and wrote many Tamil works on Śaiva doctrines; but later on the saint Mahārya initiated him into Vaiṣṇavism and taught him *aṣṭāṅga-yoga*, through which he realized the great truths of Vaiṣṇavism. He then wrote many works in Tamil on Vaiṣṇavism. Bhakti-sāra also wrote a scholarly work, refuting the views of other opponents, which is known as *Tattvārtha-sāra*. Bhakti-sāra also used to practise *aṣṭāṅga-yoga* and was learned in all the branches of Indian philosophy. Bhakti-sāra had a disciple named Kanikṛṣṇa, who wrote many extremely poetical verses or hymns in adoration of Viṣṇu. Kula-śekhara Peru-māl is also said to have practised *yoga*.

rīkākṣa Uyyakoṇḍār is supposed to have very much influenced the character of Kurukānātha, who in the end entered into *yoga* and died. Rāma Miśra was born in the city of Saugandhakulya, in a Brahmin family, and was a pupil of Puṇḍarīkākṣa. The name of Puṇḍarīkāksa's wife was Āṇḍāḷ. Puṇḍarīkākṣa asked Rāma Miśra (Manakkal-lambej) to teach Yāmuna all that he was taught. Yāmuna, however, was not born during the life of Puṇḍarīkākṣa, and Puṇḍarīkākṣa only prophesied his birth in accordance with the old prophecy of Nāthamuni. Rāma Miśra had four disciples, excluding Yāmuna, of whom Lakṣmī was the most prominent[1]. He used to stay in Śrīraṅgam and expound the doctrines of the Vedānta.

Yāmunācārya, otherwise called Āḷavandār, son of Īśvaramuni and grandson of Nāthamuni, was born probably in A.D. 918 and is said to have died in A.D. 1038. He learned the Vedas from Rāma Miśra, and was reputed to be a great debater[2]. Becoming a king, he was duly married and had two sons named Vararaṅga and Śoṭṭhapūrṇa. He lived happily for a long time, enjoying his riches, and took no notice of Rāma Miśra. But Rāma Miśra with some difficulty obtained access to him and availed himself of the opportunity to teach him the *Bhagavad-gītā*, which aroused the spirit of detachment in him, and he followed Rāma Miśra to Śrīraṅgam and, renouncing everything, became a great devotee[3]. One of the last

[1] (1) Taivattuk-k-arasu-Nambi; (2) Gomathattut-tiruvinnagar-appan; (3) Sirup-pullur-udaya-Pillai; (4) Vangi-puratt-acchi. (See *The Life of Rāmānuja*, by Govindāchāryar, p. 14.)

[2] The *Prapannāmṛta* relates a story of Yāmuna's debating power at the age of twelve. The king of the place had a priest of the name of Akkaialvan, who was a great debater. Yāmuna challenged him and defeated him in an open debate held in the court of the king. He was given half the kingdom as a reward. He seems to have been very arrogant in his earlier days, if the wording of his challenge found in the *Prapannāmṛta* can be believed. The words of challenge run as follows:

ā śailād adri-kanyā-caraṇa-kisalaya-nyāsa-dhanyopakaṇṭhād
ā rakṣo-nīta-sītā-mukha-kamala-samullāsa-hetoś ca setoḥ
ā ca prācya-pratīcya-kṣiti-dhara-yuga tadarkacandrāvataṃsān
mīmāṃsā-śāstra-yugma-śrama-vimala-manā mṛgyatāṃ mādṛśo'nyaḥ
Ch. III.

[3] A story is told in the *Prapannāmṛta* that, when Yāmuna became a king and inaccessible to him, Rāma Miśra was concerned how he could carry out the commands of his teachers and initiate Yāmuna to the path of devotion. He got in touch with Yāmuna's cook, and for six months presented some green vegetables (*alarka-śāka*) which Yāmuna very much liked. When, after the six months, the king asked how the rare vegetables found their way into the kitchen, Rāma Miśra stayed away for four days praying to Raṅganātha, the deity, to tell him how he could approach Yāmuna. In the meanwhile the king missed the green vegetables and asked his cook to present Rāma Miśra when next he should come to the kitchen. Rāma Miśra was thus presented to Yāmuna.

instructions of Rāma Miśra was to direct him to go to Kurukānātha (Kurugai-kkaval-appan) and learn from him the *aṣṭāṅga-yoga*, which had been left with him (*Kurukā*) by Nāthamuni for Yāmuna. Yāmuna had many disciples, of whom twenty-one are regarded as prominent. Of these disciples, Mahāpūrṇa belonged to the Bhāradvāja *gotra*, and had a son named Puṇḍarīkākṣa and a daughter named Attutayi. Another disciple, called Śrīśailapūrṇa, was known also by the name Tātācārya[1]. Another of his disciples, Goṣṭhīpūrṇa, was born in the Pāṇḍya country, where also, in the city of Śrimadhurā, was born another of Yāmuna's disciples, Mālādhara. In the city of Maraner in the Pāṇḍya country was born another disciple, Maraner Nambi, a *śūdra* by caste; a further disciple, Kāñcīpūrṇa, who was also of the *śūdra* caste, was born in the city of Punamallī. Yāmuna used to invest all his disciples with the five Vaiṣṇava *saṃskāras*, and he also converted the Cola king and queen to the same faith and made over the kingdom he had hitherto enjoyed to the service of the deity Raṅganātha of Śrīraṅgam. Śrīśailapūrṇa, or Bhūri Śrīśailapūrṇa, or Mahāpūrṇa had two sons, two sisters and two daughters. The elder sister, Kāntimatī, was married to Keśava Yajvan, also called Āsuri Keśava, Rāmānuja's father, and the second sister, Dyutimatī, was married to Kanalākṣa Bhaṭṭa, and a son was born to them called Govinda. Kureśa, who was long in association with Rāmānuja, was born of Ananta Bhaṭṭa and Mahādevī, and this Kureśa was the father of Anantācārya, writer of the *Prapannāmṛta*[2]. Dāśarathi was born of Ananta Dīkṣita, of Vādhūla *gotra*, and Lakṣmī. Dāśarathi had a son called Kaṇḍaḍanātha, who was also called Rāmānujadāsa. They are all associates of Rāmānuja, who had seventy-four prominent disciples.

Yāmuna was very fond of Nāmm'-āṛvār's works, the doctrines of which were often explained to the people. Yāmuna wrote six works: (i) *Stotra-ratnam*, in adoration to the deity Varada; (ii) *Catuḥ-ślokī*; (iii) *Āgama-prāmāṇya*; (iv) *Siddhi-traya*; (v) *Gītārtha-saṃgraha*; (vi) *Mahā-puruṣa-nirṇaya*[3]. Of these the *Siddhi-traya* is the most important, and the section on Yāmuna in this volume has been based almost entirely on it. The *Āgama-prāmāṇya* is a work in which he tries to establish the high antiquity and undisputed

[1] *Prapannāmṛta*, Ch. 113, p. 440.

[2] *Ibid.* Ch. 150, p. 450. Anantācārya, called also Ananta Sūri, was the pupil of Śailaraṅgeśa-guru. He reveres also Ramyajāmātṛ-mahā-muni.

[3] See Veṅkaṭanātha's introduction to the *Gītārtha-saṃgraha-rakṣā*.

authority of the Pañcarātra literature, which is supposed to be the canon of the Śrīvaiṣṇavas. The *Stotra-ratnam*, *Catuḥ-ślokī* and *Gītārtha-saṃgraha* were all commented upon by various persons, but the most important of the commentaries is that of Veṅkaṭanātha[1]. The *Stotra-ratnam* consists of sixty-five verses in which Yāmuna describes the beauty of the Lord Kṛṣṇa, as set forth in the Purāṇas, and confesses to Him the deep affliction of all his sins and guilt, frailties and vices, and asks for forgiveness of them. He also describes the greatness of the Lord as transcendent and surpassing the greatness of all other deities, as the supreme controller and upholder of the universe. He narrates his own complete surrender to Him and entire dependence on His mercy. If the mercy and grace of the Lord be so great, there is none so deserving of mercy in his wretchedness as a sinner. If the sinner is not saved, the mercy of the Lord becomes meaningless. The Lord requires the sinner in order to realize Himself as the all-merciful. Yāmuna further describes how his mind, forsaking everything else, is deeply attracted to the Lord; and the sense of his supreme helplessness and absolute abnegation[2]. The devotee cannot bear any delay in his communion with God, and is extremely impatient to meet Him; it is galling to him that God should heap happiness after happiness on him and thus keep him away. The fundamental burden of the hymns is an expression of the doctrine of *prapatti*; this has been very clearly brought out in the commentary of Veṅkaṭanātha. It is said that it was after reading these hymns that Rāmānuja became so deeply attracted to Yāmuna. The *Catuḥ-ślokī* consists of only four verses in praise of *Śrī* or *Lakṣmī*[3].

In the *Gītārtha-saṃgraha* Yāmuna says that the means to the

[1] The commentary on the *Catuḥ-ślokī* by Veṅkaṭanātha is called *Rahasya-rakṣā*, and the commentary on the *Stotra-ratnam* goes also by the same name. The commentary on the *Gītārtha-saṃgraha*, by Veṅkaṭanātha, is called *Gītārtha-saṃgraha-rakṣā*.

[2] Two specimen verses may be quoted from the *Stotra-ratnam*:

na dharma-niṣṭho'smi na cā' tma-vedī na bhaktimāṃs tvac-caraṇā-ravinde
a-kiñcano nā'nya-gatiś śaraṇya tvat-pāda-mūlaṃ śaraṇaṃ prapadye.
Śl. 22.

na ninditaṃ karma tad asti loke
sahasraśo yan na mayā vyadhāyi
so'ham vipākā-vasare mukunda
krandāmi sampraty a-gatis tavāgre. *Śl.* 23.

[3] Veṅkaṭanātha, in his commentary on the *Catuḥ-ślokī*, discusses the position of Lakṣmī according to the Vaiṣṇava tradition. Lakṣmī is regarded as a being

attainment of the ultimate goal of life is devotion, which is produced as a result of the performance of scriptural duties and the emergence of self-knowledge[1]. According to Yāmuna, *yoga* in the *Gītā* means *bhakti-yoga*. So the ultimate object of the *Gītā* is the propounding of the supreme importance of *bhakti* (devotion) as the ultimate object, which requires as a precedent condition the performance of the scriptural duties and the dawning of the true spiritual nature of the self as entirely dependent on God.

It is related in the *Prapannāmṛta* that Yāmuna was anxious to meet Rāmānuja, but died immediately before Rāmānuja came to meet him. So Rāmānuja could only render the last homage to his dead body.

Rāmānuja[2].

It has already been said that Mahāpūrṇa (Nambi), disciple of Yāmuna, had two sisters, Kāntimatī and Dyutimatī, of whom the former was married to Keśava Yajvan or Āsuri Keśava of Bhūtapurī and the latter to Kamalākṣa Bhaṭṭa. Rāmānuja (Ilaya Perumal), son of Keśava Yajvan, was born in A.D. 1017. He received his training, together with his mother's sister's son Govinda Bhaṭṭa, from Yādavaprakāśa, a teacher of Vedānta of great reputation. The details of Yādavaprakāśa's views are not known, but it is very probable that he was a monist[3]. Before going to study with

different from Nārāyaṇa, but always associated with Him. He thus tries to refute all the views that suppose Lakṣmī to be a part of Nārāyaṇa. Lakṣmī should also not be identified with *māyā*. She is also conceived as existing in intimate association with Nārāyaṇa and, like a mother, exerting helpful influence to bring the devotees into the sphere of the grace of the Lord. Thus Lakṣmī is conceived to have a separate personality of her own, though that personality is merged, as it were, in the personality of Nārāyaṇa and all His efforts, and all her efforts are in consonance with the efforts of Nārāyaṇa (*parasparā-nukūlatayā sarvatra sāmarasyam*). On the controversial point whether Lakṣmī is to be considered a *jīva* and therefore atomic in nature, the problem how she can then be all-pervasive, and the view that she is a part of Nārāyaṇa, Veṅkaṭanātha says that Lakṣmī is neither Jīva nor Nārāyaṇa, but a separate person having her being entirely dependent on God. Her relation to Nārāyaṇa can be understood on the analogy of the relation of the rays to the sun or the fragrance to the flower.

[1] *sva-dharma-jñāna-vairāgya-sādhya-bhakty-eka-gocaraḥ*
nārāyaṇaḥ paraṃ brahma gītā-śāstre samuditaḥ
Gītārtha-saṃgraha, verse 1.

[2] Most of the details of Rāmānuja's life are collected from the account given in the *Prapannāmṛta* by Anantācārya, a junior contemporary of Rāmānuja.

[3] Yādava held that Brahman, though by its nature possessing infinite qualities, yet transforms itself into all types of living beings and also into all kinds of inanimate things. Its true nature is understood when it is realized that it is one

Yādavaprakāśa, Rāmānuja was married at the age of sixteen, by his father, who died shortly afterwards. His teacher Yādavaprakāśa lived in Kāñcī. So Rāmānuja left Bhūtapurī his native place with his family and went to Kāñcī. In the early days of his association with Yādavaprakāśa, it is said that Yādavaprakāśa became annoyed with him, because he had cured the daughter of a certain chief of the place from possession by a spirit, which his teacher Yādavaprakāśa had failed to do. Shortly after this there was a difference of opinion between Yādava and Rāmānuja on the interpretation of certain Upaniṣad texts, which Yādava interpreted in the monistic manner, but Rāmānuja on the principle of modified dualism. Yādava became very much annoyed with Rāmānuja and arranged a plot, according to which Rāmānuja was to be thrown into the Ganges while on a pilgrimage to Allahabad. Govinda divulged the plot to Rāmānuja, who was thus able to wander away from the company and retire to Kāñcī, after suffering much trouble on the way. While at Kāñcī he became associated with a devout person of the *śūdra* caste, called Kāñcīpūrṇa. Later Rāmānuja was reconciled to his teacher and studied with him. When Yāmuna once came to Kāñcī he saw Rāmānuja at a distance among the students of Yādava marching in procession, but had no further contact with him, and from that time forward was greatly anxious to have Rāmānuja as one of his pupils. Rāmānuja again fell out with his teacher on the meaning of the text *kapyāsam puṇḍarīkam* (*Chāndogya*, p. 167). As a result of this quarrel, Rāmānuja was driven out by Yādava. Thenceforth he became attached to the worship of Nārāyaṇa on Hastiśaila in Kāñcī, where he first heard the chanting of the *Stotra-ratnam* of Yāmuna by Mahāpūrṇa, his maternal uncle and pupil of Yāmuna. From Mahāpūrṇa Rāmānuja learnt much of Yāmuna and started for Śrīraṅgam with him. But before he could reach Śrīraṅgam Yāmuna died. It is said that after his death three fingers of Yāmuna were found to be twisted and Rāmānuja thought that this signified three unfulfilled desires: (1) to convert the people to the *prapatti* doctrine of Vaiṣṇavism, making them well versed in

in spite of its transformation into diverse forms of animate and inanimate entities —*anye punar aikyāvabodha-yāthātmyaṃ varṇayantaḥ svābhāvika-niratiśaya-parimitodāra-guṇa-sāgaraṃ brahmaiva sura-nara-tiryak-sthāvara-nāraki-svargy-āpavargi-caitanyaika-svabhāvaṃ sva-bhāvato vilakṣaṇam avilakṣaṇaṃ ca viyad-ādi-nānā-vidhā-mala-rūpa-pariṇāmā-spadaṃ ceti pratyavatiṣṭhante.* Rāmānuja, *Vedārtha-saṃgraha*, p. 15, printed at the Medical Hall Press, 1894.

the works of the Āṛvārs; (2) to write a commentary to the *Brahma-sūtra* according to the Śrīvaiṣṇava school; (3) to write many works on Śrīvaiṣṇavism. Rāmānuja, therefore, agreed to execute all these three wishes[1]. He returned to Kāñcī and became attached to Kāñcīpūrṇa, the disciple of Yāmuna, as his teacher. Later he set out for Śrīraṅgam and on the way was met by Mahāpūrṇa, who was going to Kāñcī to bring him to Śrīraṅgam. He was then initiated by Mahāpūrṇa (the *ācārya*), according to the fivefold Vaiṣṇava rites (*pañca-saṃskāra*). Rāmānuja, being annoyed with his wife's discourteous treatment with Mahāpūrṇa's wife, and also with people who came to beg alms, sent her by a ruse to her father's house, and renounced domestic life when he was about 30 or 32 years of age. After establishing himself as a *sannyāsin*, his teaching in the Śāstras began with Dāśarathi, son of his sister[2], and Kuranātha, son of Anantabhaṭṭa. Yādavaprakāśa also became a disciple of Rāmānuja[3]. Eventually Rāmānuja left for Śrīraṅgam and dedicated himself to the worship of Raṅgeśa. He learnt certain esoteric doctrines and *mantras* from Goṣṭhīpūrṇa who had been initiated into them by his teacher. Later on Rāmānuja defeated in discussion a Śaṅkarite named Yajñamūrti, who later became his disciple and wrote two works in Tamil called *Jñāna-sāra* and *Prameya-sāra*[4]. He now had a number of well reputed disciples such as Bhaktagrāma-pūrṇa, Marudha-grāma-pūrṇa, Anantārya, Varadācārya and Yajñeśa. Rāmānuja first wrote his *Gadya-traya*. He then proceeded to the Śāradā-maṭha with Kureśa, otherwise called Śrīvatsāṅka Miśra or Kuruttāḷvan, procured the manuscript of the *Bodhāyana-vṛtti*, and started towards Śrīraṅgam. The keepers of the temple, however, finding the book missing, ran after him and

[1] *Prapannāmṛta*, IX, p. 26. The interpretation of this passage by Govindācārya and Ghoṣa seems to me to be erroneous; for there is no reference to Śaṭhakopa here. Kureśa, or Śrīvatsāṅka Miśra, had two sons; one of them was baptized by Rāmānuja as Parāśara Bhaṭṭārya and the other as Rāmadeśika. Rāmānuja's maternal cousin, Govinda, had a younger brother, called Bāla Govinda, and his son was baptized as Parāṅkuśa-pūrṇārya.

[2] The name of Dāśarathi's father is Anantadīkṣita.

[3] His baptismal name was Govindadāsa. After his conversion he wrote a book entitled *Yati-dharma-samuccaya*. This Govindadāsa must be distinguished from Govinda, son of the aunt of Rāmānuja, who had been converted to Śaivism by Yādavaprakāśa and was reconverted to Śrīvaiṣṇavism by his maternal uncle Śrīśailapūrṇa, pupil of Yāmuna. Govinda had married, but became so attached to Rāmānuja that he renounced the world. Śrīśailapūrṇa wrote a commentary on the *Sahasra-gīti*. Rāmānuja had another disciple in Puṇḍarīkākṣa, Mahāpūrṇa's son.

[4] His baptismal names were Devarāṭ and Devamannātha.

took it away. Fortunately, however, Kureśa had read the book during the several nights on the way, had remembered its purport and so was able to repeat it. Rāmānuja thus dictated his commentary of *Śrī-bhāṣya*, which was written down by Kureśa[1]. He also wrote *Vedānta-dīpa*, *Vedānta-sāra* and *Vedārtha-saṃgraha*. The *Śrī-bhāṣya* was written probably after Rāmānuja had made extensive tours to Tirukkovalur, Tirupati, Tirupputkuḷi, Kumbhakoṇam, Aḷagārkoil, Tiruppullani, Āṛvār-Tirunagari, Tirukkurungudi, Tiruvaṇpariśāram, Tiruvaṭṭar, Tiruvanandapuram, Tiruvallikeṇi, Tirunirmalai, Madhurantakam and Tiruvaigundipuram[2]. Later on he made extensive tours in Northern India to Ajmir, Mathurā, Brindāvan, Ayodhyā and Badarī, defeating many heretics. He also went to Benares and Purī and at the latter place established a *maṭha*. He forcibly tried to introduce the Pañcarātra rites into the temple of Jagannātha, but failed. According to the *Rāmānujārya-divya-charitai*, the *Śrī-bhāṣya* was completed in 1077 śaka or A.D. 1155, though two-thirds of the work were finished before the Cola persecution began. But this date must be a mistake; for Rāmānuja died in 1059 śaka or A.D. 1137[3]. The eyes of Mahāpūrṇa (Periyalnāmbi) and Kureśa were put out by the Cola king Koluttuṅga I, probably in the year 1078–1079, and this must be the date when Rāmānuja was forced to take refuge in the Hoysala country. It was in A.D. 1117, on the death of Koluttuṅga I, that Rāmānuja again returned to Śrīraṅgam, where he met Kureśa and finished the *Śrī-bhāṣya*[4]. In a *Madhva* work called *Chalāri-smṛti* it is said that in 1049 śaka, that is A.D. 1127, it was already an established work[5]. It is therefore very probable that the *Śrī-bhāṣya* was completed between A.D. 1117 and 1127. Gopī-nātha Rāu thinks that it was completed in A.D. 1125.

Rāmānuja fled in the garb of an ordinary householder from

[1] Rāmānuja had asked Kureśa to check him if he were not correctly representing the *Bodhāyana-vṛtti*, and in one place at least there was a difference of opinion and Rāmānuja was in the wrong.

[2] See Gopī-nātha Rāu's Lectures, p. 34, footnote.

[3] See *Ibid.*

[4] *Rāmānujārya-divya-charitai* (a Tamil work), p. 243, quoted in Gopīnātha Rāu's Lectures.

[5] *kalau pravṛtta-bauddhā'-di-mataṃ rāmānujaṃ tathā*
śake hy eko-na-pañcāśad-adhikā-bde sahasrake
nirākartuṃ mukhya-vāyuḥ san-mata-sthāpanāya ca
ekā-daśa-śate śāke viṃśaty-aṣṭa-yuge gate
avatīrṇaṃ madhva-guruṃ sadā vande mahā-guṇam.
Chalāri-smṛti, quoted in Gopī-nātha Rāu's Lectures, p. 35.

Śrīraṅgam to Toṇḍāṇuṛ, to escape from the persecution of Koluttuṅga I or Rājendracola, otherwise called Kṛmikanṭha, a Śaiva king. He was successful in converting the Jain king Bittideva of the Hoysala country, who was renamed Viṣṇuvardhanadeva after the *Vaiṣṇava* fashion. Mr Rāu says that this conversion took place some time before A.D. 1099[1]. With the help of this king he constructed the temple Tirunarayanapperumāl at Melukot (Yādavādri), where Rāmānuja lived for about twelve years[2]. According to the *Rāmānujārya-divya-charitai* Rāmānuja lived for eleven years after his return to Śrīraṅgam (some time after the death of Koluttuṅga I in 1118) and died in A.D. 1137. He thus enjoyed an extraordinary long life of one hundred and twenty years, which was spread over the reigns of three Cola kings, Koluttuṅga I (A.D. 1070–1118), Vikrama Cola (A.D. 1118–1135), and Koluttuṅga II (A.D. 1123–1146)[3]. He had built many temples and *maṭhas* in his lifetime, and by converting the temple superintendent of Śrīraṅgam got possession of the whole temple.

Rāmānuja's successor was Parāśara Bhaṭṭārya, son of Kureśa, who wrote a commentary on the *Sahasra-gīti*. Rāmānuja had succeeded in securing a number of devoted scholars as his disciples, and they carried on his philosophy and forms of worship through the centuries. His religion was catholic, and, though he followed the rituals regarding initiation and worship, he admitted Jains and Buddhists, Śūdras and even untouchables into his fold. He himself was the pupil of a Śūdra and used to spend a long time after his bath in the hut of an untouchable friend of his. It is said that he ruled over 74 episcopal thrones, and counted among his followers 700 ascetics, 12,000 monks and 300 nuns (Keṭṭi ammais). Many kings and rich men were among his disciples. Kureśa, Dāśarathi, Naḍāḍur Āṛvān and the Bhaṭṭāra were dedicated to scholarly discourses. Yajñamūrti performed the function of the priest; one disciple was in charge of the kitchen; Vaṭapūrṇa or Andhrapūrṇa and Gomaṭham Siṭiyāṛvān were in charge of various kinds of personal service; Dhanurdāsa was trea-

[1] Mr Rice, however, says in the *Mysore Gazetteer*, vol. I, that the conversion took place in 1039 śaka or A.D. 1117. But Rāu points out that in the *Epigraphia Carnatica* we have inscriptions of Biṭṭideva as early as śaka 1023 (No. 34 Arsiker), which call him *Viṣṇu-vardhana*.

[2] The general tradition is that Rāmānuja kept away from Śrīraṅgam for a total period of twelve years only; but Rāu holds that this period must be about twenty years, of which twelve years were spent in Yādavādri.

[3] *Śrī Rāmānujācārya*, by S. K. Aiyangar, M.A. Natesan and Co., Madras.

surer; Ammaṅgi of boiled milk; Ukkal Āṟvān served meals; Ukkal-ammal fanned, and so on[1]. Rāmānuja converted many Śaivas to Vaiṣṇavism, and in the conflict between the Śaivas and the Vaiṣṇavas in his time; though he suffered much at the hands of the Cola king Kṛmikanṭha who was a Śaiva, yet Kṛmikanṭha's successor became a Vaiṣṇava and his disciple, and this to a great extent helped the cause of the spread of Śrīvaiṣṇavism.

The sources from which the details of Rāmānuja's life can be collected are as follows: (1) *Divya-sūri-charitai*, written in Tamil by Garuḍavāha, a contemporary of Rāmānuja; (2) *Gurū-paramparā-prabhāvam*, written in *maṇipravāla* in the early part of the fourteenth century by Pinb'-aṟagiya Perū-māl Jīyar; (3) Pillai Lokam-jīyar's *Rāmānujārya-divya-charitai*, written in Tamil; (4) Āṇbillai Kaṇḍāḍaiyappan's brief handbook of Āṟvārs and Aṟagiyas called *Periya-tiru-muḍiy-aḍaiva*, written in Tamil; (5) *Prappannāmṛta*, by Anantācārya, a descendant of Andhrapūrṇa, and pupil of Śailaraṅgeśa-guru; (6) the commentaries on the *Tiru-vāy-moṟi* which contain many personal reminiscences of the Aṟagiyas; (7) other epigraphical records.

The Precursors of the Viśiṣṭādvaita Philosophy and the contemporaries and pupils of Rāmānuja.

The *bhedābheda* interpretation of the *Brahma-sūtras* is in all probability earlier than the monistic interpretation introduced by Śaṅkara. The *Bhagavad-gītā*, which is regarded as the essence of the Upaniṣads, the older *Purāṇas*, and the *Pañcarātra*, dealt with in this volume, are more or less on the lines of *bhedābheda*. In fact the origin of this theory may be traced to the *Puruṣa-sūkta*. Apart from this, Dramiḍācārya, as Yāmuna says in his *Siddhi-traya*, explained the *Brahma-sūtra*, and that it was further commented upon by Śrīvatsāṅka Miśra. Bodhāyana, referred to by Rāmānuja as *Vṛtti-kāra* and by Śaṅkara as Upavarṣa, wrote on the *Brahma-sūtras* a very elaborate and extensive *vṛtti*, which formed the basis of Rāmānuja's *bhāṣya*[2]. Ānandagiri also refers

[1] *The Life of Rāmānuja*, by Govindāchāryar, p. 218.

[2] Veṅkaṭanātha in his *Tattva-ṭīkā* says "*Vṛtti-kārasya Bodhāyanasyai'va hi Upavarṣa iti syān nāma.*" In his *Seśvara-mīmāṃsā*, however, he refutes the view of Upavarṣa, for in the *Vaijayantī* lexicon Kṛtakoṭi and Halabhūti are said to be names of Upavarṣa.

See also the second volume of the present work, p. 43 *n*.

to *Drāviḍa-bhāṣya* as being a commentary on the *Chāndogy Upaniṣad*, written in a simple style (*ṛju-vivaraṇa*) previous to Śaṅkara's attempt. In the *Saṃkṣepa-śārīraka* (III. 217–27) a writer is referred to as Ātreya and *Vākya-kāra*, and the commentator Rāmatīrtha identifies him with Brahmanandin. Rāmānuja, in his *Vedārtha-saṃgraha*, quotes a passage from the *Vākya-kāra* and also its commentary by Dramiḍācārya[1]. While the *Vākya-kāra* and Dramiḍācārya, referred to by Rāmānuja, held that Brahman was qualified, the Dramiḍācārya who wrote a commentary on Brahmānandin's work was a monist and is probably the same person as the Draviḍācārya referred to by Ānandagiri in his commentary on Śaṅkara's *bhāṣyopodghāta* on the *Chāndogya Upaniṣad*. But the point is not so easily settled. Sarvajñātma muni, in his *Saṃkṣepa-śārīraka*, refers to the *Vākya-kāra* as a monist. It is apparent, however, from his remarks that this *Vākya-kāra* devoted the greater part of his commentary to upholding the *pariṇāma* view (akin to that of Bhāskara), and introduced the well known example of the sea and its waves with reference to the relation of Brahman to the world, and that it was only in the commentary on the sixth *prapāṭhaka* of the *Chāndogya* that he expounded a purely monistic view to the effect that the world was neither existent nor non-existent. Curiously enough, the passage referred to Sarvajñātma muni as proving decidedly the monistic conclusion of Ātreya *Vākya-kāra*, and his commentator the Dramiḍācārya is referred to by Rāmānuja in his *Vedārtha-saṃgraha*, as being favourable to his own view. Rāmānuja, however, does not cite him as Brahmanandin, but as *Vākya-kāra*. The commentator of the *Vākya-kāra* is referred to by Rāmānuja also as Dramiḍacārya. But though Sarvajñātma muni also cites him as *Vākya-kāra*, his commentator, Rāmatīrtha, refers to him as Brahmanandin and the *Vākya-kāra's* commentator as Drāviḍācārya, and interprets the term "*Vākya-kāra*" merely as "author." Sarvajñātma muni, how-

[1] *Vedārtha-saṃgraha*, p. 138. The *Vākya-kāra's* passage is "*yuktaṃ tad-guṇopāsanād*," and Dramiḍācārya's commentary on it is "*yady-api sac-citto na nirbhugna-daivataṃ guṇa-gaṇam manasā'nudhāvet tathā'py antar-guṇām eva devatāṃ bhajata iti tatrā'pi sa-guṇai'va devatā prāpyata iti*." The main idea of these passages is that, even if God be adored as a pure qualityless being, when the final release comes it is by way of the realization of God as qualified.

MM.S. Kuppusvāmī Śāstrī, M.A., identifies Dramiḍācārya with Tirumaṛiṣai Pirān, who lived probably in the eighth century A.D. But the reasons adduced by him in support of his views are unconvincing. See *Proceedings and Transactions of the Third Oriental Conference*, Madras, 1924, pp. 468–473.

ever, never refers to Brahmanandin by name. Since the passage quoted in the *Saṃkṣepa-śārīraka* by Sarvajñātma muni agrees with that quoted by Rāmānuja in his *Vedārtha-saṃgraha*, it is certain that the *Vākya-kāra* referred to by Sarvajñātma muni and Rāmānuja, and the Dramiḍācārya referred to by Sarvajñātma, Rāmānuja and Ānandagiri are one and the same person. It seems, therefore, that the *Vākya-kāra's* style of writing, as well as that of his commentator Dramiḍācārya, was such that, while the monists thought that it supported their view, the Śrīvaiṣṇavas also thought that it favoured them. From Sarvajñātma muni's statement we understand that the *Vākya-kāra* was also called Ātreya, and that he devoted a large part of his work in propounding the *bhedābheda* view. Upavarṣa is also referred to by Śaṅkara as a reputed exponent of the Mīmāṃsā philosophy and the *Brahma-sūtra*; and as having been the author of one *tantra* on Mīmāṃsā and another on the *Brahma-sūtra*[1]. Our conclusion, therefore, is that we have one *Vākya-kāra* who wrote a commentary on the *Chāndogya Upaniṣad*, and that he had a commentator who wrote in a clear and simple style and who was known as Dramiḍācārya, though he wrote in Sanskrit and not in Tamil. If we believe in Rāmatīrtha's identification, we may also believe that his name was Brahmanandin. But, whoever he may be, he was a very revered person in the old circle, as the epithet "*bhagavān*" has been applied to him by Sarvajñātma muni. Regarding Upavarṣa we may say that he also was a very revered person, since Śaṅkara applies the epithet "*bhagavat*" to him, and quotes him as an ancient authority in his support. He seems to have flourished sometime before Śabara Svāmin, the great Mīmāṃsā commentator[2]. Ānandagiri and Veṅkaṭanātha, in the fourteenth century, identify Upavarṣa with the *Vṛtti-kāra*, and Veṅkaṭanātha further identifies

[1] *ata eva ca bhagavato' pavarṣeṇa prathame tantre ātmā-stitvā-bhidhāna-prasaktau śārīrake vyakṣyāma ity uddhāraḥ kṛtaḥ*. Śaṅkara's *bhāṣya* on *Brahma-sūtra*, III. 3. 53.

Govindānanda, in his *Ratna-prabhā*, identifies Upavarṣa with the *Vṛtti-kāra*. Ānandagiri also agrees with this identification. In the *Brahma-sūtra-bhāṣya*, I. I. 19 and I. 2. 23, Śaṅkara refutes views which are referred to as being those of the *Vṛtti-kāra*. What can be gathered of the *Vṛtti-kāra's* views from the last two passages, which have been regarded by the commentator Govindānanda as referring to the *Vṛtti-kāra*, is that the world is a transformation of God. But we can never be certain that these views refuted by Śaṅkara were really held by the *Vṛtti-kāra*, as we have no other authority on the point except Govindānanda, a man of the thirteenth or fourteenth century.

[2] Śavara, in his *bhāṣya* on the *Mīmāṃsā-sūtra*, I. I. 5, refers to Upavarṣa with the epithet "*bhagavān*" on the subject of *sphoṭa*.

him in a conjectural manner with Bodhāyana. Even if Upavarṣa was the *Vṛtti-kāra*, it is doubtful whether he was Bodhāyana. On this point we have only the conjectural statement of Veṅkaṭanātha referred to above. Śaṅkara, in his commentary on the *Brahma-sūtra*, I. 3. 28, refers again to Upavarṣa in support of his refutation of the *sphoṭa* theory[1]. But this point is also indecisive, since neither Śaṅkara nor the Śrīvaiṣṇavas admit the *sphoṭa* theory. There seems, however, to be little evidence. We are therefore not in a position to say anything about Upavarṣa, the *Vṛtti-kāra* and Bodhāyana[2]. If the testimony of the *Prapannāmṛta* is to be trusted, Bodhāyana's *Vṛtti* on the *Brahma-sūtra* must have been a very elaborate work, and Dramiḍācārya's work on the *Brahma-sūtra* must have been a very brief one. This was the reason why Rāmānuja attempted to write a commentary which should be neither too brief nor too elaborate.

Now we have in MS. a small work called *Brahma-sūtrārha-saṃgraha* by Śaṭhakopa, and we do not know whether this is the Dramiḍa commentary referred to in the *Prapannāmṛta*. Yāmuna, in his *Siddhi-traya*, refers to a *bhāṣya-kāra* and qualifies him as "*parimita-gambhīra-bhāṣiṇā*," which signifies that it was a brief treatise pregnant with deep sense. He further says that this *bhāṣya* was elaborated by Śrīvatsāṅka-Miśra. The views of these two writers were probably consonant with the views of the Śrīvaiṣṇava school. But Yāmuna mentions the name of Taṅka, Bhartṛ-prapañca, Bhartṛmitra, Bhartṛhari, Brahmadatta, Śaṅkara and Bhāskara. An account of Bhartṛprapañca's interpretation of the *Brahma-sūtra* has been given in the second volume of the present work. An account of Bhāskara's view has been given in the present volume. Nothing is definitely known about the interpretations of Ṭaṅka, Bhartṛmitra, Bhartṛhari and Brahmadatta, except that they were against the views of the Śrīvaiṣṇavas.

Rāmānuja, in his *bhāṣya* on the *Brahma-sūtra*, says that Bodhāyana wrote a very elaborate work on the *Brahma-sūtra* and that

[1] *varṇā eva tu śabdāḥ iti bhagavān upavarṣaḥ*. Śaṅkara's commentary on the *Brahma-sūtra*, I. 3. 28.

Deussen's remark that the entire discussion of *sphoṭa* is derived from Upavarṣa is quite unfounded. According to *Kathā-sarit-sāgara* Upavarṣa was the teacher of Pāṇini.

[2] Śavara, also, in his commentary on the 5th sūtra of the *Mīmāṃsā-sūtra*, I. I. 5, refers to a *Vṛtti-kāra*, a Mīmāṃsā writer prior to Śavara. The fact that in the *bhāṣya* on the same *sūtra* Śavara refers to bhagavān Upavarṣa by name makes it very probable that the *Vṛtti-kāra* and Upavarṣa were not the same person.

this was summarized very briefly by the older teachers. He says, further, that in making his *bhāṣya* he has closely followed the interpretation of the *Sūtra*, as made by Bodhāyana[1]. Rāmānuja also owes a great debt of gratitude to Yāmuna's *Siddhi-traya*, though he does not distinctly mention it in his *bhāṣya*. It is said that Yāmuna had a large number of disciples. Of these, however, Mahāpūrṇa, Goṣṭhīpūrṇa, Mālādhara, Kāñcīpūrṇa, Śrīśailapūrṇa, also called Tātācārya (Rāmānuja's maternal uncle), and Śrīraṅganāthagāyaka were the most important. Śrīśailapūrṇa's son Govinda, the cousin and fellow-student of Rāmānuja with Yādavaprakāśa, became later in life a disciple of Rāmānuja[2]. Of the seventy-four prominent disciples of Rāmānuja, Praṇatārtihara of Ātreya *gotra*, Kureśa or Śrīvatsāṅka Miśra, Dāśarathi, Andhrapūrṇa or Vaṭapūrṇa, Varadaviṣṇu, Yatiśekhara-bhārata, Yādava-prakāśa or Govinda and Yajñamūrti are the most important[3]. Of these Dāśarathi of Vādhūla *gotra* and Varadaviṣṇu or Varadaviṣṇu Miśra were the sister's sons of Rāmānuja. Varadaviṣṇu was better known as Vātsya Varadaguru. Kureśa or Śrīvatsāṅka Miśra had a son by Āṇḍāḷ, called Parāśara Bhaṭṭārya, who defeated the Vedāntin Mādhavadāsa and afterwards became the successor of Rāmānuja[4]. Parāśara Bhaṭṭārya had a son called Madhya Pratoli Bhaṭṭārya or Madhya-vīthi Bhaṭṭārya. Kureśa had another son named Padmanetra; Padmanetra's son was called Kurukeśvara[5]. Kurukeśvara's son was Puṇḍarīkākṣa, and his son was Śrīnivāsa. Śrīnivāsa had a son Nṛsiṃhārya. They belonged to the Śrīśaila lineage, probably from the name of Bhūri Śrī Śailapūrna, Kureśa's father. Nṛsiṃhārya had a son called Rāmānuja. Rāmānuja had two sons,

[1] Sudarśana Sūrī, in his commentary on the *bhāṣya* called the *Śruta-prakāśikā*, explains the word "*pūrvācārya*" in Rāmānuja's *bhāṣya* as *Dramiḍa-bhāṣya-kārādayaḥ*. On the phrase *bodhāyana-matā'nusāreṇa sūtrā-kṣarāṇi vyākhyāyante*, he says "*na tu svo-tprekṣitamatā-ntareṇa sūtrā-kṣarāṇi sūtra-padānāṃ prakṛti-pratyaya-vibhāgā-nuguṇaṃ vadāmaḥ na tu svot-prekṣitā-rtheṣu sūtrāṇi yathā-kathañ cit dyotayitavyāni.*"

[2] It is interesting to note that Yāmuna's son Vararaṅga later on gave instruction to Rāmānuja and had his younger brother Sottanambi initiated as a disciple of Rāmānuja. Vararaṅga had no son. He had set the *Sahasra-gīti* to music. *Prapannāmṛta*, 23. 45.

[3] Rāja Gopalacariyar also mentions the name of Tirukurugaipiran Pillai as a prominent disciple of Rāmānuja. He wrote a commentary on Nāmm'āṛvār's *Tiru-vāymoḷi*.

[4] Kureśa had another son named Śrī Rama Pillai or Vyāsa Bhaṭṭār.

[5] It is rather common in South India to give one's son the name of his grandfather.

Nṛsiṃhārya and Raṅgācārya, who lived probably in the fifteenth century. Rāmānuja's disciple, Yajñamūrti, was an exceedingly learned man. When Rāmānuja accepted him as a disciple, he changed his name to Devarāṭ or Devamannātha or Devarāja and had a separate maṭha established in Śrīraṅgam for him. Yajñamūrti had written two very learned works in Tamil, called *Jñāna-sāra* and *Prameya-sāra*. Rāmānuja had four of his disciples, Bhaktagrāma-pūrṇa, Marudha-grāma-pūrṇa, Anantārya and Yajñeśa, initiated into Vaiṣṇavism by Yajñamūrti[1]. Another pupil of Rāmānuja, Tiruku-rugai-piran Pillai, wrote a commentary of Nāmm'āṛvār's *Tiru-vāy-moṛi*. Praṇatārtihara Pillan, another pupil of Rāmānuja, of Ātreya *gotra*, had a son Rāmānuja, a disciple of Naḍaḍur Ammal of the lineage of Vātsya Varada[2]. This Rāmānuja, alias Padmanābha, had a son called Śrī Rāmānuja Pillan, a disciple of Kidambi Rāmā-nuja Pillan. This Padmanābha had a son called Rāmānuja Pillan and a daughter Totārambā, who was married to Anantasūri, the father of Veṅkaṭanātha. Rāmānuja's other disciple and nephew, Dāś-arathi, of Vādhūla *gotra*, had a son called Rāmānuja, who had a son called Toḍappā or Vāraṇādrīśa or Lokārya or Lokācārya. After Parāśara Bhaṭṭārya the Vedānti Mādhavadāsa, called also Nanjiar, became his successor. Mādhavadāsa's successor was Nambilla or Namburi Varadārya or Lokācārya. He had two wives Āṇḍal and Śrīraṅganāyakī and a son called Rāmānuja[3]. Nambilla's other name was Kalijit or Kalivairī. Now Vāraṇādrīśa became a disciple of Nambilla or the senior Lokācārya. Vāraṇādrīśa was known as Pillai Lokācārya. Namburi Varada had a pupil called Mādhava. Varada had a son called Padmanābha who had a disciple called Rāmā-nujadāsa. Rāmānujadāsa had a son called Devarāja, who had a son called Śrīśailanātha, and Śrīśailanātha had a pupil called Saumya Jāmātṛ muni or Ramyajāmātṛ muni, also called Varavara muni or Yatīndrapravaṇa or Manavalamahāmuni or Periya-jiyar. It is said that he was the grandson of Kattur-āṛagiya-vanavalapillai. All these people were influenced by the *Sahasra-gīti-vyākhyā* of Kureśa. Namburi Varadārya, otherwise called Kalijit, had two other pupils called Udak-pratoḷi-kṛṣṇa, and Kṛṣṇa-samāhbhaya, also called Kṛṣṇapāda. Kṛṣṇapāda's son Lokācārya was a pupil of

[1] See *Prapannāmṛta*, Ch. 26.

[2] See Govindāchāryar's *Life of Rāmānuja*.

[3] He wrote two works called *Sārā-rtha-saṃgraha* and *Rahasya-traya*. *Prapannāmṛta*, 119/3.

Kalijit, and Kṛṣṇapāda himself. Kṛṣṇapāda's second son was Abhirāma-Varādhīśa.

Rāmānuja's brother-in-law Devarāja, of Vātsya *gotra*, had a son called Varadaviṣṇu Miśra or Vātsya Varada, who was a pupil of Viṣṇucitta, a pupil of Kureśa. This Vātsya Varada was a great writer on Vedāntic subjects. Kureśa had a son called Śrī Rama Pillai, or Vedavyāsa Bhaṭṭa, who had a son called Vādivijaya, who wrote *Kṣamā-ṣoḍaśī-stava*. Vādivijaya had a son called Sudarśana Bhaṭṭa, who was a pupil of Vātsya Varada, a contemporary of Varadaviṣṇu. Sudarśana Bhaṭṭa was the famous author of the *Śruta-prakāśikā*. The celebrated Aṇṇayācārya also was a pupil of Pillai Lokācārya, the pupil of Kalijit. Śrīśaila Śrīnivāsa, or Śrīśailanātha, was the son of Aṇṇayācārya. Ramyajāmātṛ muni had a number of disciples, such as Rāmānuja, Paravastu Prativādibhayaṅkara Aṇṇayācārya, Vanamamalai-jiyar, Periya-jīyar, Koyilkaṇḍādaiaṇṇan, etc.[1] Of Veṅkatanātha's pupils two are of most importance: his son Nainārācārya, otherwise called Kumāra-Vēdānta-deśika, Varadanātha or Varadaguru, who wrote many Vedāntic works, and Brahmatantra-jiyar. Parakāladāsa and Śrīraṅgācārya were probably pupils of Kṛṣṇapāda, or Kṛṣṇasūri, the pupil of Kalijit or Namburi Varadārya. Abhirāma Varādhīśa was a pupil of Rāmānuja, son of Saumya Jāmātṛ muni. The pontifical position of Śrīvaiṣṇavism was always occupied in succession by eminent men in different important *maṭhas* or temples, and there arose many great preachers and teachers of Vedānta, some of whom wrote important works while others satisfied themselves with oral teachings. The works of some of these have come down to us, but others have been lost. It seems, however, that the *Viśiṣṭā-dvaita* philosophy was not a source of perennial inspiration for the development of ever newer shades of thought, and that the logical and dialectical thinkers of this school were decidedly inferior to the prominent thinkers of the Śaṅkara and the Madhva school. There is hardly any one in the whole history of the development of the school of Rāmānuja whose logical acuteness can be compared with that of Śrīharṣa or Citsukha, or with that of Jayatīrtha or Vyāsatīrtha. Veṅkaṭanātha, Meghanādāri or Rāmānujācārya, called also Vādihaṃsa, were some of the most prominent writers of this school; but even with them philosophic

[1] The Tamil names of some of the disciples have been collected from the *Life of Rāmānujācārya* by Govindāchāryar.

criticism does not always reach the highest level. It was customary for the thinkers of the Śaṅkara and the Madhva schools in the fourteenth, fifteenth and sixteenth centuries to accept the concepts of the new School of Logic of Mithilā and Bengal and introduce keen dialectical analysis and criticism. But for some reason or other this method was not adopted to any large extent by the thinkers of the Śrīvaiṣṇava school. Yet this was the principal way in which philosophical concepts developed in later times.

In dealing with the names of teachers of the Rāmānuja school, one *Guru-paramparā* mentions the name of Paravādibhayaṅkara, who was a pupil of Ramyajāmātṛ muni and belonged to the Vātsya *gotra*. Prativādibhayaṅkara was the teacher of Śaṭhakopa Yati. The treatise speaks also of another Ramyajāmātṛ muni, son of Anantārya, grandson of Prativādibhayaṅkara and pupil of Śriveṅkaṭeśa. It also mentions Vedāntaguru, of the Vātsya *gotra*, a pupil of Ramyajāmātṛ muni and Varadārya; Sundaradeśika, of the Vātsya *gotra*, son of Prativādibhayaṅkara; Aparyātmāmṛtācārya, son of Śrīveṅkaṭaguru and grandson of Prativādibhayaṅkara. This Veṅkaṭācārya had a son called Prativādibhayaṅkara. Ramyajāmātṛ muni had a son called Śrīkṛṣṇa-deśika. Puruṣottamārya, of the Vātsya *gotra*, was the son of Śrīveṅkaṭācārya. Śrīkṛṣṇa-deśika had a son called Ramyajāmātṛ muni, who had a son called Kṛṣṇa Sūri. Anantaguru had a son called Veṅkaṭa-deśika. Śrīnivāsaguru was pupil of Veṅkatārya and Vātsya Śrīnivāsa, who had a son called Anantārya. It is unnecessary to continue with the list, as it is not very useful from the point of view of the development of the Śrīvaiṣṇava school of philosophy or literature. The fact that the names of earlier teachers are reverently passed on to many of those who succeeded them makes it difficult to differentiate them one from the other. But the history of the school is unimportant after the sixteenth or the early part of the seventeenth century, as it lost much of its force as an intellectual movement. In the days of the Āṛvārs the Śrīvaiṣṇava movement was primarily a religious movement of mystic and intoxicating love of God and self-surrender to Him. In the days of Rāmānuja it became intellectualized for some time, but it slowly relapsed into the religious position. As with Śaṅkara, and not as with Madhva, the emphasis of the school has always been on the interpretations of Vedic texts, and the intellectual appeal has always been subordinated to the appeal to the Upaniṣadic texts and their interpretations. The chief opponents of the Rāmānuja school were the Śaṅkarites, and we may read many works in which copious references are made by writers of the Śaṅkara school who attempted to refute the principal points of the *bhāṣya* of Rāmānuja, both from the point of view of logical argument and from that of interpretations of the Upaniṣadic texts. But unfortunately, except in the case of a few later works of little value, no work of scholarly refutation of the views of Rāmānuja by a Śaṅkarite is available. The followers of Rāmānuja also offered slight refutation of some of the doctrines of Bhāskara, Jādava-prakāśa, and Madhva and the Śaivas. But their efforts were directed mainly against Śaṅkara.

It has already been noted that Rāmānuja wrote a *bhāṣya* on the *Brahma-sūtra*, *Vedārtha-saṃgraha*, *Vedānta-sāra* and *Vedānta-dīpa*, a commentary on the *Śrīmad-bhagavad-gītā*, *Gadya-traya*, and *Bhagavad-ārādhana-krama*[1]. According to traditional accounts, Rāmānuja was born in A.D. 1017 and died in 1137. The approximate dates of the chief events of his life have been worked out as follows: study with Yādavaprakāśa, 1033; first entry into Śrīraṅgam to see Yāmuna, 1043; taking holy orders, 1049; flight to Mysore for fear of the Cola king's persecution, 1096; conversion of Biṭṭi-deva, the Jain king of Mysore, the Hoysala country, 1098; installing the temple God at Melukot, 1100; stay in Melukot, up to 1116; return to Śrīraṅgam, 1118; death, 1137[2]. His nephew and disciple Dāśarathi and his disciple Kureśa were about fifteen or sixteen years junior to him[3]. Rāmānuja's *bhāṣya*, called also *Śrī-bhāṣya*, was commented on by Sudarśana Sūri. His work is called *Śruta prakāśikā*, and is regarded as the most important commentary on the *Śrī-bhāṣya*.

[1] *viṣṇv'arcā-kṛtam avanotsukojñānaṃ śrīgītā-vivaraṇa-bhāṣya-dīpa-sārān*
tad gadya-trayam akṛta prapanna-nityā-nuṣṭhāna-kramam api yogi-rāṭ pravandhān. *Divya-sūri-Caritai.*

Reference to the *Vedārtha-saṃgraha* of Rāmānuja is also found in the same work.

ity uktvā nigama-śikhā'rtha-saṃgrahā-khyam
bhinnas tāṃ kṛtim urarīkriyā-rtham asya.

[2] Govindāchāryar's *Life of Rāmānuja*. Yāmuna, according to the above view, would thus have died in 1042, corresponding with the first visit of Rāmānuja to Śriraṅgam; but Gopī-nātha Rāu thinks that this event took place in 1038. The date of the Cola persecution is also regarded by Gopī-nāthaRāu as having occurred in 1078–79, which would correspond to Rāmānuja's flight to Mysore; and his return to Śrīraṅgam must have taken place after 1117, the death of the Cola king Koluttuṅga. Thus there is some divergence between Govindācārya and Gopī-nātha Rāu regarding the date of Rāmānuja's first visit to Śrīraṅgam and the date of his flight to Mysore. Gopī-nātha Rāu's views seem to be more authentic.

[3] Apart from the *Sahasra-gīti-bhāṣya*, Kuresá wrote a work called *Kureśa-vijaya*.

Rāmānuja Literature.

As already noted, the principal commentary on Rāmānuja's *bhāṣya*, was the *Śruta-prakāśikā* by Sudarśana Sūri. Even before this *Śruta-prakāśikā* was written, another commentary, called *Śrī-bhāṣya-vivṛti*, was written by Rāma-miśra-deśika, a disciple of Rāmānuja, under his own direction. This work was written in six chapters and was not a commentary in the ordinary sense, but a study of the principal contents of Rāmānuja's *bhāṣya*. This Rāma Miśra was a different man from Rāma Miśra, the teacher of Yāmuna. The *Śruta-prakāśikā* had a further study, entitled *Bhāva-prakāśikā*, by Vīrarāghavadāsa. Criticisms of this work were replied to in a work called *Bhāṣya-prakāśikā-dūṣaṇoddhāra* by Śaṭhakopācārya, a writer of the sixteenth century. The *Śruta-prakāśikā* had another commentary, called *Tūlikā*, by Vādhūla Śrīnivāsa, a writer who probably belonged to the fifteenth century. The contents of the *Śruta-prakāśikā* were summarized in a work called *Śruta-prakāśikā-sāra-saṃgraha*. The *bhāṣya* of Rāmānuja was further commented on in the *Tattva-sāra*, by Vātsya Varada, a nephew of Rāmānuja. The name of the commentator's father was Devarāja, and his mother was Kamalā, a sister of Rāmānuja. He was a pupil of Śrīviṣṇucitta, a disciple of Kureśa. This *Tattva-sāra* provoked a further criticism, called *Ratna-sāriṇī*, by Vīra-rāghava-dāsa, son of Vādhūla Narasiṃha-guru and pupil of Vādhūla Varadaguru, son of Vādhūla Veṅkaṭācārya. He also himself wrote a commentary on the *Śrī-bhāṣya*, called *Tātparya-dīpikā*. Vīra-rāghava-dāsa lived probably in the later half of the fourteenth or the beginning of the fifteenth century. Rāmānuja's views were also collected together in a scholarly manner in a work called *Naya-mukha-mālikā*, by Apyaya-dīkṣita, who was born in the middle of the sixteenth century. Rāmānuja's *bhāṣya* is also dealt with by the famous Veṅkaṭanātha, in his work *Tattva-ṭīkā*. The *Śrī-bhāṣya* had another commentary called *Naya-prakāśikā*, by Meghanādāri, a contemporary of Veṅkaṭanātha of the fourteenth century[1]. A further commentary is

[1] Meghanādāri's great work, *Naya-dyu-maṇi*, has been treated in detail in a later section. He was the son of Ātreyanātha and his mother's name was Adhvaranāyikā. He had three brothers, Hastyadrinātha or Vāraṇādrīśa, Varadarāṭ, and Rāma Miśra. This Vāraṇādrīśa should not be confused with Dāśarathi's grandson, who was of Vādhūla *gotra*. Meghanādāri's other works are *Bhāva-prabodha* and *Mumukṣū-pāya-saṃgraha*.

called *Mita-prakāśikā*, by Parakāla Yati, probably of the fifteenth century. Parakāla Yati had a disciple called Raṅga Rāmānuja, who wrote a study of the *Śri-bhāṣya*, called *Mūla-bhāva-prakāśikā*. One Śrīnivāsācārya also criticized the *Śrī-bhāṣya* in *Brahma-vidyā-kaumudī*. It is difficult to guess which Śrīnivāsa was the author of the work, there being so many Śrīnivāsas among the teachers of the Rāmānuja school. Campakeśa, disciple of Veṅkaṭanātha, also dealt with the *Śrī-bhāṣya*. Śuddhasattva Lakṣmaṇācārya also wrote on the *Śrī-bhāṣya*, a work entitled *Guru-bhāva-prakāśikā* which was based upon the *Guru-tattva-prakāśikā* of Campakeśa. This work was in reality a commentary on the *Śruta-prakāśikā*. The author was the son of Śuddhasattva Yogīndra. He descends from the line of Rāmānuja's mother's sister, in which there were born eighteen teachers of Vedānta; he was the pupil of Saumya Jāmātṛ muni and flourished probably in the latter half of the sixteenth century. This *Guru-bhāva-prakāśikā* was commented on in the *Guru-bhāva-prakāśikā-vyākhyā*. Sudarśana Sūri also seems to have written a commentary on the *Śrī-bhāṣya*, called *Śruti-dīpikā*. Śrīnivāsa, the son of Tātayārya and Lakṣmī-devi, of Śriśaila lineage and pupil of Aṇṇayārya and Koṇḍinna Śrīnivāsa-dīkṣita, wrote another digest on the *Śrī-bhāṣya*, called *Tattva-mārtaṇḍa*. He probably lived in the latter half of the fifteenth or the beginning of the sixteenth century. The name of his grandfather was Aṇṇa-guru. He wrote *Ṇatva-darpaṇa*, *Bheda-darpaṇa*, *Siddhānta-cintāmaṇi*, *Sāra-darpaṇa*, and *Virodha-nirodha*[1]. He is also known as Śrīśaila Śrīnivāsa, and he wrote other books, e.g. *Jijñāsā-darpaṇa*, *Naya-dyu-maṇi-dīpikā*, and *Naya-dyu-maṇi-saṃgraha*. The *Naya-dyu-maṇi* of *Naya-dyu-maṇi-dīpikā* is not to be confused with the *Naya-dyu-maṇi* of Meghanādāri; for it is a summary in verse of Rāmānuja's *bhāṣya* with a commentary in prose. The *Naya-dyu-maṇi-saṃgraha* is a work in

[1] In his *Virodha-nirodha* he makes reference to a *Mukti-darpaṇa* (MS. p. 82), *Jñāna-ratna-darpaṇa* (MS. p. 87), and in his *Bheda-darpaṇa* (MS. p. 96) he refers to his *Guṇa-darpaṇa*. In his *Virodha-nirodha* he makes further reference to his other works, *Advaita-vana-kuṭhāra* and *Bheda-maṇi* (MS. p. 37), to his *Bheda-darpaṇa* (MS. p. 68), and to his *Sāra-darpaṇa* (MS. p. 66) and *Tattva-mārtaṇḍa* (MS. p. 87). His *Sāra-darpaṇa* gives the principal contents of Rāmānuja's philosophy. In his *Virodha-nirodha* (MS. p. 37) he refers to a *Virodha-bhañjana*, by his elder brother Aṇṇayārya and to his own *Siddhānta-cintāmaṇi* (MS. p. 12). In referring to his elder brother he says that his *Virodha-nirodha* is largely a rearrangement of the arguments adduced by him in his *Virodha-bhañjana*, some of which had been elaborated and others condensed and rearranged in his *Virodha-nirodha*. The *Virodha-nirodha* is thus admitted by the author to have been based materially on *Virodha-bhañjana* by Aṇṇayārya, his elder brother.

prose on the *bhāṣya* of Rāmānuja, and the first four *sūtras* intended to refute the criticisms made by his opponents. The *Naya-dyu-maṇi-saṃgraha* is a much smaller work than the *Naya-dyu-maṇi*, which is often referred to by the author for details. It makes constant reference to objections against Rāmānuja without mentioning the name of the critic. In the *Naya-dyu-maṇi* the author has made detailed discussions which are summarized by him in this work[1]. Thus Śrīnivāsa wrote three works *Naya-dyu-maṇi*, *Naya-dyu-maṇi-saṃgraha*, and *Naya-dyu-maṇi-dīpikā*. In his *Siddhānta-cintāmaṇi* Śrīnivāsa tries mainly to uphold the theory that Brahman is the only cause of all creation, animate and in-animate. In this work he tries to refute at every point the theory of Brahma-causality, as held by Śaṅkara.

Again, Deśikācārya wrote a commentary on the *Śrī-bhāṣya*, called *Prayoga-ratna-mālā*. Nārāyaṇamuni wrote his *Bhāva-pradīpikā*, and Puruṣottama his *Subodhinī* also as commentaries on the *Śrī-bhāṣya*. These writers probably lived some time about the seventeenth century. Vīra-rāghava-dāsa also criticized the *Śrī-bhāṣya* in the *Tātparya-dīpikā*. His name has already been mentioned in connection with his study, *Ratna-sāriṇī*, on Vātsya Varada's *Tattva-sāra*. Śrīnivāsa Tātācārya wrote his *Laghu-prakāśikā*, Śrī-vatsāṅka Śrīnivāsa his *Śrī-bhāṣya-sārārtha-saṃgraha*, and Śaṭhakopa hia *Brahma-sūtrārtha-saṃgraha* as commentaries on the *Śrī-bhāṣya*. These writers seem to have flourished late in the sixteenth century. Śrīvatsāṅka Śrīnivāsa's work was further summarized by Raṅgā-cārya in his *Śrīvatsa-siddhānta-sāra*. Appaya-dīkṣita, of the middle of the seventeenth century, wrote a commentary on the *Brahma-sūtras*, called *Naya-mukha-mālikā*, closely following the ideas of Rāmānuja[2]. Raṅga Rāmānuja also wrote a commentary, called

[1] *bhāṣyā-rṇavam avatīrṇo vistīrṇaṃ yad avadaṃ Naya-dyumaṇau*
saṃkṣipya tat paroktīr vikṣipya karomi toṣaṇaṃ viduṣām.
Naya-dyu-maṇi-saṃgraha, MS.

The general method of treatment followed in the book is to indulge in long discussions in refutation of the views of opponents and to formulate, as conclusion, the positive contentions of the *Viśiṣṭā-dvaita* theory on the special points of interest. Thus at the end of a long discussion on the *Brahma-sūtra*, I. I. 2, he says: *rāddhāntas tu na janmā'dīnāṃ viśeṣaṇatve viśesya-bheda-prasaṅgaḥ, avirud-dhaviśeṣaṇānām āśraya-bhedakatvāt na caivaṃ viśeṣaṇatvā-vacchedena na vyāvar-takatva-bhaṅgaḥ tad-an-āśraya-jīvādi-vyāvartakatvenaiva tad-asiddheḥ.* (*Naya-dyu-maṇi*, MS. p. 126.)

[2] *Lakṣmaṇārya-hṛdayā'nusāriṇī likhyate Naya-mālikā.*
Naya-mukha-mālikā, printed in Kumbakonam, 1915, p. 3.

Śārīraka-śāstrārtha-dīpikā, on the *Brahma-sūtra*, following the interpretations of Rāmānuja. His *Mūla-bhāva-prakāśikā*, a commentary on the *Śrī-bhāṣya*, has already been referred to in this section. He wrote also a commentary on the *Nyāya-siddhāñjana* of Veṅkaṭanātha, called *Nyāya-siddhāñjana-vyākhyā*. He was a pupil of Parakāla Yati and probably lived in the sixteenth century. He wrote also three other works, called *Viṣaya-vākya-dīpikā*, *Chāndagyopaniṣad-bhāṣya*, and *Rāmānuja-siddhānta-sāra*. Rāmānujadāsa, called also Mahācārya, lived probably early in the fifteenth century, and was a pupil of Vādhūla Śrīnivāsa. This Vādhūla Śrīnivāsa, author of the *Adhikaraṇa-sārārtha-dīpikā*, must be an earlier person than Śrīnivāsadāsa, author of the *Yatīndra-mata-dīpikā*, who was a pupil of Mahācārya. Mahācārya wrote a work called *Pārāśarya-vijaya*, which is a thesis on the general position of the Rāmānuja Vedānta. He wrote also another work on the *Śrī-bhāṣya* called *Brahma-sūtra-bhāṣyopanyāsa*. Mahācārya's other works are *Brahma-vidyā-vijaya*, *Vedānta-vijaya*, *Rahasya-traya-mīmāṃsā*, *Rāmānuja-carita-culuka*, *Aṣṭādaśa-rahasyārtha-nirṇaya*, and *Caṇḍa-māruta*, a commentary on the *Śata-dūṣaṇī* of Veṅkaṭanātha. He should be distinguished from Rāmānujācārya, called also Vādihaṃsāmbuvāha, uncle of Veṅkaṭanātha.

There is a work called *Śrī-bhāṣya-vārttika*, which, unlike most of those above, has already been printed; but the author does not mention his name in the book, which is composed in verse. Senānātha, or Bhagavat Senāpati Miśra, who is an author of later date, wrote *Śārīraka-nyāya-kalāpa*. Vijayīndra Bhikṣu was the author of *Śārīraka-mīmāṃsā-vṛtti*, and Raghunāthārya of *Śārīraka-śāstra-saṃgati-sāra*. Sundararāja-deśika, an author of the sixteenth century, wrote a simple commentary on the *Śri-bhāṣya* called *Brahma-sūtra-bhāsya-vyākhyā*. Veṅkaṭācārya, probably an author of the sixteenth century, wrote *Brahma-sūtra-bhāṣya-pūrva-pakṣa-saṃgraha-kārikā* in verse. This Veṅkaṭācārya was also known as "Prativādībhakeśarī." He also composed *Ācārya-pañcāśat*. Campakeśa, who has already been referred to, wrote a commentary on the *Śrī-bhāṣya*, called *Śrī-bhāṣya-vyākhyā*. Veṅkaṭanāthārya wrote a work called *Śrī-bhāṣya-sāra*. Śrīvatsāṅka Śrīnivāsācārya was the author of *Śrī-bhāṣya-sārārtha-saṃgraha*. Śrīraṅgācārya composed *Śrī-bhāṣya-siddhānta-sāra* and Śrīnivāsācārya wrote a work called *Śrī-bhāṣyopanyāsa*. There are two other commentaries, called

Brahma-sūtra-bhāṣya-saṃgraha-vivaraṇa and *Brahma-sūtra-bhāṣyārambha-prayoyana-samarthana*; but the names of the authors are missing in the manuscripts. Veṅkaṭanātha, of the thirteenth century, wrote *Adhikaraṇa-sārāvalī*, and Maṅgācārya Śrīnivāsa, *Adhikaraṇa-sārārtha-dīpikā*. Varadārya or Varadanāṭha, son of Veṅkaṭanātha, wrote a commentary on the *Adhikaraṇa-sārāvalī* called *Adhikāra-cintāmaṇi*. There is another work on similar subjects called *Adhikaraṇa-yukti-vilāsa*; but, though the author offers an adoration to Śrīnivāsa, he does not mention his name and it is difficult to discover who this Śrīnivāsa was. Jagannātha Yati wrote a commentary on the *Brahma-sūtra* on the lines of Rāmānuja's *bhāṣya*, and it was called *Brahma-sūtra-dīpikā*. It will thus be seen that Rāmānuja's *bhāṣya* inspired many scholars and thinkers and a great literature sprang up on its basis. But it must be noted with regret that this huge critical literature on Rāmānuja's *bhāṣya*, is not in general of much philosophical importance. Rāmānuja's *Vedārtha-saṃgraha* was commented on by Sudarśana Sūri of the fourteenth century, in *Tātparya-dīpikā*. He was the son of Vāgvijaya, or Viśvajaya, and pupil of Vātsya Varada. In addition to his study of Rāmānuja's *bhāṣya* already referred to, he wrote a *Sandhyā-vandana-bhāṣya*. Rāmānuja's *Vedānta-dīpa* (a brief commentary on the *Brahma-sūtra*) was dealt with by Ahobila Raṅganātha Yati, of the sixteenth century. Rāmānuja's *Gadya-traya* was criticized by Veṅkaṭanātha, and Sudarśanācārya also wrote a commentary; Kṛṣṇapada, a later author, also wrote another commentary. Rāmānuja's commentary on the *Gītā* also was commented on by Veṅkaṭanātha. The *Vedānta-sāra* was a brief commentary on the *Brahma-sūtra* by Rāmānuja himself, based on his *Śrī-bhāṣya*.

Rāmānujācārya, called also Vādihaṃsāmbuvāhācārya of Ātreya *gotra*, son of Padmanābha and maternal uncle of Veṅkaṭanātha, lived in the thirteenth or fourteenth century; he wrote an important work, called *Naya-kuliśa* or *Nyāya-kuliśa*, which has been noticed before. He composed also *Divya-sūri-prabhāva-dīpikā*, *Sarva-darśana-śiromaṇi*, and *Mokṣa-siddhi*, to which he himself refers in his *Nyāya-kuliśa*[1]. It might seem that the *Nyāya-kuliśa* was one of the earliest logical or ontological treatises of the *Viśiṣṭā-dvaita* school; but we find that there were other treatises of this type

[1] I have not been able to procure a MS. of the *Mokṣa-siddhi*, and, so far as I can guess, the book is probably lost.

written during this period and even earlier than Rāmānuja. Thus Nāthamuni wrote a *Nyāya-tattva*, in which he refuted the logical views of Gautama and founded a new system of Logic. Viṣṇucitta, a junior contemporary of Rāmānuja, wrote two works, *Prameya-saṃgraha* and *Saṃgati-mālā*. Varadaviṣṇu Miśra, who flourished probably in the latter half of the twelfth century, or the beginning of the thirteenth century, wrote a *Māna-yāthātmya-nirṇaya*. Varada Nārāyaṇa Bhaṭṭāraka, who flourished before Veṅkaṭanātha, also wrote a *Prajñā-paritrāṇa*[1]. Parāśara Bhaṭṭāraka, who also probably lived in the thirteenth century, wrote a *Tattva-ratnākara*[2]. These works have been referred to by Veṅkaṭanātha in his *Nyāya-pariśuddhi*; but the manuscripts were not available to the present writer. Vātsya Varada's works have been mentioned in a separate section.

Veṅkaṭanātha, called also Vedānta-deśika, Vedāntācārya, and Kavitārkikasiṃha, was one of the most towering figures of the school of *Viśiṣṭādvaita*. He was born at Tupple in Kanjivaram in A.D. 1268. His father was Ananta Sūri, his grandfather's name was Puṇḍarīkākṣa, and he belonged to the Viśvāmitra *gotra*; his mother was Totārambā, sister of Ātreya Rāmānuja, otherwise called Vādi-kalahaṃsāmbuvāhācārya. He studied with his uncle Ātreya Rāmānuja, and it is said that he accompanied him to Vātsya Varadācārya's place, when he was five years old. The story goes that even at such an early age he showed so much precocity that it was predicted by Vātsya Varada that in time he would be a great pillar of strength for the *Viśiṣṭā-dvaita-vāda* school and that he would repudiate all false systems of philosophy[3]. It appears that he also studied with Varadārya himself[4]. It is said that he used to live by *uñcha-vṛtti*, receiving alms in the streets, and spent all his life in

[1] He is said to have written another work, called *Nyāya-sudarśana*, mentioned in the introduction to the *Tattva-muktā-kalāpa* (Mysore, 1933).

[2] He also wrote another work, called *Bhagavad-guṇa-darpaṇa*.

[3] *utprekṣyate budha-janair upapatti-bhūmnya*
ghaṇṭā hareḥ samajaniṣṭa jaḍātmanī'ti
pratiṣṭhāpita-vedāntaḥ pratikṣipta-bahir-mataḥ
bhūyās traividya-mānyas tvaṃ bhūri-kalyāṇa-bhājanam.

It is said that he was blessed by Varadācārya in the aforesaid verse, in which he describes Veṅkaṭanātha as an incarnation of the bell of God. *Vaiṣṇavite Reformers of India*, by T. Rajagopalachariar.

[4] *śrutvā rāmānujāryāt sad-asad-api tatas tattva-muktā kalāpaṃ*
vyātānīd veṅkaṭeśo varada-guru-kṛpā-lambhito-ddāma-bhūmā.
Tattva-muktā-kalāpa, śl. 2.

writing philosophical and religious works. In the *saṃkalpa-sūryodaya* he says that at the time when he was writing that work he had finished the *Śrī-bhāṣya* for the thirtieth time. While he lived in Kāñcī and Śrīraṅgam, he had to work in the midst of various rival sects, and Pillai Lokācārya, who was very much senior to him in age and was the supporter of the Teṅgalai school, against which Veṅkaṭanātha fought, wrote a verse praising him. Scholars are in general agreement that Veṅkaṭanātha died in 1369, though there is also a view that he died in 1371. He enjoyed a long life and spent much of his time in pilgrimage to various northern countries such as Vijayanagara, Mathurā, Brindāban, Ayodhyā, and Purī. The story of Vidyāraṇya's friendship with Veṅkaṭanātha may be true or false; but we know that Vidyāraṇya was acquainted with the *Tattva-muktā-kalāpa*, and he quotes from it in his account of the *Viśiṣṭā-dvaita* view in *Sarva-darśana-saṃgraha*. When Veṅkaṭanātha was middle-aged, Sudarśana Sūri, writer of the *Śruta-prakāśikā*, was already an old man, and it is said that he called Veṅkaṭanātha to Śrīraṅgam and handed over to him his commentary on the *Śrī-bhāṣya*, so that it might get a greater publicity. Veṅkaṭanātha himself also wrote a commentary on the *Śrī-bhāṣya*, called the *Tattva-ṭīkā*. Though an extremely kind man of exemplary and saintly character, he had many enemies who tried to harass and insult him in countless ways. A great difference in interpretation of the nature of *prapatti*, or self-surrender to God, was manifested at this time in the writings of different Śrīvaiṣṇava scholars. Two distinct sects were formed, based mainly on the different interpretation of the nature of *prapatti*, though there were minor differences of a ritualistic nature, such as the marks on the forehead, etc. Of these two sects, the leader of the Vaḍakalai was Veṅkatanātha, and that of the Teṅgalai was Pillai Lokācārya. Later on Saumya Jāmātṛ muni became the accepted leader of the Teṅgalai school. Though the leaders themselves were actuated by a spirit of sympathy with one another, yet their followers made much of these little differences in their views and constantly quarrelled with one another, and it is a well known fact that these sectarian quarrels exist even now.

It was during Veṅkaṭanātha's life that Malik Kafur, a general of 'Alā-ud-dīn, invaded the Deccan in 1310. He easily conquered the countries of Warangal and Dvārasamudra and pushed to the extreme south, spreading devastation and plundering everywhere.

In 1326 the Mahomedans invaded Śrīraṅgam and pillaged the city and the temple. About 1351 the Hindu Kingdom in Vijayanagar was established by King Bukka I. When the Mahomedans pillaged the temple of Śrīraṅgam, the temple-keepers had fled away to Madurā with the God Raṅganātha, who was established in Tirupati and was worshipped there. Bukka's son Kampana began to make conquest in the south and eventually Gopana, a general of Kampana, succeeded in restoring Raṅganātha to Śrīraṅgam. This affair has been immortalized by a verse composed by Veṅkaṭanātha, which is still written on the walls of the temple of Śrīraṅgam, though certain authorities think that the verse was not by him, but is only attributed to him. This story is found in a Tamil work, called *Kavilologu*, and is also recorded in the Vaḍakalai *Guru-paramparā* of the fifteenth century. During the general massacre at Śrīraṅgam, Veṅkaṭanātha hid himself among the dead bodies and fled ultimately to Mysore. After having spent some years there he went to Coimbatore, and there he wrote his *Abhīti-stava*, in which he makes references to the invasion of the Mahomedans and the tragic condition at Śrīraṅgam. When he heard that by Gopana's endeavours Raṅganātha was restored to Śrīraṅgam he went there and wrote a verse applauding his efforts[1].

Veṅkaṭanātha was a prolific writer on various subjects and also a gifted poet. In the field of poetry his most important works are the *Yādavābhyudaya*, *Haṃsa-saṃdeśa*, *Subhāṣita-nīvi*, and *Saṃkalpa-sūryodaya*, an allegorical drama in ten acts. The *Yādavābhyudaya* was a work on the life of Kṛṣṇa, which was commented upon by no less a person than Appaya-dīkṣita. The *Subhāṣita-nīvi*, a didactic poem, was commented upon by Śrīnivāsa Sūri of the

[1] *ānīyā'nīla-śṛṅga-dyuti-racita-jagad-rañjanād añjanā'dreś*
ceñcyām ārādhya kañ cit samayam atha nihatyod'dhanuṣkāns tuluṣkān
lakṣmī-bhumyāv'ubhābhyāṃ saha nija-nagare sthāpayan raṅganāthaṃ
samyag-varyāṃ saparyāṃ punar akṛta yaśo-darpaṇaṃ goppaṇā-ryaḥ.

The verse appears in *Epigraphica Indica*, vol. VI, p. 330.

This fact has also been recorded in Doḍḍyācārya's *Vedānta-deśika-vaibhava-prakāśikā* and *Yatīndra-pravaṇa* in the following verse:

jitvā tuluṣkān bhuvi goppanendro
raṅgā-dhipaṃ sthāpitavān sva-deśe
ity'evam ākarṇya guruḥ kavīndro
dhṛṣṭavad yas tam ahaṃ prapadye.

According to the commentary, the aforesaid *Vaibhava-prakāśikā*, Veṅkaṭanātha was born in 1269 and died in 1369. Goppaṇārya's reinstallation of Śrīraṅganātha took place in 1371.

Śrīśaila lineage, son of Veṅkaṭanātha. He lived in all probability in the fifteenth century. Veṅkaṭanātha's other poem was *Haṃsa-sandeśa*. In his *Saṃkalpa-sūryodaya* he dramatically describes, after the pattern of the *Prabodha-candro-daya*, the troubles and difficulties of the human soul in attaining its final perfection. He wrote about thirty-two adoration hymns such as the *Haya-grīva-stotra*, and *Deva-nāyaka-pañcāśát* and *Pādukā-sahasra-nāma*. He also wrote many devotional and ritualistic pieces, such as the *Yajñopavīta-pratiṣṭhā*, *Ārādhana-krama*, *Hari-dina-tilaka*, *Vaiśvadeva-kārikā*, *Śrī-pañca-rātra-rakṣā*, *Sac-caritra-rakṣā* and *Nikṣepa-rakṣā*. He also collected from various sources the verses regarding the doctrine of *prapatti*, and wrote the *Nyāsa-viṃśati* and a further work based on it, called the *Nyāsa-tilaka*, which was commented upon by his son Kumāra-Vēdānta-deśika in a work called *Nyāsa-tilaka-vyākhyā*. Due notice of his *Pañcarātra-rakṣā* has been taken in the section on *Pañcarātra* of the present volume. He wrote also a work called *Śilpārtha-sāra*, two works on medicine called *Rasa-bhaumāmṛta* and *Vṛkṣa-bhaumāmṛta*, a Purāṇika geography called *Bhū-gola-nirṇaya*, and a philosophical work called *Tattva-muktā-kalāpa* in verse with his own commentary on it called *Sarvārtha-siddhi*, which have been noticed in some detail in the special section on Veṅkaṭanātha. This work has two commentaries, called *Ānanda-dāyinī* or *Ānanda-vallarī* (in some manuscripts) or *Nṛsiṃha-rājīya* and *Bhāva-prakāśa*, of which the latter is of an annotative character. The commentary called *Ānanda-dāyinī* was written by Vātsya Nṛsiṃhadeva, son of Narasiṃha-sūri, and Totārambā and Devarāja Sūri. Nṛsiṃhadeva's maternal grandfather was Kauśika-Śrībhāṣya-Śrīnivāsa, who was also his teacher. He had another teacher, named Appayācārya. This Devarāja Sūri was probably the author of the *Vimba-tattva-prakāśikā* and *Caramopāya-tātparya*. Nṛsimḥadeva's other works were *Para-tattva-dīpikā*, *Bheda-dhikkāra-nyakkāra*, *Maṇi-sāra-dhikkāra*, *Siddhānta-nirṇaya*, a commentary on Veṅkaṭanātha's *Nikṣepa-rakṣā*, called *Nṛsiṃha-rājīya*, and a commentary on the *Śata-dūṣaṇī*. This Nṛsiṃhadeva lived probably in the sixteenth century. The commentary called *Bhāva-prakāśa* was written by Navyaraṅgeśa. He describes himself as a disciple of Kalijit; but this must have been a different Kalijit from the well-known Lokācārya; for the *Bhāva-prakāśikā* commentary, as it refers to the topics of the *Ānanda-dāyinī*, is a later one. It must have been written late in the sixteenth or at the beginning of the seventeenth century.

Veṅkaṭanātha also wrote the *Nyāya-pariśuddhi*, a comprehensive logical work of the *Viśiṣṭā-dvaita* school. It was criticized by Śrīnivāsadāsa, son of Devarājācārya, who was a disciple of Veṅkaṭanātha. He may have been an uncle and teacher of Nṛsiṃhadeva, author of the *Ānanda-dāyinī*. His commentary was called *Nyāya-sāra*. The *Nyāya-pariśuddhi* had two other commentaries, *Nikāśa*, by Śaṭhakopa Yati, a disciple of Ahovila and *Nyāya-pariśuddhi-vyākhyā*, written by Kṛṣṇatātācārya.

Veṅkaṭanātha wrote a work supplementary to the *Nyāya-pariśuddhi*, called *Nyāya-siddhā-ñjana*, the contents of which have been noted in the separate sections on Veṅkaṭanātha. He also wrote another work called *Para-mata-bhaṅga*, and a polemical work called *Śata-dūṣaṇī*. The name *Śata-dūṣaṇī* signifies that it contains a hundred refutations; but actually, in the printed text available to me, I can trace only forty. The best-known commentary, by Rāmānujadāsa, pupil of Vādhūla Śrīnivāsa, is called *Caṇḍa-māruta*. All important discussions contained in the *Śata-dūṣaṇī*, which are directed mainly against the Śaṅkara school, have been duly noticed in a different section. It had another commentary, by Nṛsiṃharāja, which is also called *Caṇḍa-māruta*, and another, by Śrinivāsācārya, called *Sahasra-kiraṇī*.

Veṅkaṭanātha, in addition to his *Tattva-ṭīkā* commentary on the *Śrī-bhāṣya*, wrote a summary of the general topics of the *Śrī-bhāṣya* discussion, called *Adhikaraṇa-sārāvali*, which was commented upon by his son Kumāra Vedantācārya or Varadanātha, in a work called *Adhikaraṇa-sārāvali-vyākhyā* or *Adhikaraṇa-cintāmaṇi*. He also wrote two small pamphlets, called *Cakāra-samarthana* and *Adhikaraṇa-darpaṇa*; a commentary on the *Īśopaniṣat*; one on Yāmuna's *Gītārtha-saṃgraha*, called *Gītārtha-saṃgraha-rakṣā*, and a commentary on Rāmānuja's *Gītā-bhāṣya*, called *Tātparya-candrikā*. He also criticized Rāmānuja's *Gadya-traya*, in a work called *Tātparya-dīpikā*, and wrote commentaries on Yāmuna's *Catuḥ-ślokī* and *Stotra-ratnākara*, which are called *Rahasya-rakṣā*. In addition he composed thirty-two works in the *maṇi-pravāla* style, some of which have been translated into Sanskrit. These works are *Sampradāya-pariśuddhi*, *Tattva-padavī*, *Rahasya-padavī*, *Tattva-navanītam*, *Rahasya-navanītam*, *Tattva-*

mātṛkā, *Rahasya-mātṛkā*, *Tattva-sandeśa*, *Rahasya-sandeśa*, *Rahasya-sandeśa-vivaraṇa*, *Tattva-ratnāvali*, *Tattva-ratnāvali-saṃgraha*, *Rahasya-ratnāvalī*, *Rahasya-ratnāvalī-hṛdaya*, *Tattva-traya-culuka*, *Rahasya-traya-culuka*, *Sāra-dīpa*, *Rahasya-traya-sāra*, *Sāra-sāra*, *Abhaya-pradāna-sāra*, *Tattva-śikhā-maṇi*, *Rahasya-śikhā-maṇi*, *Añjali-vaibhava*, *Pradhānā-śataka*, *Upakāra-saṃgraha*, *Sāra-saṃgraha*, *Virodha-parihāra*, *Muni-vāhana-bhoga*, *Madhura-kavi-hṛdaya*, *Parama-pāda-sopāna*, *Para-mata-bhaṅga*, *Hastigiri-māhātmya*, *Draviḍopaniṣat-sāra*, *Draviḍopaniṣat-tātparyāvali* and *Nigama-parimala*. The last three are works summarizing the instructions of the Āṛvārs. He was the author of twenty-four poems in the Tamil language[1].

Veṅkaṭanātha also wrote a small pamphlet called *Vādi-traya-khaṇḍana*, in which he tried to refute the views of Śaṅkara, Yādavaprakāśa, and Bhāskara. Most of the arguments are directed against Śaṅkara, whereas the views of Yādavaprakāśa and Bhāskara were but slightly touched. He also wrote two works on Mīmāṃsā, called *Mīmāṃsā-pādukā* and *Seśvara-mīmāṃsā*. In the last work Veṅkaṭanātha tries to interpret the *Mīmāṃsā-sūtra* of Jaimini in a manner different from that of Śabara. His main intention was to interpret the *Mīmāṃsā-sūtra* in such a manner that it might not be in conflict with the *Brahma-sūtra*, but might be regarded as a complementary accessory to the teachings of the *Brahma-sūtra*. Thus, in interpreting the first *sūtra* of Jaimini, he says that the injunction of reading the Vedas is satisfied with the mere study of the Vedas. The injunction does not include an enquiry into the meaning of the texts and a study of the Mīmāṃsā, which comes out of the natural desire for knowing the meanings of the texts and their applications. The study of the Mīmāṃsā may therefore be undertaken even after the final bath of the *brahma-cārin*. Thus, a man may, after finishing his obligatory studies as a *brahma-cārin* in the house of his teacher, still continue to live there for the study of Mīmāṃsā, but the latter is no part of his obligatory duty. Again, in defining the nature of *dharma*, Veṅkaṭanātha says that *dharma* is that which contributes to our good and is also in accordance with the injunctions[2]. Though

[1] The list of these Tamil works, which were not accessible to the present writer, has been collected from the introduction to the Mysore edition of the *Tattva-muktā-kalāpa*.

[2] *Codanā-lakṣaṇatva-viśeṣitam evārthe sādhanatvaṃ dharma-lakṣaṇam. Īśvara-mīmāṃsā*, p. 18.

the word *dharma* may be otherwise used by some persons, yet its accepted meaning, as defined above, remains unaltered. The instructions of the *Smṛtis*, *Purāṇas*, *Pañcarātras*, *Brahma-sūtras*, etc., are to be regarded as *dharma*, as being based upon the Vedas, which are their source. The validity of the nature of *dharma* cannot be determined by a reference to any other *pramāṇa* than the scriptural texts. In all matters of doubt and dispute the *Mīmāṃsā-sūtra* should be interpreted in such a manner that it does not come in conflict with the views of Bādarāyaṇa, who was the teacher of Jaimini.

Veṅkaṭanātha's son was also a great writer on Vedānta. He was called Kumāra Vedāntācārya, Varadārya or Varadanātha or Varada Deśikācārya or Varadarāja Sūri or Varadanāyaka Sūri or Varada-guru. He wrote a *Tattva-traya-culuka-saṃgraha*, a work in Sanskrit prose, in which he summarizes the contents of the Tamil *Tattva-traya-culuka* of Veṅkaṭanātha, describing the fundamental Śrīvaiṣṇava doctrines regarding soul, matter and God[1]. His other works are *Vyavahāraika-satyatva-khaṇḍana*, *Prapatti-kārikā*, *Rahasya-traya-culuka*, *Carama-guru-nirṇaya*, *Phala-bheda-khaṇḍana*, *Ārādhana-saṃgraha*, *Adhikaraṇa-cintāmaṇi*, *Nyāsa-tilaka-vyākhyā*, *Rahasya-traya-sārārtha-saṃgraha*. The last three works are commentaries on Veṅkaṭanātha's *Adhikaraṇa-sārāvali*, *Nyāsa-tilaka*, and *Rahasya-traya-sāra*. Varadārya lived till the end of the fourteenth or the beginning of the fifteenth century.

Meghanādāri lived probably in the twelfth and the early thirteenth centuries. He was closely associated with his elder brother Rāma Miśra, a pupil of Rāmānuja. He wrote a *Naya-prakāśikā*, a commentary on the *Śrī-bhāṣya*, *Bhāva-prabodha*, *Mumukṣū-pāya-saṃgraha*, and *Naya-dyu-maṇi*. The last work is one of the most recondite works on the *Viśiṣṭā-dvaita* school of thought, and its main contents have been noted in a separate section. He was the son of Ātreyanātha and Adhvara-nāyikā. He had three brothers, Hastyadrinātha, Varadarāṭ, and Rāma Miśra.

Rāmānujadāsa or Mahācārya wrote a *Brahma-sūtra-bhāṣyopa-nyāsa*, a commentary on the *Śrī-bhāṣya*. He wrote also a *Pārāśarya*, in which he tried to show that the commentaries of Śaṅkara, Madhva and others were not in consonance with the *Sūtras* of

[1] It is also called *cid-acid-īśvara-tattva-nirūpaṇa*, or *Tattva-traya*.

Bādarāyaṇa. Some account of this will be found in the fourth volume of the present work. He also wrote a *Rāmānuja-carita-culuka*, *Rahasya-traya-mīmāṃsā-bhāṣya*, and *Caṇḍa-māruta*, a learned commentary on the *Śata-dūṣaṇī* of Veṅkaṭanātha. Sudarśanaguru wrote a commentary on his *Vedānta-vijaya*, called *Maṅgala-dīpikā*. He wrote a big treatise called *Vedānta-vijaya*, which was divided into several more or less independent, though inter-related parts. The first part is *Gurūpasatti-vijaya*, in which the methods of approaching the teacher are discussed. The manuscript is fairly voluminous, containing 273 pages, and the modes of discussion are on the basis of Upaniṣadic texts. The second part is called *Brahma-vidyā-vijaya* (a MS. containing 221 pages), in which he tries to prove, on the basis of Upaniṣadic texts, that Brahman means Nārāyaṇa and no other deity. The third part, called *Sad-vidyā-vijaya*, contains seven chapters and is philosophical and polemical in spirit. I have in a later section given an account of its principal contents. The last part is called *Vijayollāsa* (a MS. of 158 pages), in which he seeks to prove that the Upaniṣads refer to Nārāyaṇa alone. I have not been able to trace the fourth part. Sudarśanaguru wrote a commentary on this *Vedānta-vijaya*. This Sudarśana is different from Sudarśanācārya. He wrote also an *Advaita-vidyā-vijaya*, a work in three chapters, based principally on Upaniṣadic texts. The three chapters are *Prapañca-mithyātva-bhaṅga*, *Jīveśvaraikya-bhaṅga*, and *Akhaṇḍārthatva-bhaṅga*. He also composed another work, called *Upaniṣad-maṅgala-dīpikā*, which was not accessible to the present writer. He describes himself sometimes as a pupil of Vādhūla Śrīnivāsa and sometimes as a pupil of his son Prajñānidhi. He lived probably in the fifteenth century. He was the disciple of Vādhūla Śrīnivāsa, who wrote the *Tūlikā* commentary on the *Śruta-prakāśikā*.

Raṅga Rāmānuja Muni lived probably in the fifteenth century. He was the disciple of Vātsya Anantārya, Tātayārya, and Parakāla Yati or Kumbha-koṇa Tātayārya. He wrote a commentary on the *Śrībhāṣya*, called *Mūla-bhāva-prakāśikā*, and one on the *Nyāya-siddhāñjana*, called *Nyāya-siddhāñjana-vyākhyā*. He also wrote a *Dramiḍopaniṣad-bhāṣya*, *Viṣaya-vākya-dīpikā*, *Rāmānuja-siddhānta-sāra*, a commentary on the *Chāndogyo-paniṣad*, called *Chandogyo-paniṣad-prakāśikā*, and one on the *Bṛhad-āraṇyako-paniṣat-prakāśikā*. He wrote an independent commentary on the *Brahma-sūtra*, called *Śārīraka-Śāstrārtha-dīpikā*. Aufrecht reports, in his *Catalogus Catalogorum*, that he wrote also the following works (which, however, are not accessible to the present writer): *Upaniṣad-vākya-vivaraṇa*, *Upaniṣat-prakāśikā*, *Upaniṣad-bhāṣya*, *Draviḍopaniṣat-sāra-ratnāvalī-vyākhyā*, *Kaṭhavally-upaniṣat-prakāśikā*, *Kauśitakopaniṣat-prakāśikā*, *Taittirīyopaniṣat-prakāśikā*, *Praṣnopaniṣat-prakāśikā*, *Māṇḍūkyopaniṣat-prakāśikā*, *Muṇḍakopaniṣat-prakāśikā*, *Śvetāśvataropaniṣat-prakāśikā*, *Śruta-bhāva-prakāśikā*, *Guru-bhāva-prakāśikā*[1].

Raṅga Rāmānuja's teacher, Parakāla Yati, otherwise called Kumbha-koṇa Tātayārya, wrote the following works: *Draviḍa-śruti-tattvārtha-prakāśikā*, *Tiruppalāṇḍu-vyākhyana*, *Tiruppalavai-vyākhyāna*, *Kaṇṇinnuṇ-śirattāmbu-vyākhyāna*, *Adhikāra-saṃgraha-vyākhyā*. He wrote also a *Vijayīndra-parājaya* in refutation of the *Para-tattva-prakāśikā* of Vijayīndra.

Śrīnivāsadāsa, of the lineage of Mādhava, son of Devarājācārya and a pupil of Veṅkaṭanātha, wrote a *Nyāya-sāra*, a commentary on the *Nyāya-pariśuddhi*, and also a commentary called *Śata-dūṣaṇī-vyākhyā-sahasra-kiraṇī*. It is possible that the Śrīnivāsadāsa who wrote the *Viśiṣṭā-dvaita-siddhānta*, *Kaivaly-śata-duṣaṇī*, *Durupadeśa-dhikkāra*, *Nyāsa-vidyā-vijaya*, *Mukti-śabda-vicāra*, *Siddhy-upāya-sudarśana*, *Sāra-niṣkarṣa-ṭippanī* and *Vādādri-kuliśa* is the same as the author of the *Nyāya-sāra*. He lived late in the fourteenth and in the fifteenth century. This Śrīnivāsa must be distinguished from Śrīśaila Śrīnivāsa, whose works have been treated in a separate section. Śrīśaila Śrīnivāsa also lived probably in the fifteenth century.

We have another Śrīnivāsa, who wrote an *Adhikaraṇa-sārārtha-dīpikā*. On some interpretations of the colophon he may probably be styled as Vādhūla Śrīnivāsa, in which case he would be the teacher of Mahācārya[2].

There is another Śrīnivāsa, who was the pupil of Mahācārya, alias Rāmānujadāsa, and son of Govindārya. He wrote a commentary on the *Śruta-prakāśikā* and also the *Yatīndra-mata-dīpikā*, or *Yati-pati-mata-dīpikā*. The author says that in writing this elementary treatise on the fundamental principle and doctrines of Śrīvaiṣ-

[1] See Aufrecht's *Catalogus Catalogorum*, pp. 488–9.

[2] On the other interpretation the adjective Vādhūla-kula-tilaka applies to his teacher *Samara-puṅgavācārya*. This Śrīnivāsa was known also as Maṅgācārya Śrīnivāsa.

ṇavism he collected his materials from a large number of ancient treatises.[1]

The book *Yatīndra-mata-dīpikā* contains ten chapters. The first chapter enumerates the different categories, gives the definition of perception and shows how other sources of knowledge, such as memory, recognition, and non-perception, can all be included within this definition. It then gives a refutation of the various theories and establishes the theory of *sat-khyāti*. It denies the claim of verbal cognition to be regarded as a case of perception, refutes the definition of indeterminate cognition, and does not admit the possibility of any inference regarding God.

In the second chapter the writer defines "inference," classifies it and enumerates the rules regarding the validity of it and also gives a list of fallacies that may arise out of the violation of these rules. He includes analogy (*upamiti*) and proof by implication (*arthāpatti*) in the definition of inference and names the different modes of controversy.

In the third chapter we get the definition of "verbal testimony." The authority of the scriptures is established, and an attempt has been made to show that all words convey the sense of Nārāyaṇa the Lord.

The fourth chapter is longer than all the others. The author here refutes the categories of the *Nyāya* school of thought such as the universals, the relation of inherence, the causality of the atoms, and gives his own view about the genesis of the different categories, the mind-stuff, the body, the senses, the five primordial elements of earth, air, heat, water, sky, and so on.

The fifth chapter gives an account of time and establishes its all-pervasive and eternal nature. The sixth chapter enumerates the eternal, transcendental attributes of pure *sattva*, which belongs both to *īśvara* and *jīva*.

The seventh chapter is more philosophical. It contains a de-

[1] *evaṃ Drāviḍa-bhāṣya—Nyāya-tattva—Siddhi-traya—Śri-bhāsya—Dīpa-sāra—Vedārtha-saṃgraha—Bhāṣya-vivaraṇa—Saṃgīta-mālā—Sad-artha-saṃkṣepa, Śruta-prakāśika—Tattva-ratnākara—Prajñā-paritrāṇa—Prameya-saṃgraha—Nyāya-kuliśa—Nyāya-sudarśana—Māna-yāthātmya-nirṇaya—Nyāya-sāra—Tattva-dīpana—Tattva-nirṇaya—Sarvārtha-siddhi—Nyāya-pariśuddhi—Nyāya-siddhāñjana—Paramata-bhaṅga—Tattva-traya-culuka—Tattva-traya-nirūpaṇa—Tattva-traya-pracaṇḍa-māruta—Vedānta-vijaya—Pārāśaryya-vijayā'di-pūrvā'cārya-prabandhā-nusāreṇa jñātavyārthān saṃgṛhya bālabodhārthaṃ Yatīndra-mata-dīpikā-khya-śārīraka-paribhāṣāyāṃ te pratipāditāḥ. Yatīndra-mata-dīpikā*, p. 101.

tailed discussion as to how knowledge may be both an attribute and a substance, so that it may be a quality of the self and also constitute its essence. Attempts are here made to show that all mental states, including that of feeling, can be reduced to that of knowledge. Devotion and the attitude of self-surrender are discussed and the three courses, knowledge, action, and devotion, are elaborated. The writer also brings out the futility of the means of salvation prescribed by other systems of thought.

In the eighth chapter the author enumerates the attributes common to both *jīva* and *īśvara*, and deals at great length with the true nature of the individual self, refuting the theory of the Buddhists on this point. He gives also a description of the devotees and their twofold classification, and enumerates the attributes of the emancipated *jīvas*.

The ninth chapter is devoted to the definition of God, and establishes Him as the instrumental, material and the accessory cause of the world. It refutes the theory of *māyā* of the monists (*advaitins*) and gives an account of the fivefold aspects of God such as *vibhavas*, *avatāras*, etc. The tenth chapter enumerates and defines ten categories other than substance, such as the *sattva*, *rajas*, *tamas*, *śabda*, *śparsa*, and the relation of contact, etc.

There was another Śrīnivāsadāsa, of the Āṇḍān lineage, who was author of a *Natva-tattva-paritrāṇa*. He tried to prove that the word Nārāyaṇa is not an ordinary compound word, but a special word which stands by itself indicative of the name of the highest God. There was yet another Śrīnivāsa, called Śrīnivāsa Rāghavadāsa and Caṇḍa-māruta, who wrote a *Rāmānuja-siddhānta-saṃgraha*.

This Śrīnivāsa again must be distinguished from another Śrīnivāsa of the lineage of Śaṭhamarṣana, who wrote at least one work known to the present writer, *Ānanda-tāratamya-khaṇḍana*. In this small treatise he tries to refute, by a reference to scriptural passages, the view that there are differences in the state of salvation.

A few other Śrīnivāsas and their works are also known to the present writer, and it is possible that they flourished in the fifteenth or the sixteenth century. These are Śrīvatsāṅka Miśra, who wrote a small work called *Śrī-bhāṣya-sārārtha-saṃgraha*; Śrīnivāsa Tātārya, who wrote *Laghu-bhāva-prakāśikā*; Śrīśaila Yogendra, who wrote a work called *Tyāga-śabdārtha-ṭippanī*; Śrīśaila Rāghavārya, grandson of Veṅkaṭanātha, who wrote a *Vedānta-kaustubha*; Śrīśailadāsa, son of Raṅgadāsa, who wrote *Siddhānta-saṃgraha*; Sundararājadeśika, author of *Brahma-sūtra-bhāṣya-vyākhyā* (an elementary commentary). These minor writers flourished probably in the sixteenth, seventeeth and eighteenth centuries.

Śrīnivāsa-dīkṣita, son of Śrīśaila Śrīnivāsa Tātayārya, grandson of Aṇṇayārya, and a pupil of Ācārya-dīkṣita, wrote a work called *Virodha-varūthinī-pramāthinī*. This must be distinguished from the *Virodha-varūthinī-pramāthinī* of Raṅgācārya dealt with in a different section. Śrīnivāsa-sudhī also wrote *Brahma-jñāna-nirāsa*, which records the controversy which the author had with Tryambaka Paṇḍita, a follower of Saṅkara. It generally follows a line of argument adapted in the *Śata-dūṣaṇī* in refuting the monistic Vedānta of Śaṅkara. It is difficult to say whether the works *Naya-maṇikalikā*, *Lakṣmaṇārya-siddhānta-saṃgraha*, and *Hari-guṇa-maṇimālā* should be attributed to this author or to the Śrīnivāsa who wrote the *Virodha-nirodha*.

Sudarśana Sūri, who lived in the thirteenth and fourteenth centuries, of the lineage of Hārita, son of Vāgvijaya and pupil of Vātsya Varada, has been already mentioned. He wrote a treatise on the commentary of Rāmānuja from whose works all succeeding writers drew their inspiration. The title of his commentary is *Śruta-prakāśikā*, which incorporates, often word for word, what he heard from his teacher Vātsya Varada[1]. He also wrote a *Sandhyā-vandana-bhāṣya*, *Vedānta-saṃgraha-tātparya-dīpikā*, a commentary on the *Vedārtha-saṃgraha* of Rāmānuja, and another work, called *Śruta-pradīpikā*. He was often called Vedavyāsa Bhaṭṭārya. This Sudarśana must be distinguished from Sudarśanaguru who wrote a commentary on the *Vedānta-vijaya* of Mahācārya. Śaṭhakopa muni, who was a pupil of Śaṭhāri Sūri and often known as Śaṭhakopa Yati, lived probably towards the end of the sixteenth century. He wrote the following works: *Brahma-lakṣaṇa-vākyārtha-saṃgraha*, *Brahma-śabdārtha-vicāra*, *Vākyārtha-saṃgraha*, *Brahma-sūtrārtha-saṃgraha*, *Brahma-lakṣaṇa-vākyārtha*, *Divya-prabandha* and *Bhāva-prakāśikā-dūṣaṇoddhāra*. The last work is an attempt at

[1] *gurubhyo' rthaḥ śrutaḥ śabdais tat-prayuktaiś ca yojitaḥ*
saukaryāya bubhūtsūnāṃ saṃkalayya prakāśyate.
Introductory verses to the *Śruta-prakāśikā*.

refutation of the criticism of the *Bhāva-prakāśikā*, a commentary on *Śruta-prakāśikā*, by Varada Viṣṇu Sūri.

Ahobila Raṅganātha Yati, who flourished at the beginning of the fifteenth century, wrote a *Nyāsa-vivṛti*, in which he deals with the topics of *nyāsa* as expounded in Veṅkaṭanātha's *Nyāsa-tilaka*. Ādivarāha Vedāntācārya wrote a *Nyāya-ratnāvalī*. Kṛṣṇatātācārya, who flourished in the fifteenth century and belonged to the Śrīśaila lineage, wrote a commentary on the *Nyāya-pariśuddhi*, called *Nyāya-pariśuddhi-vyākhyā* and some small treatises called *Dūrārtha-dūrīkaraṇa*, *Brahma-sabdārtha-vicāra* and *Natva-candrikā*. Kṛṣṇa-pāda-lokaguru, probably of the same century, wrote a *Rahasya-traya-mīmāṃsā-bhāṣya*, *Divya-prabandha-vyākhyā*, *Catuḥ-ślokī-vyākhyā*, and a number of Tamil works. Campakeśa, of the fifteenth century, wrote a *Guru-tattva-prakāśikā*, and a *Vedānta-kaṇṭako-ddhāra*. In the last work he tried to refute the criticisms of the Śrī-bhāṣya[1]. He was a pupil of Veṅkaṭanātha. Another Tātācārya, who was grandfather of Veṅkaṭādhvarī, the author of the *Viśva-guṇādarśa*, wrote a *Tātācārya-dina-caryā*. He was the maternal uncle of Appaya-dīkṣita. Again, Deśikācārya, who wrote the *Prayoga-ratna-mālā* as a commentary on the *Śrī-bhāṣya*, also wrote a book on the commentary on Veṅkaṭanātha's *Pañyikā* on the *Taittirīyopaniṣat*, which was called the "*Asti-brahmeti-śruty-artha-vicāra*." Doḍḍayācārya, who lived probably in the fifteenth century, wrote a *Parikara-vijaya*, often referred to in Mahācārya's works, and a life of Veṅkaṭanātha, called *Vedānta-deśika-vaibhava-prakāśikā*. Nārāyaṇa muni wrote a *Bhāva-pradīpikā*, *Gītārtha-saṃgraha*, *Gītā-sāra-rakṣā*, *Gītā-saṃgraha-vibhāga*, *Rahasya-traya-jīvātu*. He was the son of Śrīśaila Tātayārya, grandson of Anantārya and pupil of Rāmānujācārya, probably Mahācārya. He lived perhaps late in the fifteenth century. Nṛsiṃharāja, who wrote a commentary on the *Śata-dūṣaṇī*, called *Śata-dūṣaṇī-vyākhyā*, was probably the same person who wrote an *Ānanda-dāyiṇī* on the *Tattva-muktā-kalāpa*. Nṛsiṃhasūri, a much later writer, wrote a *Śarīra-bhāvādhikaraṇa-vicāra* and *Tat-kratu-nyāya-vicāra*. Para-

[1] Śuddhasattvalakṣaṇārya wrote a work called *Guru-bhāva-prakāśikā* as a commentary on the *Śruta-prakāśikā*, which he based upon the *Guru-tattva-prakāśikā* of Campakeśa. He was the disciple of Śuddhasattvācārya, son of Saumya Jāmātṛ muni. In his commentary he constantly refers to the *Tūlikā* commentary of Vādhula Śrīnivāsa. He lived probably in the sixteenth century, and may have been a contemporary of Mahācārya.

vastu Vedāntācārya, son of Ādivarāhācārya, composed a *Vedānta-kaustubha*. Puruṣottama wrote a commentary on the *Śrī-bhāṣya* called *Subodhinī*, and Bhagavat Senāpati Miśra wrote a *Śārīraka-nyāya-kalā*.

Pela Puradeśika wrote a work called *Tattva-bhāskara*. It is divided into two parts, in the first of which he tries to ascertain the meaning of *māyā* and elucidates the nature of God on the basis of Dravidian and Sanskrit texts. The second part is of a ritualistic nature. Raṅgarāja, who lived probably in the sixteenth century, was the author of *Advaita-vahiṣkāra*. Raṅganāthācārya wrote an *Aṣṭādaśa-bheda-vicāra*, *Puruṣārtha-ratnākara*, *Vivādārtha-saṃgraha*, *Kāryādhikaraṇa-veda* and *Kāryādhikaraṇa-tattva*. The contents of the last two works have been dealt with in a different section. He lived perhaps in the sixteenth century, and was a pupil of Saumya Jāmātṛ muni. A Rāmānuja called Vedānta Rāmānuja wrote a *Divya-sūri-prabhāva-dīpikā* and a *Sarva-darśana-śiromaṇi*. Rāmānujadāśabhikṣu wrote *Sauri-rāja-caraṇāravinda-śaraṇā-gati-sāra*, and Rāma Subrahmaṇyasāstrī *Viṣṇu-tattva-rahasya*. These two writers flourished probably in the seventeenth or late in the sixteenth century.

Ātreya Varada wrote a *Rahasya-traya-sāra-vyākhyā*, a commentary on Veṅkaṭanātha's *Rahasya-traya-sāra*. Varadadāsa wrote *Nyāsa-vidyā-bhūṣaṇa* and Vādi Keśarī Miśra the following: *Adhyātma-cintā*, *Tattva-dīpa-saṃgraha-kārikā*, *Tattva-dīpa* and *Rahasya-traya-kārikā*. These small works are of little value. Only the *Tattva-dīpa* contains some philosophical materials inspired by the *Śruta-prakāśikā* of Sudarśana. Vīra-rāghava-dāsa, son of Vādhūla Narasiṃha and pupil of Vādhūla Varadaguru, produced a commentary on the *Śrī-bhāṣya*, called *Tātparya-dīpikā*, and one on Vātsya Varada's *Tattva-sāra*, called *Ratna-sāriṇī*. Veṅkaṭa Sudhī wrote a voluminous work in four chapters, called *Siddhānta-ratnāvali*, in which he tried to prove that Nārāyaṇa and not Śiva is the supreme Lord and the cause of the world, and dealt with many sectarian doctrines which are of no philosophical value. He was the pupil of Veṅkaṭanātha and son of Tātācārya of Śaṭhamarṣaṇa lineage. Some notice of the work will be taken in the section on *Pañcarātra*. Veṇkaṭadāsa, called also Vucci Veṅkaṭācārya, the third son of Aṇṇayārya, of Śaṭhamarṣaṇa lineage, composed a work called *Vedāntakārikāvali*. Veṅkaṭādhvarī wrote a work called *Yati-*

prativandana-khaṇḍana, Ayyaṇṇa wrote *Vyāsa-tātparya-nirṇaya* and Aṇṇavāyyaṅgācārya, *Tṛṃśa-praśno-ttara*, *Kesara-bhūṣaṇa* and *Śrī-tattva-darpaṇa*. Gopālatāta wrote *Śatakoṭi-dūṣaṇa-parihāra*, Govindācārya *Pramāṇa-sāra* and Jagannātha Yati *Brahma-sūtra-dīpikā*. Devanātha wrote *Tattva-nirṇaya*, Dharmakureśa *Rāmānuja-nava-ratna-mālikā*, Nīlameghatātācārya *Nyāsa-vidyārtha-vicāra*, Raṅgācārya *Śrīvatsa-siddhānta-sāra*, Raghunāthācārya *Bāla-sarasvatī* and *Saṅgati-sāra*. Rāghavācārya wrote *Rahasya-traya-sāra-saṃgraha*, Rāmanātha Yogī *Sadā-cāra-bodha*, Rāmānuja *Gāyatrī-śata-dūṣaṇī* and Tirumalācārya of Bharadvāja lineage *Ṇattvopapatti-bhaṅga*.

Aṇṇayārya, brother of Śrīśaila Śrīnivaśa, wrote *Saptati-ratna-mālikā*, *Vyavahārikatva-khaṇḍana-sāra*, *Mithyātva-khaṇḍana*, *Ācārya-viṃśati*, *Ānanda-tāratamya-khaṇḍana*. Appaya-dīkṣita of the sixteenth century commented on the *Brahma-sūtra* in accordance with the views of Rāmānuja, in a work called *Naya-mukha-mālikā*. Anantārya of the nineteenth century wrote a number of works of which the following have been published: *Ṇattva-tattva-vibhūṣaṇa*, *Śatakoṭi-khaṇḍana*, *Nyāya-bhāskara*, *Ācāra-locana* (a refutation of widow-remarriage), *Śāstrārambha-samarthana*, *Samāsa-vāda*, *Viṣayatā-vāda*, *Brahma-śakti-vāda*, *Śāstraikya-vāda*, *Mokṣa-kāraṇatā-vāda*, *Nirviśeṣa-pramāṇa-vyudāsa*, *Saṃvin-nānātva-samarthana*, *Jñāna-yāthārthya-vāda*, *Brahma-lakṣaṇa-vāda*, *Īkṣaty-adhikaraṇa-vicāra*, *Pratijñā-vāda*, *Ākāśādhikaraṇa-vicāra*, *Śrībhāṣya-bhāvāṅkura*, *Laghu-sāmānādhikaraṇya-vāda*, *Guru-sāmānādhikaraṇya-vāda*, *Śārīra-vāda*, *Siddhānta-siddhāñjana*, *Vidhi-sudhākara*, *Sudarśana-sura-druma*, *Bheda-vāda*, *Tat-kratu-nyāya-vicāra*, *Dṛśyatvā-numāna-nirāsa*. These treatises are mostly short papers, though a few are more elaborate. The *Nyāya-bhāskara* is a refutation of the *Gauḍa-brahmānandī* commentary on the *Advaita-siddhi*, in refutation of the *Nyāyāmṛta-taraṅginī*. It consists of twelve topics, and the refutations are mostly of a scholastic nature following the style of the new school of logic in Bengal which found fault with the definitions of their opponents. Some of the most important works of this writer have been referred to in the relevant places of this work.

The Influence of the Āṟvārs on the followers of Rāmānuja.

We have already referred to the *Divya-prabandhas*, written by the Āṟvārs in Tamil, which exerted a profound influence on all teachers of the Śrīvaiṣṇava school[1]. Kureśa (Tirukkurukaippiran Pillai) wrote a commentary of 6000 verses on a selection of Nāmm'-āṟvār's one thousand verses called the *Sahasra-gīti*. Parāśara Bhaṭṭārya wrote a commentary of 9000 verses. Under the directions of Kalijit (Lokācārya) Abhaya-prada-rāja wrote a commentary of 24,000 verses. Kṛṣṇapāda, pupil of Kalijit, wrote another commentary of 3600 verses. Saumya Jāmātṛ muni wrote 12,000 verses interpreting the views of Nāmm'-āṟvār. The commentaries of Abhaya-prada-rāja on the *Divya-prabandhas* helped the later teachers to understand the esoteric doctrine of the later works. The commentaries on the *Divya-prabandhas* written by Saumyajāmātṛ muni, the younger brother of Pillai Lokācārya, had already become rare in the time of Abhirāma Varācārya, the translator of the *Upadeśa-ratna-mālā* and the grandson of Saumya Jāmātṛ muni.

It is thus seen that Parāśara Bhaṭṭārya, the successor of Rāmānuja in the pontifical chair, and his successor Vedāntī Mādhava, called also Nanjiyar, and his successor Namburi Varadarāja, called also Kalijit or Lokācārya I, and his successor Pillai Lokācārya, all wrote works dealing not so much with the interpretation of Rāmānuja's philosophy, as with the interpretation of devotion as dealt with in the *Sahasra-gīti* and the *Divya-prabandhas*. Their writings are mostly in Tamil, only a few have been translated into Sanskrit,

[1] These *Divya-prabandhas* are four thousand in number. Thus Poygaiy-āṟvār wrote *Muḍal-tiru-vantādi* of 100 stanzas; Bhūtatt'-āṟvār, *Iraṇḍam-tiru-vantādi* of 100 stanzas; Pēy-āṟvār, *Munṟām-tiru-vantādi* of 100 stanzas; Tiru-maṟiṣai Pirān, *Nān-mukam Tiru-vantādi* and *Tiru-chaṇḍa-vruttam* of 96 and 120 stanzas respectively; Madhura-kaviy-āṟvār wrote *Kaṇṇinuṇ-śiruttāmbu* of 11 stanzas; Nāmm'-āṟvār wrote *Tiru-vruttam* of 100 stanzas, *Tiru-vāśiriyam*, *Periya-tiru-vantādi* of 87 stanzas and *Tiru-vāy-moṟi* of 1102 verses; Kula-śēkhara Perumāl wrote *Perumāl-tirumoḷi* of 105 stanzas, *Periy-āṟvār-tiruppalāṇḍu* and *Periy-āṟvār-tirumoṟi* of 12 and 461 stanzas, Āṇḍal, *Tiruppāvai* and *Nācchiyār-tirumoḷi* of 30 and 143 stanzas; Toṇḍar-aḍi-poḍiy-āṟvār, *Tiru-paḷḷiy-eṟuchi* and *Tiru-mālai* of 10 and 45 stanzas respectively; Tiru-pān-āṟvār, *Amalanādi-piṟān* of 10 stanzas; Tiru-maṅgaiy-āṟvār wrote *Periya-tirumoḷi* of 1084 verses, *Tiru-kkurundāṇḍakam* of 20 stanzas, *Tiruneḍundāṇḍakam* of 30 stanzas, *Tiruveḷukūr-tirukkai* of 1 stanza, *Śiriya-tirumaḍal* of 77 stanzas and *Periya-tirumaḍal* of 148 stanzas, thus making a total of 4000 verses in all. They are referred to in the *Upadeśá-ratna-mālā* of Saumya Jāmātṛ muni (junior) and in its introduction by M. T. Narasimhiengar.

and in the present work notice is taken only of the Sanskrit works of these writers (mostly in the manuscript form) which have been available to the present writer. Both Pillai Lokācārya and Saumya Jāmātṛ muni, called also Vādikeśarī, were sons of Kṛṣṇapāda, but this Saumya Jāmātṛ muni must be distinguished from a later Saumyajāmātṛ muni, called also Yatīndrapravaṇācārya, who was a much more distinguished man. Parāśara Bhaṭṭārya was probably born before A.D. 1078 and he died in A.D. 1165. He was succeeded by Vedāntī Mādhava or Nanjiyar, who was succeeded by Namburi Varadarāja or Lokācārya I. He was succeeded by Pillai Lokācārya, a contemporary of Veṅkaṭanātha, and Śruta-prakāśikācārya or Sudarśana Sūri. It was in his time that the Mahomedans attacked Śrīraṅgam. as has already been mentioned in connection with our account of Veṅkaṭanātha. The Mahomedans were expelled from Śrīraṅgam by Goppaṇārya, and the image of Raṅganātha was re-installed in A.D. 1293. It was at this time that the famous Saumya Jāmātṛ muni (junior) was born. The senior Saumya Jāmātṛ muni, younger brother of Pillai Lokācārya, called also Vādikesarī, wrote some commentaries on the *Divya-prabandhas*, a work called *Dīpa-prakāśa*, and *Piyaruli-ceyalare-rahasya*. He is referred to by the junior Saumya Jāmātṛ muni, called also Varavara muni, in his *Upadeśa-ratna-mālā*, *Tattva-traya-bhāṣya* and *Śrīvacana-bhūṣaṇa-vyākhyā*. We cannot be sure whether the *Adhyātma-cintāmaṇi*, in which Vādhūla Śrīnivāsa is adored as his teacher, was written by Saumya Jāmātṛ muni. Mahācārya also described himself as a pupil of Vādhūla Śrīnivāsa, and, if the senior Saumya Jāmātṛ and Mahācārya were pupils of the same teacher, Mahācārya must have lived in the fourteenth century. If, however, the junior Saumya Jāmātṛ wrote the *Adhyātma-cintāmaṇi*, Mahācārya will have to be placed at a later date.

The present writer has been able to trace only three books in Sanskrit by Pillai Lokācārya: *Tattva-traya*, *Tattva-śekhara*, and *Śrīvacana-bhūṣaṇa*[1]. The *Tattva-traya* is a very useful compendium of the Śrīvaiṣṇava school of thought, in which the nature of the inanimate (*acit*), the souls, God and their mutual relations are dealt

[1] Some of his other works are *Mumukṣu-ppaḍi*, *Prameya-śekhara*, *Nava-ratna-mālā*, *Tani-praṇava*, *Prapanna-paritrāṇa*, *Yādṛcchika-ppaḍi*, *Dvayam*, *Artha-pañcaka*, *Sāra-saṃgraha*, *Paranda-paḍi*, *Saṃsāra-sāmrājyam*, *Śriyaḥ-pati-ppaḍi*, *Caramam*, *Arcir-ādi*, *Nava-vidha-sambandha*. *Vide* footnote in *Tattva-śekhara*, p. 70.

with. There is an excellent commentary by Varavara muni. The *Tattva-śekhara* is a work in four chapters. The first chapter quotes scriptural evidences in support of the view that Nārāyaṇa is the highest God and the ultimate cause; in the second chapter he describes the nature of self by reference to scriptural testimony. The same description of the nature of self is continued in the third chapter. In the fourth chapter he deals with the ultimate goal of all souls, self-surrender to God. He says that the ultimate *summum bonum* (*puruṣārtha*) consists in the servitude (*kaiṅkarya*) to God roused by love of Him (*prīti-kārita*), due to the knowledge of one's own nature and the nature of God in all His divine beauty, majesty, power and supreme excellence. Not all servitude is undesirable. We know in our ordinary experience that servitude through love is always pleasurable. In the ordinary idea of emancipation, a man emphasizes his own self and his own end. This is therefore inferior to the *summum bonum* in which he forgets his own self and regards the servitude of God as his ultimate end. Lokācārya then refutes the various other conceptions of the ultimate goal in other schools of philosophy. He also refutes the conception of the *summum bonum* as the realization of one's own nature with a sense of supreme subordination (*para-tantratvena svā-nubhava-mātraṃ na puruṣārthaḥ*). This is also technically called *kaivalya* in the Śrīvaiṣṇava system. Our ultimate end is not cessation of pain, but enjoyment of bliss. Positive bliss is our final aim. It is held that in the emancipation as described above the individual realizes himself in close association with God and enjoys supreme bliss thereby; but he can never be equal to Him. Bondage (*bandha*) is true and the removal of bondage is also true. *Prapatti*, or self-surrender to God, is regarded as a means to cessation of bondage. This *prapatti* may be direct (*a-vyavahita*) and indirect (*vyavahita*). In the first case the self-surrender is complete and absolute and done once for all[1]. The in-

[1] *Prapatti* is defined as follows:

bhagavad-ājñātivartana-nivṛtti-bhagavad-ānukūlya-sarva-śaktitvā-nusandhāna-prabhṛti-sahitaḥ yacñā-garbho vijṛmbha-rūpa-jñāna-viśeṣaḥ; tatra jñeyākāra īśvarasya nirapekṣa-sādhanatvaṃ jñānākaro vyavasāyā-tmakatvam; etac ca śāstrārthatvāt sakṛt kartavyam. Tattva-śekhara, p. 64.

Just as the Śaṅkarites hold that, once the knowledge regarding the unity of the individual with Brahman dawns through the realization of the meaning of such texts, there remains nothing to be done. So here also the complete self-surrender to God is the dawning of the nature of one's relation to God, and, when this is once accomplished, there is nothing else to be done. The rest remains with God in His adoption of the devotee as His own.

direct *prapatti* is the continual meditation on God through love of Him, along with the performance of the obligatory duties and the non-commission of prohibited actions. This is decidedly the lower stage; the more deserving ones naturally follow the first method.

The main contents of Pillai Lokācārya's *Śrī-vacana-bhūṣaṇa* follow in a separate section in connection with the account of the commentary on it and sub-commentary by Saumya Jāmātṛ muni (junior) and Raghūttama. The *Śrīvacana-bhūṣaṇa* consists of 484 small sentences longer than the *Sūtra*-phrases, but often shorter than ordinary philosophical sentences. Lokācārya followed this style in his other works also, such as his *Tattva-traya* and *Tattva-śekhara.*

Ramya-jāmātṛ muni or Saumya Jāmātṛ muni, called also Maṇavālama muni or Periya-jīyar, was the son of Tikaḻakkiḍandān-tirunāvīruḍaiyāpiṟān-Tātar-aṇṇar, a disciple of Pillai Lokācārya and grandson of Kollikavaladasar, who was also a disciple of Pillai Lokācārya. He was born in the Tinnevelly district in A.D. 1370 and lived for seventy-three years, that is till A.D. 1443. He first obtained training from Śrīśaileśa, called also Tiru-maṟai Āṟvār, in Tiru-vāy-moṟi. One of the first works of his early youth was a poem called *Yati-rāja-viṃśati*, in honour of Rāmānuja, which is incorporated and published in Varavara muni's *Dina-caryā.* On account of his deep devotion for Rāmānuja he was also known as Yatīndra-pravaṇa, and wrote a commentary on a short life of Rāmānuja called *Prapanna-sāvitrī* or *Rāmānuja-nuṟandādi* of *Tiruvarangatt-amudanār.* After completing his studies under Śrīśaileśa he remained at Śrīraṅgam and studied the commentaries on the *Divya-prabandhas*, the *Śrīvacana-bhūṣaṇa* and other *Drāviḍa Vedānta* works. In his study of the *Divya-prabandhas* and the *Gītā-bhāṣya* he was helped by his father Tatar-āṇṇar. He also studied with Kidambi-Tirumalai-Nayinār, called also Kṛṣṇadeśika, the *Śrī-bhāṣya* and *Śruta-prakāśikā.* He also studied the *Ācārya-hṛdaya* with Aṇṇayācārya, called also Devarājaguru, of Yādavādri. He renounced the world, became a *sannyāsin*, and attached himself to the Pallava-maṭha at Śrīraṅgam, where he built a *vyākhyāna-maṇḍapa*, in which he used to deliver his religious lectures. He was very proficient in the *Draviḍa Vedānta*, produced many works in the *maṇi-pravāla* style (mixture of Sanskrit and Tamil), and had hundreds of followers. He had a son, called Rāmānujārya, and a grandson, called Viṣṇucitta. Of his pupils eight were very famous: Bhaṭṭanātha, Śrīnivāsa-yati, Devarājaguru, Vādhūla Varada Nārāyaṇa-guru, Prativādibhayaṅkara, Rāmānujaguru, Sutākhya, and Śrī-vānācala Yogīndra. These eight disciples were great teachers of *Vedānta*[1]. He taught the *Bhāṣya* to Raṅgarāja. There were many ruling chiefs in South India who were his disciples. Among his works the following are noteworthy, *Yati-rāja-viṃśati*, *Gītā-tātparya-dīpa*, a Sanskrit commentary on the *Gīta*, *Śrī-bhāṣyā-ratha*, *Taittirīyo-paniṣad-bhāṣya*, *Para-tattva-nirṇaya*. He wrote also commentaries on the *Rahasya-traya*, *Tattva-traya* and *Śrī-vacana-bhūṣaṇa* of Pillai Lokācārya and the *Ācārya-hṛdaya* of the senior Saumya Jāmātṛ muni, called also Vādikeśarī, brother of Pillai Lokācārya; commentaries on *Priyālvar-tiru-moṟi*, *Jñāna-sāra* and *Prameya-sāra* of Devarāja, and the *Sapta-gāthā* of Viṟāmśoḷai-ppillai; glosses on the authorities quoted in the *Tattva-traya*, *Śrīvacana-bhūṣaṇa*, and commentaries on the *Divya-prabandha* called the *Iḍu*; many Tamil verses, such as *Tiruvāymoṟi-nuṟundādi*, *Ārtti-prabandha*, *Tiruvārādhana-krama*, and many Sanskrit verses. He occupied a position like that of Rāmānuja, and his images are worshipped in most Vaiṣṇava temples in South India. Many works were written about him, e.g. *Varavara-muni-dina-caryā*, *Varavara-muni-śataka*, *Varavara-muni-kāvya*, *Varavara-muni-campu*, *Yatīndra-pravaṇa-prabhāva*, *Yatīndra-pravaṇa-bhadra-campu*, etc. His *Upadeśa-ratna-mālā* is recited by Śrivaiṣṇavas after the recital of the *Divya-prabandha*. In his *Upadeśa-ratna-mālā* he gives an account of the early Āṟvārs and the Āṟagiyas. It was translated into Sanskrit verse by his grandson Abhirama-varācārya, whose *Aṣṭādaśa-bheda-nirṇaya* has already been noted in the present work. He also wrote another book called *Nakṣatra-mālikā* in praise of Śaṭhakopa[2].

Though Mr Narasimhiengar says that a commentary on the *Śrīvacana-bhūṣaṇa* was written by Saumya Jāmātṛ muni (junior) in the *maṇipravāla* style, yet the manuscript of the commentary, with a sub-commentary on it by Raghūttama, which was available to the present writer, was a stupendous volume of about 750 pages, all written in Sanskrit. The main contents of this work will appear in a separate section.

[1] See *Prapannāmṛta*, Ch. 122.

[2] The present writer is indebted for some of his information regarding the works of Saumya Jāmātṛ muni to M. T. Narasimhiengar's Introduction to the English translation of the *Upadeśa-ratna-mālā*.

CHAPTER XIX

THE PHILOSOPHY OF YĀMUNĀCĀRYA

THOUGH in later days Bodhāyana is regarded as the founder of the Vaiṣṇava systems, yet, as his commentary on the *Brahma-sūtras* is not now available, we may look upon Yāmuna as being the earliest of the latter-day Vaiṣṇava philosophers. We hear that many other people, such as Taṅka, Dramiḍa and Bharuchi, wrote in accordance with the teachings contained in the commentary of Bodhāyana, endeavouring to refute the views of other systems of thought. Dramiḍa wrote a *Bhāṣya* which was elaborated by Śrīvatsāṅka Miśra and is frequently referred to by Yāmuna. The sage Vakulābharaṇa, called Śaṭhakopācārya, also wrote an elaborate treatise in the Tamil language on the *bhakti* creed, but this also is hardly available now. Thus the history of modern Vaiṣṇavism should, for all practical purposes, begin with Yāmunācārya, who flourished during the latter part of the tenth and the earlier part of the eleventh century. Yāmunācārya was said to be the preceptor of Mahāpurṇa from whom the great Rāmānuja had his initiation. So far as I am aware, Yāmuna wrote four books, namely, *Siddhi-traya*, *Āgama-prāmāṇya*, *Puruṣa-ninṇaya*, and *Kāśmīrāgama.* Of these only the first two have been printed.

Yāmuna's doctrine of Soul contrasted with those of others.

We have seen that from the Cārvākas to the Vedāntists there had been many schools of philosophy and each of them had its own theory of soul. We made but a scanty reference to Cārvākism in the first volume, and we have generally omitted the discussions against Cārvākism in which other systems usually indulged. The most important of the doctrines held by the Cārvākas is that there is no self other than the body; some of them, however, regarded the senses as the self, and others as *Manas.* They held that there were only four elements and that out of them life and consciousness sprang forth. Our notion of self also referred to the body, and there was no separate soul, apart from the body. The Cārvāka literature has, however, vanished from India, and we can know only from references in other works that their original writings were also in the form of *sūtras*[1].

Yāmuna's philosophy was directly opposed to the doctrine of the Cārvākas. It is best therefore that we should deal here with Yāmuna's theory of soul in connection with the pretensions of the Cārvākas. Yāmuna takes his stand on the notion of self-consciousness. He says that our preception "I know" distinctly points to the self as the subject, as distinguished from the perception of the body as "this is my body," which is closely akin to other objective perceptions such as "this is a jug," "this is a piece of cloth." When I restrain my senses from external objects and concentrate myself on myself, I have still the notion of my self as "I," which arises in me without the least association of my hands or feet or any other parts of the body. The body as a whole cannot be said to be indicated by my perception, when none of the parts of the body shine forth in it. Even when I say "I am fat," "I am lean," the notion of "I" does not refer to the external fat or lean body, but to some mysterious entity within me with which the body is wrongly associated. We should not forget that we also say "this is my body" as we should say "this is my house," where the body is spoken of as being different from the self as any external object. But it may be objected that we also say "my self" (*mamātmā*); but this is only a linguistic usage which expresses that difference, whereas the entity perceived is just the same and identical. The confusion which is felt in the fact that the notion of "I" refers to the body is due to this, that the self has no perceivable shape or form as have ordinary external objects (such as jug, cloth, etc.), by virtue of which they are distinguished from one another. Those who are not sufficiently discriminating cannot rest content with the formless self, and consequently confuse the soul with the body, more particularly because they find that corresponding to any and every desire of the soul there is a corresponding change of the body. They think that, since, corresponding to any mental change, such as new feeling, thought, or desire, there is a corresponding physical or physiological change of the body, there is no other soul different from the body. But, if

[1] The first *sūtra* of Bṛhaspati is *atha tattvaṃ vyākhyāsyāmaḥ*; the second is *prithivy-ap-tejo-vāyur iti tattvāni* and the third is *tebhyaś caitanyaṃ kiṇvādi-bhyo mada-śaktivat.*

we try to find out by a deeper self-introspection what we mean by "I," we find that it is an entity, as the subject, as the "I," as distinct from the objects which are not self and which are indicated as this or that. Had the notion "I know" referred to the body, the bodily parts would surely have been manifested in the notion, as external objects shine forth in all external perception as this or that. But it is not so; on the contrary, by introspection I find that the self is an entity which is independent in itself, and all other things of the world are for the sake of my self; I am the enjoyer, whereas everything else is the object of my enjoyment; I am not for the sake of any body; I am an end in myself and never a means for anything else (*a-parārtha*). All combinations and collocations are for the sake of another, whom they serve; the self is neither the result of any collocation nor does it exist for the sake of serving another.

Moreover, consciousness cannot be regarded as being a product of the body. Consciousness cannot be thought to be like an intoxicating property, the product of the four elements; for the combination of the four elements cannot produce any and every sort of power. There is a limit to the effects that a certain cause can produce; in the production of the intoxicating property it is the atoms which happen to possess that property; intoxication is not to be compared with consciousness; nor has it any similarity to any physical effect; nor can it be thought that there are atoms in which the property of consciousness is generated. Had consciousness been the result of any chemical change, such as we find in the production of the red colour by the combination of lime with catechu, there would have been particles of consciousness (*caitanya*) produced, and our consciousness would then have been the sum total of those particles of consciousness, as in the case of any material chemical product; the red colour produced by the combination of lime with catechu belongs to an object every particle of which is red; so, if consciousness had been a chemical product of the material of this body, there would have been generated some particles of consciousness, and thus there would have been perceptions of many selves in accordance with each particle of consciousness, and there would be no identity of consciousness and experience. Thus it must be admitted that consciousness belongs to an entity, the soul, which is different from the body.

Nor can consciousness belong to the senses; for, if it belonged to each of the senses, then that which was perceived by one sense (e.g. the eye) could not be perceived by another sense (e.g. the touch), and there would not rise the consciousness "I touch that which I had seen before." If all the senses together produced consciousness, then we could not perceive anything with one sense (e.g. the eye), nor could we have any consciousness, or the memory of the object of any particular sense after that sense was lost; when a man was blinded, he would lose all consciousness, or would never remember the objects which he had seen before with his eyes.

Nor can the *manas* be regarded as *ātman*; for it is only an organ accepted as accounting for the fact that knowledge is produced in succession and not in simultaneity. If it is said that the *manas* may be regarded as being a separate organ by which it can know in succession, then practically the self, or *ātman*, is admitted; the only difference being this, that the Cārvākas call *manas* what we (Yāmuna and his followers) call *ātman*.

The *Vijñānavādin* Buddhists held that knowledge, while self-manifesting, also manifested the objects and so knowledge should be regarded as the self (*ātman*). Against these Buddhists Yāmuna held that, if any permanent seat of knowledge was not admitted, then the phenomenon of personal identity and recognition could not be explained by the transitory states of self-manifesting knowledge; if each knowledge came and passed, how could one identify one's present experiences with the past, if there were only flowing states of knowledge and no persons? Since there was no permanence, it could not be held that any knowledge persisted as an abiding factor on the basis of which the phenomenon of self-identity or recognition could be explained. Each knowledge being absent while others came, there was no chance of even an illusion of sameness on grounds of similarity.

The doctrine of the Śaṅkara school, that there is one qualityless permanent pure consciousness, is regarded by Yāmuna as being against all experience. Thus, consciousness is always felt as belonging to a person and as generated, sustained for a time, and then lost. At the time of deep sleep we all cease to possess knowledge, and this is demonstrated by our impression on waking that we have slept for so long, without consciousness. If the *antaḥkaraṇa*, which the Advaitins regard as the substratum of the notion of "I," had been submerged during the sleep, then there could not have been on waking the notion that "I slept so long." Nobody has ever experienced any pure knowledge. Knowledge as such must belong to somebody. The Śaṅkarites say that the rise of knowledge means the identity of the knowledge with the objects at the time. But this is not so; for the truth of the knowledge of an object is always with reference to its limitations of time and space and not to the intrinsic quality of the thing or the knowledge. The assertion also that knowledge is permanent is without any foundation; for whenever any knowledge arises it always does so in time and under the limitations of time. Nobody has ever experienced any knowledge divested of all forms. Knowledge must come to us either as perception or as inference, etc.; but there cannot be any knowledge which is absolutely devoid of any forms or modifications and absolutely qualityless. The Śaṅkarites regard the self as pure consciousness or *anubhūti*, but it is apparent that the self is the agent of *anubhūti*, or the knower, and not knowledge or pure consciousness. Again, as in Buddhism, so in Śaṅkarism, the question of recognition remains unsolved; for recognition or personal continuity of experience means that the knower existed in the past and is existing even now —as when we say, "I have experienced this"—but, if the self is pure consciousness only, then there cannot be any perceiver persisting in the past as well as in the present, and the notion "I have experienced this" is not explained, but only discarded as being illusory. The consciousness of things, however, is never generated in us as "I am consciousness," but as "I have the consciousness of this"; if all forms were impure impositions on pure consciousness, then the changes would have taken place in the consciousness, and instead of the form "I have consciousness" the proper form of knowledge ought to have been "I am consciousness." The Śaṅkarites also hold that the notion of the knower is an illusory imposition on the pure consciousness. If that be so, the consciousness itself may be regarded as an illusory imposition; if it is said that the pure consciousness is not an imposition, since it lasts till the end—the stage of emancipation—then, since the result of right knowledge (*tattva-jñāna*) is this, that the self ceases to be a knower, false knowledge should be welcomed rather than such a right knowledge. The notion "I know" proves the self to be a knower and apart from a knower so manifested no pure consciousness can be experienced. The notion "I" at once distinguishes the knower from the body, the senses, the *manas*, or even the knowledge. Such a self is also called a *sākṣī* (perceiver), as all objects are directly perceived by it.

The *Sāṃkhya* view is that it is the *ahaṅkāra* or *buddhi* which may be regarded as the knower; for these are but products of *prakṛti*, and thus non-intelligent in themselves. The light of pure consciousness cannot be regarded as falling on them and thereby making them knowers by the reflection of its light; for reflection can only happen with reference to visible objects. Sometimes it is held by the Śaṅkarites that true consciousness is permanent and unchangeable, that the ego (*ahaṅkāra*) derives its manifestation from that and yet reveals that in association with itself, just as a mirror or the surface of water reflects the sun; and, when these limitations of *ahaṅkāra*, etc., are merged during deep sleep, the self shines forth in its own natural light and bliss. This also is unintelligible; for if the *ahaṅkāra*, etc., had all been manifested by the pure consciousness, how can they again in their turn manifest the consciousness itself? Actually it cannot be imagined what is the nature of that manifestation which pure consciousness is made to have by the *ahaṅkāra*, since all ordinary analogies fail. Ordinarily things are said to be manifested when obstructions which veil them are removed, or when a lamp destroys darkness, or when a mirror reflects an object; but none of these analogies is of any use in understanding how consciousness could be manifested by *ahaṅkāra*. If, again, consciousness requires something else to manifest it, then it ceases to be self-manifesting and becomes the same as other objects. It is said that the process of knowledge runs on by successive removals of *ajñāna* from the consciousness. *Ajñāna* (*na-jñāna*—not knowledge) may be understood as absence of knowledge or as the moment when some knowledge is going to rise, but such an *ajñāna* cannot obstruct consciousness; the Śaṅkarites hold, therefore, that there is an indefinable positive *ajñāna* which forms the stuff of the world. But all this is sheer nonsense. That which manifests anything cannot make that thing appear as a part of itself, or as its own manifestation. The ego, or *ahaṅkāra*, cannot also manifest another consciousness (which is different from it) in such a way that that consciousness shall appear as its own manifestation. So it has to be admitted that the self is not pure consciousness, but the self-conscious ego which appears in all our experience. The state of deep sleep (*suṣupti*) is often put forward as an example of pure consciousness being found unassociated with other limitations of ego, etc. But this is not possible, as we have already seen. Moreover, when the later experience of the waking moment testifies that "I did not know anything," it can well be urged that there was no pure consciousness during deep sleep; but that the ego existed is proved by the fact that at the waking moment the perception which identifies the ego (*ahaṅkāra*) as the self, also testifies that the ego as the self had persisted during deep sleep. The self which shines forth in us as the ego therefore remains the same during deep sleep; but it has no knowledge at that time. After rising from deep sleep we feel "I did not know anything, I did not know even myself." The Śaṅkarites assert the experience that during deep sleep there is no knowledge even of the ego. This, however, is hardly true; for the perception "I did not know even myself" means that during deep sleep all the personal associations (e.g. as belonging to a particular family, as occupying a particular position, etc.) were absent, and not that the ego itself was absent. When the self is conscious of itself, there is the notion of the "I," as in "I am conscious of myself." During deep sleep also, when no other objects are manifested, there is the self which is conscious of itself as the ego or the "I." If during emancipation there was no consciousness as the self, the ego, the "I," then it is the same almost as the absolute nihilism of the Buddhists. The sense of "I," the ego, is not a mere quality extraneously imposed on the self, but the very nature of the self. Even knowledge shines forth as a quality of this ego or "I," as when we say "I know it." It is the "I" who possesses the knowledge. Knowledge thus appears to be a quality of the "I." But no experience of ours ever demonstrates that "I" is a quality of pure knowledge. We say "I have this knowledge" and not that the knowledge has the "I." If there is no "I," no one who experiences, no subject who is existent during emancipation, who would strive to attain emancipation? If even the "I" is annihilated after emancipation, who would care to take all the trouble, or suffer the religious restraints, etc., for such an undesirable state? If even "I" should cease to exist, why should I care for such a nihilistic state? What am I to do with pure consciousness, when "I" ceases to exist? To say that "I" is such an object as "you" or "he" or "this" or "that," and that this "I" is illuminated by pure consciousness, is preposterously against all experience. The "I" manifests of itself without the help of any other manifesting agency, now as well as during emancipation; for the manifestation of the self has always the sole form of "I"; and, if during emancipation the self manifests, it must do so as "I." From the sacred texts also we find that the emancipated sages, Vāmadeva and Manu, thought of their own selves as the "I." Even God is not devoid of this notion of His personality as "I," as is attested by the Upaniṣad sayings, in which He declares: "I have created this world." The notion of "I" is false when it is identified with the body and other extraneous associations of birth, social rank, etc., and when it gives rise to pride and boastfulness. It is this kind of *ahaṅkāra* which has been regarded as false in the scriptures. The notion "I," when it refers to the self, is, indeed, the most accurate notion that we can have.

All our perceptions of pleasure and pain also are manifested as qualities of the "I," the self. The "I" manifests itself to itself and hence must be regarded as being of non-material stuff (*ajaḍa*). The argument, that since the notion of "I" is taken along with knowledge (*sahopalambha*), knowledge alone exists, and that "I" is not different from it, may well be repudiated by turning the table and with the same argument declaring that "I" alone exists and that there is no knowledge. All persons experience that knowledge is felt to be as distinct from the "I," the knower, as the known object. To say that self is self-manifesting by nature is not the same thing as to say that the self is knowledge by nature; for the self is independent of knowledge; knowledge is produced as a result of the perceptual process involving sense-contact, etc.; the self is the knower, the "I," which knows things and thereby possesses knowledge.

The "I," the knower, the self, manifests itself directly by self-consciousness; and hence those who have attempted to demonstrate the self by inference have failed to do so. Thus, the Naiyāyikas think that the self is proved as that in which qualities such as knowledge, desire, pleasure, pain, etc., inhere. But, even though by such an inference we may know that there is something in which the qualities inhere, it cannot be inferred therefrom that this thing is the self in us. Since nothing else is found in which knowledge, willing, etc., might inhere, it may as well be argued that knowledge, etc., are not qualities at all, or that there is no law that qualities must necessarily inhere in a thing. They are regarded as *guṇas* (qualities) only by their technical definition; and the Naiyāyikas can accept these as *guṇas*, and on that ground infer that there must be some other entity, self (which is not testified by any other proof), as the basis in which the aforesaid *guṇas* may inhere. It is hardly justifiable to accept a new substance, soul (which cannot be obtained by any other proof), simply on the ground that there must be some basis in which *guṇas* must inhere; it is the maxim of the opponents that *guṇas* must exist in some substance and that there are knowledge, willing, etc., which they are pleased to call *guṇas*; one cannot take further advantage in holding thereby that, since there is no other substance in which these so-called *guṇas* (knowledge, willing, etc.) might inhere, the existence of some other substance as the self must be inferred.

The Sāṃkhyists also make the same mistake, when they hold that all the movements of this non-intelligent *prakṛti* must be for the sake of the *puruṣa*, for whom the *prakṛti* is working. The objection to such a view is this, that even though such entities for which the *prakṛti* is working may be inferred, yet that cannot prove that those entities are not themselves also combinations of many things and objects requiring further superintendents for themselves; or that the *puruṣas* should be the same pure intelligence as they are required to be. Moreover, that alone can be the end of a certain combination of events or things, which can be in some way benefited, moved or affected by those combinations. But the *puruṣas*, as the passive pure intelligence, cannot in any way be affected by the *prakṛti*. How then can they be regarded as the end for which the *prakṛti* works? The mere illusion, the mere semblance on the part of the *puruṣa* of being affected or benefited cannot be regarded as a reality, so that by it the purposes of the movements of the *prakṛti* might be realized. Moreover, these so-called affections, or illusions of affection, themselves belong to *prakṛti* and not to the *puruṣas*; for the *puruṣas*, as pure intelligences, are without the slightest touch of modifications of the *guṇas*. All mental modifications are, according to the *Sāṃkhya*, but modifications of the *buddhi*, which, being unintelligent, cannot be subject to illusion, error, or mistake. Moreover, no explanation can be found in the supposition that the reflection of the *puruṣas* falls upon the *buddhi*; for, as the *puruṣa* is not a visible object, it cannot be reflected in the *buddhi*. If it is said that there is no real reflection, but the *buddhi* becomes like the pure intelligence, the *puruṣa*, then that also is not possible; for, if the *buddhi* is to become as qualityless as the *puruṣas*, then all mental states have to be abrogated. If it is said that the *buddhi* does not become like pure intelligence, but as if it was as intelligent as the *puruṣa*, then that also is not possible; for *puruṣa* is according to the *Sāṃkhya* pure intelligence, not intelligent. There is no intelligent knower in the *Sāṃkhya*, and that is its trouble. If it is said that what is meant by the belief that *puruṣa* is the end of all *guṇa*-movements is simply this, that, though it is absolutely incapable of any change or transformation, yet by its very presence it sets the *guṇas* in motion and is thus the end for which all the *guṇa* modifications take place, just as if the *puruṣa* were a king for whom the whole dominion works and fights. But since the *puruṣa*, unaffected by them, is only the seer of them all, this also is not possible; for the analogy does not hold, since the king is really benefited by the movements of the people of his dominions but the *puruṣa*, which merely implies seeing, cannot be regarded as a seer.

The nature of the self, as we have described it, is also attested by the verdict of the *Upaniṣads*. This self is directly revealed in its own notion as "I," and pleasure, pain, attachment, antipathy are but its states, which are also revealed along with the revelation of its own self as the "I." This self is not, however, perceived by any of the senses or even by the organ *manas*, as Kumārila supposed. For the question arises as to when, if the self is believed to be perceived by the *manas*, that takes place? It cannot take place precisely at the moment when the knowledge of an object arises; for then the notions of the self and the objects, as they occur at the same moment, could not so appear that one (the self) was the cognizer or determiner, and the others (the objects) were the cognized or the determined. If the knowledge of the objects and the self arose at two different moments as separate acts, it would be difficult to conceive how they could be related as cognizer and cognized. So it cannot be held that the self, though it always manifests itself to us in self-consciousness, could yet be perceived by any of the senses or the *manas*. Again, Kumārila held that knowledge was a new product, and that when, as a result of certain sense activities, knowledge or the *jñāna* movement was generated in us, there was also produced an illumination (*jñātatā* or *prākaṭya*) in objects in association with the self, and that from such an illumination the *jñāna-kriyā* or knowledge movement could be inferred, and the self, as being the possessor of this knowledge, could be perceived by the *manas*. But such a theory that the self is conscious not by itself, but by an extraneous introduction of knowledge, is hardly acceptable; for no one imagines that there exists in him such a difference when he perceives a thing which he had not before that perception. Moreover, since the act of knowledge did not directly reveal the self, there might also be doubts as to whether the self knew things or not, and the self would not shine forth directly in all conscious experience, as it is found to do.

Again, some hold that the self is known from the objective consciousness and not directly by itself. It is easy to see that this can hardly be accepted as true; for how can objective consciousness, which refers to the objects, in any way produce the consciousness of the self? According to this view it is difficult to prove even the existence of knowledge; for this, since it is not self-manifested, requires something else to manifest it; if it is thought that it is self-manifesting, then we should expect it to be manifested to all persons and at all times. It may be said that, though knowledge is self-manifesting, yet it can be manifested only in connection with the person in whom it inheres, and not in connection with all persons. If that be so, it really comes to this, that knowledge can become manifested only through its connection with a someone who knows. If, in answer to this, it is said that knowledge does not require its connection with a person for its own existence, but only for its specific illumination as occurring with reference to a certain subject and object, then that cannot be proved. We could have accepted it if we had known any case in which pure consciousness or knowledge had been found apart from its specific references of subject and object. If it is still asserted that consciousness cannot be separated from its self-manifesting capacities, then it may also be pointed out that consciousness is never found separated from the person, the subject, or the knower who possesses it. Instead of conceding the self-manifesting power to the infinite number of states of consciousness, is it not better to say that the self-manifestation of consciousness proceeds from the self-conscious agent, the subject and determiner of all conscious experiences? Even if the states of consciousness had been admitted as self-manifesting, that would not explain how the self could be self-manifesting on that account. If, however, the self, the knower of all experiences, be admitted as self-manifesting, then the manifestation of the conscious experiences becomes easily explained; for the self is the perceiver of all experiences. All things require for their manifestation another category which does not belong to their class; but since also there is nothing on which the self can depend for its consciousness, it has to be admitted that the self is a self-manifesting intelligent entity. Thus the jug does not require for its manifestation another jug, but a light, which belongs to an altogether different class. The light also does not require for its manifestation another light, or the jug which it manifests, but the senses; the senses again depend on consciousness for the manifestation of their powers. Consciousness, in its turn, depends upon the self; without inhering in the self it cannot get itself manifested. The self, however, has nothing else to depend upon; its self-manifestation, therefore, does not depend on anything else.

The states of consciousness have thus to be regarded as being states of the self, which by its connection with different objects manifests them as this or that consciousness. Knowledge of this or that object is thus but different states of consciousness, which itself again is a characteristic of the self.

If consciousness had not been an inseparable quality or essential characteristic of the self, then there might have been a time when the self could have been experienced as being devoid of consciousness; a thing which is so related with another thing that it never exists without it must necessarily be an essential and inseparable characteristic thereof. It cannot be said that this generalization does not hold, since we are conscious of our self in connection with the body, which is not an essential characteristic of the self; for the consciousness of the self as "I," or as "I know," is not necessarily connected with a reference to, or association with, the body. Again, it cannot be said that, if consciousness were an essential and inseparable characteristic of the self, then the states of unconsciousness in deep sleep and swoon could not be explained; for there is nothing to prove that there is no consciousness of the knowing self during those so-called stages of unconsciousness. We feel on waking that we had no consciousness at the time because we cease to have any memory of it. The reason therefore why states of unconsciousness are felt in the waking stage to be so is this, that we have no memory of those states. Memory is only possible when certain objects are apprehended and the impression of these objects of consciousness is left in the mind, so that through them the object of memory may be remembered. During deep sleep no objects are perceived, and no impressions are left, and, as a result, we cease to have any memory of those states. The self then remains with its characteristic self-consciousness, but without the consciousness of anything else. The self-conscious self does not leave any impression on the organs of the psychosis, the *manas*, etc., as they all then cease to act. It is easy to understand that no impression can be made upon the self; for, if it could and if impressions had been continually heaped on the self, then such a self could never manage to get rid of them and could never attain emancipation. Moreover, it is the characteristic of the phenomenon of memory that, when a perception has once been perceived, but is not being perceived continually, it can be remembered now, when those past impressions are revived by association of similar perceptions. But the self-conscious self has always been the same and hence there cannot be any memory of it. The fact that on waking from deep sleep one feels that one has slept happily does not prove that there was actually any consciousness of happiness during deep sleep; it is only a happy organic feeling of the body resulting from sound sleep which is interpreted or rather spoken of as being the enjoyment of happiness during deep sleep. We say, "I am the same as I was yesterday," but it is not the self that is remembered, but the particular time association that forms the content of memory.

Perception of objects is generated in us when consciousness comes in contact with the physical objects in association with this or that sense of perception. It is on that account that, though the self is always possessed of its self-consciousness, yet it is only when the consciousness of the self is in touch with an external object in association with a sense-organ that we get that particular sense-perception. This self is not all-pervading, but of an atomic size; when it comes in association with any particular sense, we acquire that particular sense-perception. This explains the fact that no two perceptions can be acquired simultaneously: where there is an appearance of simultaneity, there is only a succession of acquirement so rapid that changes cannot be noticed. Had the soul been all-pervading, we should have had the knowledge of all things at once, since the soul was in touch with all things. Thus it is proved that the self has consciousness as its essential characteristic; knowledge or consciousness is never produced in it, but when the obstructions are removed and the self comes into touch with the objects, the consciousness of these objects shines forth.

God and the World.

As we have already noted, the Mīmāṃsists do not admit the existence of *Īśvara*. Their antitheistic arguments, which we have not considered, can be dealt with here in contrast to Yāmuna's doctrine of *Īśvara*. They say that an omniscient *Īśvara* cannot be admitted, since such an assumption cannot be proved, and there are, indeed, many objections to the hypothesis. For how can such a perception of omniscience be acquired? Surely it cannot be acquired by the ordinary means of perception; for ordinary perception cannot give one the knowledge of all things present and past, before and far beyond the limits of one's senses. Also the perception of Īśvara generally ascribed to the Yogins cannot be admitted; for it is impossible that the Yogin should perceive past things and things beyond the limits of his senses, by means of his sense-organs. If mind (*antaḥkaraṇa*) be such that it can perceive all sense-objects without the aid of the senses, then what is the use at all of the senses? Of course it is true that by great concentration one can perceive things more clearly and distinctly; but no amount of concentration or any other process can enable a man to hear by the eye or to perceive things without the help of the senses. Omniscience is therefore not possible, and we have not by our senses seen any such omniscient person as Īśvara. His existence cannot be proved by inference; for, since He is beyond all perceptible things, there cannot be any reason (*hetu*) which we could perceive as being associated with Him and by reason of which we could make Him the subject of inference. It is urged by the Naiyāyikas that this world, formed by collocation of parts, must be an effect in itself, and it is argued that, like all other effects, this also must have taken place under the superintendence of an intelligent person who had a direct experience of world materials. But this is not necessary; for it may very well be conceived that the atoms, etc., have all been collocated in their present form by the destinies of men (*adṛṣṭa*)—according to the *karma*, of all the men in the world. The *karmas* of merit and demerit exist in us all, and they are moulding the world-process, though these cannot be perceived by us. The world may thus be regarded as a product of the *karmas* of men and not of *Īśvara*, whom no one has ever perceived. Moreover, why should *Īśvara*, who has no desire to satisfy, create this world? This world, with all the mountains, rivers and oceans, etc., cannot be regarded as an effect produced by any one.

Yāmuna follows the method of the *Nyāya* and tries to prove that the world is an effect, and, as such, must have been produced by an intelligent person who had a direct knowledge of the materials. He also has a direct knowledge of the *dharma* (merit) and *adharma* (demerit) of men, in accordance with which He creates the whole world and establishes an order by which every man may have only such experiences as he deserves. He, by His mere desire, sets all the world in motion. He has no body, but still He carries on the functioning of His desire by His *manas*. He has to be admitted as a person of infinite knowledge and power; for otherwise how could He create this world and establish its order?

The Śaṅkarites had held that, when the Upaniṣads say that nothing exists but one Brahman, it means that Brahman alone exists and the world is false; but that is not the sense. It means simply that there is no other Īśvara but Īśvara, and that there is none else like Him. When the Upaniṣads declare that Brahman is all that we see and that He is the sole material of the world, it does not mean that everything else does not exist and that the qualityless Brahman is the only reality. If I say there is one sun, it does not mean that He has no rays; if I say there are the seven oceans, it does not mean that the oceans have no ripples, etc. The only meaning that such passages can have is that the world has come out of Him, like sparks from fire, and that in Him the world finds its ultimate rest and support; from Him all things of the world—the fire, the wind, the earth—have drawn their powers and capacities, and without His power they would have been impotent to do anything. If, on the contrary, it is held that the whole world is false, then the whole experience has to be sacrificed, and, as the knowledge of Brahman also forms a part of this experience, that also has to be sacrificed as false. All the Vedānta dialectic employed to prove that the perception of difference is false is of very little use to us; for our experience shows that we perceive differences as well as relations. We perceive the blue colour, the lotus, and also that the lotus has the blue colour; so the world and the individuals may also be conceived in accordance with the teaching of the Upaniṣads as being inseparably related to Him. This meaning is, indeed, more legitimate than the conception which would abolish all the world manifestation, and the personality of all individual persons, and would remain content only to indicate the identity of their pure intelligence with the pure intelligence of Brahman. There is not any pure, all-absorbing, qualityless intelligence, as the Śaṅkarites assert; for to each of us different and separate ideas are being directly manifested, e.g. our feelings of individual pleasures and pains. If there were only one intelligence, then everything should have shone forth simultaneously for all times. Again, this intelligence is said to be both Being (*sat*), intelligence (*cit*), and bliss (*ānanda*). If this tripartite form be accepted, it will naturally destroy the monistic doctrine which the Śaṅkarites try to protect so zealously. If, however, they assert that these are not separate forms or qualities, but all three represent one identical truth, the Brahman, then that also is not possible; for how can bliss be the same as intelligence? Pleasure and intelligence are experienced by all of us to be entirely different. Thus, in whichever way we try to scrutinize the Śaṅkarite doctrines, we find that they are against all experiences and hardly stand the strain of a logical criticism. It has, therefore, to be admitted that our notions about the external world are correct and give us a true representation of the external world. The manifold world of infinite variety is therefore not merely an illusory appearance, but true, as attested by our sense-experience.

Thus the ultimate conclusion of Yāmuna's philosophy demonstrates that there are, on the one side, the self-conscious souls, and, on the other, the omniscient and all powerful Īśvara and the manifold external world. These three categories are real. He hints in some places that the world may be regarded as being like sparks coming out of Īśvara; but he does not elaborate this thought, and it is contradicted by other passages, in which Īśvara is spoken of as the fashioner of the world system, in accordance with the Nyāya doctrine. From the manner in which he supports the Nyāya position with regard to the relation of Īśvara and the world, both in the *Siddhi-traya* and in the *Āgama-prāmāṇya*, it is almost certain that his own attitude did not differ much from the *Nyāya* attitude, which left the duality of the world and *Īśvara* absolutely unresolved. It appears, therefore, that (so far as we can judge from his *Siddhi-traya*) Yāmuna's main contribution consists in establishing the self-consciousness of the soul. The reality of the external world and the existence of *Īśvara* had been accepted in previous systems also. Yāmuna thus gives us hardly any new ideas about *Īśvara* and His relation to the souls and the world. He does not make inquiry into the nature of the reality of the world, and rests content with proving that the world-appearance is not false, as the Śaṅkarites supposed. He says in one place that he does not believe in the existence of the partless atoms of the Naiyāyikas. The smallest particle of matter is the *trasareṇu*, the specks of dust that are found to move in the air when the sun's rays come in through a chink or hole. But he does not say anything more than this about the ultimate nature of the reality of the manifold world or how it has come to be what it is. He is also silent about the methods which a person should adopt for procuring his salvation, and the nature and characteristics of that state.

Yāmuna, in his *Āgama-prāmāṇya*, tried to establish that the *Pañca-rātra-saṃhitā* had the same validity as the Vedas, since it was uttered by Īśvara himself. Viṣṇu, or Vāsudeva, has been praised in the *Purusa-sūkta* and in other places of the Vedas as the supreme Lord. The *Pāśupata-tantra* of the Śaivas is never supported by the Vedas, and thus the validity of the *Pāśupata-tantra* cannot be compared with that of the *Pañcarātra-saṃhitā*.

God according to Rāmānuja, Veṅkaṭanātha and Lokācārya.

Bhāskara had said that, though *Īśvara* is possessed of all good qualities and is in Himself beyond all impurities, yet by His *Śakti* (power) He transformed Himself into this world, and, as all conditions and limitations, all matter and phenomena are but His power, it is He who by His power appears as an ordinary soul and at last obtains emancipation as well. Rāmānuja holds that on this view there is no essential form of Brahman which transcends the limits of all bonds, the power (*Śakti*) which manifests itself as all phenomena. Brahman, being always associated with the power which exists as the world-phenomena, becomes necessarily subject to all the defects of the phenomenal world. Moreover, when a *Śakti*, or power of Brahman, is admitted, how can Brahman be said to suffer any transformation? Even if the *Śakti* (power) be regarded as its transformation, even then it cannot be accepted that it (*Brahman*) should combine with its *Śakti* to undergo a worldly transformation.

Another Vedāntist (probably Yādavaprakāśa, the Preceptor of Rāmānuja in his early days) held that Brahman, in its own essence, transformed itself into the world; this theory also is open to the objection that the Brahman, being transformed into the world, becomes subject to all the impurities and defects of the world. Even if it is held that in one part it is transcendent and possesses innumerable good qualities and in another suffers from the impurities associated with its transformation into the world, then also that which is so impure in one part cannot have its impurity so counterbalanced by the purity of its other half that it can be called *Īśvara*.

Rāmānuja, therefore, holds that all the changes and transformations take place in the body of the *Īśvara* and not in His essence. So *Īśvara*, in His pure essence, is ever free from all impurities, and the possessor of all the best qualities, untouched by the phenomenal disturbances with which His body alone is associated. The matter which forms the stuff of the external world is not what the *Sāṃkhya* calls the *guṇa* substances, but simply the *prakṛti* or the primeval causal entity, possessing diverse qualities which may be classified under three different types—the *sattva*, the *rajas* and the *tamas*. This *prakṛti*, however, in its fine essence, forms the body of *Īśvara* and is moved into all its transformations by *Īśvara* Himself. When He withholds *prakṛti* from all its transformations and annuls all its movement, we have the state of *pralaya*, in which *Īśvara* exists in the *kāraṇa* or causal state, holding within Him the *prakṛti* in its subtle state as His body. *Prakṛti* is a body as well as a mode (*prakāra*) of *Īśvara*, and, when it is in a manifested condition, we have the state of creation. *Prakṛti* undergoes its transformations into *tan-mātra*, *ahaṅkāra*, etc.; but these are yet the subtle substance forming parts of *Īśvara*'s body. The transformations through which *prakṛti* passes in the origination of *tan-mātra*, *ahaṅkāra*, etc., are not the results of the collocation of the *guṇa* reals, as we saw in the case of the *Sāṃkhya*, but may be regarded as the passing of *prakṛti* through different stages, each stage being marked out by the special character of the *prakṛti* while passing through that stage. The word *guṇa* here has then its ordinary meaning of quality; and it is supposed that the *prakṛti*, as it is moved by *Īśvara*, continues to acquire new qualities. The present state of the world also represents *prakṛti* in a particular state wherein it has acquired the qualities which we note in the phenomenal world of ours.

We have seen before that the existence of *Īśvara* was inferred by Yāmuna on Nyāya lines. But Rāmānuja thinks that there is as much to be said in favour of the existence as against it. Thus he says that, even supposing that the hills, etc., are effects, it cannot be said that they were all created by one person; for even all jugs are not made by the same person; *Īśvara* may also be denied, after the *Sāṃkhya* mode, and it may be imagined that in accordance with the *Karma* of men the world arose out of a combination of the original *guṇas*. There is thus as much to be said against the existence of *Īśvara* as in favour of it. Rāmānuja holds that *Īśvara* cannot be proved by inference, but is to be admitted on the authority of the sacred texts[1]. The Nyāya and Yoga, moreover, conceived *Īśvara* to be only the *nimitta-kāraṇa*, or instrumental cause; but according to Rāmānuja *Īśvara* is all-pervading in all space and in all time. This all-pervasiveness of God does not mean that His reality is the only reality everywhere, or that He is identical with the world-reality, and all else is false. It means, as Sudarśanācārya has said in his *Śruta-prakāśikā* on the *Rāmānuja-bhāṣya*, 2nd *sūtra*, that there is no measure with which He may be limited by any spatial relation. Varada and Nārāyaṇa, however, and Veṅkaṭanātha, agree in interpreting all-pervasiveness as the absence of any limit to His good qualities (*iyad-guṇaka iti pariccheda-rahitaḥ*)[2]. There is nothing else than *Īśvara*'s body, so by His body also he may be conceived as pervading the whole world. Thus, *Īśvara* is not only *nimitta-kāraṇa* but also *upādāna-kāraṇa*, or material cause as well. Veṅkaṭa establishes in some detail that the highest *Īśvara* is called Nārāyaṇa and His power, as presiding over matter and souls, is called *Lakṣmī*. *Īśvara* has His *manas*, and His eternal senses do not require any body or organs for their manifestation. Veṅkaṭa also mentions three modified forms of manifestation of Lord Vāsudeva, namely Saṃkarṣaṇa, Pradyumna and Aniruddha. This *vyūha* doctrine of the *Pañcarātra* has been briefly discussed in Varavara's *bhāṣya* on the *Tattva-traya* of Lokācārya. These three, Saṃkarṣaṇa, Pradyumna, and Aniruddha,

[1] See Rāmānuja's *Bhāṣya*, 3rd *sūtra*.
[2] See *Nyāya-siddhāñjana* of Veṅkaṭanātha.

are said to be the three different forms of Vāsudeva, by which He controls the individual souls (*jīva*), the *manas* and the external world. That form of activity by which the *jīvas* were separated from the *prakṛti* at the beginning of the creation is associated with a form of *Īśvara* called Saṃkarṣaṇa. When this separating activity passes and dominates over men as their *manas* and ultimately brings them to the path of virtue and good, it is said to be associated with a form of *Īśvara* called Pradyumna. Aniruddha is that form of *Īśvara* by which the external world is generated and kept in order, and in which our experiences and attempts to attain right knowledge are fulfilled. These forms are not different *Īśvara*, but are imagined according to the diversity of His function. *Īśvara*'s full existence is everywhere; He and His forms are identical. These forms are but manifestations of the power of Vāsudeva and are therefore called *Vibhava*. Such manifestations of His power are also to be found in great religious heroes such as Vyāsa, Arjuna, etc. Lokācārya, in describing Him further, says that in His real essence *Īśvara* is not only omniscient, but this omniscience is also associated with complete and eternal joy. His knowledge and powers do not suffer any variation or comparison, as they are always the very highest and the most inconceivable by any one else. He moves us all to action and fulfils our desires according to our *karmas*. He gives knowledge to those who are ignorant, power to those who are weak, pardon to those who are guilty, mercy to the sufferers, paternal affection and overlooking of guilt to those who are guilty, goodness to those who are wicked, sincerity to the crooked, and goodness of heart to those who are wicked at heart. He cannot bear to remain separated from those who do not want to be separated from Him, and puts Himself within easy reach of those who want to see Him. When he sees people afflicted, He has mercy on them and helps them. Thus all His qualities are for the sake of others and not for Himself. His affection for us is of a maternal nature, and out of this affection He neglects our defects and tries to help us towards the ideal of good. He has created this world in Himself, not in order to satisfy any wants but in a playful manner, as it were through mere spontaneity (*līlā*). As in creation, so in keeping the created world in order, and in dissolution, His playful spontaneity upholds everything and brings about everything. Dissolution is as much of His play as creation. All this is created in Himself and out of Himself.

Viśiṣṭā-dvaita doctrine of Soul according to Rāmānuja and Veṅkaṭanātha.

The existence of souls as separate self-conscious entities, in contradistinction to the doctrines of other systems, had been established by Yāmuna, as we have shown in some detail in our section on his doctrine of soul. The soul is atomic in its size, as we have already found stated by Yāmuna. Barada, Viṣṇu Miśra and Veṅkaṭanātha held that in the ordinary phenomenal state its knowledge expands and contracts. At the time of emancipation it has its highest expansion in which it pervades the whole world. The cause of its contraction and expansion is its *karma*, which is also called *avidyā*. Rāmānuja, in his *Vedānta-dīpa*, indulged in the simile of the ray of a lamp in explaining the rise of knowledge in different parts of the body, despite the atomic soul being located in only one part. The soul exists in one part of the body and spreads out its knowledge over all other parts of the body, like the rays of a lamp. Rāmānuja says that *Īśvara* allows the individual self-conscious souls to perform whichever action they have a desire to attempt. Movement is possible only through the approval by *Īśvara* of the desires of individual souls. The self-conscious souls desire things according to their own free will, and in this they are not hampered by *Īśvara*; *Īśvara* always allows the individual souls to act, i.e. to move their limbs according to their desires. This is a sort of occasionalism, which holds that, in every action which I am performing, I am dependent on *Īśvara*'s will. I can move my limbs because He wishes it. Apart from this general law that *Īśvara* is a supporter of all actions, there are some exceptions of particular favour and disfavour. To those who are particularly attached to Him He is more favourably disposed, and by His grace generates in them such desires that they adopt actions by which they may easily win Him. Into those who are particularly opposed to Him He imports such desires that they are led farther away from Him[1]. *Īśvara* exists in us all as the inner controller. This inner controller is represented by our individual soul. This individual soul is free in all its desires, knowledge, and attempts[2]. This freedom of will, knowledge, etc., is given to us all by *Īśvara*, and He also arranges that the movements in the material world may take place in ac-

[1] See Varavara's commentary on the *Tattva-traya*.

[2] See Rāmānuja's *Bhāṣya*, II. 3. 40, 41.

cordance with our desires. Thus He not only gives us freedom of will, but also helps the realization of that will in the external world, and ultimately grants good and evil fruits according to our good and evil deeds[1]. Thus *Īśvara*'s control over us does not rob us of our freedom of will. Even His favour and disfavour consist in the fulfilment of a devotee's eager desire to be associated with Him, and His disfavour consists in fulfilling the desire of a confirmed sinner, leading him away into worldly pleasures farther from Him. The self is often called *jñāna*, or consciousness, because of the fact that it is as self-revealing as consciousness[2]. It reveals all objects, when it comes in touch with them through its senses. The souls are, however, all held in *Īśvara*. Rāmānuja had spoken of the souls only as being the body of *Īśvara*; but Lokācārya and Varavara further hold that, as the external material objects exist for the sake of the souls, so the souls exist for the *Īśvara*; as Man is the end for which the external objects of enjoyment exist, so *Īśvara* is the end (*śeṣa*) for which Man exists as the object of His control and support (*śeṣī*).

The self, though pure in itself, becomes associated with ignorance and worldly desires through coming into touch with matter (*acit*). *Avidyā*, or ignorance, here means want of knowledge, misapplication of characteristics, false knowledge, etc. This ignorance, or *avidyā*, which is the cause of many worldly desires and impure instincts, is generated by the association of the souls with matter; when this association is cut away, the self becomes divested of the *avidyā* and emancipated[3].

Rāmānuja says in his *Vedārtha-saṃgraha* that *Īśvara* grants emancipation from worldly bonds to a person, when he, after acquiring true knowledge from the *śāstras* according to the instruction of good teachers, engages himself every day in self-control, penance, purity; practises forgivingness, sincerity, charity, non-injury; performs all the obligatory and ceremonial duties; refrains from prohibited actions, and afterwards surrenders himself completely to the Lord; praises Him, continually thinks of Him, adores Him, counts His names, hears of His greatness and goodness, speaks of it, worships Him, and has all the darkness of his soul removed

[1] See Rāmānuja's *Bhāṣya*, XI. 3. 40, 41.
[2] See Rāmānuja's *Bhāṣya*, II. III. 29, 30.
[3] See Varavara's commentary on the *Tattva-traya*, *Cit-prakaraṇa*.

by His grace. The ordinary obligatory and ceremonial duties have to be performed; all the highest ethical virtues have to be practised and a true knowledge attained from the *śāstras*. It is only when a man has thus qualified himself that he can ultimately attain emancipation from all worldly bonds by supreme self-surrender and *bhakti* to the Lord. *Bhakti*, or devotion, with Rāmānuja means continual thinking of Him. Without it pure knowledge cannot give us emancipation. The special feature of *bhakti* is this, that by it a man loses all interest in everything else than that which is done for the sake of the dearest. Finally *bhakti* is not with Rāmānuja feeling, but a special kind of knowledge (*jñāna-viśeṣa*) which seeks to ignore everything that is not done for the sake of *Īśvara*, the dearest to us all[1].

Veṅkaṭanātha says that the performance of *karmas* makes a man fit to inquire into true knowledge, and the acquirement of true knowledge makes a man fit to attain devotion, or *bhakti*. When a man is fit to inquire after true knowledge, he may give up the *karmas*. *Bhakti* is, according to Veṅkaṭanātha, the feeling of joy (*prīti*) in the adorable, and not mere knowledge. Emancipation as *sāyujya* (sameness of quality) with *Īśvara* is the result of such *bhakti*. In this state of *sāyujya*, the human soul participates in the qualities of omniscience, bliss, etc., of *Īśvara*. The human soul cannot, of course, wholly participate with *Īśvara*, and such of His qualities as the power of creating and controlling the world, or of granting emancipation to human souls, remain ever with *Īśvara* alone. Human souls can participate only in His knowledge and bliss and can be as omniscient and as blissful as He. In this state of emancipation Man remains in an eternal and infinite blissful servitude to *Īśvara*. This servitude to *Īśvara* is not painful in the least, like other services. When a man forgoes all his personal vanity and merges all his independence in His service, and considers himself as His servant whose only work is to serve Him, this is indeed the state of bright joy. Veṅkaṭanātha, however, further differentiates this *Vaiṣṇava* emancipation, as the thinking of the *Īśvara* as the most supreme, and thereby deriving infinite joy, from the other type of *kaivalya*, in which Man thinks of himself the Brahman and attains *kaivalya*. There also the association with *avidyā* and the world is indeed destroyed, and the man is reduced to oneness; but

[1] See *Vedārtha-saṃgraha*, p. 146.

this is hardly a desirable state, since there is not here the infinite joy which the *Vaiṣṇava* emancipation can bring. Rāmānuja has written of *mukti* as a state which a man can acquire when he is divested of all *avidyā*, and has the natural intuition of the Supreme Soul and his relations with Him. He had distinguished this state from that *mukti* in which a man is divested of all *karmas* and realizes himself in himself, as obstructing the qualities of *Īśvara* from him. This *kaivalya*, or realization of one's own self as the highest, is thus distinctly a lower emancipation. It is not out of place to say that Veṅkaṭanātha had pushed *bhakti* and the human goal of *mukti* distinctly further on to the side of feeling, by defining *bhakti* as a feeling of joy and *mukti* as servitude to *Īśvara*.

Acit or Primeval Matter: the *Prakṛti* and its modifications.

Proceeding to describe the nature of matter, Veṅkaṭanātha tries to disprove the Nyāya-Vaiśeṣika theory of atoms. The smallest particle of matter is that which is visible in the sun's rays coming in through a chink or hole. The imagination of still finer particles, which may be called dyads or atoms, is not attested by experience; for these cannot be perceived. They cannot be compared to the small invisible pollen of flowers which makes the air carrying it fragrant; for these small particles possess the quality of smell, whereas atoms are subtle particles which do not possess any perceivable characteristic. Even inference cannot establish these atoms; for, if we suppose that particles when divided could be further divided until we could arrive at the limit of division, beyond which no division was possible, and that these subtlest particles could be called atoms, this would be impossible, for the atoms of Nyāya and Vaiśeṣika are not only the smallest particles but they are considered to have a special kind of measure (*pārimāṇḍalya*) as their characteristic, and this we have no data for inferring. If only the smallness is the criterion, we may better stop at the *trasa-reṇu* (the dust particles in the air). There are also other objections against the atomic theory, such as have been propounded by Śaṅkarācārya, that the partless atoms cannot come into touch with other atoms or form together into one whole, or that the *pārimaṇḍalya* measure of the *paramāṇu* should not generate a different kind of measure in the dyad (*dvy-aṇuka*), or that the dyad ought not to generate quite another kind of measure in the *trasa-reṇu*. The world cannot thus be accepted as due to the conglomeration of atoms or *trasa-reṇus*. *Prakṛti* containing the three qualities of *sattva*, *rajas* and *tamas* has thus to be admitted as the primal matter. The state of it just preceding *ahaṇkāra* and just following its state as *prakṛti* (the state in which, all its three qualities being the same, there is no manifestation of any particular quality) is called *mahat*. The next state, which follows *mahat* and precedes the senses, is called *ahaṇkāra*. The *mahat* and *ahaṇkāra* are not subjective states of *buddhi* or ego, as some Śāṃkhyists would think, but are two successive cosmic stages of the *prakṛti*, the primeval cosmic matter. The *ahaṇkāra* is of three kinds, *sāttvika*, *rājasa* and *tāmasa*. The senses are not products of elements, as the Vaiśeṣika supposed, but represent the functional cognitional powers in association with the eye, nose, skin, etc. It is *manas* whose states are variously called imagination, determination, etc. Lokācārya describes *prakṛti* as being of three kinds, namely (1) that which contains the purest *sattva* characters and forms the material of the abode of *Īśvara*; (2) that which contains the threefold characters of *sattva*, *rajas* and *tamas* and forms the ordinary world for us. This is the field of *Īśvara*'s play. It is called *prakṛti* because it produces all transformations, *avidyā* because it is opposed to all true knowledge, and *māyā* because it is the cause of all diverse creations. As we have mentioned before, the *guṇas* of *prakṛti* are its qualities, and not the *Sāṃkhya* reals. Creation is produced by the rise of opposite qualities in the *prakṛti*. The *tan-mātras* are those states of matter in which the specific elemental qualities are not manifested. The order of the genesis of the *tan-mātras* is described by some as follows: first the *bhūtādi*, from it *śabda-tan-matra*, and from that the *ākāśa*; again, from *ākāśa* comes *sparśa-tan-mātra* (vibration-potential), followed by *vāyu*; from *vāyu* comes the *rūpa-tan-mātra* (light-potential) and from that *tejas* (light and heat); from *tejas* comes *rasa-tan-mātra* (taste-potential), and thence water; from water comes *gandha-tan-mātra* (smell-potential), and from that earth. Other theories of the genesis of the *bhūtas* are also described, but we omit them here, as they are not of much value. Varavara says that time is regarded as the *prakṛti* without its *sattva* quality, but Veṅkaṭanātha speaks of time as existing in the nature of *Īśvara* as a special form of His manifestation. Space (*dik*) is not an entity different from *ākāśa*, which offers room for the movement of things. *Ākāśa* is not a mere vacuity or non-occupiedness, but a positive entity.

Thus it is seen that the indeterminate matter of *prakṛti*, with its three qualities, passes through many stages and at last exhibits the phenomenal world, which produces happiness and misery in accordance with a man's destiny (*adṛṣṭa*) and good or bad deeds. The force of *adṛṣṭa* is not a separate entity, but the favour and disfavour of *Īśvara*, which works in accordance with the good or bad deeds of men.

CHAPTER XX

PHILOSOPHY OF THE RĀMĀNUJA SCHOOL OF THOUGHT

Śaṅkara and Rāmānuja on the nature of Reality as qualified or unqualified.

ŚAṄKARA says that Brahman, as pure intelligence (*cin-mātram*) entirely divested of any kind of forms, is the ultimate reality (*paramārtha*), and that all differences of the knower, the known, and the diverse forms of cognition are all imposed on it and are false. Falsehood with him is an appearance which ceases to exist as soon as the reality is known, and this is caused by the defect (*doṣa*), which hides the true nature of reality and manifests various forms. The defect which produces the false world appearance is ignorance or nescience (*avidyā* or *māyā*), which can neither be said to be existent nor non-existent (*sad-asad-anirvacanīyā*), and this ceases (*nivṛtta*) when the Brahman is known. It is, indeed, true that in our ordinary experience we perceive difference and multiplicity; but this must be considered as faulty, because the faultless scriptures speak of the one truth as Brahman, and, though there are the other parts of the Vedas which impose on us the performance of the Vedic duties and therefore imply the existence of plurality, yet those texts which refer to the nature of Brahman as one must be considered to have greater validity; for they refer to the ultimate, whereas the Vedic injunctions are valid only with reference to the world of appearance or only so long as the ultimate reality is not known. Again, the scriptures describe the Brahman as the reality, the pure consciousness, the infinite (*satyaṃ jñānam anantaṃ brahma*); these are not qualities which belong to Brahman, but they are all identical in meaning, referring to the same differenceless identical entity, absolutely qualityless—the Brahman.

Rāmānuja, in refuting the above position, takes up first the view of Śaṅkara that the Brahman as the ultimate reality is absolutely unqualified (*nirviśeṣa*). He says that those who assert that reality can be unqualified have really no means of proving it; for all proofs are based on the assumption of some qualified character. This unqualifiedness could not be directly experienced, as they believe;

for there can be no experience without the assumption of some qualified character, since an experience, being my own unique experience, is necessarily qualified. Even if you tried to prove that one's own experience, which is really qualified in nature, is unqualified, you would have to pick up some special trait in it, in virtue of which you would maintain it was unqualified; and by that very fact your attempt is defeated, for that special trait would make it qualified. Intelligence is itself self-revealing, and by it the knower knows all objects. It may also be shown that even during sleep, or swoon, the experience is not characterless. Even when the Brahman is said to be real, pure consciousness, and infinite, it means that these are the characters of Brahman and it is meaningless to say that they do not indicate some character. The scriptures cannot testify to the existence of any characterless reality; for they are a collection of words arranged in order and relation, and each word is a whole, comprising a stem and a suffix, and the scriptures therefore are by nature unable to yield any meaning which signifies anything that is characterless. As regards perception, it is well established that all determinate perception (*sa-vikalpa-pratyakṣa*) manifests an entity with its characters; but even indeterminate perception (*nirvikalpa-pratyakṣa*) manifests some character for its indeterminateness means only the exclusion of some particular character; and there can be no perception which is absolutely negative regarding the manifestation of characters. All experiences are embodied in a proposition—"This is so"—and thus involve the manifestation of some characters. When a thing is perceived for the first time, some specific characters are discerned; but, when it is perceived again, the characters discerned before are revived in the mind, and by comparison the specific characters are properly assimilated. This is what we call determinate perception, involving the manifestation of common characters or class characters as distinguished from the perception of the first moment which is called indeterminate perception. But it does not mean that indeterminate perception is not the perception of some specific characters. Inference is based on perception and as such must necessarily reveal a thing with certain characteristics; and so not one of the three sources of our knowledge, perception, scriptures and inference, can reveal to us any entity devoid of characteristics.

It is urged by Śaṅkara and his followers that perception refers to pure being and pure being alone (*śan-mātra-grāhī*); but this can never be true, since perception refers to class-characters and thus necessarily involves the notion of difference; even at that one particular moment of perception it grasps all the essential characteristic differences of a thing which distinguish it from all other objects. If perception had reference only to pure being, then why should it manifest to us that "here is a jug," "here is a piece of cloth"; and, if the characteristic differences of a thing are not grasped by perception, why are we not contented with a buffalo when we need a horse? As pure being they are all the same, and it is being only which, it is urged, is revealed by perception. Memory would not then distinguish one from the other, and the cognition of one thing would suffice for the cognition of everything else. If any distinctive differences between one cognition and another is admitted, then that itself would baffle the contention of the characterlessness of perception. Moreover, the senses can grasp only their characteristic special feature, e.g. the eye, colour, the ear, sound, and so on, and not differencelessness. Again, Brahman is said to be of the nature of pure being, and, if the same pure being could be experienced by all the senses, then that would mean that Brahman itself is experienced by the senses. If this were so, the Brahman would be as changeable and destructible as any other objects experienced by the senses, and this no one would be willing to admit. So it has to be granted that perception reveals difference and not pure characterlessness.

Again, it has been argued that, since the experience of a jug, etc., varies differently with different space and time, i.e. we perceive here a jug, there a piece of cloth, and then again at another moment here a toy and there a horse, and we have not the one continuous experience of one entity in all space and time, these objects are false. But why should it be so? There is no contradiction in the fact that two objects remain at the same place at two different points of time, or that two objects remain at two different places at one and the same point of time. Thus there is nothing to prove that the objects we perceive are all false, and the objects are by nature pure being only.

Again, it has been urged that experience or intuition (e.g. as involved in perception) is self-revealing (*svayaṃ-prakāśa*); but this is true only with reference to a perceiver at the particular time of his perception. No intuition is absolutely self-revealing. The experience of another man does not reveal anything to me, nor does a past experience of mine reveal anything to me now; for with reference to a past experience of mine I only say "I knew it so before," not "I know it now." It is also not true that no experience can be further experienced; for I can remember my own past experience or can be aware of it, as I can be aware of the awareness of other persons; and, if the fact that one awareness can be the object of another would make it cease from being an experience or intuition (*saṃvid* or *anubhūti*), then there would be no *anubhūti* or experience at all. If a man could not be aware of the experiences of others, he could use no speech to express himself or understand the speech of other people, and all speech and language would be useless. That jug, etc., are not regarded as intuition or experience is simply because their nature is altogether different therefrom and not because they can be objects of cognition or experience; for that would be no criterion at all.

It is again urged that this intuition or experience (*anubhūti* or *saṃvid*) is never produced, since we do not know any stage when it was not in existence (*prāg-abhāvādy-abhāvād utpattir nirasyate*). It is also urged that any experience or awareness cannot reveal any state in which it did not exist; for how can a thing reveal its own absence, since it cannot exist at the time of its absence? Rāmānuja, in reply to such a contention on Śaṅkara's side, debates why it should be considered necessary that an experience should reveal only that which existed at the same time with it; for, had it been so, there would be no communication of the past and the future. It is only sense-knowledge which reveals the objects which are existing at the time when the senses are operating and the sense-knowledge is existing; but this is not true with regard to all knowledge. Memory, inference, scriptures, and intuitive mystic cognition (*yogi-pratyakṣa*) of sages can always communicate events which happened in the past or will happen in the future. Arguing in the same way, one could say that even in the case of the experience of ordinary objects such as jug, etc., it can be said that the perception which reveals their presence at any particular time does not reveal their existence at all times. That they are not so revealed means that the revelation of knowledge (*saṃvid* or *anubhūti*) is limited by time. If revelation of knowledge were not itself limited in time, then the objects revealed by it would also not be limited in time, which would be the same thing as to say that these objects, such as jug, etc., are all eternal in nature; but they are not. This sort of argument may also be applied to the revelation of knowledge in inference; and it may well be argued that, since the objects must be of the same type as the knowledge which reveals them, then, if the knowledge is not limited in time and is eternal, the objects also will be eternal. For there can be no knowledge without an object. It cannot be said that at the time of sleep, drunkenness, or swoon, the pure experience is experienced as such without there being an object. If the pure experience were at that time experienced as such, one would remember this on waking; for except in the case of experiences at the time of universal destruction (*pralaya*), and in the period when one's body is not in existence, all that is experienced is remembered. No one, however, remembers having experienced an experience at the time of sleep or swoon, so that no such pure revelation of knowledge exists at that time. What Rāmānuja maintains here, as will be shown later on, is that during sleep or swoon we have a direct experience of the self and not the pure formless experience of the revelation of pure consciousness. Thus there cannot be any state in which knowledge is pure revelation without an object. Hence it cannot be argued that, because knowledge does not reveal the state in which it did not exist, it must always be in existence and never be produced; for as each cognition is inseparably associated with its object, and as all objects are in time, knowledge must also be in time.

Again, the argument that, since knowledge is unproduced, it cannot suffer any further modification or change, is false. Granting for the sake of argument that knowledge is unproduced, why should it on that account be necessarily changeless? The negation preceding a particular production (*prāga-bhāva*) is beginningless, but it is destroyed. So is the *avidyā* of the Śaṅkarites, which is supposed to be beginningless and yet to be suffering all kinds of changes and modifications, as evidenced by its false creations of the world-appearance. Even the self, which is beginningless and destructionless, is supposed to be associated with a body and the senses, from which it is different. This apprehension of a difference of the self from *avidyā* means a specific character or a modification, and if this difference is not acknowledged, the self would have to be considered identical with *avidyā*. Again, it is meaningless to say that pure intelligence, consciousness, experience or intuition (*anubhūti* or *saṃvid*), is pure self-revelation; for, were it so, why should it be called even self-revelation, or eternal, or one? These are different characters, and they imply a qualified character of the entity to which they belong. It is meaningless to say that pure consciousness is characterless; for at least it has negative characters, since it is distinguished from all kinds of material, non-spiritual or dependent objects which are considered to be different from this pure consciousness. Again, if this pure consciousness is admitted to be proved as existing, that must itself be a character. But to whom is it proved? It must be to the self who knows, and in that case its specific character is felt by the self who is aware of it. If it is argued that the very nature of the self-revelation of consciousness is the self, then that would be impossible; for knowledge implies a knower who is different from the knowledge which reveals certain objects. The knower must be permanent in all his acts of knowledge, and that alone can explain the fact of memory and recognition. The consciousness of pleasure, pain and of this or that object comes and goes, whereas the knower remains the same in all his experiences. How then can the experience be identified with the person who experiences? "I know it," "just now I have forgotten it"—it is in this way that we all experience that our knowledge comes and goes and that the phases are different from ourselves. How can knowledge or consciousness be the same as the knower or the self?

It is held that the self and ego or the entity referred to by "I" are different. The entity referred to by "I" contains two parts, a self-revealing independent part as pure consciousness, and an objective, dependent non-self-revealed part as "myself," and it is the former part alone that is the self, whereas the latter part, though it is associated with the former, is entirely different from it and is only expressed, felt, or manifested by virtue of its association with the former. But this can hardly be admitted. It is the entity referred to by "I" which is the subjective and individual self and it is this which differentiates my experience from those of others. Even in liberation I am interested in emancipating this my individual self, for which I try and work and not in a so-called subject-object-less consciousness. If "I" is lost, then who is interested in a mere consciousness, whether that is liberated or not? If there is no relation with this ego, the self, the "I," no knowledge is possible. We all say "I know," "I am the knower"; and, if this individual and subjective element were unsubstantial and false, what significance would any experience have? It is this ego, the "I," which is self-luminous and does not stand in need of being revealed by anything else. It is like the light, which reveals itself and in so doing reveals others as well. It is one whole and its intelligent nature is its self-revealing character. So the self-luminous self is the knower and not a mere revelation. Revelation, cognition or knowledge means that something is revealed to someone, and so it would be meaningless to say that the self and the knowledge are identical. Again, it has been maintained that self is pure consciousness; for this pure consciousness alone is what is non-material (*ajaḍa*) and therefore the spirit. But what does this non-materiality mean? It means with the Śaṅkarites an entity whose nature is such that its very existence is its revelation, so that it does not depend on anything else for its revelation. Therefore, pleasures, pain, etc., are also self-revealing. There cannot be a toothache which is present and yet is not known; but it is held that pleasures and pains cannot be revealed, unless there is a knower who knows them. Well the same would be true for knowledge even. Can consciousness reveal itself to itself? Certainly not; consciousness is revealed always to a knower, the ego or the self. As we say "I am happy," so we say "I know." If non-materiality (*ajaḍatva*) is defined as revealing-to-itself in the above sense, such non-materiality does not belong to consciousness even. It is the ego, the "I," that is always self-revealed to itself by its very existence, and it must therefore be the self, and not the pure consciousness, which stands as much in need of self-revelation as do the pains and pleasures. Again, it is said that, though pure consciousness (*anubhūti*) is in itself without any object, yet by mistake it appears as the knower, just as the conch-shell appears by illusion as silver. But Rāmānuja contends that this cannot be so; for, had there been such an illusion, people would have felt "I am consciousness" as "this is silver." No one makes such a mistake; for we never feel that the knowledge is the knower; but, as a matter of fact, we always distinguish the two and feel ourselves different from the knowledge—as "I know" (*aham anubhavāmi*).

It is argued that the self as changeless by nature cannot be the agent of the act of cognition and be a knower, and therefore it is only the changeful modifications of *prakṛti*, the category of *ahaṅkāra*, to which can be ascribed the capacity of being a knower. This *ahaṅkāra* is the inner organ (*antaḥkaraṇa*) or mind, and this alone can be called a knower; for the agency of an act of cognition is an objective and dependent characteristic, and, as such, cannot belong to the self. If the agency and the possibility of being characterized by the notion of ego could be ascribed to the self, such a self would have only a dependent existence and be non-spiritual, like the body, since it would be non-self-revealing. Rāmānuja, in answer to such an objection, says that, if the word *ahaṅkāra* is used in the sense of *antaḥkaraṇa*, or the mind, as an inner organ, then it has all the non-spiritual characteristics of the body and it can never be considered as the knower. The capacity of being a knower (*jñātṛtva*) is not a changeful characteristic (*vikriyātmaka*), since it simply means the possession of the quality of consciousness (*jñāna-guṇāśraya*), and knowledge, being the natural quality of the eternal self, is also eternal. Though the self is itself of the nature of consciousness (*jñāna-svarūpa*), yet, just as one entity of light exists both as the light and as the rays emanating from it, so can it be regarded both as consciousness and as the possessor of consciousness (*maṇi-prabhṛtīnāṃ prabhāśrayatvam iva jñanāśrayatvam api aviruddham*). Consciousness, though unlimited of itself (*svayam aparicchinnam eva jñānam*), can contract as well as expand (*saṅkoca-vikāśārham*). In an embodied self it is in a contracted state (*saṅkucita-svarūpam*) through the influence of actions (*karmaṇā*), and is possessed of varying degrees of expansion. To the individual it is spoken of as having more or less knowledge[1], according as it is determined by the sense-organs. Thus one can speak of the rise of knowledge or its cessation. When there is the rise of knowledge, one can certainly designate it as the knower. So it is admitted that this capacity as knower is not natural to the self, but due to *karma*, and therefore, though the self is knower in itself, it is changeless in its aspect as consciousness. But it can never be admitted that the non-spiritual *ahaṅkāra* could be the knower by virtue of its being in contact with consciousness (*cit*); for consciousness as such can never be regarded as a knower. The *ahaṅkāra* also is not the knower, and therefore the notion of the knower could not be explained on such a

[1] *Śrī-bhāṣya*, p. 45.

view. It is meaningless to say that the light of consciousness falls on the non-spiritual *ahaṅkāra* through contiguity; for how can the invisible consciousness transmit its light to the non-spiritual *ahaṅkāra*?

Even in sleep one feels the self as "I"; for on waking one feels "I have slept happily." This also shows that during sleep it is the "I" that both knew and felt happy. It has to be admitted that there is a continuity between the "I" before its sleep, the "I" during its sleep, and the "I" after its sleep; for after waking the "I" remembers all that it had experienced before its sleep. The fact that one also feels "I did not know anything all this time" does not mean that the "I" had no knowledge at all; it means only that the "I" had no knowledge of objects and things which it knows on waking. There can be no doubt that the "I" knew during the sleep, since even a Śaṅkarite would say that during dreamless sleep the self (*ātman*) has the direct intuitive perception (*sākṣī*) of ignorance (*ajñāna*), and no one can have any direct intuitive perception without also being a knower. Thus, when after sleep a man says "I did not know even myself, I slept so well," what he means is that he did not know himself with all the particulars of his name, caste, parentage, etc., as he knows when he is awake. It does not mean that he had absolutely no knowledge at all. Even on liberation the entity denoted by "I" (*aham-artha*) remains; for it is the self that is denoted. If there is no one to feel or to know in the state of liberation, who is it that is liberated, and who is to strive for such a liberation? To be revealed to itself is self-consciousness and implies necessarily the knower as the "I" that knows, and therefore the notion of "I" denotes the self in its own nature as that which knows and feels. But the entity denoted by the notion of "I" (*aham-artha*) should be distinguished from the non-spiritual category of mind or the *antaḥkaraṇa*, which is but a modification of *prakṛti* or the false feeling of conceit, which is always regarded as bad and is the cause of the implication of insult towards superior persons and this is clearly due to ignorance (*avidyā*).

The next point of discussion raised by Rāmānuja in this connection, to prove his point that there is no reality which can be regarded as characterless and unqualified in any absolute sense, is in the attempt that he makes to refute Śaṅkara's contention that the scriptures give us sufficient ground for acknowledging such a reality, and their authority is to be considered as the highest and as absolutely irrefutable. Śaṅkara had urged that the testimony of the scriptures was superior to that of perception. But the scriptures are based on the assumption of plurality, without which no language is possible. These are for that reason false. For the superiority that is ascribed to the scriptures was due to their teaching of the doctrine that all plurality and difference are false, and that the reality is absolutely differenceless; but yet since the meaning and the expressions of the scriptures are themselves based on the assumption of difference, how can the teaching of the scriptures be anything but false? Again, since they are as faulty as perception on account of their assumption of plurality, why should they be regarded as having an authority superior to perception? When the scriptures are based on error, what is communicated by them must likewise be erroneous, though it may not be directly contradicted by experience. If a man who is absolutely out of touch with all men has an eye-disease which makes him see things at a great distance double, then his vision of two moons in the sky, though it may not be contradicted by his or any one else's experience, is yet false. So, when there is defect, the knowledge produced by it must be false, whether it is contradicted or not. Hence, *avidyā* being false, the Brahman communicated by it through its manifested forms, the scriptures, must also be false. And one may well argue, that, since Brahman is the object of knowledge produced by means tainted by *avidyā*, it is false, just as the world is false (*Brahma mithyā avidyādy-utpanna-jñāna-viṣayatvāt prapañcavat*). In anticipation of such objections Śaṅkara urges that even false dreams can portend real good or bad happenings, or an illusory sight of a snake may cause real death. Rāmānuja's answer to this is that what is meant by saying that dreams are false is that there is some knowledge, corresponding to which there are no objects; so there is knowledge in illusion and real fear due to such knowledge, but the corresponding external object does not exist. So in these cases also the communication of truth, or a real thing, or a real fact, is not by falsehood, but real knowledge; for no one doubts that he had knowledge in his dream or in his illusion. So far as the fact that there was knowledge in dream is concerned, dreams are true, so that it is useless to say that in dreams falsehood portends real fact.

Thus, from whatever point of view it may be argued, it is impossible to prove that the reality is characterless and differenceless, whether such a reality be pure being, or a unity of being, intelligence and bliss, or pure intuitional experience, and such a contention will so much cripple the strength of the scriptures that nothing can be proved on their authority and their right to supersede the authority of perception can hardly be established. But the scriptures also do not speak of any characterless and unqualified reality. For the texts referring to Brahman as pure being (*Ch.*, VI. 2. 1), or as transcendent (*Muṇḍ.*, I. 1. 5), or where the Brahman is apparently identified with truth and knowledge (*Tait.*, II. 1. 1), can actually be proved to refer to Brahman not as qualityless, but as possessing diverse excellent qualities of omniscience, omnipotence, all-pervasiveness, eternality and the like. The denial of qualities is but a denial of undesirable qualities (*heya-guṇān pratiṣidhya*). When Brahman is referred to in the scriptures as one, that only means that there is no second cause of the world to rival him; but that does not mean that His unity is so absolute that He has no qualities at all. Even where Brahman is referred to as being of the essence of knowledge, that does not mean that such an essence of knowledge is qualityless and characterless; for even the knower is of the essence of knowledge, and, being of the essence of knowledge, may as well be considered as the possessor of knowledge, just as a lamp, which is of the nature of light, may well be regarded as possessing rays of light[1].

Refutation of Śaṅkara's *avidyā*.

It is urged by Śaṅkara that the self-luminous differenceless one reality appears as the manifold world through the influence of defect (*doṣa*). This defect, called *avidyā*, hides its own nature and produces various appearances and can neither be described as being nor as non-being: for it cannot be being, since then the illusion and the realization of its being an error would be inexplicable, and it cannot be non-being since then the world-appearance, as well as its realization as being wrong, would be inexplicable.

[1] *jñāna-svarūpasyaiva tasya jñānā-śrayatvaṃ maṇi-dyumaṇi-pradīpā-divad ity uktam eva. Śrī-bhāṣya*, p. 61.

The above is based on the discussions in the *Śrī-bhāṣya* known as *mahā-pūrva-pakṣa* and *mahā-siddhānta*. *Śrī-bhāṣya*, p. 10 *et seq.*

Rāmānuja, in refuting *avidyā*, says that this *avidyā* is impossible since it must lean on some other thing for its support (*āśraya*), and it is clear that individual souls cannot be its support, since they themselves are regarded as being the products of *avidyā*. The Brahman also cannot be its support; for it is self-luminous consciousness and is hence opposed to *avidyā*, which is regarded as being liable to be recognized as illusory as soon as the true knowledge dawns. It cannot be argued that it is only the knowledge that Brahman is of the nature of pure knowledge, and not pure knowledge forming the essence of Brahman, that destroys *avidyā*; for there is no difference between these two, between knowledge as the essence of Brahman and knowledge as removing *avidyā*. The nature of Brahman that is revealed by the knowledge that Brahman is of the nature of pure knowledge is already present in His pure self-luminous nature, which must necessarily on that account destroy *avidyā*[1]. Moreover, in accordance with Śaṅkara's view, Brahman, being of the nature of pure intuition, cannot further be the object of any other knowledge, and hence the nature of Brahman should not be further the object of any other concept. So, if knowledge is to be opposed to ignorance or *avidyā*, it must be in its own essence as it is, in itself, and so Brahman, as pure knowledge, ought to be opposed to *avidyā*. Moreover, to say that Brahman, which is of the nature of pure self-illumination, is hidden by *avidyā* is to say that the very nature of Brahman is destroyed (*svarūpa-nāśa*); for, since pure self-illumination is never produced, its concealment can only mean that it is destroyed, since it has no other nature than pure self-illumination. Again, if the contentless pure self-luminous intuition is said to assume diverse forms on account of the defect of *avidyā*, which is supported by it, then the question may be asked, whether this defect is real or unreal. If it is real, then the monism fails, and, if it is unreal, then the question arises, how is this unreal defect brought about? If it is brought about by some other defect, then, that also being unreal, the same question will again arise, and hence there will be a vicious infinite (*anavasthā*). If it is held that even without any real basis one unreal defect may be the cause of another unreal defect and so on in a beginningless series, then we

[1] Sudarśana Sūri says here that, if there is such a difference between Brahman as essence and Brahman as destroying *avidyā*, that would mean that one form of Brahman is different from its other form, or, in other words, that it is qualified. *Śruta-prakāśikā*, Pandit edition, Benares, vol. IX, p. 658.

virtually have nihilism (*Mādhyamika-pakṣa* or *Śūnya-vāda*)[1]. If, to escape these criticisms, it is held that the defect is the very essence of intuition (*anubhūti*) or Brahman, then, Brahman being eternal, the defect also will be eternal, and emancipation, or the cessation of the world-appearance, will never take place. Again, this *avidyā* is said to be indefinable, being different from both the existent and the non-existent (*sad-asad-vilakṣana*). But how can this be? A thing must be either existing or not existing; how can there be anything which is neither existing nor not-existing?

Referring to the arguments of the Śaṅkarites in favour of the existence of *ajñāna* (nescience) as a positive entity and as directly perceived in such perceptions as "I am ignorant," "I do not know myself or any others," Rāmānuja says that such perceptions refer only to the non-existence of the knowledge of an object prior to its apprehension (*prāga-bhāva*). Rāmānuja argues that the ignorance perceived cannot refer to its specific and determinate object; for, if it did, then the object would be known and there would be no ignorance at all; and if the *ajñāna* does not refer to any specific object, how can the *ajñāna* or ignorance, standing by itself, be perceived or realized? If it is urged that *ajñāna* refers to indistinct (*a-viśada-svarūpa*) knowledge, then also it may be said that this

[1] Sudarśana Sūri here points out that the Śaṅkarites try to evade the vicious infinite in three ways: firstly, those who think that ignorance (*avidyā*) is associated with *jīva* (*jīvā-jñāna-vādī*) explain it by affirming it so as to involve an infinite series like the seed-and-the-shoot (*vijāṅkura*), but not a vicious infinite; since on their view *jīva* is produced by *avidyā* and *avidyā* is again produced by *jīva* (*avidyāyāṃ jīvaḥ jīvāda vidyā*). Those again who think that *avidyā* belongs to Brahman (*Brahmā-jñāna-vādī*) hold that *avidyā* is by nature beginningless and the irrationality or unreasonableness of its nature is nothing surprising. As regards the beginninglessness of *avidyā* in an infinite series (*pravāha-nāditva*) of *jīva* and *avidyā* and *avidyā* and *jīva* as propounded in the first view of the *jīvā-jñāna-vādins*, the refutation of it by those who hold that the *ajñāna* belongs to Brahman is enough. For they have pointed out that such a view goes against the universally accepted doctrine of the eternity of souls, since it held that the souls came out through *avidyā* and *avidyā* through souls. The other view, that the illusory series is by itself beginningless, is no better; for, if one illusion were the basis of another illusion in a beginningless series, this would be practically identical with the nihilistic philosophy. Moreover, even if the illusion is admitted to be beginningless in nature, then also that must await some other root primary cause (*mūla-doṣāpekṣā*) from which this successive series of illusions springs, and from that another, and so there will arise the vicious infinite. If no such root cause is awaited, the world-appearance may itself be regarded as *avidyā*, and there will be no need to suppose the existence of any root cause as *avidyā*. Again, if *avidyā* is held to be irrational in nature, why should it not affect the emancipated souls and also Brahman? If it is answered that it does not do so because the emancipated souls and Brahman are pure, then that means that this *avidyā* is rational and wise and not irrational. *Śruta-prakāśikā*, in Pandit, vol. IX, pp. 636–665.

may be regarded as the absence of the rise of distinct knowledge. Thus, even if a positive ignorance is admitted, it must somehow be related to something else to which it refers. In whatever way one may attempt to explain *ajñāna* (ignorance), either as want of knowledge, or as other than knowledge, or as opposed to knowledge, it can be made possible only by a knowledge of the very fact of which it will be the opposite. Even darkness has to be conceived as being opposed to light; and hence one must have knowledge of light in order to understand darkness, as being opposed to it. But the *ajñāna* (ignorance) of the Śaṅkarites cannot stand by itself, and so must show its content by a reference to the object or entity of which there is ignorance. Therefore, in the aforesaid experiences, "I am ignorant," "I do not know myself or any one else," it should be admitted that what is felt is this want of rise of knowledge and not any positive ignorance, as the latter is equally found to be relative to the object and the subject and has no advantage over the former. Moreover, the Brahman, which is ever free and ever the same pure self-luminous intelligence, cannot at any time feel this ignorance or *avidyā*. It cannot hide Brahman; for Brahman is pure intelligence, and that alone. If it is hidden, that amounts to the destruction of Brahman. Again, if Brahman can perceive *ajñāna*, it can as well perceive the world appearance; if by hiding Brahman the *ajñāna* makes itself perceived by Brahman, then such *ajñāna* cannot be removed by true knowledge, since it has the power of concealing knowledge and of making itself felt by it. Further, it cannot be said that *avidyā* hides the Brahman only partially; for Brahman has no part. So the above experience of "I did not know anything," as remembered in the awakened state and referring to experiences of deep sleep, is not the memory of *ajñāna* or ignorance directly experienced in deep sleep (*suṣupti*), but an inference during the awakened state of not having any knowledge during deep sleep on account of there being no memory[1]. Inference also is unavailing for proving the existence of any *ajñāna*; for not only would such premises of inference involve a faulty reason, but no proper example could be found which could satisfy the claim of reason by a reference to any known case where a similar thing happens. More-

[1] *ato na kiñcid avediṣam iti jñānaṃ na smaraṇaṃ kintu asmaraṇa-liṅgakaṃ jñanā-bhāva-viṣayam anumiti-rūpam. Śruta-prakāśikā*, p. 178. (Nirṇayasāgar ed. (916).)

over, it is quite easy to formulate other series of inferences to disprove the possibility of such *ajñāna* as is accepted by the Śaṅkarites[1].

Rāmānuja's theory of Illusion—All knowledge is Real.

Rāmānuja says that all illusion may briefly be described as perception in which a thing appears to be different from what it is (*anyasya anyathāvabhāsaḥ*). It is unreasonable to imagine that the illusory content of perception must be due to no cause, or is something wholly unperceived or wholly unknown (*atyantā-paridṛṣṭā-kāraṇaka-vastu-kalpanā-yogāt*). If such a wholly chimerical thing is imagined to be the content of illusory perception, then it must be inexpressible or indescribable (*anirvacanīya*); but no illusory object appears as indescribable; it appears as real. If it appeared as an inexpressible entity, there would be neither illusion nor its correction. So it has to be admitted that in all illusions (e.g. in conch-shell-silver illusion) one thing (e.g. the conch-shell) appears in another form (e.g. silver). In all theories of illusion, whatever may be the extent of their error, they have ultimately to admit that in all illusions one thing appears in the form of another. Speaking against the Śaṅkarites, it may be asked, he urges, how is their inexpressible (*anirvacanīya*) silver produced? The illusory perception cannot be the cause; for the perception follows only the production of the indescribable silver and cannot precede it to be its cause. It cannot be due to the defects in our sense-organs; for such defects are subjective and therefore cannot affect the nature of objective reality or object. Moreover, if it is inexpressible and indescribable, why should it appear under certain circumstances in the specific form of a particular kind of appearance, silver? If it is urged that this is due to the fact of there being a similarity between silver and conch-shell, it may again be asked whether this similarity is real or unreal. It cannot be real, since the content is illusory; it cannot be unreal since it has reference to real objects (e.g. the real silver in a shop). So such a theory of illusion is open to many criticisms.

Rāmānuja seems to have himself favoured the *anyathā-khyāti* theory of illusion, and says that there will be no explanations of contradiction of knowledge involved in illusory knowledge, or of consequent failure of behaviour as suggested by such knowledge,

[1] *Śruta-prakāśikā*, pp. 178–180.

unless error is ultimately explained as the wrongful appearance of one thing as another. He also says that all the other theories of illusion (except possibly the *yathārtha-khyāti* view, as suggested in the *Śruta-prakāśikā* commentary—*yathārtha-khyāti-vyatirikta-pakṣeṣu anyathā-khyāti-pakṣaḥ prabalaḥ*) would ultimately have to accept the analysis of error as the wrongful appearance of one thing as another (*khyāty-antarāṇām tu sudūram api gatvā anyathāva-bhāsaḥ āśrayaṇīyaḥ—Rāmānujabhāṣya*). Rāmānuja further points out that even the *akhyāti* theory of illusion (i.e. illusion considered as being due to the non-apprehension of the difference between the presentation of the "this" of the conch-shell and the memory of silver) is a form of *anyathā-khyāti*; for ultimately here also one has to accept the false identification of two characters or two ideas. Veṅkaṭanātha, commenting on this point in his *Nyāya-pariśuddhi*, says that the appearance of one thing as another is the indispensable condition of all errors, but the non-apprehension of difference must always be granted as an indispensable condition which must exist in all cases of false identification and has therefore the advantage of a superior simplicity (*lāghava*); yet the *anyathā-khyāti* theory gives the proper and true representation of the nature of illusion, and no theory of illusion can do away with the need of admitting it as a correct representation of the phenomenon of illusion. So Veṅkaṭa-nātha says that Rāmānuja, while he agrees with the *anyathā-khyāti* view as a theory of illusion, yet appreciates the superior simplicity of the *akhyāti* view as giving us the indispensable condition of all forms of illusion.

But, though Rāmānuja himself prefers the *anyathā-khyāti* view of illusion, he could not very well pass over the *yathārtha-khyāti* view, as advocated by the senior adherents and founders of the school of thought which he interpreted, viz. Bodhāyana, Nātha-muni and Varada Viṣṇu Miśra. Rāmānuja is thus faced with two different theories, one that he himself advocated and the other that was advocated by his seniors. Fortunately for him, while his own theory of *anyathā-khyāti* was psychological in character, the other theory of *yathārtha-khyāti* was of an ontological character, so that it was possible for one to hold the one view psychologically and the other view ontologically. Rāmānuja, therefore, offers the *yathārtha-khyāti* view as an alternative. Veṅkaṭanātha says that this *yathārtha-khyāti* view can only be put forward as a theory based on scriptural evidence, but cannot be supported as a philosophical theory which can be experienced and therefore as a scientific theory of illusion. We have to make up our minds between the two plausible alternative theories of *anyathā-khyāti* and *akhyāti*.

Rāmānuja, to distinguish the *yathārtha-khyāti* theory of his seniors, whom he refers to by the term "Vedic school" (*veda-vidāṃ matam*), develops this view in a number of verses and says that he understands on the strength of the scriptural texts that the material world was created by the intermingling of the three elements, fire, water and earth, so that in each object there are all the three elements. When a particular element predominates in any material object, it is found to possess more qualities of that element and is designated by its character, though it still holds the qualities of other elements in it. Thus it may in some sense be said that all things are in all things. A conch-shell possesses also the qualities of *tejas*, or silver, and it is on that account that it may be said to resemble silver in some sense. What happens in the case of illusion is that through defects of organs, etc., the qualities or characters in a conch-shell representing other elements are not noticed and hence the perception can only grasp the qualities or characters of silver existing in the conch-shell, and the conch-shell is perceived as silver. So the knowledge of silver in a conch-shell is neither false, nor unreal, but is real, and refers to a real object, the silver element existing in the conch-shell[1]. In this view of illusion all knowledge is regarded as referring to a real object (*yathārtha-khyāti*)[2]. The difference between this view and that of Prabhākara is this, that, while Prabhākara was content with the negative condition of non-apprehension of the difference between the present perception of a glittering conch-shell and the memory of silver in the shop as the cause of the illusion, and urges that knowledge is real either as perception or as the memory, and that illusion has been the result of non-apprehension of the distinction of the two, Rāmānuja is more radical, since he points out that the perception of silver in a

[1] See *Śruta-prakāśikā*, pp. 183–6.

[2] According to Sudarśana Sūri this view is the traditional view (*sāmpra dāyika*) accepted by Bodhāyana, Nāthamuni, Rāma Miśra and others, which Rāmānuja, as a faithful follower of that school, had himself followed. Thus, Rāmānuja says:

yathā-rthaṃ sarva-vijñānam iti veda-vidāṃ matam
śruti-smṛtibhyaḥ sarvasya sarvā-tmatva-pratītitaḥ.

Bhāṣya and *Śruta-prakāśikā*, p. 183.

conch-shell is due to the real perception of the element of silver in a conch-shell and the non-apprehension owing to defects (*doṣa*) of the other elements present in it which would have shown its difference from silver. So what is called the illusory perception of silver in the conch-shell has a real objective basis to which it refers.

Dreams are explained by Rāmānuja as being creations of God, intended to produce corresponding perceptions in the minds of the dreamers. The case of the appearance of a conch-shell as yellow to a person with jaundiced eyes is explained by him as due to the fact that yellow colour emanates from the bile of his eyes, and is carried to the conch-shell through the rays of the eyes which turn the white shell yellow. The appearance of the conch-shell as yellow is therefore a real transformation of the conch-shell, noticed by the eye of a jaundiced person, though this transformation can be noticed only by him and not by other persons, the yellow being very near his eyes[1].

The *akhyāti* and the *yathārtha-khyāti* views agree in holding that the imposed idea has a real basis as its object. But, while the former holds that this real basis is a past presentation, the latter holds that it is given as a presentation along with the object, i.e. the silver element, being mixed up with the conch-shell element, is also presented to the senses, but owing to some defects of circumstances, organs of sight, etc., the conch-shell, which ought to be the main part, is not perceived. Thus, it is only the silver part that forms the presentation, and hence the error. So non-perception of the conch-shell part is common to both the views; but, while the *akhyāti* view holds that the silver part is only a reproduced image of past experience, the *yathārtha-khyāti* view grounds itself on the *trivṛt-karaṇa* texts of the Upaniṣads and holds that the silver part is perceived at the time. But Sudarśana Sūri refers to the views of other teachers (*kecid ācāryāḥ*) and says that the *trivṛt-karaṇa* view may well explain the misapprehension of one element (*bhūta*) for another; but in the cases of misapprehension due to similarity *trivṛt-karaṇa* is not of much use, for *trivṛt-karaṇa* and *pañcī-karaṇa*

[1] Other types of errors or illusions are similarly explained by Rāmānuja as having a real objective existence, the error being due to the non-apprehension of other elements which are objectively existent and associated with the entity which is the object of illusory perception, but which owing to defects are not perceived. See *ibid.* pp. 187, 188.

can explain the intermixture of *bhūtas*, but not of the *bhautikas*, or the later modifications of the five elements into the varied substances such as conch-shell and silver, which are mutually misapprehended for each other on account of their similarity. It has, therefore, to be maintained that in these *bhūta*-modifications also the *trivṛt-karaṇa* principle applies to a certain extent; for here also the molecules or atoms of things or substances are made up of large parts of some *bhūta*-modification and smaller parts of one or more of other *bhūta*-modifications. The conch-shell molecules are thus made up of large parts of conch-shell material and smaller parts of the silver material, and this explains the similarity of the one element to the other. The similarity is due to the real presence of one element in the other, and is called the *pratinidhi-nyāya*, or the maxim of determining similarity by real representation. So in all cases of misapprehension of one thing as another through similarity there is no misapprehension in the strict sense, but a right apprehension of a counterpart in the other object constituting the basis of the similarity, and the non-apprehension of the bigger and the larger part which held the counterpart coeval with it. It is because the conch-shell contains a major part of conch-shell element (*śukty-aṃśa*) and only a minor part of silver that it passes as conch-shell and not as silver. Conch-shell cannot serve the purpose of silver, despite the silver element in it, on account of the obstruction of the major part of the conch-shell element; and it is also on account of this that under normal circumstances the silver element in it is hidden by the conch-shell element, and we say that we perceive conch-shell and not silver. When it is said that this is conch-shell and not silver (*nedaṃ rajataṃ*), the "not silver" has no other meaning than that of the conch-shell, the apprehension of which dispelled the idea of silver. It is the conch-shell that is designated in its negative aspect as "not silver" and in its positive aspect as conch-shell.

Rāmānujācārya, alias Vādihaṃsāmbuvāhācārya, the maternal uncle of Veṅkaṭanātha, seems to support the Rāmānuja method of *sat-khyāti* by showing that all the other three rival theories of illusion, such as that of *anyathā-khyāti*, *akhyāti*, and the *anirvacanīya-khyāti*, cross each other and are therefore incompatible. But he takes great pains to show that the *sat-khyāti* theory may be supported on the basis of the logical implications involved in both the *anyathā-khyāti* and the *akhyāti* types of realism. He starts the discussion by taking for granted the *akhyāti* type of realism and its logical implications. He holds that it also would ultimately lead to *anyathā-khyāti*, and that therefore (excepting the *sat-khyāti*), of all the *khyātis*, *anyathā-khyāti* is perhaps the best. He says in his *Nyāya-kuliśa* that, since the way of knowledge requires that the sense-organs should reach their objects, even in illusory perception there must be some objects which they reach; for they could not convey any knowledge about an object with which they were not in contact[1]. The defect (*doṣa*) cannot account for the production of new knowledge, for it only serves to obstruct anything from being perceived or known. Defects only obstruct the course of the natural sequence of cause and effect[2], just as fire would destroy the natural shooting powers of seeds[1]. Moreover, taking the old example of the conch-shell–silver, it may be asked how, if there was no silver at all objectively present, there could be any knowledge of such an absolutely non-existing thing? Since our awareness cannot refer to non-existing entities, all forms of awareness must guarantee the existence of corresponding objects. What happens in the case of the illusion of conch-shell–silver is that there is memory of silver previously experienced and the "this," which is experienced at the time of the illusion; and it is on account of the defects (*doṣa*) that it is not grasped that the silver is only a memory of past experience, while it is only the "this" in front of us that is experienced at the time (*doṣāt pramuṣita-tadavamarśaḥ*)[3].

Vādihaṃsāmbuvāha, weighing the various arguments of the rival theories of *anyathā-khyāti* and *akhyāti*, deals with the arguments of the *anyathā-khyāti* view which holds that it is the conch-shell that appears as silver. As against the objections raised by such a view in opposition to the *akhyāti* view, viz., if each thing is different from every other thing, how can an illusion be explained as being due to the non-apprehension of the difference between the silver remembered and the "this" perceived directly in experience? Arguing in its favour, he says that the difference which is not

[1] *indriyāṇāṃ prāpya-kāritvena aprāptā-rtha-prakāśana nupapatteḥ. Nyāya-kuliśa*, Madras Govt. Oriental MS. No. 4910.

[2] *doṣāṇāṃ kārya-vighāta-mātra-hetutvena kāryā-ntaro-pajanakatvā-yogāt, na hy agni-saṃspṛṣṭasya kalama-vījasya aṅkuro-tpādane sāmarthyam asti. Ibid.*

[3] *idam iti puro-vastuni anubhavaḥ rajatam iti ca pūrvā-nubhūta-rajata-viṣayā smṛtiḥ. Ibid.*

apprehended here consists of that characteristic which exists in things by virtue of which one thing is not confused with or misapprehended as another thing, and it is the non-apprehension of this differentiating characteristic that causes the misapprehension of the conch-shell as silver (*saṃsarga-virodhi-vaidharmya-viśeṣa-rūpa-bhedā-grahaḥ pravṛtti-hetuḥ*)[1]. But the real objections to holding this *akhyāti* view of illusion to be ultimately sufficient consists in the fact that it cannot do away with the necessity of the synthetic operation (*saṃsarga-vyāpāra*) consisting of a thing being regarded as such-and-such, as found in all discussions of disputants, in all our behaviours and concepts of error and illusion. This forces us to accept the *anyathā-khyāti* view as an unavoidable and ultimate explanation[2]. Vādihaṃsāmbuvāha urges that, since the silver is felt to be in that which is only a piece of conch-shell, this must imply the imposition of the one on the other (which is the essential part of *anyathā-khyāti*). Just as in the real perception of a piece of silver the object before us is experienced as silver, so in the conch-shell–silver illusion, the object before us is experienced as silver,

[1] Madras Govt. MS. No. 4910.

[2] Like the seniors referred to by Rāmānuja, Prabhākara also considers all knowledge to be valid (*yathārthaṃ sarvam eve'ha vijñānam iti*, *Prakaraṇa-pañcikā*, p. 32), though the former does so on ontological grounds and the latter on psychological and experiential grounds. Śālikanātha, representing Prabhākara's view, says that, whatever is the content of awareness, that alone is known, and at the time of the conch-shell–silver illusion, what is known is "this is silver," but there is no knowledge of conch-shell, since it is not the content of awareness at the time. Thus it cannot be said that the illusory knowledge consists of knowing the conch-shell as silver, but of the "this" as silver; for, when there is the knowledge of illusory silver, there is no knowledge of conch-shell. What happens in illusory perception is that through defects the differentiating characteristics of the conch-shell are not apprehended and the conch-shell is perceived only in its general character as an object. Then there is memory of silver, and through a defect in the mental process (*mano-doṣāt*) the silver is not remembered with its original association of time and place as that silver which was perceived there, but is simply remembered as an image of silver (*tad-ity-aṃśa-parāmarśa-vivarjitam*). Though there is no such definite experience that I remember silver, yet the idea of silver has to be admitted to be due to memory; for it cannot be due either to perception or to inference or to any other source of knowledge. Thus, through the elimination of all other sources of knowledge, silver has to be admitted to be due to memory (*ananya-gatitaḥ smṛtir atrā'vagamyate*). On account of the absence of a feeling that I remember a past experience, the memory of silver cannot be distinguished from a percept; for it is only these facts that distinguish a present percept from a reproduced image; and so we fail to differentiate between this memory and the actual perception of some object before us (the differentiating characteristics of which are entirely lost to us through defects of sense-organs or the like). On account of the non-apprehension of the distinction, these two different kinds of awareness themselves produce the illusion of a direct and immediate perception of silver which is not there at the time, and even tempt us to

and here also it is the conch-shell that appears as silver. When the illusion is dispelled, we say that "this is not silver"; this cannot mean the mere presence of the conch-shell, but it must mean the denial of the imposition that was made previously. For, if negations could be treated as positive entities, then there would be no difference between positives and negatives (*bādhyasya vidhi-rūpatve vidhi-niṣedha-vyatyāsaṃ ca niṣedhe bādha iti tulyārthatvāt*)[1]. The *akhyāti* view speaks of non-apprehension of absence of association (e.g. of conch-shell–silver, *asaṃsargāgraha*) to be the cause of illusion. It may well be asked, What is this absence of association? It cannot be the mere thing itself; for, had it been so, we should expect that the thing itself (say the conch-shell) is not perceived and this alone constitutes error, which is impossible. Moreover, the silver is felt to be in front of us as the object we perceive and not as something which we remember. We know that, when we perceive illusorily that "this is silver," there is the perception of a false association (*bādhaka-saṃsarga-grahaṇam*); but the concept of non-apprehension of difference (*bhedāgraha*) never seems to be practically realized in experience. If we inquire into the nature of what constitutes falsity or contradiction (e.g. in conch-shell–silver), we find that it is not the fact that a conch-shell when burnt becomes ash while silver, when burnt, may be made into a finger-ring that constitutes error, but the fact that what was believed to be capable of being rendered into a finger-ring by being put into fire cannot be so done (*yadi tv-aṅgulīyakādi-hetutayābhimatasya vyavahārasya bhasma-hetutvako hy atra viśeṣaḥ*). If this is what is really meant by falsehood, it is nothing but the apprehension of the cause of one kind of action as being another cause (*anya-hetu-vyavahāro 'nya-hetutayāvagataḥ*). This will be *anyathā-khyāti*; for, if even here it is urged to be non-apprehension of difference, then

stretch our hands to pick it up, as if there were a real piece of silver before us. (See *Prakaraṇa-pañcikā*, Ch. IV, *Naya-vīthi*.)

Sudarśana Sūri, commenting on the *akhyāti* view in his *Śruta-prakāśikā* in connection with his commentary on the *yathārtha-khyāti* view of Rāmānuja's seniors, says that the *akhyāti* view has the advantage of superior simplicity or the minimum assumption, viz. that in illusion only an indefinite object is seen, and the distinction between this and the image roused in memory by it is not apprehended. This has to be admitted in all theories of illusion, and in addition other assumptions have to be made.

[1] *Nyāya-kuliśa* of Vādihaṃsāmbuvāha Rāmānujācārya, Govt. Oriental MS. No. 4910.

the experience in such cases of the belief of one thing as another is not explained[1]. In all such cases the final appeal must be made to experience, which attests all cases of illusion as being the appearance of one thing as another[2].

But though Vādihaṃsāmbuvāhācārya thus tries to support the *anyathā-khyāti* view of illusion, yet he does not dismiss the *akhyāti* view of error curtly, but admits that it may also properly explain facts of illusion, when looked at from another point of view. For, if there was not the non-apprehension of difference between silver and conch-shell, the conch-shell could not be mistaken as silver. So, even in *anyathā-khyāti*, there is one element of *akhyāti* involved; for in order that one may behave towards a piece of conch-shell in the same way as one would do to a piece of silver, it is necessary that one should not be able to distinguish between what one sees before one and what one remembers. But, though the negative fact of *akhyāti*, i.e., non-apprehension of difference, may be regarded in many cases as a necessary stage, yet the positive fact of association (*saṃsarga*) or synthesis has to be admitted as an indispensable process, connecting the different elements constituting a concrete perception. The root-cause of all our behaviour and action, being of the nature of synthetic association, it would be wrong to suppose that non-apprehension of difference could by itself be made a real cause of our actions (*na ca mūla-bhūte saṃsarga-jñāne pravṛtti-kāraṇe siddhe tad-upajīvino nirantara-jñānasya pravṛttihetutvam iti yuktaṃ vaktum*)[1]. Although Vādihaṃsāmbuvāha spends all his discussions on the relative strength of *akhyāti* and *anyathā-khyāti* as probable theories of illusion, yet he refers to the view of illusion mentioned by Rāmānuja that all things are present in all things and that therefore no knowledge is illusory. He considers this view as the real and ultimately correct view. But, if this were so, all his discussions on the *akhyāti* and *anyathā-khyāti* theories of illusion would be futile. Vādihaṃsāmbuvāha does not, however, attempt to show how, if this theory be admitted, the other theories of *akhyāti* or *anyathā-khyāti* could be sup-

[1] *yadi cā'trā'pi bhedā-grahaḥ śaraṇaṃ syāt tato'bhimāna-viśeṣa-kṛta-bādha-vyavasthā na sidhyet.* Govt. Oriental MS. No. 4910.

[2] *katham ayaṃ loka-vyavahāro vṛtta iti, na hi kañcid upādhim anālambya loke śabda-prayogo'vakalpyate, tasmād bādhya-bādhaka-bhāvā-nyathā-nupapattyā anyathā-khyāti-siddhiḥ. Ibid.*

[3] *Ibid.*

ported[1]. He further criticizes the *anirvacanīya-khyāti* (illusion as the indescribable creation of, say, the appearance of silver in the conch-shell–silver illusion), a view of illusion as held by the Śaṅkarites, in the stereotyped form with which we are already familiar.

Anantācarya, a writer of the nineteenth century, laid stress on the view of illusion which held that all things were contained in all things, and hence the perception of conch-shell as silver was neither false knowledge nor non-apprehension of the difference between what is perceived and what is remembered; for the perception "this is silver" is a complex of two perceptions, "this" and "silver." Had not this been a case of actual perception, we should not have felt as if we perceived the "this" before us as "silver." The function of *doṣa* (defect) was only to hide the conch-shell part (mixed up with the silver part) from perception. To say that all perceptions have objective entities corresponding to them (*yathārtha*) does not mean that things are as they are perceived, but it means that it is not true that what is perceived has not an objective basis corresponding to it[2]. That sort of *tejas*-substance which forms the material cause of silver certainly exists in the elemental *tejas*, and, the earth-particles forming the material cause of conch-shells being present in the elemental earth-substances, these substances get mixed in the primitive stage of compounding by *trivṛt-karaṇa*, and this explains the presence of the objective substratum of silver in the illusory perception of silver[3]. It is evident, argues Anantācārya, that conch-shell cannot appear as silver; for, since conch-shell is not silver, how can it appear as silver? In order properly to account for the perceptual experience "this is silver," it is necessary to assume that the two constituents, "this" and "silver," of the complex "this is silver" are both perceptually determined; for it is only in this way that one can justify the perception "I perceive this silver."

[1] *yady api bhūtānāṃ pañcīkaraṇa-labdha-paraspara-vyāptyā śuktikāyām api sādṛśyāt rajatai-kadeśo vidyata eva iti siddhāntaḥ tathāpi na vidyata iti kṛtvā cintyate vādy-udāharaṇa-prasiddhy-anurodhāya.* Govt. Oriental MSS. No. 4910.

[2] *tad-viṣayaka-jñāna-sāmānyaṃ viśeṣyāvṛtti-dharma-prakārakatvā-bhāvavad iti yathārthaṃ sarva-vijñānam. Jñāna-yāthārthya-vāda*, MSS. No. 4884.

[3] *yādṛśa-dharmā-vacchinnāt tejo'ṃśād rajatā-rambhaḥ tādṛśa-dharmā-vacchinnānām apy aṃśānāṃ mahā-bhūtātmake tejasi sattvena śukty-ārambhakatā-vacchedaka-dharmā-vacchinnānāṃ pārthiva-bhāgānām api mahā-pṛthivyāṃ sattvena tayoḥ mahā-bhūta-trivṛt-karaṇa-daśāyām eva melanā-sambhavācchukty-ādau rajatā-sad-bhāvo-papatteḥ. Ibid.*

This is an answer to the already noted objection raised by the *Śruta-prakāśikā*.

Failure of theistic proofs.

The existence of God can be known by the testimony of the scriptures (*śāstra-pramāṇaka*), and by that alone. All other proofs which seem to demonstrate the existence of God ultimately fail to do so, since suitable counter-arguments may always be successfully arrayed to destroy the efficacy of such arguments.

God cannot be perceived either by any of the sense-organs or by the mind; for the former can make known only those objects with which they have come in contact, and the latter (excepting in the direct communication of feelings like pleasure, pain, etc.) cannot make external objects known to us without depending on the sense-organs. Further, God cannot be perceived by the special perception of saints (*yogi-pratyakṣa*); for these are of the nature of memory, and do not convey any facts previously unknown through the senses. The saints can perceive only what has been already perceived, though these may not be present to the senses at the time. Objects too small for the senses cannot be perceived; for there cannot be any sense-contact with them. No reason can be perceived by means of which a necessary inference could be drawn regarding the existence of a supreme person who has a direct acquaintance with all things and the power of making them all. The ordinary argument that is offered is from effect to cause—since the world is "effect" (*kārya*), it must have a cause, a maker, who has direct acquaintance with all its materials and their utility and enjoys them. The world is "effect" because, like all effects, it is made up of parts (*sāvayava*); like a healthy human body, therefore, it is under the guidance and superintendence of one person and one alone. But the point is that the two cases are not analogous. The human body is neither produced nor maintained in existence by its superintendent, the soul. The production of the body of a person is due to the *adṛṣṭa* (unseen effects of deeds) not only of that person, but also of beings who are benefited or in some way connected with it. Its existence as connected parts is due to the union of its parts, and does not depend for that on the living person who superintends it. Its existence as living is wholly unique and cannot be found in the case of the world as a whole. The superintendence of one person need not be considered as the invariable cause of all movements; for it is well known that many persons unite their efforts to move some heavy object which could not otherwise be moved.

Moreover, if such a maker of the universe is to be admitted, could not the making of the world be better ascribed to one or more individual souls? They have a direct acquaintance with the materials of the world. It is not necessary that the maker should be acquainted with the inner efficiencies or power of things; for it is enough if the objects containing those powers are directly known. We see also that in all examples of making, such as the making of a jug, a cloth, or the like, the maker is an ordinary human being. Since the inference of the existence of a cause of the world is inspired by these examples, it will be only fair to assume that the maker of the universe belongs to the same class of beings as the makers of the ordinary mundane effects, such as a jug or a cloth. Thus, instead of assuming a supreme being to be the maker of the universe, we might as well assume an individual soul to be the maker of the universe. Hence it is difficult to prove the existence of God by inference. Ordinarily inferences are applied for the knowing of an object which may also be known in other ways, and in all such cases the validity of any inference is tested by these. But in the case of the application of inference for the knowing of God this is not possible; for God cannot be known by any other direct or indirect method. So the application of inference is not of any use here, since there is nothing which can test the validity of the inference or can determine that inference in a particular way and in that way alone. Therefore, since all sorts of inferences can be made from diverse propositions, it is not possible to determine that any particular kind of inference would be more acceptable than any other.

There are some who would still want to support the cosmological argument on the ground that no less than a supreme person, entirely different from the individual persons, could be regarded as the maker of this vast universe; for the individuals cannot have the power of perceiving subtle things, or things which are obstructed from our view, or things which are far away. Thus it is necessary to hold that the maker of the universe must be a being of unlimited powers. From the effect we infer its cause; and again from the nature of the effect we infer the nature of the cause. So, if the cause of the universe is to be inferred, then only such a cause can be inferred as really has the unlimited powers required for producing such an effect. It is irrelevant to infer such a cause as cannot produce it. Also the unessential conditions of ordinary causes need not be imported by suggesting that, just as in the case of ordinary human beings there must be a body and also instruments by which they can operate and produce the effect, so also in the case of the supreme cause it might be expected that He should have a body and should have instruments by which He could operate. This cannot be; for we know that many effects are wrought by sheer force of will and desire (*saṅkalpa*) and neither will nor desire needs a body for its existence, since these are generated not by body, but by mind (*manas*). The existence of *manas* also is independent of the existence of body; for the mind continues to exist even when it is dissociated from body. Since limited beings, who are under the sway of virtue and vice, are unable to produce this manifold universe of such wonderful and diverse construction, it has to be admitted that there exists a supreme person who has done it. Moreover, since the material cause is seen in all known examples to be entirely different from the cause as agent or doer, there cannot be a Brahman which is both the material cause (*upādāna-kāraṇa*) and the cause as agent (*nimitta-kāraṇa*) of this universe.

To this, however, it may be replied that it is admitted that the world is effect and that it is vast, but it is not known that all parts of this vast world originated at one time and from one person. Not all jugs are made at one time and by one person. How can any room be made for an unknown supreme person and the possibility be ruled out that different individual souls, by virtue of special merit and special powers, should at different times create the different parts of the world, which now appear as one unified whole created by one person at one time? It is quite possible that the different parts of the world were created at different times and will similarly be destroyed at different times. To imagine the existence of one such supreme person who could create all this manifold may well be regarded as almost chimerical. From the fact that the world is effect all that can be argued is that it must have been produced by an intelligent being, but there is nothing to infer that it is necessarily the creation of *one* intelligent being. This infinite universe could not have sprung into being at any one moment, and there is no proof that it did so. And, if it came into being gradually, it may well be supposed that there were many intelligent beings who brought it into being gradually. Moreover, God, being absolutely complete in Himself, could not be conceived as having any need to effect such a creation, and He has neither body nor hands with which He could create. It is true that mind does not die with the body, but it is not found in any active state when it is not associated with the body. If it is admitted that God has a body, then He cannot be eternal. If His body could be eternal, though having parts, then on the same grounds the world too might be regarded as eternal. If the world is admitted to have come into being by His mere wish, that would be so strange as to be entirely dissimilar to all known cases of cause and effect. So, if one has to argue the existence of God as cause of the world on the basis of the analogy of known causes and effects as experienced by us, and if such a God is endowed with all the attributes with which He is generally associated, and with strange ways of creating this world, He must be such a cause as could never be inferred on the basis of the similarity of known causes and their modes of creating the effect. Thus, God can never be proved by inference. His existence has to be admitted on the testimony of scriptural texts and of that alone.

Bhāskara and Rāmānuja.

Every careful reader of Bhāskara and Rāmānuja must have noticed that Rāmānuja was largely indebted for his philosophical opinions and views to Bhāskara, and on most topics their doctrines are more or less the same. It is possible that Rāmānuja was indebted for his views to Bodhāyana or other Vaiṣṇava writers, but, however that may be, his indebtedness to Bhāskara also was very great, as a comparative study of the two systems would show. However, the two systems are not identical, and there is an important point on which they disagree. Bhāskara believed that there is Brahman as pure being and intelligence, absolutely formless, and the causal principle, and Brahman as the manifested effect, the world. According to Bhāskara there is no contradiction or difficulty in such a conception, since all things have such a dual form as the one and the many or as unity and difference. "Unity in difference" is the nature of all things. Rāmānuja, however, holds that difference and unity cannot both be affirmed of the same thing. Thus, when we affirm "this is like this," it is not true that the same entity is both the subject and the predicate. For example, when "this" in the above proposition stands for a cow, the predicate "like this" stands for its particular and unique description of bodily appearance. The latter is only the attribute of the former and determines its nature and character. There is no meaning in asserting the identity of the subject and the predicate or in asserting that it is the same entity that in one form as unity is "subject" and in another form as difference is the predicate. Bhāskara argues that the conditions and the conditioned (*avasthā-taadvasthaś ca*) are not wholly different; nor are the substance and its attributes, the cloth and the whiteness, entirely different. There are no qualities without substance and no substance without qualities. All difference is also unity as well. The powers or attributes of a thing are not different from it; the fire is the same as its power of burning and illuminating. So everything is both unity and difference, and neither of them may be said to be wholly reducible to the other. But Rāmānuja maintains that all propositions are such that the predicate is an attribute of the subject. The same attributive view is applicable to all cases of genus and species, cause and effect, and universals and individuals. The "difference" and the "unity" are not two independent forms of things which are both real; but the "difference" modifies or qualifies the nature and character of the "unity," and this is certified by all our experience of complex or compound existence[1]. According to Rāmānuja the affirmation of both unity and difference of the same entity is self-contradictory. The truth of "difference" standing by itself is not attested by experience; for the difference of quality, quantity, etc., always modifies the nature and character of the subject as "unity," and it is this alone that is experienced by us.

Bhāskara urges that, though there is the twofold Brahman as the manifested many and as the unmanifested formless identity of pure being and intelligence, it is only the latter that is the object of our highest knowledge and worship. Rāmānuja, however, denies this formless and differenceless Brahman and believes in the qualified complex Brahman as the transcendent and immanent God holding within Him as His body the individual souls and the world of matter. Regarding the relation of Brahman and the individual souls (*jīva*) Bhāskara says that a *jīva* is nothing but Brahman

[1] *Vādi-traya-khaṇḍana.*

narrowed by the limitations of the mind substance (*antaḥkaraṇopādhy-avacchinna*). When it is said that *jīva* is a part (*aṃśa*) of Brahman, it is neither in the sense of part or of cause that the word "*aṃśa*" is used, but in the technical sense of being limited by the limitation of mind. This limitation is not false or unreal, and it is on account of it that the individual souls are atomic. According to Rāmānuja "difference" is felt as a result of ignorance and the difference is therefore unreal. With Rāmānuja the identity of Brahman with the individual souls is the last word. The apparent difference of imperfection, finiteness, etc., between the individual souls and the perfection and infiniteness of Brahman is due to ignorance (*avidyā*), and is found to be false as soon as the souls realize themselves to be forming the body of Brahman itself. "Difference" as such has no reality according to Rāmānuja, but only modifies and determines the character of the identical subject to which it refers. The subject and its character are identical. Bhāskara considers identity and difference as two modes, both of which are alike independently true, though they are correlated to each other. In criticism of Bhāskara it is said that, if the limitations of Brahman were also true, then they would wholly limit Brahman, since it has no parts, and thus it would be polluted in its entirety. This objection to Bhāskara's view in some of its subtle aspects is made with dialectical skill by Rāmānuja[1]. But it does not appear that it has much force against Bhāskara, if we admit his logical claim that unity and plurality, cause and effect, are two modes of existence of the same reality and that both these forms are equally real. It does not seem that the logical position of Bhāskara has been sufficiently refuted.

Rāmānuja also speaks of Brahman as being identical with individual souls or the material world and yet different therefrom, but only in the sense in which a character or a part may be said to be at once identical with and different from the substance possessing the character or the whole to which the part is said to belong. The individual souls and the inanimate creation cannot stand by themselves independently, but only as parts of Brahman. So from the fact that they are parts of Brahman their identity (*abheda*) with Brahman becomes as primary as their difference (*bheda*), inasmuch

[1] Rāmānuja's *Bhāṣya*, pp. 265, 266, with the *Śruta-prakāśikā*, Nirṇayasāgara Press, Bombay, 1916.

as the substance may be considered to be different from its attributes[1]. The main difference that remains on this point between Bhāskara and Rāmānuja is this, that Bhāskara does not think it necessary to introduce the conception of body and parts, or substance and attributes. According to his doctrine Brahman is immanent and transcendent at the same time, identity and difference can be affirmed of a thing at one and the same time; and this can be illustrated from the cases of cause and effect, or substance and attributes, etc.

Ontological position of Rāmānuja's Philosophy.

The entire universe of wondrous construction, regulated throughout by wonderful order and method, has sprung into being from Brahman, is maintained by Him in existence, and will also ultimately return to Him. Brahman is that to the greatness of which there is no limitation. Though the creation, maintenance and absorption of the world signify three different traits, yet they do not refer to different substances, but to one substance in which they inhere. His real nature is, however, His changeless being and His eternal omniscience and His unlimitedness in time, space and character. Referring to Śaṅkara's interpretation of this *sūtra* (I. I. 2), Rāmānuja says that those who believe in Brahman as characterless (*nirviśeṣa*) cannot do justice to the interpretation of this attribute of Brahman as affirmed in *Brahma-sūtra* I. I. 2; for instead of stating that the creation, maintenance and absorption of the world are from Brahman, the passage ought rather to say that the illusion of creation, maintenance, and absorption is from Brahman. But even that would not establish a characterless Brahman; for the illusion would be due to *ajñāna*, and Brahman would be the manifester of all *ajñāna*. This it can do by virtue of the fact that it is of the nature of pure illumination, which is different from the concept of materiality, and, if there is this difference, it is neither characterless nor without any difference[2].

This raises an important question as regards the real meaning

[1] *jīvavat-pṛthak-siddhy-anarha-viśeṣaṇatvena acid-vastuno brahmā-ṃśatvaṃ; viśiṣṭa-vastv-eka-deśatvena abheda-vyavahāro mukhyaḥ, viśeṣaṇa-viśeṣyayoḥ svarūpa-svabhāva-bhedena bheda-vyavahāro'pi mukhyaḥ. Śrī-bhāṣya*, III. 2. 28.

[2] *jagaj-janmādi-bhramo yatas tad brahme' ti svot-prekṣā-pakṣe'pi na nirviśeṣa-vastu-siddhiḥ, etc. Ibid.* I. I. 2.

of Śaṅkara's interpretation of the above *sūtra*. Did he really mean, as he is apparently stated by Rāmānuja to have said, that that from which there is the illusion of creation, etc., of the world is Brahman? Or did he really mean Brahman and Brahman by itself alone is the cause of a real creation, etc., of the world? Śaṅkara, as is well known, was a commentator on the *Brahma-sūtras* and the Upaniṣads, and it can hardly be denied that there are many passages in these which would directly yield a theistic sense and the sense of a real creation of a real world by a real God. Śaṅkara had to explain these passages, and he did not always use strictly absolutist phrases; for, as he admitted three kinds of existence, he could talk in all kinds of phraseology, but one needed to be warned of the phraseology that Śaṅkara had in view at the time, and this was not always done. The result has been that there are at least some passages which appear by themselves to be realistically theistic, others which are ambiguous and may be interpreted in both ways, and others again which are professedly absolutist. But, if the testimony of the great commentators and independent writers of the Śaṅkara school be taken, Śaṅkara's doctrine should be explained in the purely monistic sense, and in that alone. Brahman is indeed the unchangeable infinite and absolute ground of the emergence, maintenance and dissolution of all world-appearance and the ultimate truth underlying it. But there are two elements in the appearance of the world-phenomena—the ultimate ground, the Brahman, the only being and truth in them, and the element of change and diversity, the *māyā*—by the evolution or transformation of which the appearance of "the many" is possible. But from passages like those found in Śaṅkara's *bhāṣya* on the *Brahma-sūtra*, I. I. 2, it might appear as if the world-phenomena are no mere appearance, but are real, inasmuch as they are not merely grounded in the real, but are emanations from the real: the Brahman. But, strictly speaking, Brahman is not alone the *upādāna* or the material cause of the world, but with *avidyā* is the material cause of the world, and such a world is grounded in Brahman and is absorbed in Him. Vācaspati, in his *Bhāmatī* on Śaṅkara's *bhāṣya* on the same *sūtra* (*Brahma-sūtra*, I. I. 2), makes the same remark[1]. Prakāśātman, in his *Pañca-pādikā-vivaraṇa*, says that the creative functions here spoken of do

[1] *avidyā-sahita-brahmo'pādānaṃ jagat brahmaṇy evāsti tatraiyva ca līyate. Bhāmatī*, I. I. 2.

not essentially appertain to Brahman and an inquiry into the nature of Brahman does not mean that he is to be known as being associated with these qualities[1]. Bhāskara had asserted that Brahman had transformed Himself into the world-order, and that this was a real transformation—*pariṇāma*—a transformation of His energies into the manifold universe. But Prakāśātman, in rejecting the view of *pariṇāma*, says that, even though the world-appearance be of the stuff of *māyā*, since this *māyā* is associated with Brahman, the world-appearance as such is never found to be contradicted or negated or to be non-existing—it is only found that it is not ultimately real[2]. *Māyā* is supported in Brahman; and the world-appearance, being transformations of *māyā*, is real only as such transformations. It is grounded also in Brahman, but its ultimate reality is only so far as this ground or Brahman is concerned. So far as the world-appearances are concerned, they are only relatively real as *māyā* transformations. The conception of the joint causality of Brahman and *māyā* may be made in three ways; that *māyā* and Brahman are like two threads twisted together into one thread; or that Brahman, with *māyā* as its power or *śakti*, is the cause of the world; or that Brahman, being the support of *māyā*, is indirectly the cause of the world[3]. On the latter two views *māyā* being dependent on Brahman, the work of *māyā*—the world—is also dependent on Brahman; and on these two views, by an interpretation like this, pure Brahman (*śuddha-brahma*) is the cause of the world. Sarvajñātma muni, who also thinks that pure Brahman is the material cause, conceives the function of *māyā* not as being joint material cause with Brahman, but as the instrument or the means through which the causality of pure Brahman appears as the manifold and diversity of the universe. But even on this view the stuff of the diversity is the *māyā*, though such a manifestation of *māyā* would have been impossible if the ground-cause, the Brahman, had been absent[4]. In discerning the nature of the causality of Brahman, Prakāśātman says that the monistic doctrine of Vedānta is upheld by the fact that apart from

[1] *na hi nānā-vidha-kārya-kriyāveśātmakatvaṃ tat-prasava-śakty-ātmakatvaṃ vā jijñāsya-viśuddha-brahmāntargataṃ bhavitum arhati. Pañca-pādikā-vivaraṇa*, p. 205.

[2] *sṛṣṭeś ca svopādhau abhāva-vyāvṛttatvāt sarve ca sopādhika-dharmāḥ svāśrayopādhau abādhyatayā satyā bhavanti sṛṣṭir api svarūpeṇa na bādhyate kintu paramā-rthā-satyatvā-ṃśena. Ibid.* p. 206.

[3] *Ibid.* p. 212.

[4] *Saṅkṣepa-śārīraka*, I. 332, 334, and the commentary *Anvayārtha-prakāśikā* by Rāmatīrtha.

the cause there is nothing in the effect which can be expressed or described (*upādāna-vyatirekeṇa kāryasya anirūpaṇād advitīyatā*)[1]. Thus, in all these various ways in which Śaṅkara's philosophy has been interpreted, it has been universally held by almost all the followers of Śaṅkara that, though Brahman was at bottom the ground-cause yet the stuff of the world was not of real Brahman material, but of *māyā*; and, though all the diversity of the world has a relative existence, it has no reality in the true sense of the term in which Brahman is real[2]. Śaṅkara himself says that the omniscience of Brahman consists in its eternal power of universal illumination or manifestation (*yasya hi sarva-viṣayāvabhāsana-kṣamaṃ jñānaṃ nityam asti*). Though there is no action or agency involved in this universal consciousness, it is spoken of as being a knowing agent, just as the sun is spoken of as burning and illuminating, though the sun itself is nothing but an identity of heat and light (*pratatauṣṇya-prakāśepi savitari dahati prakāsayatīti svātantrya-vyapadeśa-darśanāt...evam asaty api jñāna-karmaṇi Brahmaṇas tad aikṣata iti kartṛtva-vyapadeśa-darśanāt*). Before the creation of the world what becomes the object of this universal consciousness is the indefinable name and form which cannot be ascertained as "this" or "that"[3]. The omniscience of Brahman is therefore this universal manifestation, by which all the creations of *māyā* become the knowable contents of thought. But this manifestation is not an act of knowledge, but a permanent steady light of consciousness by which the unreal appearance of *māyā* flash into being and are made known.

Rāmānuja's view is altogether different. He discards the view of Śaṅkara, that the cause alone is true and that all effects are false.

[1] *Pañca-pādikā-vivaraṇa*, p. 221.

[2] Prakāśātman refers to several ways in which the relation of Brahman and *māyā* has been conceived, e.g. Brahman has *māyā* as His power, and the individual souls are all associated with *avidyā*; Brahman as reflected in *māyā* and *avidyā* is the cause of the world (*māyā-vidyā-pratibimbitaṃ brahma jagat-kāraṇaṃ*); pure Brahman is immortal, and individual souls are associated with *avidyā*; individual souls have their own illusions of the world, and these through similarity appear to be one permanent world; Brahman undergoes an apparent transformation through His own *avidyā*. But in none of these views is the world regarded as a real emanation from Brahman. *Pañca-pādikā-vivaraṇa*, p. 232.

Regarding the question as to how Brahman could be the cause of beginningless Vedas, Prakāśātman explains it by supposing that Brahman was the underlying reality by which all the Vedas imposed on it were manifested. *Ibid.* pp. 203, 231.

[3] *kiṃ punas tat-karma? yat prāg-utpatter Īśvara-jñānasya viṣayo bhavatīti. tattvānyatvābhyām anirvacanīye nāma-rūpe avyākṛte vyācikīrṣite iti brūmaḥ. Śaṅkara-bhāṣya*, I. I. 5.

One of the reasons adduced for the falsity of the world of effects is that the effects do not last. This does not prove their falsehood, but only their destructible or non-eternal nature (*anityatva*). When a thing apparently existing in a particular time and space is found to be non-existing at that time or in that space, then it is said to be false; but, if it is found to be non-existing at a different place and at a different time, it cannot be called false, it is only destructible or non-eternal. It is wrong to suppose that a cause cannot suffer transformation; for the associations of time, space, etc., are new elements which bring in new factors which would naturally cause such transformation. The effect-thing is neither non-existent nor an illusion; for it is perceived as existing in a definite time and place after its production from the cause until it is destroyed. There is nothing to show that such a perception of ours is wrong. All the scriptural texts that speak of the world's being identical with Brahman are true in the sense that Brahman alone is the cause of the world and that the effect is not ultimately different from the cause. When it is said that a jug is nothing but clay, what is meant is that it is the clay that, in a specific and particular form or shape, is called a jug and performs the work of carrying water or the like; but, though it does so, it is not a different substance from clay. The jug is thus a state of clay itself, and, when this particular state is changed, we say that the effect-jug has been destroyed, though the cause, the clay, remains the same. Production (*utpatti*) means the destruction of a previous state and the formation of a new state. The substance remains constant through all its states, and it is for this reason that the causal doctrine, that the effect exists even before the operation of causal instruments, can be said to be true. Of course, states or forms which were non-existent come into being; but, as the states have no existence independently from the substance in which they appear, their new appearance does not affect the causal doctrine that the effects are already in existence in the cause. So the one Brahman has transformed Himself into the world, and the many souls, being particular states of Him, are at once one with Him and yet have a real existence as His parts or states.

The whole or the Absolute here is Brahman, and it is He who has for His body the individual souls and the material world. When Brahman exists with its body, the individual souls and the material world in a subtler and finer form, it is called the "cause" or Brahman in the causal state (*kāraṇāvasthā*). When it exists with its body, the world and souls in the ordinary manifested form, it is called Brahman in the effect state (*kāryāvasthā*)[1]. Those who think that the effect is false cannot say that the effect is identical with the cause; for with them the world which is false cannot be identical with Brahman which is real[2]. Rāmānuja emphatically denies the suggestion that there is something like pure being (*san-mātra*), more ultimately real than God the controller with His body as the material world and individual souls in a subtler or finer state as cause, as he also denies that God could be regarded as pure being (*san-mātra*); for God is always possessed of His infinite good qualities of omniscience, omnipotence, etc. Rāmānuja thus sticks to his doctrine of the twofold division of matter and the individual souls as forming parts of God, the constant inner controller (*antar-yāmin*) of them both. He is no doubt a *sat-kārya-vādin*, but his *sat-kārya-vāda* is more on the Sāṃkhya line than on that of the Vedānta as interpreted by Śaṅkara. The effect is only a changed state of the cause, and so the manifested world of matter and souls forming the body of God is regarded as effect only because previous to such a manifestation of these as effect they existed in a subtler and finer form. But the differentiation of the parts of God as matter and soul always existed, and there is no part of Him which is truer or more ultimate than this. Here Rāmānuja completely parts company with Bhāskara. For according to Bhāskara, though God as effect existed as the manifested world of matter and souls, there was also God as cause, Who was absolutely unmanifested and undifferentiated as pure being (*san-mātra*). God, therefore, always existed in this His tripartite form as matter, soul and their controller, and the primitive or causal state and the state of dissolution meant only the existence of matter and souls in a subtler or finer state than their present manifest form. But Rāmānuja maintains that, as there is difference between the soul and the body of a person, and as the defects or deficiencies of the body do not affect the soul, so there is a marked difference between God, the Absolute controller, and His body, the individual souls and the world of matter, and the defects

[1] *Śrī-bhāṣya*, pp. 444, 454, Bombay ed., 1914.

[2] This objection of Rāmānuja, however, is not valid; for according to it the underlying reality in the effect is identical with the cause. But there is thus truth in the criticism, that the doctrine of the "identity of cause and effect" has to be given a special and twisted meaning for Śaṅkara's view.

of the latter cannot therefore affect the nature of Brahman. Thus, though Brahman has a body, He is partless (*niravay ava*) and absolutely devoid of any *karma*; for in all His determining efforts He has no purpose to serve. He is, therefore, wholly unaffected by all faults and remains pure and perfect in Himself, possessing endless beneficent qualities.

In his *Vedārtha-saṃgraha* and *Vedānta-dīpa*, Rāmānuja tried to show how, avoiding Śaṅkara's absolute monism, he had also to keep clear of the systems of Bhāskara and of his own former teacher Yādavaprakāśa. He could not side with Bhāskara, because Bhāskara held that the Brahman was associated with various conditions or limitations by which it suffered bondage and with the removal of which it was liberated. He could also not agree with Yādavaprakāśa, who held that Brahman was on the one hand pure and on the other hand had actually transformed itself into the manifold world. Both these views would be irreconcilable with the Upaniṣadic texts.

Veṅkaṭanātha's treatment of *pramāṇa*.

As the nihilistic Buddhists (*śūnya-vādī* or *mādhyamika*) are supposed to deny the valid existence of any fact or proposition, so the Śaṅkarites also may be supposed to suspend their judgment on all such questions. In the preliminary portions of his *Khaṇḍana-khaṇḍa-khādya*, in answer to the question whether all discussions (*kathā*) must presuppose the previous admission of validity and invalidity as really referring to facts and propositions, Śrīharṣa says that no such admission is indispensable; for a discussion can be conducted by the mutual agreement of the contending persons to respect certain principles of reality or unreality as decided by the referee (*madhyastha*) of the debate, without entering into the question of their ultimate validity. Even if validity or invalidity of certain principles, facts, or propositions, were admitted, then also the mutual agreement of the contending persons to these or other principles, as ruled by the referee, would be an indispensable preliminary to all discussions[1]. As against these views Veṅkaṭanātha,

[1] *na ca pramāṇādīnāṃ sattā'pi ittham eva tābhyām aṅgīkartum ucitā; tādṛśa-vyavahāra-niyama-mātreṇaiva kathā-pravṛtty-upapatteḥ. pramāṇādi-sattām abhyupetyā'pi tathā-vyavahāra-niyama-vyatireke kathā-pravṛttiṃ vinā tattva-nirṇayasya jayasya vā abhilaṣitasya kathakayor aparyavasānāt, etc. Khaṇḍana-khaṇḍa-khādya*, p. 35.

the best-reputed philosopher of the Rāmānuja school, seeks to determine the necessity of the admission of validity (*prāmāṇya*) or invalidity (*a-prāmāṇya*) as naturally belonging to certain proportions or facts, as a preliminary to our quest of truth or objective and knowable facts. If the distinction of valid and invalid propositions is not admitted, then neither can any thesis be established, nor can practical affairs run on. But, though in this way the distinction between valid and invalid propositions has to be admitted on the basis of its general acceptance by people at large, yet their real nature has still to be examined. Those who deny such a distinction can have four alternative views, viz. that all propositions are valid, that all propositions are invalid, that all propositions mutually contradict one another, or that all propositions are doubtful. If all propositions are valid, then the negation of such a proposition is also valid, which is self-contradictory; if they are all invalid, then even such a proposition is invalid and hence no invalidity can be asserted. As to the third alternative, it may be pointed out that invalid propositions can never contradict the valid ones. If one valid proposition restricts the sphere of another valid proposition, this does not mean contradiction. A valid proposition has not to depend on other propositions for making its validity realized; for a valid proposition guarantees its own validity. Lastly, if you doubt everything, at least you do not doubt that you doubt; so then you are not consistent in saying that you doubt everything; for at least in one point you are certain, viz. that you doubt everything[1]. Thus it has to be admitted that there are two classes of propositions, valid and invalid. But, though the general distinction between valid and invalid propositions be admitted, yet proper inquiry, investigation, or examination, is justified in attempting to determine whether any particular proposition is valid or invalid. That only is called a *pramāṇa* which leads to valid knowledge.[2] In the case of perception, for example, those which would lead to valid knowledge would be defectless eyes, mind-contact as attention, proper proximity of the object, etc., and these would jointly constitute *pramāṇa*. But in the

[1] This remark naturally reminds one of Descartes—*sarvaṃ sandigdham iti te nipuṇasyāsti niścayaḥ, saṃśayaś ca na sandigdhaḥ sandigdhādvaita-vādinaḥ. Nyāya-pariśuddhi.* p. 34. Chowkhamba s.s.

[2] A distinction is here made between *karaṇa-prāmāṇya* and *āśraya-pramāṇya* (*pramāśrayasya īśvarasya prāmāṇyam aṅgīkṛtam*). *Nyāya-sāra* commentary on *Nyāya-pariśuddhi* by Śrīnivāsa, p. 35.

case of testimony it is the faultlessness of the speaker that constitutes the validity of the knowledge. The scriptures are valid because they have been uttered by God, Who has the right knowledge of things. The validity of the Vedas is not guaranteed by absence of defect in our instruments of knowledge. Whatever that may be, the ultimate determination of *pramāṇa* is through *pramā*, or right knowledge. That by which one can have right knowledge is *pramāṇa*. Vedas are valid, because they are uttered by God, Who has right knowledge. So it is the rightness of knowledge that ultimately determines the validity of *pramāṇa*[1].

Vātsya Śrīnivāsa, a successor of Veṅkaṭanātha of the Rāmānuja school, defines *pramāṇa* as the most efficient instrument amongst a collocation of causes forming the immediate, invariable and unconditional antecedents of any right knowledge (*pramā*). Thus, in the case of perception, for example, the visual organ is a *pramāṇa* which leads to right visual knowledge, through its intermediary active operation (*avāntara-vyāpāra*)—the sense-contact of the eye with its objects[2]. Jayanta, the celebrated Nyāya writer, had, however, expressed a different view on the point in his *Nyāya-mañjarī*. He held that no member in a collocation of causes producing the effect could be considered to be more efficient or important than the other members. The efficiency (*atiśaya*) of the causal instruments means their power of producing the effect, and that power belongs to all the members jointly in the collocation of causes; so it is the entire collocation of causes producing right knowledge that is to be admitted as its instrument or *pramāṇa*[3]. Even subject and object cannot be regarded as more important; for they manifest themselves only through the collocating causes producing the desired relation between the subject and the object[4]. With Nyāya this

[1] *karaṇa-prāmāṇyasya āśraya-prāmāṇyasya ca jñāna-prāmāṇyā-dhīna-jñānatvāt tad ubhaya-prāmāṇya-siddhy-artham api jñāna-prāmāṇyam eva vicāraṇīyam. Nyāya-sāra*, p. 35.

[2] *pramā-karaṇaṃ pramāṇam ity uktam ācāryaiḥ siddhānta-sāre pramotpādaka-sāmagrī-madhye yad atiśayena pramā-guṇakaṃ tat tasyāḥ kāraṇam; atiśayaś ca vyāpāraḥ, yad dhi yad janayitvaiva yad janayet tat tatra tasyāvāntara-vyāpāraḥ. sākṣātkāri-pramāyā indriyaṃ kāraṇam indriyā-rtha-saṃyogo 'vāntara-vyāpāraḥ.* Rāmānuja, *Siddhānta-saṃgraha*. Govt. Oriental MS. No. 4988.

[3] *sa ca sāmagry-antar-gatasya na kasyacid ekasya kārakasya kathayituṃ pāryate, sāmagryās tu so'tiśayaḥ suvacaḥ sannihitā cet sāmagrī sampannam eva phalam iti. Nyāya-mañjarī*, p. 13.

[4] *sākalya-prasāda-labdha-pramiti-sambandha-nibandhanaḥ pramātṛ-prameyayor mukhya-svarūpa-lābhaḥ. Ibid.* p. 14.

collocation of causes consists of ideational and non-ideational (*bodhābodha-svabhāva*) factors[1].

If the view of the *Vedānta-paribhāṣā* is to be accepted, then the Śaṅkarite view also is very much like the Rāmānuja view on this point; for both Dharmarājādhvarīndra and Rāmakṛṣṇa agree in defining *pramāṇa* as the instrument of right knowledge. In the case of visual perception or the like the visual or the other sense organs are regarded as *pramāṇa*; and the sense-contact is regarded as the operation of this instrument.

The difference between the Nyāya view and the Rāmānuja view consists in this, that, while the Nyāya gives equal importance to all members of the collocation, the Rāmānuja view distinguishes that only as the instrumental cause which is directly associated with the active operation (*vyāpāra*). Even the Śaṅkarites agree with such a productive view of knowledge; for, though they believe consciousness to be eternal and unproduced, yet they also believe the states of consciousness (*vṛtti-jñāna*) to be capable of being produced. Both the Rāmānuja and the Śaṅkara beliefs accept the productive view of knowledge in common with the Nyāya view, because with both of them there is the objective world standing outside the subject, and perceptual knowledge is produced by the sense-organs when they are in operative contact with the external objects. A distinction, however, is made in the Rāmānuja school between *kāraṇa* (cause) and *karaṇa* (important instrument), and that cause which is directly and intimately associated with certain operations leading to the production of the effect is called a *karaṇa*[2]. It is for this reason that, though the Rāmānuja view may agree regarding the *sāmagrī*, or collocation as causes, in some sense it regards only the sense-organ as the chief instrument; the others are accessories or otherwise helpful to production.

There are Buddhists also who believe that it is the joint collocation of mental and extra-mental factors of the preceding moment which produce knowledge and external events of the later moment; but they consider the mental factors to be directly producing knowledge, whereas the extra-mental or external objects are mere accessories or exciting agents. Knowledge on this view is determined

[1] *bodhā-bod a-svabhāvā sāmagrī pramāṇam. Nyāya-mañjarī*, p. 15.

[2] *tat-kāraṇānāṃ madhye yad atiśayena kāryotpādakaṃ tat karaṇam. Rāmānuja-siddhānta-saṃgraha.* Govt. Oriental MS. No. 4988.

a priori from within, though the influence of the external objects is not denied. With reference to the operation of causality in the external world, they believe that, though the mental elements of the present moment influence them as accessories, immediate causal operation is to be sought among the external objects themselves. The mental and extra-mental elements of the preceding moment jointly determine every phenomenon of the later moment in the world, whether mental or physical; but in the determination of the occurrence of knowledge, the mental factors predominate, and the external factors are accessories. In the determination of external phenomena mental elements are accessories and the external causes are immediate instruments. Thus, in the production of knowledge, though the specific external objects may be regarded as accessory causes, their direct and immediate determinants are mental elements[1].

The idealistic Buddhists, the *vijñāna-vādins*, who do not distinguish between ideas and their objects, consider that it is the formless ideas that assume different forms as "blue," "red," etc.; for they do not believe in any external objects other than these ideas, and so it is these ideas in diverse forms and not the sense-organs or other collocations which are called *pramāṇas*. No distinction is here made between *pramāṇa* and *pramāṇa-phala* or the result of the process of *pramāṇa*[2]. They, however, fail to explain the difference that exists between the awareness and its object.

The *Mīmāṃsaka* school of Kumārila thinks that, following the soul-sense-mind-object contact, there is a process or an act (*jñāna-vyāpāra*) which, though not directly perceived, has to be accepted as an operation which immediately leads to the manifestation of objects of knowledge (*artha-dṛṣṭatā* or *viṣaya-prakāśatā*). It is this unperceived, but logically inferred, act of knowledge or *jñāna-*

[1] *jñāna-janmani jñānam upādāna-kāraṇam arthaḥ sahakāri-kāraṇam artha-janmani ca artha upādāna-kāraṇaṃ jñānaṃ sahakāri-kāraṇam. Nyāya-mañjarī*, p. 15.

The objection against this view as raised by Jayanta is this, that, if both mental and physical entities and events are determined by the joint operation of mental-physical entities of the preceding moments, we ask what determines the fact that one is mental and the other physical, that one is perceiver and the other perceived.

[2] *nirākārasya bodha-rūpasya nīla-pītādy-aneka-viṣaya-sādhāraṇatvād janakatvasya ca cakṣur-ādāv api bhāvenā'tiprasaṅgāt tad-ākāratva-kṛtam eva jñāna-karma-niyamam avagacchantaḥ sākāra-vijñānaṃ pramāṇam. . .arthas tu sākāra-jñāna-vādino na samasty eva. Ibid.* p. 16.

vyāpāra that is called *pramāṇa*[1]. Jayanta, of course, would not tolerate such an unperceived operation or act of knowledge; for, according to Nyāya, the only kind of action that is accepted is the molecular motion or vibration (*parispanda* or *calana*) produced by a collocation of causes (*kāraka-cakra*)[2].

The Jains, however, repudiate the idea of the combined causality of the collocation, or of any particular individual cause such as any sense-organ, or any kind of sense-contact with reference to sense-knowledge, or of any other kind of knowledge. Thus Prabhācandra contends in his *Prameya-kamala-mārtaṇḍa* that none of the so-called individual causes or collocations of causes can lead to the production of knowledge. For knowledge is wholly independent and self-determined in leading us to our desired objects or keeping us away from undesirable objects, and in no sense can we attribute it to the causal operation of the sense-organs or collocations of sense-organs and other entities. Thus knowledge (*jñāna*) should itself be regarded as *pramāṇa*, leading us to our desired objects[3].

The whole point in these divergent views regarding *pramāṇas* consists in the determination of the nature of the relation of the sense-organs, the objects and other accessory circumstances to the rise of knowledge. As we have seen, knowledge is in the Rāmānuja view regarded as the product of the operation of diverse causal entities, among which in the case of sense-perception the sense-organs play the most important, direct and immediate part. Both the Jains and the idealistic Buddhists (though they have important and most radical differences among themselves) agree in holding the view of self-determination of knowledge independent of the sense-organs or the operation of objective entities which become the objects of knowledge and are revealed by it.

1 *nānyathā hy artha-sadbhāvo dṛṣṭaḥ sann upapadyate*
jñānaṃ cennetyataḥ paścāt pramāṇam upajāyate.
Śloka-vārttika, *Śūnya-vāda*, 178.

Jayanta also says *phalānumeyo jñāna-vyāpāro jñānādi-śabda-vācyaḥ pramāṇam*. *Nyāya-mañjarī*, p. 17.

2 *tasmāt kāraka-cakreṇa calatā janyate phalam,*
na punaś calanād anyo vyāpāra upalabhyate. *Ibid.* p. 20.

3 *tato'nya-nirapekṣatayā svārtha-paricchinnaṃ sādhakatamatvāt jñānam eva pramāṇam*. *Prameya-kamala-mārtaṇḍa*, p. 5.

Veṅkaṭanātha's treatment of Doubt.

Veṅkaṭanātha defines doubt as the appearance of two or more alternatives (which are in themselves incompatible) owing to the non-perception of their specific contradictory qualities and the perception of some general characteristics common to them both; e.g. when a tall thing only is seen, which may be either a man or a stump, both of which it could not be, they being entirely different from one another. So the two alternatives are not to be entirely different, and from what is seen of the object it cannot be known that it must be the one and not the other, and this causes the doubt. Veṅkaṭanātha tries to justify this analysis of doubt by referring to other earlier authorities who regarded doubt as an oscillating apprehension in which the mind goes from one alternative to another (*dolā-vegavad atra sphuraṇa-kramaḥ*), since it would be contradictory that the same object should be two different things at the same time. The author of the *Ātma-siddhi* has therefore described it as the loose contact of the mind with two or more things in quick succession (*bahubhir-yugapad a-dṛḍha-saṃyogaḥ*). Doubt may arise either from the apprehension of common characteristics—such as from tallness, whether the object perceived be a tree-stump or a man—or from not having been able to decide between the relative strength of the various opposite and different possibilities suggested by what is perceived or otherwise known (*a-gṛhyamāna-bala-tāratamya-viruddhā-neka-jñāpako-pasthāpanam iha-vipratipattiḥ*). So, whenever there are two or more possibilities, none of which can be ruled out without further verification, there is doubt[1].

[1] The Nyāya analysis of doubt, as found in *Vātsyāyana's bhāṣya*, I. II. 23, is as follows: When the common characteristics of two possible things are noticed, but not the specific quality which would decide for the one or the other, the anguish of the mind in determining or deciding in favour of the one or the other is called doubt. Doubt may also arise from conflicting opinions (*vipratipatteḥ*), e.g., some say that there is a soul, while others hold that there is no soul. Doubt may also arise from the perception of determining qualities (production through division, *vibhāgajatva*) which a thing (e.g. sound) has in common with other things (e.g. substance, attributes, and actions). Doubt may arise from perception of things which may be illusorily perceived even when non-existent (e.g. water in mirage), out of a desire for certainty and also from a non-perception of things (which may yet be there, though non-evident), out of a desire to discover some traits by which one could be certain whether the thing was there or not. The special contribution of Veṅkaṭanātha consists in giving a general analysis of doubt as a state of the mind instead of the specification of the five specific forms of doubt. Veṅkaṭanātha points out that doubt need not be of five kinds only but

Thus, doubt arises between a true and a false perception as when I perceive a face in the mirror, but do not know whether it is a real face or not until it is decided by an attempt to feel it by touch. So, between valid and invalid inference, when I judge from smoke that the hill is on fire, and yet through not perceiving any light doubt that it is on fire; between opposition of scriptural texts, "*jīva* has been said to be different from Brahman and to be one with it," whether then the *jīva* is different from Brahman or one with it; between conflicting authorities (e.g. the *Vaiśeṣika* philosophers and the Upaniṣadic doctrines) such as "are the senses material or are they the products of the ego?" Between perception and inference (e.g. in the case of the illusory perception of yellow conch-shell, the perceiving of it as yellow and the inferring that it could not be yellow because it is a conch-shell and hence the doubt, whether the conch-shell is white or yellow, and so forth).

In referring to the view of Varadanārāyaṇa in his *Prajñā-paritrāṇa*, Veṅkaṭanātha says that the threefold division of doubt that he made, due to perception of common characteristics, apprehension of different alternatives, and the opposition of scholars and authorities, is in imitation of the Nyāya ways of looking at doubt[1], for the last two forms were essentially the same. Veṅkaṭanātha further refutes the Nyāya view of doubt in which Vātsyāyana, in explaining *Nyāya-sūtra*, I. II. 23, says that there can be doubt even from special distinguishing qualities. Thus, earth has smell as a distinctive characteristic which is not possessed either by eternal substances, such as self, or by non-eternal substances, such as water, etc.; and there can naturally be a doubt whether earth, being different from eternal substances, is non-eternal, or whether, being different from non-eternal substances, it is eternal. Veṅkaṭanātha points out that here doubt does not take place owing to the fact that earth possesses this distinguishing quality. It is simply because the possession of smell is quite irrelevant to the determination of eternity or non-eternity, as it is shared by both eternal and non-

can be of many kinds which, however, all agree in this, that in all states of doubt there is an oscillation of the mind from one alternative to another, due to the indetermination of the relative strength of the different possible alternatives on account of the perception of merely certain common characteristics without their specific determining and decisive features.

1 *sādhāraṇā-kṛter dṛṣṭyā'nekā-kāra-grahāt tathā*
vipaścitāṃ vivādāc ca tridhā saṃśaya iṣyate.
Prajñā-paritrāṇa, quoted in *Nyāya-pariśuddhi*, p. 62.

eternal substances. Doubt would continue until a distinguishing characteristic, such as is possessed by eternal or non-eternal substances alone, is found in earth (*vyatireki-nirūpaṇa-vilambāt*), on the strength of which it could be determined whether it is eternal or not. Veṅkaṭanātha, in various illustrations, shows that doubt consists essentially of an oscillation of the mind, due to indecision between two possible alternatives. He would admit even such inquiries as "What may be the name of this tree?" as doubt, and not mere indecision or want of knowledge (*an-adhyavasāya*). Such inquiries can rightly be admitted as doubts; for they involve doubt regarding two or more alternative names, which are vaguely wavering in the mind and which are followed by a desire to settle or decide in favour of one or the other. So here also there is a want of settlement between two alternatives, due to a failure to find the determining factor (*avacchedakā-darśanāt an-avacchinna-koṭi-viśeṣaḥ*). Such a state of oscillation might naturally end in a mental reckoning in favour of or against the possible or probable alternatives, which is called *ūha* (but which must be distinguished from *ūha* as ***tarka*** in connection with inference), which leads to the resolution of doubt into probability[1]. However, Anantārya, a later writer of the Rāmānuja school, further described doubt as being a state of mind in which one perceived only that something lay before him, but did not notice any of its specific features, qualities or characters (***puro-vṛtti-mātram a-gṛhīta-viśeṣaṇam anubhūyate***). Only the two alternatives (e.g. "a tree stump or a man"—***sthāṇu-puruṣau***) are remembered. According to the *Sarvārtha-siddhi*, the imperfect observation of something before us rouses its corresponding subconscious impression (*saṃskāra*), which, in its turn, rouses the subconscious impressions leading to the simultaneous revival in one sweep of memory of the two possible alternatives of which neither could be decided upon[2]. The point disputed in this connection is between a minority party of interpreters, who think that the perception of something in front of us rouses an impression which in its turn rouses two different subconscious impressions leading to

[1] *ūhas tu prāyaḥ puruṣeṇā'nena bhavitavyam ity-ādi-rūpa eka-koṭi-saha-carita-bhūyo-dharma-darśanād anudbhūtā-nya-koṭikaḥ sa eva.*

Nyāya-pariśuddhi, p. 68. Chowkhamba.

[2] *puro-vṛtty-anubhava-janita-saṃskāreṇa koṭi-dvayo-pasthiti-hetu-saṃskārā-bhyāṃ ca yugapad-eka-smaraṇaṃ saṃśaya-sthale svīkriyata iti sarvā-rtha-siddhau uktam.* Anantārya's *Jñāna-yāthārthya-vāda*. Govt. Oriental MS. No. 4884.

one memory joining up the two alternative entities (e.g. tree-stump and man), and a majority party, who think that the perception of something in front of us leads directly to the memory of two different alternatives, which is interpreted as doubt. The former view, by linking up the two memories in one act of knowledge, supposes the oscillating movement to be one act of judgment and so holds the opinion that in doubt also there is the false substitution of one judgment for another, which is in accordance with the *anyathā-khyāti* (illegitimate substitution of judgments) theory of illusion. The latter view, which holds that there are two separate memories of the two possible alternatives, interprets Rāmānuja as an upholder of realism of knowledge (*jñāna-yāthārthya-vāda*), or the view that whatever is known or perceived has an objective and a real basis.

Error and Doubt according to Veṅkaṭanātha.

Error is defined by Veṅkaṭanātha as occurring when one or more incompatible characters are predicted of an entity without any notion of their incompatibility or contradictions. It is generally due to a wrong psychological tendency in association with other vicious perceptual data, as in the case of the perception of the conch-shell as yellow, the perception of one big moon as small and two, the relativistic (*anekānta*) assertion of contradictory predicates with reference to one thing or the predication of both reality and unreality in regard to world-appearance by the Śaṅkarites[1]. Doubt, on the other hand, occurs when a perceived characteristic is not incompatible in predication with regard to two or more entities which are felt to be exclusive and opposed to one another, and which therefore cannot both at the same time be affirmed. This state is therefore described by some as an oscillatory movement of the mind from one pole to another. Decision results from a unipolar and firm direction of mind to one object; doubt results from a multipolar oscillation, as has been set forth in the *Ātma-siddhi*. Absence of firmness of the direction of the mind is due to the natural constitution of mind, which has necessarily to reject a particular alternative before it can settle down in its opposite. Bhaṭṭārakaguru repeats the same idea in his *Tattva-ratnākara*, when he defines

[1] See *Nyāya-pariśuddhi*, pp. 54–5.

doubt as the association of two contrary or contradictory qualities with any particular entity. Doubt, according to Veṅkaṭanātha, is of two kinds: from *samāna-dharma* and from *vipratipatti*, i.e. when different indications point to two or more conclusions and the relative strength of these indications cannot be conclusively decided. The condition of doubt in the first case is the uncertainty caused by the fact that two contrary possibilities, the relative strength of which cannot be determined on account of certain similar traits (*samāna-dharma-vipratipattibhyām*), claim affirmation. Thus, when we see something tall before us, two possibilities may arise—the tall object may be a man or a post, since both these are tall. When the relative strength of the different sources of knowledge, e.g. perception, illusion, inference, testimony, etc., leading to different conclusions (*a-gṛhyamāṇa-bala-tāratamya*) cannot be determined, both claim affirmation with regard to the same object or conclusion, and doubt arises as to which is to be accepted. Thus, when one sees in the mirror the image of one's face, which is not corroborated by touch, there arises the doubt as to the reality of the reflection. Again, there may be a doubt arising from two possible inferences regarding the existence of fire in the hill from smoke, and its possible non-existence from the existence of light. Again, as there are texts in the Upaniṣads some of which are monistic and others dualistic, a doubt may arise as to which is the right view of the Upaniṣads, and so forth. Doubt may also arise from two opposing contentions, such as those of the atomists and the Upaniṣadists regarding the question as to whether the senses have sprung from matter or from the ego. It may also arise regarding the opposing assertions of two ordinary individuals; between perception (e.g. illusory perception of conch-shell as yellow) and inference which indicates that the conch-shell cannot be yellow; between perception of the self as an embodied being and the scriptural testimony concerning the self as atomic.

Doubt may also arise between inferential knowledge of the world as atomic and the scriptural knowledge of the world as having Brahman as its substance. The Naiyāyikas, however, think that doubt can also arise regarding the two different contentions of opposing parties[1]. Veṅkaṭanātha points out that both the *Nyāya-*

[1] *samānā-neka-dharmo-papatter vipratipatter upalabdhy-anupalabdhy-avy-avasthātaś ca viśeṣā-pekṣo vimarśaḥ saṃśayaḥ. Nyāya-sūtra*, I. I. 23. The in-

sūtra and the *Prajñā-paritrāṇa* are wrong in giving the perception of similar traits (*samāna-dharma*) and of special characteristics (*aneka-dharma*) as two independent reasons for the origin of doubt[1]. The explanation given with regard to the doubt arising from a special characteristic such as odorousness is that, as this characteristic is not possessed by non-eternal substances, one may be led to think of including earth under eternal substances; and, again, as this characteristic is not to be found in any of the eternal substances, one may be led to include earth under non-eternal substances. But the doubt here is due not to the perception of a special characteristic, but to the delay of the mind in determining the ultimate differentia (*vyatireki-nirupaṇa-vilambāt*) which may justify one in including it under either of them. Odorousness as such is not an indispensable condition of either eternality, or non-eternality; so naturally an inquiry arises regarding such common features in eternal or non-eternal substances as may be possessed by the odorous earth and may lead to a classification. The doubt here is due not to the fact that odorousness is a special characteristic of earth, but to the fact that earth possesses such characteristics as are possessed by eternal things on the one hand and by non-eternal things on the other. Even when it is urged that the odorous character distinguishes earth from eternal and non-eternal

terpretation given by Uddyotakara is that in all cases of doubt there are three factors, viz. knowledge of the (1) common or (2) special features, (3) opposite assertions and contending persons associated with a non-determinate state of mind due to the want of definite realization of any of the contrary possibilities, and a hankering to know the differentia. Uddyotakara thinks that doubt can arise not only from a conflict of knowledge, but also from a conflict of opinions of contending persons, *vipratipattiḥ* being interpreted by him as *vādi-vipratipattiḥ*. This view is also held by the *Prajñā-paritrāṇa* by Varadaviṣṇu Miśra, as is evident from the following *śloka*:

sādhāraṇā-kṛter dṛṣṭyā-nekā-kāra-grahāt tathā,
vipaścitāṃ vivādāc ca tridhā saṃśaya iṣyate.
Prajñā-paritrāṇa, quoted in the *Nyāya-pariśuddhi*, p. 61.

This view is criticized by Veṅkaṭanātha as a blind acceptance of the *Nyāya* view.

[1] As an example of doubt arising from perception of similar traits, Vātsyāyana gives the example of man and post, in which the common traits (viz. height, etc.) are visible, but the differentia remains unnoticed. The example given by him of doubt arising from perception of special characteristics is that odorousness, the special character of earth, is not characteristic of *dravya* (substance), *karma* (action), and *guṇa* (quality), and this may rouse a legitimate doubt as to whether earth is to be classed as substance, quality, or action. Similarly, from the special characteristic of odorousness of earth a doubt may arise as to whether earth is eternal or non-eternal, since no other eternal or non-eternal thing has this characteristic.

substances and that this is the cause of doubt, it may be pointed out that doubt is due not to this distinguishing characteristic, but to the fact that earth possesses qualities common to both eternal and non-eternal substances. There are some who think that doubt through *vipratipatti* (i.e. through uncertainty arising from reasoned assertions of contending persons) may also be regarded as a case of doubt from *samāna-dharma* (i.e. perception of similar traits), because the opposed assertions have this similarity amongst themselves that they are all held as true by the respective contending persons. Veṅkaṭanātha, however, does not agree with this. He holds that doubt here does not arise merely on the strength of the fact that the opposed assertions are held as true by the contending persons, but because of our remembering the diverse reasons in support of such assertions when the relative strength of such reasons or possibilities of validity cannot be definitely ascertained. Thus, *vipratipatti* has to be accepted as an independent source of doubt. Doubt arises generally between two possible alternatives; but there may be cases in which two doubts merge together and appear as one complex doubt. Thus, when it is known that one or other of two persons is a thief, but not which of them, there may be a doubt—"this man or that man is a thief". In such a case there are two doubts: "this man may or may not be a thief" and "that man may or may not be a thief," and these merge together to form the complex doubt (*saṃśaya-dvaya-samāhāra*). The need of admitting a complex doubt may, however, vanish, if it is interpreted as a case where the quality of being a thief is doubted between two individuals. Doubt, however, involves in it also an assertory aspect, in so far as it implies that, if one of the alternatives is ruled out, the other must be affirmed. But, since it cannot be ascertained which of them is ruled out, there arises the doubt. There is, however, no opposition between doubt and the assertory attitude; for all doubts imply that the doubtful property must belong to one or other of the alternatives[1].

But there may be cases in which the two alternatives may be such that the doubtful property is not in reality affirmable of either of them, and this is different from those cases in which the alternatives are such that, if the doubtful property is negated of the one,

[1] *sarvasminn api saṃśaye dharmy-aṃśādau nirṇayasya dustyajatvāt. Nyāya-pariśuddhi*, p. 66.

it is in reality affirmable of the other. From these two points of view we have further twofold divisions of doubt. Thus, when a volume of smoke arising from a heap of grass on fire is subject of doubt as being either an elephant or a hill, in this case negation of one alternative does not imply the actual affirmation of the other. Uncertainty (*an-adhyavasāya*, e.g. "what may be the name of this tree?") cannot be regarded as an independent state of mind; for this also may be regarded as a case of doubt in which there is uncertainty between a number of possible alternative names with which the tree may be associated. It seems, however, that Vēnkaṭanātha has not been able to repudiate satisfactorily the view of those who regard uncertainty or inquiry as a separate state of mind. *Ūha* (in the sense of probability such as "that must be a man") does not involve any oscillation of the mind between two poles, but sets forth an attitude of mind in which the possibility of one side, being far stronger, renders that alternative an object of the most probable affirmation and so cannot be classed as doubt. Where such a probable affirmation is brought about through perception, it is included under perception, and when through inference it is included under inference.

Veṅkaṭanātha, following Rāmānuja, admits only three *pramāṇas*, viz. perception, inference, and scriptural testimony. Rāmānuja, however, in his commentary on the *Gītā*[1], includes intuitive yogic knowledge as a separate source of knowledge; but Veṅkaṭanātha holds that intuitive yogic knowledge should be included under perception, and its separate inclusion is due to the fact that the yogic perception reveals a special aspect of perception[2]. Correct memory is to be regarded as a valid *pramāṇa*. It should not be classed as an independent source of knowledge, but is to be included within the *pramāṇa* which is responsible for memory (e.g. perception)[3].

Meghanādāri, in discussing the claim of memory to be regarded as *pramāṇa*, says that memory satisfies the indispensable condition of *pramāṇa* that it must not depend upon anything else for its self-manifestation; for memory, being spontaneous, does not depend

[1] *jñānam indriya-liṅgā-gama-yogajo vastu-niścayaḥ. Gītā-bhāṣya*, 15. 15.

[2] Viṣṇucitta also, in his *Prameya-saṃgraha*, holds that Rāmānuja admitted only three *pramāṇas*.

[3] This view has been supported by Bhaṭṭārakaguru in his *Tattva-ratnākara*. Varadaviṣṇu Miśra, in his *Prajñā-paritrāṇa*, includes *divya* (i.e. intuitive knowledge through the grace of God) and *svayaṃ-siddha* (natural omniscience) as separate sources of knowledge, but they are also but modes of perception.

upon anything else for its manifestation. It is true, no doubt, that the revelation of objects in memory depends upon the fact of their having been perceived before, but the functioning of memory is undoubtedly spontaneous[1]. But it may be argued that, since the objects revealed in memory can never be manifested if they were not perceived before, memory, though partly valid in so far as its own functioning is concerned, is also invalid so far as the revelation of the object is concerned, since this depends on previous perception and cannot, therefore, be regarded as spontaneous manifestation, which is the indispensable condition of a *pramāṇa*. To this Meghanādāri's reply is that the criticism is not sound; for the spontaneous manifestation is also at the same time revelation of the object remembered, and hence the revelation of the remembered object does not depend on any other condition. Memory, therefore, is valid both in its own manifestation and in the revelation of its object. It may be pointed out in this connection that the revelation of knowledge necessarily implies the revelation of the object also. The revelation of the object should not, therefore, be regarded as depending on any other condition, it being spontaneously given with the revelations of knowledge[2].

In many other systems of philosophy the definition of a *pramāṇa* involves the condition that the object apprehended should be such that it was not known before (*an-adhigatā-rtha-gantṛ*), since in these systems memory is excluded from the status of *pramāṇa*. Meghanādāri objects to this. He says that the condition imposed does not state clearly whether the apprehension of the object which is intended to be ruled out should be of the perceiver or of other persons. In the case of permanent objects such as the self or the sky these have all been perceived by many persons, and yet the validity of the perception or inference of the present knower is not denied[3]. It also cannot be said that the object of valid perception or inference should be such that it has not been perceived before by the present perceiver; for when a person seeks to find out an object which he knew before and perceives it, such a perception would be invalid; and similarly, when an object perceived by the eye is re-perceived

[1] *sva-sphuraṇe pramāṇā-ntara-sā-peksatvā-bhāvāt. viṣaya-sphuraṇa eva hi-smṛteḥ pūrvā-nubhūta-bhāvā-pekṣā.* Meghanādāri's *Naya-dyu-maṇi.*

[2] *jñāna-sphūrtivad viṣayasyāpi sphūrtiḥ. Ibid.*

[3] *sthāyitvenā-bhimatā-kāśā-deḥ pūrvair avagatatva-saṃbhavāt tad-viṣayā-numānāder aprāmāṇya-prasaṅgāt. Ibid.*

by touch, the tactile perception will be invalid[1]. The reply is often given (e.g. Dharmarājādhvarīndra in his *Vedānta-pari-bhāṣā*) that, when an object known before is again perceived, it has a new temporal character, and so the object may be regarded as new and thus its later perception may be regarded as valid. Meghanādāri's criticism against this is that, if the new temporal character can constitute the newness of the object, then all objects will be new, including memory. Hence there will be nothing which would be ruled out by the condition that the object must be new (*an-adhigatārtha-gantṛ*).

There are others who hold that the validity of a *pramāṇa* of any particular sense-knowledge, or of inference, is conditioned by the fact of its being attested by the evidence of other senses, as in the case where a visual perception is corroborated by the tactile. These philosophers regard corroboration (*a-visaṃvāditva*) as an indispensable condition of the validity of *pramāṇa*. Meghanādāri criticizes this by pointing out that on such a view the validity of each *pramāṇa* would have to depend upon others, and thus there would be a vicious circle[2]. Moreover, the determinate knowledge of the Buddhists, which is corroborative, would, under the supposition, have to be regarded as a *pramāṇa*.

Unlike Veṅkaṭanātha, Meghanādāri holds that Rāmānuja admitted five *pramāṇas*, viz. perception, inference, analogy, scripture and implication.

Perception is defined by Veṅkaṭanātha as direct intuitive knowledge (*sākṣātkāri-pramā*). This may be regarded either as a special class of cognition (*jāti-rūpa*) or knowledge under special conditions (*upādhi-rūpa*). It is indefinable in its own nature, which can only be felt by special self-consciousness as perception (*jñāna-svabhāva-viśeṣaḥ svātma-ṣākṣikaḥ*). It may be negatively defined as knowledge which is not generated by other cognitions, as in the case of inference or verbal knowledge and memory[3]. Varadaviṣṇu also, in his *Māna-yāthātmya-nirṇaya*, has defined perception as clear and

[1] *sva-viditasyā'rthasya sattvā-nveṣaṇe pratyakṣā-der a-prāmāṇya-prasaṅgāc cakṣuṣā dṛṣṭa-viṣaye dravye sparśanasyā'prāmāṇya-prasaṅgāt.* Meghanādāri's *Naya-dyu-maṇi.*

[2] *pramāṇā-ntarasyā-py avisaṃvā'dā-rthaṃ pramāṇā-ntarā-nveṣaṇenā-navasthā. Ibid.*

[3] *jñāna-karaṇaja-jñāna-smṛti-rahitā matir aparokṣam.* Veṅkaṭanātha's *Nyāya-pariśuddhi*, pp. 70–71. This view has also been supported in the *Prameya-saṃgraha* and *Tattva-ratnākara.*

vivid impression (*pramāyā āparokṣyaṃ nāma viśadā-vabhāsatvam*). Clearness and vividness with him mean the illumination of the special and unique features of the object, as different from the appearance of generic features as in the case of inference or verbal knowledge.

Meghanādāri also defines perception as direct knowledge of objects (*artha-paricchedaka-sākṣāj-jñānaṃ*). The directness (*sākṣāttva*) consists in the fact that the production of this knowledge does not depend on any other *pramāṇas*. It is, no doubt, true that sense-perception depends upon the functioning of the senses, but this is no objection; for the senses are common causes, which are operative as means in the perception of the *hetu*, even in inference[1]. The directness of perceptual knowledge, as distinguished from inference, is evident from the fact that the latter is produced through the mediacy of other cognitions[2]. Meghanādāri criticizes the definition of perception as vivid impression (*viśadā-vabhāsa*), as given by Varadaviṣṇu Miśra, on the ground that vividness is a relative term, and even in inference there are different stages of vividness. Clearness of awareness, "*dhī-sphuṭatā*," also cannot be regarded as defining perception; for all awarenesses are clear so far as they are known. The definition of perception as sense-knowledge is also open to criticism; for in that case it would only apply to indeterminate (*nirvikalpa*) knowledge, in which certain specific characters of the object are imprinted through the functioning of the senses, but which it did not carry further for the production of determinate knowledge (*savikalpa*).

Both Veṅkaṭanātha and Meghanādāri hold that the pure objective substance without any character or universals is never apprehended by sense-perception. Following Rāmānuja, they hold that objects are always apprehended with certain characters at the very first instance when they are grasped by the visual sense; otherwise it is difficult to explain how in the later instance they are apprehended in diverse characters. If they were not apprehended in the first instance, they could not have been known in the later

[1] *indriyāṇāṃ sattā-kāraṇatvena karaṇatvā-bhāvāt. Naya-dyu-maṇi.*

[2] The word *sākṣāttva* is explained by some as *svarūpa-dhī* (its own awareness). But such an explanation is exposed to criticism; for even inferential knowledge reveals some features of the object. If *svarūpa* is taken to mean "nothing but the nature of the object," then the definition would not be applicable even to perception; for perception reveals not merely the object, but also its relation to other objects, and thereby transcends the limit of the object merely as it is.

instance in their fullness in a related manner. So it has to be admitted that they were all grasped in the first instance, but could not manifest themselves in their fullness in the short span of the first moment. In the *Vedārtha-saṃgraha* of Rāmānuja the determinateness of all perceptions has been illustrated by the case of their apprehension of universals at the first moment of perception. This has led some interpreters to think that the apprehension of determinate characters in the first moment of perception applies only to the universals on account of the fact that it involves the assimilation of many individuals in one sweep which must be started at the very first moment in order that it may be manifested in its full form in the second moment. But Meghanādāri holds that the apprehension of other characters also, such as colours, etc., has specific differences when the object is near or at a distance. This involves the grasping of diverse shades of colour in one colour-perception, and thus they also are apprehended at the first moment of perception, on the same grounds which led to the affirmation of the apprehension of universals at the first moment of perception.

It is objected that the concept of determinateness or relatedness (*viśiṣṭatva*) of all knowledge is incomprehensible and indefinable. What exist are the two relata and the relation. The relatedness cannot be identical with them or different; for we do not know "relatedness" as an entity different from the two relata and the relation. Also relatedness cannot be defined either as the manifestation of two entities in one cognition or the appearance of two cognitions without any break or interval; for in a concrete specific illustration, as in such awareness as "jug-and-pot," though two different cognitions have appeared without any break, they have not lost their unique separateness, as may well be judged by the duality implied in such awareness. Thus, there is no way in which the concept of determinateness, as distinguished from that of the relata and the relation, can be arrived at.

To this Meghanādāri's reply is that, in such a sentence as "bring a white cow," the verb refers to a qualified being, the "white cow," and not to the separate elements, "the whiteness" and "the cow." Both the relation and the relata are involved in the determinate conception, the "white cow." In contactual perception, such as "a man with a stick," the contactual relation is directly perceived. The conception of a determinate being is not thus different from the relation and the relata, but implies them. The relations and the relata thus jointly yield the conception of a determinate being[1]. The unifying trait that constitutes determinateness is not an extraneous entity, but is involved in the fact that all entities in this world await one another for their self-manifestation through relations, and it is this mutual awaitedness that constitutes their bond of unity, through which they appear connectedly in a determinate conception[2]. It is this mutual awaitedness of entities that contributes to their apprehension, as connected in experience, which is simultaneous with it, there being no mediation or arresting of thought of any kind between the two[3]. The fact that all our perceptions, thoughts and ideas always appear as related and connected is realized in universal experience. All linguistic expressions always manifest the purport of the speech in a connected and related form. Had it not been so, communication of ideas through our speech would have been impossible.

Nirvikalpa knowledge is a cognition in which only some fundamental characters of the object are noted, while the details of many other characters remain unelaborated[4]. *Savikalpa* knowledge, on the other hand, is a cognition of a number of qualities and characters of the object, together with those of its distinctive features by which its differentiation from other objects is clearly affirmed[5].

On the analogy of visual perception, the perception of other senses may be explained. The relation of *samavāya* admitted by the Naiyāyikas is discarded by the Rāmānuja view on account of the difficulty of defining it or admitting it as a separate category. Various relations, such as container and contained, contact and the like, are revealed in experience in accordance with the different directions in which things await one another to be related; and

[1] *na ca pratyekaṃ viśiṣṭatā-pātaḥ militānām eva viśiṣṭatvāt. Naya-dyu-maṇi.*

[2] *eka-buddhi-viṣayatā-rhāṇāṃ padā-rthānām anyo-nya-sāpekṣa-svarūpatvaṃ militatvaṃ. Ibid.*

[3] *viśiṣṭatva-dhī-viṣayatve ca teṣāṃ sāpekṣatvaṃ ca yaugapadyāt tatra virāmā-pratīteḥ sāpekṣatā siddhā ca. Ibid.*

[4] *nirvikalpakaṃ ca ghaṭā-der anullekhitā-nuvṛtti-dharma-ghaṭatvā-di-katipaya-viśeṣaṇa-viśiṣṭatayā-rthā-vacchedakaṃ jñānam. Ibid.*

[5] *ullekhitā-nuvṛtty-ādi-dharmakā-neka-viśeṣaṇa-viśiṣṭatayā sākṣād-vastu-vya-vacchedakaṃ jñānaṃ savikalpakam. Ibid.*

Veṅkaṭanātha however defines *savikalpa* and *nirvikalpa* knowledge as "*sa pratyavamarśa-pratyakṣaṃ savikalpakam*" and "*tad-rahitaṃ pratyakṣaṃ nirvikalpakam.*" *Nyāya-pariśuddhi*, p. 77.

these determine the nature of various relations which are perceived in sense-experience[1]. Veṅkaṭanātha also points out that the very same collocations (*sāmagrī*) that manifest the awareness of substance and attribute also manifest the awareness of relations; for, if the relations were not grasped at the first moment of perception, they could not originate out of nothing at the later moment. The relatedness being a character of entities, the awareness of entities necessarily means the awareness of relations.

Perception in the light of elucidation by the later members of the Rāmānuja School.

Rāmānuja and his followers admitted only three kinds of *pramāṇas*: perception, inference and scriptural testimony. Knowledge, directly and immediately experienced, is perception (*sākṣāt-kāriṇī pramā pratyakṣam*). The special distinguishing feature of perception is that it is not knowledge mediated by other knowledge (*jñānā-karaṇaka-jñānatvam*). Perception is of three kinds: God's perception, perception of yogins, and perception of ordinary persons. This perception of yogins includes intuitive perception of the mind (*mānasa-pratyakṣa*) or perception of sages (*ārṣa-pratyakṣa*), and the *yogi-pratyakṣa* is due to the special enlightenment of *yoga* practice. Ordinary perception is said to be of two kinds, *savikalpa*, or determinate, and *nirvikalpa*, or indeterminate. *Savikalpa pratyakṣa* is the determinate perception which involves a spatial and temporal reference to past time and different places where the object was experienced before. Thus, when we see a jug, we think of it as having been seen at other times and in other places, and it is this reference of the jug to other times and other places, and the

[1] *atas tat-smbandhād vastuta upādhito vā'dhārā-dheya-bhāva-vastv-antaram eva. evaṃ ca kalpanā-lāghavam. sa ca guṇā-di-bhedād anekaḥ na ca tat-sambandha-smbahdhinos sambandhā-ntara-kalpanāyām anavasthā. anyo-nya-sāpekṣa-svarūpatva-rūpo-pādhi-vyatirekeṇā'rthā-ntarā-bhāvāt. Naya-dyu-maṇi* MS.

The *nirvikalpaka* is the knowledge involving the notion of certain positive features and rousing the subconscious memory resulting in the first moment of perception through the direct operation of the sense. *Savikalpaka* knowledge involves the noting of differences consequent upon the operation of memory. They are thus defined by Viṣṇuacitta:

saṃskāro-dbodha-sahakṛte-ndriya-janyaṃ jñānaṃ savikalpakam iti eka-jātīyeṣu prathama-piṇḍa-grahaṇaṃ dvitīyā-di-piṇḍa-grahaṇeṣu prathamā-kṣa-san-nipātajaṃ jñānaṃ nirvikalpakam iti.

And in the *Tattva-ratnākara*:

viśeṣaṇānāṃ svā-yoga-vyāvṛttir avikalpake
savikalpe'nya-yogasya vyāvṛttiḥ saṃjñinā tathā.

Nyāya-pariśuddhi, p. 82.

associations connected with it as involved in such reference, that constitutes the determinate character of such perceptions, by virtue of which they are called *savikalpa*[1]. A perception, however, which reveals the specific character of its object, say a jug as a jug, without involving any direct references to its past associations, is called indeterminate perception or *nirvikalpa jñāna*[2]. This definition of *nirvikalpa* perception distinguishes the Rāmānuja conception of *nirvikalpa* knowledge from the types formulated by many other systems of Indian philosophy.

It is now obvious that according to Rāmānuja philosophy both the *savikalpa* and the *nirvikalpa* knowledges are differentiated and qualified in their nature, referring to objects which are qualified in their nature (*ubhaya-vidham api etad viśiṣṭa-viṣayam eva*)[3]. Veṅkaṭa says that there is no evidence whatsoever of the existence of indeterminate and unqualified knowledge, at even its first stage of appearance, as is held by the Naiyāyikas; for our experience is entirely against them, and even the knowledge of infants, dumb persons, and the lower animals, though it is devoid of concepts and names, is somehow determinate since the objects stand as signs of things liked or disliked, things which they desire, or of which they are afraid[4]. For if these so-called indeterminate perceptions of these animals, etc., were really absolutely devoid of qualitative colouring, how could they indicate the suitable attractive or repulsive behaviour? The Naiyayikas urge that all attribute-substance-complex or determinate knowledge (*viśiṣṭa-jñāna*) must first be preceded by the knowledge of the simpler element of the attribute; but this is true only to a limited extent, as in the case of acquired perception. I see a piece of sandal to be fragrant; fragrance cannot be seen, but the sight of the colour, etc., of a piece of sandal and its recognition as such suggest and rouse the nasal impressions of fragrance, which is then directly associated with

[1] *tatrā'nuvṛtti-viṣayakaṃ jñānaṃ savikalpakam anuvṛttiś ca saṃsthāna-rūpa-jāty-āder aneka-vyakti-vṛttitā, sā ca kālato deśataś ca bhavati. Rāmānuja-siddhānta-saṃgraha*, MS. No. 4988.

[2] *ekasyāṃ vyaktau ghaṭatva-prakārakam ayaṃ ghaṭa iti yaj jñānaṃ janyate tan nirvikalpakam. Ibid.*

[3] *Nyāya-pariśuddhi*, p. 77.

[4] *bāla-mūka-tiryag-ādi-jñānānāṃ anna-kaṇṭaka-vahni-vyāghrā-di-śabda-vaiśiṣṭyā-navagāhitve'pi iṣṭa-dvaiṣyatā-vacchedakā-nnatvā-hitva-kaṇṭakatvā-di-prakārā-vagāhitvam asti. Nyāya-sāra* commentary on *Nyāya-pariśuddhi* by Śrīnivāsa, p. 78.

vision. Here there must first be the perception of the attributes of the sandal as perceived by the visual organ, as rousing sub-conscious impressions of fragrance associated with the nasal organ and giving rise to its memory, and finally associating it with the attributes perceived by the visual organ. But in the perception of attribute and substance there is no necessity of assuming such a succession of the elements constituting a complex; for the data which give rise to the perception of the attribute and those which give rise to the perception of substance are presented to the senses simultaneously and are identically the same (*eka-sāmagrī-vedya-viśeṣaṇeṣu tan-nirapekṣatvāt*)[1]. The main point of this discussion consists in our consideration of the question whether relations are directly perceived or not. If relations are regarded as being the very nature of the things and attributes that are perceived (*svarūpa-sambandha*), then, of course, the relations must necessarily be perceived with the perceived things and attributes at the first moment of sight. If the relation of attributes to things be called an inherent inseparable relation (*samavāya*), then this, being an entity, may be admitted to be capable of being grasped by the eye; and, since it constitutes the essence of the linking of the attributes and the thing, the fact that it is grasped by the eye along with the thing and the attribute ought to convince us that the relatedness of attribute and thing is also grasped by the eye. For, if it is admitted that *samavāya* is grasped, then that itself makes it unexceptionable that the attribute and things are grasped, as the former qualifying the latter. Like the attribute and the thing, their relation as constituting their relatedness is also grasped by the senses (*dharmavad dharmivac ca tat-sambandhasyā'py aindriyakatvā-viśeṣeṇa grahaṇa-sambhavāt*)[2]. For, if the relation could not be grasped by the senses at the time of the perception of the thing and the object, it could not be grasped by any other way at any other time.

In the *savikalpa* perception, the internal impressions are roused in association with the visual and other senses, and they co-operate with the data supplied by the sense-organs in producing the inner act of analysis and synthesis, assimilation and differentiation, and

[1] *Nyāya-pariśuddhi*, p. 78: *surabhi-candanaṃ so'yam ghaṭa ity-ādi-jñāneṣu saurabhatā-ṃśe cakṣuṣaḥ sva-vijātīya-saṃskāra-janyāyāḥ smṛter viśeṣaṇa-pratyāsattitayā apekṣaṇe'pi cakṣur-mātra-janye ghaṭa-jñāne tad-apekṣāyā abhāvāt. Nyāya-sāra*, p. 78.

[2] *Ibid.* p. 79.

mutual comparison of similar concepts, as involved in the process of *savikalpa* perception. What distinguishes it from memory is the fact that memory is produced only by the rousing of the subconscious impressions of the mind, whereas *savikalpa* perception is produced by the subconscious impressions (*saṃskāra*) working in association with the sense-organs[1]. Though the roused subconscious impressions co-operate with sense-impressions in *savikalpa* perception, yet the *savikalpa* can properly be described as genuine sense-perception.

It may be pointed out in this connection that difference is considered in this system not as a separate and independent category, but as apprehended only through the mutual reference to the two things between which difference is realized. It is such a mutual reference, in which the affirmation of one makes the affirmation of the other impossible, that constitutes the essence of "difference" (*bheda*)[2].

Veṅkaṭanātha strongly controverts the Śaṅkarite view of *nirvikalpa pratyakṣa* in the case where a perception, the materials of which are already there, is made on the strength of auditory sensation in the way of scriptural instructions. Thus, when each of ten persons was counting upon leaving himself out of consideration, and counting nine persons instead of ten, another observer from outside pointed out to the counting person that he himself was the tenth. The Śaṅkarites urge that the statement or affirmation "thou art the tenth" is a case of direct *nirvikalpa* perception. But Veṅkaṭanātha points out that, though the entity indicated by "thou" is directly perceived, the proposition itself cannot be directly perceived, but can only be cogitated as being heard; for, if whatever is heard can be perceived, then one can also perceive or be directly acquainted with the import of such propositions as "thou art virtuous"—*dharmavāṃs tvam*. So the mental realization of the import of any proposition does not mean direct acquaintance by perception. It is easy to see how this view controverts the Śaṅkarite position, which holds that the realization of the import of the proposition "thou art that"—*tat tvam asi*—constitutes direct ac-

[1] *smṛtāv iva savikalpake saṃskārasya na svātantryeṇa kāraṇatvaṃ yena pratyakṣatvaṃ na syāt kintu indriya-sahakāritayā tathā ce'ndriya-janyatvena pratyakṣam eva savikalpakam. Nyāya-sāra* p. 80.

[2] *yad-graho yatra yad-āropa-virodhī sa hi tasya tasmād bhedaḥ. Nyāya-pariśuddhi*, p. 86.

quaintance with the identity of self and Brahman by perception (*pratyakṣa*)[1].

It has already been pointed out that *nirvikalpa* perception means a determinate knowledge which does not involve a reference to past associations of similar things (*anuvṛtty-aviṣayaka-jñāna*), and *savikalpa* perception means a determinate knowledge which involves a reference to past association (*anuvṛtti-viṣayaka*). This *anuvṛtti*, or reference to past association, does not mean a mere determinateness (e.g. the perception of a jug as endowed with the specific characteristics of a jug—*ghaṭatva-prakārakam ayaṃ ghaṭaḥ*), but a conscious reference to other similar objects (e.g. jugs) experienced before. In *savikalpa* knowledge there is a direct perception by the visual organ of the determinate characters constituting a complex of the related qualities, the thing and the relatedness; but that does not mean the comprehension or realization of any universals or class concepts involving a reference to other similar concepts or things. Thus, the visual organs are operative equally in *savikalpa* and *nirvikalpa*, but in the former there is a conscious reference to other similar entities experienced before.

The universals or class concepts are not, however, to be regarded as a separate independent category, which is comprehended in *savikalpa* perception, but a reference or assimilation of similar characteristics. Thus, when we refer to two or more cows as possessing common characteristics, it is these common characteristics existing in all individual cows that justify us in calling all these animals cows. So, apart from these common characteristics which persist in all these individual animals, there is no other separate entity which may be called *jāti* or universal. The commonness (*anuvṛtti*) consists in similarity (*susadṛśatvam eva gotvā-dīnām anuvṛttiḥ*)[2]. Similarity is again defined as the special cause (*asādhāraṇa-kāraṇa*) which justifies our regarding two things as similar which exist separately in these things and are determined by each other. The application of a common name is but a short way of signifying the fact that two things are regarded as similar. This similarity is of two kinds: similarity of attributes (*dharma-sādṛśya*) as in substances, and similarity of essence (*svarūpa-sādṛśya*)

[1] *ata eva tat tvam-asy-ādi-śabdaḥ sva-viṣaya-gocara-pratyakṣa-jñāna-janakaḥ ...ity-ādy-anumānāni nirastāni. Nyāya-pariśuddhi*, p. 89.

[2] *ayaṃ sāsnādimān ayam api sāsnādimān iti sāsnādir eva anuvṛtta-vyavahāra-viṣayo dṛśyate. Rāmānuja-siddhānta-saṃgraha*, MS. No. 4988.

as in all other categories of qualities which are not substance (*a-dravya*)[1].

In perception two kinds of sense-contact are admitted: sense-contact with the object (*saṃyoga*) and sense-contact with the qualities associated with the object (*saṃyuktā-śraya*). Thus, the perception of a jug is by the former kind of contact, and the perception of its qualities is by the latter[2].

Veṅkaṭanātha's treatment of Inference.

Inference according to the Rāmānuja school is very much the same as inference according to the Naiyāyikas. Inference is the direct result of *parāmarśa*, or knowledge of the existence of reason (associated with the knowledge of its unblemished and full concomitance with the probandum) in the object denoted by the minor term[3]. Inference is a process by which, from a universal proposition which includes within it all the particular cases, we can make an affirmation regarding a particular case.[4] Inference must therefore be always limited to those cases in which the general proposition has been enunciated on the basis of experience derived from sensible objects and not to the affirmation of ultra-sensual objects—a reason which precludes Rāmānuja and his followers from inferring the existence of Īśvara (God), who is admitted to be ultra-sensual (*atīndriya*) (*ata eva ca vayam atyantā-tīndriya-vastv-anumānaṃ necchāmaḥ*)[5].

As formulated by the traditional view of the school, the principle of concomitance (*vyāpti*) holds that what in the range of time or space is either equal or less than another is called the "pervaded" (*vyāpya*) or the *hetu*, while that which in the range of time or space is either equal or greater than it, is called *vyāpaka* or the probandum[6]. But this view does not cover all cases of valid con-

[1] MSS. No. 4988.

[2] The sense-contact with remote objects can take place in the case of the visual and the auditory organs by means of a mysterious process called *vṛtti*. It is supposed that these senses are lengthened as it were (*āpyāyamāna*) by means of their objects. *Ibid.*

[3] *parāmarśa-janyā pramitir anumitiḥ. Ibid.*

[4] *parāmarśa* means *vyāpti-viśiṣṭa-pakṣa-dharmatā-jñānaṃ sarva-viśeṣa-saṃgrāhi-sāmāñya-vyāpti-dhīr api viśeṣā-numiti-hetuḥ. Nyāya-pariśuddhi*, p. 97.

[5] *Ibid.*

[6] *deśataḥ kālato vā'pi samo nyūno'pi vā bhavet*
sva-vyāpyo vyāpakastasya samo vā'py adhiko'pi vā.

Ibid. p. 100.

comitance. The example given for spatial and temporal co-existence is that between date-juice (*rasa*) and sweetness (*guḍa*), or between the shadow thrown by our bodies and the specific position of the Sun. But such spatio-temporal co-existences do not exhaust all cases, as, for example, the sunset and the surging of the sea. This led the later Rāmānujas to adopt a stricter definition of concomitance as unconditional and invariable association (*nirupādhikatayā niyataḥ sambandho vyāptiḥ*)[1].

Regarding the formation of this inductive generalization or concomitance, we find in *Tattva-ratnākara*, an older authority, that a single observation of concomitance leading to a belief is sufficient to establish a general proposition[2]. But Veṅkaṭanātha urges that this cannot be so and that a wide experience of concomitance is indispensable for the affirmation of a general proposition of concomitance.

One of the important points in which Rāmānuja logic differs from the Nyāya logic is the refusal on the part of the former to accept *kevala-vyatireki* (impossible-positive) forms of inference, which are admitted by the latter. Thus, in the *kevala-vyatireki* forms of inference (e.g. earth is different from other elements on account of its possession of smell) it is argued by the Nyāya logic that this difference of earth with other elements, by virtue of its possession of the specific property of smell not possessed by any other element, cannot be proved by a reference to any proposition which embodies the principle of agreement in presence *anvaya*. This view apparently seems to have got the support of the earlier Rāmānuja logicians such as Varadaviṣṇu Miśra and Bhaṭṭārakaguru (in his *Tattva-ratnākara*); but both Veṅkaṭanātha (in his *Nyāya-pariśuddhi*) and the author of the *Rāmānuja-siddhānta-saṃgraha* point

[1] *Nyāya-pariśuddhi.*

[2] *sambandho'yaṃ sakṛd grāhyaḥ pratīti-sva-rasāt tathā*
pratītayo hi sva-rasād dharma-dharmy-avadhīn viduḥ.
Tattva-ratnākara MS.

The author of the *Tattva-ratnākara* urges that, since the class-concept (e.g. of *dhūma-dhūmatva*) is associated with any particular instance (e.g. of smoke), the experience of any concomitance of smoke and fire would mean the comprehension of the concomitance of the class-concept of smoke with the class-concept of fire. So through the experience of any individual and its class-concept as associated with it we are in touch with other individuals included within that class-concept —*sannihita-dhūmādi-vyakti-saṃyuktasya indriyasya tad-āśrita-dhūmatvādiḥ saṃyuktā-śritaḥ, tad-āśrayatvena vyakty-antarāṇi saṃyuktāni,* etc. *Nyāya-pariśuddhi*, p. 105. (Chowkhamba.)

out that, since Yāmuna rejects the *kevala-vyatireki* form of argument in his lecture on *Ātma-siddhi*, it is better to suppose that, when the previous authors referred to spoke of *kevala-vyatireki* as a form of inference, it was not admission of their acceptance of it, but only that they counted it as being accepted by the Nyāya logicians[1]. The author of the *Rāmānuja-siddhānta-saṃgraha* points out that it may very well be brought under *anvaya-vyatireki*. Thus we may argue "body is earthly by virtue of its possession of smell; for whatever possesses smell is earthly and whatever does not possess smell is not earthly." So in this form it may be put forward as a *anvaya-vyatireki* form of argument. The possession of smell (*gandhavattva*) may very well be put forth as "reason" or *hetu*, the presence of which determines earthiness and the absence of which determines non-earthiness or difference from non-earthiness.

Rāmānuja logic admits the necessity of "*tarka*" (cogitation regarding the relative possibilities of the alternative conclusions by a dialectic of contradictions) as an indispensable means of inferential conclusions. Regarding the number of propositions, Veṅkaṭanātha says that there is no necessity of admitting the indispensable character of five propositions. Thus it must depend on the way in which the inference is made as to how many propositions (*avayava*) are to be admitted. It may be that two, three, four or five propositions are deemed necessary at the time of making an inference. We find it said in the *Tattva-ratnākara* also that, though five propositions would make a complete statement, yet there is no hard and fast rule (*aniyama*) regarding the number of propositions necessary for inference[1].

Veṅkaṭanātha urges that inference is always limited to perceptible objects. Things which entirely transcend the senses cannot be known by inference. Inference, though irrefragably connected with perception, cannot, on that account, be regarded as a mode of perception; for the knowledge derived from perception is always indirect (*a-parokṣa*). Inference cannot also be regarded as due to memory; for it always reveals new knowledge. Further, it cannot be said to be a form of mental intuition, on account of the fact that inference works by rousing the subconscious impressions of the mind; for such impressions are also found to be active in percep-

[1] *Nyāya-pariśuddhi* and *Rāmānuja-siddhānta-saṃgraha.*
[2] *Ibid.*

tion, and on that analogy even perception may be called mental intuition.

Vyāpti (concomitance) may be defined as that in which the area of the probandum (*sādhya*) is not spatially or temporally less than (*a-nyūna-deśa-kāla-vṛtti*) that of the reason, *hetu*—and reason is defined as that, the area of which is never wider than that of the probandum (*a-nadhik-deśa-kāla-niyataṃ vyāpyam*). As an illustration of spatial and temporal co-existence (*yaugapadya*) Veṅkatanātha gives the instance of sugar and sweetness. As an illustration of temporal co-existence (*yaugapadya*) he gives the example of the measure of the shadow and the position of the sun. As a case of purely spatial co-existence he gives the instance of heat and its effects. Sometimes, however, there is concomitance between entities which are separate in space and time, as in the case of tides and their relation to the sun and the moon[1].

Such a concomitance, however, between the probandum and the reason can be grasped only by the observation of numerous instances (*bhūyo-darśana-gamya*), and not by a single instance, as in the case of Śaṅkara Vedānta as expounded by Dharmārājādhvarīndra. Bhaṭṭārakaguru, in his *Tattva-ratnākara*, in explaining the process by which the notion of concomitance is arrived at, says that, when in numerous instances the concomitance between the probandum and the reason is observed, the result of such observation accumulates as subconscious impressions in favour of the universal concomitance between all cases of probandum and all cases of the reason, and then in the last instance the perception of the concomitance rouses in the mind the notion of the concomitance of all probandum and all reason through the help of the roused subconscious impressions previously formed. Veṅkaṭanātha admits concomitance through joint method of Agreement and Difference (*anvyaya-vyatireki*) and by pure Agreement (*kevalā-nvayi*), where negative instances are not available. Ordinarily the method of difference contributes to the notion of concomitance by demonstrating that each and every instance in which the probandum does not occur is also an instance in which the reason does not occur. But in the case of *kevalā-nvayi* concomitance, in which negative instances

[1] *vyāpti* is thus defined by Veṅkaṭanātha—*atre'daṃ tattvaṃ yādṛg-rūpasya yad-deśa-kāla-vartino yasya yādṛg-rūpeṇa yad-deśa-kāla-vartinā yenā'vinā-bhāvaḥ tad idam avinā-bhūtaṃ vyāpyam. tat-pratisambandhi-vyāpakam iti. Nyāya-pariśuddhi*, pp. 101–102.

are not available, the non-existence of the reason in the negative instance cannot be shown. But in such cases the very non-existence of negative instances is itself sufficient to contribute to the notion of *kevalā-nvayi* concomitance. The validity of *kevalā-nvayi* concomitance is made patent by the fact that, if the reason remains unchanged, the assumption of a contrary probandum is self-contradictory (*vyāhata-sādhya-viparyayāt*), and this distinguishes it from the forms of *kevalā-nvayi* arguments employed by Kulārka in formulating his *Mahā-vidyā* doctrines.

Rāmānuja's own intention regarding the types of inference that may be admitted seems to be uncertain, as he has never definitely given any opinion on the subject. His intention, therefore, is diversely interpreted by the thinkers of his school. Thus, Meghanādāri gives a threefold classification of inference: (1) of the cause from the effect (*kāraṇā-numāna*); (2) of the effect from the cause (*kāryā-numāna*); and (3) inference by mental association (*anubhavā-numāna*—as the inference of the rise of the constellation of Rohiṇī from the Kṛttikā constellation). As an alternative classification he gives (1) the joint method of agreement and difference (*anvaya-vyatireki*); (2) inference through universal agreement in which no negative instances are found (*kevalā-nvayi*); and (3) inference through exclusion, in which no positive instances are found (*kevala-vyatireki*). Bhaṭṭārakaguru and Varadaviṣṇu Miśra, who preceded Veṅkaṭanātha in working out a consistent system of Rāmānuja logic, seem also to admit the three kinds of inference, viz. *anvayi*, *kevalā-nvayi*, and *kevala-vyatireki*, as is evident from the quotation of their works *Tattva-ratnākara* and *Māna-yāthātmya-nirṇaya*. Veṅkaṭanātha, however, tries to explain them away and takes great pains to refute the *kevala-vyatireki* form of argument[1]. His contention is that there can be no inference through mere negative concomitance, which can never legitimately lead to the affirmation of any positive character when there is no positive proposition purporting the affirmation of any character. If any such positive proposition be regarded as implied in the negative proposition, then also the contention that there can be inference from purely negative proposition fails. One of the conditions of validity

[1] Veṅkaṭanātha points out that Yāmunācārya, also the accredited teacher of Rāmānuja, did not admit the *kevala-vyatireki* form of inference in his *Siddhi-traya*.

of inference is that the *hetu* or reason must exist in the *sa-pakṣa* (that is, in all such instances where there is the *sādhya*), but in the *vyatireki* form of inference, where there are no positive instances of the existence of the *hetu* and the *sādhya* excepting the point at issue, the above condition necessarily fails[1]. The opponent might say that on the same analogy the *kevalā-nvayi* form of argument may also be denied; for there negative instances are found (e.g. *idaṃ vācyaṃ prameyatvāt*). The reply would be that the validity of a *kevalā-nvayi* form of argument is attested by the fact that the assumption of a contrary conclusion would be self-contradictory. If the contention of the opponent is that the universal concomitance of the negation of the *hetu* with the negation of the *sādhya* implies the absolute coincidence of the *hetu* and the *sādhya*, then the absolute coincidence of the *hetu* and the *sādhya* would imply the absolute coincidence of the opposites of them both. This would imply that from the absolute coincidence of the *hetu* and the *sādhya* in a *kevalā-nvayi* form of inference the absolute coincidence of their opposites would be demonstrable. This is absurd[2]. Thus, the Naiyāikas, who admit the *kevalā-nvayi* inference, cannot indulge in such ways of support in establishing the validity of the *kevala-vyatireki* form of argument. Again, following the same method, one might as well argue that a jug is self-revealing (*sva-prakāśa*) because it is a jug (*ghaṭatvāt*); for the negation of self-revealing character (*a-sva-prakāśatva*) is found in the negation of jug, viz. the cloth, which is impossible (*yan naivaṃ tan naivaṃ yathā paṭaḥ*). Thus, merely from the concomitance of two negations it is not possible to affirm the concomitance of their opposites. Again, in the above instance—*anubhūtir ananubhāvyā anubhūtitvāt* (immediate intuition cannot be an object of awareness, because it is immediate intuition)—even the existence of *an-anubhāvyatva* (not being an object of awareness) is doubtful; for it is not known to exist anywhere else than in the instance under discussion, and therefore, from the mere case of

[1] The typical forms of *vyatireki* inference are as follows: *anubhūtir an-anubhāvyā anubhūtitvāt, yan naivaṃ tan naivaṃ yathā ghaṭaḥ. pṛthivī itarebhyo bhidyate gandhavattvāt yan naivaṃ tan naivaṃ yathā jalam.* In the above instance *an-anubhāvyatva* (non-cognizability) belongs only to immediate intuition. There is thus no *sa-pakṣa* of *anubhūti* where *an-anubhāvyatva* was found before.

[2] *idaṃ vācyaṃ prameyatvāt* (this is definable, because it is knowable) would, under the supposition, imply that the concomitance of the negation of *vācyatva* and *prameyatva*, viz. *avācyatva* (indefinable) and *aprameyatva* (unknowable), would be demonstrable; which is absurd, since no such cases are known.

concomitance of the negation of *an-anubhāvyatva* with the negation of *anubhūti* the affirmation of *an-anubhāvyatva* would be inadmissible. Moreover, when one says that that which is an object of awareness (*anubhāvya*) is not immediate intuition, the mere affirmation of the negative relation makes *anubhūti* an object of awareness in a negative relation, which contradicts the conclusion that *anubhūti* is not an object of awareness. If, again, the character that is intended to be inferred by the *vyatireki anumāna* is already known to exist in the *pakṣa*, then there is no need of inference. If it is known to exist elsewhere, then, since there is a *sa-pakṣa*[1], there is no *kevala-vyatireki* inference. Even if, through the concomitance of the negation of the *hetu* and the *sādhya*, the *sādhya* is known to exist elsewhere outside the negation of the *hetu*, its presence in the case under consideration would not be demonstrated. Again, in the instance under discussion, if, from the concomitance of the negation of not being an object of awareness and the negation of immediate intuition, it is argued that the character as not being an object of awareness (*a-vedyatva*) must be present somewhere, then such conclusion would be self-contradictory; for, if it is known that there is an entity which is not an object of awareness, then by that very fact it becomes an object of awareness. If an existent entity is ruled out from all possible spheres excepting one, it necessarily belongs to that residual sphere. So it may be said that "willing, being an existent quality, is known to be absent from all spheres excepting the self; it, therefore, necessarily belongs thereto." On such an interpretation also there is no necessity of *vyatireki anumāna*; for it is really a case of agreement (*anvaya*); and it is possible for us to enunciate it in a general formula of agreement such as "an existent entity, which is absent from all other spheres excepting one must necessarily belong to that residual sphere." Again, in such an instance as "all-knowingness (*sarva-vittva*), being absent in all known spheres, must be present somewhere, as we have a notion of it, and therefore there must be an entity to which it belongs, and such an entity is God," we have the well known ontological argument which is of *vyatireki* type. Against such an inference it may well be contended with justice that the notion of

[1] *sa-pakṣa* are all instances (outside the instance of the inference under discussion) where the *hetu* or reason is known to co-exist with the *sādhya* or probandum.

a hare's horn, which is absent in all known spheres, must necessarily belong to an unperceived entity which is obviously false.

It may be contended that, if the *vyatireki* inference is not admitted, then that amounts to a denial of all defining characters; for a defining character is that which is absent everywhere except in the object under definition, and thus definition is the very nature of *vyatireki* inference. The obvious reply to this is that definition proceeds from the perception of special characteristics which are enunciated as the defining characteristics of a particular object, and it has therefore nothing to do with *vyatireki* inference[1]. It may also be urged that defining characteristics may also be gathered by joint method of agreement and difference, and not by a *vyatireki* inference as suggested by the opponents. In such an instance as where knowability is defined as that which is capable of being known, no negative instances are known but it still remains a definition. The definition of definition is that the special characteristic is existent only in the object under definition and nowhere else (*a-sādhāraṇa-vyāpako dharmo lakṣaṇam*)[2]. In the case where a class of objects is defined the defining class-character would be that which should exist in all individuals of that class, and should be absent in all other individuals of other classes. But when an individual which stands alone (such as God) is defined, then we have no class-character, but only unique character which belongs to that individual only and not to a class. Even in such cases, such a defining character differentiates that entity from other entities (*Brahmā*, *Śiva*, etc.) with which, through partial similarity, He might be confused. Thus, the definition is a case of agreement of a character in an entity, and not a negation, as contended by those who confuse it with *vyatireki* inference. Therefore, the *kevala-vyatireki* form of inference cannot be supported by any argument.

On the subject of propositions (*avayava*) Veṅkaṭanātha holds that there is no reason why there should be five propositions for all inference. The dispute, therefore, among various logicians regarding the number of propositions that can be admitted in an inference is meaningless; for just so many propositions need be admitted for an inference as are sufficient to make the inference appeal to the

[1] *arthā-sādhāraṇā-kāra-pratipatti-nibandhanam*
sajātīya-vijātīya-vyavacchedeṇa lakṣaṇam.
Tattva-ratnākara, quoted in *Nyāya-pariśuddhi*, p. 143.

[2] *Nyāya-pariśuddhi*, p. 145.

person for whom it may be intended. Thus, there may be three, four, or five propositions, according to the context in which the inference appears.

In addition to inference Veṅkaṭanātha also admits *śabda*, or scriptural testimony. No elaboration need be made here regarding the *śabda-pramāṇa*, as the treatment of the subject is more or less the same as is found in other systems of philosophy. It may be remembered that on the subject of the interpretation of words and sentences the Naiyāikas held that each single element of a sentence, such as simple words or roots, had its own separate or specific sense. These senses suffer a modification through a process of addition of meaning through the suffixes of another case-relation. Viewed from this light, the simple constituents of sentences are atomic, and gradually go through a process of aggregation through their association with suffixes until they grow into a total meaning of the sentence. This is called the *abhihitā-nvaya-vāda*. The opposite view is that of *anvitā-bhidhāna-vāda*, such as that of Mīmāṃsaka, which held that no sentence could be analysed into purely simple entities of meaning, unassociated with one another, which could go gradually by a process of aggregation or association. Into however simple a stage each sentence might be capable of being analysed, the very simplest part of it would always imply a general association with some kind of a verb or full meaning. The function of the suffixes and case-relations, consists only in applying restrictions and limitations to this general connectedness of meaning which every word carries with itself. Veṅkaṭanātha holds this *anvitā-bhidhāna-vāda* against the *abhihitā-nvaya-vāda* on the ground that the latter involves the unnecessary assumption of separate specific powers for associating the meaning of the simplest word-elements with their suffixes, or between the suffixed words among themselves and their mutual connectedness for conveying the meaning of a sentence[1]. The acceptance of *anvitā-bhidhāna* was conducive to the philosophy of Rāmānuja, as it established the all-connectedness of meaning (*viśiṣṭā-rtha*).

Rāmānuja himself did not write any work propounding his views of logic consistent with his system of philosophy. But Nāthamuni had written a work called *Nyāya-tattva*, in which he criticized

[1] *abhihitā-nvayaye hi padānāṃ padā-rthe padā-rthānaṃ vākyā-rthe padānāṃ ca tatra iti śakti-traya-kalpanā-gauravaṃ syāt. Nyāya-pariśuddhi*, p. 369.

the views of Gotama's logic and revised it in accordance with the *Viśiṣṭā-dvaita* tradition. Viṣṇucitta wrote his *Saṅgati-mālā* and *Prameya-saṃgraha*, following the same lines, Bhaṭṭārakaguru wrote his *Tattva-ratnākara*, and Varadaviṣṇu Miśra also wrote his *Prajñā-paritrāṇa* and *Māna-yāthātmya-nirṇaya*, working out the views of *Viśiṣṭā-dvaita* logic. Veṅkaṭanātha based his *Nyāya-pariśuddhi* on these works, sometimes elucidating their views and sometimes differing from them in certain details. But, on the whole, he drew his views on the *Viśiṣṭā-dvaita* logic from the above writers. His originality, therefore, in this field is very limited. Meghanādāri, however, seems to differ very largely from Veṅkaṭanātha in admitting *Upamāna* and *arthāpatti* as separate *pramāṇas*. He has also made some very illuminating contributions in his treatment of perception, and in his treatment of inference he has wholly differed from Veṅkaṭanātha in admitting *vyatireki anumāna*.

Meghanādāri admits *upamāna* as a separate *pramāṇa*. With him *upamāna* is the *pramāṇa* through which it is possible to have the knowledge of similarity of a perceived object with an unperceived one, when there was previously a knowledge of the similarity of the latter with the former. Thus, when a man has the knowledge that the cow which he perceives is similar to a bison, and when later on, roaming in the forest, he observes a bison, he at once notes that the cow which he does not perceive now is similar to a bison which he perceives. This knowledge, Meghanādāri contends, cannot be due to perception, because the cow is not before the perceiver; it also cannot be due to memory, since the knowledge of similarity dawns before the reproduction of the cow in the mind. Meghanādāri holds that no separate *pramāṇa* need be admitted for the notion of difference; for the knowledge of difference is but a negation of similarity. This interpretation of *upamāna* is, however, different from that given in Nyāya, where it is interpreted to mean the association of a word with its object on the basis of similarity, e.g. that animal is called a bison which is similar to a cow. Here, on the basis of similarity, the word "bison" is associated with that animal. Meghanādāri tries to explain this by the function of recognition, and repudiates its claim to be regarded as a separate *pramāṇa*[1]. He also admits *arthāpatti* as a separate *pramāṇa*. *Arthāpatti* is generally translated as "implication," where a certain hypothesis, without the

[1] See MS. *Naya-dyu-maṇi*. Chapter on *Upamāna*.

assumption of which an obscured fact of experience becomes inexplicable, is urged before the mind by the demand for an explanation of the observed fact of experience. Thus, when one knows from an independent source that Devadatta is living, though not found at his house, a natural hypothesis is urged before the mind that he must be staying outside the house; for otherwise either the present observation of his non-existence at his house is false or the previous knowledge that he is living is false. That he is living and that he is non-existent at his house can only be explained by the supposition that he is existing somewhere outside the house. This cannot be regarded as a case of inference of the form that "since somewhere-existing Devadatta is non-existent at his house, he must be existent somewhere else; for all somewhere-existing entities which are non-existent at a place must be existent elsewhere like myself." Such an inference is meaningless; for the non-existence of an existing entity in one place is but the other name of its existing elsewhere. Therefore, the non-existence of an existing entity in one place should not be made a reason for arriving at a conclusion (its existence elsewhere) which is not different from itself. *Arthāpatti* is thus to be admitted as a separate *pramāṇa*.

Epistemology of the Rāmānuja School according to Meghanādāri and others.

Veṅkaṭanātha, in his *Nyāya-pariśuddhi*, tries to construct the principles of Logic (*Nyāya* or *Nīti*) on which Rāmānuja's system of philosophy is based. He was not a pioneer in the field, but he followed and elaborated the doctrines of *Viśiṣṭā-dvaita* logic as enunciated by Nāthamuni, the teacher of Yāmuna, in his work called *Nyāya-tattva*, and the works of Parāśara Bhaṭṭa on the subject. Regarding the system of Nyāya propounded by Gotama, Veṅkaṭa's main contention is that though Gotama's doctrines have been rejected by Bādarāyaṇa as unacceptable to right-minded scholars, they may yet be so explained that they may be made to harmonize with the true Vedantic doctrines of *Viśiṣṭā-dvaita*. But the interpretations of Gotama's Nyāya by Vātsyāyana take them far away from the right course and have therefore to be refuted. At any rate Veṅkaṭa, like Viṣṇucitta, is not unwilling to accept such doctrines of Gotama as are not in conflict with the Vedānta view. Thus, there may be a divergence of opinion regarding the sixteenfold classification of logical categories. There can be no two opinions regarding the admission of the fact that there are at least certain entities which are logically valid; for if logical validity is denied, logic itself becomes unfounded. All our experiences assume the existence of certain objective factors on which they are based. A general denial of such objective factors takes away the very root of experience. It is only when such objective factors are admitted to be in existence in a general manner that there may be any inquiry regarding their specific nature. If everything were invalid, then the opponent's contention would also be invalid. If everything were doubted, then also it would remain uncontradictory. The doubt itself cannot be doubted and the existence of doubt would have to be admitted as a decisive conclusion. So, even by leading a full course of thoroughgoing doubt, the admission of the possibility of definite conclusion becomes irresistible[1]. Therefore, the contention of the Buddhists that there is nothing valid and that there is nothing the certainty of which can be accepted, is inadmissible. If, therefore, there are things of which definite and valid knowledge is possible, there arises a natural inquiry about the means or instruments by which such valid knowledge is possible. The word *pramāṇa* is used in two senses. Firstly, it means valid knowledge; secondly, it means instruments by which valid knowledge is produced. *pramāṇa* as valid knowledge is defined by Veṅkaṭa as the knowledge which corresponds to or produces a behaviour leading to an experience of things as they are (*yathā-vasthita-vyavahārā-nuguṇam*)[2]. The definition includes behaviour as an indispensable condition of *pramāṇa* such that, even though in a particular case a behaviour may not actually be induced, it may yet be *pramāṇa* if the knowledge be such that it has the capacity of producing a behaviour which would tally with things as they are[3]. The definition

[1] *vyavahāro hi jagato bhavaty ālmbane kvacit*
na tat sāmānyato nāsti kathantā tu parīkṣyate
sāmānya-niścitā-rthena viśeṣe tu bubhutsitam
parīkṣā hy ucitā sve-ṣṭa-pramāṇo-tpādanā-tmikā...
. . . .
sarvaṃ sandigdham iti te nipuṇasyā'sti niścayaḥ
saṃśayaś ca na sandigdhaḥ sandigdhā-dvaita-vādinaḥ.
Nyāya-pariśuddhi, p. 31 (Chowkhamba edition).

[2] *Nyāya-pariśuddhi*, by Veṅkaṭanātha, p. 36.

[3] *anuguṇa-padaṃ vyavahāra-janana-svarūpa-yogya-paraṃ tenā'janita-vyavahāre yathā-rtha-jñāna-viśeṣe nā'vyāptiḥ.* Śrīnivāsa's *Nyāya-sāra* on *Nyāya-pariśuddhi*, p. 36.

of *pramāṇa* as knowledge leading to a behaviour tallying with facts naturally means the inclusion of valid memory within it. An uncontradicted memory is thus regarded as valid means of knowledge according to the Rāmānuja system[1]. Veṅkaṭa urges that it is wrong to suppose the illicit introduction of memory as the invariable condition of illusion, for in such illusory perception as that of yellow conch-shell, there is manifestly no experience of the production of memory. The conch-shell directly appears as yellow. So in all cases of illusions the condition that is invariably fulfilled is that one thing appears as another, which is technically called *anyathā-khyāti.* But it may as well be urged that in such an illusion as that of the conch-shell–silver, the reason why the conch-shell appears as the silver is the non-apprehension of the distinction between the subconscious image of the silver seen in shops and the perception of a shining piece before the eyes, technically called *akhyāti*. Thus, in all cases of illusion, when one thing appears as another there is this condition of the non-apprehension of the distinction between a memory image and a percept. If illusions are considered from this point of view, then they may be said to be primarily and directly due to the aforesaid psychological fact known as *akhyāti*. Thus, both these theories of illusion have been accepted by Rāmānuja from two points of view. The theory of *anyathā-khyāti* appeals directly to experience, whereas the *akhyāti* view is the result of analysis and reasoning regarding the psychological origin of illusions[2]. The other theory of illusion (*yathārtha-khyāti*), which regards illusions also as being real knowledge, on the ground that in accordance with the *pañcī-karaṇa* theory all things are the result of a primordial admixture of the elements of all things, is neither psychological nor analytical but is only metaphysical, and as such does not explain the nature of illusions. The illusion in such a view consists in the fact or apprehension of the presence of such silver in the conch-shell as can be utilized for domestic or ornamental purposes, whereas the metaphysical explanation only justifies the perception of certain primordial elements of silver in the universal admixture of the elements of all things in all things.

[1] *smṛti-mātrā-pramāṇatvaṃ na yuktam iti vakṣyate*
abādhita-smṛiter loke pramāṇatva-parigrahāt.
Nyāya-pariśuddhi, p. 38.

[2] *idaṃ rajatam anubhavāmī'ty ekatvenai'va pratīyamānāyāḥ pratīter grahaṇa-smaraṇā-tmakatvam anekatvaṃ ca yuktitaḥ sādhyamānaṃ na pratīti-patham ārohati. Nyāya-sāra*, p. 40.

In refuting the *ātma-khyāti* theory of illusion of the Buddhists, Veṅkaṭa says that if the idealistic Buddhist can admit the validity of the different awarenesses as imposed on the one fundamental consciousness, then on the same analogy the validity of the perceived objects may also be admitted. If the different subjective and objective awarenesses are not admitted, then all experiences would be reduced to one undifferentiated consciousness, and that would be clearly against the Buddhistic theory of knowledge. The Buddhist view that entities which are simultaneously apprehended are one, and that therefore knowledge and its objects which are apprehended simultaneously are one, is wrong. Knowledge and its objects are directly apprehended as different, and therefore the affirmation of their identity is contradicted in experience. The Mādhyamika Buddhists further hold that, just as in spite of the falsehood of the defects (*doṣa*), illusions happen, so in spite of the falsehood of any substratum or any abiding entity, illusions may appear as mere appearances without any reality behind them. Against such a view, Veṅkaṭa says that whatever is understood by people as existent or non-existent has always a reference to a reality, and mere phenomena without any basis or ground on reality are incomprehensible in all our experience. Hence the pure phenomenalism of the Mādhyamika is wholly against all experience[1]. When people speak of non-existence of any entity, they always do it with some kind of spatial or temporal qualification. Thus, when they say that the book does not exist, they always qualify this non-existence with a "here" and a "there" or with a "now" or a "then." But pure unqualified non-existence is unknown to ordinary experience[2]. Again all positive experience of things is spatially limited (e.g. there is a jug "here"); if this spatial qualification as "here" is admitted, then it cannot be held that appearances occur on mere nothing (*nir-adhiṣṭhāna-bhramā-nupapattiḥ*). If, however, the limitation of a "here" or "there" is denied, then no experience is possible (*pratīter apahnava eva syāt*).

Criticizing the *a-nirvacanīya* theory of illusion of the Vedāntists Veṅkaṭanātha says that when the Śaṅkarites described all things as

[1] *loke bhāvā-bhāva-śabdayos tat-pratītyoś ca vidyamānasyai'va vastunaḥ avasthā-viśeṣa-gocaratvasya pratipāditatvāt. prakārā-ntarasya ca loka-siddha-pramāṇā-viṣayatvād ity-arthaḥ. Nyāya-sāra*, p. 46.

[2] *sarvo'pi niṣedhaḥ sa-pratiyogiko niyata-deśa-kālaśca pratīyate. Nīrūpadhir niyata-deśa-kāla-pratiyogi-viśeṣaṇa-rahito niṣedho na pratīyate iti. Ibid.* p. 46.

indefinable (*a-nirvacanīya*), the word "indefinable" must mean either some definite trait, in which case it would cease to be indefinable, or it might mean failure to define in a particular manner, in which case the Śaṅkarites might as well accept the Rāmānuja account of the nature of the universe. Again when the Śaṅkarites are prepared to accept such a self-contradictory category as that which is different both from being and non-being (*sad-asad-vyatirekaḥ*), why cannot they rather accept things as both existent and non-existent as they are felt in experience? The self-contradiction would be the same in either case. If, however, their description of the world-appearance as something different from being and non-being is for the purpose of establishing the fact that the world-appearance is different both from chimerical entities (*tuccha*) and from Brahman, then Rāmānujists should have no dispute with them. Further, the falsity of the world does not of itself appeal to experience; if an attempt is made to establish such a falsity through unfounded dialectic, then by an extension of such a dialectic even Brahman could be proved to be self-contradictory. Again the assertion that the world-appearance is non-existent because it is destructible is unfounded; for the Upaniṣads speak of Brahman, the individual souls and the *prakṛti* as being eternal. The Śaṅkarites also confuse destruction and contradiction (*na cai'kyaṃ nāśa-bādhayoḥ*)[1].

The followers of Patañjali speak of an illusory comprehension through linguistic usage in which we are supposed to apprehend entities which have no existence. This is called *nirviṣaya-khyāti*. Thus, when we speak of the head of Rāhu, we conceive Rāhu as having an existence apart from his head, and this apprehension is due to linguistic usage following the genitive case-ending in Rāhu, but Veṅkaṭa urges that it is unnecessary to accept a separate theory of illusion for explaining such experience, since it may well be done by the *akhyāti* or *anyathā-khyāti* theory of illusion, and he contends that he has already demonstrated the impossibility of other theories of illusion.

Meghanādāri, however, defines *pramāṇa* as the knowledge that determines the objects without depending on other sources of knowledge such as memory[2].

[1] *Nyāya-pariśuddhi*, pp. 48–51.

[2] "*tatrā'nya-pramāṇā-napekṣam artha-paricchedakaṃ jñanaṃ pramāṇam, artha-paricchede'nya-pramāṇa-sāpekṣa-smṛtāv ativyāpti-parihāre'nya-pramāṇā-napekṣam iti.*" *Naya-dyu-maṇi*, Madras Govt. Oriental MS.

Though knowledge is self-revealing (*sva-mūrtāv api svayam eva hetuḥ*), and though there is a continuity of consciousness in sleep, or in a state of swoon, yet the consciousness in these stages cannot reveal objects of cognition. This is only possible when knowledge is produced through the processes known as *pramāṇa*. When we speak of the self-validity of knowledge, we may speak of the cognition as being determined by the objects that it grasps (*artha-paricchinnaṃ pramāṇam*). But when we speak of it from the perceptual point of view or from the point of view of its determining the objects of knowledge, we have to speak of knowledge as determining the nature of objects (*artha-paricchedaka*) and not as being determined by them. Knowledge may thus be looked at from a subjective point of view in self-validity of cognition (*svataḥ-prāmāṇya*). Then the self-validity refers to its content which is determined by the objects of comprehension. It has also to be looked at from the objective point of view in all cases of acquirement of knowledge and in our behaviour in the world of objects, and then the knowledge appears as the means by which we determine the nature of the objects and measure our behaviour accordingly. The definition of knowledge as that which measures the nature of objects (*artha-pariccheda-kāri jñānaṃ pramāṇam*), as given by Meghanādāri is thus somewhat different from that given by Veṅkaṭa, who defines it as that which corresponds to or produces a behaviour leading to an experience of things as they are (*yathā-vasthita vyavahārā-nuguṇam*). In the case of Veṅkaṭa, knowledge is looked at as a means to behaviour and it is the behaviour which is supposed to determine the nature of correspondence. In Meghanādāri's definition the whole question of behaviour and of correspondence is lost sight of, or at least put in the background. The emphasis is put on the function of knowledge as determining the objects. The supposition probably is that in case of error or illusion also the real object is perceived, and the illusion is caused through the omission of other details, a correct perception of which would have rendered the illusion impossible. We know already that according to the *yathārtha-khyāti* theory of Rāmānuja there are elements of all things in all things, according to the Upaniṣadic theory of "*trivṛt-karaṇa*" and its elaboration in the *pañcī-karaṇa* doctrine. What happens therefore in illusion (e.g. the conch-shell-silver) is that the visual organ is in contact with the element of silver that forms one of the constituents of the conch-shell. This element of silver no doubt is infinitesimally small as compared with the overwhelmingly preponderating parts—the conch-shell. But on account of the temporary defect of the visual organ or other distracting circumstances, these preponderating parts of the conch-shell are lost sight of. The result is that knowledge is produced only of the silver elements with which the sense-organ was in contact; and since the conch-shell element had entirely dropped out of comprehension, the silver element was regarded as being the only one that was perceived and thus the illusion was produced. But even in such an illusion the perception of silver is no error. The error consists in the non-perception of the preponderating part—the conch-shell. Thus, even in illusory perception, it is undoubtedly a real object that is perceived. The theory of *anyathā-khyāti* is that illusion consists in attributing a quality or character to a thing which it does not possess. In an indirect manner this theory is also implied in the *yathārtha-khyāti* theory in so far that here also the characters attributed (e.g. the silver) to the object of perception (*purovarti vastu*) do not belong to it, though the essence of illusion does not consist in that, and there is no real illusion of perception. Meghanādāri thus holds that all knowledge is true in the sense that it has always an object corresponding to it, or what has been more precisely described by Anantācārya that all cognitive characters (illusory or otherwise) universally refer to real objective entities as objects of knowledge[1]. We have seen that Veṅkaṭa had admitted three theories of illusion, namely, *anyathā-khyāti*, *akhyāti* and *yathārtha-khyāti*, from three different points of view. This does not seem to find any support in Meghanādāri's work, as he spares no effort to prove that the *yathārtha-khyāti* theory is the only theory of illusion and to refute the other rival theories. The main drift of Meghanādāri's criticism of *anyathā-khyāti* consists in the view that since knowledge must always refer to an object that is perceived, it is not possible that an object should produce a knowledge giving an entirely different content, for then such a content would refer to no object and thus would be chimerical (*tuccha*). If it is argued that the object is present elsewhere, then it might be contended that since the presence of the object can be determined

1 "*Tat-tad-dharma-prakāraka-jñānatva-vyāpakaṃ tat-tad-dharmavad-viśeṣyakatvam iti yathā'rthaṃ sarva-vijñānam iti.*" Anantācārya, *Jñāna-yāthārthya-vāda* (MS.).

only by the content of knowledge, and since such an object is denied in the case of illusory perception where we have such a knowledge, what is the guarantee that the object should be present in other cases? In those cases also it is the knowledge that alone should determine the presence of the object. That is to say, that if knowledge alone is to be the guarantor of the corresponding object, it is not right to say in two instances where such knowledge occurs that the object exists in one case and not in the other[1].

In refuting the *anirvacanīya-khyāti* Meghanādāri says that if it is supposed that in illusions an indefinable silver is produced which is mistaken for real silver, then that is almost the same as the *anyathā-khyāti* view, for here also one thing is taken as another. Moreover, it is difficult to explain how the perception of such an indefinable silver would produce the real desire for picking it up which is possible only in the case of the perception of real silver. A desire which can be produced by a real object can never be produced by a mere illusory notion. Nor can there be any similarity between a mere illusory notion and the real shining entity, viz. silver[2]. The so-called indefinable silver is regarded either as being of the nature of being and non-being, or as different from being and non-being, both of which are impossible according to the Law of Contradiction and the Law of Excluded Middle. Even if it be admitted for the sake of argument that such an extra-logical entity is possible, it would be difficult to conceive how it could have any similarity with such a positive entity as ordinary silver. It cannot be admitted that this complex of being and non-being is of the nature of pure vacuity, for then also it would be impossible to conceive any similarity between a vacuum entity and real silver[3].

[1] *na ca tadbajjñāne'stviti vācyam. tad-ākārasya satyatve bhrāntitvā-nupapattiḥ asattve tu na tasya jñānā-kāratā. tucchasya vastv-ākāratā-nupapatteḥ. tad-ākāratve ca khyātir eva tucche'ti śuktikādau na rajatā-rthi-pravṛttiḥ.* Meghanādāri, *Naya-dyu-maṇi* (MS.).

The general drift of Meghanādāri's theme may be summed up in the words of Anantācārya in his *Jñāna-yāthārthya-vāda* (MS.) as follows: "*tathā ca rajatatvaṃ śukti-niṣṭha-viṣayatā-vacchedakatvā-bhāvavat śukty-avṛttitvāt yo yad-avṛttiḥ sa tan-niṣṭha-dharma-nirūpitā-vacchedakatvā-bhāvavān iti sāmānya-vyāptau daṇḍa-niṣṭha-kāraṇatā-vacchedakatvā-bhāvavad daṇḍā-vṛtti ghaṭatvādikaṃ dṛṣṭāntaḥ.*"

[2] "*tasyā'nirvācya-rajatatayā grahaṇād viparīta-khyāti-pakṣa-pātaḥ... samyag-rajata-dhīr hi pravṛtti-hetuḥ... tasya pratīty-ātmaka-vastv-ātmakayor bhāsvaratvā-di-sādṛśyā-bhāvāt.*" *Ibid.*

[3] *ekasya yugapat sad-asadā-tmaka-viruddha-dharmavattvā-nupapatteḥ. tad-upapattāv api sādṛśyā-nupapatteśca...śūnya-vastuni pramāṇā-bhāvāt. tat-sad-bhāve'pi tasya rajata-sādṛśyā-bhāvācca tato na pravṛttiḥ. Ibid.*

Again it is said that the illusory silver is called indefinable (*anirvacanīya*) because it is different from pure being such as the self which is never contradicted in experience (*ātmano bādhā-yogāt*) and from non-being such as the chimerical entities like the hare's horn which can never be objects of knowledge (*khyāty-ayogāt*). But in reply to this it may very well be urged that the being of the self cannot itself be proved, for if the self were the object of knowledge it would be as false as the world appearance; and if it were not it could not have any being. It cannot also be said to have being because of its association with the class concept of being, for the self is admitted to be one, and as such cannot be associated with class concept[1]. Again want of variability cannot be regarded as a condition of reality, for if the cognitive objects are unreal because they are variable, the knower himself would be variable on account of his association with variable objects and variable relations, and would therefore be false. Again being (*sattā*) is not as universal as it is supposed to be, for it is different from the entities (jug, etc.) to which it is supposed to belong and also from negation in the view that holds negation to be a positive category[2]. If the self is regarded as self-luminous, then it may also be contended that such self-luminosity must be validly proved; and it may also be urged that unless the existence of the self has already been so proved its character cannot be proved to be self-luminous.[3]

Again the *akhyāti* view is liable to two different interpretations, in both of which it may be styled in some sense as *yathārtha-khyāti*. In the first interpretation the illusion is supposed to be produced in the following manner: the visual organ is affected by the shining character of something before the eyes, and this shining character, being of the same nature as that of the silver, the shining character of the silver is remembered, and since it is not possible to dis-

[1] *tasya dṛśyatvā-nabhyupagame śaśa-viṣāṇā-dī-sāmyam. ātmanaḥ prameyatā ca ne'ṣṭe'ti, na tatas tat-sattā-siddhiḥ. tad-abhyupagatau ca prapañcavanmithyātvaṃ...ātma-vyakter ekatvā-bhimānāt tad-vyatirikta-padārthasyā'sattvā-bhimānācca sattā-samavāyitvā-nupapatteḥ.* Meghanādāri, *Naya-dyu-maṇi.*

[2] *atha ghaṭa-paṭā-di-bhedānāṃ vyāvartamānatvenā'pāramārthyam...ātmano'pi ghaṭa-paṭādi-sarva-padārthebhyo vyāvartamānatvān mithyātvā-pattiḥ...abhivyañjakā-pāramārthye'bhivyañgyā-pāramārthyam...na ca sattvasyai'va samasta-padārtheṣv anuvartamānaṃ pāramārthyam. ghaṭādayo'pi tad-apekṣayā vyāvartante...abhāvasya padārthā-ntarbhāve'pi tatra sattā-nabhyupagamāt sarva-padārthā-nuvṛtty-abhāvāt. Ibid.*

[3] *na ca tasya svayaṃ-prakāśatvān na pramāṇā-pekṣe'ti svayaṃ-prakāśatvasyā'pi pramāṇā-dhīnatvāt pramāṇā-ntara-siddhā-tmanaḥ svayaṃ-prakāśatvasya sādhyatvācca. na hi dharmy-aprasidhau dharma-sādhyatā. Ibid.*

tinguish whether this shining character belongs to silver or to something else, and since the object in front is associated with such an undiscriminated shining character, the shining character cannot be treated as a mere self-ejected idea, but has to be taken as having its true seat in that something before the eye; thus, the notion of silver is a result of a true perception. It would have been a false perception if the conch-shell had been perceived as silver, but in such a perception it is not the conch-shell, but "this" in front, that is perceived as silver. The general maxim is that the idea which corresponds to any particular kind of behaviour is to be regarded as a true representation of the object experienced in such a behaviour (*yad-artha-vyavahārā-nuguṇā ya dhīḥ sā tad-arthā*). This maxim has its application here inasmuch as the "this" in front can be experienced in practical behaviour as such, and the silvery character has also a true reference to real silver. So the notion "this silver" is to be regarded as a complex of two notions, the "this" and the "silver." Thus, the perception involved in the above interpretation is a true perception according to the *akhyāti* view. In the above explanation it is contended that just as the two different notions of substance and quality may both appear in the same concept, so there cannot be any difficulty in conceiving of a legitimate unity of two different notions in one illusory perception as "this silver." Such a fusion is possible on account of the fact that here two notions occur in the same moment and there is no gap between them. This is different from the *anyathā-khyāti* view, in which one thing is supposed to appear as another. The objections against this view are: firstly, that a defect cannot possibly transmute one thing into another; secondly, if illusions be regarded as the appearance of one thing as another, then there is scope for such a fear, even in those cases which are regarded as correct perception; for all knowledge would be exposed to doubt, and this would land us in scepticism. If, therefore, it is suggested that illusion is due to a non-comprehension of the difference between the presence of a conch-shell and the memory-image of silver, that also would be impossible. For if "difference" means only the different entities (*bhedo vastu-svarūpam-eva*), then non-comprehension of difference (which is regarded as the root-cause of illusion in the present view) would mean the comprehension of the identity of the memory-image and the percept, and that would not account for the qualified concept where one notion (e.g. the silver) appears as qualifying the other notion (the "this" before the eye). Moreover, if two independent notions which are not related as substance and quality be miscomprehended as one concept, then any notion could be so united with any other notion, because the memory-images which are stored in our past experiences are limitless. Again the silver that was experienced in the past was experienced in association with the space in which it existed, and the reproduction of the silver and memory would also be associated with that special spatial quality. This would render its mis-association with the percept before the perceiver impossible on account of the spatial difference of the two. If it is contended that through the influence of defects the spatial quality of the memory-image is changed, then that would be the *anyathā-khyāti* theory, which would be inadmissible in the *akhyāti* view. Again since all sensible qualities must be associated with some kind of spatial relation, even if the original spatial quality be transmuted or changed, that would be no reason why such a spatial image should be felt as being in front of the perceiver. It must also be said that the distinctive differences between the memory-image and the percept are bound to be noted; for if such a distinctive difference were not noted, the memory-image could not be distinguished as "silver-image." It cannot also be said that though the percept can be distinguished from the memory-image the latter cannot be distinguished from the former, for the discriminative character is a constituent of both, and it is nothing but the white shining attribute. If it is urged that the spatial and other distinctive qualities are not noted in the memory-image and it appears merely as an image, then it may well be objected that any and every memory-image may be confused with the present percept, and even a stone may appear as silver.

Since both the *a-nirvacanīya-khyāti* and the *akhyāti* are in some sense *yathārtha-khyāti*, Meghanādāri refuted these two theories of illusion and attempted to show that the *yathārtha-khyāti* would be untenable in these views. Now he tries to show that all other possible interpretations of *yathārtha-khyāti* are invalid. The fundamental assumption of *yathārtha-khyāti* is that all knowledge must correspond to a real object like all right knowledge[1]. Thus, in other

[1] *vipratipannaḥ pratyayo yathā-rthaḥ pratyatvāt, sampratipanna-pratyaya-vaditi. Naya-dyu-maṇi*, p. 140 (MS.).

interpretations, the *yathārtha-khyāti* or the correspondence theory, might mean that cognition is produced by a real object or by the objective percept or that it means uncontradicted experience. The first alternative is untenable because even in the illusion of the conch-shell–silver the notion of silver has been produced by a real object, the conch-shell; the second view is untenable, for the object corresponding to the illusory percept of silver is not actually present in the conch-shell according to other theories; and so far as the operation of the memory impression of the silver as experienced in the past is concerned (*pūrvā-nubhūta-rajata-saṃskāra-dvārā*) its instrumentality is undeniable both in right and in illusory cognitions. The third alternative is untenable because contradiction refers to knowledge or judgment and not to things themselves. If it is said that the cognition refers to the illusory appearance and hence it is the illusory entity existing outside that is the object of perception, the obvious objection would be that perception refers to a non-illusory something in front of the perceiver, and this cannot be obviated. If non-illusory something is a constituent in the cognition, then it would be futile to say that the mere illusory perceptual form is all that can be the object of perception.

It cannot also be said that the illusory perception has no object (*nirviṣaya-khyāti*) and that it is called cognition, because, though it may not itself be amenable to behaviour as right cognitions are, it is similar to them by producing an impression that it also is amenable to behaviour, just as autumn clouds, which cannot shower, are also called clouds. The illusory cognition has for its content not only the illusory appearance but also the non-illusory "this" to which it objectively and adjectively refers. The truth, however, is that it is not indispensable for constituting the objectivity of a cognition that all the characters of the object should appear in the cognition; if any of its characters are manifested, that alone is sufficient to constitute the objectivity of an entity with regard to its cognition. The position, therefore, is that all cognitions refer and correspond to certain real entities in the objective world, and this cannot be explained on any other theory than on the supposition of a metaphysico-cosmological theory akin to the theory of *homoiomeriae*.

Anantācārya, in his *Jñāna-yāthārthya-vāda*, more or less repeats the arguments of Meghanādāri when he says that no cognition can be possible without its being based on a relation of correspondence to an objective entity. The content of knowledge must therefore have a direct correspondence with the objective entity to which it refers. Thus, since there is a perception of silver (in the illusory perception of conch-shell-silver), it must refer to an objective substratum corresponding to it[1]. The Mīmāṃsā supposition that errors are produced through non-discrimination of memory-image and perception is also wrong, because in that case we should have the experience of remembering silver and not of perceiving it as an objective entity before us[2]. Both Meghanādāri and Anantācārya take infinite pains to prove that their definition of error applies to all cases of illusions of diverse sorts, including dreams, into the details of which it is unnecessary for our present purposes to enter[3].

The Doctrine of Self-validity of Knowledge.

Pramāṇa, or valid knowledge, is defined as the cognition of objects as they are (*tathā-bhūtā-rtha-jñānaṃ hi pramāṇam ucyate*), and *apramāṇa*, or invalid knowledge, is described as cognition representing a wrong notion of an object (*a-tathā-bhūtā-rtha-jñānaṃ hi a-pramāṇam*). Such a validity, it is urged by Meghanādāri, is manifested by the knowledge itself (*tathātvā-vadhāraṇā-tmakaṃ prāmāṇyam ātmanai'va niścīyate*). This does not expose it to the criticism that knowledge, being passive, cannot at the same moment be also regarded as active, determining its own nature as valid (*na ca karma-kartṛtā-virodhaḥ*); for since it is of the nature of a faithful representation of the object, the manifestation of its own nature as such is an affirmation of its validity. If knowledge had no power by itself of affirming its own validity, there would be no way by which such a validity could be affirmed, for the affirmation of its validity by any other mediate process, or through any other instrumentality, will always raise the same question as to how the testimony of those processes or instruments can be accepted. For on such a supposition, knowledge not being self-valid, each such testimony has to be

[1] *tathā ca rajatatvaṃ śukti-niṣṭha-viṣayatā-vacchedakatvā-bhāvavat śukty-avṛttitvāt yo yad-avṛttiḥ sa tan-niṣṭha-dharma-nirūpitā-vacchedakatvā-bhāvavā-niti. Jñāna-yāthārthya-vāda* (MS.).

[2] *rajata-smaraṇe idaṃ-padārtha-grahaṇa-rūpa-jñāna-dvaya-kalpane rajataṃ smarāmī'ti tatrā'nubhava-prasaṅgaḥ, na tu rajataṃ paśyāmīti, sākṣāt-kāratva-vyañjaka-viṣayatāyāḥ smaraṇe'bhāvāt. Ibid.*

[3] (*a*) *Ibid.* (*b*) Meghanādāri, *Naya-dyu-maṇi*.

corroborated by another testimony, and that by another, and this will lead us to infinite regress.

In repudiating other views Meghanādāri points out that if validity is admitted as belonging to the collocative causes of knowledge (involving the self, the senses, and the object), then even the object would have to be regarded as a *pramāṇa*, and there would be no *prameya* or object left. Again, if affirmation is regarded as being of the nature of awareness, then even memory-knowledge has to be regarded as valid, since it is of the nature of awareness. Further, if affirmation of validity be of the nature of power, then such power, being non-sensible, has to be manifested by some other means of knowledge. If, again, validity is supposed to be produced by the causes of knowledge, then the dictum of the self-manifestation of validity would have to be given up. Uncontradicted behaviour also cannot be regarded as a definition of validity, for in that case even memory has to be regarded as valid by itself. It cannot also be defined as merely knowledge as such, for knowledge, not being able to turn back on itself to apprehend its own validity, would have to depend on something else, and that would imply the affirmation of validity through extraneous reference (*parataḥ-prāmāṇya*). Again in those cases where the cause of error is known, the cognition, though known as erroneous, irresistibly manifests itself to us (e.g. the movement of the sun). The assumption that all knowledge is associated with its validity is inapplicable to such cases. If, again, it is held that, whenever a later cognition rejects the former, we have a clear case as to how the invalidity of the previous cognition is demolished by the valid knowledge of a later moment; it may be urged that, when the generic knowledge of an object is replaced by a cognition of details, we have a case when one cognition replaces another, though it does not involve any criticism of the former knowledge.

In the Bhāṭṭa view, where it is supposed that when the object attains its specific cognized character its knowledge as an internal operation is inferred, both validity and invalidity ought to depend upon the objects. If, however, it is urged that the notion of validity shows itself in the faultless character of the instruments and condition of cognition, that would also imply the notion of validity as of extraneous origin. In the Prābhākara view, where knowledge is supposed to reveal the knower, the object and knowledge in one sweep, we have a much better case in so far that here knowledge has not to depend on anything extraneous. In this case self-invalidity may apply only to memory which has to depend on previous perception. To this the Nyāya objection is that since memory is also knowledge, and since all knowledge is self-revealing, the Prābhākaras ought consistently to admit the self-validity of memory.

Meghanādāri holds that all these objections against the self-validity of knowledge are invalid; for if the knowledge of the validity of any cognition has to depend on other *pramāṇas*, then there is an infinite regress. If, however, an attempt is made to avoid the regress by admitting the self-validity of any later *pramāṇa*, then it virtually amounts to the admission of self-validity (*anavasthā-parihārāya kasyacit svatastvā-ṅgīkāre ca na parataḥ-prāmāṇyam*). It may be urged that we are not necessarily prompted to action by a consciousness of validity, but through the probability of the same which is sought to be tested (*ajñātatayā jñātatayai'va*) by our efforts in the direction of the object. But in such a supposition there is no meaning in the attempt of our opponents in favour of the doctrine of the validity of cognition through extraneous means (*parataḥ-prāmāṇya*), for such a supposition is based on the view that our efforts are produced without a previous determination of the validity of cognition. When we see that a person, having perceived an object, makes an effort towards it, our natural conclusion is that he has, as the basis of the effort, a knowledge of the validity of his perception, for without it there can be no effort. It is hopeless to contend that there is validity of cognition in such cases without the knowledge of validity, for validity of knowledge always means the consciousness of such validity. The fact is that what constitutes a *pramāṇa* constitutes also its validity. It is wrong to think that validity appertains to anything else outside the cognition in question. When we see fire, its validity as a burning object is grasped with the very notion of fire and does not wait for the comprehension of any supersensible power or burning capacity of fire. The comprehension of fire as a burning object involves the knowledge of its association with its burning capacity. The knowledge of the burning capacity by itself cannot induce any action on our part, for we are always led to act by the comprehension of objects and not by their capacities. It is, therefore, wrong to separate the capacity from the object and speak of it as the cause of our effort. So the cognition of a *pramāṇa* involves with it its validity. Thus validity cannot be dissociated from the cognition of the object[1]. Further, validity cannot be defined as uncontradictedness, for if that test is to be applied to every knowledge it would lead to infinite regress. If, however, the knowledge of the validity of any cognition has to depend upon the knowledge of the defectlessness or correctness of the means and conditions of cognition, then, since validity of such knowledge has to depend upon another knowledge for the correctness of the means and condition, and that upon another, there is obviously an infinite regress. Since knowledge normally corresponds to the object, ordinarily there should not be any fear of any error arising from the defects of the causes and conditions of such knowledge; it is only in specific cases that such doubts may arise leading to special inquiries about the correctness or incorrectness of the means and conditions of knowledge. If there is an inquiry as to the validity of every knowledge, we should be landed in scepticism. Thus, validity means the manifestation of any form of content not awaiting the confirmation by other means of knowledge (*pramāṇā-ntarāṇapekṣayā'rthā-vacchinnattvam*), and such a conviction of validity is manifested along with the cognition itself. Memory, however, depends upon a prior cognition, and as such the conviction of its validity depends upon the validity of a prior knowledge, and hence it cannot be regarded as self-valid.

Rāmānujācārya, the teacher and maternal uncle of Veṅkaṭanātha, anticipates the objection that if self-validity of cognition is to be

[1] Rāmānujācārya, the maternal uncle of Veṅkaṭanātha, anticipates an objection that perceptual cognition reveals only the content (*vastu*). The revelation of such a content does not also involve the knowing relation which must necessarily be of a very varied nature, for a knowledge may refer to a content in infinitely diverse relation. The revelation of the mere content, therefore, without the specific knowing relation, does not involve the judgmental form, though the truth of this content may be ascertained at a later moment when it is reduced to a judgmental form as "I know it." There is no possibility of the affirmation of any validity at the moment of the revelation of the content. In reply to this, Rāmānujācārya says that the revelation of a content necessarily implies all its knowing relations in a general manner; and therefore, by the mode of its revelation at any particular moment, the mode of its specific knowing relation at any particular moment is grasped along with the content. Thus, since the revelation of the content implies the specific knowing relation, all cognitions may be regarded as implicitly judgmental, and there cannot be any objection to the self-validity of such knowledge.

If the content and knowledge were regarded as entirely distinct, as they must be, and if the knowing relation were not given implicitly along with the content, then all knowledge would be contentless, and as such any future attempt to relate them would be impossible. *Nyāya-kuliśa* (MS.).

admitted, then no doubt could arise with reference to any cognition[1]. The reply of Rāmānujācārya is that all cognitions are associated with a general conviction of their self-validity, but that does not prevent the rise of doubt in a certain specific direction. Self-validity in this view means that all cognitions produce by themselves a general conviction regarding their validity, though it does not rule out misapprehension in a specific direction[2].

The Ontological categories of the Rāmānuja School according to Veṅkaṭanātha.

(*a*) *Substance.*

Veṅkaṭanātha in his *Nyāya-siddhāñjana* and *Tattva-muktā-kalāpa*, tries to give a succinct account of the different categories, admitted or presumed, in the philosophy of Rāmānuja which the latter did not bring prominently to the view of his readers. The main division is that of the substance (*dravya*) and that which is non-substance (*adravya*). Substance is defined as that which has states (*daśāvat*) or which suffers change and modification. In admitting substance he tries to refute the Buddhist view that there is no substance, and all things are but a momentary conglomeration of separate entities which come into being and are destroyed the next moment. The Vaibhāṣika Buddhists say that there are four ultimate sense-data, viz. colour, taste, touch, and smell, which are themselves qualities and are not themselves qualities of anything. These can be grasped by our specific senses[3]. The Vātsīputriya school includes sound as a separate sense-data which can be perceived by the ear. Against this Veṅkaṭa urges that in all perception we have a notion that we touch what we see; such a perception cannot be false, for such a feeling is both invariable and uncontradicted in experience (*svārasika-bādhā-dṛṣter ananyathā-siddheśca*). Such a perception implies recognition (*pratyabhvjñā*) involving the notion that it is a permanent entity in the objective field which is perceived by a constant and unchangeable perceiver, and that the two sense-qualities refer to one and the same object. This recognition does not refer merely to the colour sensation, for the colour

[1] *sāmānyasya svato-graheṇā'bhyāsa-daśo-tpanna-jñāne tat-saṃśayo na syāt. Tattva-cintā-maṇi* (A.S. B), p. 184.

[2] *Nyāya-kuliśa*, p. 27 (MS.).

[3] *evam āhur vaibhāṣikāḥ nirādhārā nirdharmakāśca rūpādayaś catvāraḥ padārthāḥ. Tattva-muktā-kalāpa, Sarvārtha-siddhi*, p. 8.

sensation does not involve the tactile; nor does it refer merely to the tactile, as that does not involve colour. Perception, therefore, refers to an entity to which both the colour and the tactile qualities belong. Such a perception of recognition also repudiates the Buddhist view of the conglomeration of entities. For such a view naturally raises the question as to whether the conglomeration is different from or the same as the entities that conglomerate. In the latter case there cannot be any recognition of the object as one entity to which both the colour and the tactile quality belong. In the former case, when conglomeration is regarded as extraneous to the conglomerated entities, such a conglomeration must either be positive or negative. In the first alternative it amounts virtually to an admission of substances, for the assumption of the existence of merely the complex characters is inadmissible, since there cannot be anything like that which is neither a substance, nor quality, nor a qualifying relation. In the second alternative, if the conglomeration (*saṃghāta*) is non-existent, then it cannot produce the recognition. If conglomeration be defined as absence of interval between the perceived qualities, then also, since each sense quality has an appeal only to its own specific sense-organ, it is impossible that the perception of two different sense-qualities by two different organs should point to a common entity. Conglomeration cannot also be defined as spatial identity, for it must also involve temporal identity in order to give the notion of conglomeration. It cannot also be said that time and space are identical, for such a view which is true of momentariness, will be shown to be false by the refutation of momentariness. Space cannot also be of the nature of *ākāśa*, which in the Buddhist view means unobstructedness and is not a positive concept. Space cannot also be regarded as material identity with the sense-qualities, for the different sense-qualities are regarded as the unique nature of different moments[1]. If it means that the different sensible qualities have but one material behind them, that amounts to the admission of substance[2]. If the sensible qualities be regarded as a conglomeration on account of their existence in the same material object, then the material object would have to be described as a conglomeration by virtue of the existence of its elemental entities

[1] *na co'pādāna-rūpaḥ sparśa-rūpādīnāṃ bhinna-svalakṣaṇo-pādānatvā-bhyupagamāt. Tattva-muktā-kalāpa, Sarvārtha-siddhi*, p. 9.

[2] *eko-pādānatve tu tad eva dravyam. Ibid.*

in some other entity and that again in some other entity, and thus we have a vicious infinite. It cannot also be urged that the tactile sensation is inferred from the colour sensation, for such an inference would involve as its pre-condition the knowledge of the concomitance of the colour datum and the tactile, which is not possible unless they are known to belong to the same object. Neither can it be urged that the tactile and the colour-data are mutually associated; this gives rise to the notion that what is seen is touched, for the two sensations are known to be different in nature and originate through different sense-organs. It cannot also be said that our apperception that we touch what we see, being due to the operation of our instinctive root-desire (*vāsanā*), is false, for proceeding on the same analogy and following the *Yogācāra* view, one may as well deny all external data. If it is said that the sense-data are never contradicted in experience and thus that the idealistic view is wrong, then it may as well be pointed out that our notion that we experience an object to which colour and the tactile sensations belong is also never contradicted in experience. If it is urged that such an experience cannot be proved to be logically valid, then it may be proved with equal force that the existence of external sense-data cannot be logically proved. Therefore, our ordinary experience that the object as a substance is the repository of various sense-qualities cannot be invalidated. The view that all the other four elements, excepting air (*vāyu*), are themselves of diverse nature and are hence perceived as coloured, as touchable, etc., and that they are capable of being grasped by different senses is also false, as it does not necessarily involve the supposition that they are the repository of different sense-qualities; for experience shows that we intuit the fact that the objects are endowed with qualities. No one perceives a jug as being merely the colour-datum, but as an object having colour. It is also impossible that one neutral datum should have two different natures; for one entity cannot have two different natures. If it is said that two different qualities can abide in the same object, then that amounts to the admission of a substance in which different qualities inhere. It is also wrong to suppose that since the colour-datum and the tactile are grasped together they are identical in nature, for in the case of one error where a white conch-shell appears as yellow, the conch-shell is grasped without its white character, just as the yellow colour is grasped without its corresponding object. And it cannot be said that a separate yellow conch-shell is produced there; for such a view is directly contradicted in experience when we perceive the yellow colour and assert its identity with the conch-shell by touch. So, by the simultaneity of perception, coherence of qualities in an object is proved and not identity.

Moreover, even the Buddhists cannot prove that the tactile and the colour sensations occur simultaneously. If this were so, the testimony of the two different senses naturally points to the existence of two different characters. When an object is near we have a distinct perception of it, and when it is at a distance perception is indistinct. This distinctness or indistinctness cannot refer merely to the sense-character, for then their difference as objects would not be perceived. It cannot also refer to the size (*parimāṇa*), for the notion of size is admitted to be false by the Buddhists. Under the circumstances, it is to be admitted that such perceptions should refer to the objects.

The Buddhists are supposed to urge that if qualities are admitted to be separate from the substance, then it may be asked whether these qualities (*dharma*) have further qualities themselves or are without quality. In the latter alternative, being qualitiless, they are incapable of being defined or used in speech. In the former alternative, if qualities have further qualities, then the second grade qualities would have to be known by further qualities adhering to it, and that again by another, and thus we have a vicious infinite. Again, qualitiness (*dharmatva*) would itself be a quality. And it cannot be said that qualitiness is the very nature of quality, for a thing cannot be explained by having reference to itself. If qualitiness is something different from the quality, then such a concept would lead us in infinite regress. To this Veṅkaṭa's reply is that all qualities are not qualitiless. In some cases quality appears as itself qualified, as testified by experience. In those cases where a quality is not demonstrable with particularizing specification, such as "this quality is so and so" (*ittham-bhāva*), it does not depend for its comprehension on any other quality. Such qualities may be illustrated in the case of all abstract qualities and universals, and the opposite may be illustrated in the case of adjectival qualities such as the word "white" in the case of "white horse." There may be further specification regarding the nature of whiteness in the white horse, whereas when the word "whiteness" stands by itself any inquiry regarding its further specification becomes inadmissible. Logically, however, there may be a demand of further specification in both the cases and the fear of an infinite regress, but it is not felt in experience[1]. Moreover, one might imagine a vicious infinite in the necessity of having an awareness of an awareness, and then another and so on, but still this is only hyper-logical; for the awareness, in manifesting itself, manifests all that needs be known about it, and there is actually nothing gained by continuing the series. Thus a quality may be supposed to have further qualities, but whatever could be manifested by these may be regarded as revealed by the quality itself[2]. Again the assertion that if qualities are themselves without quality then they are unspeakable would involve the Buddhists themselves in a great difficulty when they described the nature of all things as unique; for obviously such a uniqueness (*svalakṣaṇya*) is without quality, and if that which has no quality cannot be described, then its specification as unique or *svalakṣaṇa* is impossible[3].

It may be urged that a quality may belong to that which has no quality or to that which has it. The former alternative would imply the existence of an entity in its negation which is impossible; for then everything could exist everywhere, and even the chimerical entities, which are not regarded as existing anywhere, would be regarded as existing. In the other alternative a quality would exist in a quality, which is an absurd conception, being only a circular reasoning (*ātmāśraya*). The reply of Veṅkaṭa to this is that he does not hold that the quality belongs to the locus of its negation or to that which has it already, but he holds that a qualified entity possesses the quality not as a qualified entity but as taken apart from it[4]. It cannot be urged that this virtually implies the old objection of the existence of a quality in the locus of its negation. To this Veṅkaṭa's reply is that the special feature of a qualified entity does

[1] *udāhṛteṣu niyatā-niyata-niṣkarṣaka-śabdeṣu jāti-guṇādeḥ pradhānatayā nirdeśe'pi santi kecit yathā-pramāṇam ittham-bhāvāḥ tvayā'pi hetu-sādhyā-di-dharmāṇāṃ pakṣa-dharmatvā-di-dharmāḥ svīkāryā anavasthā ca kathañcid upaśamanīyā. Tattva-muktā-kalāpa, Sarvārtha-siddhi*, p. 16.

[2] *svīkṛtañca saṃvedana-saṃvedane śabda-śabdādau sva-para-nirvāhakatvam. Ibid.*

[3] *kiñca sva-lakṣaṇā-dīnāṃ jātyā-dīnāñca samvṛti-siddhānāṃ nirdharmakatve'pi kathañcid abhilāpārhatvaṃ tvayāpi grāhyam. Ibid.*

[4] *vastutas' tad-viśiṣṭe viśeṣye tad viśiṣṭa-vṛty-abhāve tac-chūnye vṛtti syād eva. Ibid.* p. 17.

not belong to any of its constituents, and qualities of any of the constituents may not belong to the constituted entity[1]. If by the hyper-logical method the manner of the subsistence of a quality in a qualified entity is criticized, then it might lead to the view that the conception of qualified entity is without any sufficient ground, or self-contradictory, or that such a conception is itself inadmissible. All such views are meaningless, for the wildest criticism of opponents would involve the very notion of qualified entity in the use of their logical apparatus. So it has to be admitted that qualities adhere in qualified entities and that such an adherence does not involve infinite regress.

(*b*) *Criticism of the Sāṃkhya Inference for Establishing the Existence of Prakṛti.*

Veṅkaṭanātha admits the doctrine of *prakṛti* as the theory of materiality, but he thinks that such a doctrine can be accepted only on the testimony of scriptures and not on inference. He therefore criticizes the Sāṃkhya inference as follows. Neither *prakṛti* nor any of its evolutes such as *mahat*, *ahaṃkāra*, *tanmātras*, etc., can be known through perception. Neither *prakṛti* nor any of its evolutes can also be known by inference. The Sāṃkhyists hold that the effect has the same qualities as the cause. The world of effects, as we find it, is pleasurable, painful or dulling (*mohātmaka*); so its cause also must have, as its nature, pleasure, pain and a feeling of dullness. To this the question naturally arises regarding the relation of the causal qualities with the effects. They cannot be identical—the whiteness of the cloth is not identical with the thread of which it is made; the effect as a substance is not identical with causal qualities, for the white and the cloth are not identical. Further it cannot be said that the identity of the cause and the effect means merely that the effect is subordinate to the cause, as when one says that the effect, cloth, exists only in the *samavāya* relation in the cause and in no other form (*adṛṣṭer eva tantu-samavetatvāt paṭasya tantu-guṇatvoktiḥ*), for the obvious reply is that the Sāṃkhya itself does not admit the *samavāya* relation or any ultimate distinction between the whole and the part. If it is said that all that is intended is that the effect exists in the cause, then it may be pointed out that merely by such an affirmation nothing is gained; for that would not explain

[1] *na ca ghaṭavati bhūtale vartamānānāṃ guṇādīnāṃ ghaṭe'pi vṛtter adṛṣṭeḥ. Tattva-muktā-kalāpa, Sarvārtha-siddhi*, p. 18.

why the causal matter (*prakṛti*) should have the nature or qualities as the effect substance (*na kāraṇā-vasthasya sukha-duḥkhā-dyā-tmakatva-siddhiḥ*). If it is held that the effect shares the qualities of the cause, then also it is against the normal supposition that the effect qualities are generated by the cause qualities; and, moreover, such a supposition would imply that the effect should have no other quality than those of the cause. It cannot also be said that the effect is of the same nature as the cause (*sajātīya-guṇavattvam*), for the Sāṃkhyists admit the *mahat* to be a different category existent in the *prakṛti* as its cause (*vilakṣaṇa-mahatvā-dy-adhikaraṇatvād*). If it is held that the effect must have only qualities similar to the cause, then they may be admitted with impunity; if the effect has all its qualities the same as those of the cause, then there will be no difference between the effect and the cause. If, again, it is held that only certain specific traits which are not inappropriate in the cause can be supposed to migrate to the effect, and that the relation of the transmission of qualities from cause to the effect can thus be limited by a specific observation of the nature of the essential trait of the cause, then such cases in which living flies are produced from inanimate cow-dung would be inexplicable as cases of cause and effect[1].

The Sāṃkhyists are supposed to argue that if pure intelligence were supposed naturally to tend to worldly objects, then there would be no chance of its attaining liberation. Its association, therefore, must needs be supposed through the intermediary of some other category. This cannot be the senses, for even without them the mind alone may continue to imagine worldly objects. Even when the mind is inactive in sleep, one may dream of various objects. And this may lead to the assumption of the category of ego or *ahaṃkāra*; and in dreamless sleep, when the operation of this category of *ahaṃkāra* may be regarded as suspended, there is still the functioning of breathing, which leads to the assumption of another category, viz. *manas*. But as this has a limited operation, it presupposes some other cause; if that cause is also regarded as limited, then there would be an infinite regress. The Sāṃkhyists, therefore, rest with the assumption that the cause of *mahat* is unlimited, and this is *prakṛti* or *avyakta*. The reply of Veṅkaṭa

[1] *mṛt-suvarṇā-divat-kārya-viśeṣa-vyavasthāpaka-kāraṇa-svabhāva-sājātya-vivakṣāyāṃ gomaya-makṣikā-dy-ārabdha-vṛścikā-diṣu vyabhicārāt. Tattva-muktā-kalāpa, Sarvārtha-siddhi*, p. 22.

to this is that the association of pure intelligence with worldly objects is through the instrumentality of *karma*. It is also not possible to infer the existence of *Manas* as a separate category through the possibility of the thinking operation, for this may well be explained by the functioning of the subconscious root-impressions; for even the assumption of mind would not explain the thinking operation, since *manas*, by itself, cannot be regarded as capable of producing thought. *Manas*, being merely an instrument, cannot be regarded as playing the role of a substance of which thought may be regarded as a modification. In the state of dream also it is not necessary to assume the existence of a separate category of *ahaṃkāra* to explain dream experiences, for this may well be done by mind working in association with subconscious root-impression. The breathing operation in deep, dreamless sleep may also be explained by ordinary bio-motor functions, and for this there is no necessity for the assumption of *mahat*.

It is also wrong to suppose that the cause must be of a more unlimited extent than the effect, for it is not testified in ordinary experience, in which a big jug is often found to be made out of a lump of clay of a smaller size. It is also wrong to suppose that whatever is found to abide in an effect must also be found in its cause (*na hi yad yenā'nugatam tat tasya kāraṇam iti niyamaḥ*), for the various qualities that are found in a cow are never regarded as its cause. Following the same assumption, one would expect to find a separate cause of which the common characteristics of the *prakṛti* and its evolutes are the effects, and this would involve the admission of another cause of the *prakṛti* itself (*vyaktā-vyakta-sādhāraṇa-dharmāṇāṃ tad-ubhaya-kāraṇa-prasaṅgāt tathā ca tattvā-dhikya-prasaṅgaḥ*). Thus, the argument that an effect must have as its cause qualitative entities that inhere in it is false. The earthiness (*mṛttva*) which inheres in the jug is not its cause, and the earthy substance (*mṛd-dravya*) which shows itself in its unmodified form or its modified form as jug cannot be said to be inherent in the jug. Again the argument that things which are related as cause and effect have the same form is also false; for if this sameness means identity, then no distinction can be made between cause and effect. If this sameness means the existence of some similar qualities, then there may be such similarity with other things (which are not cause and effect) as well. Again applying the same analogy to the Sāṃkhya doctrine of *puruṣas* (which are admitted to have the common characteristic of intelligence), the Sāṃkhyists may well be asked to hold a new category as the cause of the *puruṣas*. Further, two jugs which are similar in their character are not for that reason produced from the same lump of clay; and, on the other hand, we have the illustration of production of effects from an entirely different cause, as in the case of production of insects from cow-dung. Thus, from our experiences of pleasure, pain, and dullness it does not follow that there is a common cause of the nature of pleasure, pain, and dullness, for these experiences can in each specific instance be explained by a specific cause, and there is no necessity to admit a separate common cause of the nature of three *guṇas*. If for the explanation of the ordinary pleasurable and painful experiences a separate pleasure-and-pain complex be admitted as the cause, then there may be further inquiry regarding this pleasure-and-pain complex and this will lead to infinite regress. Again if the three *guṇas* are regarded as the cause of the world, then that would not lead to the affirmation that the world is produced out of one cause; for though the three *guṇas* may be in a state of equilibrium, they may still be regarded as having their special contribution in generating the varied types of effects. Thus, the *triguṇa* or the *prakṛti* of the Sāṃkhya can never be proved by inference. The only mode of approach to the doctrine of *prakṛti* is through the scriptures. The three *guṇas* rest in the *prakṛti*, and in accordance with the gradual prominence of *sattva*, *rajas*, and *tamas*, three kinds of *mahat* are produced. From these three types of *mahat* three kinds of *ahaṃkāras* are produced. Out of the first type (i.e. *sāttvika ahaṃkāra*) the eleven senses are produced. Out of the last type (viz. the *tāmasa ahaṃkāra*) the *tanmātras* (also called the *bhūtādi*) are produced. The second type of *ahaṃkāra* (called *rājasa ahaṃkāra*) behaves as an accessory for the production of both the eleven senses and the *bhūtādi*. There are some who say that the conative senses are produced by *rājasa ahaṃkāra*. This cannot be accepted, as it is against the scriptural testimony. The *tanmātras* represent the subtle stage of evolution between the *tāmasa ahaṃkāra* and the gross elemental stage of the *bhūtas*[1]. The *śabda-tan-mātra* (sound-

[1] *bhūtānām avyavahita-sūkṣmā-vasthā-viśiṣṭaṃ dravyaṃ tanmātraṃ dadhi-rūpeṇa pariṇamamānasya payaso madhyamā-vasthāvad bhūta-rūpeṇa pariṇamamānasya dravyasya tataḥ pūrvā kācid avasthā tanmātrā. Nyāya-siddhāñjana*, p. 25.

potential) is produced from *bhūtādi*, and from it the gross elemental sound is produced. Again the *rūpa-tanmātra* (light-heat-potential) is produced from the *bhūtādi* or the *tāmasa ahaṃkāra*, and from the *rūpa-tanmātra* (light-heat-potential) gross light-heat is produced, and so on. Lokācārya, however, says that there is another view of the genesis of the *tanmātra* and the *bhūta* which has also the support of the scriptures and cannot therefore be ignored. This is as follows: *śabda-tanmātra* is produced from the *bhūtādi* and the *ākāśa* is produced from the *śabda-tanmātra* (sound-potential); the *ākāśa* again produces the *sparśa-tanmātra* (the touch-potential) and air is produced from the touch-potential. Again from air heat-light-potential (*rūpa-tanmātra*) is produced and from heat-light-potential *tejas* (heat-light) is produced; from *tejas*, *rasa-tanmātra* (taste-potential) is produced, and from it water. From water again the *gandha-tanmātra* (smell-potential) is produced, and from it the earth[1].

The view is explained by Varavara on the supposition that just as a seed can produce shoots only when it is covered by husks, so the *tanmātras* can be supposed to be able to produce further evolutes only when they can operate from within the envelope of the *bhūtādi*[2].

The process of evolution according to the said interpretation is as follows. *Śabda-tanmātra* is produced from *bhūtādi* which then envelops it, and then in such an enveloped state *ākāśa* is produced. Then from such a *śabda-tanmātra*, *sparśa-tan-mātra* is produced which

[1] This view seems to be held in the *Viṣṇu-purāṇa*, I. 3. 66, etc. where it is distinctly said that the element of *ākāśa* produces *sparśa-tanmātra* (touch-potential). Varavara, however, in his commentary on the *Tattvatraya* of Lokācārya, wishes to point out that according to Parāśara's commentary this has been explained as being the production of *tanmātras* from *tanmātras*, though it clearly contradicts the manifest expressions of the *Viṣṇu-purāna* when it states that *tanmātras* are produced from the *bhūtādi*. He further points out that in the Mahābhārata (*Śāntiparva Mokṣadharma*, Ch. XXX) the *vikāras* or pure modifications are described as sixteen and the causes (*prakṛti*) as eight. But in this counting the sixteen *vikāras* (eleven senses and the five categories—*śabda*, etc.), the distinction between the five *tanmātras* and the five elements has not been observed on account of there not being any essential difference, the grosser stages being only modified states of the subtler ones (*tanmātrāṇām bhūtebhyaḥ svarūpa-bhedā-bhāvāt avasthā-bheda-mātrattvāt*). According to this interpretation the eight *Prakṛtis* mean the *prakṛti*, the *mahat*, the *ahaṃkāra* and five categories of *ākāśa*, etc., in their gross forms. The five categories included under the sixteen *vikāras* are the *tanmātras* which are regarded as modifications of the elemental states of the *bhūtas*.

[2] *yathā tvak-śūnya-vījasyā'ṃkura-śaktir nāsti,*
tathā'varaṇa-śūnyasyo'ttara-kārya-śaktir nāstīti bhānāt
kāraṇa-guṇaṃ vino'ttaro-ttara-guṇa-viśeṣeṣu. . . .
sva-viśeṣasyo'kta-guṇā-tiśayā-nupapatteḥ.
Varavara's *bhāṣya* on *Tattvatraya*, p. 58.

envelops the *śabda-tanmātra*. The *sparśa-tanmātra*, as enveloped by the *śabda-tanmātra*, produces the *vāyu* through the accessory help of *ākāśa*. Then from this *sparśa-tanmātra* the *rūpa-tanmātra* is produced. The *rūpa-tanmātra* in its turn envelops the *sparśa-tanmātra* and then from the *rūpa-tanmātra*, as enveloped by the *sparśa-tanmātra*, *tejas* is produced through the accessory help of *vāyu*. Again the *rasa-tanmātra* is produced from the *rūpa-tanmātra*, which again envelops the *rasa-tanmātra*. From the *rasa-tanmātra* enveloped by the *rūpa-tanmatra* water is produced through the accessory help of *tejas*. From the *rasa-tanmātra* the *gandha-tanmātra* is produced which again, enveloped by *rasa-tanmātra*, produces earth through the accessory help of water[1].

Varavara points out that in the *Tattva-nirūpaṇa* another genesis of creation is given which is as follows. *Śabda-tan-mātra* is produced from *bhūtādi* and as a gross state of it *ākāśa* is produced. The *bhūtādi* envelops the *śabda-tanmātra* and the *ākāśa*. From the transforming *śabda-tan-mātra*, through the accessory of the gross *ākāśa* as enveloped by *bhūtādi*, the *sparśa-tanmātra* is produced and from such a *sparśa-tanmātra vāyu* is produced. The *śabda-tan-mātra* then envelops both the *sparśa-tanmātra* and the *vāyu*, and from the transforming *sparśa-tanmātra*, through the accessory of *vāyu* as enveloped by *śabda-tanmātra*, the *rūpa-tanmātra* is produced. From the *rūpa-tanmātra*, similarly, *tejas* is produced, and so on. In this view, in the production of the *sparśa* and other *tanmātras* the accessory help of the previous *bhūtas* is found necessary.

As Veṅkaṭanātha accepts the view that the gross *bhūta* of *ākāśa* acts as accessory to the production of the later *bhūtas*, he criticizes the Sāṃkhya view that the gross *bhūtas* are produced from the synthesis of *tanmātras*[2]. The Sāṃkhyists, again, think that the evolution of the different categories from *prakṛti* is due to an inherent teleology and not to the operation of any separate agent. Veṅkaṭa, however, as a true follower of Rāmānuja, repudiates it and asserts that the evolving operation of the *prakṛti* can only proceed through the dynamic operation of God Himself.

[1] Varavara's *bhāṣya* on *Tattvatraya*, p. 59.

[2] *sāṃkhyāstu pañchā'pi tanmātrāṇi sākṣāt-tāmasā-haṃkāro-tpannāni tatra śabda-tanmātram ākāśā-rambhakam itarāṇi tu tanmātrāṇi pūrva-pūrva-tanmātra-sahakṛtāny uttaro-ttara-bhūtā-rambhakānī'ty āhuḥ tad asat. ākāśād vāyur ity-ādy-ananyathā-siddho-pādānakrama-viśeṣā-bhidhāna-darśanāt. Nyāya-siddhāñjana*, pp. 25–26.

(*c*) *Refutation of the Atomic Theory of Nyāya in relation to Whole and Part.*

In refuting the *Nyāya* view that the parts attach themselves to each other and thereby produce the whole, and ultimately the partless atoms combine together to form a molecule, Veṅkaṭa introduces the following arguments. So far as the association of the wholes through their parts (beginning from the molecules) through the association of the parts are concerned, Veṅkaṭa has nothing to object. His objection is against the possibility of an atomic contract for the formation of molecules. If the atoms combine together through their parts, then these parts may be conceived to have further parts, and thus there would be infinite regress. If these parts are regarded as not different from the whole, then the different atoms could well be regarded as occupying the same atomic space, and thus they would not produce a conglomeration bigger in size than the constituent atoms. Further, it is not possible to imagine that there should be wholes without the parts also being present. Proceeding in this way, if the atomic combination cannot account for the origin of bigger measures, the possibility of objects of different magnitude through conglomeration (e.g. a hill or a mustard seed) would be inexplicable. If it is said that parts refer to the different sides of an atom, then also it might be urged that a partless atom cannot have sides.

It is held that knowledge, though one, can refer to many, though it is partless. It may also be urged in this connection that if it refers to all objects in their entirety, then the constituent entities would not be referred to separately, and it cannot also refer to the objects separately in parts, for then intelligence itself would not be partless. The Naiyāyika may also, on this analogy, urge that any solution that the idealist may find to his difficulty also applies to the atomic theory. To this the obvious answer of the idealist is that in the case of intelligence, experience testifies that though one and partless it can refer to many, and the Naiyāyikas have no such advantage to show in their favour, for the Naiyāyikas do not admit that in any case wholes may combine except through their parts. The objection cannot be laid against the Buddhist theory of conglomeration (*saṅghāta*), for there such conglomeration is not due to contact. The Naiyāyikas may be supposed to raise an objection regarding the association of all-pervasive entities (*vibhu*) with finite objects; such an association has to be admitted, for otherwise the association of the self or the *ākāśa* with objects cannot be explained; it is not also possible to hold that all pervasive entities have parts. So ultimately it has to be admitted that the partless all-pervasive entities have contact with finite objects, and if their procedure is accepted, then the same might explain the contact of partless atoms. To this Veṅkaṭa's reply is that the illustration of the contact of all-pervasive entities with finite objects might well be thrown in our face, if we had attempted to refute the view that wholes had no specific qualities; but our main object is to show the inconsistency to which the Naiyāyikas are exposed when they apply their theory that all combinations of wholes must be through parts to the combination of the supposed partless atoms. As a matter of fact, the error lies in the assumption that the atoms are partless. If it is supposed that division of particles must ultimately take us to partless atoms, the obvious reply is that from the division of parts we could not go to the partless, the better way being the acceptance of the smallest visible particles called the *trasareṇu*. If it is urged that if *trasareṇu* is the atom, then it must be invisible, the obvious reply is that there is no such general concomitance between atomic nature and invisibility. The better course, therefore, is to accept the *trasareṇu* as ultimate particles of matter. There is, therefore, no necessity to admit *dvyaṇuka* also.

Veṅkaṭanātha further objects to the Nyāya doctrine of the formation of wholes (*avayavī*) from parts (*avayava*) and points out that if this is to be admitted, then the weight of an object must be due to the weight of the atoms; but the Naiyāyikas hold that the atoms have no weight. The proper view therefore is that the effect, or the so-called whole, is to be regarded as being only a modified condition of the parts. The causal operation in such a view is justified in producing the change in the condition of the causal object and not in producing a new object in the effect or the whole as is supposed by the Naiyāyikas. Again in the consideration of the production of the wholes from parts, when the thread is regarded as the cause of the production of the whole, the cloth, it may be observed that in the process of the production we find various accretions through the gradual addition of one thread after another. In each such addition we have separate wholes, since the process may easily be stopped anywhere; and in such a view we have the addition of a part to a whole for the production of another whole. This is obviously against the Nyāya view, which would not lend any support to the doctrine that the addition of parts to wholes would produce other wholes. The Naiyāyikas urge that if a whole as a different entity from the parts be not admitted, and if a whole be regarded as nothing more than a collection of atoms, then, the atoms being invisible, the wholes would be invisible. The production of gross wholes not being admitted, the supposed explanation that there is an illusion of grossness in the atoms would also be inadmissible[1]. The question now is what is meant by grossness. If it means a new measure, then it is quite admissible in the Rāmānuja view in which the production of separate wholes is not admitted; for just as the atomists would think of the production of the new wholes from atoms, so the Rāmānujist may also agree to the production of a new measure (*parimāṇa*). If the Naiyāyikas object to this and urge that the production of a new measure from the atomic is inadmissible, then they may as well be asked how they would also account for the notion of plurality in a collection of separate entities, each of which may be regarded as one in itself. If it is said that the conception of number as plurality proceeds from a mental oscillation incorporating the diversity, then it may also be argued that from the absence of any such oscillation there may be a failure in noting the separateness which may give rise to a notion of gross measure. Moreover, there is nothing incongruous in the fact that if individuals are not visible the collection may be visible. If the grossness is supposed to mean the occupation of more spatial units than the individual entities, then also it is not inadmissible; for in a collection of small particles they are cognized as occupying different spatial units. If it is urged that since no separate wholes are admitted to be produced the gross dimension cannot be perceptible, the obvious reply is that the perception of grossness has no connection with the perception of wholes. Even before the dyad is produced the combining atoms have to be admitted as occupying more space in their totality than in their individual capacity; for otherwise they in their totality could not produce a bigger dimension. Thus, there is no reason for admitting the production of wholes separate from the parts. Under the same specific

[1] *sthūla-dravyā-bhāve cā'ṇu-saṁhatau sthūlatvā-dhyāso na siddhyet. Sarvārtha-siddhi*, p. 46.

kind of combination of threads in which the Naiyāyikas think that a cloth could be produced, the Rāmānujists think that the threads under the selfsame condition are the cloth and there is no separate production of cloth[1]. But it should not be thought that any slight change in the condition of an object would mean that thereby there is a new object so long as the object remains sufficiently unchanged to be recognized as the same for all practical purposes. The causal operation, according to the Rāmānujists, only brings about new changes of conditions and states in the already existent causal substance. This is thus different from the Sāṃkhya theory of *sat-kārya-vāda*, according to which the effect is already existent in the cause even before the causal operation is set in motion. Veṅkaṭa, therefore, criticizes the Sāṃkhya theory of *sat-kārya-vāda*.

(*d*) *Criticism of the Sāṃkhya Theory of Sat-kārya-vāda.*

The Sāṃkhya is wrong in supposing that the effect (e.g. the jug) was pre-existent in its cause (e.g. earth), for had it been so the causal operation would have been fruitless. The Sāṃkhya may, however, say that the causal operation serves to manifest what was potentially existing in the cause; the function of causal operation is thus manifestation and not production. This, however, is wrong, for manifestation (*vyaṅga*) and production (*kārya*) are two different words having two different concepts. Manifestation can occur only in the operation of a manifesting agent with the help of its accessories in making an object manifested with regard to a particular sense-organ in a particular place where the manifesting agent exists[2]. It would first be proved that the pre-existent effect is manifested and not produced; only then would it have been worth while to inquire into the conditions of the causal operation to see whether it satisfied the necessary conditions of a manifesting agent. But the Sāṃkhya can hardly succeed in showing that it is so. The Sāṃkhyist says that the effect is pre-existent before the causal

[1] *yadi saṃsṛṣṭās tantava eva paṭas tatas tantu-rāśimātre'pi paṭa-dhīḥ syād ity āha saṃsargāder iti. na hi tvayā'pi tantu-saṃsarga-mātraṃ paṭasyā'samavāyi-kāraṇam iṣyate tathā sati kuvindā-di-vyāpāra-nairapekṣya-prasaṅgāt ato yādṛśāt saṃsarga-viśeṣād avayavī tavo'tpadyate tādṛśa-saṃsarga-viśiṣṭās tantavaḥ paṭa iti kvā'tiprasaṅgaḥ. Sarvārtha-siddhi*, p. 48.

[2] *kārya-vyaṅgya-śabdau ca vyavasthita-viṣayau loke dṛṣṭau kāraka-vyañjaka-bhedaś ca kārakaṃ samagram apy ekam utpādayati vyañjakantu sahakāri-sampannaṃ samāne-ndriya-grāhyāni samāna-deśa-sthāni tādṛśāni sarvāṇyapi vyanakti. Ibid.* pp. 55–56.

operation; but the causal operation is itself an effect, and if their previous assertion is correct then it was non-existent when the effect was non-manifested. If the causal operation was also existent at the time of the existence of the cause, then the effect would also have been present in the cause in a manifested state. The Sāṃkhya says that what is non-existent cannot be produced, and this implies that a thing is existent because it can be produced, which is, on the face of it, self-contradictory. The theory that the effect is pre-existing in the cause could have been admitted as a last resort if there were no other theory available, but the ordinary notion of causality as invariable and immediate antecedent is quite sufficient to explain the phenomenon of production. Therefore, there is no necessity for such a chimerical theory. Again instead of holding that the effect is nothing more than the potential power in the cause, it is much better to say that the cause has such power by which it can produce the effect under certain conditions[1]. Again it may be thought about the instrumental and other accessory agents that if they lead to the generation of effort, as indeed they do, they should also be accepted as subtle potential states of the effect. But this is not admitted by the Sāṃkhyist, for according to him it is only the material cause which is regarded as the potential effect. Otherwise even the *puruṣa*, which, teleologically, is to be regarded as the instrumental cause of the world phenomenon, has to be regarded as a part of *prakṛti*. Again consider the destructive agents. Are the destructible effects already present in the destructible agent? It cannot be so, for they are entirely opposed to each other. If it were not so, it could not destroy it[2]. If it were not so and yet if it would be destroyed by the destructive agent, then everything could be destroyed by everything.

Turning to the function of the material cause, it may be pointed out that it cannot be defined as that from which an effect is produced (*tajjanyatva*); for then even an instrumental cause would be included in the material cause. Nor can it be regarded as a modification (*tadvikāratva*), for then the effect would be only the quality of the cause, and there would be no difference between the cause

[1] *yathā sarveṣu dravyeṣu tilā eva taila-garbhāḥ sva-kāraṇa-śaktyā sṛjyante tathā tat-tat-kārya-niyata-pūrva-bhāvitayā tat-tad-utpādaka-svabhāvās te te bhāvās tathai've'ti svīkāryam. Sarvārtha-siddhi*, p. 59.

[2] *nāśakeṣu ca nāśya-vṛttir asti na vā. asti cet bahnau tūlavad virodhaḥ na cet kathaṃ tadeva tasya nāśakam. Ibid.* p. 60.

and the effect. But we see that the cloth is different from threads[1]. If the effect is regarded as identical with the cause on the ground that though there cannot be any contact between the effect and the cause yet the former is never outside the latter, the obvious reply is that in the view that the effect is not a substance there need not be any contact, and if it is a property of the cause it is never beside it[2]. On the view that the effect is a manifestation, it may be asked whether such a manifestation is eternal or itself an effect. In the former case no causal operation is necessary for the manifestation. In the latter case, if the manifestation be regarded as a separate effect, then it virtually amounts to a partial sacrifice of *sat-kārya-vāda*. If for the manifestation of a manifestation causal operation is necessary, then that will lead to a vicious infinite. Moreover, if manifestation is itself regarded as an effect, then since it did not exist before, its coming into being would involve the sacrifice of *sat-kārya-vāda*.

It may be urged that the production of an effect is not of the nature of the effect itself, for one always speaks of an effect as being produced. Thus the effect is different from production. If this is admitted, then what is the difficulty in accepting the view that the effect may be manifested? If the word production be considered more logical, then with regard to it also there may be the same question, whether a production is produced or manifested, and in the former case there would be infinite regress, and in the latter no necessity for the causal operation. With regard to the manifestation also there would be the same difficulty as to whether it is produced or manifested, and in both cases there would be vicious infinite. The reply to this is that production means the operation of the causal agents, and if this operation be again admitted to be produced by the operation of its own causal constituent, and that by another, there is no doubt an infinite regress, but it is not vicious and is admitted by all. When there is a movement of a specific nature in the thread, we say a cloth is produced, or rather at the very first moment of such a movement involving the cloth-state of the thread

[1] *tad-dharmatva-hetū-kta-doṣād eva ubhayatra paṭā-vasthā tantvā-tmā na bhavati tantubhyo bhinnatvāt ghaṭavad iti prati-prayogasya śakyatvācca. Sarvārtha-siddhi*, p. 60.

[2] *tādātmya-virahe'pi anyatarasyā'dravyatvāt saṃyogā-bhāvaḥ tad-dharma-svabhāvatvād eva aprāpti-parihārāt iti anyathā-siddhasya asādhakatvāt. Ibid.* p. 61.

we say that a cloth is produced[1]. It is for this reason that we can speak of an effect as being produced. Such a production has no further production.

(*e*) *Refutation of the Buddhist Doctrine of Momentariness.*

The Buddhists hold that the theory of causal efficiency proves that whatever is existent must be momentary; for the same efficiency cannot be produced again and again. So, in accordance with each efficiency or the production of effects, a separate entity has to be admitted. Since the efficiency at two different moments cannot be identical, the entities producing them also cannot be identical. Since the different characters that are supposed to belong to the same object represent different efficiencies, their attribution to the same object is also erroneous. Therefore, there are as many different entities as there are different character points in a particular moment (*yo yo viruddha-dharmā-dhyāsavān sa sa nānā*). To this Veṅkaṭanātha's reply is that things are not associated with diverse opposite characters, and that though in certain cases, e.g. the flowing river or the flame of a lamp, changing entities may show the appearance of an unchanging whole, there are undeniable cases of true recognition in all such cases where we perceive that it is the same thing which we both see and touch. The fact that in such cases subconscious impressions may also be working should not be exaggerated to such an extent as to lead us to believe that recognition is a mere affair of memory. Recognition is a case where perception predominates, or at the worst it may be said to be a joint complex of memory and perception. The objection that the presence of memory falsifies recognition is wrong, for not all memory is false. It is also wrong to think that memory is only subjective and as such cannot lead us to an objective determination; for memory is not only subjective but has also an objective reference involving the time character of the objects as past. Again the Buddhists say that the association of many characters to an object is wrong, for each character-point represents the efficiency of a momentary unit, and that, therefore, the association of many characters in recognition is false. To this Veṅkaṭa's reply is that if each momentary unit

[1] *yadā hi tantvā-dayaḥ vyāpriyante tadā paṭa utpadyate iti vyavaharanti ādya-kṣaṇā-vacchinna-paṭatvā-vasthai-va vā paṭo'tpattir ucyate sai'va tadavasthasyo'tpattir iti bhāṣyam api tad-abhiprāyam eva. Sarvārtha-siddhi*, p. 62.

is by itself capable of producing any effect, it ought to do it by its own nature, and it ought not to wait for the assistance of other accessories. Following the same analogy, even the unique nature of any momentary unit would not be the same with any other unique nature of any other moment, and thus the idea of identity would be impossible and would land us in nihilism. It is, therefore, wrong to suppose that there is a separate entity corresponding to each and every character unit[1]. The Buddhists are supposed to urge further that the experience of recognition identifies a past moment with a present, which is impossible. The reply of Veṅkaṭa is that though it would be absurd to connect a past moment with the present, there is no incongruity in associating them with an entity which has lived through the past and is also persisting in the present moment[2]. It is true that the affirmation of a past time in the present is contradictory, but the real mystery of the situation is that one time appears as many under diverse conditions (*upādhi*). In such cases the contradiction arises in associating the different conditions in each other's conditioned time unit, but this does not imply that the reference to the different conditions and time is inadmissible; for had it been so, even the concept of a successive series of moments would be inadmissible, since the notion of successive moments implies a reference of before and after, and hence in some way or other it brings together the past, the present and the future. If this be not admitted, the very concept of momentariness would have to be sacrificed[3]. If it is urged that momentariness (*kṣaṇa-sambandhitva*) means the unique self-identity of any entity, then that leads us to no new knowledge. Thus, the mere association of the past with the present leads us to no temporal self-contradiction.

Again the Buddhists are supposed to urge that perception refers

[1] *viruddhānāṃ deśa-kālā-dya-samāhita-virodhatvena sva-lakṣaṇasyā'pi virud-dha-śata-kṣuṇṇatayā nānātve tat-kṣodānāṃ ca tathā tathā kṣode kiñcid apy ekaṃ na siddhyet tad-abhāve ca kuto nai'kam iti mādhyamika-matā-pātaḥ. Sarvārtha-siddhi*, p. 66.

[2] *kāla-dvayasyā'nyonyasminn-abhāve'pi tad-ubhaya-sambandhini vastuny a-bhāvā-bhāvāt yas tu tasmin vastuny asambaddha kālaḥ tasya tatra sadbhāvaṃ na brūmaḥ. Ibid.* p. 68.

[3] *pūrvā-para-kāla-yogo hi viruddhaḥ sveno'pādhinā'vacchinnasyai'kasya kāla-syā'vāntaro-pādhibhir nānātve'pi tat-tad-upādhīnām eva tat-tad-avāntarakā-ladvayānvaya-virodhaḥ anyā-pekṣayā pūrvā-para-kālayor anyasya viruddhatve kṣana-kālasyā'py anyā-pekṣayā paurvāparyāt tat-kāla-vartitvam api vastuno viruddhyeta. Ibid.*

only to the present moment. It can never lead us to the comprehension of the past. Our notion, therefore, that things existent in the past are persistent in the present is an illusion due to the operation of the subconscious root-impressions which ignore difference between the past and the present, and impose the former on the latter, as silver is imposed on conch-shell. The reply of Veṅkaṭa to this is that perception demonstrates only the presence of an object in the present moment as against its absence; but it does not on that account deny its existence in the past. Just as "this" indicates the presence of an object in the present moment, the perceptual experience "that is this" demonstrates the persistence of the object in the past and in the present[1]. If it is urged that perception reveals its object as a present entity, then the Buddhist theory of perception as indeterminate (*nirvikalpa*), which cannot reveal the object as qualified by the temporal character as present, falls to the ground. If it is urged that perception reveals the existence of the object at the moment of the perceptual revelation, then also it is impossible in the Buddhist view, for the momentary object with which the sense-organ was in touch has ceased to exist by the time knowledge was produced. So, in whichever way the Buddhist may take it, he cannot prove that perception reveals an object only as present; whereas in the Rāmānuja view, since the sense-contact, the object as associated with it, and the temporal element associated with them, are continuous, the mental state is also continuous and as such the perception reveals the object as that with which the sense was in contact. Even after the cessation of the sense-contact, the mental state, indicating the perception of the object with which the sense was in contact, is comprehended[2].

Again if it is argued that whatever is invariably produced from anything must also be produced unconditionally without awaiting any causal operation, then it must be said that when leaves and flowers grow from a plant they do so unconditionally, which is absurd. Moreover, when in a series of momentary entities one entity follows another, it must do so without awaiting any cause; then, on the one hand, since each of the preceding entities has no

[1] *yathā idam iti tat-kāla-sattā gṛhyate tathā tad idaṃ iti kāla-dvaya-sattvam api pratyakṣeṇai'va gṛhītam. Sarvārtha-siddhi*, p. 69.

[2] *asman-mate tv indriya-samprayogasya tad-viśiṣṭa-vastunas tad-upahita-kālāṃśasya ca sthāyitvena dhī-kṣanānuvṛttau tad-viṣayatayā pratyakṣo-dayāt samprayogā-nantara-kṣaṇe dhīr api nirvartyate. Ibid.* p. 70.

special function to fulfil, it is without any causal efficiency and as such is non-existent; and, on the other hand, since each succeeding entity rises into being without waiting for any cause, it may rise into being in the preceding moment as well, and if this is so there would be no series at all. Again it is argued that since whatever is produced must necessarily be destroyed, destruction as such is unconditioned and takes place without awaiting any cause. Negation can be unconditioned only when it is an implication of position which as such is never produced but is always associated with any and every position (e.g. cow implies the negation of a horse). But negations which are produced always depend on certain causes which can produce them just as much as any positive entity, as in the case of the destruction of a jug by the stroke of a stick. If it is argued that the stroke of a stick does not produce any destruction but only starts a new series of existence in the form of the particles of the jug, then also there are many other illustrations (e.g. the blowing out of a flame) in which the explanation of the starting of a new series is not available. If it is argued that negation is mere nothing and as such does not depend on a cause like chimerical entities, e.g. the lotus of the sky, such an explanation would be meaningless; for negations or destructions are conditioned in time just as are any positive entities, and as such are different from chimerical entities (*pratiyogivad eva niyata-kālatayā pramitasya atyanta-tucchatā-yogāt*). If negations be regarded as similar to chimerical entities, then the former would be as beginningless as the latter, and, if this were so, then there would be no positive entities, all being beginningless negations. If negation were chimerical, then even at the time of negation there could be the positive entities, for negation being chimerical could not condition anything and this would amount to the persistence of all entities and cannot be acceptable to momentarists like the Buddhists. If negations were devoid only of certain specific characters, then they would be like the unique-charactered entities (*svalakṣaṇa*) which are also devoid of certain specific characters. If they were devoid of all characters (*sarva-svabhāva-viraha*), then they could have no place in a proposition which must affirm some predicate of them. If it is said that negation has a character as such, then that being its character it would not be devoid of any character. If such negations were not pre-existent, then their coming into being must depend on some causal operation. If they were pre-existent, then there would not be any positive entities (*prāk-sattve tu bhāvā-pahnavaḥ*).

If it is urged that the effect-moment as destruction is simultaneous with the cause-moment, then the positive entity and its destruction would occur at the same moment; and if this were so, there is no reason why the destruction should not precede the positive entity. If destruction is admitted to appear at a moment succeeding that of the production of the positive moment, then the destruction would not be unconditioned. If the sequence of the positive entity and its destruction be with reference to the positive entity itself and not to its production, then the positive entity would be the cause of the destruction. It cannot be said that destruction is conditioned only by the position, for its dependence on other accessory agents cannot be repudiated. It cannot be argued that the production of a moment is also its destruction, for that would be self-contradictory. It is sometimes maintained that difference does not constitute destruction, and hence the rise of a different-charactered moment does not imply the destruction of the previous moment. The destruction of a moment has thus to be regarded as a separate fact, and as such it is involved and inherent in the very production of a moment[1]. To this the reply is that a different-charactered entity must also be regarded as the destruction of the previous entity, for otherwise it would be impossible to assign any cause to the rise of such a different-charactered entity. If, again, the destruction be the very essence of an entity, then such an essence might as well manifest itself at the time of the rise of the present entity, and thus reduce it to the negation which would mean the universal negation of all things. If it is urged that an entity produces its own destruction by itself, then it would be meaningless to hold that destruction is unconditional; and if it is thus conditioned by itself, it would be idle to suppose that it does not depend on any other condition, for there is no means of knowing it. If it is admitted that an entity produces its own destruction with the help of other accessories, then the doctrine of momentariness fails. It has also been shown before that the affirmation of momentariness is distinctly contradicted by the phenomenon of recognition

[1] *yad yato bhidyate na tat tasya dhvaṃsaḥ yathā rūpasya rasaḥ. dhvaṃsas tu kasyacid eva bhavati iti tad-ātmakaḥ. ataḥ svo-tpattāv eva svātmani dhvaṃse sannihite kathaṃ kṣaṇā-ntaraṃ prāpnuyāt. Sarvārtha-siddhi*, p. 72.

as elaborated above. Again when the momentarist says that all things are momentary, how does he explain the fact that the effect-moment is caused by the cause-moment? If causation means nothing more than immediate succession, then the universe at a particular moment is caused by the universe at the preceding moment. The problem is whether such immediacy of succession is by itself competent to produce the effect-moment or needs the accessories of space and time. If such accessories are not necessary, then spatial co-existence or concomitance (as in the case of smoke and fire) ought not to lead to any inference. If such accessories are awaited, then it would mean that whatever is produced at any unit of space has also its cause in that unit of space and that unit of time. On such a view the effect-moment would be in the space and time of the cause, and thus the cause-space or cause-time would be co-extensive in two moments. If this were admitted, then the momentarist might as well admit that the cause persists in two moments. So, the momentarist who does not admit persisting time and space cannot also admit that any sequence should be conditioned by them. If it is said that a cause-moment starts its effect in the very space or time in which it exists, then there would be no unity of the series between the cause and the effect; and, by supposition, they are regarded as having different sets of moments for themselves. There might be superimposition but no unity of the series. If the unity of the series be not admitted, then the expectation that just as when a cotton-seed is dyed there is redness in the cotton, so in the moral sphere whenever there is the *vāsanā* or root-inclination there is also its fruit, fails. The co-existence of the causal-moment and the effect-moment does not imply the unity that is expected in a normal cause and effect relation, and it would therefore be difficult to say that such an effect has such a cause, for the momentaristic theory cannot establish the bond between cause and effect.

Let us now analyse the concept of momentariness. It may mean the fact that (1) an entity is associated with a moment (*kṣaṇa-sambandhavattva*), or (2) association with a momentary unit of time (*kṣaṇa-kāla-sambandhatvaṃ*), or (3) existence for only one moment (*kṣaṇa-mātra-vartitva*), or (4) absence of relation with two moments (*kṣaṇa-dvaya-sambandha-śūnyatva*), or (5) identity with the moment of time (*kṣaṇa-kālatvaṃ*), or (6) being determinant of the moment-character (*kṣaṇa-pādhitvaṃ*). The first alternative is inadmissible, for even those who believe in persistent entities admit that such entities, since they persist in time, are associated with a moment. The second alternative is inadmissible because the Buddhists do not believe in any separate category of time apart from the *kṣaṇa*[1]. On such an admission, again, an entity as time which is beyond a *kṣaṇa* has to be virtually accepted, which contradicts the doctrine of momentariness. The third alternative is directly contradicted in the experience of recognition which testifies to the fact that we touch what we see. The fourth view is also for the same reason contradicted in experience; and if any supposed entity which is not itself a *kṣaṇa* is not associated with two time-moments, then it can have only a chimerical existence, and, curiously enough, the Buddhists often compare all existent entities with chimerical objects[2]. The fifth alternative is also inadmissible, for just as an entity exists in a unit of space and cannot be identical with it, so also it cannot be identical with the time in which it exists, and it is directly contradicted in experience. The sixth alternative is also inadmissible for the reason that if objects were in their own nature determinants of moments, then there would be nothing to explain our notion of temporal succession[3]; and all our experiences depending on such a succession would be contradicted. If things did not persist in time and were absolutely destroyed without leaving any trace (*niranvaya-vināśaḥ*), then the ordinary experience of the world in which things are done for the purpose of reaping their benefits could not be explained. The man who had done some work would not wait a moment for his reward. In the Rāmānuja view persistence of the self is well explained in self-consciousness. The theory that such a self-consciousness refers only to the succeeding terms produced in the series of the *ālaya-vijñāna* is only a theory which has no verification, and such a theory is directly contradicted by the well attested maxim that the experience of one individual cannot be remembered by another (*nā'nya-dṛṣṭaṃ smaraty anyaḥ*). There is also no way in which the

[1] *kālam evā'nicchatas te ko'sau kṣaṇa-kālaḥ kaś ca tasya sambandhaḥ. Sarvārtha-siddhi*, p. 74.

[2] *yasminnanityatā nāsti kāryatā'pi na vidyate tasmin yathā kha-puspādāviti śakyaṃ hi bhāṣitum. Ibid.* p. 75.

[3] *yadā hi ghaṭā-dayaḥ svarūpeṇa kṣano-pādhayaḥ syuḥ kāla-tāratamya-dhīḥ kutrā'pi na bhavet. Ibid.*

terms of the *ālaya-vijñāna* series may be associated with volitional notions.

If the momentariness of entities means that they are modified or conditioned by moments, then also the question arises if they are not themselves momentary, how can they be conditioned by moments? If the conditioning by moments means that causal collocations represent only the previous moment of the effect (*kārya-prāga-bhāva-samanvita*), then it may be urged by the opponent that it would be difficult to refute such momentariness. On the side of the opponent it may be further said that the criticism that the conglomeration of the causes is something different from, or identical with the conglomerating entities, cannot be made; for, in either case, since such an entity would, according to the Rāmānujists, be a persisting one, it would not condition a moment. The reply is that conglomeration can neither mean relation nor the related entities; for the word "conglomeration" cannot apply specifically to each of the entities, and as such it is to be admitted that the causal entities, collected together by some condition, represent the conglomeration. If such entities are regarded as determining the moment, then they must necessarily be persistent. If it is held that the combining condition is the condition of the *kṣaṇa*, then the reply is that the production must be due to the joint operations of the combining conditions and the specific collocating entities. Of these the combining condition is not momentary, and since the collocating entities would stay till they were combined, they are also not momentary. The condition of the *kṣaṇa* seems, therefore, to be the last accessory agent or operation which associates with it the previous entities or operations and thereby behaves as the condition of the moment immediately antecedent to the effect. There is thus nothing momentary in it. Time being unlimited in its nature cannot be parcelled out in moments. The supposed moments can be attributed to an operation or an existing entity only for specifying particular states or conditions for practical purposes; but an entity that exists, exists in time, and thus outgrows the limits of a previous or later moment. So, though a specific unit of time may be regarded as momentary, the entity that exists, therefore, is not momentary in the nature of its own existence. Since the Buddhists do not admit time, they are not justified in speaking of momentary time in which things are supposed to exist. Nor are they justified in holding that nature in itself suffers change in every moment, for that virtually amounts to the existence of a persisting entity which suffers modification[1].

The Buddhist assumption that things are destroyed entirely, and there are no elements in them that persist (*niranvaya-vināśa*), on the analogy that flames are destroyed without leaving any trace of their existence, is false. For, from various other instances, e.g. the case of jugs, cloth, etc., we find that their destruction means only a change of state and not entire annihilation; and from this analogy it is reasonable to suppose that the elements of the flame that are destroyed are not completely annihilated but persist in invisible forms. Even when a flame is destroyed, the tip of the wick is felt to be slightly warm, and this is certainly to be interpreted as a remnant of the heat possessed by the flame. If the last stage in the destruction of an entity be regarded as lapsing into entire annihilation, it would have no causal efficiency and as such would be non-existent. If the last stage is non-existent, then its previous stage also would have no causal efficiency and would be non-existent, and so on. This would lead to universal non-existence.

(*f*) *Refutation of the Cārvāka criticism against the Doctrine of Causality.*

The problem of causality naturally brings in the question of time relation between the cause and the effect, i.e. whether the effect precedes the cause, or whether the cause precedes the effect, or whether they are simultaneous. If the effect precedes the cause, then it would not depend upon causal operation for its existence and it would then be an eternally existent entity like space. If it is not existent, then it cannot be brought into existence by any means, for a non-existent entity cannot be produced. If the effect were produced before the cause, then the so-called "cause" could not be its cause. If the cause and effect were simultaneous, then it would be difficult to determine which is the cause and which the effect. If the cause precedes the effect, then, again, it may be asked whether the effect was already existent or beside it. If it is already existent, there is no need of causal operation, and that which is to happen

[1] *sarva-kṣaṇikatvaṃ sādhayitum upakramya sthira-dravya-vṛtti-kṣaṇika-vikāravad iti kathaṃ dṛṣṭāntayema teṣu ca na tvad-abhimataṃ kṣaṇikatvaṃ pradīpā-di vad āśutara-vināśitva-mātreṇa kṣaṇikato-kteḥ. Sarvārtha-siddhi*, p. 77.

later cannot be considered to be co-existent with that which was at a prior moment. If the effect was not co-existent with the cause, then what would be the bond which would determine why a particular cause should produce a particular effect and not others? Since production cannot be synonymous with what is produced, it must be different from it. Being a different entity, it may be demanded that production should have a further production, and that another, and this will lead to infinite regress.

To these objections Veṅkaṭanātha's reply is that the opposition of negation with position can hold good only with reference to the same unit of time and space. Therefore, the non-existence of the effect at a prior moment has no opposition to its existence at a later moment. That there is a relation between the cause of a prior moment and the effect of a later moment can be directly experienced. Such a relation is, of course, not contact, but one of dependence, of one another, as prior and later, as is perceived in experience. The dialectical criticism that production, being a separate entity, demands a further production and so forth cannot be applied to the Rāmānuja view; for here the effect is regarded as only a modified condition or state of the cause. The effect depends upon the cause in the sense that it is identical with it as being its state[1]. Identity here, of course, does not mean oneness but identity in difference. The objection that no bond can be established in difference is found contradicted in our experience of cause and effect, and in many other cases, e.g. in the instance where a speaker tries to produce a conviction in his hearers who are different from him. The objection that a cause can be called a cause only by virtue of its doing some operation (*kiñcit-kara*) and that its causality towards that operation must again involve the effectuation of some other operation, and thus there is an infinite regress, is invalid; for the existence of a number of operations (as given in experience) in producing an effect cannot lead to a vicious infinite, for only those operations which are revealed in experience can be accepted as having happened. In the case of spontaneous production (*dvārā-ntara-nirapekṣa*), there is no necessity to admit any series of operations as the causality as invariable antecedent is directly given in

[1] *na hi vayam abhivyaktiṃ vā kāraṇa-samavāyā-dikaṃ vā janme'ti brūmaḥ. kintū'pādānā-vasthā-viśeṣaṃ tasya kāryā-vasthā-sāmānādhikaraṇya-vyapadeśaḥ tādātmyena tad-āśraya-vṛtteḥ. Sarvārtha-siddhi*, p. 80.

experience. The objection that a cause is a cause because it produces the effect involves the previous existence of the effect, and hence the futility of the causal operation is invalid; for causality means the happening of an operation suitable to the becoming of the effect[1]. This does not involve the prior existence of the effect, since the happening of the operation leading to the effect refers to the effect not as an existing fact but as anticipated in the mind of the observer (*kurvattva-nirūpaṇaṃ tu bhāvinā'pi kāryeṇa buddhyā-rohiṇā siddheḥ*). The objection that if effect was a nature of the cause then it would be already there, and if it was not it could not come into being at any time, is also invalid on the supposition that there is an invariable uniformity of relationship (*niyata-pratisambandhika-svabhāvatā eva*). The effect entity is numerically and characteristically different from the cause entity, but yet the former and the latter are related to one another as mutually determining each other (*anyo-nya-nirūpyatayā*). The objection, that since the separate entities in a causal conglomeration cannot produce the effect, the conglomeration as a whole could not produce the effect, is invalid; for the capacity of the individual entities is defined in terms of their capacity in joint production (*samuditānāṃ kārya-karatvam eva hi pratyekam api hi śaktiḥ*). The further objection that since the cause is destroyed on its way to produce the effect, it (cause) itself being destroyed, ought not to be able to produce the effect, is not valid; for the production of the effect requires only the existence of the cause at a prior moment (*pūrva-kṣaṇa-sattvam eva hi kāraṇasya kāryo-payogi*).

Again it is urged that the concept of invariable priority which determines causation is itself indeterminable, for time as duration has no quality in itself. Priority and posteriority therefore have to be determined by other imposed conditions (*upādhi*), and the causal phenomena could be regarded as such an imposed condition. If this is so, priority and posteriority, which are in this view supposed to originate from causal conditions, cannot be regarded as determining causality. Again if conditions are supposed to split up time as pure duration into succession, then, since time is not regarded as discrete, the supposed conditions would have to refer to the whole of time, in which case there would be no succession.

[1] *bhāvi-kāryā-nuguṇa-vyāpāravattvam eva kāraṇasya kurvattvam. Sarvārtha-siddhi*, p. 81.

Moreover, if the conditions were to refer to certain parts, discrete time has first to be accepted[1]. The reply to the above objection is that if by the force of the above argument time as succession is not admitted, then if things are in time they are eternal, and if they are not, they are chimerical; which is absurd. The objector is again supposed to urge that, all universals being eternally existing, priority and posteriority can never be referred mutually among them, or between them and individuals. Where the rise of the constellation Rohiṇī is inferred from the rise of the constellation Kṛttikā, priority and posteriority are not between the two. The reply is to be found in the experience that such a qualified entity is produced from such other qualified entity where the universal and the individual merge together in a complex whole—a qualified entity[2]. Definite causal relations with definite effects are known from large experience of invariable antecedence between them, and this repudiates the idea of any denial of the uniformity of causal relation relating specific cause to specific effect. The notion of the plurality of causes is also therefore repudiated for the same reason. Where the same effect seems to be produced by different causes it is due to mal-observation and non-observation. A closer observation by experts reveals that though certain effects may be apparently similar yet they have specificity in their individual nature. By virtue of such specificity, each one of them can be referred to its own determinate cause. The negation-antecedent-to-being (*prāgabhāva*) cannot by itself be regarded as determining the effect, for such negations in themselves, being beginningless, could not explain the occasion of an effect's coming into being. Moreover, such negations involve in some form or other the effect to which it would give rise as its constituent; for, otherwise it could not be referred to or defined as a negation-antecedent-to-being of the effect. If an effect, being existent, be without any cause, it would be eternal; and if it be non-existent without any cause, then it would be chimerical. If the effect could happen by fits and starts, then its uniform dependence upon the immediate and invariable ante-

[1] *kāle ca pūrvattvam upādhi-kṛtaṃ sa ca upādhir yady ayam eva tadā tad-adhīnaṃ kālasya pūrvattvaṃ kālā-dhīnañco'pādher ity anyonyā-śrayaḥ. anyā-pekṣāyāṃ cakrakam anavasthā'pi kālasya kramavad upādhi-sambandha-bhedād bhedaśca kṛtsnai-ka-deśa-vikalpa-duḥstha iti. Sarvārtha-siddhi*, p. 82.

[2] *etad-dharmakād etad-dharmakam upajātam iti jāty-upādhi-kroḍī-kṛta-rūpeṇa vyaktiṣu niyama-siddheḥ. Ibid.* p. 83.

cedents could not be explained. Thus the doctrine of causality stands unimpeached by any of the objections brought forward by the Cārvākas.

(g) *The Nature of the Senses according to Veṅkaṭanātha.*

The Naiyāyikas think that the visual organ has for its material cause the eight elements, for though it cannot perceive any other sense-data it can grasp colours like a lamp; and, following a similar course of argument, they hold that the tactile organ is made up of air, the gustatory organ, of water, the smell-organ, of earth, and the auditory organ, of space-element (*ākāśa*). Veṅkaṭanātha's main objection is directed against viewing the senses as the specific and most important instruments of the corresponding perceptions on the ground that in the act of perception many accessories, such as the subject, object, light, sense-organ, sense-contact, absence of obstruction, and other accessories participate in such a manner that it is impossible to single out the sense-organ as being the most important instrument (*karaṇa*). Even if the sense-faculties be regarded as different from the sense-organs, they may be considered as the special ways of the ego-hood (*ahaṃkāra*), and this is testified by scriptural texts. Merely on the ground that the visual sense-faculty can perceive colours, it would be wrong to argue that this sense-faculty is made up of the same element as colour; for the visual sense-faculty is not by itself responsible for the colour-perception. The special predominance of the visional organ over other accessories in colour-perception, by which its affinity with the colour element may be shown, cannot be established.

Veṅkaṭa urges that the same reasons that lead to the acceptance of the five cognitive senses lead also to the admission of the five conative senses and *manas* (mind). The function of the cognitive senses is believed to be of a special kind by which the senses can operate only in a special manner and under special conditions, and the same applies also to the conative senses. These are as much associated with the subtle body as the cognitive senses, and the view of Yādavaprakāśa that the conative senses came into being with this body and were destroyed with its destruction is regarded as false[1]. *Manas*, being a part of the evolution of *prakṛti*, cannot be regarded as all-pervasive. The ordinary argument that that which,

[1] *Nyāya-siddhāñjana*, p. 24.

being eternal, is not the material constituent of any other thing is all-pervasive, is faulty, for this is directly contradicted by the testimony of the scriptures, and according to the Rāmānuja view atoms are not the ultimate constituent of things. Again the argument that that which is devoid of specific qualities, like time, is all-pervasive is also untenable, for according to the Rāmānuja view there is nothing which is devoid of specific quality. The argument that since mind can remember very distant experiences it is all-pervasive is also faulty, for such remembrances are due to the contact of mind with specific subconscious root-impressions.

The senses are to be regarded as subtle (*sūkṣma*) or atomic, and yet by their functioning or in association with other things they may behave as being spread out[1]. It is for this reason that in the bodies of animals of different dimensions the same senses may spread over smaller or larger areas through such functions without which they have to be admitted as becoming larger or smaller according to the dimensions of the bodies in which they may operate. If *manas* is all-pervasive, or if it occupies the span of the body, then the cognition by all the five senses may arise at one moment. The senses are regarded by Veṅkaṭa as abiding in the heart, whence they move through respective nerves to the particular sense-organs.

The sense operates by its function called *vṛtti*, which moves almost with the speed of light and grasps its object. There is thus a gradual operation of the sense-function passing from one place to another which, on account of its high speed, seems to be operative with regard to the object near at hand and also at a distance. This produces the appearance of simultaneous perception. The same process also holds good in the case of auditory perception. Since, according to the Rāmānuja school, senses are immaterial, their functions also are to be described as immaterial[2].

[1] *siddhe'pi hy aṇutve vikāsatayā vṛtti-viśeṣa-dvārā'pyāyaka-pracayād vā pṛthutvam aṅgīkāryam. Sarvārtha-siddhi*, p. 98.

[2] According to the Sāṃkhya view, where also the senses are regarded as immaterial, the *vṛtti* is regarded as their transformation in the form of the object and not contact. The Yoga view, however, as explained by Bhikṣu, is that the *citta* passes through the senses and comes in contact with the object and is transformed into its form in association with the senses. The transformation, therefore, is not of the *citta* alone but of the *citta* together with the senses.

(*h*) *The Nature of* ākāśa *according to Veṅkaṭanātha.*

Veṅkaṭa tries to establish in some detail the supposed fact that the *ākāśa* is perceived by the visual organ, as in our well attested experience in perceiving the blue sky or the scarlet sky in the evening and also the movement of the birds through the sky. He denies the position that the existence of *ākāśa* can only be inferred through movements, for the *ākāśa* exists even in thick walls where no movement is possible. *Ākāśa* is not its pure vacuity; its existence is manifested by its non-obstruction to the movements of animals. Some of the Buddhists and the Cārvākas argue that there are only four elements and that *ākāśa* is only the negation (*āvaraṇā-bhāva*). We do not perceive any *ākāśa* in a wall, but when it is split up we say that we perceive *ākāśa.* Such an *ākāśa* cannot be anything but a negation of obstruction; for if this is not admitted, then there is no negation of obstruction anywhere, all such cases being explainable on the supposition of *ākāśa.* It is this negation of obstruction, pure vacuity, which produces the illusion of some positive entity like a mirage. Such experiences may well be illustrated in those instances where the negation of pain is experienced as pleasure and negation of light as blue darkness. We are all familiar with the fact that mere linguistic usage sometimes produces an idea without there being an entity behind it, when someone says "the sharp horn of a hare."

To this Veṅkaṭa's reply is that the existence of categories can only be justified by an appeal to experience, and we all have a positive experience of *ākāśa*. What we call negation is also a positive entity. The very negative concept can well be regarded as a positive notion. It is useless to argue that the negative concept differs from all positivity, for each specific category has its own special notion, and it is futile to argue why a particular entity should have its own peculiar concept[1]. A negation is always defined as the absence of the positive entity of which the negation is affirmed. The positivity of *ākāśa* is established by its positive experience. The view that there is no *ākāśa* in occupied space is wrong, for when the occupying object is cut asunder we perceive the *ākāśa* and we affirm of it the negation of occupation. Thus the negation of occupation (*āvar-*

[1] *nā'bhāvasya niḥsvabhāvatā abhāva-svabhāvatayai'va tat-siddheḥ svānya-svabhāvatayā siddhis tu na kasyā'pi. na ca svena svabhāvena siddhasya para-svabhāva-virahād asattvam atiprasaṅgāt. Sarvārtha-siddhi*, p. 113.

aṇā-bhāvā) is the predicate which is affirmed of the positive entity *ākāśa*, for in our experience of *ākāśa* we perceive that there is no occupation (*āvarṇa*) in the *ākāśa* (*ihā'varaṇaṃ nāsti*). If this is not admitted, then such perceptions as "Here is an object" would be inexplicable, for the word "here" would have no meaning if it were mere absence of negation. If, again, *ākāśa* was absent in an occupying object, it would be unreasonable to define *ākāśa* as the absence of such an object; since nothing exists in itself, everything would on the above analogy become its own negation[1]. The fact that *ākāśa* sometimes seems to show the false appearance of a surface is due also to the fact that it is an entity on which certain qualities are illusorily imposed. If it were mere nothing, there could have been no predication of false qualities to it. When it is said that the negation of pain is falsely conceived as pleasure, the fact is that the so-called negation is only another kind of positivity[2]. In the case of chimerical entities such as the sharp hare's horn there is an affirmation of horn in the hare, and when the horn is known there is a deliberation in our mind whether our notion of sharpness is true or false. The affirmation of sharpness, therefore, is not on mere negation. The falsity of chimerical predication also consists of affirming a predicate to a subject which in the course of nature it does not possess, and there is nothing like pure falsity or non-existence in such notions. When one says that there is no occupation here he must show the locus where the occupation is denied or negated; for a negation implies a locus. The locus of the negation of occupation would be pure space (*ākāśa*). If the negation of occupation meant absolute non-existence, then that would land us in nihilism. If the occupation (*āvaraṇa*) did exist anywhere or did not exist anywhere, then in either case the production or destruction of such occupation would be undemonstrable; for an existent thing is never produced nor destroyed and a non-existent thing is neither produced nor destroyed. Thus, for these and other considerations, *ākāśa*, which is neither eternal nor all-pervasive, has to be regarded as a separate positive entity and not as mere negation of occupation. *Dik* or the quarter of the sky, north, south, etc., should

[1] *na tv ākāśa-mātram āvaraṇeṣv avidyamānatayā tad-abhāva ākāśa iti cā'yuktaṃ sarveṣāṃ svasminn avidyamānatayā svā-bhāvatva-prasaṅgāt. Sarvārtha-siddhi*, p. 114.

[2] *duhkhā-bhāve sukhā-ropāt abhāvasya bhāvā-nyatva-mātram eva hy asatvaṃ siddhaṃ tena ca svarūpa-sann evā'sau. Ibid.*

not be regarded as separate entities, but it is the sky, or *ākāśa*, which appears as different kinds of *dik* on account of its association with different conditions of the perceiver and the perceived space-relations.

(*i*) *Nature of Time according to Veṅkaṭanātha.*

Time is eternal and beginningless, for any conception in which it might be held that time were produced would involve the view that time was non-existent before its production. This, as it is easy to see, involves a notion of before and after, and as such it may be presumed that without the assumption of time even the production of time cannot be perceived. Time is directly perceived as a quality of all perceived entities. If time is regarded as being only inferable, then since it is intimately associated with all perceptible things the non-apprehension of time by direct perception would mean that the perceived objects also are not directly apprehended but known by inference. Even those who deny the separate existence of time explain it as an unreal notion of things in relation with the movement of the sun. Thus, the category of time, whether it is admitted as real or unreal, is taken as a quality or mode of perceived things and is apprehended along with them. There is no other time than what is conceived as before and after, as modes of our experience. It may be argued that with the exception of recognition all our experiences relate to the present and as such in the apprehension of objects by perception there is no notion of before and after which constitutes time, so there is no direct perception of time. To this the suggested discussion is whether, when objects are apprehended, they are apprehended as present or not, or whether only the notion of "the present" is apprehended without any association of any other object. Such views are directly contradicted in such experience as "I see this," where the object is demonstrated as being perceived at the present time. Perception thus refers both to the object and to its temporal character as present. It cannot be said that the temporal character is only illusorily imposed upon the perceived object; for in that case it must be shown that the temporal character was at least somewhere perceived or known independently by itself. It is argued that the sense-characters are perceived as "present," and this notion of the "present" is illusorily imposed upon time. To this it may be replied that in the passing series of the momentary sense-characters it is impossible to point out anything as "present," since these are only perceived as "before" and "after"; by the time anything could be designated as "present" it is already past. Thus the point of time as present is undemonstrable. If the time as present may be affirmed of any sense-character, it may be affirmed of time itself. Again if time were non-existent, what is the use of assuming its imposition? If it is held that there is only the imposition of time-conception without any entity of which it is affirmed, then it would become the blind phenomenalism of the nihilists. In the Rāmānuja view of things it is possible somehow to affirm the notion as "present" of time just as it is affirmed of the sense-characters. It cannot be said that time is merely a character of the sensibles, and that there is no other entity as time apart from these sensibles; for the temporal character of the sensibles as "present" is only possible on the assumption that there is such a thing as "present" time. Again if the "present" is denied, then that would mean universal negation, for the past and future are never perceived by us. Moreover, the present cannot be conceived as something different or unrelated and independent of the past and the future. If the past and the future were regarded as constituting the present, then our experience would only be related to the past and the future and there would be no possibility for any of our present afflictions. "Present" thus may be regarded as that series of operations which has begun but has not as yet ended in fruition.

Though time is one and eternal it can appear as limited and many, like all other objects which, though they may remain as one, may yet be supposed to be many and different in respect of the states through which they may seem to pass by virtue of the various conditional qualities (*upādhi-sambandha*) with which they may be associated. Though this view may be regarded as sufficient in explaining the notion of limited time, yet there are others who think that unless time itself is supposed to be constituted of moments through which time as changeable may be apprehended, the association of conditions to explain the notion of limitation will be impossible; for such an association presupposes the fact of limitation in time to which alone the conditions could be referred. Thus, Yādavaprakāśa holds that time is beginningless and endless, and continually transforms itself through moments by which the divisions of time as hours, days and nights can be spanned; through which again the transformation of all changeable objects can be measured[1]. In this view the conditions are relative from the point of view of each person, who collects the passing time-units and forms his own conceptions of minutes, hours and days from his own point of calculation according to his own needs. A valid objection, however, may be raised against such a view when it is pointed out that the criticism that was made against the association of conditional qualities to partless time may also be raised against the present view in which time is regarded as constituted of parts as moments. For it may well be said that the parts would require further parts for associating the conditional qualities; and if it does, there would be a vicious infinite and if it does not, then it will be admitted that the whole of a moment would not require a specification of parts for the association of conditional qualities. If the whole of a moment does not stand in need of any specification of parts for such association, why should time as a whole require it? The explanation that the association of a conditional quality with a part means its association with the whole on the analogy of the association of qualities in a substance is equally applicable to partless time. Veṅkaṭa points out that though the moments are adventitiously conceived on account of the variety of conditional qualities, time in itself is eternal. "Eternal" means that it is never destroyed. Time is thus co-existent with God. It is a material cause with reference to its own modifications and is the efficient cause with reference to everything else. The scriptural pronouncements that God is all-pervading can be harmonized with the all-pervading character of time by conceiving it to be co-existent with God.

(*j*) *The Nature of Soul according to Veṅkaṭanātha.*

Veṅkaṭanātha first tries to establish the existence of the soul as different from the body, and in this connection tries to refute the well-known Cārvāka arguments which do not admit the existence of a soul as different from the body to which the former may be supposed to belong. The main emphasis of Veṅkaṭa's arguments lies in the appeal to the testimony of our experience which manifests the body as a whole and its parts as belonging to an "I," as

[1] *yādavaprakāśair apy abhyupagato' yaṃ pakṣaḥ kālo' nādy-ananto'jasra-kṣaṇa-pariṇāmī muhūrtā-horātrā-di-vibhāga-yuk sarveṣāṃ pariṇāma-spanda-hetuḥ. Sarvārtha-siddhi*, pp. 148–149.

when we say "my body," "my head," etc. He says that though we have various parts of one body and though some of these may be destroyed, yet in spite of such variations they are all supposed to belong to one unchangeable unity, the self, which seems to persist through all changes of time. If the experiences belonged to the different parts of the body, then on the removal of any of the limbs the experiences which are associated with that limb could not be remembered; for it cannot be admitted that there is a transmission of experiences from one limb to another. Even a mother's experience cannot be shared by the fœtus. It cannot also be supposed that the experiences of the different limbs are somehow collected as impressions in the heart or brain; for it can neither be directly perceived, nor is there a datum which can lead to such an inference. Moreover, if there is a continual accumulation of impressions in the heart or brain, such a matter of conglomeration would be different at each moment through dissipation and aggregation of its constituent impressions, and as such it would be impossible to explain the fact of memory through such a changing entity[1].

The unified behaviour of an individual cannot also be regarded as being due to the co-operation of a number of individual units of consciousness; for, in that case there must be individual purposes in each of them, leading to a conflict, and if they have no such purposes, there is no reason why they should co-operate together. If it is assumed that these individual constituent conscious-entities are naturally such that they are engaged in serving one another without any conflict, then the more normal possibility would be that, having no natural attachment or antipathy, they would cease to act, and this would result in a cessation of all activities on the part of the constituted individual as a whole. Again whenever an animal is born it is perceived as endowed with certain instinctive tendencies towards certain action, such as sucking the mother's breast, which demonstrates its attachment in that direction and necessarily presupposes an experience of that kind in a previous birth. This shows that there is a self which is different and distinct from the body and its parts. The experiences and their root-impressions

[1] *sarva-bodhaiś ca hṛt-kośe saṃskārā-dhānam ityapi*
na dṛṣṭaṃ na ca tat-kḷptau liṅgaṃ kim api dṛśyate
ṅa ca saṃskāra-kośas te saṅghātā-tmā prati-kṣaṇaṃ
pracayā-pacayābhyāṃ syād bhinnaḥ smartā'tra ko bhavet.
Sarvārtha-siddhi, p. 153.

also explain the diversity of intellectual powers, tendencies and inclinations[1].

It cannot also be held that the units of consciousness of the different parts of the body are in themselves too subtle and potential to manifest themselves in their individual capacity, but they may yet co-operate together jointly to manifest the consciousness of the individual as a whole; for even the smallest molecular animals are found to be endowed with behaviouristic action. Moreover, if the units of consciousness emanating from the different parts of the body are admitted to be only potentially conscious, then it is absurd to suppose that they will be able to produce actual consciousness by mere conglomeration.

Again consciousness is a quality and as such it must await a substratum to which it would belong, but in the view in which consciousness is supposed to be material, the fundamental distinction between a quality and a substance is not observed[2]. It cannot also be held that consciousness is but a special modification of certain of the bodily elements, for this would only be a theory, which cannot be attested by any experience. Again to such of the Cārvākas as admit the validity of inference, it may be urged that the body is a matter-complex; and, being but a conglomeration and sensible, is material like any other material object, whereas consciousness, being something entirely different from the body by virtue of its being consciousness, is also entirely distinct from it. The ordinary illusory notion which confuses the self with the body can be explained in diverse ways. The objector may say that if from such notions as "my body," "my hand," etc., it is argued that the self is something different from the body, then from such expressions as "my self" one may as well argue that the self has a further self. To this Veṅkaṭa's reply is that such expressions as "my hand" and "my body" are like such other expressions as "my house" and "my stick," where the distinction between the two things is directly apprehended. In such an expression as "my self" we have a linguistic usage in which the possessive case can be explained only in the sense of ideality, having only such an imaginary distinction between the two terms as may be in the mind of the observer at the

[1] *evaṃ manuṣyā-di-śarīra-prāpti-daśāyām adṛṣṭa-viśeṣāt pūrva-janmā-nubhava-saṃskāra-bhedair evam abhiruci-bhedāś ca yujyante. Sarvārtha-siddhi*, pp. 153–154.

[2] *nanu caitanyam iti na kaścid guṇaḥ, yasyā'dhāro'pekṣyaḥ kintu yā'sau yuṣmākaṃ caitanya-sāmagrī sai'va caitanya-padārthaḥ syāt. Ibid.* p. 154.

moment and due to his emphasizing a difference from a conditional point of view. Veṅkaṭa holds that further arguments may also be brought forward by the Cārvākas[1], to which effective replies may be given. But instead of going into a big chain of arguments and counter arguments the most effective way is to appeal to the testimony of scripture which in its self-validity affirms both positively and by implication the existence of the permanent self as distinct from the body. The testimony of the scriptures cannot be rebutted or refuted by mere speculative arguments.

There is a view that consciousness belongs to the senses and that cognitions through the different senses are integrated together in the same body, and it is by that means that an object perceived by the eye is also identified as the same entity as that grasped by the tactile apprehension. Another view is that the pleasurable, painful feelings associated with sense-cognitions can themselves attract or repulse an individual to behave as a separate entity who is being attracted or repelled by a sense-object. Veṅkaṭa objects to such a doctrine as being incapable of explaining our psychological experience in which we feel that we have touched the very thing that we have seen. This implies that there is an entity that persists over and above the two different cognitions of the two senses; for the

[1] The additional arguments of the Cārvākas are as follows:

When one says "I, a fat person, know," it is difficult to say that the fatness belongs to the body and the knowledge to some other entity. If the expression "my body" seems to imply that the body is different, the expression "I am fat" demonstrates the identity of the body and the self. What is definitely perceived cannot be refuted by inference, for in that case even fire could be inferred as cold. Perception is even stronger than scriptures and so there is no cause of doubt in our experience; therefore there is no reason to have recourse to any inference for testing the perceptual experience. The Sāṃkhya argument, that those which are the results of aggregation must imply some other entity for which the aggregation has been named (just as a bedstead implies someone who is to lie on the bed), is ineffective; for the second-grade entity for which the first-grade conglomeration is supposed to be intended may itself await a third grade entity, and that another, and this may lead to a vicious infinite. To stop this vicious infinite the Sāṃkhya thinks that the self does not await for any further entity. But instead of arbitrarily thinking the self to be ultimate, it is as good to stop at the body and to think that the body is its own end. The argument that a living body must have a soul because it has life is false, for the supposed self as distinct from the body is not known to us by other means. One might as well say that a living body must have a sky-lotus because it has life. The Cārvāka ultimately winds up the argument and says that the body is like an automatic machine which works by itself without awaiting the help of any other distinct entity presiding over it, and is the result of a specific modification of matter (*ananyā-dhiṣṭhita-svayaṃ-vāhaka-yantra-nyāyād vicitra-bhūta-pariṇati-viśeṣa-sambhavo'yaṃ deha-yantraḥ*). *Sarvārtha-siddhi*, p. 157.

visual and the tactile sense-organs are limited to the apprehension of their own peculiar sense-data or sensibles, and none of them is competent to affirm the identity of the object through two different sense-appearances or sense-characteristics. Veṅkaṭa further says that the view that the impressions of the various senses accumulate in the heart, and that it is through such an integration of experiences in the heart that there is an appearance of one concrete individual, is wrong; for no such centre of integration of impressions inside our bodies is known to us, and if such a centre in the body is to be admitted there is no harm in admitting a separate soul in which these impressions inhere[1].

Consciousness also cannot be regarded as the self, for consciousness is an experience and as such must belong to some individual separate and distinct from it. In the passing conscious states there is nothing that abides and persists which can integrate the past and present states in itself and develop the notion of the person, the perceiver. Therefore, it has to be admitted that there is a conscious ego to which all cognitions and experiences belong. Such an ego is self-luminous in the sense that it is always manifest by itself to itself and not merely the locus of self-knowledge. Such a self-revealing ego is present even in our dreamless sleep, and this is attested by later recollections in which one feels "I slept happily"; and it is not contradicted by any experience. Even when one is referred to by another as "you" or "this," the ego in the latter is all the time self-manifested as "I." Such an ego refers to the soul which is a real agent and experiencer of pleasure and pain and a cognizer of all cognitions and as such is a real moral agent and is therefore distinguished from other kindred souls by its specific efforts leading to specific kinds of deeds and their fruits. The efforts, however, of the individual agents are themselves pre-determined by the resulting fruits of actions in previous births, and those by other actions of other previous births. Those who say that efforts lead to no efforts contradict themselves in all the practical behaviour which presupposes a belief in the efficacy of efforts. Only such of the efforts as are directed towards the attainment of the impossible or towards objects which require no effort are found

[1] *tvad-iṣṭa-saṃskāra-kośe mānā-bhāvāt, anekeṣām aham-arthānām eka-śarīra-yoge ca tataś ca varaṃ yatho-palambham ekasminn aham-arthe sarvais saṃskārā-dhānam. Sarvārtha-siddhi*, p. 160.

to be ineffective, whereas all other efforts are attended with fruition.

Veṅkaṭa urges that the theory which holds that there is but one Brahman which appears as many by its association with different minds is false; for we know that the same individual is associated with different bodies in the series of his transmigrations, and such an association with different bodies cannot produce any difference in the individual. And if this is so, that is, if association with different bodies cannot induce a difference in the individual, there is no reason why one Brahman should become many by its association with different minds. Again the view that holds that the individuals, though really different from one another, are so far identical that they are all but parts of pure Being—the Brahman—is equally false; for if the Brahman is thus one with the individual, it should also be exposed to all its sufferings and imperfections, which is absurd.

Brahmadatta held that Brahman alone is eternal and unborn and the individual souls are born out of it. Veṅkaṭa criticizes this view and propounds the theory that the souls are all uncreated and unborn. They are to be regarded as permanent and eternal; for if they are believed to be changing during the continuance of their body, then the continuity of purposive activity will be inexplicable. If they are destroyed with the death of the body, then the *karma* theory and all theories of moral responsibility have to be given up.

The soul, however, is not all-pervasive; for the Upaniṣads speak of it as going out of the body. The argument for all-pervasiveness of the soul as given by the *Naiyāyikas* is as follows. Virtue and vice are associated with a particular soul and may produce such changes in the material world, even in distant places, as would conduce to the enjoyment or suffering of that particular individual; and since virtue and vice are associated with a particular soul, they could not produce their effects on a distant place unless the soul, their locus, is co-extensive with those places. This, however, does not apply to the Rāmānujists, for according to them virtue and vice are only terms which mean that God has either been pleased or displeased owing to the particular kinds of deeds of an individual, and God's pleasure or displeasure has no limitations of operation[1].

[1] *iha hi dharmā-dharma-śabdaḥ karma-nimitte-śvara-prīti-kopa-rūpa-buddhi-dyotakaḥ. asti hi śubhe tv asau tuṣyati duṣkṛte tu na tuṣyate' sau paramaḥ śarīrī iti. Sarvārtha-siddhi,* p. 179.

From the opponent's point of view, even if the self is regarded as all-pervasive, that would not explain the happening of favourable or unfavourable effects; for though the self may be co-extensive with those distant places, yet its *adṛṣṭa* or unseen merit occurs not throughout the entire pervasive self, but only in a part of it, and as such, since it is not in touch with the place where the effect will happen, it cannot very well explain it.

(*k*) *The Nature of Emancipation according to Veṅkaṭanātha.*

Veṅkaṭanātha says that an objection has been raised by some that if individuals had been in the state of bondage from beginningless time, there is no reason why they should attain emancipation at some future date. To this the reply is that it is admitted by all that there is every hope that at some time or other there will be such a favourable collocation of accessories that our *karma* will so fructify that it will lead us out of bondage, through the production of sight of discrimination and disinclination, to enjoyment of all kinds that it may give God an opportunity to exercise His mercy. Thus, though all are in a state of bondage from beginningless time, they all gradually find a suitable opportunity for attaining their emancipation. Thus, God extends His grace for emancipation only to those who deserve it by reason of their deeds, and it is theoretically possible that there should be a time when all people would receive their salvation and the world process would cease to exist. Such a cessation of the world-process will be due to His own free will, and thus there is not the slightest reason for fear that in such a state there will have been any obstruction to God's free and spontaneous activity from extraneous sources. Man is led to the way of emancipation by his experience of suffering, which nullifies the pleasure of our mundane life. He feels that worldly pleasures are limited (*alpa*) and impermanent (*asthira*) and associated with pain. He thus aspires to attain a stage in which he can get unlimited pleasure unmixed with suffering. Such an emancipation can be brought about only through the love of God (*bhakti*). *Bhakti*, however, is used here in the sense of meditation or thinking with affection[1]. Such a *bhakti* also produces knowledge, and such a

[1] *mahanīya-viṣaye prītir bhaktiḥ prīty-ādayaś ca jñāna-viśeṣā iti vakṣyate sneha-pūrvam anudhyānaṃ bhaktiḥ. Sarvārtha-siddhi*, p. 190.

knowledge is also included in *bhakti*[1]. *Bhakti* is defined here as unceasing meditation (*dhruvā-nusmṛti*), and this therefore has to be continually practised. The Śaṇkarite view that emancipation can be attained by mere knowledge is false. In the Upaniṣads knowledge means unceasing meditation, and this has to be continued and only then can it be regarded as *upāsanā*, which is the same as *bhakti*[2].

The performance of the prescribed duties is helpful to the production of knowledge in the sense of *bhakti* by counteracting the wrong influence of such *karmas* as are antagonistic to the rise of true knowledge. Thus the prescribed duties are not to be performed along with the practice of *bhakti*, and they are not both to be regarded as joint causes of emancipation; but the performance of duties is to be interpreted as helping the rise of *bhakti* only by removing the obstructive influences of other opposing *karmas*[3]. The performance of scriptural duties including sacrifices is not incompatible with devotional exercises, for the gods referred to in the Vedic sacrifices may also be regarded as referring to Brahman, the only god of the *Vaiṣṇavas*. The absolutely (*nitya*) and the conditionally (*naimittika*) obligatory duties should not be given up by the devotee, for mere cessation from one's duties has no meaning; the real significance of the cessation from duties is that these should be performed without any motive of gain or advantage. It is wrong to suppose that emancipation can be attained only by those who renounce the world and become ascetics, for a man of any caste (*varṇa*) and at any stage of life (*āśrama*) may attain it provided he follows his normal caste duties and is filled with unceasing *bhakti* towards God.

It is well to point out in this connection that duties are regarded as threefold. Those that are absolutely obligatory are called *nitya*. No special good or advantage comes out of their performance, but their non-performance is associated with evil effects. Those that are obligatory under certain circumstances are called *naimittika*. If these duties are not performed under those special circumstances, sin will accrue, but no special beneficial effects are produced by

[1] *bhakti-sādhyaṃ prāpaka-jñānam api bhakti-lakṣaṇo-petam. Sarvārtha-siddhi*, p. 191.

[2] *ekasminn eva viṣaye vedano-pāsana-śabdayoḥ vyatikareṇo'pakramo-pasaṃhāra-darśanāc ca vedanam eva upāsanatayā viśeṣyate... sā mukti-sādhanatayo'ktā hi vittiḥ bhakti-rūpatva-paryanta-viśeṣaṇa-viśiṣṭā. Ibid.* pp. 191–192.

[3] *Ibid.* pp. 194–195.

their performance. Those duties which are to be performed only if the person is desirous of attaining special kinds of pleasurable ends such as residence in Heaven, the birth of a son, and the like, are called *kāmya*. Now a man who wishes to attain emancipation should give up all the *kāmya* duties and refrain from all actions prohibited in the scriptures, but he should perform the *nitya* and the *naimittika* duties. Though the performance of the *nitya* and the *naimittika* duties is associated with some kind of beneficial results, inasmuch as such performance keeps away the evil and the sinful effects which would have resulted from their non-performance, yet these, being fruits of a negative nature, are not precluded for a person who intends to attain emancipation. For such a person only the performance of such actions as bring positive pleasures is prohibited. When it is said that actions of a devotee should have no motive, this does not mean that it includes also actions which are performed with the motive of pleasing God; for actions with motive are only such actions as are performed with motives of one's own pleasure, and these are always associated with harmful effects[1].

It has already been said that the *naimittika* duties should be performed; but of these there are some which are of an expiatory nature, called *prāyaścitta*, by which the sinful effects of our deeds are expiated. A true devotee should not perform this latter kind of expiatory duties, for the meditation of God with love is by itself sufficient to purge us of all our sins and indeed of all our virtues also; for these latter, as they produce heavenly pleasures as their effects, obstruct the path of emancipation as much as do our sins. All that narrows our mind by associating it with narrow ends is to be regarded as sinful. Judged from this point of view even the so-called meritorious actions (*puṇya*) are to be regarded as harmful to a devotee who intends to attain emancipation[2]. Virtue (*dharma*) can be regarded as such only relatively, so that actions which are regarded as virtuous for ordinary persons may be regarded as sinful for a person inspired with the higher ambition of attaining emancipation[3]. For a true devotee who has attained the knowledge

[1] *anarthā-vinā-bhūta-sukha-kāmanāto nivṛttaṃ karma niṣkāmam. Sarvārtha-siddhi*, p. 202.

[2] *tad evaṃ dhī-saṅkocaka-karma-dhvaṃse dhī-vikāśa eva brahmā-nubhūtiḥ. Ibid.* p. 220.

[3] *sa eva dharmaḥ so'dharmas taṃ taṃ prati naraṃ bhavet*
pātra-karma-viśeṣeṇa deśa-kālāvapekṣya ca. *Ibid.* p. 221.

of Brahman and is pursuing the meditation of God, sinful or virtuous actions are both inefficacious, the older ones being destroyed by the meditation itself and the new ones incapable of being associated with him—the wise man.

The eschatological conception of the Rāmānuja school as explained by Veṅkaṭa is that the soul of the true devotee escapes by a special nerve in the head (*mūrdhanya-nāḍī*) and is gradually lifted from one stage to another by the presiding deities of fire, day, white fortnight, the vernal equinox, year, wind, the sun, the moon, lightning, Varuṇa, Indra and Prajāpati, who are appointed by God for the conducting of the departed devotee[1].

The state of final emancipation is regarded as the rise of the ultimate expansion of the intellect. But though this is a state which is produced as a result of devotional exercises, yet there is no chance that there would ever be a cessation of such a state, for it is the result of the ultimate dissociation of all causes, such as sins or virtues, which can produce a contraction of the mind. Therefore, there can never be a falling off from this state.

An emancipated person can assume bodies at his own will. His body is not a source of bondage to him, for only those whose bodies are conditioned by their *karma* may be supposed to suffer bondage through them. The state of emancipation is a state of perfect bliss through a continual realization of Brahman, to whom he is attached as a servant. This servitude, however, cannot beget misery, for servitude can beget misery only when it is associated with sins. The emancipated person is omnipotent in the sense that God is never pleased to frustrate the fulfilment of his wishes.

The emancipated person regards all things as being held in Brahman as its parts and as such no mundane affair can pain him, though he may have the knowledge that in the past many things in the world caused him misery.

Veṅkaṭa denied the possibility of attaining emancipation in this life, for the very definition of emancipation is dissociation from life, sense-organs and the body generated by *karma*. So when we hear of *jīvanmukta* or those emancipated in their lifetime, it is to be interpreted to mean a state similar to the state of emancipation. The contention of the Advaitins that the principal *avidyā* vanishes with knowledge, yet that its partial states may still continue binding

[1] *Sarvārtha-siddhi*, pp. 226–227.

the emancipated person with a body, is false. For if the principal *avidyā* has vanished, its states cannot still continue. Moreover, if they do continue in spite of the knowledge, it is impossible to imagine how they will cease at the death of the emancipated person.

God in the Rāmānuja School.

We have seen that according to Rāmānuja the nature and existence of God can be known only through the testimony of the scriptures and not through inference. Veṅkaṭa points out that the Sāṃkhya theory that the world-creation is due to the movement of *prakṛti*, set in operation through its contiguity with the *puruṣas*, is inadequate; for the Upaniṣads definitely assert that just as the spider weaves its net, so does God create the world. The scriptures further assert that God entered into both the *prakṛti* and the *puruṣaṣ*, and produced the creative movement in them at the time of creation[1]. The Yoga view of God—that He is only an emancipated being who enters into the body of Hiraṇyagarbha or adopts some such other pure body—is also against all scriptural testimony. It is also idle to think that the world-creation is the result of the co-operative activity of the emancipated spirits, for it is much against the scriptural testimony as also against the normal possibility, since there cannot be such an agreement of wish among the infinite number of emancipated beings that would explain the creation of the world by unobstructed co-operation. Thus, on the strength of the scriptural testimony it has to be admitted that God has engaged Himself in world-creation, either for the good of the created beings or through His own playful pleasurable activity. The enjoyment of playful activity is not to be explained as anything negative, as avoidance of ennui or langour, but as a movement which produces pleasure of itself[2]. When we hear of God's anger, this is not to be regarded as indicating any disappointment on God's part, for He is ever complete in Himself and has nothing to attain or to lose. So God's anger is to be interpreted simply as meaning His desire to punish those who deserve punishment.

[1] *prakṛtiṃ puruṣam cai'va praviśyā'tme-cchayā hariḥ.*
kṣobhayāmāsa saṃprāpte sarga-kāle vyayā-vyayau.
Sarvārtha-siddhi, p. 252.

[2] *krīḍā-yogād arati-yogaḥ tad-abhāvād vā tad-abhāvaḥ syāt, mai'vaṃ krīḍā hi prīti-viśeṣa-prabhavaḥ svayam-priyo vyāpāraḥ. Ibid.* p. 255.

According to the Rāmānuja system the individual souls and the material world form the body of God (*śarīra*). Anantārya of the Śeṣārya family, following Veṅkaṭa's treatment of this doctrine in the *Nyāya-siddhā-ñjana*, elaborates upon the same and enters into a critical analysis of the conception and significance of the notion of the body of God, which is not unworthy of our notice. He refuses to accept the view that the notion of body (*śarīra*) involves a class-concept (*jāti*); for though the notion of a body is found applicable in each specific instance of a body, the existence of such a notion is always associated with one or other of those specific instances and as such it does not justify the assumption of the existence of a separate category as a self-existent universal bodiness. All that one can say is that there is a universal notion of bodiness associated with the individual bodies[1]. All notions of class-concepts may therefore be explained in the same manner as notions which are associated with particular kinds of groupings in their aggregate characters, and in this way they may be regarded as somewhat similar to collective notions such as an army or assembly[2]. Vātsya Śrīnivāsa, however, in his *Rāmānuja-siddhānta-saṃgraha*, explains the notion of class-concepts as being based upon the notion of close similarity of collocative groupings. He says that when two collocative groupings are both called cow, nothing more is seen than those individual collocative groupings. That they are both called cow is due to the fact of close similarity (*sausādṛśya*) subsisting between those groupings[3]. Thus there is no other entity apart from

[1] *na ce'daṃ śarīram idaṃ śarīram ity anugata-pratītir eva tat-sādhikā, anugatā-pratīteḥ bādhaka-virahe jāti-sādhakatvād iti vācyaṃ, siddhānte anugata-pratīteḥ saṃsthāna-viṣayakatvena tad-atirikta-jāti-sādhakatvā-sambhavāt.* Anantārya, *Śarīra-vāda* (MS.).

[2] *eka-jātīyam iti vyavahārasya tat-tad-upādhi viśeṣeṇo-papatteḥ, rāśi-sainya-pariṣad-araṇyā-diṣv aikya-vyavahārādivat, upādhiś cā'yam anekeṣām eka-smṛti-samārohaḥ. Nyāya-siddhā-ñjana*, p. 180.

[3] *ayaṃ sāsnā-dimān ayam api sāsnā-dimān iti sāsnā-dir eva anuvṛtta-vyavahāra-viṣayo dṛśyate, anuvṛtta-dhī-vyavahāra-viṣayas tad-atirikto na kaś cid api dṛśyate. tasmād ubhaya-sampratipanna-saṃsthānenai 'va susadṛśo-pādhi-vaśād anugata-dhī-vyavahāro-papattāv atirikta-kalpane mānā-bhāvāt, susadṛśatvam eva gotvā-dīnāṃ anuvṛttiḥ. Rāmānuja-siddhānta-saṃgraha* (MS.).

Vātsya Śrīnivāsa defines close similarity as the special character which may be regarded as the cause of the apprehension of generality amidst differences (*pratiyogi-nirūpya-prativyakti-vilakṣaṇa-viṣaya-niṣṭha-sadṛśa-vyavahāra-sādhāraṇa-kāraṇa-dharma-viśeṣaḥ sausādṛśyam*). This similarity leads to the application of names to similar objects. When it subsists between two substances, we call it similarity of character (*dharma-sādṛśya*). When it subsists between entities other than substances (*a-dravya*) we call it similarity of essence (*sva-rūpa-sādṛśya*).

our notion of universality arising from specific similarity of similar groupings (*tāvad-viṣayaka-jñana-rūpa-jāti-viṣayakatvā-ṅgīkāreṇa*).

Anantārya refers to the definition of *śarīra* in the *Rāmānuja-bhāṣya* as that which is liable to be held or controlled in its entirety for the purpose of spirit, and is thus merely a means to its end (*cetanasya yad dravyaṃ sarvā-tmanā svārthe niyantuṃ dhārayituṃ śakyaṃ tac ceṣṭai-ka-svarūpañca tat tasya svarūpaṃ*). Sudarśanācārya, the author of the *Śruta-prakāśikā*, interprets this definition as meaning that when the movement of anything is wholly determined by the desire or will of any spirit and is thus controlled by it, the former is said to be the body of the latter (*kṛti-prayukta-svīya-ceṣṭā-sāmānyakatva-rūpa-niyāmyatvaṃ śarīra-pada-pravṛtti-nimittam*)[1]. When it is said that this body belongs to this soul, the sense of possession (*ādheyatva*) is limited to the fact that the movements in general of that body are due to the will of that spirit or soul[2]. A servant cannot be called the body of his master on the same analogy, for only some of the movements of the servant are controlled by the will of the master. The assumption that underlies the above definition is that the movement in the animal and vegetable bodies presided over by individual souls and in the inanimate objects presided over by God is due to the subtle will-movements in these specific souls, though they may not always be apprehended by us[3].

But anticipating the objection that there is no perceptual evidence that the physico-biological movements of bodies are due to subtle volitions of their presiding souls, a second definition of *śarīra* has been suggested in the *bhāṣya* of Rāmānuja. According to this definition a body is said to be that which may as a whole be held fast and prevented from falling by the volitional efforts of a spirit[4]. But an objection may still be raised against such a definition, as it cannot explain the usage which regards the souls as being the

[1] *Śarīra-vāda* (MS.).

[2] *etaj-jīvasye'daṃ śarīram ity-ādau ādheyatvaṃ tasya ca śarīrā-padārthai-kadeśe kṛtau anvayād vā taj-jīva-niṣṭha-kṛti-prayukta-svīya-ceṣṭā-sāmānyakam idam iti bodhaḥ. Ibid.*

[3] *jīva-śarīre vṛkṣādau īśvara-sarīre parvatādau ca sūkṣmasya tat-tat-kṛti-prayukta-ceṣṭā-viśeṣasya aṅgīkārān na śarīra-vyavahāra-viṣayatvā-nupapattiḥ. Ibid.*

[4] *yasya cetanasya yad dravyaṃ sarvā-tmanā dhārayituṃ śakyaṃ tat tasya śarīram iti kṛti-prayukta-sva-pratiyogika-patana-pratibandhaka-saṃyoga-sāmānya-vattvaṃ sarīra-pada-pravṛtti-nimittam. Ibid.*

bodies of God (*yasyā'tmā śarīram*). The souls have no weight and as such it is absurd to suppose that God prevents them from falling down, and in that way they are related to Him as bodies. The definition may therefore be modified to the extent that a body is that which is wholly held together in a contactual relation with a particular spirit through its own volition[1]. But a further objection may also be raised against this modification, for the definition, even so modified, fails to include time and other entities which are all-pervasive. Now the contactual relation subsisting between two all-pervasive entities is held to be eternal and uncaused. So the contactual relation of God with time and the like cannot be held to be caused by the volition of God, and if this be held to be the connotation of the body, time, etc., cannot be regarded as the body of God. So a different definition has been given which states that a body is a substance which is wholly dependent upon and subservient to a spirit. Dependence and subserviency are to be understood in the sense of productivity of a special excellence. Now, in the present context the special excellence which is produced in the spirit is its determination either as a cause or as an effect. When Brahman is regarded as cause, such causality can be understood only in relation to its association with the subtle constituents of matter and individual souls, and its evolution into the effect-stage as the manifold world is intelligible only through the transformation of the subtle matter-constituents in gross material forms and the spirits as endeavouring towards perfection through their deeds and rebirths. Brahman as such, without its relation to matter and souls, can be regarded neither as cause nor as effect. That it can be viewed as cause and effect is only because it is looked at in association with the causal or the effectuated states of matter and souls. The latter, therefore, are regarded as His body because they by their own states serve His purpose in reflecting Him as cause and effect.

The definition, however, needs a further modification in so far as the determining relation of the body is such that there is never a time when such a relation did not subsist. The relation conceived in this way (*apṛthak-siddha*) is not something extraneous, but is a defining constituent of both the body and the soul, i.e. so long as either of them exists they must have that relation of the

[1] *Patana-pratibandhakatvaṃ parityajya kṛti-prayukta-sva-pratiyogika-saṃyoga-sāmānyasya śarīra-pada-pravṛtti-nimittatva-svīkāre'pi kṣati-virahāt. Śarīra-vāda.*

determiner and the determined (*yāvat sattvam asambandhanā-rthayor evā'pṛthak sambandhā-bhyupagamāt*)[1]. Thus, even the emancipated souls are associated with bodies, and it is held that with death the body associated with the living soul is destroyed; the so-called dead body is not the body with which the living soul was in association[2]. But it may again be objected that the soul also determines the actions and efforts of the body and being inseparably connected with it, the soul may also be called the body of the body according to the definition. To meet this objection the definition is further modified, and it is held that only such inseparable relation as determines the causality or effectness in association with the production of knowledge can be regarded as constituting the condition of a body. The whole idea is that a body, while inseparably connected with the soul, conditions its cognitive experiences, and this should be regarded as the defining characteristic of a body[3]. This definition of *Śarīra* is, of course, very different from the Nyāya definition of "body" (*śarīra*) as the support (*āśraya*) of effort (*ceṣṭā*), senses (*indriya*), and enjoyment (*bhoga*)[4]. For in such a definition, since there may be movement in the furthest extremities of the body which is not a direct support of the original volition of the soul, the definition of the notion of support has to be so far extended as to include these parts which are in association with that which was directly moved by the soul. Extending this principle of indirect associations, one might as well include the movement of objects held in the hand, and in that case the extraneous objects might also be regarded as body, which is impossible. The defence of the Naviyāyikas would, of course, be by the

[1] *Śarīra-vāda*, p. 8 (MS.).

[2] *mṛta-śarīrasya jīva-sambandha-rahitatayā'pi avasthāna-darśanena yāvat-sattvam asambandhā-narhatva-virahād iti cet na pūrva-śarīratayā'vasthitasya dravyasya cetana-viyogā-nantara-kṣaṇe eva nāśā-bhyūpagamena anupapatti-virahāt. Ibid.*

[3] *tac-cheṣatvaṃ hi tan-niṣṭhā-tiśayā-dhāyakatvaṃ, prakṛte ca tan-niṣṭhā-tiśayaḥ kāryatva-kāraṇatvā-nyatara-ūpo jñānā-vacchinnā-nuyogitākā-pṛthak-siddhi-sambandhā-vacchinna-kāryatva-kāraṇatvā-nyatarā-vacchedakatvaṃ śarīra pada-pravṛtti-nimittam ityarthaḥ. Ibid.*

Brahman as associated with subtle matter and spirits is the cause, and as associated with gross matter and the souls passing through diverse gross states may be regarded as effect. The subtle and the gross states of matter and spirits may thus be regarded as determining the causal and effect states of the Brahman. —*sūkṣma-cid-acid-viśiṣṭa-brahmaṇaḥ kāraṇatvāt sthūla-cid-acid-viśiṣṭasya ca tasya kāryatvāt brahma-niṣtha-kāryatva-kāraṇatvā-nyatarā-vacchedakatvasya prapañca-sāmānye sattvāt. Ibid.*

[4] *Ceṣṭe-ndriyā-rthā-śrayaḥ śarīram. Nyāya-sūtra*, I. I. II.

introduction of the relation of inseparable coherence (*samavāya*) in which the parts of a body are connected together in a way different from any other object. But it has already been pointed out that the *samavāya* relation is not admitted by the Rāmānujists.

Brahman may be regarded as the material cause of the world through its body as *prakṛti* and the souls. Though a material cause, it is also the instrumental cause just as the individual souls are the efficient causes of their own experiences of pleasure and pain (through their own deeds), of which, since the latter inhere in the former, they may be regarded as their material causes. On the other hand, God in Himself, when looked at as apart from His body, may be regarded as unchangeable. Thus, from these two points of view God may be regarded as the material and efficient cause and may also be regarded as the unchanging cause.

Bhāskara and his followers hold that Brahman has two parts, a spirit part (*cidaṃśa*) and a material part (*acidaṃśa*), and that it transforms itself through its material part and undergoes the cycles of *karma* through the conditions of such material changes. Bhāskara thinks that the conditions are a part of Brahman and that even in the time of dissolution they remain in subtle form and that it is only in the emancipated stage that the conditions (*upādhi*), which could account for the limited appearance of Brahman as individual souls, are lost in Brahman. Veṅkaṭa thinks that the explanation through the conception of *upādhi* is misleading. If the *upādhi* constitutes *jīvas* by mere conjunction, then since they are all conjoined with God, God Himself becomes limited. If the conception of *upādhi* be made on the analogy of space within a jug or a cup, where space remains continuous and it is by the movement of the conditioning jugs or cups that the space appears to be limited by them, then no question of bondage or emancipation can arise. The conception of *upādhi* cannot be also on the analogy of the container and the contained, as water in the jug, since Brahman being continuous and indivisible such a conception would be absurd. The *upādhis* themselves cannot be regarded as constitutive of individual souls, for they are material in their nature. Yādavaprakāśa holds that Brahman is of the nature of pure universal being (*sarvā-tmakaṃ sad-rūpaṃ brahma*) endowed with three distinct powers as consciousness, matter and God, and through these powers it passes through the various phenomenal changes which are held up in it and at the same time are one with it, just as one ocean appears in diverse forms as foam, billows and waves. Veṅkaṭa says that instead of explaining the world-creation from these makeshift points of view, it is better to follow the scriptures and regard Brahman as being associated with these changes through its body. It is wrong also to regard God, world and spirit as being phenomenal modifications of one pure being as Kātyāyana does[1]. For the scriptures definitely assert that God and the changeless Brahman are one and identical. If the transformation is regarded as taking place through the transformation of the powers of Brahman, then the latter cannot be regarded as the material cause of the world, nor can these transformations be regarded as creations of Brahman. If it is said that Brahman is both identical and different from its powers, then such a view would be like the relative pluralism of the Jains. There is a further view that Brahman in His pure nature exists as the world, the souls and God, though these are different and though in them His pure nature as such is not properly and equally evident. Veṅkaṭa holds that such a view is contradicted by our experience and by scriptural texts. There is again another view according to which Brahman is like an ocean of consciousness and bliss, and out of the joy of self-realization undergoes various transformations, a small portion of which he transforms into matter and infuses the spiritual parts into its modifications. Thus, Brahman transforms itself into a number of limited souls which undergo the various experiences of pleasure and pain, and the whole show and procedure becomes a source of joy to Him. It is not a rare phenomenon that there are beings who derive pleasure from performing actions painful to themselves. The case of incarnations (*avatāra*) again corroborates this view, otherwise there would be no meaning in the course of misery and pain which they suffer of their own free will. Veṅkaṭa observes that this view is absolutely hollow. There may be fools who mistake painful actions for sources of pleasure. But it is unthinkable that Brahman, who is all-knowing and all-powerful, should engage in an undertaking which involves for Him even the slightest misery and pain. The misery of even a single individual is sufficient evil and the total miseries of the whole

[1] *īśvara-vyākṛta-prāṇair virāṭ-sindhur ivo'rmibhiḥ*
yat pranṛtya divā bhāti tasmai sad-brahmaṇe namaḥ.
Kātyāyana-kārikā, quoted in *Sarvārtha-siddhi*, p. 298.

world of individual selves are intolerable in the extreme. Therefore, how can Brahman elect to shoulder all this misery of His own free choice without stultifying Himself? The case of incarnations is to be understood as that of actors on the stage. Further, this view contradicts the testimony of all scriptures. Veṅkaṭa thinks that the view of his school is free from all these objections, as the relation of the Brahman and individuals is neither one of absolute identity nor one of identity and difference but one of substance and adjuncts. The defects in the adjuncts cannot affect the substance nor can the association between them be a source of pollution to Brahman, the substance, because association becomes so only when it is determined by *karma*[1].

On the theological side Veṅkaṭa accepts all the principal religious dogmas elaborated in the *Pañcarātra* works. God is, of course, omniscient, omnipotent and all-complete. His all-completeness, however, does not mean that He has no desires. It only means that His desires or wishes are never frustrated and His wishes are under His own control[2]. What we call our virtue and sins also proceed through His pleasure and displeasure. His displeasure does not bring any suffering or discomfort. But the term "displeasure" simply indicates that God has a particular attitude in which He may punish us or may not extend His favour.

The scriptural injunctions are but the commands of God. There is no separate instrumental as *apūrva* or *adṛṣṭa* which stands between the performance of deeds and their fruition and which, while it persists when the deeds are over, brings about the effects of these actions. But God alone abides and He is either pleased or displeased by our actions and He arranges such fruits of actions as He thinks fit[3]. The scriptures only show which kinds of actions will be pleasing to God and which are against His commands. The object of the scriptural sacrifices is the worship of God, and all the different deities that are worshipped in these sacrifices are but the different names of God Himself. All morality and religion are thus

[1] *asman-mate tu viśeṣaṇa-gatā doṣā na viśeṣyaṃ spṛśanti, aikya-bhedā-bhedānaṅgīkārāt, akarma-vaśya-saṃsargaja-doṣāṇām asambhavācca. Tattva-muktā-kalāpa*, p. 302.

[2] *āpta-kāma-śabdas tāvad īśitur eṣṭavyā-bhāvam icchā-rāhityaṃ vā na brūte ...iṣṭaṃ sarvam asya prāptam eva bhavatīti tātparyaṃ grāhyam...sarva-kārya-viṣaya-pratihatā-nanyā-dhīne-chāvān īśvaraḥ, jīvas tu na tathā. Ibid.* p. 386.

[3] *tat-tat-karmā-caraṇa-pariṇate-śvara-buddhi-viśeṣa eva adṛṣṭam. Ibid.* p. 665.

reduced in this system to obedience to God's commands and the worship of Him. It is by God's grace that one can attain emancipation when there is an ultimate expansion of one's intellect, and by continual realization of the infinite nature of God one remains plunged as it were in an ocean of bliss compared with which the so-called worldly pleasures are but sufferings[1]. It is not ultimately given to man to be virtuous or vicious by his own efforts, but God makes a man virtuous or vicious at His own pleasure or displeasure, and rewards or punishes accordingly; and, as has already been said, virtue and vice are not subjective characters of the person but only different attitudes of God as He is pleased or displeased. Whomsoever He wishes to raise up He makes perform good actions, and whomsoever He wishes to throw down He makes commit sinful actions. The final choice and adjudgment rests with Him, and man is only a tool in His hands. Man's actions in themselves cannot guarantee anything to him merely as the fruits of those actions, but good or bad fruits are reaped in accordance with the pleasure or displeasure of God[2].

Dialectical criticism against the Śaṅkara School.

The readers who have followed the present work so far must have noticed that the chief philosophical opponents of the Śrī Vaiṣṇava school of thought were Śaṅkara and his followers. In South India there were other religious opponents of the Śrī Vaiṣṇavas, Śaivas and the Jainas. Mutual persecution among the Śrī Vaiṣṇavas, Śaivas and the Jainas is a matter of common historical knowledge. Conversion from one faith to another also took place under the influence of this or that local king or this or that religious teacher. Many volumes were written for the purpose of proving the superiority of Nārāyaṇa, Viṣṇu or Kṛṣṇa to Śiva and *vice versa*. Madhva and his followers were also opponents of the Śrī Vaiṣṇavas, but there were some who regarded the philosophy of the Madhvas as more or less akin to the Śrī Vaiṣṇava thought.

[1] *Tattva-muktā-kalāpa*, pp. 663, 664.

[2] *sa evainam bhūtiṃ gamayati, sa enaṃ prītaḥ prīṇāti eṣa eva sādhu karma kārayati taṃ kṣipāmy ajasram aśubhā-nityā-di-bhiḥ pramāṇa-śataiḥ īśvara-prīti-kopābhyāṃ dharmā-dharma-phala-prāptir avagamyate. Ibid.* p. 670.

There were others, however, who strongly criticized the views of Madhva, and Mahācārya's *Pārāśarya-vijaya* and Parakāla Yati's *Vijayīndra-parājaya* may be cited as examples of polemical discussions against the Madhvas. The Śrī Vaiṣṇavas also criticized the views of Bhāskara and Yādavaprakāśa, and as examples of this the *Vedārtha-saṃgraha* of Rāmānuja, or the *Vāditraya-khaṇḍana* of Veṅkaṭa may be cited. But the chief opponents of the Śrī Vaiṣṇava school were Śaṅkara and his followers. The *Śata-dūṣaṇī* is a polemical work of that class in which Veṅkaṭanātha tried his best to criticize the views of Śaṅkara and his followers. The work is supposed to have consisted of one hundred polemical points of discussion as the name *Śata-dūṣaṇī* (century of refutations) itself shows. But the text, printed at the Śrī Sudarśana Press, Conjeeveram, has only sixty-six refutations, as far as the manuscripts available to the present writer showed. This printed text contains a commentary on it by Mahācārya alias Rāmānujadāsa, pupil of Vādhūla Śrīnivāsa. But the work ends with the sixty-fourth refutation, and the other two commentaries appear to be missing. The printed text has two further refutations—the sixty-fifth and sixty-sixth—which are published without commentary, and the editor, P. B. Anantācārya, says that the work was completed with the sixty-sixth refutation (*samāptā ca Śata-dūṣaṇī*). If the editor's remark is to be believed, it has to be supposed that the word *Śata* in *Śata-dūṣaṇī* is intended to mean "many" and not "hundred." It is, however, difficult to guess whether the remaining thirty-four refutations were actually written by Veṅkaṭa and lost or whether he wrote only the sixty-six refutations now available. Many of these do not contain any new material and most of them are only of doctrinal and sectarian interest, with little philosophical or religious value, and so have been omitted in the present section, which closes with the sixty-first refutation. The sixty-second refutation deals with the inappropriateness of the Śaṅkara *Vedānta* in barring the Śūdras from Brahma-knowledge. In the sixty-third, Veṅkaṭa deals with the qualifications of persons entitled to study *Vedānta* (*adhikāri-viveka*), in the sixty-fourth with the inappropriateness of the external garb and marks of the ascetics of the Śaṅkara school, in the sixty-fifth with the prohibition of association with certain classes of ascetics, and in the sixty-sixth with the fact that Śaṅkara's philosophy cannot be reconciled with the *Brahma-sūtra*.

First Objection. The view that Brahman is qualityless cannot give any satisfactory account of how the word Brahman can rightly denote this qualityless entity. For if it is qualityless it cannot be denoted by the term Brahman either in its primary sense or in any secondary sense of implication (*lakṣaṇā*); for if the former is not possible, the second is also impossible, since an implicative extension of meaning can take place only when in any particular content the primary meaning becomes impossible. We know also from the scriptural testimony that the word Brahman is often used in its primary meaning to denote the Great Being who is endowed with an infinite number of excellent qualities. The fact that there are many texts in which an aspect of qualitylessness is also referred to cannot be pushed forward as an objection, for these can all be otherwise explained, and even if any doubt arises the opponent cannot take advantage of it and assert that Brahman is qualityless. It is also not possible to say that the word Brahman denotes the true Brahman only by implication, for the scriptures declare the realization of the meaning of the word Brahman as being one of direct perception. So in the opponent's view of Brahman, the word Brahman would be rendered meaningless.

Second Objection. There cannot be any inquiry regarding Brahman according to Śaṅkara's interpretation of the term as a qualityless something. Śaṅkara says that Brahman is known in a general manner as the self in us all; the inquiry concerning Brahman is for knowing it in its specific nature, i.e. whether it is the body endowed with consciousness, the overlord, pure self, or some other entity regarding which there are many divergences of opinion. Veṅkaṭa urges that if the self-revelation of Brahman is beginningless it cannot depend on our making any inquiry about it. All that depends on causes and conditions must be regarded as an effect and in that sense Brahma-revelation would be an effect which is decidedly against Śaṅkara's intention. Thus, therefore, an inquiry regarding the general and specific nature of Brahman cannot deal with its own real pure nature. If, therefore, it is urged by the Śaṅkarites that this inquiry does not concern the real nature of Brahman, but only a false appearance of Brahman (*upahita-svarūpa*), then the knowledge derived from this inquiry would also be of this false appearance and nothing would be gained by this false knowledge. Again, when Brahman is partless and self-revealing, there cannot be any meaning in knowing it in a general manner or in a specific manner, for no such distinction can be made in it. It must be known in its entirety or not known at all; there cannot be any distinction of parts such that there may be scope for different grades of knowledge in it. All inquiry (*jijñāsā*) however must imply that its object is known generally but that greater detail is sought; since Śaṅkara's unqualified homogeneous Brahman cannot be the object of such an inquiry, no such Brahman can be sought. Therefore, an inquiry can only be regarding a qualified object about which general or special knowledge is possible. The Śaṅkarites cannot legitimately urge that a distinction of general and specific knowledge is possible in their view; for it may be maintained that, though the Brahman may be known in a general manner, there is room for knowing it in its character as different from the illusory appearances, since if Brahman has no specific nature it is not possible to know it in a general manner (*nirviśeṣe sāmānya-niṣedhaḥ*). If it is urged that the knowledge of the world-appearance as false is the knowledge of Brahman, then there would be no difference between Vedānta and the nihilism of Nāgārjuna.

Third Objection. Veṅkaṭa here introduces the oft-repeated arguments in favour of the doctrine of the theory of *Jñāna-karma-samuccaya* as against the view of Śaṅkara that a wise man has no duties.

Fourth Objection. Veṅkaṭa here says that all errors and illusions do not vanish merely by the knowledge that all world-appearance is false. The performance of the scriptural duties is absolutely necessary even when the highest knowledge is attained. This is well illustrated in the ordinary experience of a jaundiced person where the illusion of yellow is not removed merely by the knowledge of its falsity but by taking medicines which overcome the jaundice. Ultimate salvation can be obtained only by worshipping and adoring God the supreme Lord and not by a mere revelation of any philosophical wisdom. It is impossible to attain the final emancipation merely by listening to the unity texts, for had it been so then Śaṅkara himself must have attained it. If he did so, he would have been merged in Brahman and would not have been in a position to explain his view to his pupils. The view that the grasping of the meaning of the unity texts is an immediate perception is also untenable, for our ordinary experience shows that scriptural knowledge is verbal knowledge and as such cannot be regarded as immediate and direct perception.

Fifth Objection. Śaṅkara's reply to the above objection is that though the final knowledge of the identity of all things with self be attained yet the illusion of world-appearance may still continue until the present body be destroyed. To this Veṅkaṭa asks that if *avidyā* be destroyed through right knowledge, how can the world-appearance still continue? If it is urged that though the *avidyā* be destroyed the root-impressions (*vāsanā*) may still persist, then it may be replied that if the *vāsanā* be regarded as possessing true existence then the theory of monism fails. If *vāsanā* is regarded as forming part of Brahman, then the Brahman itself would be contaminated by association with it. If *vāsanā* is, however, regarded as a product of *avidyā*, then it should be destroyed with the destruction of *avidyā*. Again, if the *vāsanā* persists even after the destruction of *avidyā*, how is it to be destroyed at all? If it can be destroyed of itself, then the *avidyā* may as well be destroyed of itself. Thus there is no reason why the *vāsanā* and its product, the world-appearance, should persist after the destruction of *avidyā* and the realization of Brahma-knowledge.

Seventh Objection. Śaṅkara and his followers say that the utterance of the unity text produces a direct and immediate perception of the highest truth in the mind of a man chastened by the acquirement of the proper qualifications for listening to the Vedāntic instructions. That the hearing of the unity texts produces the immediate and direct perception of the nature of self as Brahman has to be admitted, since there is no other way by which this could be explained. To this Veṅkaṭa replies that if this special case of realization of the purport of the unity texts be admitted as a case of direct perception through the instrumentality of verbal audition only because there is no other means through which the pure knowledge of Brahman could be realized, then inference and the auditory knowledge of other words may equally well be regarded as leading to direct perception, for they also must be regarded as the only causes of the manifestation of pure knowledge. Moreover, if the causes of verbal knowledge be there, how is that knowledge to be prevented, and how is the direct and immediate perception to be produced from a collocation of causes which can never produce it? Any knowledge gained at a particular time cannot be regarded as the revelation of one individuated consciousness which is identical with all knowledge of all times or of all persons, and therefore the words which may lead to any such knowledge cannot be regarded as producing any such immediate realization (*āparokṣya*). If it is held that there is no other cause leading to the realization of pure consciousness apart from what leads to the apprehension of the specific forms of such consciousness, then the same is true of all means of knowledge, and as such it would be true of inference and of verbal expressions other than the unity texts. It is not possible therefore to adduce for the unity texts claims which may not be possessed by other ordinary verbal expressions and inferential knowledge. In the case of such phrases as "You are the tenth," if the person addressed had already perceived that he was the tenth, then the understanding of the meaning of such a phrase would only mean a mere repetition of all that was understood by such a perception; if, however, such a person did not perceive the fact of his being the tenth person, then the communication of this fact was done by the verbal expression and this so far cannot be regarded as direct, immediate or perceptual. It may be noted in this connection that though the object of knowledge may remain the same, yet the knowledge attained may be different on account of the ways of its communication. Thus, the same object may be realized perceptually in some part and non-perceptually in another part. Again, though Brahman is admittedly realized in direct perception, yet at the time of its first apprehension from such verbal phrases as "Thou art he" it is a verbal cognition, and at the second moment a realization is ushered in which is immediate and direct. But if the first cognition be not regarded as direct and immediate, why should the second be so? Again, the position taken by Śaṅkara is that since disappearance of the falsity of world-appearance cannot be explained otherwise, the communication imparted by the understanding of the unity texts must be regarded as being immediate; for falsehood is removed by the direct and immediate realization of the real. But the world is not false; if it is regarded as false because it is knowable, then Brahman, being knowable, would also be false. Again, if the world-appearance be regarded as false, there is no meaning in saying that such an appearance is destroyed by right knowledge; for that which never exists cannot be destroyed. If it is held that the world-appearance is not destroyed but only its knowledge ceases, then it may be pointed out that a false knowledge may cease naturally with the change of one's mental state, just as the illusion of false silver may cease in deep dreamless sleep, or it may be removed by inferential and other kinds of cognition. There is no necessary implication that false knowledge must be removed only by direct and immediate knowledge. Again, if it is held that the cessation of the world-appearance means the destruction of its cause, then the reply is that no direct realization of reality is possible unless the cause itself is removed by some other means. So long as there is a pressure on the retina from the fingers there will be the appearance of two moons. Thus it is meaningless to suppose that it is only by direct and immediate perception that the falsity of the world-appearance would cease. If the removal of the falsity of world-appearance simply means that the rise of a knowledge is contradictory to it, then that can be done even by indirect knowledge, just as the false perception of two moons may be removed by the testimony of other persons that there is only one moon. But not only is the world not false and therefore cannot be removed, but verbal knowledge cannot be regarded as leading to immediate perception; even if it did, there must be other accessory conditions working along with it, just as in the case of visual perception, attention, mental alertness, and other physical conditions are regarded as accessory factors. Thus, mere verbal knowledge by itself cannot bring about immediate realization. Nor is it correct to suppose that perceptual knowledge cannot be contradicted by non-perceptual knowledge, for it is well known that the notion of one continuous flame of a lamp is negated by the consideration that there cannot be a continuous flame and that what so appears is in reality but a series of different flames coming in succession. Thus, even if the realization of the purport of unity texts be regarded as a case of direct perception, there is no guarantee that it could not be further contradicted by other forms of knowledge.

Tenth Objection. In refuting the reality of pure contentless consciousness, Veṅkaṭa urges that even if such a thing existed it could not manifest by itself its own nature as reality, for if it did it could no longer be regarded as formless; since if it demonstrated the falsity of all content, such content would be a constituent part of it. If its reality were demonstrated by other cognitions, then it was obviously not self-luminous. Then, again, it may be asked, to whom does this pure consciousness manifest itself? The reply of the Śaṅkarites is that it does not reveal itself to this or that person but its very existence is its realization. But such a reply would be far from what is normally understood by the term manifestation, for a manifestation must be for some person. The chief objection against the existence of a contentless consciousness is that no such thing can be experienced by us and therefore its priority and superiority or its power of illuminating the content imposed upon it cannot also be admitted. The illustration of bliss in the deep dreamless sleep is of no use; for if in that state the pure contentless consciousness was experienced as bliss, that could not be in the form of a subjective experience of bliss, as it could not be called contentless. A later experience after rising from sleep could not communicate to the perceiver that he was experiencing contentless consciousness for a long period, as there is no recognition of it and the fact of recognition would be irreconcilable to its so-called contentless character.

Eleventh Objection. In attempting to refute the existence of indeterminate knowledge (*nirvikalpa*) Veṅkaṭa says that the so-called indeterminate knowledge refers to a determinate object (*nirvikalpakam api saviśeṣa-viṣayakameva*). Even at the very first moment of sense-contact it is the object as a whole with its manifold qualities that is grasped by the senses and it is such an object that is elaborated later on in conceptual forms. The special feature of the *nirvikalpa* stage is that in this stage of cognition no special emphasis is given to any of the aspects or qualities of the object. If, however, the determinate characters did not in reality form the object of the cognition, such characters could never be revealed in any of the later stages of cognition and the *nirvikalpa* could never develop into the *savikalpa* state. The characters are perceived in the first stage, but these characters assume the determinate form when in the later moments other similar characters are remembered. Thus a pure indeterminate entity can never be the object of perception.

Twelfth Objection. The contention of the Śaṅkarite is that perception is directly concerned with pure being, and it is through nescience that the diverse forms are later on associated with it, and through such association they also seemingly appear as being directly perceived. Veṅkaṭa says that both being and its characters are simultaneously perceived by our senses, for they form part of the same object that determines our knowledge. Even universals can be the objects of our direct knowledge: it is only when these universals are distinguished from one another at a later moment that a separate mental operation involving its diverse functions becomes necessary. Again, if perception only referred to indeterminate being, how then can the experience of the diverse objects and their relative differentiation be explained?

Thirteenth Objection. In refuting the view of the Śaṅkara school that the apprehension of "difference" either as a category or as a character is false, Veṅkaṭa says that the experience of "difference" is universal and as such cannot be denied. Even the much-argued "absence of difference" is itself different from "difference" and thus proves the existence of difference. Any attempt to refute "difference" would end in refuting identity as well; for these two are relative, and if there is no difference, there is no identity. Veṅkaṭa urges that a thing is identical with itself and different from others, and in this way both identity and difference have to be admitted.

Fourteenth Objection. The Śaṅkarites say that the world-appearance, being cognizable, is false like the conch-shell–silver. But what is meant by the assertion that the world is false? It cannot be chimerical like the hare's horn, for that would be contrary to our experience and the Śaṅkarite would not himself admit it. It cannot mean that the world is something which is different from both being and non-being, for no such entity is admitted by us. It cannot also mean that the world-appearance can be negated even where it seems to be real (*pratipanno-pādhau niṣedha-pratiyogitvam*), for if this negation cannot further be negated, then it must be either of the nature of Brahman and therefore false as world-appearance or different from it. The first alternative is admitted by us in the sense that the world is a part of Brahman. If the world-appearance can be negated and it is at the same time admitted to be identical with Brahman, then the negation would apply to Brahman itself. If the second alternative is taken, then since its existence is implied as a condition or explication of the negation, it itself cannot be denied. It cannot also be said that falsity means the appearance of the world in an entity where it does not exist (*svā-tyantā-bhāva-samāna-dhikaraṇatayā pratīyamānatvam*), for such a falsity of the world as not existing where it appears cannot be understood by perception, and if there is no perception for its ground no inference is also possible. If all perception is to be regarded as false, all inference would be impossible. It is said that world-appearance is false because it is different from the ultimate reality, the Brahman. Veṅkaṭa, in answer to this, says that he admits the world to be different from the Brahman though it has no existence independent and separable from it. Still, if it is argued that the world is false because it is different from reality, the reply is that there may be different realities. If it is held that since Brahman alone is real, its negation would necessarily be false, then the reply is that if Brahman is real its negation is also real. The being or reality that is attributed by Veṅkaṭa to the world is that it is amenable to proof (*prāmāṇika*). Truth is defined by Rāmānuja as that which is capable of being dealt with pragmatically (*vyavahāra-yogyatā sattvaṃ*), and the falsity of the assertion that the world is false is understood by the actual perception of the reality of the world. Again, the falsity of the world cannot be attempted to be proved by logical proof, for these fall within the world and would therefore be themselves false. Again, it may be said that Brahman is also in some sense knowable and so also is the world; it may be admitted for argument's sake that Brahman is not knowable in an ultimate sense (*pāramārthika*), so the world also is not knowable in an ultimate sense; for, if it were, the Śaṅkarite could not call it false. If that is so, how could the Śaṅkarite argue that the world is false because it is knowable, for in that case Brahman would also be false?

Sixteenth Objection. Again, it may be argued that the objects of the world are false because, though being remains the same, its content always varies. Thus we may say a jug exists, a cloth exists, but though these so-called existents change, "being" alone remains unchanged. Therefore the changeable entities are false and the unchangeable alone is real. Now it may be asked: what is the meaning of this change? It cannot mean any difference of identity, for in that case Brahman being different from other entities could be regarded as false. If, however, Brahman be regarded as identical with the false world, Brahman itself would be false, or the world-appearance would be real being identical with the real Brahman. Spatial or temporal change can have nothing to do with determining falsehood; the conch-shell–silver is not false because it does not exist elsewhere. Brahman itself is changeable in the sense that it does not exist as unreal or as an entity which is neither being nor non-being. Change cannot here legitimately be used in the sense of destruction, for, even when the illusion of conch-shell–silver is discovered, no one says that the conch-shell–silver is destroyed (*bādha-vināśayor viviktatayai'va vyutpatteḥ*). Destruction (*vināśa*) is the dissolution of an entity, whereas *vādha* or contradiction is the negation of what was perceived. In such phrases as "a jug exists" or "a cloth exists," the existence qualifies jug and cloth, but jug and cloth do not qualify existence. Again, though Brahman abides everywhere, it does not cause in us the cognition "jug exists" or "cloth exists." Again, temporal variation in existence depends upon the cause of such existence, but it cannot render the existence of anything false. If non-illumination at any particular time be regarded as the criterion of falsehood, then Brahman also is false for it does not reveal itself before the dawn of emancipation. If it is held that Brahman is always self-revealing, but its revelation remains somehow hidden until emancipation is attained, then it may be said with the same force that the jug and the cloth also remain revealed in a hidden manner in the same way. Again, the eternity of illumination, or its uncontradicted nature, cannot be regarded as a criterion of reality, for it is faultlessness that is the cause of the eternity of self-illumination, and this has nothing to do with determining the nature of existence. Since the ordinary things, such as a jug or a cloth, appear as existent at some time, they are manifestations of the self-illumination and therefore real.

An opposite argument may also be adduced here. Thus, it may be said that that which is not false does not break its continuity or does not change. Brahman is false, for it is without any continuity with anything else, and is different from everything else.

Seventeenth Objection. The Śaṅkarites hold that since it is impossible to explain the existence of any relation (whatever may be its nature) between the perceiver and the perceived, the perceived entity or the content of knowledge has to be admitted as false. In reply to this Veṅkaṭa says that the falsity of the world cannot be adduced as a necessary implication (*arthāpatti*), for the establishment of a relation between the perceiver and the perceived is possible not by denying the latter but by affirming it. If, however, it is said that since the relation between the perceiver and the perceived can be logically proved chimerical, the necessary deduction is that the perceived entity is false. To this the reply is that the falsity of the relation does not prove the falsity of the relata; the relation between a hare and a horn may be non-existent, but that will not indicate that both the hare and the horn are themselves non-existent. Following that argument, the perceiver might just as well be declared as false. If, however, it is contended that the perceiver, being self-luminous, is self-evident and cannot therefore be supposed to be false, the reply is, that even if, in the absence of the act of perceiving, the perceiver may be regarded as self-revealing, what harm is there in admitting the perceived to have the same status even when the perceiver is denied? If, however, it is said that the cognition of objects cannot be admitted to be self-established in the same way as the objects themselves, it may be asked if consciousness is ever perceived to be self-revealed. If it is said that the self-revealing character of consciousness can be established by inference, then by a counter-contention it may be held that the self-revealing character of the universe can also be proved by a suitable inference. It may again be questioned whether, if the Śaṅkarite wishes to establish the self-revealing nature of Brahman by inference, its objectivity can be denied, and thus the original thesis that Brahman cannot be the object of any process of cognition must necessarily fail.

The Śaṅkarite may indeed contend that the followers of Rāmānuja also admit that the objects are revealed by the cognition of the self and hence they are dependent on the perceiver. The reply to such a contention is that the followers of Rāmānuja admit the existence of self-consciousness by which the perceiver himself is regarded as cognized. If this self-consciousness is regarded as false, then the self-luminous self would also be false; and if this self-consciousness be admitted as real, then the relation between them is real. If the self-revealing consciousness be regarded as impossible of perception and yet real, then on the same analogy the world may as well be regarded as real though unperceived.

The objection that the known is regarded as false, since it is difficult logically to conceive the nature of the relation subsisting between the knower and the known, is untenable, for merely on account of the difficulty of conceiving the logical nature of the relation one cannot deny the reality of the related entity which is incontestably given in experience. Therefore the relation has somehow to be admitted. If relation is admitted to be real because it is experienced, then the world is also real because it is also experienced. If the world is false because it is inexplicable, then falsity itself would be false because it is inexplicable.

The objection that there can be no relation between the past and the future is groundless, for the very fact that two things exist in the present time would not mean that they are necessarily related, e.g. the hare and the horn. If, however, it is said that it may be true that things which exist in the present time are not necessarily related, yet there are certain entities at present which are related, so also there are certain things in the present which are related with certain other things in the past and the future. It is no doubt true that the relation of contact is not possible between things of the present and the future, but that does not affect our case, for certain relations exist between entities at present, and certain other relations exist between entities in the present and the future. What relations exist in the present, past and future have to be learnt by experience. If spatial contiguity be a special feature of entities at present, temporal contiguity would hold between entities in present, past and future. However, relation does not necessarily mean contiguity; proximity and remoteness may both condition the relation. Relations are to be admitted just as they are given by experience, and are indefinable and unique in their specific nature. Any attempt to explain them through mediation would end in a conflict with experience. If an attempt is made to refute all relations as such on the ground that relations would imply further relations and thus involve a vicious infinite, the reply is that the attempt to refute a relation itself involves relation and therefore according to the opponent's own supposition stands cancelled. A relation stands by itself and does not depend on other relations for its existence.

Eighteenth Objection. In refuting the view of the Śaṅkarites that self-luminous Brahman cannot have as an object of illumination anything that is external to it, Veṅkaṭa argues that if nescience be itself inherent in Brahman from beginningless time, then there would be no way for Brahman to extricate itself from its clutches and emancipation would be impossible. Then the question may be asked, whether the *avidyā* is different from Brahman or not. If it be different, then the monism of the Śaṅkara philosophy breaks down; if it be non-different, then also on the one hand Brahman could not free itself from it and on the other hand there could be no evolution of the *avidyā* which has merged itself in the nature of the Brahman, into the various forms of egoism, passions, etc. If this *avidyā* be regarded as false and therefore incapable of binding the free nature of Brahman, the objection may still be urged that, if this falsehood covers the nature of Brahman, how can it regain its self-luminosity; and if it cannot do so, that would mean its destruction, for self-luminosity is the very nature of Brahman. If the *avidyā* stands as an independent entity and covers the nature of Brahman, then it would be difficult to conceive how the existence of a real entity can be destroyed by mere knowledge. According to Rāmānuja's view, however, knowledge is a quality or a characteristic of Brahman by which other things are known by it; experience also shows that a knower reveals the objects by his knowledge, and thus knowledge is a characteristic quality of the knower by which the objects are known.

Nineteenth Objection. In refuting the view of Śaṅkara that ignorance or *avidyā* rests in Brahman, Veṅkaṭa tries to clarify the concept of *ajñāna*. He says that *ajñāna* here cannot mean the absolute negation of the capacity of being the knower; for this capacity, being the essence of Brahman, cannot be absent. It (*ajñāna*) cannot also mean the ignorance that precedes the rise of any cognition, for the Śaṅkarites do not admit knowledge as a quality or a characteristic of Brahman; nor can it mean the negation of any particular knowledge, for the Brahman-consciousness is the only consciousness admitted by the Śaṅkarites. This *ajñāna* cannot also be regarded as the absence of knowledge, since it is admitted to be a positive entity. The *ajñāna* which can be removed by knowledge must belong to the same knower who has the knowledge and must refer to the specific object regarding which there was absence of knowledge. Now since Brahman is not admitted by the Śaṅkarites to be knower, it is impossible that any *ajñāna* could be associated with it. The view that is held by the members of the Rāmānuja school is that the individual knowers possess ignorance in so far as they are ignorant of their real nature as self-luminous entities, and in so far as they associate themselves with their bodies, their senses, their passions, and other prejudices and ideas. When they happen to discover their folly, their ignorance is removed. It is only in this way that it can be said to be removed by knowledge. But all this would be impossible in the case of Brahman conceived as pure consciousness. According to the view of Rāmānuja's school, individual knowers are all in their essential natures omniscient; it is the false prejudice and passions that cover up this omniscience whereby they appear as ordinary knowers who can know things only under specific conditions.

Twentieth Objection. Veṅkaṭa, in refuting the definition of immediate intuition (*anubhūti*) as that which may be called immediate perception without being further capable of being an object of awareness (*avedyatve sati aparokṣa-vyavahāra-yogyatvam*), as given by Citsukhācārya in his *Tattva-pradīpikā*, raises certain objections against it as follows. It is urged by the Śaṅkarites that if the immediate intuition be itself an object of further cognitive action, then it loses its status as immediate intuition and may be treated as an object like other objects, e.g. a jug. If by the words "immediate intuition" it is meant that at the time of its operation it is self-expressed and does not stand in need of being revealed by another cognition, then this is also admitted by Rāmānuja. Furthermore, this intuition at the time of its self-revelation involves with it the revelation of the self of the knower as well. Therefore, so far as this meaning of intuition is concerned, the denial of self-revelation is out of place.

The words "immediate intuition" (*anubhūti*) are supposed to have another meaning, viz. that the intuition is not individuated in separate individual cognitions as limited by time, space or individual laws. But such an intuition is never experienced, for not only do we infer certain cognitions as having taken place in certain persons or being absent in them, but we also speak of our own cognitions as present in past and future, such as "I know it," "I knew it" and the like, which prove that cognitions are temporally limited. It may be asked whether this immediate intuition reveals Brahman or anything else; if it reveals Brahman, then it certainly has an object. If it is supposed that in doing so it simply reveals that which has already been self-expressed, even then it will be expressive of something though that something stood already expressed. This would involve a contradiction between the two terms of the thesis *avedyatve sati aparokṣa-vyavahāra-yogyatvam*, for, following the arguments given above, though the Brahman may be regarded as immediate, yet it has been shown to be capable of being made an object of intuition. If on the other alternative this intuition expresses something else than Brahman, that would bring the opponent to a conclusion not intended by him and contradictory as well.

Just as one may say that one knows a jug or a cloth or an orange, so one may say that one knows another man's awareness or one's own. In this way an awareness can be the object of another awareness just as another object. Again, if one cannot be aware of another man's awareness, the use of language for mental understanding should cease.

If the immediate intuition itself cannot be made an object of awareness, that would mean that it is not known at all and consequently its existence would be chimerical. It cannot be urged that chimerical entities are not perceivable because they are chimerical, but entities do not become chimerical because they cannot be perceived, for the concomitance in the former proposition is not conditional. The Śaṅkarites would not hold that all entities other than immediate intuition are chimerical. It may also be held that chimerical entities are not immediate intuition because they are chimerical; but in that case it may also be held that these objects (e.g. a jug) are not immediate intuition because of their specific characters as jug, etc. The whole point that has to be emphasized here is that the ordinary objects are other than immediate intuition, not because they can be known but because of their specific characters. The reason that an entity cannot be called immediate intuition if it can be known is entirely faulty[1].

If, again, Brahman is manifest as only immediate intuition, then neither the scriptures nor philosophy can in any way help us regarding the nature of Brahman.

Twenty-first Objection. The Śaṅkarites deny the production of individual cognitions. In their view all the various forms of so-called cognitions arise through the association of various modes of *avidyā* with the self-luminous pure consciousness. In refuting this view Veṅkaṭa urges that the fact that various cognitions arise in time is testified by universal experience. If the pure consciousness be always present and if individual cognitions are denied, then all

[1] *Śata-dūṣaṇī*, II. 78.

objects ought to be manifested simultaneously. If, however, it is ascertained that though the pure consciousness is always present yet the rise of various cognitions is conditioned by other collocating causal circumstances, the reply is that such an infinite number of causal conditions conditioning the pure consciousness would be against the dictum of the Śaṅkarites themselves, for this would be in conflict with their uncompromising monism. Now if, again, it is held that the cognitive forms do really modify the nature of pure consciousness, then the pure consciousness becomes changeable, which is against the thesis of Śaṅkara. If it is held that the forms are imposed on pure consciousness as it is and by such impositions the specific objects are in their turn illuminated by consciousness, then the position is that in order that an object may be illuminated such illumination must be mediated by a false imposition on the nature of pure consciousness. If the direct illumination of objects is impossible, then another imposition might be necessary to mediate the other false impositions on the nature of pure consciousness, and that might require another, and this would result in a vicious infinite. If the imposition is not false, then the consciousness becomes changeable and the old objection would recur. If, however, it is urged that the objects are illuminated independent of any collocating circumstances and independent of any specific contribution from the nature of the pure consciousness, then all objects (since they are all related to pure consciousness) might simultaneously be revealing. If, again, all cognitions are but false impositions on the nature of pure consciousness, then at the time of an illusory imposition of a particular cognition, say, a jug, nothing else would exist, and this would bring about nihilism. It may also be asked, if the Śaṅkarite is prepared to deny the world on account of the impossibility of any relation subsisting between it and the perceiver, how can he launch himself into an attempt to explain the relation of such a world with Brahman?

On the other hand, the experience of us all testifies to the fact that we are aware of cognitions coming into being, staying, passing away, and having passed and gone from us; except in the case of perceptual experience, there is no difficulty in being aware of past and future events; so the objection that the present awareness cannot be related to past and future events is invalid. The objection that there cannot be awareness of past or future entities because they are not existing now is invalid, for past and future entities also exist in their own specific temporal relations. Validity of awareness consists in the absence of contradiction and not in the fact of its relating to an entity of the present moment, for otherwise an illusory perception of the present moment would have to be considered as valid. Thus, since it is possible to be aware of an awareness that was not there but which comes into being both by direct and immediate acquaintance and by inference, the view of the Śaṅkarites denying the origination of individual awareness is invalid. In the view of Rāmānuja, knowledge is no doubt admitted to be eternal; yet this knowledge is also admitted to have specific temporal characters and also specific states. Therefore, so far as these characters or states are concerned, origination and cessation would be possible under the influence of specific collocative circumstances. Again, the objection that since pure consciousness is beginningless it cannot suffer changes is invalid, for the Śaṅkarites admit *avidyā* also as beginningless and yet changeable. It may also be pointed out in this connection that the so-called contentless consciousness is never given in experience. Even the consciousness in dreamless sleep or in a swoon is related to the perceiver and therefore not absolutely contentless.

Twenty-second Objection. It is urged by the Śaṅkarites that the pure consciousness is unchanging because it is not produced. If, however, the word unchanging means that it never ceases to exist, it may be pointed out that the Śaṅkarites admit *ajñāna* to be unproduced and yet liable to destruction. Thus there is no reason why a thing should not be liable to destruction because it is not produced. If it is urged that the destruction of *avidyā* is itself false, then it may be pointed out with the same force that the destruction of all things is false. Moreover, since the Śaṅkarites do not admit any change to be real, the syllogism adduced by them that an entity which is unproduced is not changeable falls to the ground. The difference between Śaṅkara's conception of Brahman and that of Rāmānuja is that according to the former Brahman is absolutely unchangeable and characterless, and according to the latter the Brahman is the absolute, containing within it the world and the individual beings and all the changes involved in them. It is unchangeable only in so far as all the dynamical change rises from within and there is nothing else outside it which can affect it. That is, the absolute, though changeable within it, is absolutely self-contained and self-sustained, and is entirely unaffected by anything outside it.

Twenty-third Objection. The Śaṅkarites urge that since consciousness is unproduced it cannot be many, for whatever is many is produced, e.g. the jug. If it is a pure consciousness which appears as many through the conditioning factors of *avidyā*, it may be asked in this connection whether, if the pure consciousness cannot be differentiated from anything else, it may as well be one with the body also, which is contrary to Śaṅkara's thesis. If, however, it is replied that the so-called difference between the body and the pure consciousness is only a false difference, then it would have to be admitted and that would militate against the changeless character of Brahman as held by the Śaṅkarites. Again, if the real difference between the body and the pure consciousness be denied, then it may be urged that the proposition following from it is that things which in reality differ are produced (e.g. the jug); but according to the Śaṅkarites jug, etc., are also not different from Brahman, and thus a proposition like the above cannot be quoted in support. Moreover, since the *avidyā* is unproduced, it follows that according to the maxim of the Śaṅkarites it would not be different from Brahman which, however, the Śaṅkarites would undoubtedly be slow to accept. It cannot also be held that an awareness does not differ from another awareness on the supposition that different awarenesses are but seeming forms imposed upon the same consciousness, for so long as we speak of difference we speak only of apparent difference and of apparent divergent forms; and if the apparent divergent forms are admitted, it cannot be said that they are not different. Again, it is urged that the same moon appears as many through wavy water, so it is the same awareness that appears as many, though these are identically one. To this the reply is that the analogy is false. The image-moon is not identical with the moon, so the appearances are not identical with awareness. If it is said that all image-moons are false, then on the same analogy all awarenesses may be false and then if only one consciousness be true as a ground of all awarenesses then all awarenesses may be said to be equally true or equally false. Again, as to the view that the principle of consciousness as such does not differ from individual cognitions, such a position is untenable, because the Rāmānujists do not admit the existence of an abstract principle of consciousness; with them all cognitions are specific and individual. It may be pointed out in this connection that according to the Rāmānujists consciousness exists in the individuals as eternal qualities, i.e. it may suffer modification according to conditions and circumstances.

Twenty-fourth Objection. In objecting to the unqualified character of pure consciousness Veṅkaṭa says that to be unqualified is also a qualification. It differs from other qualities only in being negative. Negative qualifications ought to be deemed as objectionable as the positive ones. Again, Brahman is admitted by the Śaṅkarites to be absolute and unchangeable, and these are qualifications. If it is replied that these qualifications are also false, then their opposite qualifications would hold good, viz. Brahman would be admitted as changeable. Again, it may be asked how this unqualified character of Brahman is established. If it is not established by reason, the assumption is invalid; if it is established by reason, then that reason must exist in Brahman and it will be qualified by it (the reason).

Twenty-fifth Objection. Veṅkaṭa denies the assumption of the Śaṅkarites that consciousness is the self because it reveals it to itself on the ground that if whatever reveals it to itself or whatever stands self-revealed is to be called the self, then pleasure and pain also should be identical with the self, for these are self-revealed. Veṅkaṭa further urges that the revelation of knowledge is not absolutely unconditional because revelation is made to the perceiver's self and not to anything and everything, a fact which shows that it is conditioned by the self. It may also be pointed out that the revelation of knowledge is not made to itself but to the self on one hand and to the objects on the other in the sense that they form constituents of knowledge. Again, it is testified by universal experience that consciousness is different from the self. It may also be asked whether, if consciousness be identical with the self, this consciousness is unchangeable or changeable. Would later recognition be impossible? In the former alternative it may further be asked whether this unchanging consciousness has any support or not; if not, how can it stand unsupported? If it has a support, then that support may well be taken as the knower, as is done by the Rāmānujists. It may also be pointed out here that knowledge being a character or a quality cannot be identified with that (viz. the self) which possesses that character.

Twenty-sixth Objection. The Śaṅkarites assert that the self is pure consciousness. Therefore the perception of self as "I" is false, and therefore this notion of "I" is obsolete both in dreamless sleep and emancipation. To this Veṅkaṭa's reply is that if the notion of "I" is obsolete in dreamless sleep, then the continuity of self-consciousness is impossible. It is no doubt true that in dreamless sleep the notion of the self as "I" is not then manifestly experienced, but it is not on that account non-existent at the time, for the continuity of the self as "I" is necessarily implied in the fact that it is experienced both before the dreamless sleep and after it. Since it is manifestly experienced both before and after the dreamless sleep, it must be abiding even at the time of the sleep. And this self-consciousness itself refers to the past and the present as a continuity. If this ego-notion was annihilated during the dreamless sleep, then the continuity of experience could not be explained (*madhye cā'hama-rthā-bhāve saṃskāra-dhārā-bhāvāt, pratisandhānā-bhāva-prasaṅgaś ca*). It is a patent fact that in the absence of the knower neither ignorance nor knowledge can exist. It cannot also be said that the continuity of experience is transmitted to pure consciousness or *avidyā* during the dreamless sleep; for the pure consciousness cannot be a repository of experiences, and if *avidyā* is the repository it would be the knower, which is impossible; and the fact of recognition would be unexplainable, for the experience associated with *avidyā* cannot be remembered by the entity to which the ego-notion refers. Moreover, the experience of a man rising from sleep who feels "I slept happily so long" indicates that the entity referred to by the ego-notion was also experienced during the sleep. Even the experience referring to the state in dreamless sleep as "I slept so soundly that I even did not know myself" also indicates that the self was experienced at that time as being ignorant of its specific bodily and other spatial and temporal relations. It cannot be contended that the entity denoted by the ego-notion cannot abide even in emancipation, for if there was no entity in emancipation no one would attempt to attain to this stage. The existence of pure qualityless consciousness at the time of emancipation would mean the annihilation of the self, and no one would ever be interested in his own self-destruction. Moreover, if the entity denoted by the ego-notion is not a real entity, then the view (often put forward by the Śaṅkarites) that the entity denoted by the ego-notion is often falsely identified with the body or the senses would be meaningless. If the illusion be due to a false imposition of false appearances, such as the body or the senses, on the pure consciousness, then that cannot be called the delusion of the ego-entity as the body and the senses. It cannot also be said that in the experience of the self as "I" there are two parts, the pure consciousness which is eternal and real and the egohood which is a mere false appearance. For if it is so in the ego-experience it might also be so in other experiences as objectivity as this or that. Moreover, if this is so, what is there to distinguish the specific experience as subjectivity from the experience as objectivity? What is it that constitutes the special feature of subjectivity? Thus it may be confidently stated that the ego-entity is the real nature of the self.

Twenty-seventh Objection. It is urged by the Śaṅkarites that the notion of the self as the knower is false because the ultimate reality, being the self-luminous Brahman, is absolutely unchangeable. The attribution of the characteristic of being a knower would be incompatible with this nature. To this it may be replied that if the fact of being a knower is regarded as a changeable character, then being or self-luminosity would also be a character, and they also would be incompatible with this nature. The change of the states of knowledge does not in any way affect the unchangeable nature of the self, for the self is not changed along with the change of the cognitions.

Twenty-eighth Objection. It is well known that the Śaṅkarites conceive of pure consciousness which is regarded as the witness (*sākṣin*), as it were, of all appearances and forms that are presented to it, and it is through its function as such a witness that these are revealed. It is through this *sākṣi*-consciousness that the continuity of consciousness is maintained, and during dreamless sleep the blissfulness that is experienced is also made apparent to this *sākṣi*-consciousness. The Rāmānujists deny this *sākṣi*-consciousness because it is unnecessary for them; its purpose is served by the functions of a knower whose consciousness is regarded as continuous in the waking state, in dreams, and also in dreamless sleep. Veṅkaṭa urges that the manifestation of blissfulness which is one with pure consciousness is implied by the very nature of pure consciousness as self-revealed. It may also be pointed out that the sensuous pleasures cannot be manifested during dreamless sleep; if this is so, why should a *sākṣi*-consciousness be admitted for explaining the experience of blissfulness during dreamless sleep? Since Brahman is not admitted to be a real knower, the conception of *sākṣin* is not the same as that of a knower. It cannot also be a mere revelation; for if it be a revelation of itself as Brahman, then the mediation of the function of *sākṣi*-consciousness is unnecessary, and if it be of *avidyā*, then through its association Brahman would be false. It cannot be that the functioning of the *sākṣi*-consciousness is one with the nature of Brahman, and yet that partakes of the nature of *avidyā*; for it cannot both be identical with Brahman and the *avidyā*. If the functioning of the *sākṣi*-consciousness be false, a number of other *sākṣins* is to be admitted, leading to a vicious infinite. Thus in whatsoever way one may try to conceive of the *sākṣi*-consciousness, one fails to reconcile it either with reason or with experience.

Twenty-ninth and thirtieth Objections. Veṅkaṭa urges that the Śaṅkarites are wrong in asserting that scriptural testimony is superior in validity to perceptual experience. As a matter of fact, scriptural knowledge is not possible without perceptual experience. Therefore scriptures are to be interpreted in such a way that they do not come into conflict with the testimony of perceptual knowledge. Therefore, since the perception proves to us the reality of the many around us, the scriptural interpretation that would try to convince us of their falsity is certainly invalid. The Śaṅkarites further urge and adduce many false illustrations to prove the possibility of attaining right knowledge through false means (e.g. the fear that arises from the perception of false snakes, representations of things that are made by letters, and the combinations of letters which are combinations of lines). But Veṅkaṭa's reply to it is that in all those cases where falsehood is supposed to lead us to truth it is not through falsehood that we come to truth but from one right knowledge to another. It is because the lines stand as true symbols for certain things that they are represented by them, and it is not possible to adduce any illustration in which falsehood may be supposed to lead us to truth. If, therefore, scriptures are false (in the ultimate sense) as Śaṅkarites would say, it would be impossible for them to lead us to the true Brahma-knowledge.

Thirty-first Objection. The view of the Śaṅkarites that the emancipation may be attained by right knowledge even in this life before death, called by them *Jīvanmukti* or emancipation in life, is denied by the Rāmānujists, who hold that emancipation cannot be attained by right knowledge but by right actions and right feelings associated with right knowledge, and consequently emancipation is the result. Real separation of the association of the worldly things from the self can only come about after the body ceases to exist. Veṇkaṭa points out that, so long as the body remains, perception of the ultimate truth as one is impossible, for such a person is bound to be aware of the existence of the body and its manifold relations. If it be said that though the body persists yet it may be regarded as absolutely false or non-existent, then that would amount to one's being without any body and the distinction of emancipation in life and emancipation in death would be impossible.

Thirty-second Objection. The Śaṅkarites assert that *ajñāna* or ignorance, though opposed to knowledge, is a positive entity as it is revealed as such by perception, inference and scriptural testimony. Veṅkaṭa, in refusing this, says that if *ajñāna* be regarded as opposed to knowledge, it can only be so if it negates knowledge, i.e. if it be of the nature of negation. Such a negation must then obviously refer to a content of knowledge; and if this be admitted then the content of knowledge must have been known, for otherwise the negation cannot refer to it. To this the Śaṅkarites are supposed to say that the negation of knowledge and the content to which it refers are two independent entities such that the experience of the negation of knowledge does not necessarily imply that the content should be known. Therefore it is wrong to say that the negation of knowledge is a contradiction in terms. To this the obvious reply is that as in the case of a negation, where the presence of the object of negation contradicts a negation, so when there is a negation of all contents of knowledge the presence of any content necessarily contradicts it. So the experience that "I do not know anything" would be contradicted by any knowledge whatsoever. If it is urged that a negation of knowledge and its experience may be at two different moments so that the experience and the negation may not be contradictory, the reply is that perceptual experience always grasps things which are existent at the present time. Though in the case of the supposed perception of *ajñāna* during dreamless sleep the experience of *ajñāna* may be supposed to be known by inference, and in cases of such perception as "I am ignorant," "I do not know myself or anything else," there is obviously perceptual experience of *ajñāna*. It is, therefore, impossible that "I" should perceive and be at the same time ignorant. Perception of ignorance would thus be absurd. Again, the experience of a negation necessarily must refer to a locus, and this implies that there is a knowledge of the locus and that this would contradict the experience of a universal negation which is devoid of all knowledge. It may, however, be urged that the perception of ignorance is not the experience of a negation, but that of a positive entity, and so the objections brought forward in the above controversy would not apply to it.

To this the reply is that the admission of a positive category called *ajñāna* which is directly experienced in perception may imply that it is of an entity which is opposed to knowledge; for the negative particle "*a*" in "*ajñāna*" is used either in the sense of absence or negation. If it does so, it may well be urged that experience of opposition implies two terms, that which opposes and that to which there is an opposition. Thus, the experience of *ajñāna* would involve the experience of knowledge also, and, therefore, when the opposite of *ajñāna* shines forth, how can *ajñāna* be perceived? It is clear, therefore, that no advantage is gained by regarding *ajñāna* as a positive entity instead of a mere negation. The conception of a positive *ajñāna* cannot serve any new purpose which is not equally attainable by the conception of it as negation of knowledge. If a positive entity is regarded as able to circumscribe or limit the scope of manifestation of Brahman, a negation also may do the same. The Śaṅkarites themselves admit that knowledge shines by driving away the ignorance which constituted the negation-precedent-to the production of (*prāga-bhāva*) knowledge, and thus in a way they admit that *ajñāna* is of the nature of negation. The supposed experience of dullness (*mugdho'smi*) involves in it the notion of an opposition. The mere fact that the word "dull" (*mugdha*) has no negative particle in it does not mean that it has no negative sense. Thus, a positive ignorance cannot be testified by perception.

It has been suggested that the existence of *ajñāna* may be proved by inference on the supposition that if light manifests itself by driving away darkness, so knowledge must shine by driving away positive ignorance. Now inference is a mode of knowledge and as such it must drive away some ignorance which was hiding its operation. Since this *ajñāna* could not manifest itself, it must imply some other *ajñāna* which was hiding it, and without driving which it could not manifest itself, and there would thus be infinite regress. If the *ajñāna* be regarded as hiding, then the inference may as well be regarded as destroying the ignorance directly. Whenever a knowledge illuminates some contents, it may be regarded as dispelling the ignorance regarding it. The scriptural texts also do not support the conception of a positive *ajñāna*. Thus, the concept of a positive *ajñāna* is wholly illegitimate.

Fortieth Objection. The supposition that the *ajñāna* rests in the individual *jīvas* and not Brahman is also false. If the *ajñāna* is supposed to rest in the individual in its own real essence (i.e. as Brahman), then the *ajñāna* would virtually rest in Brahman. If it is supposed that *ajñāna* rests in the individual *jīvas*, not in their natural state but in their ordinarily supposed nature as suffering rebirth, etc., then this amounts to saying that the *ajñāna* is associated with the material stuff and as such can never be removed; for the material limitations of an individual can never have a desire to remove the *ajñāna*, nor has it the power to destroy it. Again, it may be asked whether the *ajñāna* that constitutes the difference of individual *jīvas* is one or many in different cases. In the former case in the emancipation of one, *ajñāna* would be removed and all would be emancipated. In the second case it is difficult to determine whether *avidyā* comes first or the difference between individual *jīvas*, and there would thus be *anyonyā-śraya*, for the Śaṅkarites do not admit the reality of difference between *jīvas*. In the theory that *ajñāna* is associated with Brahman, the difference between *jīvas* being false, there is no necessity to admit the diversity of *ajñāna* according to the diversity of *jīvas*. In any case, whether real or fictitious, *avidyā* cannot explain the diversity of the *jīvas*. Again, if the *ajñānas* which are supposed to produce the diversity of the *jīvas* be supposed to exist in the Brahman, then Brahman cannot be known. In the view that these *ajñānas* exist in the *jīvas*, the old difficulty comes in as to whether the difference of *avidyās* is primary or whether that of the *jīvas* is primary. If the difficulty is intended to be solved by suggesting that the regression is not vicious as in the case of the seed and the shoot, then it may be pointed out that in the supposition that the *ajñānas* which produce difference in *jīvas* have these as their support then there is no scope for such a regression. The seed that produces the shoot does not produce itself. If it is suggested that the *avidyā* of the previous *jīvas* produces the later *jīvas*, then the *jīvas* would be destructible. Thus, from whichever way we may try to support the view that the *avidyā* rests in individual *jīvas* we meet with unmitigated failure.

Forty-first Objection. It is said that the defect of *avidyā* belongs to Brahman. If this defect of *avidyā* is something different from Brahman, then that virtually amounts to the admission of dualism; if it is not different from Brahman, then Brahman itself becomes responsible for all errors and illusions which are supposed to be due to *avidyā*, and Brahman being eternal all errors and illusions are bound to be eternal. If it is said that the errors and illusions are produced when Brahman is associated with some other accessory cause, then about this also the old question may be raised as to whether the accessory cause or causes are different or not different from Brahman and whether real or not. Again, such an accessory cause cannot be of the nature of a negation-precedent-to the production of the true knowledge of the identity of the self and the Brahman; for then the doctrine of a positive ignorance propounded by the Śaṅkarites would be wholly unnecessary and uncalled for. Further, such a negation cannot be identical with Brahman, for then with true knowledge and with the destruction of ignorance Brahman itself would cease. Again, since everything else outside Brahman is false, if there is any such entity that obstructs the light of Brahman or distorts it (if the distortion is in any sense real), then that entity would also be Brahman; and Brahman being eternal that distortion would also be eternal. If the defect which acts as an obstructive agent be regarded as unreal and beginningless, then also it must depend on some cause and this will lead to an infinite regress; if it does not depend upon any cause, then it would be like Brahman which shines forth by itself without depending on any defect, which is absurd. If it is supposed that this defect constructs itself as well as others, then the world-creation would manifest itself without depending upon any other defect. If it is said that there is no impropriety in admitting the defect as constructing itself, just as an illusion is the same as the construction, i.e. is made by it, then the Śaṅkarites would be contradicting their own views;

for they certainly do admit the beginningless world-creation to be due to the operation of defects. If the *avidyā* is not itself an illusory imposition, then it will be either true or chimerical. If it is regarded as both an illusory construction and a product, then it would not be beginningless. If it has a beginning, then it cannot be distinguished from the world-appearance. If illusion and its construction be regarded as identical, then also the old difficulty of the *avidyā* generating itself through its own construction would remain the same. Again, if the *avidyā* appears to Brahman without the aid of any accessory defect, then it will do so eternally. If it is urged that, when the *avidyā* ceases, its manifestation would also cease, then also there is a difficulty which is suggested by the theory of the Śaṅkarites themselves; for we know that in their theory there is no difference between the illumination and that which is illuminated and that there is no causal operation between them. That which is being illuminated cannot be separated from the principle of illumination.

If it is urged that the *avidyā* is manifested so long as there is no dawning of true knowledge, then may it not be said that the negation-precedent-to the rise of true knowledge is the cause of world-appearance and that the admission of *avidyā* is unnecessary? If it is said that the negation cannot be regarded as the cause of the very varied production of world-appearances, then it can be urged with as much force that the position may also be regarded as capable of producing the manifold world-appearance. If it is held that positive defects in the eye often produce many illusory appearances, then it may also be urged on the other side that the non-observation of distinctions and differences is also often capable of producing many illusory appearances. If it is urged that negation is not limited by time and is therefore incapable of producing the diverse kinds of world-appearances under different conditions of time, and that it is for that reason that it is better to admit positive ignorance, then also it may be asked with as much force how such a beginningless ignorance unconditioned by any temporal character can continue to produce the diverse world-appearance conditioned in time till the dawning of true knowledge. If in answer to this it is said that such is the nature and character of *avidyā*, then it may well be asked what is the harm in admitting such a nature or character of "negation." This, at least, saves us from admitting a strange and uncalled for hypothesis of positive ignorance. It may be urged that negation is homogeneous and formless and as such it cannot undergo transformations of character, while *avidyā*, being a positive stuff, can pass through a series of transformations of character (*vivarta-paramparā*). In this connection it may be urged that the nature of *avidyā* is nothing but this succession of transformations of character; if it is so, then since it is the nature of *avidyā* to have a succession of diverse kinds of transformations, there may be all kinds of illusions at all times. It cannot also be regarded as an effect of transformation of character, for the *avidyā* is supposed to produce such effects. If it is urged that *avidyā* is a distinct entity by itself, different from the appearance of its character that is perceived, then also the old question would recur regarding the reality or unreality of it. The former supposition would be an admission of dualism; the latter supposition, that is, if it is false, the succession of it as various appearances conditioned by diverse kinds of time and space would presuppose such other previous presuppositions *ad infinitum*. If it is held that there is no logical defect in supposing that the previous sets of transformations determine the later sets in an unending series, it is still not necessary to admit *avidyā* in order to explain such a situation. For it may well be supposed that the different transformations arise in Brahman without depending upon any extraneous cause. The objection that such a supposition that Brahman is continually undergoing such diverse transformations of character (real or unreal) would inevitably lead to the conclusion that there is no Brahman beyond such transformations is invalid; for our perceptual experience shows that the transformatory change of a lump of clay does not invalidate its being. In such a view Brahman may be regarded as the ground of all illusory appearances. On the other hand, it is only on the assumption of false *avidyā* that one cannot legitimately affirm the existence of a basis, for the basis of falsehood would itself be false. Therefore, if Brahman be regarded as its basis, then it would itself be false and would land us in nihilism.

Again, it may well be asked whether *avidyā* shines by itself or not. If it does not, it becomes chimerical; if it does, then it may again be asked whether this shining is of the nature of *avidyā* or not. If it is, then it would be as self-shining as Brahman and there would be no difference between them. Again, if the shining character of *avidyā* belongs to Brahman, the Brahman being eternal, there would never be a time when *avidyā* would not shine. The shiningness cannot also be regarded as a character of either Brahman or the *avidyā*, for none of them is regarded as being a knower of it. If it is urged that the character as the knower is the result of an illusory imposition, then the objection is that the meaning of such an imposition is unintelligible unless the conception of *avidyā* is clarified. The character as knower is possible only on the supposition of an illusory imposition, and on the above supposition the illusory imposition becomes possible on the supposition of the knower. If it is due to Brahman, then Brahman, being eternal, the illusory impositions would also be eternal. If it be without any reason, then the entire world-illusion would be without any cause.

Again, any conception regarding the support of *avidyā* is unintelligible. If it has no support, it must be either independent like Brahman or be like chimerical entities. If it has a support and if that support be of the nature of Brahman, then it is difficult to conceive how the eternally pure Brahman can be the support of the impure *avidyā* which is naturally opposed to it. If the solution is to be found in the supposition that the impure *avidyā* is false, then it may well be urged that if it is false there is no meaning in the effort to make it cease. If it is said in reply that though it is nonexistent yet there is an appearance of it, and the effort is made to make that appearance cease, then also the reply is that the appearance is also as false as itself. If it is admitted that though false it can yet injure one's interest, then its falsehood would be only in name, for its effects are virtually admitted to be real. If Brahman in its limited or conditioned aspect be regarded as the support of *avidyā*, then since such a limitation must be through some other *avidyā* this would merely bring us into confusion. If it is held that *avidyā* has for its support an entity quite different from Brahman conditioned or unconditioned, then the view that Brahman is the support of *avidyā* has to be given up, and there would be other difficulties regarding the discovery of another support of this support. If it be said that like Brahman *avidyā* is its own support but Brahman is not its own support, then the support of *avidyā* would have no other support. If it is said that the support can be explained on the basis of conditions, then also it would be difficult to imagine how a condition of the nature of a receptacle (*ādhārā-kāro-pādhi*) can itself be without any support. If further supports are conceived, then there would be a vicious infinite. Again, if it is held that what is false does not require any support, then it may be urged that according to the Śaṅkarites the support is regarded as the basis on which the illusion occurs, and even the jug is regarded as an illusion on the ground. Moreover, this false experience of *avidyā* is not any of the illusory or limited perceptions, such as ego-experience or the experience of other mental states; for these are regarded as the effects of *avidyā*. If they are not so, then they must be due to some other defects, and these to other ones, and so there would be a vicious infinite. If it is held that *avidyā* is nothing different from its experience, then since all experience is of the nature of Brahman, Brahman itself would be false. Again, if the *avidyā* manifests itself as Brahman by hiding its (Brahman) nature, then all pure revelation being hidden and lost, *avidyā* itself, which is manifested by it, would also be naturally lost. If it be manifested as Brahman and its own nature be hidden, then Brahman alone being manifested there would be no question of bondage. It is obvious that it cannot manifest itself both as *avidyā* and as Brahman, for that would be self-contradictory, since knowledge always dispels ignorance. If it is held that just as a mirror reflects an image in which the character of the mirror and the real face is hidden, so *avidyā* may manifest itself and hide both itself and the Brahman. To this the reply is that in all cases of illusions of identity (*tādātmyā-dhyāsa*) the non-observation of the difference is the cause of the error. The cause of the illusion of the face and the mirror is the non-observation of the fact that the face is away from the mirror. But Brahman and *avidyā* are neither located in a proximate space so that it is possible to compare their illusion of identity by the illustration of other illusions which depend upon such proximity. If it is said of *avidyā*, not being a substance, that all criticism that applies to real and existent entities would be inapplicable to it, then such a doctrine would be almost like nihilism, for all criticisms against nihilism are accepted by nihilists as not invalidating their doctrine.

Forty-second Objection. It is held by the Śaṅkarites that *avidyā* and *māyā* are two distinct conceptions. *Māyā* is supposed to be that by which others are deluded, and *avidyā* is supposed to be that which deludes one's self. The word *māyā* is used in various senses but none of these seems to satisfy the usage of the word in Śaṅkarite manner. If it is supposed that the word *māyā*, of which Brahman is supposed to be the support, has this peculiarity that it manifests its various forms to others as well as deludes them, then it is hard to distinguish it from the conception of *avidyā*. If it is held that the word *avidyā* is restricted to mean the agent that causes false perceptions as in the case of conch-shell–silver, then *māyā* may also be called *avidyā*, for it also causes the false world-appearance to be perceived. There is no reason why the cause of the false perception of the conch-shell–silver should be called *avidyā* and not those relatively true cognitions which contradict such illusory perceptions. *Īśvara* also may be said to be suffering from *avidyā*, for since He is omniscient He has the knowledge of all individual selves of which falsehood is a constituent. If God has no knowledge of illusions, He would not be omniscient. It is wrong also to suppose that *māyā* is that which manifests everything else except Brahman in its nature as false; for if the Brahman knows the world-appearance as false without being under an illusion, it would still be hard to repudiate the ignorance of Brahman. If Brahman knows all things as the illusions of others, then He must know the others and as such their constituent illusions, and this would mean that Brahman is itself subject to *avidyā*. It is difficult also to conceive how one can have any cognition of falsehood without being under illusion, for falsehood is not mere non-existence but the appearance of an entity where it does not exist. If Brahman sees other people only under illusions, that does not mean that Brahman deludes others by His *māyā*. There may be a magician who would try to show his magic by mere false tricks. If the Brahman tried to show His magic by mere false reflections, He would indeed be mad. It may be supposed that the difference between *avidyā* and *māyā* is that *avidyā*, by producing illusory experiences, hurts the real interests of the perceiving selves, yet the Brahman Who perceives these illusory selves and their experiences does so through the agency of *māyā* which does not injure His interest. To this the reply is that if *māyā* does not injure anybody's interest, it cannot be called a defect. It may be objected that defects have no connection with harmful or beneficial effects but they have a relation only to truth and error. Such a view cannot be accepted, for truth and error have a pragmatic value and all that is erroneous hurts one's interests; if it were not so, nobody would be anxious to remove them.

If it is argued that *māyā* is not a defect of Brahman but a quality, then it may be said that if it were so then no one would be anxious to remove it. If, again, *māyā* were a quality of Brahman and served the purpose of such a mighty person, how could the poor individual selves dare it? And if they could, they would be able to injure the practical interests of an Omnipotent Being, for *māyā* being a quality would certainly be of great use to Him. *Māyā* cannot be destroyed by itself without any cause, for that would land us in the doctrine of momentariness. If the *māyā* were eternal and real, that would be an admission of dualism. If *māyā* be regarded as being included in Brahman, then Brahman, being only self-manifesting, and *māyā* being included within it would not have the power of producing the world-delusions which it is supposed to produce. Again, *māyā* being eternal cannot also be false. Again, if the manifestation of *māyā* from Brahman be regarded as real, then the ignorance of Brahman becomes also real; if it is a false manifestation from Brahman, then it would be meaningless to suppose that Brahman should be using the *māyā* as an instrument of play. It is absurd to suppose that Brahman would be playing with false reflected images, like a child. Again, if the *jīvas* and Brahman be identical, then it is unreasonable to suppose that the ignorance of the *jīvas* would not imply the ignorance of Brahman. If, again, the *jīvas* and the Brahman be really different, then how can there be any emancipation by the knowledge of their identity? So the conception of a *māyā* and an *avidyā* different from it is wholly incomprehensible.

Forty-third Objection. It is held by the Śaṅkarites that a knowledge of monistic identity produces emancipation. Now such a knowledge cannot be different from the Brahma-knowledge; for if it is a contentless entity, then it would be no knowledge, since the Śaṅkarites hold that knowledge can only be a mental state associated with a content (*vṛtti-rūpaṃ hi jñānaṃ saviṣayam eva iti bhavatām api siddhāntaḥ*). It cannot also be identical with Brahma-knowledge, for if such a knowledge can produce emancipation the pure Brahma-knowledge would have done the same. It may be held that in the case of the illusion of conch-shell–silver, when there is a true shining regarding the nature of the "this" in its own character, then that is equivalent to the contradiction of the illusory appearance of silver, and the manifestation of identity showing the real nature of Brahman may be regarded as contradictory to world-illusion. To this the reply is that there is no identity between the existence of the "this" as conch-shell and its appearance as silver. Thus, one knowledge may contradict the other, but in the case under review there is no new element in the notion of the identity which was not already present in the Brahma-knowledge itself. If the notion of identity be regarded as a contentful knowledge, then it would be different from the Brahma-knowledge, and being itself false it could not remove the error. The case where a thing known is again recognized is also not a proper instance for supporting the Śaṅkarite position, for here also the knowledge of recognition is not the same as the knowledge of original acquaintance, whereas the notion of identity is supposed to be the same as the Brahma-knowledge. Again, if it is supposed that a mental state of a particular content removes the illusions and produces Brahma-knowledge, then the illusions would be real entities since they were capable of being destroyed like other entities.

If it is held that the notion of identity has a reference to Brahman as limited by *avidyā*, then that will be like the manifestation of the illusory world-creations through the *sākṣi*-consciousness, and such a manifestation would not remove errors.

Again, it may be asked whether the knowledge that produces the notion that all else excepting Brahman is false can itself be regarded as constituting falsehood, for that would be self-contradictory. If the notion of the falsehood of the world-appearance be itself regarded as false, then the world would have to be regarded as real. If it is urged that as in the supposition of the death of a barren woman's son both the barren woman's son and his death are false, so here also both the world and its falsehood may be equally false. But it may be replied that in the instance put forward the falsehood of the barren woman's son and that of his death are not both false. Again, if the falsehood of the world-appearance were real, then that would imply dualism.

Again, if inferences led to the contradiction of world-appearance, then there would be no reason to suppose that the contradiction of the world-appearance would be possible only through listening to the Vedāntic texts of identity. If the contradiction of world-appearance is produced by Brahman itself, then Brahman being eternal there would be no world-illusion. Again, Brahman has been regarded as helping the process of world-illusion in its own pure nature for otherwise there would have been no illusion at all. It is a curious doctrine that though Brahman in its pure nature helps illusion, yet, in its impure nature, as the scriptural texts or the knowledge arising out of them, it would remove it. So in whichever way we may think of the possibility of a removal of *ajñāna* we are brought into confusion.

Forty-fourth Objection. The conception of the cessation of the *avidyā* is also illegitimate. For the question that arises in this connection is whether the cessation of *avidyā* is itself real or unreal. If it is unreal, then the hope that the *avidyā* is rooted out with such a cessation is baffled, for the cessation itself is a manifestation of *avidyā*. It cannot be said that the cessation of *avidyā* has as its ground a real entity, the *ātman*, for then the *ātman* will have to be admitted as suffering change. And if in any way the cessation of *avidyā* is to be regarded as having a true cause as its support, then the cessation being real there would be dualism. If it is regarded as an illusion, and there is no defect behind it, then the assumption of *avidyā* as a defect for explaining the world-illusion would be unnecessary. If it is without any further ground like *avidyā* and Brahman, then there is no meaning in associating *avidyā* with it. There is also no reason why, even after the cessation of *avidyā*, it may not rise up again into appearance. If it is suggested that the function of the cessation of *avidyā* is to show that everything else except Brahman is false and as soon as this function is fulfilled the cessation of *avidyā* also ceases to exist, then also another difficulty has to be faced. For if the cessation of *avidyā* itself ceases to exist, then that would mean that there is a cessation of cessation which means that *avidyā* is again rehabilitated. It may be urged that when a jug is produced it means the destruction of the negation-precedent-to-production (*prāga-bhāva*), and when this jug is again destroyed it does not mean that the negation-precedent again rises into being; so it may be in this case also. To this the reply is that the two cases are different, for in the above case the negation of one negation is through a positive entity, whereas there is nothing to negate the cessation of *avidyā*; so in this case the negation would be a logical negation leading to a position of the entity negated, the *avidyā*. If it is said that there is the Brahman which negates the cessation of *avidyā*, then the difficulty would be that Brahman, the negation of both *avidyā* and its cessation, being eternal, there ought to be no illusory world-creation at any time.

If the cessation of *avidyā* is not itself of illusory nature and if it is regarded as included in the being of Brahman, then Brahman being beginningless the *avidyā* should be regarded as having always remained arrested. It cannot be said that the existence of Brahman is itself the cessation of *ajñāna*, for then it would be impossible to connect the cessation of *avidyā* with the realization of the nature of Brahman as cause and effect.

If it is suggested that a mental state reflecting the nature of Brahman represents the cessation of *ajñāna* of Brahman and that this mental state may be removed by other causes, then the reply is that this would mean that such a mental state is illusory; and this implies that the cessation of *avidyā* is illusory. The criticism of such a view is given above. The cessation of *avidyā* is not real, being outside Brahman; neither real, something different from real, and unreal, for that could not lead to a real cessation. So ultimately it must be neither unreal nor something different from any of the above entities, for the cessation of positive and negative entities only are of the nature of real and unreal. *Ajñāna* is something different from real and unreal; its cessation is valid, being amenable to proofs. So the cessation has to be admitted as being something unique and different from all existent and non-existent entities. In reply it may be said that if the *ajñāna* is admitted to be like-a-non-existent entity (*asatīva*), then in both the two meanings of negation, that is, in the view that negation is but the other name of position and that negation is a separate category in itself, the admission of *avidyā* would involve dualism. If it is regarded as something chimerical, it could never show itself, and such a chimerical entity would have no opposition to the world-cycle. So the cessation of *avidyā* cannot lead to emancipation. Again, if the cessation of *avidyā* is non-existent, that would imply the existence of *avidyā*. The cessation of *avidyā* is not like the destruction of a jug which has a real existence, so that though it may appear like a non-being, yet the jug may be regarded as a positive entity. The destruction of *avidyā* is not of that nature, for it has no definite form. If it is held that the cessation of *avidyā* is of the fifth type, that is, different from existent, non-existent, existent-and-non-existent and different-from-existent-and-non-existent, then this is virtually the admission of the *mādhyamika* doctrine of indescribability of all phenomena, for it also describes the world-phenomena as being of the fifth type. There is also really no way in which such an absolutely unique and indefinable category can be related to anything else.

Forty-fifth Objection. It is argued by the Śaṅkarites that the scriptural texts cannot signify Brahman, which is devoid of all and every specific quality. To this Veṅkaṭa replies that Brahman is endowed with all specific qualities and, therefore, it is quite legitimate that texts should signify it. It is wrong also to suppose that Brahman, being self-luminous, cannot be manifested by words, for it has been shown by the Rāmānuja school that even the self-luminous can be the object of further awareness. Brahman is also sometimes described by the Śaṅkarites as the state of being qualityless, but is itself a quality since it is used adjectively to Brahman. Moreover, if Brahman could not be signified by the scriptural texts, the texts themselves would be meaningless. It is wrong also to suppose that the scriptural words refer to Brahman only in a secondary manner, just as one may point to a tree-top in order to show that the moon is visible (*śākhā-candra-darśana*); for whatever be the method, Brahman is indicated by the texts. Even a state of non-conceptual meditation (*asamprajñāta-samādhi*) is not absolutely unpredicable. In that state one cannot apply the concepts or words. If Brahman is absolutely without any character, it cannot be admitted that it should be implied or signified in a remote manner (*lakṣya*) by the scriptures. The passages which say that Brahman is beyond word (*yato vāco nivartante*) indicate only that the qualities of Brahman are infinite. Thus, it is wholly unjustifiable on the part of the Śaṅkarites to say that Brahman is not indicated by the texts.

Forty-seventh Objection. It is maintained by the Śaṅkarites that all determinate knowledge is false because it is determinate in its nature like the conch-shell–silver. If all that is determinate is false, then since all distinctions must involve determinateness they would all be false and thus ultimately we have monism. The futility of such a position is shown by Veṅkaṭa, who points out that such an inference involves determinate concepts in all its limbs, and would thus be absolutely unwarrantable according to the thesis itself. Moreover, if the determinate knowledge is false, the indeterminate would also be false for want of corroboration. It is wrong also to suppose that determinate perceptions are false for want of corroborative evidence from other awarenesses; for an illusion may be further corroborated by other illusions and may yet be false, and the last corroborative knowledge would be false for want of further corroborations, which would lead to the falsehood of the whole set of corroborations which is dependent on it. It is also wrong to suppose that determinate conceptions do not stand the test of causal efficiency, for all our practical experiences depend on determinate notions. It cannot also be held that the conceptual cognitions involving universals are false, for they are neither contradicted nor found to be doubtful in any way. Thus, if all determinate cognitions are regarded as false, then that would lead us to nihilism and not to monism. Moreover, if the indeterminate nature of Brahman is to be inferred from the indeterminate nature of our perception of external things, then on the analogy of the falsehood of the former the latter may also be false.

Fifty-fifth Objection. The Śaṅkarites hold that all effects are false, for they seem to contradict themselves if an attempt is made to conceive the logical situation. Is the effect produced out of the cause related with it or unrelated? In the first alternative the cause and the effect, being but two relata connected together by relation, there is no reason why the effect should be produced by the cause and not the cause by the effect. If the cause produces the effect without being related to it, then anything might produce anything. Again, if the effect be different from the cause, things which are different from one another would be productive of one another. If they are identical, then one could not produce the other. If it is said that cause is that which invariably precedes and effect is that which invariably succeeds, then a thing ought to be existent before the negation-precedent-to-production. Again, if the effect be regarded as having been produced from a material cause which has undergone transformation, then it may further be asked whether these transformations are produced from other transformations, and this would lead to a vicious infinite. If the effect be regarded as produced from a cause which has not undergone any transformation, then it would abide the whole time in which the material cause remains. Moreover, an effect is like the illusory silver which is non-existent in the beginning and in the end. The production of an entity cannot be either from a positive entity or a negative entity; for an effect, say, the jug, cannot be produced from its cause, the earth-matter, without producing some change in it, that is, without negating it in some way or the other. On the other hand, if the production is regarded as being from a negation, then it will itself be a negation. So in whichever way a causal relation may be viewed, it becomes fraught with contradictions.

The reply of Veṅkaṭa to this is that the objection as to whether the effect is related to the cause in its production or unrelated to it is overcome by the view that the effect is unrelated to the cause; but that need not imply that all that is unrelated to the cause should be the effect, for mere unrelatedness does not induce the production of the effect such that the very unrelatedness will connect anything with any other thing as effect. The special powers associated with causal entity are responsible for the production of the special effects, and these can be known by the ordinary methods of agreement and difference. The relations of the causal elements among themselves are transferred to the effect. It is well known that causes produce effects of an entirely different nature, just as when a jug is produced by a stick and the potter's wheel. Even the material cause is very different from the material cause as the effect. It is indeed admitted that the effect is produced from a modified (*vikṛta*) cause, for any change in the cause, even the proximity of an accessory condition, would be a modification. But if modification or *vikāra* cannot be affirmed of the cause in the sense in which the effect is regarded as a modification, it may be said in that sense that the effect is produced from an unmodified cause. It would be wrong to suggest that any and every effect might spring from any and every unmodified cause, for an effect is produced from an unmodified cause under proper temporal conditions and the association of collocative agents. It is also wrong to suggest that in the supposition that an effect is analysable as a course of changes, the cause as the immediate antecedent would be undiscoverable; and the cause being undiscoverable the effect would also be inexplicable; for it is the effect which is recognized as perceived and this implies the existence of the cause without which it could not come into being. If it is urged that the effect is not perceived, or that it is contradicted, then the obvious reply is that both non-perception and contradiction are effects, and in denying effects through them the criticism becomes self-contradictory.

When a material cause is changed into an effect, there are certain parts of it which remain unchanged, even when that effect is changed into other objects called effects, and there are some characters which are formed only in certain effects. Thus, when gold is changed into a bangle and the bangle into a necklace, the persisting qualities of gold continue the same both in the bangle and in the necklace; but the special form of the bangle does not pass into that of the necklace. Again, the objection that if the effects were already existent in the cause, then there is no necessity of the causal operation as has elsewhere been repudiated, and it has also been pointed out that the assertion that all effects are false like conch-shell–silver is false, for these effects are not found to be contradicted like these illusory appearances. It is wrong also to suggest that because an effect does not exist in the beginning or in the end it also does not exist in the middle, for its existence in the middle is directly experienced. It may also be suggested on the other hand that because an effect exists in the middle it must also exist in the beginning and in the end.

It is suggested by the Śaṅkarites that all notions of difference as effects are illusorily imposed upon one permanent entity which permeates through all so-called different entities, and that it is this permeating entity which is real. Against such a supposition the Śaṅkarites may be asked to discover any entity that permeates both through Brahman and *avidyā*. It would be wrong to suggest that Brahman is both in itself and in the *avidyā*; for Brahman cannot have any dual entity, and also cannot be illusorily imposed upon itself.

The suggestion that since the unity of a flame is perceived to be false all perception is false is obviously wrong, for in the former case the illusion is due to the rapid coalescing of similar flames, but this does not apply to all perception.

In the sense of substance (*dravya*) an effect exists in the cause, but in the sense of an effect-state the effect does not exist in the cause. The objections of the Śaṃkhyists that if the effect-state did not exist in the cause it could not be produced and that similarly anything could be produced from anything are futile, for the effects are produced by specific powers which manifest themselves as effects in definite spatial and temporal conditions.

A question is asked whether the effects are produced from a positive or a negative entity, that is, whether when the effects are produced they are produced as states of a substance which persists through them or not. Veṅkaṭa's reply is that the substance persists; only states and conditions change when the effect is produced. For in the production of an effect there is change only in the causal state and not in the causal substance. There is thus an agreement between the cause and the effect only so far as the substance is concerned and not with reference to their states; for it is by the negation of the causal state that the effect-state arises. It is sometimes suggested that since an effect is neither permanently existing nor permanently non-existing it must be false. But this suggestion is obviously wrong, for the fact that an entity may be destroyed at a later moment does not mean that it was non-existent at the moment when it was perceived. Destruction means that an entity which was existent at a particular moment was non-existent at another. Contradiction means that a thing is non-existent even when it is perceived. Mere non-existence is not destruction, for the negation-precedent-to-production might also be called destruction since it is also non-existent. Non-existence at a later point of time also does not mean destruction, for then even chimerical entities might also be called destruction. The case of conch-shell–silver is not a case of destruction, for clearly that is a case of contradiction in experience. Thus, if the concepts of production, destruction and non-existence be analysed, then it will be found that the concept of effect can never be regarded as illusory.

Fifty-seventh Objection. It is said that Brahman is of the nature of pure bliss (*ānanda*); but it may well be said that in whichever sense the word *ānanda* may be used it will not be possible to affirm that Brahman is of the nature of pure bliss. For if *ānanda* means an entity the awareness of which induces an agreeable experience, then Brahman will be knowable. If it means merely an agreeable experience, then Brahman would not be pure indeterminate consciousness. If it means a mere agreeable attitude, then duality will be implied. If it means negation of pain, then Brahman would not be positive and it is well admitted on all hands that Brahman is neutral. Moreover, according to the Śaṅkarites themselves the state of intuition of Brahman is regarded as a positive state like the state of dreamless sleep. Thus, in whichever way one may look at the problem the assertion that the indeterminate Brahman is of the nature of pure bliss becomes wholly unwarrantable.

Fifty-eighth Objection. The eternity of Brahman cannot be maintained, if it is regarded as indeterminate. If eternity means existence in all times, then *avidyā* also would be eternal; for it is also associated with all time, and time is itself regarded as its product. If it is urged that association with all time does not mean existence in all time, then it is wrong to regard existence in all times as a definition of eternity, for it will be enough to say that existence itself is eternal. The "inclusion of all time" as distinguished from mere existence shows the difference between existence and eternity. Eternity would thus mean existence in all time, which can be affirmed of *avidyā* also. Eternity cannot also be defined as that which does not cease in time since such a definition would apply to time also which does not cease in time. It cannot also be said that eternity means that which is not contradicted in the beginning or in the end, for then the world-appearance also would be eternal. Again, it is difficult to understand how consciousness is regarded as eternal by the Śaṅkarites, for if it is affirmed of ordinary consciousness, then that is directly against perceptual experience; and if it is affirmed of transcendental consciousness, then that is directly against experience. Further, eternity cannot be regarded as the essence, for then it would be identical with self-luminosity, and its predication, such as Brahman is eternal, would be unnecessary. If it is regarded as a knowable quality, then if such a quality existed in consciousness, consciousness would become knowable. If it did not exist in consciousness, then its knowledge would not imply the eternity of consciousness. It cannot also be said that whatever is not produced is eternal, for then negation-precedent-to-production would be eternal. If it is said that any positive entity which is not produced is eternal, then *avidyā* would also be eternal. Thus, in whichever way one may try to prove the eternity of the indeterminable pure consciousness one fails.

Sixty-first Objection. It is often asserted by the Śaṅkarites that there is a unity of the self. If by self here they mean the "ego," then clearly all the egos cannot be regarded as identical, for it is well known that the experiences of other people are never identified by us as ours. Nor can it be said that there is unity of consciousness of us all, for then each of us would know the minds of others. It is not maintainable that our underlying being is the same, for that would not mean the identity of our selves. One may think of universal existence, but that would not mean the identity of the existents. Again, the identity of the selves cannot be regarded as real since the selves (*jīvas*) themselves are regarded as unreal. If the identity of the selves be regarded as false, then there is no reason why such a doctrine should be propounded. In any case, when one has to deal with our experiential life, one has to admit the diversity of selves and there is no other proof by which their identity may be established. Thus it would be wrong to think, as the Śaṅkarites do, that there is one self.

Meghanādāri.

Meghanādāri, son of Ātreyanātha sūri, seems to be one of the earliest members of the Rāmānuja school. He wrote at least two books, *Naya-prakāśikā* and *Naya-dyu-maṇi*, both of which are still in manuscript and only the latter has been available to the present writer. Most of the important contributions of Meghanādāri on the subject of the Rāmānuja theory of the *pramāṇas* have already been discussed in some detail in connection with the treatment of that subject under Veṅkaṭanātha. Only a few of his views on other topics of Rāmānuja philosophy will therefore be given here.

Svataḥ-prāmāṇya-vāda. Veṅkaṭa, in his *Tattva-muktā-kalāpa* and *Sarvārtha-siddhi*, says that all knowledge manifests the objects as they are. Even errors are true at least so far as they point to the object of the error. The erroneousness or error is due to the existence of certain vitiating conditions[1]. When there is knowledge that there is a jug, the existence of the object is the validity (*prāmāṇya*) of it and this is made known by the very knowledge that the jug exists[2]. Even where there is the knowledge of silver in a conch-shell, there is the knowledge of the existence of the objective silver implied in that very knowledge, and thus even in erroneous knowledge there is the self-validity so far as it carries with it the existence of the object of perception[3].

Meghanādāri however, who in all probability preceded Veṅkaṭa, gives a somewhat different account of the doctrine of *svataḥ-*

[1] *jñānāñāṃ yathā-vasthitā-rtha-prakāśakatvaṃ sāmānyam eva bhrāntasyā'pi jñānasya dharmiṇy abhrāntatvāt ato vahnyā-der dāhakatvavaj jñānānāṃ prāmāṇyam svābhāvikam eva upādher maṇi-mantravad doṣo-pādhi-vaśād apramāṇatvaṃ bhramāṃśe. Sarvārtha-siddhi*, p. 554.

[2] *ghaṭo'stī' ti jñānam utpadyate tatra viṣayā-stitvam eva prāmāṇyaṃ tat tu tenaiva jñānena pratīyate ataḥ svataḥ-prāmāṇyam. Ibid.*

[3] See *Ibid.*

prāmāṇya. He says that validity (*prāmāṇya*) proceeds from the apprehension of cognition (*prāmāṇyaṃ jñāna-sattā-pratīti-kāraṇād eva*), for the validity must have a cause and no other cause is traceable[1].

The Naiyāyikas, arguing against the *svataḥ-prāmāṇya* doctrine of the Mīmāṃsakas, are supposed to say that the self-validity cannot be regarded as being produced in every case of knowledge, for the Mīmāṃsakas hold that the Vedas are eternal and thus their self-validity cannot be regarded as being produced. Self-validity cannot be regarded as produced in some cases only, for if that were the case the thesis that all cognitions are self-valid cannot stand. Therefore the proper view is that only that knowledge is self-valid which is uncontradicted in experience (*abādhita-vyavahāra-hetutvam eva jñānasya prāmāṇyam*)[2]. Self-validity cannot be regarded as a special potency, for such a potency is non-sensible and has therefore to be known by inference or some other means; neither can it be regarded as being one (*svarūpa*) with the sense-organs by which knowledge is acquired, for the existence of such sense-organs is itself inferred from mere knowledge and not from what is only true knowledge.

Arguing against the Śaṅkarites, the Naiyāyikas are supposed to say that in their view knowledge being self-luminous, there would be no way of determining validity either from uncontradicted experience or by any other means; and since, according to them, everything is false, the distinction of validity and invalidity also ought to have no place in their system, for if such distinctions are admitted it would land them in dualism. To this Meghanādāri says that if self-validity is not admitted, then the whole idea of validity has to be given up; for if validity is said to be produced from a knowledge of the proper conditions of knowledge or the absence of defects, such a knowledge has to be regarded as self-valid, for it would have to depend on some other knowledge and that again on some other knowledge, which would mean a vicious infinite. So knowledge is to be regarded as self-valid by nature and its invalidity occurs only when the defects and vitiating contributions of the causes of knowledge are known by some other means. But the method of establishing self-validity according to the followers of Kumārila is liable to criticism, for according to that system the existence of knowledge is only inferred from the fact of the revelation of the objects, and that implication cannot also further

[1] *Naya-dyu-maṇi*, p. 21 (MS.). [2] *Ibid.* p. 22.

lead to the self-validity of knowledge. The theory of self-validity that it is caused by the same constituents which produce the knowledge is also inadmissible, for the senses have also to be regarded as the cause of knowledge and these may be defective. Again, it is held that knowledge which corresponds with the object (*tathā-bhūta*) is valid and that which does not correspond with the object is invalid and that such validity and invalidity are therefore directly manifested by the knowledge itself. Meghanādāri replies that if such correspondence be a quality of the object, then that does not establish the validity of knowledge; if it is a quality of knowledge, then memory has also to be regarded as self-valid, for there is correspondence in it also. Again, the question arises whether the self-validity is merely produced or also known. In the former case the self-manifestation of self-validity has to be given up, and in the latter case the Kumārila view is indefensible for by it knowledge being itself an implication from the revelation of objects its self-validity cannot obviously be self-manifested.

Meghanādāri, therefore, contends that an intuition (*anubhūti*) carries with it its own validity; in revealing the knowledge it also carries with it the conviction of its own validity. The invalidity, on the other hand, is suggested by other sources. This intuition is in itself different from memory[1]. The whole emphasis of this contention is on his view that each cognition of an object carries with it its cognizability as true, and since this is manifested along with the cognition, all cognitions are self-valid in this sense. Such a self-validity is therefore not produced since it is practically identical with the knowledge itself. Meghanādāri points out that this view is in apparent contradiction with Rāmānuja's own definition of *svataḥ-prāmāṇya* as that which is produced by the cause of knowledge; but Rāmānuja's statement in this connection has to be interpreted differently, for the knowledge of God and the emancipated beings being eternal and unproduced any view which defines self-validity as a production from the same source from which knowledge is produced would be inapplicable to them[2].

Time. Time according to Meghanādāri is not to be regarded as a separate entity. He takes great pains to show that Rāmānuja has

[1] *anubhūtitvaṃ vā prāmāṇyam astu; tac ca jñānā-vāntara-jātiḥ; sā ca smṛti-jñāna-jātitaḥ pṛthaktayā lokataḥ eva siddhā; anubhūteḥ svasattayā eva sphūrteḥ. Naya-dyu-maṇi*, p. 31.

[2] *Ibid.* p. 38.

himself discarded the view that time is a separate entity in his commentary on the *Brahma-sūtra*, the *Vedānta-dīpa* and the *Vedānta-sāra*. The notion of time originates from the relative position of the sun in the zodiac with reference to earth. It is the varying earth-space that appears as time, being conditioned by the relative positions of the Sun[1]. This view is entirely different from that of Veṅkaṭa which will be described later on.

Karma and its fruits. According to Meghanādāri deeds produce their fruits through the satisfaction and dissatisfaction of God. Though ordinarily deeds are regarded as virtuous or vicious, yet strictly speaking virtue and vice should be regarded as the fruits of actions and these fruits are nothing but the satisfaction and dissatisfaction of God. The performance of good deeds in the past determines the performance of similar deeds in the future by producing helpful tendencies, capacities and circumstances in his favour, and the performance of bad deeds forces a man to take a vicious line of action in the future. At the time of dissolution also there is no separate *dharma* and *adharma*, but God's satisfaction and dissatisfaction produced by the individual's deeds determine the nature and extent of his sufferings and enjoyment as well as his tendencies towards virtue or vice at the time of the next creation. The fruits of actions are experienced in the Heaven and Hell and also in the mundane life, but not while the individual is passing from Heaven or Hell to earth, for at that time there is no experience of pleasure or pain, it being merely a state of transition. Again, except in the case of those sacrifices which are performed for injuring or molesting other fellow beings, there is no sin in the killing of animals in sacrifices which are performed for the attainment of Heaven or such other pleasurable purposes[2].

Vātsya Varada.

Regarding the doctrine of Vedic injunction that one should study the Vedas, Vātsya Varada in his *Prameya-mālā* holds the view, in contradistinction to the *Śabara Bhāṣya*, that Vedic injunction is satisfied only in the actual reading of the Vedic texts and that the Vedic injunction does not imply an inquiry into the mean-

[1] *sūryā-di-sambandha-viśeṣo-pādhitaḥ pṛthivyā-dideśānām eva kāla-saṃjñā. Naya-dyu-maṇi*, p. 168.

[2] *Ibid.* pp. 243–246.

ing of those texts. Such an inquiry proceeds from the normal inquisitive spirit and the desire to know the various applications in the practical performances of sacrifices. These do not form a part of the Vedic injunction (*vidhi*).

Vātsya Varada holds that the study of the Vedic injunction and the inquiry relating to Brahman form the parts of one unified scripture, i.e. the latter follows or is a continuation of the former; and he mentions Bodhāyana in his support.

Śaṅkara had thought that the study of the Mīmāṃsā was intended for a class of people but not necessarily for those who would inquire into the nature of Brahman. The Pūrva-mīmāṃsā and the Uttara-mīmāṃsā were intended for different purposes and were written by different authors. These should not therefore be regarded as integrally related as two parts of a unified work. To this Vātsya Varada, following Bodhāyana, takes exception, for he thinks that though the Pūrva-mīmāṃsā and Uttara-mīmāṃsā are written by different authors yet the two together uphold one common view and the two may be regarded as two chapters of one whole book.

Vātsya Varada also, in referring to Śaṅkara's view that the Pūrva-mīmāṃsā assumes the existence of a real world, whereas the purport of the *Brahma-sūtra* is to deny it and therefore the two cannot be regarded as having the same end in view, challenges it by affirming the reality of the world. Śaṅkara's argument, that all which is cognizable is false, would imply that even the self is false; for many Upaniṣads speak of the perceptibility of the self. His declaration of the falsity of the world would also imply that the falsehood itself is false, for it is a part of the world. Such an argument ought to be acceptable to Śaṅkara, for he himself utilized it in refuting the nihilists.

Regarding the denial of the category of difference by the Śaṅkarites Vātsya Varada says that the opponent cannot by any means deny that difference is perceived, for all his arguments are based on the assumption of the existence of difference. If there were no difference, there would be no party and no view to be refuted. If it is admitted that the category of difference is perceived, then the opponent has also to admit that such a perception must have its own peculiar and proper cause. The real point in the conception of difference is that it constitutes its other as a part of itself. An object in its own nature has twofold characteristics, the characteristic of its universal similarity with other things of its class and the characteristic in which it differs from others. In its second characteristic it holds its others in itself. When it is said that a thing is different it does not mean that the difference is identical with the thing or but another name for the thing, but what is meant is that a thing known as different has an outside reference to other entities. This outside reference to other entities, when conceived along with the object, produces the perception of difference.

The conception of difference involves the conception of negation as involved in the notion of otherness. If this negation is different in nature from the object which is conceived as "different" or as the "other" of other objects, then since this negation cannot be directly known by perception "difference" also cannot be known directly by perception. The *Viśiṣṭā-dvaita* theory admits that "difference" can be directly perceived. In order to prove this point Vātsya Varada gives a special interpretation of "negation" (*abhāva*). He holds that the notion of negation of an entity in another entity is due to the latter's being endowed with a special character as involving a reference to the former. The notion of negation thus proceeds from a special modified character of an object in which the negation is affirmed. There are many Śaṅkarites who regard negation as positive, but in their case it is held to be a special category by itself which is perceived in the locus of the negation by the special *pramāṇa* of non-perception. Though positive its notion is not produced according to them by the special modified nature of the object perceived in which the negation is affirmed. But Vātsya Varada holds that the notion of negation is due to the perception of a special modified nature of the entity in which the negation is affirmed[1]. The negation revealed to us in one object as the otherness of another object means that the latter is included in a special character of the former which makes the reference as the otherness possible.

Vātsya Varada also emphasizes the view that the tests referring to Brahman as *satya*, *jñāna*, *ananta*, etc., indicate the fact of the possession of these qualities by God and that the monistic interpretation that these together refer to one identical being, the Brahman, is false. He also describes the infinite and unlimited nature of

[1] *pratiyogi-buddhau vastu-viśeṣa-dhīr evo'petā nāstī' ti vyavahāra-hetuḥ.* Varada, *Prameya-mālā*, p. 35 (MS.).

Brahman and explains the exact sense in which the world and the individuals may be regarded as the body of God and that the individuals exist for God who is their final end. He also deals in this work with certain topics regarding the external rituals, such as shaving of the head, wearing the holy thread, etc., by ascetics.

Varada, in his *Tattva-sāra*, collects some of the specially interesting points of the *Bhāṣya* of Rāmānuja and interprets them in prose and verse. Some of these points are as follows: (i) The view that the existence of God cannot be logically proved, but can be accepted only from scriptural testimony. (ii) The special interpretation of some of the important Upaniṣadic texts such as the *Kapyāsa* text. (iii) The results of the discussions of the important *adhikaraṇas* of Vedānta according to Rāmānuja. (iv) The doctrine that negation is only a kind of position. (v) The interpretation of the apparent dualistic and monistic texts. (vi) The discussion regarding the reality of the world, etc.

This *Tattva-sāra* provoked a further commentary on it called *Ratna-sāriṇī* by Vīra-rāghava-dāsa, a son of Bādhūla Narasiṃha Guru, disciple of Bādhūla Varada Guru, son of Bādhūla Veṅkaṭācārya. Some of Vātsya Varada's other works are: *Sārā-rtha-catuṣṭaya*, *Ārādhanā-saṃgraha*, *Tattva-nirṇaya*, *Prapanna-pārijāta*, *Yati-liṅga-samarthana* and *Puruṣa-ninṇaya*[1].

Rāmānujācārya II alias Vādi-Haṃsa-Navāmvuda.

Rāmānujācārya II, the son of Padmanābhārya, belonged to the Atri lineage. He was the maternal uncle of Veṅkaṭanātha, the famous writer of the Rāmānuja school. He wrote the *Nyāya-kuliśa* which has often been referred to in Veṅkaṭa's *Sarvārtha-siddhi*. He also wrote another work called *Mokṣa-siddhi*. Some of his interpretations of Rāmānuja's ideas have already been referred to in dealing with the Rāmānuja theory of knowledge as explained by Veṅkaṭa. Other contributions by him are mentioned in brief below.

Negation. Negation as a separate category is denied by Rāmānujācārya II. He thinks that negation of an entity means only another entity different from it. The negation of a jug thus means the

[1] In his *Tattva-nirṇaya* he tries to prove that all the important *Śruti* texts prove that Nārāyaṇa is the highest God. He refers in this work to his *Puruṣa-nirṇaya* where, he says, he has discussed the subject in more detail.

existence of some other entity different from it. The real notion of negation is thus only "difference." A negation is described as that which is antagonistic to a positive entity and there is thus no way in which a negation can be conceived by itself without reference to a positive entity. But a positive entity never stands in need of its specification through a reference to negation[1]. It is also well known that the negation of a negation is nothing else than the existence of positive entity. The existence of negation cannot be known either by perception, inference, or by implication. Veṅkaṭa, in further explaining this idea, says that the idea of absence in negation is derived from the association of the object of negation with a different kind of temporal or spatial character[2]. Thus, when it is said that there is no jug here, it merely means that the jug exists in another place. It is argued that negation cannot be regarded as the existence of positive entity, and it may be asked if negation cannot be regarded as negation, how can negation of negation be regarded as the existence of positive entity. Just as those who admit negation regard negation and existence of positive entity as mutually denying each other, so the Rāmānujas also regard the existence of positive entities and negations as denying each other in their different spatial and temporal characters. Thus it is not necessary to admit negation as a separate category. When an existing entity is said to be destroyed, what happens is that there is a change of state. Negation-precedent-to-production (*prāga-bhāva*) and the negation of destruction do not mean anything more than two positive states succeeding each other, and there may be an infinite series of such states. If this view is not admitted, and if the negation of destruction (*pradhvaṃsā-bhāva*) and the negation-precedent-to-production (*prāg-abhāva*) be regarded as separate categories of negation, then the destruction of negation-precedent-to-production and negation-precedent-to-production of destruction will depend upon an infinite series of negations which would lead to a vicious infinite. It is the succession of a new state that is regarded as the destruction of the old state, the former being a different state from the latter. It is sometimes held that negation is mere vacuity and has no reference to the existence of positive entity. If that were so, then on the one hand

[1] *athā'bhāvasya tad-rūpaṃ yad-bhāva-pratipakṣatā nai'vam adyā'py asau yasmād bhāvo-ttīrṇena sādhitaḥ. Nyāya-kuliśa.* MS.

[2] *tat-tat-pratiyogi-bhāva-sphuraṇa-sahakṛto deśa-kālā-di-bheda eva svabhāvāt nañ-prayogam api sahate. Sarvārtha-siddhi,* p. 714.

negation would be causeless and on the other it could not be the cause of anything; and so negations would thus be both beginningless and eternal. In that case the whole world would be within the grasp of negation and everything in the world would be non-existing. Thus it is unnecessary to admit negation as a separate category. The difference of one positive entity from another is regarded as negation.

Another problem that arises in this connection is that if negation is not admitted as a separate category how can negative causes be admitted. It is well known that when certain collocations of causes can produce an effect they can do so only when there are no negative causes to counteract their productive capacity. This capacity (*śakti*) is admitted in the Rāmānuja school as the collocation of accessories which helps a cause to produce the effect (*kāraṇasya kāryo-payogī sahakāri-kalāpaḥ śaktir ity ucyate*)[1]. To this Rāmānujacārya's reply is that the absence of counteracting agents is not regarded as a separate cause, but the presence of the counteracting agents along with the other accessory collocations is regarded as making those accessory collocations unfit for producing the effect. Thus there are two sets of collocations where the effect is or is not produced, and it is the difference of two collocations that accounts for the production of the effect in one case and its non-production in another; but this does not imply that absence or negation of the obstructive factors should be regarded as contributing to the causation. In one case there was the capacity for production and in another case there was no such capacity[2]. Capacity (*śakti*) is not regarded by Rāmānujācārya as a separate non-sensible (*atīndriya*) entity, but as an abstract specification of that which produces any effect (*śakti-gata-jāty-anabhyupagame tad-abhāvāt śaktasya'iva jātiḥ kārya-niyāmikā na tu śakti-jātir iti*)[3].

Jāti (*universal*). Rāmānujācārya does not admit any *jāti* or universal in the sense of any abstract generality of individuals. Accord-

[1] *Sarvārtha-siddhi*, p. 685.

[2] *siddha-vastu-virodhī ghātakaḥ sādhya-vastu-virodhī pratibandhakaḥ, katham yadi kārye tad-viruddhatvam iti cen na; ittham kāryam kāraṇa-pauṣkalye bhavati, tad-apauṣkalye na bhavati, apauṣkalyaṃ ca kvacit kāraṇānām anyatama-vaikalyāt kvacit śakti-vaikalyāt iti bhidyate, yadyapi śaktir na kāraṇaṃ tathā'pi śaktasyai'va kāraṇatvāt viśeṣaṇā-bhāve'pi viśiṣṭā-bhāva-nyāyena kāraṇā-bhāvaḥ. tad-ubhaya-kāraṇena prāg-abhāva-sthitī-karaṇāt kārya-virodhī'ti pratibandhako bhavati; tatra yathā kāraṇa-vaikalya-dṛṣṭa-rūpeṇa kurvato'bhāvaḥ kāraṇaṃ na syāt; tathā śakti-vighnitaḥ yo hi nāma pratibandhakaḥ kāraṇaṃ kiñcid vināśya kāryaṃ pratibadhnāti na tasyā'bhāvaḥ kāraṇam iti siddham. Nyāya-kuliśa.* MS.

[3] *Ibid.*

ing to him any unified assemblage of parts similar to such other assemblages of parts (*susadṛśa-saṃsthāna*) is called a universal[1].

Veṅkaṭa, a follower of Rāmānujācārya, defines *jāti* as mere similarity (*sausādṛśya*). Criticizing the Naiyāyika theory of *jāti* he says that if that which manifests universals is itself manifested through universals, then these universals should have to be manifested by others which have to be manifested by further universals and this would lead to a vicious infinite. If to avoid such a vicious infinite it is held that the second grade parts that manifest a *jāti* (universal) do not require a further *jāti* for their manifestation, then it is better to say that it is the similar individuals that represent the notion of *jāti* and that it is not necessary to admit any separate category as *jāti*. It is clear that the notion of universals proceeds from qualities or characters in which certain individuals agree, and if that is so it should be enough to explain the notion of universals. It is these characters, the similarity of which with the similar characters of other individuals is remembered, that produce the notion of universals[2]. When some parts or qualities are perceived in some things they of themselves naturally remind us of other similar parts in other things and it is this fact, that the two mutually stand, one beside the other, in the mind, which is called similarity[3]. It is inexplicable why certain qualities or characters remind us of others and it can only be said that they do so naturally; and it is this fact that they stand beside each other in the mind which constitutes their similarity as well as their universal. There is no other separate category which may either be called similarity (*sādṛśya*) or universal. There is not, however, much difference between Rāmānujācārya's definition of universals and Veṅkaṭa's definition of it, for though the former defines it as any assemblages that are similar and the latter as similarity, yet the very conception of similarity of Veṅkaṭa involves within it the assemblage of parts as its constituent; for the notion of similarity according to Veṅkaṭa is not

[1] *Nyāya-kuliśa.* MS.

[2] *kecid dhī-saṃsthāna-bhedāḥ kvacana khalu mithas sādṛśyarūpā bhānti yair bhavadīyaṃ sāmānyam abhivyajyate ta eva sausādṛśya-vyavahāra-viṣaya-bhūtāḥ sāmānya-vyavahāraṃ nirvahantu; tasmāt teṣāṃ sarveṣām anyonya-sāpekṣai-ka-smṛti-viṣayatayā tat-tad-ekāvamarśas tat-tajjātīyatvā-vamarśaḥ. Sarvārtha-siddhi,* p. 704.

[3] *yady apy ekaikasthaṃ sāsnā-di-dharma-svarūpaṃ tathā'pi tan-nirupadhi-niyataiḥ svabhāvato niyataiḥ tais tais sāsnā-dibhir anya-niṣṭhais sa-pratidvand-vikaṃ syāt; idam eva anvonya-sa-pratidvandvika-rūpaṃ sādṛśya-śabda-vācyam abhidhīyate. Ibid.*

anything abstract, but it means the concrete assemblages of parts that stand beside one another in memory. Veṅkaṭa, however, points out that the notion of "universal" does not necessarily mean that it can be with regard to assemblages of parts only, for in case of those partless entities, such as qualities, there cannot be any assemblage of parts, yet the notion of universals is still quite applicable. It is for this reason that Veṅkaṭa makes "similarity" only as the condition of "universals" and does not include assemblages of parts (*saṃsthāna*) as is done by Rāmānujācārya.

Svataḥ-prāmāṇya (*self-validity*). It is sometimes argued that as in all things so in the determination of validity and invalidity the application of the methods of agreement and difference is to be regarded as the decisive test. The presence of qualities that contribute to validity and the absence of defects that make any perception invalid is to be regarded as deciding the validity or invalidity of any perception. To this Rāmānujācārya says that the ascertainment of qualities that contribute to validity cannot be determined without an assurance that there are no defects, and the absence of defects cannot also be known without the knowledge of the presence of qualities that contribute towards validity; and so, since they mutually depend upon each other, their independent determination is impossible. Thus the suggestion is that there is neither the determination of validity nor invalidity, but there is doubt. To this the reply is that unless something is known there cannot be any doubt. So there is a middle stage before the determination of validity or invalidity. Before it is known that the knowledge corresponds with the object or does not do so, there must be the manifestation of the object (*artha-prakāśa*) which, so far as it itself is concerned, is self-valid and does not depend for its validity upon the application of any other method; for it is the basis of all future determinations of its nature as true or false. So this part of knowledge—the basic part—the manifestation of objects—is self-valid. It is wrong to say that this knowledge is in itself characterless (*niḥsvabhāva*), for it is of the nature of the manifestation of an objective entity like the determination of tree-ness before its specific nature as a mango or a pine tree[1]. The knowledge of the contri-

[1] *yathā-rtha-paricchedaḥ prāmāṇyam ayathā-rtha-paricchedaḥ aprāmāṇyaṃ kathaṃ tad-ubhaya-parityāge artha-pariccheda-siddhiḥ iti cen na, aparityājyatvābhyupagamāt. tayoḥ sādhāraṇam eva hy artha-paricchedaṃ brūmaḥ śiṃśapā-palāśā-diṣu iva vṛkṣatvam. Nyāya-kuliśa.* MS.

butory qualities is not the cause of validity, but when validity is determined they may be regarded as having contributed to the validity. The self-validity is of the knowledge (*jñāna*) and not of its correspondence (*tathātva*). If the correspondence were also directly revealed, then there can never be any doubt regarding such correspondence. When the followers of Kumārila say that knowledge is self-valid, they cannot mean that knowledge itself imparts the fact that there has been a true correspondence, for they do not admit that knowledge is self-revealing. They have therefore admitted that there are some other means by which the notion of such validity is imparted. The validity of those will again have to depend upon the validity of other imparting agents, and there will thus be a vicious infinite. For the determination of validity one is bound to depend on the ascertainment by corroboration and causal efficiency. If validity thus depends upon the ascertainment of contributory qualities, then there is no self-validity. The Vedas also cannot be self-valid in this view. If there are no defects in them because they have not proceeded from any erring mortals, then they have no contributory qualities also because they have not proceeded (according to the Mīmāṃsā view) from any trustworthy person. So there may legitimately be a doubt regarding their validity. The truth of any correspondence depends upon something other than the knowledge itself, e.g. the falsehood of any mis-correspondence. If it depended merely on the cause of the knowledge, then even a false knowledge would be right. For establishing the validity of the Vedas, therefore, it has to be admitted that they have been uttered by an absolutely trustworthy person. Knowledge does not manifest merely objectivity but a particular thing or entity and it is valid so far as that particular thing has been manifested in knowledge[1]. The validity of knowledge thus refers to the thing in its general character as the manifestation of a particular thing and not regarding its specific details in character[2]. Such a validity, however, refers only to the form of the knowledge itself and not to objective corroboration[3]. Whatever may be doubtful in it is to be ascertained by contributory qualities, corroboration and the like, and when the

[1] *yad dhi jñāne vidyate tad eva tasya lakṣaṇam ucitaṃ vastu-prakāśatvam eva jñāne vidyate na tu viṣaya-prakāśatvaṃ yato vijñāne samutpanne viṣayo' yam iti nā' bhāti kintu ghaṭo' yam iti. Nyāya-kuliśa.* MS.

[2] *jñānānāṃ sāmānya-rūpaṃ eva prāmāṇyaṃ na vaiśeṣikaṃ rūpam. Ibid.*

[3] *tasmād bodhā'tmakatvena prāptā buddheḥ pramāṇatā. Ibid.*

chances of error are eliminated by other sources the original validity stands uncontradicted.

Saprakāśatva (*self-luminosity*). Rāmānujācārya first states the Naiyāyika objection against self-luminosity. The Naiyāyikas are supposed to argue that things are existent but they become knowable only under certain conditions and this shows that existence (*sattā*) is different from cognition or its self-illumination (*prakāśa*). Arguing from the same position it may be said that knowledge as an existent entity is different from its illumination as such[1]. If knowledge itself were self-revealing, then it would not depend upon any conditioning of it by its contiguity or relationing with objects and as such any individual cognition would mean universal cognition. If, on the other hand, knowledge requires a further conditioning through its relationing with objects, then knowledge would not be self-revealing. Further, knowledge being partless, there cannot be any such conception that one part of it reveals the other. In the case of partless entities it is not possible to conceive that knowledge should be self-revealing, for it cannot be both an agent and an object at the same time. Again, if knowledge were self-revealing, then the difference between consciousness and its re-perception through introspection cannot be accounted for. Further, it must be remembered that the difference between one cognition and another depends upon the difference of its objective content. Apart from this there is no difference between one cognition and another. If the objective content was not a constituent of knowledge, then there would be no difference between the illumination of knowledge as such and the illumination of an object. If knowledge were by itself self-illuminating, then there would be no place for objects outside it and this would bring us to absolute idealism. So the solution may be either on the Mīmāṃsā lines that knowledge produces such a character in the objective entity that by that cognized character of objects cognition may be inferred, or it may be on *Nyāyā* lines that knowledge manifests the objects. Thus it has to be admitted that there must be some kind of cognitive relation between the object and its knowledge, and it would be the specific nature of these relations that would determine the cognitive character in each case. Now it may again be asked whether this cognitive relation is only object-pointing or

[1] *sarvasya hi svataḥ sva-gocara-jñānā-dhīnaḥ prakāśaḥ saṃvidām api tathai'va abhyupagantum ucitaḥ. Nyāya-kuliśa.* MS.

whether it is object-knowledge-pointing. In the former case the object alone would be manifested and in the latter case knowledge would be its own object, which is again absurd. If knowledge manifested the object without any specific relation, then any knowledge might manifest any object or all objects. Knowledge implies a cognitive operation and if such an operation is not admitted knowledge cannot be manifested, for the very objectivity of knowledge implies such an operation. Hence the conclusion is that as knowledge manifests other objects so it is also manifested by a further cognition of re-perception. When one says "I perceive it," it is not a case of mere knowledge-manifestation but a re-perception of having perceived that particular object. So knowledge is manifested by a further re-perception and not by itself. To this Rāmānujācārya raises an objection: it may be asked whether this re-perception of knowledge takes place in spite of the absence of any desire to re-perceive on the part of the knower or as the result of any such desire. In the former case, since the re-perception takes place automatically, there will be an infinite series of such automatic re-perceptions. In the latter case, i.e. when the re-perception takes place in consequence of a desire to do so, then such a desire must be produced out of previous knowledge and that would again presuppose another desire, and that another knowledge, and there would thus be a vicious infinite. To this the *Naiyāyika* reply is that the general re-perception takes place without any desire, but the specific re-perception occurs as a result of a desire to that effect. This ordinary re-perception of a general nature follows as a natural course, for all mundane people have always some knowledge or other throughout the course of their experience. It is only when there is a desire to know some specific details that there is a specific mental intuition (*mānasa-pratyakṣa*) to that effect.

To this Rāmānujācārya's reply is that in the case of an ordinary existent thing there is a difference between its existence as such and its manifestation of knowledge, for it always depends upon specific relations between itself and knowledge; but in the case of a self-luminous entity where no such relations are needed there is no difference between its existence and its manifestation. The fire illuminates other objects but it does not need any other assistance to manifest itself. It is this that is meant by self-luminosity. Just as no entity depends upon any other entity of its own class for its manifestation, so knowledge also does not need assistance from knowledge for its manifestation. The relations that are needed for the manifestation of other objects are not needed for the manifestation of knowledge itself[1]. Knowledge thus being self-luminous helps our behaviour directly but does not depend upon anything else for lending such assistance. It is against all experience that knowledge for its manifestation requires some other knowledge, and if it has no support in our experience there is no justification for making such an extraordinary theory that any knowledge for its manifestation should require the operation of another knowledge. That only can be called an object of knowledge which though existent remains unmanifested. But it cannot be said that there was knowledge which was not known, for a cognition would not last like other objective entities awaiting the time when it might be manifested. In the case of a past knowledge which is merely inferred now, there is no notion of that knowledge, so one can always draw a distinction between the known and the unknown. If only the object were illuminated and not the knowledge of it, no one would fail for a moment to perceive that. If knowledge were merely inferred from its effect, everyone would have so experienced it, but no one has a moment's hesitation in discriminating between what is known and unknown. It is again wrong to say that knowledge arises only after inquiry, for in the present knowledge whatever is sought to be known is known directly, and in the past knowledge also there is no such inference that there was knowledge because it is remembered, but the past knowledge directly appears as memory; for if that is called an inference, then even re-perception may be regarded as an inference from memory.

Again, a thing that exists without being an object of knowledge at the same time is liable to erroneous manifestation on account of the presence of defects in the collocation conditioning the knowledge, but knowledge itself is never liable to error, and consequently it has no existence apart from being known. Just as there cannot be any doubt whether a pleasure or a pain is experienced, so there cannot be any doubt about knowledge, and this shows that whenever there is knowledge it is self-manifested. When one knows an object one is also sure about one's knowledge of it. Again, it is

[1] *jñānam ananyā-dhīna-prakāśam artha-prakāśakatvāt dīpavat. Nyāya-kuliśa.* MS.

wrong to suppose that if knowledge is self-manifested then there would be no difference between itself and its objective content, for the difference is obvious; knowledge in itself is formless, while the object supplies the content. Two entities which appear in the same manifestation, such as quality and substance, things and their number, are not on that account identical. It cannot also be said that knowledge and its object are identical because they are simultaneously manifested, for the very fact that they are simultaneously manifested shows that they are two different things. Knowledge and the object shine forth in the same manifestation and it is impossible to determine which of them shines before or after.

The self also is to be regarded as being of the nature of knowledge from the testimony of the scriptures. Self being of the nature of knowledge is also self-luminous, and it is not therefore to be supposed that it is cognized by mental intuition (*mānasa-pratyakṣa*).

Rāmānujadāsa alias Mahācārya.

Rāmānujadāsa, called also Mahācārya, was the pupil of Bādhūla Śrīnivāsācārya. He is not, however, to be confused with Rāmānujācārya II, the son of Padmanābhārya and the maternal uncle of Vedānta-deśika—who was also known as Vādi-haṃsa-navāmbuda. He wrote at least three books: *Sad-vidyā-vijaya*, *Advaita-vijaya*, and *Parikara-vijaya*.

In his *Sad-vidyā-vijaya*, in refuting the Śaṅkarite doctrine that the existence of positive nescience (*bhāva-rūpā-jñāna*) can be known by the different *pramāṇas* of perception, inference and implication, he says that intuitive experience of ignorance, such as "I am ignorant," cannot be regarded as an experience of nescience as such in its entirety (*kṛtsnā-jñāna-pratītis tāvad asiddhā*), for it can never refer to all objects as negativing all knowledge. A perceptual mental state of the *antaḥkaraṇa* is not admitted by the Śaṅkarites to refer to entities past and gone. Even when a man intuits that he is ignorant, there is at that stage an illumination of his own ego and the fact of his being ignorant, and it cannot be said that in such an experience the nescience in its entirety has been illuminated, for the ego is also illuminated at the time. If nescience in its entirety is not illuminated, then the nescience is only illuminated with reference to particular objects, and if that is so the assumption of a positive nescience is useless. Again, if nescience or want of knowledge refers to a particular object, then there is a knowledge of that object implied in it; and therefore nescience as such is not experienced and a supposition of a positive nescience is no better than the ordinarily accepted view that in such cases there is only a negation of the knowledge of an object except in deep dreamless sleep. In all other stages all experiences of ignorance refer to the negation of knowledge of particular objects. All cases of ignorance mean that their objects are known only in a general manner, but not in their specific details. Again, it cannot be said that nescience is regarded as positive merely to denote that it is of the nature of a stuff that is opposed to knowledge in general (*jñāna-sāmānya-virodhī*); for in such experiences as "I am ignorant" there is the knowledge of the subject to which the ignorance belongs and also some general content regarding which there is the ignorance. Further, since the nescience has the pure consciousness as its support and since the mind (*antaḥkaraṇa*) is not regarded as its support, how can the experience "I am ignorant" be said to refer to the experience of this stuff? If it be held that since the mind is an illusory construction on the pure consciousness which is the support of the nescience (*ajñāna*), the latter may appear as a mental function, for both the ego and the nescience, being illusory impositions on the pure consciousness, may shine forth from the same identical basis of consciousness. The reply is that such an explanation is obviously wrong, for if both the ego-consciousness and the *ajñāna* shone forth from the same basic consciousness, the latter could not appear as the predicate of the former. If the one pure consciousness manifests both the ego and the *ajñāna*, they would not appear as different and arranged in a definite subject-predicate order. Again, if it is held that the *ajñāna* shines only as a predicative to the ego because they are based on pure consciousness, then how can such an *ajñāna* refer to the objective things (which are independent impositions on pure consciousness) in such experiences as "I do not know a jug?" If it is said that since there is the one identical consciousness on which the objective entities, the *ajñāna* and the ego-entity, are all imposed, and the *ajñāna* is always in relation with the objective entities, then it may be said that even when a jug is known, the *ajñāna*, being in relation with other entities (such as cloth) and through them with the pure consciousness underlying them, is also in relation with the pure consciousness on which the jug is a construction. As such it would also be in relation with the jug, with the result that there would be the experience that the jug is not known. It may be argued that the very fact of the positive perception of the jug may be an obstacle to the association of *ajñāna* with it. To this the reply is that just as when one says "I do not know this tree" there is knowledge regarding the "this" and ignorance regarding the nature of the tree, so here also there may be a partial knowledge and ignorance in different aspects of the same jug. In cases of doubt one has to admit knowledge and ignorance subsisting in the same entity, and this is true in all cases of inquiry where a thing may be known in a general way and yet remain unknown so far as its specific details are concerned.

Again, it is wrongly contended by the Śaṅkarites that during deep dreamless sleep there is a direct intuition of *ajñāna*; for if *ajñāna* were then known in its own nature as such, a man could not wake up and remember that he knew nothing. He should then have remembered that he had a direct intuition of *ajñāna*. If during deep dreamless sleep the pure consciousness illuminated *ajñāna*, it must have also illuminated all known and unknown things in the world, which is absurd, for then these would have been remembered during the waking period. It cannot be said that during deep dreamless sleep only *ajñāna* is manifested and nothing else, for according to the testimony of waking consciousness time is also perceived during dreamless sleep which accounts for the memory of the waking stage "so long I did not know anything." Further, if it is held that whatever is illuminated by pure *sākṣi*-consciousness (i.e. without passing through the *vṛtti* stage) then the *ajñāna* also would not be remembered. If it is held that the objects of *ajñāna* only are not illuminated by the *sākṣi*-consciousness but only the *ajñāna*, then that could not account for the memory in the waking stage "I did not know anything," where "anything" definitely refers to some object of *ajñāna*. Moreover, if the above supposition were correct, then the pure bliss could not be illuminated during dreamless sleep and remembered later in the waking stage. If in reply to this it were contended that certain specific characters were remembered during the waking period in addition to the *ajñāna* because they were represented through the modes of *avidyā*, the reply is that instead of assuming that there were specific modes of *avidyā* one might as well admit them to be due to mental modes or states, and the experience of *ajñāna* might well be accounted for as being the experience of absence of knowledge. Since absence of knowledge is acceptable to all, there is no justification for admitting a new entity such as a positive *ajñāna*.

Again, in the case of loss of memory of a perceived object, a person might say that he did not know the object, but that does not prove that while he knew the object he had an intuition of the *ajñāna* of that object. After an illusory perception of conch-shell-silver one says "I did not know silver so long"; and how is this to be explained? Moreover, when one sees an object at the present moment, one may say "I did not know this object so long." How is this to be explained? The obvious reply is that in all such cases we infer only that there was an absence of knowledge of those entities. In the instance under discussion also we may hold the same view and say that we infer that during dreamless sleep we had no knowledge. But we cannot say that we then intuited directly a positive *ajñāna*. The Śaṅkarites say that the existence of *ajñāna* as a positive stuff can be proved by inference also, for according to them just as light manifests things by removing the positive stuff of darkness, so knowledge also manifests things by removing the *ajñāna* stuff that was hiding them. In refuting this, Mahācārya enters into a long discourse of formal and scholastic criticism of the Śaṅkarite mode of syllogism which cannot appropriately be treated here. The main point that is worthy of our notice here and which has a philosophical significance is the view of the Rāmānuja school that the illumination of things by knowledge does not presuppose that some positive stuff of *ajñāna* must have been removed. The Śaṅkarites object that unless *ajñāna* is admitted as a separate stuff, hiding the pure bliss of the self, it is difficult to explain emancipation. To this Mahācārya's reply is that emancipation can well be explained as cessation of bondage. People are as anxious to gain positive pleasure as to remove negative pain. It is wrong to suppose that unless the bondage were false it could not be removed, for it is well known that the effects of poison can be removed by the meditation of the mythical bird Garuda. So worldly bondage can also be removed by the meditation of God, though it be real. Meditation as knowledge can remove not only ignorance but also the real fact of bondage. Emancipation may thus be regarded as the eternal manifestation of bliss and it is not indispensably necessary that all manifestation of bliss or happiness must be associated with a body like other ordinary bodily pleasure[1].

The Śaṅkarites say that since the unchangeable self cannot be the material cause of the world phenomena nor anything else, it comes by implication that there must be an *ajñāna* stuff which is the material cause of the world, for it is only such a material cause that can explain the *ajñāna* characteristics of the world-phenomena. Brahman has often been designated as the material cause of the world, and this is true only so far as it is the basic cause (*adhiṣṭhāna-kāraṇa*), the pure being that underlies all phenomena. The *ajñāna* is the changing material cause (*pariṇāmi-kāraṇa*), and as such the world participates in the nature of *ajñāna* in its characters.

To this Mahācārya's reply is that even though the world-creation may be supposed to be false, that does not necessarily imply the assumption of a positive *ajñāna*. Thus the illusory silver is produced without any cause, or the self may be regarded as the material cause of the world-creation, which though partless may appear as the world through error. It cannot be said that a false effect must have a false entity as its cause, for no such generalization can be made. The presence of the common characteristic of falsehood cannot determine the supposition that a false entity must necessarily be the cause of a false effect, for there must be other common characteristics in other respects too and there is certainly no absolute similarity of characteristics between the cause and the effect[2]. Moreover, an effect does not necessarily possess the same identity of existence as its changing material cause; it is therefore not impossible for the Brahman to be the material cause of the world, though its purity may not be found in the world. If the Brahman is regarded as the *pariṇāmi-kāraṇa* of the world, it cannot of course have the same identical existence as the world, but if an entity can show itself in another form we may call it a *pariṇāmi-kāraṇa*, and it is not necessary for it to have the same existence as that effect. Thus, destruction and the cessation of *avidyā* are both regarded as

[1] *Sad-vidyā-vijaya*, pp. 39–75 (MSS.).

[2] *nanu upādāno-pādeyayoḥ sālakṣaṇya-niyama-darśanād eva tat-siddhir iti cet sarvathā sālakṣaṇyasya mṛd-ghaṭayoḥ apy adarśanāt yat kiñcit sārūpyasya śukti-rajatā-dāv api padārthatvā-dinā satvāt. Ibid.* p. 77.

effects and yet they have not the same existence as their causes[1]. It cannot therefore be argued that if Brahman be regarded as the *pariṇāmi-kāraṇa* of the world, the world would thereby be as real as Brahman. Again, the non-appearance of the Brahma-character of the world may well be explained as being due to the influence of *karma*. Even for explaining the non-appearance of the Brahma-character of the world the assumption of an *ajñāna* is not necessary. It is also not necessary to define emancipation as the cessation of *ajñāna*, for that stage, being itself a state of bliss, can thereby be regarded as an object of our efforts, and the supposition of *avidyā* and its cessation is wholly groundless.

Mahācārya also made a vigorous effort to show by textual contents that the existence of *avidyā* as a positive ignorance is not admitted in the Vedic scriptures.

In the second chapter Mahācārya attempts to show that there is no necessity to admit an *ajñāna* as an independent hiding stuff. The Śaṅkarites argue that though the self is experienced in the notion of our ego, yet the self is not expressed in our ego-experience as identical with Brahman as the fullness of bliss, and for this it is necessary to admit that there is an *ajñāna* stuff which hides the pure character of Brahman. To this Mahācārya's reply is that since *ajñāna* is regarded as beginningless its hiding capacity will also be eternal and no emancipation is possible; and if Brahman could be hidden, it will cease to have its own nature as self-luminous and will be ignorant. Moreover, the experience is of the form "I am ignorant" and as such the *ajñāna* seems to have reference only to the ego. If it is held that the existence of the veil is admitted only to explain the limited appearance of Brahman through mind (*antaḥkaraṇa*), then it may well be pointed out that the limited appearance of Brahman as ego may well be explained through the limitation of the *antaḥkaraṇa* through which it manifests itself, and for that it is not necessary to admit a separate veil of *ajñāna*.

Again it may be asked whether the veiling is identical with *ajñāna* or different from it. In the former case it would ever remain

[1] *yad uktaṃ brahmaṇaḥ pariṇāmitayā upādānatve pariṇāmasya pariṇāmi-samāna-sattākatva-niyamena kāryasyā'pi satyatva-prasaṅga iti. tatra kiṃ pariṇāma-śabdena kārya-mātraṃ vivakṣitam, uta rūpā-ntarā-pattiḥ; dhvaṃsasya avidyā-nivṛtteśca pariṇāmi-samāna-sattākatvā-bhāvāt na hi tad-rūpeṇa pariṇāmi kiñcid asti. na dvitīyaṃ rūpā-ntarā-patteḥ pariṇāmi-mātra-sāpekṣatvāt gauraveṇa sva-samāna-sattāka-pariṇāmy-apekṣā-bhāvāt. Sad-vidyā-vijaya*, p. 77.

unmanifested, and the manifestation of the world-appearance would be impossible. If the veiling is something different from *ajñāna*, then since that something is not in any way related with pure consciousness its operation would not explain the world-illusion. If this veiling is supposed to render the *ajñāna* indefinable, then it may be asked if this veiling is something different from *ajñāna* or identical with it; in the latter case it would not depend on it and in the former case it is meaningless to regard *ajñāna* as antagonistic to Brahman. Thus, since the limitations through which the Brahman manifests itself are sufficient to explain the limited appearance of Brahman as world-objects, it is unnecessary to admit a separate *ajñāna*.

Again, if *ajñāna* can veil the pure *sākṣi*-consciousness, then the whole world would be blind and there would be no knowledge at all. If the *sākṣi*-consciousness cannot be veiled, then the Brahman also cannot be veiled. Further, if Brahman is always self-luminous, then it can never be hidden by *ajñāna*. If it is said that the self-luminosity of Brahman means that it cannot be the object of cognition (*a-vedyatva*) or of immediacy (*aparokṣa*), then it is unnecessary to indulge in the conception of veiling, for the non-cognizability is neither of the two. Again, the Śaṅkarites hold that the *ajñāna* hides the bliss part of Brahman but not the part of its consciousness. This is obviously impossible, for they hold that bliss and pure consciousness are identical; and if that were so, how can the bliss part be covered without covering also the part of consciousness, and how can one identical partless being, the Brahman, be divided into two parts of which one is covered while the other is not? Again, if the self is admitted to be of the nature of pure bliss, and if our love of pleasure is explained as being due to the illusory construction of the ego on this self, then since all things of the world are but illusory impositions on the self, all things in the world would be dear to us and even pain would be pleasurable.

In the third chapter Mahācārya refutes the Śaṅkarite theory of the support of *ajñāna*. It is held by some exponents of the Śaṅkara school that the *ajñāna*-constituents of the objects are supported in the pure consciousness underlying these objects. Though there are the modifications of these *ajñāna* entities, yet they may have relation with our ego-consciousness, for both the ego and the objects are but the states of a ground-*ajñāna*. To this Mahācārya says that if all objects of the world have separate and different *ajñāna* materials as their causes, then it is wrong to suppose that the illusory silver is produced by the *ajñāna* of the conch-shell. It would be much better to say that the *ajñāna* of the subject (*pramātā*) as it comes out with the *antaḥkaraṇa* has produced the illusory silver. Again, if the *ajñāna* of the conch-shell is regarded as beginningless, it is meaningless to regard it as being a modification of a ground-*ajñāna*, and if it is not regarded as a mode its perception cannot be explained.

There are again others who hold that the *ajñāna* constituting an external object in some sense subsists in the subject as well and thus there may be a connection between the subject and the object. To this Mahācārya says that such a view is impossible, for the consciousness underlying the object is different from that underlying the subject; and if it is held that pure consciousness is ultimately one, then all objects ought to be illuminated just as much as any particular object is illuminated at the time of any particular cognition. Again, if the consciousness underlying the objects and the subject is without any distinction, why should a man know himself to be ignorant when he says "I am ignorant"? There is no reason why this feeling of ignorance should be felt in the subject and not in the object when the consciousness underlying them are one and the same. Moreover, in that case where one person knows an object, there would be a knowledge of that object with all persons.

There are again others who say that the *ajñāna* constituent of the conch-shell has the consciousness underlying the ego-experience as its support and the consciousness underlying the conch-shell as its object. To this Mahācārya says that the *ajñāna* supported by the consciousness underlying the ego-experience cannot undergo transformation, and, if this is so, it cannot explain the diverse objects.

There are others again who think that when a man says that he does not know the conch-shell his ignorance refers to the root-*ajñāna*; for though the *ajñāna* refers to the pure consciousness, that being identical with the pure consciousness underlying the conch-shell, the *ajñāna* also refers to the conch-shell and may be so apprehended. One has also to admit that the illusory silver is also made up of the stuff of *ajñāna*, for since the illusory silver appears in perception, it must have some stuff as its material cause.

To this Mahācārya's reply is that if the apperception of self-ignorance has a reference to the root-*ajñāna*, there is no justification for admitting separate *ajñānas* constituting the stuff of the objects. It cannot be suggested that the existence of such *ajñāna* may be proved by the fact that each perception implies the cessation of a particular *ajñāna*, for the disappearance of such an *ajñāna* is only a matter of inference, and it may as well be assumed that it does not mean anything more than that a particular cognition follows only the absence of that particular knowledge. A negation-precedent-to-a-production is always destroyed by the production of a particular entity. When one says "I did not know the jug long, but I know it now," the cessation of the absence of knowledge or the *ajñāna* has a direct and immediate reference to the subject, the knower. But the removal of the *ajñāna* hiding the objects is only a matter of inference from the fact of cognition, and it can never be immediate or intuitive. Again, if the root-*ajñāna* is supposed to veil the pure consciousness as underlying the objects, it is unnecessary to suppose the existence of separate *ajñānas* hiding the objects. If it is supposed that the pure consciousness underlying the objects, being identical with Brahman, which is referred to by the root-*ajñāna*, may appear in consciousness as being limited under the object-appearance, it may be asked how on account of the association of the root-*ajñāna* the object may appear to be unknown even when it is known. Again, the root-ignorance implied in such an experience as "I do not know" cannot belong to the mind (*antaḥkaraṇa*), for it is a material object and it cannot belong to the self-shining pure consciousness. Being what it is, it cannot be ignorant about itself.

Further, it may well be said that though the self is manifested in self-consciousness yet it often appears as associated with the body, and though objects may generally be known as "knowable" yet their specific nature may not be known and it is this that often leads to doubt; all these are inexplicable except on the assumption of ignorance. They may all be admitted, but even then the assumption that *ajñāna* acts as a veiling agent is wholly unwarrantable. Uncertainty (*anavadhāraṇa*) and veiling (*āvaraṇa*) are not one and the same thing. In the appearance of water in a mirage there may be doubt due to uncertainty, and it cannot be denied that there is all the appearance of water which could not have been if the so-called *ajñāna* had veiled it. Nor can it be said that the uncertainty is due to the veiling, for it may well be urged that since veiling cannot manifest itself either as being or as self-luminous, it is itself a mere consequence or result of the factor of uncertainty. If it is urged that the factor of indefiniteness or uncertainty itself constitutes the nature of veiling (*anavadhāraṇatvam eva āvaraṇam*), then it may be said that the fact that the individual ego is not felt to be identical is regarded as being due to the veiling operation; but that does not mean that there is any uncertainty in our experience as the limited individual. If there were any such uncertainty, then ego-experience would not have stood as an indubitable fact. Again, if *ajñāna* be itself of the nature of uncertainty, then there is no meaning in ascribing a separate veiling character to it. If it is held that *ajñāna* is supported only by pure consciousness, then there would be no reason why the individual selves should pass through the cycles of birth and rebirth, for such *ajñāna* would have no association with the individual selves. If it is urged that the same consciousness manifests itself through the individual self, then it may also be urged that since the consciousness underlies both the individuals and God, God may equally well be supposed to undergo the cycle of birth and rebirth[1].

It is sometimes said that it is the mind (*antaḥkaraṇa*) which experiences pleasure and pain and it is this that constitutes bondage. The mind itself being an illusory construction on the pure consciousness, the characters of the mind are felt to belong to the consciousness. To this Mahācārya's reply is that if the bondage belonged to the mind, then the pure consciousness cannot be supposed to suffer bondage. For if the suffering of bondage is due to the false notion of the identification of the pure consciousness with the mind, the bondage is not due to mind but to that false notion. In a similar manner Mahācārya enters into a criticism of many alternative interpretations that are offered by various writers of the Śaṅkara school in support of the existence of *ajñāna* and such of its relations as may explain the world creation, and finally tries to establish his view that in whichever way the relation of *ajñāna* may be conceived it is fraught with diverse kinds of contradictions which baffle explanation.

Again, in the fourth chapter Mahācārya contends that the

[1] *ajñānasya caitanya-mātrā-śrayatve jīve saṃsāra-hetutā na syāt vaiyadhikaraṇyāc caitanyasyai'va jīve-śa-vibhāgāt sāmānādhikaraṇye īśvarasyā'pi saṃsāra-prasaṅgaḥ. Sad-vidyā-vijaya*, p. 107 (MS.).

avidyā cannot be regarded as ultimately real (*pāramārthikī*) for then there would be no monism. It cannot be regarded as the stuff of all that is cognized in practical experience (*vyavahārikī*), for then it could not be called the stuff of illusory experiences. It is sometimes urged that even from false things, such as a false fear, there may be real illness or even death, and so even from ignorance there can be real knowledge. Mahācārya points out that this analogy is false, for even in the above instances it is knowledge that produces the said results. If *avidyā* is false, then all its material transformations must also be false, for the effect is always identical with the cause. It is urged that since the world-objects are false their knowledge must also be false; then the Brahman, which is the knowledge which is itself a product of *avidyā*, is also false.

Further, if *ajñāna* be regarded as one, then with the knowledge of conch-shell all *ajñāna* should cease; for without the cessation of *ajñāna* the conch-shell could not have been known. It cannot be said that with the knowledge of the conch-shell only the veil hiding it has been removed and that the *ajñāna* did not cease, for experience testifies to the disappearance of *ajñāna* and not that of the veil. Thus one is forced to admit the existence of many *ajñānas*. For if it is held that knowledge removes only the veil, then even the last emancipating knowledge would also remove only a particular veil and that would not result in the destruction of the ultimate *ajñāna*. Again, *ajñāna* is defined as that which is destroyed by knowledge (*jñāna*). If that is so, it is obviously wrong to define knowledge as being itself a product of *ajñāna*. The effect cannot destroy the causal entity. Again, if at the time of emancipation of a man the *ajñāna* is supposed to be destroyed, such an *ajñāna* if it is one only would be wholly destroyed and there would be no other *ajñāna* left which could bind the other unemancipated individuals. It is supposed that *ajñāna* must be false, for it is destroyed by knowledge, but at the same time it is admitted that the *ajñāna* is destroyed by the true scriptures (*śruti*), and when a thing is destroyed by another real and true entity the former cannot be regarded as false.

Again, *avidyā* is sometimes defined as something the cessation of which can be produced by knowledge (*jñānajanya*). Now Brahman is itself the cessation of *avidyā*, but it is not produced by knowledge. If knowledge is regarded as a means to the cessation of knowledge (*jñānasādhyatvāt*), then it does not necessarily mean that it has produced the cessation (*na ca sva-janyatvam eva sva-sādhyatvam*). If the two concepts are regarded as identical, then the relationing of *avidyā* to which *avidyā* may be regarded as a means would also have to be admitted as being produced by *avidyā*, which is reasoning in a circle[1]. Arguing on the same analogy, one might as well say that the cessation of the relationing with *avidyā* depends on the cessation of *avidyā*, but in that case since the cessation of *avidyā* itself means a relationing with *avidyā* it becomes a tautology only.

Again, in order to differentiate any ordinary erroneous view, which is removed by right knowledge from *avidyā*, it has been defined as being beginningless yet destructible by knowledge. Now, it may be asked, what is the nature of this knowledge which destroys *avidyā*? Does it mean pure consciousness or only mental states? If it is pure consciousness, then it cannot destroy the root-impressions (*saṃskāra*); for it is only the mental states (*vṛtti*) which can destroy the mental root-impressions, and if *avidyā* is a beginningless *saṃskāra* it cannot be removed by knowledge as pure consciousness and thus the assumption of its being beginningless serves no useful purpose. The second supposition, that knowledge which destroys *avidyā* is only a mental state, cannot also be correct, for it is held that knowledge as mental state can remove only the veil of *ajñāna* but not the *ajñāna* itself. If it is said that the mental state removes both the veil and the *ajñāna*, then the definition of *ajñāna* as that which can be removed by knowledge becomes too wide, as it would also signify the veil (*āvaraṇa*) which is not intended to be covered within the definition of *ajñāna*. Again, if *ajñānas* are regarded as many, then such cognitive states can remove only the *ajñānas* veiling the ordinary objects, and cannot therefore be applied to one undifferentiated *ajñāna*-whole which can be removed only by the intuition of the partless real, for this knowledge would not be a mental state which is always limited[2]. Here also the *ajñāna* must be supposed to be hiding the nature of Brahman, and the cessation of the *ajñāna* is directly consequent upon the cessation of the veil. So, firstly, the direct cause of the cessation of the *ajñāna* is not knowledge but the removal of the veil; secondly, it is the removal of the veil that is caused by the knowledge, and so it is this that ought to be called *ajñāna* according to the definition, for the veil is both beginningless and destructible by knowledge.

[1] *Sad-vidyā-vijaya*, p. 116. [2] *Ibid.*

Mahācārya enters into a series of further criticisms of the definition of *avidyā* which are more or less of a scholastic nature and may therefore be omitted here.

In the fifth chapter Mahācārya disputes the possibility that the *avidyā* is illuminated or manifested. If *avidyā* was self-manifesting, then it would be real and spiritual like the Brahman. If the manifestation of Brahman were the manifestation of the manifestation of the *avidyā*, then the former being eternal the manifestation of the *avidyā* would also be eternal; yet *avidyā* is always regarded as existing only so long as it shines, and therefore as false (*mithyārthasya pratibhāsa-samāna-kālīnatva-niyamāt*). If the manifestation (*prakāśa*) of *avidyā* be regarded as its non-distinguishingness (*abheda*) with the manifestation of Brahman, then so long as the manifestation of Brahman remains, the *avidyā* would also remain and hence *avidyā* itself would be eternal. Again, if it is urged that, when the *avidyā* ceases, its non-distinguishingness with the Brahma-manifestation would also cease, and hence Brahman would be eternal and *avidyā* would be destructible, a further difficulty may be pointed out to this contention, namely, that if the *avidyā* be indistinguishable from the Brahma-manifestation, then either the latter would be false or the former real. It would be absurd to suggest in reply that, though different, they have an identical being (*bhinnatve saty abhinnas-attākatvam*). The criticisms suggested herein will apply to the doctrine if the illumination of *avidyā* be explained as the manifestation of Brahman, as limited by *avidyā* (*avidyā-vacchinnaṃ brahma-svarūpam avidyā-prakāśaḥ*) or as conditioned by it or reflected through it.

In the next chapter Mahācārya tries to show the incompatibility of the conception that *avidyā* may be brought to an end. He says that pure consciousness cannot be supposed to destroy *avidyā*. Then *avidyā* can never exist, for the pure consciousness is eternally existing and as such by itself destroys *avidyā* and no other effort is necessary. If pure consciousness cannot destroy *avidyā*, it cannot do so when reflected through a mental state (*vṛtti-prativimbitam*), for it is not more than the unlimited consciousness (*caitanyād adhika-viṣayatvā-bhāve tadvad eva nivarttakatvā-sambhavāt*). If the pure consciousness reflected through a *vṛtti* cannot remove *avidyā*, then it cannot do so when limited by a *vṛtti* or conditioned by it. The *vṛtti* itself also cannot remove it, for it is itself material. If it is held that the knowledge which contradicts the illusory notion brought about by the *ajñāna* destroys it and not the intuition of the reality, then if that contradiction is something identical with pure consciousness, it is the pure consciousness which is to be supposed as destroying the *ajñāna*; the objections against such a view have already been dealt with. If knowledge and *ajñāna* are different, then it is wrong to suppose that knowledge destroys *ajñāna*; for knowledge is the contradiction that is supposed to destroy *avidyā* and by supposition *avidyā* is not knowledge. Moreover, since that illumination which destroys *ajñāna* cannot be supposed to have a further veil which is removed by it, it cannot rightly be called knowledge; for knowledge according to the supposition of the Śaṅkarites operates by removing a veil. Further, this knowledge is supposed to be opposed to all things in the world, and if that is so how can it be said that by this knowledge only the *ajñāna* is destroyed? Again, if it is supposed that illusion consists in identifying everything with Brahman and knowledge is supposed to remove this false identification, then since knowledge is supposed to operate by removing a veil, it has to be supposed that *ajñāna* was veiling the false identification, and if that were so there could have been no knowledge in our world-experience.

Again, the cessation of *avidyā* is also incomprehensible in itself, for it cannot be different from the nature of Brahman; if it were there would be duality and emancipation would be impossible. If it were one with the Brahman, then being so it would exist always and there would be no scope for making any effort about it. It cannot also be said that *avidyā* and Brahman mutually negate each other; for *avidyā* has Brahman for its support and as such is not antagonistic to it.

Prapatti Doctrine as expounded in Śrīvacana-bhūṣaṇa of Lokācārya and Saumya Jāmātṛ Muni's Commentary on it.

According to the *Śrīvacana-bhūṣaṇa* the mercy of God remains always as submerged in His justice, but yet it always exists and its apprehension by us is obstructed by certain conditions. It is not produced by our efforts, for then God would not always be merciful (*anudbhūta-dayā-dy-udbhāvaka-puruṣa-kāra-sāpekṣakatve nityo-dbhūta-dayā-di-mattvaṃ vyāhataṃ syāt* 35. B.).

The mercy of God is dependent on Him and on no one else; yet there exists in Nārāyaṇa the deity Lakṣmī who is like the essence of Him or the body of Him, and who has voluntarily reconciled her will absolutely with that of Nārāyaṇa. Though in such a conception the Lakṣmī is dependent on Nārāyaṇa, yet for the devotees Nārāyaṇa and Lakṣmī go together, and for him the mercy of God is to be attributed to both Lakṣmī and Nārāyaṇa taken as a whole.

The conception of Lakṣmī is such that she is the greatest object of love for Nārāyaṇa, who has conceived her as a part of Himself, and Lakṣmī has also so identified herself with Him that there is no separate existence for her. As such Lakṣmī has not to make any special effort for bringing Nārāyaṇa in consonance with her will; for there is practically no existence of duality, and for this reason there is no necessity for devotees to cling separately to Lakṣmī. The nature of Lakṣmī is the pure essence of the mercy of God[1].

When the devotee is in a state of separation from God through the wrong conception of his own independence and separate individuality, he has to make an effort in the negative direction in forsaking his own sense of freedom and adopting God as his ultimate end. But once he has forsaken his false egoism and surrendered himself entirely to God, there is no need of further effort on his part. At such a stage through the influence of Lakṣmī all the sins of the devotee are destroyed and through her influence God extends His mercy to him[2]. Lakṣmī also rouses in the human mind through internal moral persuasion the belief in the necessity of seeking His friendship. She performs the dual function, first that of turning the minds of the people, who are under the sway of beginningless *avidyā* by which they are always being attracted by mundane interest to God; and, secondly, she also melts the heart of God Who is bent upon giving fruits in accordance with the deserts of the people, and persuades Him to extend His bliss to all people by overruling the bondage of *karma*.

The *prapatti*, as seeking the protection of God, is not restricted

[1] *devyā kāruṇya-rūpaye'ti tad-guṇa-sāratvena kāruṇyaṃ svayam eve'ti. Śrīvacana-bhūṣaṇa.* MS.

[2] *prapatter deśa-niyamaḥ kāla-niyamaḥ prakāra-niyamaḥ adhikāri-niyamaḥ phala-niyamaś ca nāsti. Śrīvacana-bhūṣaṇa-vyākhyā.* MS.

The above idea is supported in the commentary by a quotation from *Bhāradvāja-saṃhitā* which runs as follows:

brahma-kṣatra-viśaḥ śūdrāḥ striyaś cā'ntara-jātayaḥ
sarva eva prapadyeran sarva-dhātāraṃ acyutam. Ibid.

by any limiting conditions of holy or unholy places, or of any special time, or of any special mode, or of any caste restriction, or that it can produce only this or that result. When God accepts any person through *prapatti* He forgives all his faults of commission and omission. The only fault that He does not forgive is insincerity or cruelty (*kraurya*). People take to *prapatti* either because they feel helpless and know no other means of saving themselves, or because they are very wise and definitely know that this is the best means, or because they are naturally attached to God, like the Āṛvārs[1]. In the first case true knowledge and devotion are at the minimum; in the second case there is not so much ignorance but devotion also is of the normal extent. In the third case ignorance is least and attachment is at its highest and as such even true knowledge of the nature of God is engulfed as it were by an excess of attachment. In the first case the consciousness of one's own ignorance is strongest; in the second case the consciousness of one's humbleness and ignorance is equally balanced with the true knowledge of the essence of God and the relation of one's nature with Him.

The devotee who has in great love surrendered himself to God has occasional communion and detachment with Him. In the first case he is filled with ecstatic joy by coming in direct contact with God as associated with noble qualities. But at the moment of detachment the memory of that communion and ecstasy of joy is a source of dire pain. It has been related above that God's mercy is continuous and ever-flowing; but in spite of this, on account of obstructive tendencies which by investing us with a false belief in our own independence lead to the assertion of our false individuality, the course of God's mercy is obstructed. The adoption of *prapatti* removes the obstructive attitude and renders it possible for God to extend His mercy to us. In such a conception *prapatti* is to be regarded only as a negative means. The positive means (*upāya*) is God Who extends His mercy. *Prapatti* therefore should not be regarded as the cause of our deliverance. It only removes our obstructive tendencies, and cannot therefore be regarded as an element of the cause that secures our deliverance—that cause being God

[1] As an illustration of the last type a few lines from *Śrīvacana-bhūṣaṇa-vyākhyā* may be quoted: *bhakti-pāravaśyena prapannā bhagavat-prema-pauṣkalyena pādau stabdhau manaḥ śithilaṃ bhavati cakṣur bhramati pādau hastau ca niśceṣṭau ity ukta-prakāreṇa śithila-karaṇatvena sādhanā-nuṣṭhāna-yogyatā-bhāvād ananya-gatikās santas tasmin bhara-samarpaṇaṃ kṛtaṃ*. MS.

and God alone. God is thus both the means and end of attainment, and the only absolute means for the devotee to attain Him. The *prapatti* view here propounded flatly denies the necessity of any other means. The essence of *prapatti* consists in the passivity involved in the mental attitude of the devotee surrendering himself to God and thus giving occasion for God's affecting powers to affect him favourably. When the devotee ceases to concern himself with any anxiety as to how he may be saved, then God exerts His will to save him[1]. This view of God's relationship with the devotee involves within it the philosophical doctrine that the individual souls exist for God and have no end to realize for themselves. It is only through ignorance that the individual seems to possess an independent end for himself. The denial of this position through excessive love of God renders the philosophical reality of their mutual relationship realizable as a spiritual fact.

The definition of soul as consciousness and bliss and as atomic is only an external description (*taṭastha*). The internal situation (*antaraṅga*) of the relation of the individual soul with God may best be described as his servitude to Him.

The nature of emotional attachment which is associated with *prapatti* is such that the devotee by his tender love for God induces the same in Him so that the emotion of love may be regarded on the one hand as a consciousness of bliss and on the other hand as a relation in which the lover and the beloved are the constituents. The first inferior stage of *prapatti* is not always actuated by deep natural attachment, but by a sense of one's own insignificance and helplessness[2]. In the second stage called the *upeya* the devotee is so much actuated by his deep love for God that he loses all considerations for himself, and the intoxication of love may grow so deep that it may lead to the annihilation of his body. But the prospect of such an annihilation does not deter him from moving forward in the path of intoxication, for at that stage he loses all interest in the consequences of such an attachment. He is simply lost in God through intoxicating emotion. This is technically called *rāga-prāpta-prapatti*.

The relation between the devotee and God is interpreted on the analogy of the wedding of the mistress with her lover, of the

[1] *asya icchā nivṛttā cet tasye'cchā asya kāryakarī bhavati. Śrīvacana-bhūṣaṇa-vyākhyā.* MS.

[2] This is regarded as the *upāya* stage where the devotee seeks God as the means to his highest attainment.

Gopikā with Kṛṣṇa, and it is held that the deep emotion is like the erotic emotion that leads to the wedding of the bridegroom with the bride. *Bhakti* or devotion is described as a special kind of consciousness dissociated from ignorance which reveals itself in the form of a deep emotion. The devotee is supposed to pass through all the stages which a love-stricken woman would do. All the emotions of the devotee, the lover, are for rousing the pleasure of God. Just as a woman's behaviour under the influence of love is intended to bring a smile or twinkle into the eyes of her lover, so the emotion of the devotee is intended solely to please God[1]. This is regarded as *siddha-prema* or natural love. Devotees intoxicated by such a love are not necessarily subjected to any kind of code of duty. It is only those whose intoxication by love is so great that they cannot wait and pass through any such discipline as is prescribed in the *vaidhī* or the *upāya* stage of *prapatti* who are driven to embrace God as it were with their melting hearts. The ordinary rules of *prapatti* are utterly unbinding on these people. In the adoption of *prapatti* of all the three types mentioned above the personal effort (*puruṣakāra*) necessary is limited to the extent that the individual should hold himself in absolute self-surrender so that God may be inclined to accept even his faults and defects as they are and remove them by His divine grace. In the case of those who are advanced in the stage of *prapatti*—the *paramārtas*—God removes even all the *prārabdha-karmas* and grants them immediate emancipation[2].

The person who adopts the path of *prapatti* is not anxious to attain even emancipation. He has also no specific preference as to the nature of the spiritual emancipation that may be granted to him. To desire emancipation and to attach any preference to any possible state of existence involves an egoistic desire. But the person who has sincerely adopted the path of *prapatti* must annihilate altogether even the last traces of egoism. On the one side egoism means ignorance, for it is only by false knowledge that a man asserts

[1] *ajñāna-nivṛtti-pūrvaka-bhakti-rūpā-pannaṃ jñānaṃ prasādhitam. mahad-vivāha-janaka-kāmaṃ samudra-tulyatayā varddhayan megha-sadṛśa-vigraho' smat-kṛṣṇa ity evaṃ-bhūta-pravṛtti-hetor bhakter utpādako varddhakaś ca. sā eva hi tasya bhakti-pāravaśya-nivandhanā pravṛttir upāya-phalam ity ucyate.... prāpya-tvarayā strī-vratayā netra-bhramaṇena etasya sambhramā sarve mad-viṣayā'sāṃ kṛtvā evam avasthā labdhā iti tan-mukha-vikāśā-rthaṃ kṛiyamāṇa-kaiṅkaryavad upeyā-ntarbhūtā. Śrīvacana-bhūṣaṇa-vyākhyā.* MS.

[2] *evam-bhūtasya śarīra-sthiti-hetuḥ prārabdha-karme'ti na vaktuṃ śakyate sarva-pāpebhyaḥ mokṣayiṣyāmi ity anena virodhāt. Ibid.* MS.

himself as having an independent being. On the other side egoism means insincerity (*kraurya*). It has been said above that God may forgive all our sins excepting insincerity. The fundamental requirement of *prapatti* therefore consists in the annihilation of egoism. It is only through the annihilation of egoism that the perfect self-surrender required by *prapatti* is possible[1].

The four stages precedent to the attainment of the *summum bonum* through *prapatti* are as follows: (i) *jñāna-daśā*, i.e. the state in which through the instructions of the teacher the devotee attains self-knowledge in relation to God. (ii) *varaṇa-daśā*, the state in which the devotee adopts God in a spirit of helpless surrender as the only protector. (iii) *prāpti-daśā*, the state in which he realizes God. (iv) *prāpyā-nubhava-daśā*, i.e. the state in which, having realized God, he attains the *summum bonum*[2].

The doctrine of *prapatti* is, indeed, very old. It is found in the *Ahirbudhnya-saṃhitā*, *Lakṣmī Tantra*, *Bharadvāja-saṃhitā* and other *Pañca-rātra* works. The *Śrīvaiṣṇava* writers trace its origin to much older literature such as the *Taittirīyopaniṣad*, *Kaṭhopaniṣad* and the *Śvetāśvatara*, the *Mahābhārata* and the *Rāmāyaṇa*. The nature of *prapatti* in the *Ahirbudhnya-saṃhitā* has already been discussed. In the *Bharadvāja-Saṃhitā* the *prapatti* is described as self-surrender to God, and the descriptions that it gives are more or less the same as those found in the *Ahirbudhnya*. The devotee who adopts the path of *prapatti* is not exempted from the ordinary duties of a *Vaiṣṇava* or from the regular caste duties. The *Bharadvāja-saṃhitā* describes in some detail the courses of action which are favourable or unfavourable to the adoption of such a path. Rāmānuja, in his *Śaraṇā-gati-gadya*, advocates the path of *prapatti* in which the devotee seeks protection not only of *Nārāyaṇa* but also of *Lakṣmī*. But it does not appear either in the *Śaraṇā-gati-gadya* or in his commentary of the *Gītā* that a person who has adopted the path of *prapatti* is exempted from the normal caste and other duties, nor is the function of *Lakṣmī* in awarding the fruits of *prapatti* explained by him. In his explanation of the *Bhagavad-gītā* text (*sarva-dharmān parityajya*, etc., 18. 66), he says that the devotee should perform all his normal duties without any motive of

[1] *Śrīvacana-bhūṣaṇa-vyākhyā*. MS.

[2] *etad-anubhava-janita-prīti-kārita-kaiṅkaryam eva parama-puruṣā-rthaḥ. Ibid.*

attaining fruits thereby[1]. As regards the destruction of the *prārabdha-karma* also, Rāmānuja and Veṅkaṭanātha hold that though most of it is destroyed by the grace of God, yet a trace of it is left[2]. Vātsya Varada, in his *Prapanna-pārijāta*, follows the same idea. Veṅkaṭanātha also repeats the same view in his *Nyāsa-viṃśati* and *Nyāsa-tilaka*, and Aṇṇayārya, a disciple of Vedāntī Rāmānuja, follows the idea in his *Prapatti-prayoga*. Varadanātha, the son of Veṅkaṭanātha, also repeats the idea in his *Nyāsa-tilaka-vākhyā* and *Nyāsa-kārikā*. The view of Lokācārya and Saumya Jāmātṛ muni, the leaders of the *Teṅgalai* school, differs from it to the extent that while the above-mentioned *prapatti* doctrine may be true of the inferior devotees, the superior devotees who are absolutely intoxicated with God's love are through the very nature of their psychological intoxication unable to follow any of the normal duties and are entirely exempted from them. Their *prāraddha-karma* may also be entirely destroyed by God's grace. The distinction

[1] Veṅkaṭanātha in his *Tātparya-dīpikā* on *Rāmānuja-bhāṣya* on the *Gītā* (verse 18. 66) says: *etac-chlokā-pāta-pratītyā kūṭa-yuktibhiśca yathā varṇāśrama-dharma-svarūpa-tyāgā-di-pakṣo no'deti tathā upapāditam.*

[2] *sādhya-bhaktistu sā hantrī prāravddhasyā'pi bhūyasī.* (*Rahasya-rakṣā* commentary of Veṅkaṭanātha on *Śaraṇā-gati-gadya*, p. 50. Vānīvilāsa Press, 1910).

In the *Nyāsa-viṃśati* and the *Nyāsa-tilaka* as commented in the *Nyāsa-tilaka-vyākhyā* by Veṅkaṭanātha's son Varadanātha *prapatti* is defined in the same manner as that by Lokācārya. *Prapatti* is an old doctrine in Southern Vaiṣṇavism and its fundamental characters are more or less final. In the *Nyāsa-tilaka-vyākhyā* great emphasis is laid on the fact that *prapatti* as a path of approach to God is different from the path of *bhakti* and superior to it. In the *Śrīvacana-bhūṣaṇa* there is a tendency to treat *bhakti* as an intermediary way to *prapatti*. In the *Nyāsa-tilaka-vyākhyā* it is said that the chief difference between *bhakti* and *prapatti* is firstly that the former is of the nature of unbroken meditation, while the latter has to be done once for all; secondly, the *prāravdha-karma* cannot be destroyed by the former, whereas in the latter it can be so done by the grace of God; thirdly, the former needs various accessory methods of worship—continual effort and continual action—whereas in the latter we have excessive faith; fourthly, the former produces fruit after a long time whereas the latter applies only to those who want immediate fruit; fifthly, the former may have different objectives and may yield different fruits accordingly, whereas the latter being of the nature of absolutely helpless surrender produces all fruits immediately. High faith is the foundation of *prapatti*. In and through many obstacles this faith and attachment to God leads the devotee to his goal. For these reasons the path of *bhakti* is inferior to the path of *prapatti*. *Prapatti* to the teacher is regarded as a part of *prapatti* to God. The difference between the conception of *prapatti* in the *Śrīvacana-bhūṣaṇa* and the *Nyāsa-tilaka* is that the latter holds that even those who adopt the path of *prapatti* should perform the obligatory duties imposed by the scriptures and refrain from committing the acts prohibited by them; for the scriptures are the commands of God. The former however thinks that a man who adopts the path of *prapatti* by the very nature of the psychological state produced by it is unable to adhere to any programme of duties outlined by the scriptures. He therefore transcends it.

between the *Varagalai* and *Teṅgalai* schools depends largely on the emphasis given by the latter to the superior type of *prapatti*.

Kastūrī Raṅgācārya.

Kastūrī Raṅgācārya, otherwise called Śrī Raṅgasūri, was a disciple of Saumya Jāmātṛ muni and probably lived late in the fifteenth or the beginning of the sixteenth century. Rāmānuja's views do not seem to have undergone great changes of interpretation, and we do not find the emergence of different schools of interpretation as in the case of the philosophy of Śaṅkara. The followers of Rāmānuja throughout the succeeding centuries directed their efforts mostly to elucidating Rāmānuja's views and adducing new arguments for his doctrines or refuting the arguments of his opponents and finding fault with the theories of other schools. A sectarian difference, however, arose with Veṅkaṭanātha's efforts to explain the nature of devotion and the ultimate nature of emancipation and various other problems associated with it. Some external ritualistic differences can also be traced from his time. One sect[1] (*Vaḍkalai* or *Uttara-kalārya*) was led by Veṅkaṭanātha and the other school (called *Teṅgalai* or *Dakṣiṇa-kalārya*) by Lokācārya and Saumya Jāmātṛ muni.

Kastūrī Raṅgācārya wrote two works called *Kāryā-dhikaraṇa-vāda* and the *Kāryā-dhikaraṇa-tattva*, in which he discussed some of the most important differences of these two schools and lent his support to the *Teṅgalai* or the *Dakṣiṇa-kalārya* school. The discussion began on the occasion of the interpretation of Rāmānuja of a topic in the *Brahma-sūtra* (4.3.6–15) called the *Kāryā-dhikaraṇa-vāda*, in which some Upaniṣad texts raised certain difficulties regarding the attainment of absolute immortality as conditioned by wisdom or worship (*upāsanā*). Vādari says that the worship of Hiraṇyagarbha, the highest of the created beings, leads to absolute immortality; Jaimini says that only the worship of the highest Brahman can produce immortality. Bādarāyaṇa, however, rejects their views and holds that only those who regard their souls as naturally dissociated from *Prakṛti* and as parts of Brahman attain absolute immortality.

[1] *sarvāsu vipratipattiṣu purvā kakṣyā vedāntā-cārya-tad-anuvandhinām uttara-kalārya-saṃjñānām uttarā tu lokācārya-tad-anubandhināṃ dakṣiṇa-kalārya-saṃjñānām iti viveko bodhyaḥ. Kārya-kāraṇā-dhikaraṇa-vāda*, 8. 2.

Those who cannot realize their essential difference from the material qualities with which they are seemingly associated cannot attain the highest immortality and have ultimately to follow the cycles of births and rebirths. Those alone who worship Brahman with a proper apprehension of their own nature in relation to it can attain the highest immortality. The nature of this worship has been described by Raṅgācārya in accordance with the Gītā which enjoins the worship of Brahman with *śraddhā* (*śraddhā-pūrvakaṃ brahmo-pāsanam*). The word *śraddhā* ordinarily means faith. This faith undergoes a special characterization at the hands of Raṅgācārya and other thinkers of the *Teṅgalai* school. Thus it is said that the first stage is the full apprehension of the great and noble qualities of God; the second stage is the attachment produced by such apprehension; the third stage is to regard Him as the ultimate end and fulfilment of our nature; the fourth stage is to think of Him as the only dear object of our life; the fifth stage is the incapacity to bear separation from God through intense love for Him; the sixth stage is absolute faith in God as the only means of self-fulfilment; the seventh and last stage is the enkindling of the spirit in its forward movement to hold fast to Him. It is this last stage as associated with all the previous stages and as integrated with them which is called *śraddhā*. The worship of God with such faith (*śraddhā*) is also called devotion or *bhakti*. The worship of God again means intense joy in Him (*prīti-rūpo-paśāntatva-lakṣaṇam*). The mere realization of one's self as dissociated from the material elements is not sufficient. Those who follow the process of *Pañcāgni-vidyā* rest only with self-discriminative wisdom and do not take to God as the final end of self-fulfilment.

The first point of dispute between the followers of *Uttara-kalārya* and *Dakṣiṇa-kalārya* concerns the nature of emancipation called *kaivalya* which consists in self-realization as the ultimate end (*ātmā-nubhava-lakṣaṇa-kaivalyā-khya-puruṣā-rthaḥ*). Veṅkaṭanātha, the leader of the *Uttara-kalārya*, thinks that those who attain such emancipation have again to come back, i.e. such an emancipation is destructible. The *Dakṣiṇa-kalārya* sohool, however, thinks that such an emancipation is eternal. Thus Veṅkaṭa, in his *Nyāya-siddhāñjana*, says that mere realization of self as distinguished from all material elements is not sufficient, for it should also be supplemented by the knowledge that that self is a part of God and is entirely subordinate to Him, and that this view is held in the *Śrī-bhāṣya*[1]. He draws a distinction between the realization of one's own nature as bliss and the realization of the blissful nature of God. The former may happen without the latter. It has to be admitted that in the state of *kaivalya* there is an association of materiality (*acit-saṃsarga*), since the *karma* in its entirety is not destroyed in this case; for to know one's proper essence is to know oneself as a part of God and so long as this state is not attained one is under the influence of *māyā*. In the case of such a person the *māyā* obstructs his vision of God. Veṅkaṭa, however, cannot say anything definitely as to the ultimate destiny of those who attain *kaivalya*. He asserts only that they cannot attain the eternal Brahmahood. He is also uncertain as to whether they are associated with bodies or not. He is also aware that his interpretation of the nature of *kaivalya* is not in harmony with all the scriptural texts, but he feels that since some of the texts definitely support his views other texts also should be taken in that light.

Kastūrī Raṅgācārya, however, asserts that, according to the testimony of the old Draviḍa texts and also of the Gītā and such other texts, those who attain emancipation through self-knowledge attain the state of absolute immortality. The difference between liberation through self-knowledge and the liberation through one's self-knowledge in association with God is only a difference in the richness and greatness of experience, the latter being higher than the former in this respect[2]. Other points of difference between the *Uttara-kalāryas* and the *Dakṣiṇa-kalāryas* are closely connected with the point discussed above. They have been enumerated in the second chapter of *Kāryā-dhikaraṇa-vāda* and are as follows. The *Uttara-kalāryas* think that those who attain the emancipation of a self-realization as *kaivalya* pass to a higher world through other

[1] *parama-puruṣa-vibhūti-bhūtasya prāptur ātmanaḥ svarūpa-yāthātmya-vedanam apavarga-sādhana-bhūta-parama-puruṣa-vedano-payogitayā āvaśyakam. na svata eva upāyatvena ity uktam. Nyāya-siddhāñjana*, p. 82.

Veṅkaṭa also refers to Varada Viṣṇumiśra in support of his views. "*niḥśeṣa-karma-kṣayā-bhāvāt kaivalya-prāptau na muktiḥ.*"

He refers to *Saṅgati-mālā*, where Śrī Viṣṇucitta says that a person wishing to attain Brahman may commit such errors of conception that instead of attaining the true Brahmahood he may attain only the lower state of *kaivalya* just as a man performing sacrifices to attain Heaven may commit errors for which he may become a *brahma-rākṣasa* instead of attaining Heaven. *Ibid.* p. 84.

[2] *Kāryā-dhi karaṇa-vāda*, 3. 79. Kastūrī Raṅgācārya goes through a long course of references to scriptural texts, Dravidian and Sanskritic, in support of his views.

channels than those adopted by persons who attain ultimate emancipation. This is denied by the *Dakṣiṇa-kalāryas.* Secondly, the former hold that the absolute dissociation of all trace of the elements of *prakṛti* is the same as emancipation, but the latter deny it. Thirdly, the former hold that those who attain the *kaivalya* are associated with subtle material impurities and may still be regarded as attaining immortality in a remote sense; this is desired by the latter. Fourthly, the former hold that those who attain *kaivalya* remain in a place within the sphere of the material world and their state is therefore not unchangeable, but the latter deny it. Fifthly, the former hold that those who attain wisdom through the five sacrifices (*pañcāgni-vidyā*) are different from those that attain *kaivalya*, but the latter hold that they may or may not be so. Sixthly, the former hold that those who attain wisdom through the five sacrifices may remain within the sphere of the material world when they attain only self-knowledge, but when they realize the nature of their relation with Brahman they pass away beyond the sphere of the material world (*prakṛti*); the latter, however, deny this. Seventhly, the former hold that those who attain wisdom through *pañcāgni-vidyā*, those who realize the nature of their relation to God, have the same characteristics, but the latter deny it. Eighthly, the former hold that outside the sphere of the material world (*prakṛti*) there cannot be any difference in the nature of one's highest experience, but this also is denied by the latter[1].

In his *Kāryā-dhikaraṇa-tattva*, Raṅgācārya only repeats the same arguments and the topic of discussion is also the same as that in *Kāryā-dhikaraṇa-vāda*.

Śaila Śrīnivāsa.

Śaila Śrīnivāsa was the disciple of Kauṇḍinya Śrīnivāsa Dīkṣita, the son of Śrīnivāsa Tātācārya, and the brother of Anvayārya Dīkṣita. He was very much influenced by the writings of his elder brother Anvayārya and some of his works are but elaborations of the works of his elder brother who wrote many books, e.g. *Virodha-bhañjanī*, etc. Śaila Śrīnivāsa wrote at least six books: *Virodha-nirodha*, *Bheda-darpaṇa*, *Advaita-vana-kuṭhāra*, *Sāra-darpaṇa*, *Mukti-darpaṇa*, *Jñāna-ratna-darpaṇa*, *Guṇa-darpaṇa*, and *Bheda-maṇi*.

[1] *Kāryā-dhikaraṇa-vāda*, II. 7.

In his *Virodha-nirodha*, probably the last of his works, he tries mainly to explain away the criticisms that are made on the different Rāmānuja doctrines by the Śaṅkarites, and also by the writers of other Vedāntic schools—viz. that the Rāmānuja views are not strictly faithful to the scriptural texts—by showing that the scriptural texts favour the Rāmānuja interpretations and not the views of the other Vedāntic writers.

In the first chapter of the *Virodha-nirodha* Śaila Śrīnivāsa first takes up the view that the Brahman is both the material and efficient cause of the world—which he thinks is possible only in the conception that Brahman has the individual souls and the matter-stuff associated with Him (*brahmaṇi cid-acid-viśiṣṭa-rūpatām antareṇa na ghaṭate*). The Brahman remains unchanged in itself but suffers transformations through its two parts, the soul and the matter-stuff. Brahman as cause is associated with souls and the matter-stuff in their subtle forms, and when it undergoes transformation the souls expand and broaden as it were through the various intellectual states as a result of their *karma*, and the matter-stuff passes through its grosser stages as the visible material world; the portion of God as the inner controller of these two suffers transformation only so far as it is possible through its association with these two transforming entities[1]. When the scriptural texts deny the changing character of the Brahman, all that is meant by them is that it does not undergo the changes through which matter and individual souls pass through their *karma*, but that does not deny the fact that Brahman is the material cause[2]. Brahman has two parts, a substantive and a qualifying part, and it is the substantive part that through its subtle material parts becomes the transforming cause of the grosser qualifying material part. This material part being inseparable from Brahman may be regarded as subsisting in it. So also the Brahman has a spiritual part which undergoes a sort of expansion through thought-experiences and behaves as individual souls. Thus Brahman suffers modification through its physical and spiritual parts, and from this point of view God is

[1] *acid-aṃśasya kāraṇā-vasthāyāṃ śabdā-di-vihīnasya bhogyatvāya śabdā-di-mattvayā svarūpā-nyathā-bhāva-rūpa-vikāro bhavaṭi ubhaya-prakāra-viśiṣṭe niyantṛ-aṃśe tad-avastha-tad-ubhaya-viśiṣṭatā-rūpa-vikāro bhavati. Virodha-nirodha.* MS.

[2] *cid-acid-gata-karmā-dy-adhīna-vikāratvaṃ nirvikāratva-śrutir niṣedhati ity etādṛśaṃ jagad-upādānatvaṃ na sā śrutir bādhate. Ibid.*

subject to development through its two parts and through their association independently as their inner controller. Unlike Veṅkaṭa, Śaila Śrīnivāsa holds that this causal transformation is like the Sāṃkhyist causal transformation[1]; *vikāra* or change here means change of states. Brahman thus suffers change directly in the spiritual and the intellectual part and indirectly as their inner controller, though in itself it suffers no change. To the objection that if matter and spirit are regarded as suffering transformation there is no meaning in attributing causality to Brahman as qualified by them, the reply is that the causality of Brahman is admitted on the strength of scriptural testimony. So far as Brahman remains as the inner controller and does not suffer any change in itself, it is regarded as the efficient cause[2].

In the second chapter Śaila Śrīnivāsa replies to the criticisms against the Rāmānuja doctrine of soul, and says that the contraction and expansion of soul due to ignorance and increase of knowledge does not imply that it is non-eternal, for non-eternality or destructibility can be affirmed only of those who undergo accretion or decrease of parts (*avayavo-pacayā-pacayayor eva anityatva-vyāpyatayā*). Knowledge is partless and so there is no contraction or expansion of it in any real sense. What are called contraction and expansion consist in reality of its absence of relationship with objects due to the effects of *karma* or the natural extension of relations with objects like the ray of a lamp; *karma* is thus regarded as the *upādhi* (limiting condition) which limits the natural flow of knowledge to its objects and is figuratively described as contraction. It is on account of this nature of knowledge that unless obstructed by *karma* it can grasp all sensations of pain and pleasure spreading over all parts of the body, though it belongs to soul which is an atomic entity. So knowledge is all-pervading (*vibhu*)[3]. Knowledge also is eternal in its own nature though changeful so far as its states are concerned.

In the third chapter Śrīnivāsa deals with the question as to

[1] *viśiṣṭaṃ brahma kāraṇam ity uktaṃ tena kāryam api viśiṣṭaṃ eva tatra ca brahmaṇa upādānatvaṃ viśeṣaṇā-ṃśaṃ viśeṣyā-ṃśaṃ prati tatra cā'cid-aṃśaṃ prati yad-upādānatvaṃ tat sūkṣmā-vasthā-cid-aṃśa-dvārakaṃ tatra tatra dvāra-bhūtā-cid-aṃśa-gata-svarūpā nyathā-bhāva-rūpa eve vikāraḥ sa ca apṛthak-siddha-vastu-gatatvāt brahma-gato'pi...evaṃ ca sāṃkhyā-bhimato-pādānatāyāḥ siddhānte'py anapāyāt na ko'pi virodhaḥ. Virodha-nirodha.* MS.

[2] *tena tad eva advārakaṃ nimittaṃ-sad-vārakaṃ upādānam. Ibid.*

[3] *Ibid.*

whether the souls are produced or eternal, and his conclusion is that in their own nature they are unproduced, but they are produced so far as their own specific data of knowledge are concerned[1]. The production of eternal knowledge is possible only so far as its contraction and expansion are concerned, which is due to the action of the body and other accessories. It is only in this sense that knowledge though eternal in itself can be said to be suffering production through its various kinds of manifestation (*abhivyakti*).

In the fourth chapter Śrīnivāsa discusses the same question in which the Upaniṣads urge that by the knowledge of one everything is known. He criticizes the Madhva and the Śaṅkarite views and holds that the knowledge of one means the knowledge of Brahman which, being always associated with the individual souls and matter, involves the knowledge of these two entities. His exposition in this subject is based throughout on the interpretations of scriptural texts.

In the fifth chapter Śrīnivāsa explains the same question in which the individual souls can be called agents (*kartā*). Agency (*kartṛtva*) consists in an effort that may lead to the production of any action (*kāryā-nukūla kṛtimattvam*). In the Rāmānuja view effort means a particular intellectual state and as such it may well belong to the soul, and so the effort that may lead to any action also belongs to the soul which, though eternal in itself, is changeful so far as its states are concerned[2]. The agency of the individual souls, however, is controlled by God, though the fruits of the action are enjoyed by the former, for the direction of God which determines the efforts of the individuals is in accordance with their actions. This virtually means an admixture of determinism and occasionalism.

In the seventh chapter Śrīnivāsa contends that though knowledge is universal it only manifests itself in accordance with the deeds of any particular person in association with his body, and so there is no possibility that it should have all kinds of sufferings and enjoyments and should not be limited to his own series of experiences. In the eighth and ninth chapters he tries to establish

[1] *tatra niṣedhāḥ viyad-ādivat jīva-svarūpo-tpattiṃ pratiṣedhanti utpatti-vidhayaas tu svā-sādhāraṇa-dharma-bhūta-jñāna-viśiṣṭa-veṣeṇa utpattiṃ vadanti. Virodha-nirodha.* MS.

[2] *prayatnā-der buddhi-viśeṣa-rūpatayā kāryā-nukūla-kṛtimattvasy'āpi kartṛtvasya jñāna-viśeṣa-rūpatayā tasya svābhā vikatayā tad-ātmanā jīvasya jñānasya nityatve'pi tat-pariṇāma-viśeṣasya anityatvāt. Ibid.*.

the view that during emancipation the individuals are cleanly purged of all their deeds, virtues and sins, but at this stage God may be pleased to endow them with extraordinary bodies for the enjoyment of various kinds of pleasures. In the remaining nineteen chapters Śaila Śrīnivāsa introduces some of the relatively unimportant theological doctrines of the Rāmānuja system and discusses them on the basis of scriptural texts which may very well be dropped for their insignificance as philosophical contribution.

In the *Bheda-darpaṇa* also Śaila Śrīnivāsa takes some of the important doctrines where the Rāmānujists and the Śaṅkarites part company, and tries to show by textual criticism that the Rāmānuja interpretation of the scriptural texts is the only correct interpretation[1]. The work, therefore, is absolutely worthless from a philosophical point of view. In most of his other works mentioned above, Śaila Śrīnivāsa prefers to discuss the doctrines of Rāmānuja philosophy in the same style of scriptural criticism, and any account of these is therefore of very little value to students of philosophy.

Śrī Śaila Śrīnivāsa, in his *Siddhānta-cintāmaṇi*, discusses the nature of Brahma-causality. Brahman is both the instrumental (*nimitta*) and the material (*upādāna*) cause of the world. Such a Brahman is the object of our meditation (*dhyāna*). An object of meditation must have knowledge and will. A mere qualityless entity cannot be the object of meditation. In order that Brahman may be properly meditated upon it is necessary that the nature of His causality should be properly ascertained. It is no use to attribute false qualities for the sake of meditation. If the world is an illusion, then the causality of Brahman is also illusory, and that would give us an insight into His real nature. If God is the real cause of the world, the world must also be real. It is sometimes said that the same entity cannot be both a material and instrumental cause (*samavāya-samavāyi-bhinnaṃ kāraṇaṃ nimitta-kāraṇamiti*). The material cause of the jar is earth, while the instrumental cause is the potter, the wheel, etc. To this the reply is that such an objection is groundless; for it is difficult to assert that that which is an instrumental cause cannot be a material cause, since the wheel of the potter, though an instrumental cause in itself, is also the material

[1] *bhedā-bheda-śruti-vrāta-jāta-sandeha-santatāḥ*
bheda-darpaṇam ādāya niścinvantu vipaścitaḥ.
Bheda-darpaṇa. MS.

cause of its own form, colour, etc. There is thus nothing which can lead us to suppose that the material cause and the instrumental cause cannot exist together in the same entity. It may further be contended that the same entity cannot behave as the material and instrumental cause with regard to the production of another entity. To this the reply is that the internal structure of rod is both the material cause for its form as well as the instrumental cause for its destruction in association with other entities. Or it may be contended that time (*kāla*) is the cause for both the production and destruction of entities (*kāla-ghaṭa-saṃyogā-dikaṃ prati kālasya nimittatvād upādānatvācca*). To this the obvious reply would be that the behaviour of the same entity as the material and the instrumental cause is limited by separate specific conditions in each case. The association of separate specific conditions renders a difference in the nature of the cause; and therefore it would be inexact to say that the same entity is both the material and the instrumental cause. This objection, however, produces more difficulty in the conception of the causality of Brahman according to the *Viśiṣṭādvaita* theory, for in our view Brahman in His own nature may be regarded as the instrumental cause and in His nature as matter (*acit*) and souls (*cit*). He may be regarded as the material cause[1]. It is sometimes objected that if Brahman as described in the texts is changeless, how can He be associated with changes as required by the conception of Him as the material and instrumental cause, which involves the view of associating Him with a body? Moreover, the association of body (*śarīra*) with God is neither an analogy nor an imagery. The general conception of body involves the idea that an entity is called the body where it is only controlled by some spiritual substance[2]. To this the reply is that Brahman may Himself remain unchangeable and may yet be the cause of changes in His twofold body-substance. The objection is that the material world is so different from the bodies of animals that the conception of body cannot be directly applied to it. The reply is that even among animal bodies there is a large amount of diversity,

[1] *evaṃ hi brahmaṇy'api no'pādānatva-nimittatvayor virodhaḥ; tasya cid-acid-viśiṣṭa-veṣeṇa upādānatvāt svarūpeṇa nimittatvāc ca. tat-tad-avacchedaka-bheda-prayukta-tad-bhedasya tasya tatrā'pi niṣpratyūhavtāt. Siddhānta-cintāmaṇi.* MS.

[2] *yasya cetanasya yad dravyaṃ sarvā-tmanā svārthe niyāmyam tat tasya śarīram. Ibid.* This subject has been dealt with elaborately in Śrī Śaila Śrīnivāsa's *Sāra-darpaṇa.*

e.g. the body of a man and the body of a microscopic insect. Under the circumstances we are to fall upon a general definition which would cover the concept of all bodies and ignore the individual differences. The definition given above suits the concept of bodies of all living beings and applies also to the concept of the world as the body of Brahman. This is also supported by the *Śruti* texts of the *Antaryāmi-brāhmaṇa*, where the world has been spoken of as the body of God. If there is an apparent difference in our conception of body as indicated in the definition as testified by the Vedic texts, with our ordinary perception of the world which does not reveal its nature as body, the testimony of the Vedic texts should prevail; for while our perception can be explained away as erroneous, a scientific definition and the testimony of texts cannot be dismissed. Our ordinary perception is not always reliable. We perceive the moon like a small dish in size, whereas the scriptural testimony reveals its nature to us as much bigger. When there is a conflict between two sources of evidence, the decision is to be made in favour of one or the other by the canon of unconditionality (*ananyathā-siddhatva*). An evidence which is unconditional in its nature has to be relied upon, whereas that which is conditional has to be subordinated to it. It is in accordance with this that sometimes the Vedic texts have to be interpreted in such a manner that they may not contradict perceptual experience, whereas in other cases the evidence of perceptual experience has to be dismissed on the strength of scriptural testimony. It cannot also be said that the evidence of a later *pramāṇa* will have greater force, for there may be a series of errors, in which case there is no certitude in any of the later *pramāṇas*. Again, there is no force also in mere cumulation of evidence, for in the case of a blind man leading other blind men mere cumulation is no guarantee of certitude[1]. In the case of the conflict of *pramāṇas*, the dissolution of doubt and the attainment of certitude are achieved on the principle of unconditionality. That which is realized in an unconditional manner should be given precedence over what is realized only in a conditional manner[2]. Our powers of perception are limited by their own limitations and can-

[1] *na ca paratvād uttareṇa purva-bādhaḥ iti yuktaṃ dhārā-vāhika-bhrama-sthale vyabhicārāt ata eva na bhūyastvam api nirṇāyakaṃ śatā'ndha-nyāyena aprayojakatvāc ca. Siddhānta-cintāmaṇi.* MS.

[2] *ananyathā-siddhatvam eva virodhy-aprāmāṇya-vyavasthā pakatā-vacchedakam iṣyate. Ibid.*

not therefore discern whether the world may after all be the body of the transcendent Brahman, and therefore it cannot successfully contradict the testimony of the Vedic texts which declare the world to be the body of God. The Vedic texts of pure monism are intended only to deny the duality of Brahman, but it can well be interpreted on the supposition of one Brahman as associated with his body, the world. The denial of dualism only means the denial of any other being like Brahman. Thus Brahman as *cit* and *acit* forms the material cause of the world, and Brahman as idea and will as affecting these is the instrumental cause of the world. The twofold causality of Brahman thus refers to twofold conditions as stated above which exist together in Brahman[1].

In the Vedāntic texts we have expressions in the ablative case indicating the fact that the world has proceeded out of Brahman as the material cause (*upādāna*). The ablative case always signifies the materiality of the cause and not its instrumentality[2]. But it also denotes that the effect comes out of the cause and it may be objected that the world, being always in Brahman and not outside Him, the ablative expressions of the Vedāntic texts cannot be justified. To this the reply is that the conception of material cause or the signification of the ablative cause does not necessarily mean that the effect should come out and be spatially or temporally differentiated from the cause. Even if this were its meaning, it may well be conceived that there are subtle parts in Brahman corresponding to *cit* and *acit* in their manifested forms, and it is from these that the world has evolved in its manifested form. Such an evolution does not mean that the effect should stand entirely outside the cause, for when the entire causal substance is transformed, the effect cannot be spatially outside the cause[3]. It is true that all

[1] *sarva-śarīra-bhūtā-vibhakta-nāma-rūpā-vasthā panna-cid-acid-viśiṣta-veṣeṇa brahmaṇaḥ upādānatvam; tad-upayukta-saṃkalpā-di-viśiṣṭa-svarūpeṇa nimittatvaṃ ca niṣpratyūham iti nimittatvo-pādānatvayor ihā' py avacchedaka-bheda-prayukta-bhedasya durapahnavatvā ttayor ekāśraya-vṛttitvasya prāg upapāditatvāt na brahmaṇo abhinna-nimitto-pādānatve kaś cid virodhaḥ. Siddhānta-cintāmaṇi.* MS.

[2] Such as *yato vā imāni bhūtāni jāyante.*

[3] *upādānatva-sthale'pi na sarvatra loke'pi viśleṣaḥ kṛtsna-pariṇāme tad asambhavāt kintv ekadeśa-pariṇāma eve'ti tad-abhiprāyakaṃ pratyākhyānaṃ vācyam. tac ce'hā' pi sambhavati. viśiṣṭai-kadeśa-pariṇāmā-ṅgīkārāt. ato na tad-virodpaḥ; kiñca sūkṣma-cid-acid-viśiṣṭam upādānatvam iti vakṣyate tasmāc ca sthūlā-vasthasya viśleṣo yujyate viśleṣo hi na sarvā-tmanā kāraṇa-deśa-parityāgaḥ. Ibid.* MS.

material causes suffer a transformation; but in the *Viśiṣṭādvaita* view there is no difficulty, for it is held here that Brahman suffers this modification and controls it only so far as it has reference to his body, the *cit* and *acit*. God's instrumentality is through His will, and will is but a form of knowledge.

In the *Bheda-darpaṇa* Śrīnivāsa tries to support all the principal contentions of the *Viśiṣṭādvaita* theory by a reference to Upaniṣadic and other scriptural texts. In his other works mentioned above the subjects that he takes up for discussion are almost the same as those treated in *Virodha-nirodha*, but the method of treatment is somewhat different; what is treated briefly in one book is elaborately discussed in another, just as the problem of causality is the main topic of discussion in *Siddhānta-cintāmaṇi*, though it has been only slightly touched upon in *Virodha-nirodha*. His *Naya-dyu-maṇi-saṃgraha* is a brief summary in verse and prose of the contents of what the author wrote in his *Naya-dyu-maṇi*, a much bigger work to which constant references are made in the *Naya-dyu-maṇi-saṃgraha*. Śrī Śaila Śrīnivāsa wrote also another work called *Naya-dyu-maṇi-dipikā* which is bigger than *Naya-dyu-maṇi-saṃgraha*. It is probably smaller than *Naya-dyu-maṇi*, which is referred to as a big work[1]. There is nothing particular to be noted which is of any philosophical importance in *Naya-dyu-maṇi-dipikā* or *Naya-dyu-maṇi-saṃgraha*. He generally clarifies the ideas which are already contained in the *Śruta-prakāśikā* of Sudarśana Sūri. He also wrote *Oṃkāra-vādārtha*, *Ānandatāra-tamya-khaṇḍana*, *Arunādhikaraṇa-saraṇi-vivaraṇī* and *Jijñāsā-darpaṇa*. He lived probably in the fifteenth century.

Śrīnivāsa wrote first his *Sāra-darpaṇa* which was followed by *Siddhānta-cintāmaṇi*, and *Virodha-nirodha*. In fact *Virodha-nirodha* was one of his last works, if not the last. In the first chapter of this work he deals with the same subject as he did in the *Siddhānta-cintāmaṇi*, and tries to explain the nature of Brahman as the material and instrumental cause of the world. In the second chapter he tries to refute the objections against the view that the souls as associated with knowledge or rather as having their character interpreted as knowledge should be regarded as the means for God's manifestation as the world. The objector says that thought is always moving, either expanding or contracting, and as such it can-

[1] Unfortunately this *Naya-dyu-maṇi* was not available to the present writer.

not be the nature of self which is regarded as eternal. In the case of the Jains the soul is regarded as contracting and expanding in accordance with the body that it occupies, and it may rightly be objected that in such a conception the soul has to be regarded as non-eternal. But in the *Viśiṣṭādvaita* conception it is only thought that is regarded as expanding or contracting. The expansion or contraction of thought means that it conceives greater or lesser things, and this is different from the idea of an entity that grows larger or smaller by the accretion or dissociation of parts. The expansion or contraction of thought is due to one's *karma* and as such it cannot be regarded as non-eternal. Knowledge in its own nature is without parts and all-pervading; its contraction is due to the effect of one's bad deeds which is often called *māyā* or *avidyā*[1]. The *Viśiṣṭādvaitins* do not regard knowledge as produced through the collocations of conditions as the *Naiyāyikas* think, but they regard it as eternal and yet behaving as occasional (*āgantuka-dharmavattvam*) or as being produced. Earth in its own nature is eternal, and remaining eternal in its own nature suffers transformation as a jug, etc. In this way the conception of the eternity of the soul is different from the conception of knowledge as eternal, for in the case of knowledge, while remaining all-pervasive in itself, it seems to suffer transformation by virtue of the hindrances that obstruct its nature in relation to objects[2]. Universal relationship is the essential nature of knowledge, but this nature may be obstructed by hindrances, in which case the sphere of relationship is narrowed, and it is this narrowing and expansive action of knowledge which is spoken of as transformation of knowledge or as the rise or cessation of knowledge. A distinction has thus to be made between knowledge as process and knowledge as essence. In its nature as essence it is the eternal self; in its nature as process, as memory, perception, thinking, etc., it is changing. The Jaina objection on this point is that in the above view it is unnecessary to admit a special quality of *ajñāna* as the cause for this expansion or contraction of thought, for it may well be admitted that the soul itself undergoes such a

[1] *jñānasya svābhāvikam prasaraṇam aupadhikas tu saṁkocaḥ; upādhis tu prācīnaṃ karma eva. Virodha-nirodha*, pp. 39, 40 (MS.).

[2] *na hi yādṛśam ātmano nityatvam tādṛg jñānasyā'pi nityatvam abhyapugacchāmaḥ karaṇa-vyāpāra-vaiyarthy, prasaṅgāt. kintu tārkikā'dy abhimataṃ jñānasya āgantuka-dharmatvaṃ ni ākartuṃ dṛśer iva svarūpato nityatvam āgantukā'-vasthā'-śrayatvaṃ ca; tena rūpeṇa nityatvaṃ tu ghaṭatvā'-dy-avasthā-viśiṣta-veṣeṇa mṛdāderiva iṣṭam eva. Ibid.* p. 44.

transformation through the instrumentality of its deeds. To this the reply is that the Vedic texts always declare that the soul is in itself unchangeable, and if that is so the change has to be explained through the instrumentality of another factor, the *ajñāna*. Knowledge is thus to be regarded as the pure essence or nature of the soul and not as its *dharma* or character, and it is this character that is in itself universal and yet is observed to undergo change on account of obstructions. Thus, the soul in itself is eternal, though when looked at in association with its character as knowledge which is continually expanding or contracting it may seemingly appear to be non-eternal[1]. Thought in itself has no parts and therefore cannot itself be regarded as non-eternal. It is nothing but relationship, and as such the analogy of change which, in other objects, determines their non-eternity cannot apply to it.

Now there are different kinds of Upaniṣadic texts, from some of which it may appear that the soul is eternal, whereas from others it may appear that the soul is created. How can this difficulty be avoided? On this point Śrīnivāsa says that the eternity and uncreated nature of the self is a correct assertion, for the soul as such is eternal and has never been created. In its own nature also the soul has thought associated with it as it were in a potential form. Such an unmanifested thought is non-existent. But knowledge in its growing richness of relations is an after-production, and it is from this point of view that the soul may be regarded as having been created. Even that which is eternal may be regarded as created with reference to any of its special characteristics or characters[2]. The whole idea, therefore, is that before the creative action of God the souls are only potentially conscious; their real conscious activity is only a result of later development in consequence of God's creative action.

Again, the Upaniṣads assert that by the knowledge of Brahman everything else is known. Now according to the Śaṅkarite explanation the whole world is but a magical creation on Brahman which alone has real being. Under the circumstances it is impossible that

[1] *nityā-nitya-vibhāga-svarūpa-dvārakatva-svabhāva-dvārakatvābhyāṃ vyavasthita iti na kaś cid doṣaḥ. Virodha-nirodha.* MS.

[2] *svā-sādhāraṇa-dharma-bhūta-jñāna-viśiṣṭa-veṣeṇa utpattiṃ vadanti siddhasyā'pi hi vastunaḥ dharmā-ntara-viśiṣṭa-veṣeṇa sādhyatā vrīhyā-dau dṛṣṭā. Ibid.*

prāk sṛṣṭer jīvānāṃ niṣkriyatvo-ktyā ca idam eva darśitam. Ibid.

by the knowledge of Brahman, the real, there would be the knowledge of all illusory and unreal creation, for these two, the reality and the appearance, are entirely different and therefore by the knowledge of one there cannot be the knowledge of the other. In the *Viśiṣṭādvaita* view it may be said that when God as associated with his subtle body, the subtle causal nature of the souls and the material world, is known the knowledge of God as associated with the grosser development of His body as souls and the world is also by that means realized[1].

In performing the actions it need not be supposed that the eternal soul undergoes any transformation, for the individual soul may remain identically unchanged in itself and yet undergo transformation so far as the process of its knowledge is concerned. In the *Viśiṣṭādvaita* view, will and desire are regarded as but modes of knowledge and as such the psychological transformations of the mind involved in the performance of actions have reference only to knowledge[2]. It has already been shown that possibly knowledge in its essential form is unchangeable and yet unchangeable so far as its nature as process is concerned. Such an activity and performance of actions belongs naturally to the individual souls.

The *Virodha-nirodha* is written in twenty-seven chapters, but most of these are devoted to the refutation of objections raised by opponents on questions of theological dogma which have no philosophical interest. These have therefore been left out in this book.

Raṅgācārya[3].

A follower of Śaṅkara named Umā-Maheśvara wrote a work named *Virodha-varūthinī* in which he proposed to show one hundred contradictions in Rāmānuja's *bhāṣya* and other cognate

[1] *sūkṣma-cid-acic-charīrake brahmaṇi jñāte sthūla-cid-acic-charīrakasya tasya jñānam atrā' bhimatam. Virodha-nirodha.* MS.

[2] *iha prayatnāder buddhi-viśeṣa-rūpatayā kāryā-nukūla-kṛtimattvasyā'pi kartṛtvasya jñāna-viśeṣa-rūpatayā tasya svābhāvikatayā tad-ātmanā jīvasya jñānasya nityatve'pi tat-pariṇāma-viśeṣasya anityatvāc ca. Ibid.*

[3] "*śrī-rāmānuja-yogi-pāda-kamala-sthānā-bhiṣekaṃ gato jīyāt so'yam*
ananta-puruṣa-guru-siṃhāsanā-dhīśvaraḥ
śrī-raṅga-sūriḥ śrīśaile tasya siṃhāsane sthitaḥ
Ku-dṛṣṭi-dhvānta-mārtaṇḍaṃ prakāśayati samprati."

He was thus a disciple of Anantārya of the middle of the nineteenth century. At the end of his *San-mārga-dīpa* he says that it was written in refutation of Rāma Miśra's work on the subject. Rāma Miśra lived late in the nineteenth century and wrote *Sneha-pūrti.*

literature of the school, such as *Śatadūsaṇī*, etc., but through illness he lost his tongue and could offer criticisms on only twenty-seven points[1]. As a refutation of that work Raṅgācārya wrote his *Ku-dṛṣṭi-dhvānta-mārtaṇḍa.* It also appears that Annayārya's grandson and Śrīnivāsa-tāyārya's son, Śrīnivāsa-dīkṣita, also wrote a work called *Virodha-varūthinī-pramāthinī* as a refutation of *Virodha-varūthinī.* The first chapter of *Ku-dṛṣṭi-dhvānta-mārtaṇḍa* is also called *Virodha-varūthinī-pramāthinī.*

Umā-Maheśvara says that according to the view of Rāmānuja the manifold world and the individual souls (*acit* and *cit*) exist in an undivided and subtle state in Brahman, the original cause. In the state of actualized transformation, as the manifested manifold worlds and the experiencing selves, we have thus a change of state, and as Brahman holds within Himself as qualifying Him this gross transformation of the world He is associated with them. He must, therefore, be supposed to have Himself undergone change. But again Rāmānuja refers to many scriptural texts in which Brahman is regarded as unchanging.

To this the reply is that the mode in which the *cit* and the *acit* undergo transformation is different from the mode in which the all-controlling Brahman produces those changes in them. For this reason the causality of Brahman remains unaffected by the changes through which the *cit* and the *acit* pass. It is this unaffectedness of Brahma-causality that has often been described as the changelessness of Brahman. In the Śaṅkara view, the manifested world being the transformation of *māyā*, Brahman cannot on any account be regarded as a material cause of it. The Brahman of Śaṅkara being only pure consciousness, no instrumental agencies (*nimitta-kāranatā*) can be attributed to it. If Brahman cannot undergo any change in any manner and if it always remains absolutely changeless it can never be regarded as cause. Causality implies power of producing change or undergoing change. If both these are impossible in Brahman it cannot consistently be regarded as the cause. According to the Rāmānuja view, however, Brahman is not absolutely changeless; for, as producer of change it also itself undergoes a change homogeneous (*brahma-samasattāka-vikārā-ṅgīkārāt*) with

[1] Umā-Maheśvara is said to have written other works also, i.e. *Tattva-candrikā, Advaita-kāmadhenu, Tapta-mudrā-vidrāvaṇa, Prasaṅga-ratnākara,* and *Rāmāyana-tīkā.*

it. As the change is of a homogeneous nature, it may also be regarded as unchanged. The Brahman is the ultimate upholder of the world; though the worldly things have their intermediate causes, in which they may be regarded as subsisting, yet since Brahman is the ultimate and absolute locus of subsistence all things are said to be upheld in it.

Causation may be defined as unconditional, invariable antecedence (*ananyathā-siddha-niyata-pūrva-vartitā*). Brahman is certainly the ultimate antecedent entity of all things, and its unconditional character is testified by all scriptural texts. The fact that it determines the changes in *cit* and *acit* and is therefore to be regarded as the instrumental agent does not divest it of its right to be regarded as the material cause; for it alone is the ultimate antecedent substance. Brahman originally holds within itself the *cit* and the *acit* in their subtle nature as undivided in itself, and later on undergoes within itself such changes by its own will as to allow the transformation of *cit* and *acit* in their gross manifested forms. It leaves its pristine homogeneous character and adopts an altered state at least with reference to its true parts, the *cit* and the *acit*, which in their subtle state remained undivided in themselves. It is this change of Brahman's nature that is regarded as the *pariṇāma* of Brahman. Since Brahman is thus admitted to be undergoing change of state (*pariṇāma*), it can consistently be regarded as the material cause of the world. The illustration of the ocean and the waves is also consistent with such an explanation. Just as mud transforms itself into earthen jugs or earthen pots, and yet in spite of all its changes into jugs or pots really remains nothing but mud, so Brahman also undergoes changes in the form of the manifested world with which it can always be regarded as one[1]. As the jug and the pot are not false, so the world also is not false. But the true conception of the world will be to consider it as one with Brahman. The upper and the lower parts of a jug may appear to be different when they are not regarded as parts of the jug, and

[1] *vahu syāṃ prajāyeye'tyā-di-śrutibhiḥ sṛṣṭeḥ prāñ nāma-rūpa-vibhāgā-bhāvena ekatvā-vasthāpannasya sūkṣma-cid-acid-viśiṣṭa-brahmaṇaḥ paścān-nāma-rūpa-vibhāgena ekatvā-vasthā-prahāṇa-pūrvakaṃ sthūla-cid-acid-vaiśiṣṭya-lakṣaṇa-vahutvā-pattir-hi prasphuṭaṃ pratipādyate; sai'va hi brahmaṇaḥ pariṇāmo nāma; prāg-avasthā-prahāṇenā' vasthā-ntara-prāpter eva pariṇāma-sabdā-rthatvāt.... yathā sarvaṃ mṛd-dravya-vikṛti-bhūtaṃ ghaṭā-di-kārya-jātaṃ kāraṇa-bhūta-mṛd-dravyā-bhinname va na tu dravyā-ntaraṃ tathā brahmā'pi jagataḥ abhinnam eva. Ku-dṛṣṭi-dhvānta-mārtaṇḍa*, p. 66.

in that condition to consider them as two would be false; for they attain their meaning only when they are taken as the parts of one whole jug. When the Upaniṣads say that plurality is false, the import of the text is that plurality attains its full meaning only in its unified conception as parts of God, the Absolute.

The Śaṅkarites do not admit the theory of illusion as one thing appearing as another (*anyathā-khyāti*). According to them illusion consists in the production of an indefinable illusory object. Such an object appears to a person only at a particular moment when he commits an error of perception. It cannot be proved that the illusory object was not present at the time of the commission of illusory perception. Under the circumstances the absence of that object at other times cannot prove its falsity; for an object present at one time and not present at another cannot indicate its false nature. Falsity has then to be defined as relative to the perceiver at the time of perception. When the perceiver has knowledge of the true object, and knows also that one object is being perceived as another object, he is aware of the falsity of his perception. But if at the time of perception he has only one kind of knowledge and he is not aware of any contradiction, his perception at any time cannot be regarded as false. But since the dream experiences are not known to be self-contradictory in the same stage, the experience of conch-shell-silver is not known to be illusory at the time of the illusion; and as the world experience is uncontradicted at the time of our waking consciousness, it cannot be regarded as false in the respective stages of experience. The falsehood of the dream experiences therefore is only relative to the experience of another stage at another time. In such a view of the Śaṅkarites everything becomes relative, and there is no positive certainty regarding the experience of any stage. According to the Buddhists and their scriptures, the notion of Brahman is also false; and thus, if we consider their experience, the notion of Brahman is also relatively true. In such a view we are necessarily landed in a state of uncertainty from which there is no escape[1].

[1] Raṅgācārya wrote at least one other work called *San-mārga-dīpa* which, being of a ritualistic nature, does not warrant any treatment in this work.

CHAPTER XXI

THE NIMBĀRKA SCHOOL OF PHILOSOPHY

Teachers and Pupils of the Nimbārka School.

NIMBĀRKA, Nimbāditya or Niyamānanda is said to have been a Telugu Brahmin who probably lived in Nimba or Nimbapura in the Bellary district. It is said in Harivyāsadeva's commentary on *Daśa-ślokī* that his father's name was Jagannātha and his mother's name was Sarasvatī. But it is difficult to fix his exact date. Sir R. G. Bhandarkar, in his *Vaiṣṇavism, Śaivism and Minor Religious Systems*, thinks that he lived shortly after Rāmānuja. The argument that he adduces is as follows: Harivyāsadeva is counted in the *Guru-paramparā* list as the thirty-second teacher in succession from Nimbārka, and Bhandarkar discovered a manuscript containing this list which was written in Samvat 1806 or A.D. 1750 when Dāmodara Gosvāmī was living. Allowing fifteen years for the life of Dāmodara Gosvāmī we have A.D. 1765. Now the thirty-third successor from Madhva died in A.D. 1876 and Madhva died in A.D. 1276. Thus thirty-three successive teachers, on the Madhva line, occupied 600 years. Applying the same test and deducting 600 years from A.D. 1765, the date of the thirty-third successor, we have 1165 as the date of Nimbārka. This, therefore, ought to be regarded as the date of Nimbārka's death and it means that he died sometime after Rāmānuja and might have been his junior contemporary. Bhandarkar would thus put roughly eighteen years as the pontifical period for each teacher. But Pandit Kiśoradāsa says that in the lives of teachers written by Pandit Anantarām Devācārya the twelfth teacher from Nimbārka was born in Samvat 1112 or A.D. 1056, and applying the same test of eighteen years for each teacher we have A.D. 868 as the date of Nimbārka, in which case he is to be credited with having lived long before Rāmānuja. But from the internal examination of the writings of Nimbārka and Śrīnivāsa this would appear to be hardly credible. Again, in the *Catalogue of Sanskrit Manuscripts in the Private Libraries of the North Western Provinces*, Part I, Benares, 1874 (or *N.W.P. Catalogue*, MS. No. 274), *Madhva-mukha-mardana*, deposited in the

Madan Mohan Library, Benares, is attributed to Nimbārka. This manuscript is not procurable on loan and has not been available to the present writer. But if the account of the authors of the *Catalogue* is to be believed, Nimbārka is to be placed after Madhva. One argument in support of this later date is to be found in the fact that Mādhava who lived in the fourteenth century did not make any reference in his *Sarva-darśana-saṃgraha*, to Nimbārka's system, though he referred to all important systems of thought known at the time. If Nimbārka had lived before the fourteenth century there would have been at least some reference to him in the *Sarva-darśana-saṃgraha*, or by some of the writers of that time. Dr Rajendra Lal Mitra, however, thinks that since Nimbārka refers to the schools (*sampradāya*) of Śrī, Brahmā and Sanaka, he lived later than Rāmānuja, Madhva and even Vallabha. While there is no positive, definite evidence that Nimbārka lived after Vallabha, yet from the long list of teachers of his school it probably would not be correct to attribute a very recent date to him. Again, on the assumption that the *Madhva-mukha-mardana* was really written by him as testified in the *N.W.P. Catalogue*, one would be inclined to place him towards the latter quarter of the fourteenth or the beginning of the fifteenth century. Considering the fact that there have been up till now about forty-three teachers from the time of Nimbārka, this would mean that the pontifical period of each teacher was on the average about ten to twelve years, which is not improbable. An internal analysis of Nimbārka's philosophy shows its great indebtedness to Rāmānuja's system and even the style of Nimbārka's *bhāṣya* in many places shows that it was modelled upon the style of approach adopted by Rāmānuja in his *bhāṣya*. This is an additional corroboration of the fact that Nimbārka must have lived after Rāmānuja.

The works attributed to him are as follows: (1) *Vedānta-pārijāta-saurabha*. (2) *Daśa-ślokī*. (3) *Kṛṣṇa-stava-rāja*. (4) *Guru-paramparā*. (5) *Madhva-mukha-mardana*. (6) *Vedānta-tattva-bodha*. (7) *Vedānta-siddhānta-pradīpa*. (8) *Sva-dharmā-dhva-bodha*. (9) *Śrī-kṛṣṇa-stava*. But excepting the first three works all the rest exist in MS. most of which are not procurable[1]. Of these the present writer

[1] *Vedānta-tattva-bodha* exists in the *Oudh Catalogue*, 1877, 42 and VIII. 24, compiled by Pandit Deviprasad.

Vedānta-siddhānta-pradīpa and *Sva-dharmā-dhva-bodha* occur in the *Notices*

could secure only the *Sva-dharmā-dhva-bodha*, which is deposited with the Bengal Asiatic Society. It is difficult to say whether this work was actually written by Nimbārka. In any case it must have been considerably manipulated by some later followers of the Nimbārka school, since it contains several verses interspersed, in which Nimbārka is regarded as an *avatāra* and salutations are offered to him. He is also spoken of in the third person, and views are expressed as being *Nimbārka-matam* which could not have come from the pen of Nimbārka. The book contains reference to the *Kevala-bheda-vādī* which must be a reference to the Madhva school. It is a curious piece of work, containing various topics, partly related and partly unrelated, in a very unmethodical style. It contains references to the various schools of asceticism and religion.

In the *Guru-paramparā* list found in the *Har-iguru-stava-mālā* noted in Sir R. G. Bhandarkar's *Report of the Search for Sanskrit Manuscripts 1882–1883*, we find that Haṃsa, the unity of Rādhā and Kṛṣṇa, is regarded as the first teacher of the Nimbārka school. His pupil was Kumāra of the form of four *vyūhas*. Kumāra's pupil was Nārada, the teacher of *prema-bhakti* in the Tretā-yuga. Nimbārka was the pupil of Nārada and the incarnation of the power (*sudarśana*) of Nārāyaṇa. He is supposed to have introduced the worship of Kṛṣṇa in Dvāpara-yuga. His pupil was Śrīnivāsa, who is supposed to be the incarnation of the conch-shell of Nārāyaṇa. Śrīnivāsa's pupil was Viśvācārya, whose pupil was Puruṣottama, who in turn had as his pupil Svarupācārya. These are all described as devotees. Svarūpācārya's pupil was Mādhavācārya, who had a pupil Balabhadrācārya, and his pupil was Padmācārya who is said to have been a great controversialist, who travelled over different parts of India defeating people in discussion. Padmācārya's pupil was Śyāmācārya, and his pupil was Gopālācārya, who is described as a great scholar of the Vedas and the Vedānta. He had as pupil Kṛpācārya, who taught Devācārya, who is described as a great controversialist. Devācārya's pupil was Sundara Bhaṭṭa, and Sundara Bhaṭṭa's pupil was Padmanā Bhācārya. His pupil was Upendra Bhaṭṭa; the succession of pupils is in the following order:

of Sanskrit Manuscripts, by R. L. Mitra, Nos. 2826 and 1216, and the *Guru-paramparā* in the *Catalogue of Manuscripts in the Private Libraries of the N.W.P.*, Parts I–X, Allahabad, 1877–86.

Rāmacandra Bhaṭṭa, Kṛṣṇa Bhaṭṭa, Padmākara Bhaṭṭa, Śravaṇa Bhaṭṭa, Bhūri Bhaṭṭa, Madhva Bhaṭṭa, Śyāma Bhaṭṭa, Gopāla Bhaṭṭa, Valabhadra Bhaṭṭa, Gopīnātha Bhaṭṭa (who is described as a great controversialist), Keśava, Gaṅgala Bhaṭṭa, Keśava Kāśmīrī, Śrī Bhaṭṭa and Harivyāsadeva. Up to Harivyāsadeva apparently all available lists of teachers agree with one another; but after him it seems that the school split into two and we have two different lists of teachers. Bhandarkar has fixed the date for Harivyāsadeva as the thirty-second teacher after Nimbārka. The date of Harivyāsadeva and his successor in one branch line, Dāmodara Gosvāmī, has been fixed as 1750-1755. After Harivyāsadeva we have, according to some lists, Paraśurāmadeva, Harivaṃśadeva, Nārāyaṇadeva, Vṛndāvanadeva and Govindadeva. According to another list we have Svabhūrāmadeva after Harivyāsadeva, and after him Karmaharadeva, Mathuradeva, Śyāmadeva, Sevadeva, Naraharideva, Dayārāmadeva, Pūrṇadeva, Maniṣīdeva, Rādhākṛṣṇaśaraṇadeva, Harideva and Vrajabhūṣaṇasaraṇadeva who was living in 1924 and Santadāsa Vāvājī who died in 1935. A study of the list of teachers gives fairly convincing proof that on the average the pontifical period of each teacher was about fourteen years. If Harivyāsadeva lived in 1750 and Śāntadāsa Vāvājī who was the thirteenth teacher from Harivyāsadeva died in 1935, the thirteen teachers occupied a period of 185 years. This would make the average pontifical period for each teacher about fourteen years. By backward calculation from Harivyāsadeva, putting a period of fourteen years for each teacher, we have for Nimbārka a date which would be roughly about the middle of the fourteenth century.

Nimbārka's commentary of the *Brahma-sūtras* is called the *Vedānta-pārijata-saurabha* as has been already stated. A commentary on it, called the *Vedānta-kaustubha*, was written by his direct disciple Śrīnivāsa. Kesava-kāśmīrī Bhaṭṭa, the disciple of Mukunda, wrote a commentary on the *Vedānta-kaustubha*, called the *Vedānta-kaustubha-prabhā*. He also is said to have written a commentary on the *Bhagavad-gītā*, called the *Tattva-prakāśikā*, a commentary on the tenth *skanda* of *Bhāgavata-purāṇa* called the *Tattva-prakāśikā-veda-stuti-tīkā*, and a commentary on the *Taittrīya Upaniṣad* called the *Taittrīya-prakāśikā*. He also wrote a work called *Krama-dīpikā*, which was commented upon by Govinda

Bhattācārya[1]. The *Krama-dīpikā* is a work of eight chapters dealing mainly with the ritualistic parts of the Nimbārka school of religion. This work deals very largely with various kinds of *Mantras* and meditations on them. Śrīnivāsa also wrote a work called *Laghu-stava-raja-stotra* in which he praises his own teacher Nimbārka. It has been commented upon by Puruṣottama Prasāda, and the commentary is called *Guru-bhakti-mandākinī*. The work *Vedānta-siddhānta-pradīpa* attributed to Nimbārka seems to be a spurious work so far as can be judged from the colophon of the work and from the summary of the contents given in R. L. Mitra's *Notices of Sanskrit Manuscripts* (MS. No. 2826). It appears that the book is devoted to the elucidation of the doctrine of monistic Vedānta of the school of Śaṅkara. Nimbārka's *Daśa-ślokī*, called also *Siddhānta-ratna*, had at least three commentaries: *Vedānta-ratna-mañjuṣā*, by Puruṣottama Prasāda; *Laghu-māñjuṣā*, the author of which is unknown; and a commentary by Harivyāsa muni. Puruṣottama Prasāda wrote a work called *Vedānta-ratna-mañjuṣā* as a commentary on the *Daśa-ślokī* of Nimbārka, and also *Guru-bhakti-mandākinī* commentary as already mentioned. He wrote also a commentary on the *Śrī-kṛṣṇa-stava* of Nimbārka in twenty chapters called *Śruty-anta-sura-druma*, and also *Stotra-trayī*[2]. The discussions contained in the commentary are more or less of the same nature as those found in *Para-pakṣa-giri-vajra*, which has been already described in a separate section. The polemic therein is mainly directed against Śaṅkara *vedānta*. Puruṣottama also strongly criticizes Rāmānuja's view in which the impure *cit* and *acit* are regarded as parts of Brahman possessed of the highest and noblest qualities, and suggests the impossibility of this. According to the Nimbārka school the individual selves are different from Brahman. Their identity is only in the remote sense inasmuch as the individual selves cannot have any separate existence apart from God. Puruṣottama also criticizes the dualists, the Madhvas. The dualistic texts have as much force as the identity texts, and therefore on the strength of the identity texts we have to admit that the world exists in Brahman, and on the strength of the duality texts we have to

[1] This Keśava Kāśmīrī Bhaṭṭa seems to be a very different person from the Keśava Kāśmīrī who is said to have had a discussion with Caitanya as described in the *Caitanya-caritāmṛta*.

[2] The *Śrī-kṛṣṇa-stava* had another commentary on it called *Śruti-siddhānta-mañjarī*, the writer of which is unknown.

admit that the world is different from Brahman. The real meaning of the view that God is the material cause of the world is that though everything springs from Him, yet the nature of God remains the same in spite of all His productions. The energy of God exists in God and though He produces everything by the diverse kinds of manifestations of His energies, He remains unchanged in His Self[1].

Puruṣottama makes reference to Devācārya's *Siddhanta-jāhnavī*, and therefore lived after him. According to Pandit Kiśoradāsa's introduction to *Śruty-anta-sura-druma*, he was born in 1623 and was the son of Nārāyaṇa Śarmā. The present writer is unable to substantiate this view. According to Pandit Kiśoradāsa he was a pupil of Dharmadevācārya.[2] Devācārya wrote a commentary on the *Brahma-sūtras* called the *Siddhānta-jāhnavī*, on which Sundara Bhaṭṭa wrote a commentary called the *Siddhānta-setukā*.

A General Idea of Nimbārka's Philosophy.

According to Nimbārka, the inquiry into the nature of Brahman can take place only after one has studied the literature that deals with the Vedic duties leading to various kinds of beneficial results and discovered that they are all vitiated by enjoyment and cannot bring about a state of eternal bliss. After such a discovery, and after the seeker has learnt in a general manner from the various religious texts that the realization of Brahman leads to the unchangeable, eternal and ever-constant state of bliss, he becomes anxious to attain it through the grace of God and approaches his teacher with affection and reverence for instruction regarding the

[1] *yathā ca bhūmes tathā-bhūta-śakti-matyā oṣadhīnāṃ janma-mātraṃ tathā sarva-kāryo-tpādanā-rha-lakṣaṇā-cintyānnanta-sarva-śakter akṣara-padārthād brahmaṇo viśvam sambhavatī'ti; yadā sva-svā-bhāvikā-lpā-dhika-sātiśaya-śaktimadbhyo' cetanebhyas tat-tac-chaktya-nusāreṇa sva-sva-kārya-bhāvā-pattavapi apracyuta-sva-rūpatvaṃ pratyakṣa-pramāṇa-siddhaṃ, tarhy acintya-sarvā-cintya-viśvākhya-kāryo-tpādanā-rha-śaktimato bhagavata ukta-rītyā jagad-bhāvā-pattavapya-pracyuta-sva-rūpatvaṃ kim aśakyam iti. . . .śakti-vikṣepa-saṃharaṇasya pariṇāma-śabda-vācyatvā-bhiprāyeṇa kvacit pariṇāmo-ktiḥ. sva-rūpa-pariṇāmā-bhāvaś ca pārvam eva nirūpitaḥ; śakteḥ śakti-mato' pṛthak-siddhatvāt.* (*Śruty-anta-sura-druma*, pp. 73–74.)

[2] Pandit Kiśoradāsa contradicts himself in his introduction to *Vedānta-mañjuṣā* and it seems that the dates he gives are of a more or less fanciful character. Pandit Kiśoradāsa further says that Devācārya lived in A.D. 1055. This would place Nimbārka prior even to Rāmānuja, which seems very improbable.

nature of Brahman. The Brahman is Śrī Kṛṣṇa, who is omniscient, omnipotent, the ultimate cause, and the all-pervading Being. Such a Being can be realized only through a constant effort to permeate oneself with His nature by means of thought and devotion. The import of the first aphorism of the *Brahma-sūtra* consists in the imposition of such a duty on the devotee, namely, the constant effort at realizing the nature of Brahman[1]. The pupil listens to the instruction of his teacher who has a direct realization of the nature of Brahman and whose words are therefore pregnant with his concrete experience. He tries to understand the import and meaning of the instruction of his teacher which is technically called *śravaṇa*. This is indeed different from the ordinary accepted meaning of the *śravaṇa* in the Śaṅkara literature where it is used in the sense of listening to the Upaniṣadic texts. The next step is called *manana*—the process of organizing one's thought so as to facilitate a favourable mental approach towards the truths communicated by the teacher in order to rouse a growing faith in it. The third step is called *nididhyāsana*—the process of marshalling one's inner psychical processes by constant meditation leading ultimately to a permanent conviction and experiences of the truths inspired and communicated by the teacher. It is the fruitful culmination of the last process that brings about the realization of the nature of Brahman. The study of the nature of the Vedic duties, technically called *dharma*, and their inefficacy, rouses a desire for the knowledge of the nature of Brahman leading to eternal bliss. As a means to that end the pupil approaches the teacher who has a direct experience of the nature of Brahman. The revelation of the nature of the Brahman in the pupil is possible through a process of spiritual communication of which *śravaṇa*, *manana* and *nididhyāsana* are the three moments.

According to Nimbārka's philosophy which is a type of *Bhedā-bheda-vāda*, that is, the theory of the Absolute as Unity-in-difference, Brahman or the Absolute has transformed itself into the world of matter and spirits. Just as the life-force or *prāṇa* manifests itself into the various conative and cognitive sense-functions, yet keeps its own independence, integrity and difference from them,

[1] As the nature of this duty is revealed through the text of the *Brahma-sūtra*, namely, that the Brahma-hood can be attained only by such a process of *nididhyāsana*, it is called the *apūrva-vidhi*.

so the Brahman also manifests itself through the numberless spirits and matter without losing itself in them. Just as the spider spins out of its own self its web and yet remains independent of it, so the Brahman also has split itself up into the numberless spirits and matter but remains in its fullness and purity. The very existence and movement of the spirits and indeed all their operations are said to depend upon Brahman (*tad-āyatta-sthiti-pūrvikā*) in the sense that the Brahman is both the material and the determining cause of them all[1].

In the scriptures we hear of dualistic and monistic texts, and the only way in which the claims of both these types of texts can be reconciled is by coming to a position of compromise that the Brahman is at once different from and identical with the world of spirits and matter. The nature of Brahman is regarded as such that it is at once one with and different from the world of spirits and matter, not by any imposition or supposition, but as the specific peculiarity of its spiritual nature. It is on this account that this *Bhedā-bheda* doctrine is called the *svābhāvika bhedā-bheda-vāda*. In the pure dualistic interpretation of the Vedānta the Brahman is to be regarded only as the determining cause and as such the claims of all texts that speak of the Brahman as the material cause or of the ultimate identity of the spirits with the Brahman are to be disregarded. The monistic view of the Vedānta is also untenable, for a pure differenceless qualityless consciousness as the ultimate reality is not amenable to perception, since it is super-sensible, nor to inference, since it is devoid of any distinctive marks, nor also to scriptural testimony, as no words can signify it. The supposition that, just as one's attention to the moon may be drawn in an indirect manner by perceiving the branch of a tree with which the moon may be in a line, so the nature of Brahman also may be expressed by demonstrating other concepts which are more or less contiguous or associated with it, is untenable; for in the above illustration the moon and the branch of the tree are both sensible objects, whereas Brahman is absolutely super-sensible. Again, if it is supposed that Brahman is amenable to logical proofs, then also this supposition would be false; for all that is amenable to proofs or subject to any demonstration is false. Further, if it is not amenable to any proof, the Brahman would be chimerical as the

[1] Śrīnivāsa's commentary on Nimbārka's *Vedānta-pārijāta-saurabha* on *Brahma-sūtra*, I. i. 1–3.

hare's horn. If it is held that, Brahman being self-luminous, no proofs are required for its demonstration, then all the scriptural texts describing the nature of Brahman would be superfluous. Moreover, the pure qualityless Brahman being absolutely unassociated with any kind of impurity has to be regarded as being eternally free from any bondage, and thus all scriptural texts giving instruction in the methods for the attainment of salvation would be meaningless. The reply of the Śaṅkarites, that all duality though false has yet an appearance and serves practical purposes, is untenable; for when the scriptures speak of the destruction of bondage they mean that it was a real bondage and its dissolution is also a real one. Again, an illusion is possible in a locus only when it has some specific as well as some general characters, and the illusion takes place only when the object is known in a general manner without any of its specific attributes. But if the Brahman is absolutely qualityless, it is impossible that it should be the locus of any illusion. Again, since it is difficult to explain how the *ajñāna* should have any support or object (*āśraya* or *viṣaya*), the illusion itself becomes inexplicable. The Brahman being of the nature of pure knowledge can hardly be supposed to be the support or object of *ajñāna*. The *jīva* also being itself a product of *ajñāna* cannot be regarded as its support. Moreover, since Brahman is of the nature of pure illumination and *ajñāna* is darkness, the former cannot legitimately be regarded as the support of the latter, just as the sun cannot be regarded as the supporter of darkness.

The operation that results in the formation of illusion cannot be regarded as being due to the agency of *ajñāna*, for *ajñāna* is devoid of consciousness and cannot, therefore, be regarded as an agent. The agency cannot also be attributed to Brahman because it is pure and static. Again, the false appearance of Brahman as diverse undesirable phenomena such as a sinner, an animal, and the like, is inexplicable; for if the Brahman is always conscious and independent it cannot be admitted to allow itself to suffer through the undesirable states which one has to experience in various animal lives through rebirth. If the Brahman has no knowledge of such experiences, then it is to be regarded as ignorant and its claim to self-luminosity fails. Again, if *ajñāna* is regarded as an existent entity, there is the change to dualism, and if it is regarded as non-existent then it cannot hide the nature of Brahman. Further, if

Brahman is self-luminous, how can it be hidden and how can there be any illusion about it? If the conch-shell shines forth in its own nature, there cannot be any misperception of its nature as a piece of silver. Again, if the nature of Brahman is admitted to be hidden by *ajñāna*, the question that naturally arises is whether the *ajñāna* veils the nature of the Brahman as a whole or in part. The former supposition is impossible, for then the world would be absolutely blind and dark (*jagad-āndhya-prasaṅgāt*), and the latter is impossible, for the Brahman is a homogeneous entity and has no characters or parts. It is admitted by the monists to be absolutely qualityless and partless. If it is held that ordinarily only the "bliss" part of the Brahman is hidden by *ajñāna* whereas the "being" part remains unveiled, then that would mean that Brahman is divisible in parts and the falsity of the Brahman would be demonstrable by such inferences as: Brahman is false, because it has parts like the jug (*brahma mithyā sāṃśatvāt, ghaṭādivat*).

In reply to the above objections it may be argued that the objections against *ajñāna* are inadmissible, for the *ajñāna* is absolutely false knowledge. Just as an owl perceives utter darkness, even in bright sunlight, so the intuitive perception "I am ignorant" is manifest to all. Anantarāma, a follower of the Nimbārka school, raises further objections against such a supposition in his *Vedānta-tattva-bodha*. He says that this intuitively felt "I" in "I am ignorant" cannot be pure knowledge, for pure knowledge cannot be felt as ignorant. It cannot be mere egoism, for then the experience would be "the egoism is ignorant." If by "ego" one means the pure self, then such a self cannot be experienced before emancipation. The ego-entity cannot be something different from both pure consciousness and *ajñāna*, for such an entity must doubtless be an effect of *ajñāna* which cannot exist before the association of the *ajñāna* with Brahman. The reply of the Śaṅkarites that *ajñāna*, being merely false imagination, cannot affect the nature of the Brahman, the abiding substratum (*adhiṣṭhāna*), is also inadmissible; for if the *ajñāna* be regarded as false imagination there must be someone who imagines it. But such an imagination cannot be attributed to either of the two possible entities, Brahman or the *ajñāna*; for the former is pure qualityless which cannot therefore imagine and the latter is inert and unconscious and therefore devoid of all imagination. It is also wrong to suppose that Brahman as pure consciousness has no intrinsic opposition to *ajñāna*, for there can be no knowledge which is not opposed to ignorance. Therefore the Śaṅkarites are not in a position to demonstrate any entity which they mean by the intuition "I" in "I am ignorant."

The final conclusion from the Nimbārka point of view therefore is that it is inadmissible to accept any *ajñāna* as a world-principle producing the world-appearance by working in co-operation with the Brahman. The *ajñāna* or ignorance is a quality of individual beings or selves who are by nature different from Brahman but are under its complete domination. They are eternal parts of it, atomic in nature, and are of limited powers. Being associated with beginningless chains of *karma* they are naturally largely blinded in their outlook on knowledge[1].

The Śaṅkarites affirm that, through habitual failure in distinguishing between the real nature of the self and the not-self, mis-perceptions, misapprehensions and illusions occur. The objection of Anantarāma against such an explanation is that such a failure cannot be attributed either to Brahman or to *ajñāna*. And since all other entities are but later products of illusion, they cannot be responsible for producing the illusion[2].

In his commentary Śaṅkara had said that the pure consciousness was not absolutely undemonstrable, since it was constantly being referred to by our ego-intuitions. To this the objection that naturally arises is that the entity referred to by our ego-intuitions cannot be pure consciousness; for then the pure consciousness would have the characteristic of an ego—a view which is favourable to the Nimbārka but absolutely unacceptable to the Śaṅkarites. If it is held to be illusory, then it has to be admitted that the ego-intuition appears when there is an illusion. But by supposition the illusion can only occur when there is an ego-intuition[3]. Here is then a reasoning in a circle. The defence that reasoning in a circle can be avoided on the supposition that the illusory imposition is beginningless is also unavailing. For the supposition that illusions as such are beginningless is false, as it is well known that illusions

[1] *paramā-tma-bhinno'lpa-śaktis tad-adhīnaḥ sanātanas tad-aṃśa-bhūto' nādi-karmā-tmikā-vidyā-vṛta-dharma-bhūtā-jñāno jīva-kṣetrajñā-di-śabdā-bhidheyas tat-pratyayā-śraya iti. Vedānta-tattva-bodha*, p. 12.

[2] *Ibid.* p. 13.

[3] *adhyastattve tu adhyāse sati bhāsamānatvam, tasmin sati sa ity anyonyā-śraya-doṣaḥ. Ibid.* p. 14.

are possible only through the operation of the subconscious impressions of previous valid cognitions[1]. Again, the reflection of the pure consciousness in the *ajñāna* is impossible, for reflections can take place only between two entities which have the same order of existence. From other considerations also the illusion has to be regarded as illegitimate. Illusions take place as the result of certain physical conditions such as contact, defect of the organs of perception, the operation of the subconscious impressions, etc. These conditions are all absent in the supposed case of the illusion involved in the ego-intuition.

The Śaṅkarites described *māyā* as indefinable. By "indefinable" they mean something that appears in perception but is ultimately contradicted. The Śaṅkarites define falsehood or non-existence as that which is liable to contradiction. The phenomena of *māyā* appear in experience and are therefore regarded as existent. They are liable to contradiction and are therefore regarded as non-existent. It is this unity of existence and non-existence in *māyā* that constitutes its indefinability. To this Anantarāma's objection is that contradiction does not imply non-existence. As a particular object, say a jug, may be destroyed by the stroke of a club, so one knowledge can destroy another. The destruction of the jug by the stroke of the club does not involve the supposition that the jug was non-existent. So the contradiction of the prior knowledge by a later one does not involve the non-existence or falsity of the former. All cognitions are true in themselves, though some of them may destroy another. This is what the Nimbārkists mean by the *sat-khyāti* of knowledge. The theory of *sat-khyāti* with them means that all knowledge (*khyāti*) is produced by some existent objects, which are to be regarded as its cause (*sad-dhetukā khyāti*, *sat-khyāti*). According to such a view, therefore, the illusory knowledge must have its basic cause in some existent object. It is wrong also to suppose that false or non-existent objects can produce effects on the analogy that the illusory cobra may produce fear and even death. For here it is not the illusory cobra that produces fear but the memory of a true snake. It is wrong therefore to suppose that the illusory world-appearance may be the cause of our bondage.

Since illusions are not possible, it is idle to suppose that all our

[1] *adhyāso nā'nādiḥ, pūrva-pramā-hita-saṃskāra-janyatvāt. Vedānta-tattva-bodha*, p. 14.

perceptual, inferential, and other kinds of cognitions are produced as associated with an ego through sheer illusion. Right knowledge is to be regarded as a characteristic quality of the self and the production of knowledge does not need the intervention of a *vṛtti*. The *ajñāna* which prevents the flashing in of knowledge is our *karma* which is in accumulation from beginningless time. Through the operation of the sense-organs our selves expand outside us and are filled with the cognition of the sense-objects. It is for this reason that when the sense-organs are not in operation the sense-objects do not appear in cognition, as in the state of sleep. The self is thus a real knower (*jñātā*) and a real agent (*kartā*), and its experiences as a knower and as an agent should on no account be regarded as the result of a process of illusion[1].

The self is of the nature of pure consciousness, but it should yet be regarded as the real knower. The objection that what is knowledge cannot behave in a different aspect as a knower, just as water cannot be mixed with water and yet remain distinct from it, is regarded by the Nimbārkists as invalid. As an illustration vindicating the Nimbārka position, Puruṣottama, in his *Vedānta-ratna-mañjuṣā*, refers to the case of the sun which is both light and that from which light emanates. Even when a drop of water is mixed with another drop the distinction of the drops, both quantitative and qualitative, remains, though it may not be so apprehended. The mere non-apprehension of difference is no proof that the two drops have merged into identity. On the other hand, since the second drop has its parts distinct from the first one it must be regarded as having a separate existence, even when the two drops are mixed. The character as knower must be attributed to the self; for the other scheme proposed by the Śaṅkarites, that the character as knower is due to the reflection of the pure consciousness in the *vṛtti*, is inefficacious. The sun that is reflected in water as an image cannot be regarded as a glowing orb by itself. Moreover, reflection can only take place between two visible objects; neither pure consciousness nor the *antaḥkaraṇa-vṛtti* can be regarded as visible objects justifying the assumption of reflection.

The ego-intuition refers directly to the self and there is no illusion about it. The ego-intuition thus appears to be a continuous revelation of the nature of the self. After deep dreamless sleep one

[1] *Vedānta-tattva-bodha*, p. 20.

says "I slept so well that I did not know even myself." But this should not be interpreted as the absence of the ego-intuition or the revelation of the self. The experience "I did not know myself" refers to the absence of the intuition of the body and the mental psychosis, but it does not indicate that the self-conscious self had ever ceased to shine by itself. The negation involved in the denial of the perception of one's self during dreamless sleep refers to the negation of certain associations (say, of the body, etc.) with which the ego ordinarily links itself. Similar experience of negation can also be illustrated in such expressions as "I was not so long in the room," "I did not live at that time," etc., where negations refer to the associations of the ego and not to the ego. The self is not only to be regarded as expressed in the ego-intuition, but it is also to be regarded as distinct from the knowledge it has. The perception of the self continues not only in the state of dreamless sleep but also in the state of emancipation, and even God in His absolute freedom is conscious of Himself in His super-ego intuition. He is also all-Merciful, the supreme Instructor, and the presiding deity of all our understanding. Like individual selves God is also the agent, the creator of the universe. If the Brahman were not an agent by nature, then He could not have been the creator of the universe, even with the association of the *māyā* conditions. Unlike Brahman the activity of the individual souls has to depend upon the operation of the conative organs for its manifestation. The self also really experiences the feelings of pleasure and pain. The existence and agency of the human souls, however, ultimately depend on the will of God. Yet there is no reason to suppose that God is partial or cruel because He makes some suffer and others enjoy; for He is like the grand master and Lord who directs different men differently and awards suffering and enjoyment according to their individual deserts. The whole idea is that though God awards suffering and enjoyment to individuals and directs their actions according to their deserts, He is not ultimately bound by the law of *karma*, and may by His grace at any time free them from their bondage. The law of *karma* is a mechanical law and God as the superintendent decides each individual case. He is thus the dispenser of the laws of *karma* but is not bound by it[1]. The human souls are a part of the

[1] *na vayaṃ brahma-niyantṛtvasya karma-sāpekṣattvaṃ brūmaḥ, kintu puṇyā-di-karma-kārayitṛtve tat-phala-dātṛtve ca. Vedānta-ratna-mañjuṣā*, p. 14.

nature of God and as such are dependent on Him for their essence, existence, and activities (*tad-āyatta-svarūpa-sthiti-pūrvikāḥ*). God being the ultimate truth, both the human souls and inanimate nature attain their essence and existence by virtue of the fact that they are parts of Him and participate in His nature. They are therefore entirely dependent on Him for their existence and all their operations.

The individual souls are infinite in number and atomic in size. But though atomic in size they can at the same time cognize the various sensations in various parts of the body through all-pervading knowledge which exists in them as their attribute. Though atomic and partless in their nature, they are completely pervaded by God through His all-pervading nature. The atomic souls are associated with the beginningless girdle of *karma* which is the cause of the body, and are yet through the grace of God finally emancipated when their doubts are dissolved by listening to the instructions of the *śāstras* from the teachers, and by entering into a deep meditation regarding the true essence of God by which they are ultimately merged in Him. God is absolutely free in extending His mercy and grace. But it so happens that He actually extends them to those who deserve them by their good deeds and devotion. God in His transcendence is beyond His three natures as souls, the world and even as God. In this His pure and transcendent nature He is absolutely unaffected by any changes, and He is the unity of pure being, bliss and consciousness. In His nature as God He realizes His own infinite joy through the infinite souls which are but constituent parts of Him. The experiences of individuals are therefore contained in Him as constituents of Him because it is by His own *īkṣaṇa* or self-perceiving activity that the experiences of the individual selves can be accounted for. The existence and the process of all human experience are therefore contained and controlled by Him. The individual selves are thus in one sense different from Him and in another sense but constituent parts of Him. In Bhāskara's philosophy the emphasis was on the aspect of unity, since the differences were due to conditions (*upādhi*). But though Nimbārka's system is to be counted as a type of *Bhedā-bheda* or *Dvaitā-dvaita* theory, the emphasis here is not merely on the part of the unity but on the difference as well. As a part cannot be different from the whole, so the individual souls can never be different from God. But, in the state of bondage the individuals are apt to forget their aspects of unity with God and feel themselves independent in all their actions and experiences. When by absolute self-abnegation springing from love the individual feels himself to be absolutely controlled and regulated by God and realizes himself to be a constituent of Him, he loses all his interests in his actions and is not affected by them. The ultimate ideal, therefore, is to realize the relation with God, to abnegate all actions, desires and motives, and to feel oneself as a constituent of Him. Such a being never again comes within the grasp of mundane bondage and lives in eternal bliss in his devotional contemplation of God. The devotee in the state of his emancipation feels himself to be one with God and abides in Him as a part of His energy (*tat-tādātmyā-nubhava-pūrvakaṃ viśvarūpe bhagavati tac-chaktyā-tmanā avasthānam*)[1]. Thus, even in the state of emancipation, there is a difference between the emancipated beings and God, though in this state they are filled with the utmost bliss. With the true realization of the nature of God and one's relation with Him, all the three kinds of *karma* (*sañcita*, *kriyamāṇa* and *ārabdha*) are destroyed[2]. *Avidyā* in this system means ignorance of one's true nature and relationship with God which is the cause of his *karma* and his association with the body, senses and the subtle matter[3]. The *prārabdha karma*, or the *karma* which is in a state of fructification, may persist through the present life or through other lives if necessary, for until their fruits are reaped the bodiless emancipation cannot be attained[4]. Sainthood consists in the devotional state consisting of a continual and unflinching meditation on the nature of God (*dhyāna-paripākena dhruva-smṛti-para-bhakty-ākhya-jñānā-dhigame*). Such a saint becomes free from the tainting influence of all deeds committed and collected before and all good or bad actions that may be performed later on (*tatra uttara-bhāvinaḥ kriyamāṇasya pāpasya āśleṣaḥ tat-prāg-bhūtasya sañcitasya tasya nāśaḥ. Vedānta-kaustubha-prabhā*, IV. 1. 13). The regular caste duties and the duties of the various stages of life help the rise of wisdom and ought therefore always to be performed, even when the wisdom has arisen; for the flame of

[1] *Para-pakṣa-giri-vajra*, p. 591.

[2] *Ibid.* p. 598.

[3] *Ibid.*

[4] *viduṣo vidyā-māhātmyāt sañcita-kriyamāṇayor āśleṣa-vināśau, prārabdhasya tu karmaṇo bhogena vināśaḥ, tatra prārabdhasya etac charīreṇa itara-śarīrair vā bhuktvā vināśān-mokṣa iti saṃkṣepaḥ. Ibid.* p. 583.

this light has always to be kept burning (*tasmāt vidyo-dayāya svā-śrama-karmā-gnihotrā-di-rūpaṃ gṛhasthena, tapo-japā-dīni karmāṇi ūrdhva-retobhir anuṣṭheyāni iti siddham*). But the conglomeration of deeds which has started fructifying must fructify and the results of such deeds have to be reaped by the saint either in one life or in many lives as the case may be. The realization of Brahman consists in the unflinching meditation on the nature of God and the participation in Him as His constituent which is the same thing as the establishment of a continuous devotional relationship with Him. This is independent of the ontological fusion and return in Him which may happen as a result of the complete destruction of the fructifying deeds (*prārabdha karma*) through their experiences in the life of the saint (*vidyā-yoni-śarīra*) or in other lives that may follow. A saint, after the exhaustion of his fructifying deeds, leaves his gross body through the *suṣumnā* nerve in his subtle body, and going beyond the material regions (*prākṛta-maṇḍala*) reaches the border region—the river *virajā*—between the material regions and the universe of *Viṣṇu*[1]. Here he leaves aside his subtle body in the supreme being and enters into the transcendent essence of God (*Vedānta-kaustubha-prabhā*, IV. 2. 15). The emancipated beings thus exist in God as His distinct energies and may again be employed by Him for His own purposes. Such emancipated beings, however, are never sent down by God for carrying on an earthly existence. Though the emancipated beings become one with God, they have no control over the affairs of the world, which are managed entirely by God Himself[2].

Though it is through the will of God that we enjoy the dream experiences and though He remains the controller and abides in us through all stages of our experiences, yet He is never tainted by the imperfections of our experiental existence (*Vedānta-kaustubha* and its commentary *Prabha*, III. 2. 11). The objects of our experiences are not in themselves pleasurable or painful, but God makes them so to us in accordance with the reward and punishment due to us according to our good or bad deeds. In themselves the objects are

[1] *para-loka-gamane dehād utsarpaṇa-samaye eva viduṣaḥ puṇya-pāpe nira-vaśeṣaṃ kṣīyate,...vidyā hi sva-sāmarthyād eva sva-phala-bhūta-brahma-prāpti-pratipādanāya...enaṃ deva-yānena pathā gamayituṃ sūkṣma-śarīraṃ sthāpayati. Vedānta-kaustubha-prabhā*, III. 3. 27.

[2] *muktasya tu para-brahma-sādharmye'pi nikhila-cetanā-cetana-patitva-tan-niyantṛtva-tad-vidhārakatva-sarva-gatatvā-dy-asambhavāt jagad-vyāpāra-varjam aiśvaryam. Ibid.* IV. 4. 20.

but indifferent entities and are neither pleasurable nor painful (*Vedānta-kaustubha-prabhā*, III. 2. 12). The relation of God and the world is like that of a snake and its coiled existence. The coiled (*kuṇḍala*) condition of a snake is neither different from it nor absolutely identical with it. So God's relation with the individuals also is like that of a lamp and its light (*prabhā-tadvatoṛ iva*) or like the sun and the illumination (*prakāśa*). God remains unchanged in Himself and only undergoes transformation through His energies as conscious (*cic-chakti*) and unconscious (*acic-chakti*)[1]. As the individuals cannot have any existence apart from Brahman, so the material world also cannot have any existence apart from him. It is in this sense that the material world is a part or constituent of God and is regarded as being one with God. But as the nature of the material world is different from the nature of God, it is regarded as different from Him[2].

The Vedic duties of caste and stages of life are to be performed for the production of the desire of wisdom (*vividiṣā*), but once the true wisdom is produced there is no further need of the performance of the duties (*Ibid.* III. 4. 9). The wise man is never affected by the deeds that he performs. But though ordinarily the performance of the duties is helpful to the attainment of wisdom, this is not indispensable, and there are many who achieve wisdom without going through the customary path of caste duties and the duties attached to stages of life.

Controversy with the Monists by Mādhava Mukunda.

(*a*) *The Main Thesis and the Ultimate End in Advaita Vedānta are Untenable.*

Mādhava Mukunda, supposed to be a native of the village of Aruṇaghaṭī, Bengal, wrote a work called *Para-pakṣa-giri-vajra* or *Hārda-sañcaya*, in which he tried to show from various points of

[1] *ananta-guṇa-śaktimato brahmaṇaḥ pariṇāmi-svabhāvā-cic-chakteḥ sthūlā-vasthāyāṃ satyāṃ tad-antarā-tmatvena tatrā'vasthāne'pi pariṇāmasya śakti-gatatvāt svarūpe pariṇāmā-bhāvāt kuṇḍala-dṛṣṭānto na doṣā-vahaḥ apṛthak-siddhatvena abhede'pi bheda-jñāpanā-rthaḥ. Vedānta-kaustubha-prabhā,* III. 2. 29.

[2] *jīvavat pṛthak-sthity-anarha-viśeṣaṇatvena acid-vastuno brahmā-ṃśatvaṃ viśiṣṭa-vastv-eka-deśatvena abheda-vyavahāro mukhyaḥ viśeṣaṇa-viśeṣyayoḥ sva-rūpa-svabhāva-bhedena ca bheda-vyavahāro mukhyaḥ. Ibid.* III. 2. 30.

view the futility of the monistic interpretation of Vedānta by Śaṅkara and his followers.

He says that the Śaṅkarites are interested in demonstrating the identity of the individuals with Brahman (*jīva-brahmai-kya*) and this forms the principal subject-matter of all their discussions. This identity may be illusory or not. In the former case duality or plurality would be real, and in the latter case, i.e. if identity be real, then the duality presupposed in the identification must also be real[1]. It is not the case of the single point of an identity that Śaṅkarites are interested in, but in the demonstration of an identification of the individuals with Brahman. The demonstration of identity necessarily implies the reality of the negation of the duality. If such a negation is false, the identification must also be false, for it is on the reality of the negation that the reality of the identification depends. If the negation of duality be real, then the duality must also be real in some sense and the identification can imply the reality of the negation only in some particular aspect.

The objections levelled by the Śaṅkarites against the admission of "duality" or "difference" as a category are, firstly, that the category of difference (*bheda*) being by nature a relation involves two poles and hence it cannot be identical in nature with its locus in which it is supposed to subsist (*bhedasya na adhikaraṇa-svarūpatvam*). Secondly, that if "difference" is different in nature from its locus, then a second grade of "difference" has to be introduced and this would imply another grade of difference and so on *ad infinitum*. Thus we have a vicious infinite. To the first objection, the reply is that "difference" is not relational in nature with this or that individual locus, but with the concept of the locus as such (*bhūtalatvā-dinā nirapekṣatve'pi adhikaraṇātmakatvena sāpeksatve kṣater abhāvāt*)[2]. The charge of vicious infinite by the introduction of differences of differences is invalid, for all differences are identical in nature with their locus. So in the case of a series of differences the nature of each difference becomes well defined and the viciousness of the infinite series vanishes. In the instance "there is a jug on the ground" the nature of the difference of the jug is jugness, whereas in the case of the difference of the difference, the second order of

[1] *dvitīye aikya-pratiyogika-bhedasya pāramārthikatva-prasaṅgāt. Para-pakṣa-giri-vajra*, p. 12.

[2] *Ibid.* p. 14.

difference has a separate specification as a special order of differenceness. Moreover, since difference reveals only the particular modes of the objects, these difficulties cannot arise. In perceiving difference we do not perceive difference as an entity different from the two objects between which it is supposed to subsist[1]. One might equally well find such a fault of mutual dependence on the identification of Brahman with *jīva*, since it depends upon the identification of the *jīva* with the Brahman.

A further discussion of the subject shows that there cannot be any objections against "differences" on the score of their being produced, for they merely subsist and are not produced; or on the possibility of their being known, for if differences were never perceived the Śaṅkarites would not have been so anxious to remove the so-called illusions or mis-perception of differences, or to misspend their energies in trying to demonstrate that Brahman was different from all that was ıalse, material and the like; and the saint also would not be able to distinguish between what was eternal and transitory. Again, it is held that there is a knowledge which contradicts the notion of difference. But if this knowledge itself involves difference it cannot contradict it. Whatever may signify anything must do so by restricting its signification to it, and all such restriction involves difference. Even the comprehension that demonstrates the illusoriness of "difference" (e.g. this is not difference, or there is no difference here, etc.) proves the existence of "difference." Moreover, a question may be raised as to whether the notion that contradicts difference is itself comprehended as different from difference or not. In the former case the validity of the notion leaves "difference" unmolested and in the second case, i.e. if it is not comprehended as different from "difference," it becomes identical with it and cannot contradict it.

If it is contended that in the above procedure an attempt has been made to establish the category of difference only in indirect manner and that nothing has been directly said in explanation of the concept of difference, the reply is that those who have sought to explain the concept of unity have fared no better. If it is urged that if ultimately the absolute unity or identity is not accepted then

[1] *nā'py anyonyā-śrayaḥ bheda-pratyakṣe pratiyogitā-vacchedaka-stambhatvādi-prakāraka-jñānasyai'va hetutvāt na tāvad bheda-pratyakṣe bhedā-śrayād bhinnatvena pratiyogi-jñānaṃ hetuḥ. Para-pakṣa-giri-vajra*, pp. 14, 15.

that would lead us to nihilism, then it may also be urged with the same force that, differences being but modes of the objects themselves, a denial of difference would mean the denial of the objects, and this would also land us in nihilism. It must, however, be noted that though difference is but a mode of the objects which differ, yet the terms of reference by which difference becomes intelligible (the table is different from the chair: here the difference of the table is but its mode, though it becomes intelligible by its difference from the chair) are by no means constituents of the objects in which the difference exists as their mode. The Śaṅkarites believe in the refutation of dualism, as by such a refutation the unity is established. The thesis of unity is thus though, on the one hand dependent upon such refutation and yet on the other hand identical with it because all such refutations are believed to be imaginary. In the same manner it may be urged that the demonstration of difference involves with it a reference to other terms, but is yet identical in nature with the object of which it is a mode; the reference to the terms is necessary only for purposes of comprehension.

It must, however, be noted that since difference is but a mode of the object the comprehension of the latter necessarily means the comprehension of all differences existing in it. An object may be known in a particular manner, yet it may remain unknown in its differential aspects, just as the monists hold that pure consciousness is always flashing forth but yet its aspect as the unity of all things may remain unknown. In comprehending a difference between any two objects, no logical priority which could have led to a vicious circle is demanded. But the two are together taken in consciousness and the apprehension of the one is felt as its distinction from the other. The same sort of distinction has to be adduced by the monists also in explaining the comprehension of the identity of the individual souls with the Brahman, otherwise in their case too there would have been the charge of a vicious circle. For when one says "these two are not different," their duality and difference depend upon a comprehension of their difference which, while present, prevents their identity from being established. If it is held that the duality is imaginary whereas the identity is real, then the two being of a different order of existence the contradiction of the one cannot lead to the affirmation of the other. The apology that in comprehending identity no two-term reference is needed is futile, for an identity is comprehended only as the negation of the two-term duality.

Thus, from the above considerations, the main thesis of the Śaṅkarites, that all things are identical with Brahman, falls to the ground.

According to Nimbārka the ideal of emancipation is participation in God's nature (*tad-bhāvā-patti*). This is the ultimate end and *summum bonum* of life (*prayojana*). According to the Śaṅkarites emancipation consists in the ultimate oneness or identity existing between individual souls and Brahman. The Brahman in reality is one with the individual souls, and the apparent difference noticed in our ordinary practical life is due to misconception and ignorance, which impose upon us a false notion of duality. Mādhava Mukunda urges that in such a view, since the individual souls are already one with Brahman, they have nothing to strive for. There is thus really no actual end (*proyojana*) as the goal of our strivings. Mādhava Mukunda, in attempting to emphasize the futility of the Śaṅkarite position, says that, if the ultimate consciousness be regarded as one, then it would be speckled with the various experiences of individuals. It cannot be held to be appearing as different in accordance with the variety of conditions through which it appears, for in our experiences we find that though through our various cognitive organs we have various experiences they are also emphasized as belonging to one being. Variability of conditions does not necessarily imply a variety of the units of experience of individual beings, as is maintained by the Śaṅkarites. The pure and ubiquitous differenceless consciousness (*nirviśeṣa-caitanya*) cannot also be regarded as capable of being identified as one with the plurality of minds (*antaḥkaraṇa*). Again, it is admitted by the Śaṅkarites that in dreamless sleep the mind is dissolved. If that were so and if pure consciousness is regarded as being capable of manifesting itself through false identification with minds, there would be no explanation of the continuity of consciousness from day to day in the form of memory. It cannot be urged that such a continuity is maintained by the fact that minds exist in a state of potency (*saṃskārā-tmanā' vasthitasya*) in the deep dreamless sleep; for the mind in a potent state cannot be regarded as carrying impressions and memories, since in that case there would be memories even in dreamless sleep.

Further, if the experiences are supposed to belong to the states of ignorance, then emancipation, which refers only to pure consciousness, would refer to an entity different from that which was suffering from bondage. On the other hand, if the experiences belong to pure consciousness, then emancipation will be associated with diverse contradictory experiences at the same time according to the diversity of experiences.

The Śaṅkarites may urge that the conditions which bring about the experiences are associated with pure consciousness and hence in an indirect manner there is a continuity of the being that experiences and attains salvation. To this the reply is that the experiencing of sorrow is a sufficient description of the conditions. That being so, where the experiencing of sorrow does not exist, the conditions, of which it is a sufficient description, also do not exist. Thus, the discontinuity of the entities which suffer bondage and attain emancipation remains the same.

Again, since it is held that the conditions subsist in the pure consciousness, it may well be asked whether emancipation means the dissolution of one condition or many conditions. In the former case we should have emancipation always, for one or other of the conditions is being dissolved every moment, and in the latter case we might not have any emancipation at all, for all the conditions determining the experiences of infinite individuals can never be dissolved.

It may also be asked whether the conditions are associated with the pure consciousness in part or in whole. In the first alternative there would be a vicious infinite and in the second the differentiation of the pure consciousness in various units would be inadmissible.

Moreover, it may be asked whether conditions are associated with pure consciousness conditionally or unconditionally. In the former alternative there would be a vicious infinite and in the second case there would be no chance of emancipation. The theory of reflection cannot also explain the situation, for reflection is admitted only when the reflected image has the same order of existence as the object. The *avidyā* has a different order of existence from Brahman, and thus reflection of Brahman in *avidyā* cannot be justified. Again, in reflection that which is reflected and that in which the reflection takes place must be in two different places, whereas in the case of *avidyā* and Brahman the former is supposed to have Brahman as its support. The conditions (*upādhi*) cannot occupy a part of Brahman, for Brahman has no parts; nor can they occupy the whole of it, for in that case there will be no reflection.

In the Nimbārka system both the monistic and the dualistic texts have their full scope, the dualistic texts in demonstrating the difference that exists between souls and God, and the monistic texts showing the final goal in which the individuals realize themselves as constituents of Him and as such one with Him. But in the Śaṅkara system, where no duality is admitted, everything is self-realized, there is nothing to be attained and even the process of instruction of the disciple by the preceptor is unavailable, as they are all but adumbrations of ignorance.

(*b*) *Refutation of the Śaṅkara Theory of Illusion in its various Aspects.*

The Śaṅkarite doctrine of illusion involves a supposition that the basis of illusion (*adhiṣṭhāna*) is imperfectly or partly known. The illusion consists in the imposition of certain appearances upon the unknown part. The stump of a tree is perceived in part as an elongated thing but not in the other part as the stump of a tree, and it is in reference to this part that the mis-attribution of an illusory appearance, e.g. a man, is possible by virtue of which the elongated part is perceived as man. But Brahman is partless and no division of its part is conceivable. It must therefore be wholly known or wholly unknown, and hence there can be no illusion regarding it. Again, illusion implies that an illusory appearance has to be imposed upon an object. But the *avidyā*, which is beginningless, cannot itself be supposed to be an illusory appearance. Following the analogy of beginninglessness Brahman may be regarded as illusory. The reply that Brahman being the basis cannot be illusory is meaningless; for though the basis is regarded as the ground of the imposition, there is no necessary implication that the basis must also be true. The objection that the basis has an independent reality because it is the basis associated with ignorance which can become the datum of illusion is futile; because the basis may also be an unreal one in a serial process where at each stage it is associated with ignorance. In such a view it is not the pure Brahman which becomes the basis but the illusory Brahman which is associated with ignorance. Moreover, if the *avidyā* and its modifications were absolutely non-existent they could not be the subject of imposition. What really exists somewhere may be imposed elsewhere, but not that which does not exist at all. The pure chimericals like the hare's horn can never be the subjects of imposition, for that which is absolutely non-existent cannot appear at all.

Again, illusions are supposed to happen through the operation of impressions (*saṃskāra*), but in the beginningless cosmic illusion the impressions must also be beginningless and co-existent with the basis (*adhiṣṭhāna*) and therefore real. The impressions must exist prior to the illusion and as such they cannot themselves be illusory, and if they are not illusory they must be real. Again, the impressions cannot belong to Brahman, for then it could not be qualityless and pure; they cannot belong to individual souls, for these are produced as a result of illusory impositions which are again the products of the operation of impressions. Further, similarity plays an important part in all illusions, but Brahman as the ground or basis which is absolutely pure and qualityless has no similarity with anything. There cannot also be any imaginary similarity imposed upon the qualityless Brahman, for such an imaginary imposition presupposes a prior illusion. Again, all illusions are seen to have a beginning, whereas entities that are not illusory, such as the individual souls, are found to be beginningless. It is also erroneous to hold that the ego-substratum behaves as the basis of the illusion, for it is itself a product of the illusion.

Furthermore, the supposition that the world-appearance is a cosmic illusion which is related to pure consciousness in an illusory relation (*ādhyāsika-sambandha*) is unwarrantable. But the Śaṅkarites admit that the relation between the external world and the knower is brought about by the operation of the mind in modification, called *vṛtti*. Moreover, if the pure consciousness be admitted to be right knowledge or *pramā*, then its object or that which shines with it must also be right knowledge and as such it cannot be the basis of false knowledge. If the pure consciousness be false knowledge, it cannot obviously be the basis of false knowledge. The mere fact that some of the known relations, such as contact, inseparable inherence, do not hold between the object of knowledge and knowledge does not prove that their relation must be an illusory one, for other kinds of relations may subsist between them Knowledge-and-the-known may itself be regarded as a unique kind of relation. It is also wrong to suppose that all relations are false because they are constituents of the false universe, for the universe is supposed to be false because the relations are false, and hence there would be a vicious infinite. Again, the objection that, if relations are admitted to establish connection between two relata, then further relations may be necessary to relate the relation to relata and that this would lead to a vicious infinite, and also that, if relations are identical in essence with the relata, then relations become useless, is futile. The same objections would be admissible in the case of illusory relations. If it is held that, since all relations are illusory, the above strictures do not apply, then it may be pointed out that if the order of the relations be subversed, then, instead of conceiving the jug to be a product of *māyā*, *māyā* may be taken as a product of the jug. Thus, not only the Śaṅkarites but even the Buddhists have to admit the orderly character of relations. In the Nimbārka view all relations are regarded as true, being the different modes of the manifestation of the energy of God. Even if the relations be denied, then the nature of Brahman cannot be described as this or that.

(*c*) *Refutation of the Śaṇkarite View of Ajñāna.*

Ajñāna is defined as a beginningless positive entity which is destructible by knowledge (*anādi-bhāvatve sati jñāna-nivartyatvam*). The definition is unavailing as it does not apply to ignorance that hides an ordinary object before it is perceived. Nor does *ajñāna* apply to the ignorance regarding the negation of an object, since it is of a positive nature. Again, in the case of the ignorance that abides in the saint who has attained the knowledge of Brahman, the *ajñāna* is seen to persist even though knowledge has been attained; hence the definition of *ajñāna* as that which is destructible by knowledge fails. In the case of the perception of red colour in the crystal through reflection, the ignorant perception of the white crystal as red persists even though it is known to be false and due to reflection. Here also the ignorance is not removed by knowledge. It is also wrong to suppose that *ajñāna*, which is but the product of defect, should be regarded as beginningless. Moreover, it may be pointed out that all things (excluding negation) that are beginningless are also eternal like the souls and it is a curious assumption that there should be an entity called *ajñāna* which is beginningless and yet destructible. Again, *ajñāna* is often described as being different both from being and non-being, but has yet been defined as a positive entity. It is also difficult to imagine how, since negative entities are regarded as products of *ajñāna*, *ajñāna* may itself be regarded as a positive entity. Moreover, the error or illusion that takes place through absence of knowledge has to be admitted as a negative entity; but being an illusion it has to be regarded as a product of *ajñāna*.

There is no proof of the existence of *ajñāna* in the so-called perception "I am ignorant." It cannot be the pure Brahman, for then that would have to be styled impure. It cannot be a positive knowledge by itself, for that is the very point which has to be proved. Further, if in establishing *ajñāna* (ignorance) one has to fall back upon *jñāna* or knowledge, and if in establishing the latter one has to fall back upon the former, then that would involve a vicious circle. It cannot be the ego-substratum (*aham-artha*), for that is itself a product of *ajñāna* and cannot be in existence as the datum of the perception of *ajñāna*. The ego itself cannot be perceived as ignorant, for it is itself a product of ignorance. The ego is never regarded as synonymous with ignorance, and thus there is no means of proving the supposition that ignorance is perceived as a positive entity either as a quality or as a substance. Ignorance is thus nothing but "absence of knowledge" (*jñānā-bhāva*) and ought to be recognized by the Śaṅkarites, since they have to admit the validity of the experience "I do not know what you say" which is evidently nothing but a reference to the absence of knowledge which is admitted by the Śaṅkarites in other cases. There is no proof that the cases in point are in any way different from such cases of absence of knowledge. Again, if the *ajñāna* is regarded as hiding an object, then in the case of mediate knowledge (*parokṣa-vṛtti*—where according to the Śaṅkarites the *vṛtti* or the mental state does not remove the veil of *ajñāna*) one ought to feel that one is ignorant of the object of one's mediate knowledge, for the veil of *ajñāna* remains here intact[1]. Moreover, all cases of the supposed perception of ignorance can be explained as the comprehension of the absence of knowledge. In the above manner Mukunda criti-

[1] *parokṣa-vṛtter viṣayā-varakā-jñāna-nivartakatvena parokṣato jñāte'pi na jānāmī'ty anubhavā-pātāc ca. Para-pakṣa-giri-vajra*, p. 76.

cizes the theories of *ajñāna* and of the illusion in their various aspects. But as the method of the dialectic followed in these logical refutations is substantially the same as that attempted by Veṅkaṭanātha and Vyāsatīrtha which have been examined in detail it is not necessary to give a detailed study of Mukunda's treatment.

The Pramāṇas according to Mādhava Mukunda.

The followers of Nimbārka admit only three (perception, inference and testimony) out of the following eight *pramāṇas*, viz. perception (*pratyakṣa*), inference (*anumāna*), similarity (*upamāna*), scriptural testimony (*śabda*), implication (*arthāpatti*), non-perception (*anupalabdhi*), inclusion of the lower within the higher as of ten within a hundred (*sambhava*), and tradition (*aitihya*). Perception is of two kinds, external and internal. The external perception is of five kinds according to the five cognitive senses. The mental perception called also the internal perception is of two kinds, ordinary (*laukika*) and transcendent (*alaukika*). The perception of pleasure and pain is a case of ordinary internal perception, whereas the perception of the nature of self, God and their qualities is a case of transcendent internal perception. This transcendent internal perception is again of two kinds, that which flashes forth through the meditation of an entity and that which comes out of meditation on the essence of a scriptural text. The scriptural reference that the ultimate truth cannot be perceived by the mind means either that the ultimate truth in its entirety cannot be perceived by the mind or that unless the mind is duly trained by a teacher or by the formation of right tendencies it cannot have a glimpse of the transcendent realities. Knowledge is a beginningless, eternal and all-pervasive characteristic of individual selves. But in our state of bondage this knowledge is like the rays of a lamp in a closed place, in a state of contraction. Just as the rays of a lamp enclosed within a jug may go out through the hole into the room and straight through the door of the room and flood with light some object outside, so the knowledge in each individual may by the modification of the mind reach the senses and again through their modification reach the object and, having flood-lit it, may illuminate both the object and the knowledge. The *ajñāna* (ignorance) that ceases with the knowledge of an object is the partial cessation of a state of contraction leading to the flashing of knowledge. What is meant by the phrase "knowledge has an object" is that knowledge takes a particular form and illuminates it. The objects remain as they are, but they are manifested through their association with knowledge and remain unmanifested without it. In the case of internal perception the operation of the senses is not required, and so pleasure and pain are directly perceived by the mind. In self-consciousness or the perception of the self, the self being itself self-luminous, the mental directions to the self remove the state of contraction and reveal the nature of the self. So God can be realized through His grace and the removal of obstruction through the meditative condition of the mind[1].

In inference the knowledge of the existence of the *hetu* (reason) in the minor (*pakṣa*) having a concomitance (*vyāpti*) with the probandum (*sādhya*), otherwise called *parāmarśa* (*vahni-vyāpya-dhūmavān ayam evaṃ-rūpaḥ*), is regarded as the inferential process (*anumāna*) and from it comes the inference (e.g. "the hill is fiery"). Two kinds of inference, i.e. for the conviction of one's own self (*svārthānumāna*) and for convincing others (*parārthānumāna*), are admitted here; and in the latter case only three propositions (the thesis, *pratijñā*, the reason, *hetu*, and the instance, *udāharaṇa*) are regarded as necessary. Three kinds of inference are admitted, namely *kevalā-nvayi* (argument from only positive instances, where negative instances are not available), *kevala-vyatireki* (argument from purely negative instances, where positive instances are not available), and *anvaya-vyatireki* (argument from both sets of positive and negative instances). In addition to the well-known concomitance (*vyāpti*) arising from the above three ways, scriptural assertions are also regarded as cases of concomitance. Thus there is a scriptural passage to the following effect: The self is indestructible and it is never divested of its essential qualities (*avināśī vā are ātma an-ucchitti-dharmā*), and this is regarded as a *vyāpti* or concomitance, from which one may infer the indestructibility of the soul like the Brahman.[2] There are no other specially interesting features in the Nimbārka doctrine of inference.

Knowledge of similarity is regarded as being due to a separate *pramāṇa* called *upamāna*. Such a comprehension of similarity (*sādṛśya*) may be due to perception or through a scriptural assertion

[1] *Para-pakṣa-giri-vajra*, pp. 203–206. [2] *Ibid.* p. 210.

of similarity. Thus a man may perceive the similarity of the face to the moon or he may learn from the scriptures that the self and God are similar in nature and thus comprehend such similarity. This may be included within the proposition of instance or illustration in an inference (*upamānasya dṛṣṭānta-mātrā-ika-vigraha-tvenā'numānā-vayave udāharaṇe antarbhāvaḥ. Para-pakṣa-giri-vajra*, p. 254).

That from which there is a communication of the negation or non-existence of anything is regarded as the *pramāṇa* or *anupalabdhi.* It is of four kinds: firstly, the negation that precedes a production, called *prāg-abhāva*; secondly, the negation of one entity in another, i.e. the negation as "otherness," called *anyonyā-bhāva*; thirdly, the negation as the destruction of an entity, called *dhvaṃsā-bhāva*; fourthly, the negation of an entity in all times (*kālatraye'pi nastī'ti pratīti-viṣayaḥ atyantā-bhāvaḥ*). But it is unnecessary to admit *abhāva* or *anupalabdhi* as a separate *pramāṇa*, for according to the Nimbārkas negation is not admitted as a separate category. The perception of negation is nothing but the perception of the locus of the object of negation as unassociated with it. The negation-precedent (*prāg-abhāva*) of a jug is nothing but the lump of clay; the negation of destruction of a jug is nothing but the broken fragments of a jug; the negation of otherness (*anyonyā-bhāva*) is the entity tha. is perceived as the other of an another, and the negation existent in all times is nothing but the locus of a negation. Thus the *pramāṇa* of negation may best be included with perception. The *pramāṇa* of implication may well be taken as a species of inference. The *pramāṇa* of *sambhava* may well be regarded as a deductive piece of reasoning.

The Nimbārkas admit the self-validity of the *pramāṇas* (*svataḥ-prāmāṇya*) in the manner of the Śaṅkarites. Self-validity (*svatastva*) is defined as the fact that in the absence of any defect an assemblage forming the data of cognition produces a cognition that represents its nature as it is (*doṣā-bhāvatve yāvat-svā-śraya-bhūta-pramā-grāhaka-sāmagrī-mātra-grāhyatvam*)[1]. Just as the eye when it perceives a coloured object perceives also the colours and forms associated with it, so it takes with the cognition of an object also the validity of such a cognition.

The nature of God can, however, be expressed only by the

[1] *Para-pakṣa-giri-vajra*, p. 253.

scriptural texts, as the signifying powers of these texts directly originate from God. Indeed, all the powers of individual minds also are derived from God, but they cannot signify Him as they are tainted by the imperfections of the human mind. The Mīmāṃsists are wrong to think that the import of all parts of the Vedas consists in enjoining the performance of the Vedic duties, for the results of all deeds ultimately produce a desire for knowing Brahman and through it produce the fitness for the attainment of emancipation. Thus considered from this point of view the goal of the performance of all duties is the attainment of emancipation[1]. There cannot be any scope for the performance of duties for one who has realized the Brahman, for that is the ultimate fruit of all actions and the wise man has nothing else to attain by the performance of actions. Just as though different kinds of seeds may be sown, yet if there is no rain these different kinds of seeds cannot produce the different kinds of trees, so the actions by themselves cannot produce the fruits independently. It is through God's grace that actions can produce their specific fruits. So though the obligatory duties are helpful in purifying the mind and in producing a desire for true knowledge, they cannot by themselves be regarded as the ultimate end, which consists in the production of a desire for true knowledge and the ultimate union with God.

Criticism of the views of Rāmānuja and Bhāskara.

The view of Rāmānuja and his followers is that the souls and the inanimate world are associated with God as His qualities. The function of qualities (*viśeṣana*) is that by their presence they distinguish an object from other similar objects. Thus, when one says "Rāma the son of Daśaratha," the adjective "son of Daśaratha" distinguishes this Rāma from the other two Rāmas, Balarāma and Paraśurāma. But no such purpose is served by styling the individual souls and the inanimate nature as being qualities of Brahman, for they do not distinguish Him from any other similar persons; for the Rāmānujists also do not admit any other category than the conscious souls, the unconscious world and God the controller of them both. Since there is nothing to differentiate, the concept of the souls and matter as quality or differentia also fails. Another

[1] *Para-pakṣa-giri-vajra*, pp. 279–280.

function of qualities is that they help the substance to which they belong to become better known. The knowledge of souls and matter as qualities of God does not help us to know or comprehend Him better.

Again, if God be associated with matter and souls, He is found to be associated with their defects also. It may be argued whether the Brahman in which the souls and matter are held to abide is itself unqualified or qualified. In the former alternative the Rāmānujas like the Śaṅkarites have to admit the existence of an unqualified entity and a part in Brahman has to be admitted which exists in itself as an unqualified entity. If the Brahman be in part qualityless and in part associated with qualities, then it would in part be omniscient only in certain parts of itself. Again, if the pure unassociated Brahman be regarded as omniscient, then there would be one Brahman associated with omniscience and other qualities and another Brahman associated with matter and soul, and the doctrine of qualified monism would thus break down. The pure Brahman being outside the souls and matter, these two would be without a controller inside them and would thus be independent of God. Moreover, God in this view would be in certain parts associated with the highest and purest qualities and in other parts with the defiled characters of the material world and the imperfect souls. In the other alternative, i.e. if Brahman as associated with matter and souls be the ultimate substance which is qualified with matter and souls, then there would be two composite entities and not one, and God will as before be associated with two opposite sets of pure and impure qualities. Again, if God be admitted to be a composite unity and if matter and souls which are regarded as mutually distinct and different are admitted to be constituents of Him though He is different in nature from them, it is difficult to imagine how under the circumstances those constituents can be at once one with God and yet different from Him[1].

In the Nimbārka view Śri Kṛṣṇa is the Lord, the ultimate Brahman and He is the support of the universe consisting of the souls and matter which are derivative parts of Him and are absolutely under His control and thus have a dependent existence only (*para-tantra-sattva*). Entities that have dependent existence are of two kinds, the souls which, though they pass through apparent

[1] *Para-pakṣa-giri-vajra*, p. 342.

birth and death, are yet eternal in their nature and the substance of the corporeal structure that supports them, the matter. The scriptural texts that speak of duality refer to this duality that subsists between the ultimate substance, the Brahman, which alone has the independent existence, and souls and matter which have only a dependent existence. The scriptural texts that deny duality refer to the ultimate entity which has independent existence which forms the common ground and basis of all kinds of existence. The texts that try to refer to Brahman by negations (*ne'ti, ne'ti*) signify how Brahman is different from all other things, or, in other words, how Brahman is different from matter and the souls which are limited by material conditions[1]. Brahman is thus the absolute Being, the abode of all good and noble qualities, which is different from all entities having only dependent existence. The monistic texts refer to the fact, as has already been noted, that the world of matter and the infinite number of souls having but dependent existence cannot exist independent of God (*tad-apṛthak-siddha*) and are, in that sense, one with Him. They also have the essence of their being in Brahman (*brahmā-tmatva*), are pervaded through and through by it (*tad-vyāpyatva*), are supported in it and held in it and are always being completely controlled and dominated by it[2]. Just as all individual objects, a jug, a stone, etc., may be said to have substantiality (*dravyatva*) permeating through them by virtue of their being substances, so the souls and the matter may be called God by virtue of the fact that God permeates through them as their inner essence. But just as none of these individual objects can be regarded as substance *per se*, so the souls and matter cannot also be identified with God as being one with Him[3].

The Bhāskarites are wrong in asserting that the individuals are false inasmuch as they have only a false appearance through the

[1] *vastutas tu ne'ti ne'tī'ti nañbhyāṃ prakṛta-sthūla-sūkṣmatvāṃ-di-dharmavat jaḍa-vastu-tad-avacchinna-jīva-vastu-vilakṣaṇaṃ brahme'ti pratipādyate. Para-pakṣa-giri-vajra*, p. 347.

[2] *tayoś ca. brahmā-tmakatva-tan-niyamyatva-tad-vyāpyatva-tad-adhīna-sattva-tad-ādheyatva-di-yogena tad-apṛthak-siddhatvāt abhedo'pi svābhāvikaḥ. Ibid.* p. 355.

[3] *yathā ghaṭo dravyaṃ, pṛthivī-dravyam ity-ādau dravyatvā-vacchinnena saha ghaṭatvā-vacchinna-pṛthivītvā-vacchinnayoḥ sāmānādhikaraṇyaṃ mukhyam eva viśeṣasya sāmānyā-bhinnatva-niyamāt evaṃ prakṛte'pi sārvajñyā-dy-anantā-chintyā-parimita-viseṣā-vacchinnenā'paricchinna-śakti-vibhūtikena tat-padārthena para-bhrahmaṇā svā-tmaka-cetana-cetanatvā-vacchinyayos tad-ātma-rūpayos tvam-ādi-padārthayoḥ sāmānādhikaraṇyaṃ mukhyam eva. Ibid.* pp. 355–356.

limitations (*upādhi*) imposed upon the pure Brahman. The nature of the imposition of Brahman by the so-called conditions is unintelligible. It may mean that the atomic individual is the result of the imposition of the conditions on Brahman by which the Brahman as a whole appears as the individual soul or by which the Brahman is split asunder, and being thus split appears as the individual self or the Brahman as qualified by the conditions or that the conditions themselves appear as the individuals. The Brahman being homogeneous and unchangeable cannot be split asunder. Even if it can be split asunder, the individual selves being the products of such a splitting would have a beginning in time and would not thus be eternal; and it has to be admitted that on such a view Brahman has to be split up into as many infinite parts as there are selves. If it is held that the parts of Brahman as limited by the conditions appear as individual souls, then Brahman would be subject to all the defects of the conditions which could so modify it as to resolve it into parts for the production of the individual selves. Moreover, owing to the shifting nature of the conditions the nature of the selves would vary and they might have in this way spontaneous bondage and salvation[1]. If with the shifting of the conditions Brahman also shifts, then Brahman would not be partless and all-pervasive. If it is held that Brahman in its entirety becomes envisaged by the conditions, then, on the one hand, there will be no transcendent pure Brahman and, on the other, there will be one self in all the different bodies. Again, if the individuals are regarded as entirely different from Brahman, then the assertion that they are but the product of the conditioning of Brahman has to be given up. If it is held that the conditions themselves are the individuals, then it becomes a materialistic view like that of the Cārvākas. Again, it cannot be held that the conditions only cover up the natural qualities of Brahman such as omniscience, etc., for these being natural qualities of Brahman cannot be removed. Further questions may arise as to whether these natural qualities of Brahman are different from Brahman or not, or whether this is a case of difference-in-identity. They cannot be absolutely different, for that would be an admission of duality. They cannot be identical with Brahman, for then they

[1] *kiñ ca upādhau gacchati sati upādhinā svā-vacchinna-brahma-pradeśākarṣanā-yogāt anukṣaṇam upādhi-saṃyukta-pradeśa-bhedāt kṣane kṣane bandha-mokṣau syātām. Para-pakṣa-giri-vajra*, p. 357.

could not be regarded as qualities of Brahman. If it be its own essence, then it cannot be covered up, for in that case Brahman would lose all its omniscience. If it is held that it is a case of difference-in-identity, then it comes to an acceptance of the Nimbārka creed.

Again, if it is held that the so-called natural qualities of omniscience, etc., are also due to conditions, it may be asked whether such conditions are different from or identical with Brahman. In the latter alternative they would have no capacity to produce any plurality in Brahman. In the former alternative, it may be asked whether they are moved by themselves into operation or by some other entity or by Brahman. The first view would be open to the criticism of self-dynamism, the second to that of a vicious infinite, and the third to a vicious circle. Moreover, in this view, Brahman being eternal, its dynamism would also be eternal; at no time would the conditions cease to operate, and thus there would be no emancipation. The conditions cannot be regarded as false, unreal or non-existent, for then that would be an acceptance of the Nimbārka creed[1].

It may further be asked whether the conditions are imposed by certain causes or whether they are without any cause. In the former alternative we have a vicious infinite and in the latter even emancipated beings may have further bondage. Again, it may be asked whether the qualities, e.g. omniscience, that belong to Brahman pervade the whole of Brahman or whether they belong only to particular parts of Brahman. In the former view, if there is entire veiling of the qualities of Brahman there cannot be any emancipation and the whole field of consciousness being veiled by ignorance there is absolute blindness or darkness (*jagad-āndhya-prasaṅga*). In the second view the omniscience of Brahman being only a quality or a part of it the importance of Brahman as a whole fails.

Following the Bhāskara line it may be asked whether the emancipated beings have separate existence or not. If the former alternative be admitted, and if after destruction of the conditions the individuals still retain their separate existence then the view that differences are created by the conditions has to be given up (*aupādhika-bheda-vādo datta-jalāñjaliḥ syāt*). If the distinctness of the souls is not preserved in their emancipation, then their very

[1] *Para-pakṣa-giri-vajra*, p. 358.

essence is destroyed, and this would almost be the same as the *māyā* doctrine of the Śaṅkarites, who hold that the essential nature of both God and souls is destructible.

It is wrong to suppose that individuals are but parts of which a structural Brahman is constituted, for in that case, being made up of parts, the Brahman would be itself destructible. When the scriptures speak of the universe and the souls as being but a part of Brahman, the main emphasis is on the fact that Brahman is infinite and the universe is but too small in comparison with it. It is also difficult to imagine how the minds or the *antaḥkaraṇas* can operate as conditions for limiting the nature of the Brahman. How should Brahman allow these so-called conditions to mutilate its nature? It could not have created these conditions for the production of individual souls, for these souls were not in existence before the conditions were in existence. Thus the Bhāskara doctrine that the concept of distinction and unity of Brahman is due to the operation of conditions (*aupādhika-bhedābheda-vāda*) is entirely false.

According to the Nimbārka view, therefore, the unity and difference that exist between the individuals and Brahman is natural (*svābhāvika*) and not due to conditions (*aupādhika*) as in the case of Bhāskara. The coiling posture (*kuṇḍala*) of a snake is different from the long snake as it is in itself and is yet identical with it in the sense that the coiling posture is an effect; it is dependent and under the absolute control of the snake as it is and it has no separate existence from the nature of the snake as it is. The coiled state of the snake exists in the elongated state but only in an undifferentiated, unperceivable way; and is nothing but the snake by which it is pervaded through and through and supported in its entirety. So this universe of matter and souls is also in one aspect absolutely identical with God, being supported entirely by Him, pervaded through and through by Him and entirely dependent on Him, and yet in another aspect different from Him in all its visible manifestations and operations[1]. The other analogy through which the Nimbārkists try to explain the situation is that of the sun and its rays which are at once one with it and are also perceived as different from it.

[1] *yathā kuṇḍalā-vasthā-pannasya aheḥ kuṇḍalaṃ vyaktā-pannatvāt pratyakṣa-pramāṇa-gocaraṃ tad-bhedasya svābhāvikatvāt lambāyamānā-vasthāyāṃ tu sarpā-yatā-vacchinna-svarūpeṇa kuṇḍalasya tatra sattve'pi avyakta-nāma-rūpatā-pattyā pratyakṣā-gocaratvaṃ sarvā-tmakatva-tad-ādheyatva-tad-vyāpyatvā-dinā tad-apṛthak-siddhatvād abhedasyā'pi svābhāvikatvam. Para-pakṣa-giri-vajra*, p. 361.

The difference of this view from that of the Rāmānujists is that while the latter consider that the souls and the matter qualify the nature of Brahman and are in that sense one with it, the former repudiate the concept of a permanent modification of the nature of Brahman by the souls and matter.

The Reality of the World.

The Śaṅkarites hold that if the world which is of the nature of effect were real it would not be liable to contradiction at the time of Brahma-knowledge; if it were chimerical it would not appear to our sense. The world, however, appears to our senses and is ultimately liable to contradiction; it has therefore an indefinable (*anirvacanīya*) nature which is the same thing as saying that the world is false[1]. But what is the meaning of this indefinability? It cannot mean the absolutely non-existent, like the chimerical entities of the hare's horn; it cannot mean that which is absolutely non-existent, for then it would be the souls. But all things must be either existent or non-existent, for there is no third category which is different from the existent and the non-existent. It cannot also be that of which no definition can be given, for it has already been defined as indefinability (*nā'pi nirvacanā-narhattvaṃ anenai'va nirucyamānatayā asambhavāt*). It cannot be said to be that which is not the locus of non-existence, for even the chimericals are not so, and even Brahman, which is regarded as existent and which is absolutely qualityless, is not the locus of any real existence; for Brahman is only existent in its own nature and is not the locus of any other existence. If it is said that Brahman is the locus of the existence of false appearances, then that may be said to be true as well of the so-called indefinable. Brahman is not the locus of any existence that has the same status as itself. It cannot be defined as that which is not the locus of either the existent or the non-existent, for there is nothing which is the locus of absolute non-existence, since even the chimerical is not the locus of its own non-existence. Moreover, since Brahman and the chimerical have the quality of being qualityless, they may themselves be regarded as the locus of that which is both existent and

[1] *asac cen na pratīyate sac cen na vādhyate, pratīyate vādhyate ca ataḥ sad-asad-vilakṣaṇaṃ hy anirvacanīyam eva abhyūpagantavyam. Para-pakṣa-giri-vajra*, p. 384.

non-existent, and as such may themselves be regarded as indefinable.

It cannot also be said that indefinability is that of which no sufficient description can be given that "this is such" or that "this is not such," for no such sufficient description can be given of Brahman itself. There would thus be little difference between Brahman and the indefinable. If it is held that "the indefinable" is that regarding the existence of which no evidence can be put forward, then the same may be said about Brahman, because the Brahman being the conceptless pure essence, it is not possible to prove its existence by any proof.

Again, when it is said that the indefinable is that which is neither existent nor non-existent, the meaning of the two terms "existence" and "non-existence" becomes somewhat unintelligible. For "existence" cannot mean only "being" as a class concept, for such a concept does not exist either in Brahman or in the world-appearance. Existence cannot be defined as causal efficiency (*artha-kriyā-kāritva*), nor as that which is never contradicted; nor non-existence as that which is contradicted, for the world-appearance which is liable to contradiction is not supposed to be non-existent; it is said to be that which is neither existent nor non-existent. Existence and non-existence cannot also be defined as that which can or cannot be proved, for Brahman is an entity which is neither proved nor unproved. Moreover, the world-appearance cannot be said to be that which is different from all that which can be called "existent" or "non-existent," for it is admitted to have a practical existence (*vyavahārika-sattā*). Again, it cannot be urged that if the nature of anything cannot be properly defined as existent or non-existent that it signifies that such an entity must be wholly unreal (*avāstava*). If a thing is not properly describable as existent or non-existent, that does not imply that it is unreal. The nature of the final dissolution of *avidyā* cannot be described as existent or not, but that does not imply that such a dissolution is itself unreal and indefinable (*nā'nirvācyaśca tat-kṣayaḥ*).

Again, from the simple assertion that the world is liable to dissolution through knowledge, its falsity does not necessarily follow. It is wrong to suppose that knowledge destroys only false ignorance, for knowledge destroys its own negation which has a content similar to that of itself; the knowledge of one thing, say that of a jug, is removed by the knowledge of another, the subconscious impression is removed by recognition, attachment is removed by the knowledge of the defects of all worldly things and so also virtuous actions destroy sins. In the case under discussion also it may well be supposed that it is not merely the knowledge of Brahman but meditation of its nature that removes all false notions about the world. Thus, even if the bondage is real, there cannot be any objection that it cannot be cut asunder through the meditation of the nature of Brahman if the scriptures so direct. It does not follow from any legitimate assumption that what can be cut asunder or removed must necessarily be false. Again, it is well known in experience that what demolishes and what is demolished have the same status of existence; if the knowledge of Brahman can destroy our outlook of the world, that outlook must also be a real and true one. As the knowledge and the object of knowledge have the same status, the defects, as also the locus wherein the defects are imposed, have the same status; the Brahman and the *ajñāna* also have the same status and both are equally real.

Further, if what is called *ajñāna* is merely false knowledge, then even when it is removed by the realization, there is no reason why it should still persist in the stage of *jīvanmukti* or sainthood. The mere fact, therefore, that anything is removable by knowledge does not prove its falsity but only its antagonism to knowledge. So the world is real and the bondage also is real. The bondage is removed not by any kind of knowledge but by the grace of God[1]. The function of true knowledge is to awaken God to exert His grace to cut asunder the knots of bondage.

Again, all the scriptures agree in holding that the world we see around us is being protected and maintained by God. If the world were but a mere false appearance, there would be no meaning in saying that it is being maintained by God. For knowing the world-appearance to be false, He would not be tempted to make any effort for the protection and maintenance of that which is false and unreal. If God Himself is admitted to be under the influence of ignorance, He cannot be entitled to be called God at all.

Pursuing the old dialectical type of reasoning, Mādhava Mukunda urges that the sort of falsehood that is asserted of the

[1] *vastutas tu bhagavat-prasādād eva bandha-nivṛttir na prakārā'ntareṇa. Para-pakṣa-giri-vajra*, p. 388.

world can never be proved or demonstrated. One of the reasons that is adduced in favour of the falsity of the world is that it is knowable or the object of an intellectual state (*dṛśya*). But if the Vedāntic texts refer to the nature of Brahman, the due comprehension and realization of the meaning of such texts must involve the concept of the nature of Brahman as its object, and thus Brahman itself would be the object of an intellectual state and therefore false. If it is urged that the Brahman can be the object of an intellectual state only in a conditioned form and that the conditioned Brahman is admitted to be false, then the reply is that since the Brahman in its pure form can never manifest itself its purity cannot be proved. If the Brahman does not express itself in its purity through an ideational state corresponding to scriptural texts describing the nature of Brahman, then it is not self-luminous; if it is expressed through such a state, then being expressible through a mental state it is false. It cannot also be said that since all that is impure is known to be non-self-luminous it follows that all that is pure is self-luminous, for the pure being absolutely unrelationed cannot be referred to or known by way of a negative concomitance. Thus the impure is known only in itself as a positive entity and not as the opposite of the pure, for such a knowledge would imply the knowledge of purity. If, therefore, the predicate of self-luminosity is not denied of impurity as an opposite of "purity," the predicate of self-luminosity cannot also be affirmed of "purity." Moreover, if the pure Brahman is never intelligibly realizable, then there would be no emancipation, or there would be an emancipation only with the conditioned Brahman.

Moreover, if all objects are regarded as illusory impositions on pure Brahman, then in the comprehension of these objects the pure Brahman must also be comprehended. The scriptures also say: "Brahman is to be perceived with the mind and with the keen intellect" (*manasai'vā'nudraṣṭavyaṃ...dṛśyate tvagrayā buddhyā*). There are also scriptural passages which say that it is the pure Brahman which is the object of meditation (*taṃ paśyati niṣkalaṃ dhyāyamānam*).

Again, if perceivability or intelligibility determining falsehood is defined as relationing with consciousness, then since pure consciousness is supposed to have a relationing through illusion it also is liable to the charge of being perceivable. In this connection it is difficult to conceive how Brahman, which has no opposition to *ajñāna*, can have an opposing influence against it when it is in conjunction with a mental state or *vṛtti*. Instead of such an assumption it might as well be assumed that the object itself acquires an opposing influence to its own ignorance when it is in association with a mental state having the same content as itself. On such a supposition perceivability does not consist in relation with consciousness as conditioned by mental state, for the conditioning has a bearing on the object and not on the consciousness. Thus it may well be assumed that an object becomes perceivable by being conditioned by a mental state of its own content. The assumption that the *vṛtti* or the mental state must be reflected on pure consciousness is unnecessary, for it may well be assumed that the ignorance is removed by the mental state itself. An object comes into awareness when it is represented by a mental state, and in order to be aware of anything it is not necessary that the mental state, idea or representation should be reflected in consciousness. Again, if Brahman cannot be its own object, it cannot also be termed self-luminous. For self-luminous means that it is manifest to itself independently, and this involves the implication that the Brahman is an object to itself. If that which is not an object to itself can be called self-luminous, then even material objects can be called self-luminous. Moreover, in the differenceless Brahman there cannot be any immediacy or self-luminousness apart from its nature (*nirviśeṣe brahmaṇi svarūpa-bhinnā-parokṣasya abhāvena*).

In the monistic view the self is regarded as pure knowledge which has neither a subject nor an object. But that which is subject-less and object-less can hardly be called knowledge, for knowledge is that which manifests objects. If that which does not manifest objects can be called knowledge, even a jug can be called knowledge. Again, the question naturally arises whether, if knowledge be regarded as identical with the self, such knowledge is valid or invalid; if it be valid, then the *ajñāna* which shines through it should also be valid, and if it be invalid, then that must be due to some defects and there are no such defects in the self. If it is neither false nor right knowledge, it would not be knowledge at all. Again, if the world-appearance is an illusion, then it must be an imposition on the Brahman. If Brahman be the basis (*adhiṣṭhāna*) of the illusory imposition, then it must be an entity that is known in a general manner but not in its details. But Brahman is not an entity of which we can have either any general or specific knowledge. Brahman cannot therefore be regarded as the basis of the imposition of any illusion. In this connection it has further to be borne in mind that if the world were non-existent then it could not have appeared in consciousness; the chimerical entities are never perceived by anyone. The argument that even the illusory snake can produce real fear is invalid, for it is not the illusory snake that produces fear but the real knowledge of snakes that produces it. The child is not afraid of handling even a real snake, for it has no knowledge of snakes and their injurious character. Even dreams are to be regarded as real creation by God and not illusory impositions. The argument that they are false since they can only be perceived by the dreamer and not by others who are near him is invalid, for even the feelings and ideas felt or known by a person cannot be perceived by others who are near him[1].

The world is thus not an illusory imposition on the pure Brahman, but a real transformation of the varied powers of God. The difference of this view from that of Sāṃkhya is that while the Sāṃkhya believes in the transformation of certain primary entities in their entirety, the Nimbārkists believe in the transformation of the various powers of God. God Himself remains unchanged and unmodified, and it is only His powers that suffer modification and thereby produce the visible world[2].

The explanation that the world is produced through the reflection of Brahman in *māyā* or by its limitation through it is invalid, for since the *māyā* is an entity of an entirely different order, there cannot be any reflection of Brahman in it or a limitation by it. It is not possible to bind down a thief with a dream-rope.

Vanamālī Miśra.

Vanamālī Miśra, a native of Triyaga, a village within two miles of Brindavan, of Bharadvāja lineage, in his *Vedānta-siddhānta-saṃgraha*, called also *Śruti-siddhānta-saṃgraha*, gives some of the important tenets of the Nimbārka school. The work is written in the form of *Kārikās* and a commentary on it and is based on the commentary on the *Brahma-sūtra* by Nimbārka and other commentaries on it.

[1] *Para-pakṣa-giri-vajra*, p. 420.

[2] *Ibid.* p. 429.

He regards sorrow as being due to attachment to things that are outside one's own self, and the opposite of it as happiness[1]. All actions performed with a view to securing any selfish end, all performance of actions prohibited by Vedic injunctions and non-performance of duties rendered obligatory by Vedas produce sins. The opposite of this and all such actions as may please God are regarded as producing virtue. It is the power of God which is at the root of all virtue and vice which operates by veiling the qualities of God to us. This nescience (*avidyā*) is real and positive and different in different individuals. It produces the error or illusion which consists in regarding a thing as what it is not; and it is this false knowledge that is the cause of rebirth[2]. This *avidyā* is different with different individuals. It is through this *avidyā* that one gets attached to one's possession as "mine" and has also the false experience of individual freedom. In reality all one's actions are due to God, and when a person realizes this he ceases to have any attachment to anything and does not look forward for the fruits of his deeds. The *avidyā* produces the mind and its experiences of sorrows and pleasures; it also produces the false attachment by which the self regards the experiences as its own and ceases to realize its own nature as pure knowledge and bliss. Only the *videhi-muktas* enjoy this state; those in the state of *jīvanmukti* or sainthood enjoy it only to a partial extent. It is on account of attachments produced by ignorance that man is stirred to be led by the will of God. But as the ignorance is a true ignorance, so the experience of sorrow is also a true experience. All our rebirths are due to our actions performed against the mandates of the Vedas or for the fulfilment of our desires[3]. The purity of the soul is attained by the realization of the idea that all our actions are induced by God and that the performer has no independence in anything. When a person feels that it is through false association with other things, and by considering oneself as the real independent agent that one gets into trouble, one naturally loses all interest in one's actions and experience of

[1] *Śruti-siddhānta-saṃgraha*, I. 9, 10, 11.

[2] *prati-jīvaṃ vibhinnā syāt satyā ca bhāva-rūpiṇī | a-tasmiṃs tad-dhiyo hetur nidānaṃ jīva-saṃsṛtau.* || *Ibid.* I. 15.

[3] *ataḥ kāmyaṃ niṣiddhaṃ ca duḥkh-avījaṃ tyajed budhaḥ. Śruti-siddhānta-saṃgraha*, I. 63. According to Vanāmālī Miśra at death a person goes to Heaven or to Hell according to his deeds and then after enjoying the fruits of his actions or suffering therefrom he is born as plants and then as lower animals, then as *Yavanas* or *mlecchas* and then in lower castes and finally as Brahmins.

pleasure and pain, and regards all objects as being invested with harmful defects. It is this disinclination or detachment that pleases God. The process of attaining devotion is also described in the scriptures as listening to the Upaniṣads (*śravaṇa*), realizing their meaning with logical persuasion (*manana*), and continual meditation on the nature of God as an unceasing flow (*nididhyāsana*)[1]. The last can come only as a result of the first two; for meditation involves a direct realization which is not possible without the performance of *śravaṇa* and *manana*. It is only through the purification of the mind by the above processes that God is pleased and makes Himself directly intuited (*aparokṣa*) by the devotee, just as one can intuit the musical melodies and tunes through musical discipline. This direct intuition is of the very nature of one's own self. For at this stage one has no functioning of the mind. The destruction of experiential knowledge is identical with the intuition of God. This stage therefore implies the annihilation of *avidyā* or the mind[2]. It is in this way that the nature of God as bliss is realized by man in his state of supreme emancipation; but even then it is not possible for him to know all the qualities of God, for even God Himself does not know all His qualities. Such an emancipation can be realized only through the grace of God. In the state of emancipation, man exists in God just as the fish swims about in the ocean. God creates because of the spontaneity of His grace and not in order to increase His grace; so also emancipated souls dally in God out of the spontaneity of their essence as bliss and not in order to increase their bliss[3]. The nature of God is always within us, and it is only when it is directly intuited that we can attain salvation. Some people attain emancipation in this world while others attain it in the upper worlds through which they pass as a result of their deeds. But emancipation of all kinds may be defined as the existence of man in his own nature as a result of the destruction of nescience[4]. The *jīvanmuktas* or saints are those whose *avidyā* has

[1] *anyā-rtha-viṣayaḥ puro brahmā-kāra-dhiyāṃ sadā*
nididhyāsana-śabdā-rtho jāyate sudhiyāṃ hi saḥ.
Śruti-siddhānta-saṃgraha, II. 13.

[2] *brahma-gocarasya vedānta-vāsita-manasi utpannasya ā-parokṣyasya yaḥ prāga-bhavaḥ tasya abhāvo dhvaṃso jñāna-tad-dhvaṃsā-nyatara-rūpo jñāna-brahmaṇaḥ sambandhaḥ, saṃsāra-daśāyāṃ nāsti. Ibid.* II. 19.

[3] *ānando-drekato viṣṇoryathā sṛstyā-di-ceṣṭanam.*
tathā mukta-citāṃ krīḍā na tv ānanda-vivṛddhaye. Ibid. II. 37.

[4] *sva-rūpeṇa sthitir muktir ajñāna-dhvaṃsa-pūrvakam* (*Ibid.* II. 58). This *mukti* can be of four kinds: *sārūpya*, i.e. the same external form as Kṛṣṇa;

been destroyed, but who have still to suffer the effects of their *prārabdha karma*. The realization of God can destroy the *sañcita* and *kriyamāṇa karma*, i.e. previously collected *karma* and those that are performed in the present life, but not the *prārabdha karma*, i.e. the *karma* that is already in a state of fruition.

It is wrong to suppose that the attainment of a state of bliss can be desired by any person; the state desired can only be one in which a person enjoys unobstructed bliss[1]. In a state of deep dreamless sleep one can enjoy a little bliss, but not the full bliss, as the *māyāvādins* hold. There is but little difference between the *māyāvādins* and the Buddhists; the difference is only in the mode of expression[2].

The self is regarded as atomic, but its existence is definitely proved by the notion of the ego (*ahaṃ-pratyayavedya*) who enjoys all his experiences. Even though he may be dependent upon God, yet he is a real and active agent who works through the influence of *avidyā*. The existence of the self is also proved by the continuity of experiences through all stages of life. The self-love manifested in all beings for selfish ends also shows that each person feels a self or soul within himself and that this self is also different in different individuals. The difference between *jīva* and *īśvara* is that the former is of little power and little knowledge and always dependent, and the latter is omniscient, omnipotent and independent; He makes the *jīvas* work or assert their supposed independence by His *avidyā*-power. The *jīvas* are thus different from God, but as they exist in Him at the time of emancipation and as all their actions are guided by the *avidyā*-power of God, they are regarded also as being

sālokya, i.e. existence in the same sphere as God; *sāyujya*, as being merged in God; *sāmīpya*, as existence in proximity to God as associated with a particular form of Him. The merging in God called *sāyujya* should not be regarded as being unified with God. This merging is like the animals roaming in the forest. The emancipated beings are different from God, but exist in Him (*evaṃ muktvā harer bhinna ramante tatra modataḥ* (*Ibid.* II. 61). They can thus come out of God also, and we hear of them as entering in succession the bodies of Aniruddha, Pradyumna, Saṃkarṣaṇa and Vāsudeva. Such emancipated beings are not associated with the creation and destruction of the worlds, but remain the same in spite of all cosmic changes. They are like the being of *Śvetadvīpa* referred to in the Nārāyaṇīya section of the *Mahābhārata*. But they are still always under the control of God and do not suffer any sorrow on account of such control.

[1] *puruṣā-rthaṃ sukhitvaṃ hi na tv ānanda-svarūpatā. Śruti-siddhānta-saṃgraha*, II. 96.

[2] *meyato na viśeṣo'-sti māyi-saugatayor mate*
bhaṅgī-mātra-bhidā tu syāt ekasminn api darśane. Ibid. II. 136.

one with Him. The mind of the individual being a creation of God's *avidyā*, all His world experience is also due to God's activity. In His own nature as self the *jīvas*, the individuals, have the revelation of God's nature which is pure bliss. The existence of individuals in their own essential nature is therefore regarded as a state of salvation. The individuals in their essential nature are therefore of the nature of *sat*, *cit* and *ānanda*, and though atomic they can enjoy the experiences all over the body through their internal functioning just as a lamp illuminates the whole room by rays. The experience of sorrow also is possible through the expansion or dilatation of the mind (*antaḥ-karaṇa*) through the various parts of the body and by means of the help of *avidyā* by which the *jīva* wrongly identifies himself with other objects. As the relation of the self with other objects takes place through the *antaḥ-karaṇa* of each person the sphere of experience of each of the *jīvas* is limited by the functioning of his own *antaḥ-karaṇa*. The *antaḥ-karaṇa* is different in different persons.

The Upaniṣads speak of God as the all (*sarvaṃ khalv'idaṃ Brahma*), and this is due to the fact that He pervades all things and controls all things. It means that the souls are dependent on Him or maintained in Him (*tad-ādhāratva*), but it does not mean their identity with Him. God is Himself able to create all things by Himself; but for His pleasure, for His mere sportive dalliance, He takes the help of *prakṛti* and the destiny born out of the deeds of human beings as His accessories. Though God makes all persons act in the manner in which they do act, yet His directive control is regulated in accordance with the *adṛṣṭa* or the destiny of the human beings which is beginningless. The theory of *karma* doctrine herein suggested is different from that propounded by Patañjali. According to Patañjali and his commentators, the fruits of the deeds, i.e. pleasure or pain, are enjoyed by the persons while they are free to act by themselves. Here, however, the freedom of the individuals is controlled and limited by God in accordance with the previous good or bad deeds of the individual, which are beginningless. Thus in our ordinary life not only our pleasures and pains but also our power to do good or bad actions are determined by previous deeds and the consequent control of God.

CHAPTER XXII

THE PHILOSOPHY OF VIJÑĀNA BHIKṢU

A General Idea of Vijñāna Bhikṣu's Philosophy.

THE ultimate goal is not the cessation of sorrow, but the cessation of the experience of sorrow; for when in the state of emancipation one ceases to experience sorrow, the sorrow as such is not emancipated since it remains in the world and others suffer from it. It is only the emancipated individual who ceases to experience sorrow. The ultimate state of emancipation cannot be a state of bliss, for since there are no mental organs and no mind in this state there cannot be any experience of bliss. The self cannot itself be of the nature of bliss and be at the same time the experiencer of it. When it is said that self is of the nature of bliss (*ānanda*), the word bliss is there used in a technical sense of negation of sorrow.

Bhikṣu admits a gradation of realities. He holds that one is stabler and more real than the other. Since *paramātmā* is always the same and does not undergo any change or transformation or dissolution, he is more real than the *prakṛti* or *puruṣa* or the evolutes of *prakṛti*. This idea has also been expressed in the view of the Purāṇas that the ultimate essence of the world is of the nature of knowledge which is the form of the *paramātman*. It is in this essential form that the world is regarded as ultimately real and not as *prakṛti* and *puruṣa* which are changing forms; *prakṛti*, so far as it exists as a potential power in God, is regarded as non-existent but so far as it manifests itself through evolutionary changes it is regarded as existent. The state of emancipation is brought about by the dissociation of the subtle body consisting of the five *tammātras* and the eleven senses. Consequent upon such a dissociation the self as pure consciousness is merged in Brahman as the rivers mingle with the ocean, a state not one of identity but identity-in-difference. According to the Sāṃkhya, emancipation cannot be attained until the fruits of the *karmas* which have ripened for giving experiences of pleasure and pain are actually exhausted through experiencing them, i.e. even when ignorance or *avidyā* is destroyed the attainment of the emancipation is delayed until the *prārabdha karma* is finished. The Yogin, however, can enter into an objectless state of meditation (*asamprajñāta yoga*) and this wards off the possibility of experiencing the *prārabdha karma.* From the state of *asamprajñāta samādhi* he can at will pass into a state of emancipation. The state of emancipation is reached not merely by realizing the purport of the text of the Upaniṣads but by philosophic wisdom attained through a reasoned process of thought and by the successive stages of *Yoga* meditation.

The world does not emanate directly from Brahman as pure consciousness, nor are the *kāla*, *prakṛti* and *puruṣa* derived from Brahman through transformatory changes (*pariṇāma*). Had the world come into being directly from Brahman, evil and sins would have been regarded as coming into being from it. With the association of *sattva* through the beginningless will of God at the beginning of the previous cycles the Brahman behaves as *Īśvara* and brings into actual being the *prakṛti* and the *puruṣa* which are already potentially existent in God, and connects the *prakṛti* with the *puruṣa*. The moment of God's activity in bringing out the *prakṛti* and *puruṣa* may be regarded as *kāla*. In this sense *kāla* is often regarded as the dynamic agency of God. Though *puruṣas* in themselves are absolutely static, yet they have a seeming movement as they are always associated with *prakṛti*, which is ever in a state of movement. *kāla* as the dynamic agency of God is naturally associated with the movement of *prakṛti*, for both the *prakṛti* and the *puruṣa* are in themselves passive and are rendered active by the dynamic agency of God. This dynamic agency is otherwise called *kāla*, and as such it is an eternal power existing in Brahman, like the *prakṛti* and *puruṣa*. In all other forms of actual existence *kāla* is determinate and conditioned, and as such non-eternal and to some extent imaginary. It is only as the eternal power that subsists in and through all the operations of dynamic activity that *kāla* may be called eternal. The *kāla* that produces the connection of the *prakṛti* and the *puruṣa* and also produces the *mahat* is non-eternal and therefore does not exist at the time of *pralaya* when no such connection exists. The reason for this is that the *kāla* that produces the connection between *prakṛti* and *puruṣa* is a determinate *kāla* which is conditioned, on the one hand by the will of God, and, on the other, by the effects it produces. It is this determinate *kāla* that can be designated as present, past and future. But the terms present, past and future imply an evolutionary change and such a change implies activity; it is this activity as dissociated from the manifest forms of *kāla* as present, past and future that can be regarded as eternal[1].

The reference to the *Atharva-Veda*, as noted below in the footnote, will show how the conception of time in very ancient eras reveals "time" as a separate entity or energy which has brought everything into being, maintains it, and destroys everything. The God, *parameṣṭhin* Brahman or *prajāpati* is said to be derived from it. In the *Maitrī Upaniṣad* we also hear of the conception of *kāla* or time as *akāla* or timeless. The timeless time is the primordial time which is only the pure energy unmeasured and immeasurable. It appears in a measurable form when, after the production of the sun from it, it is measured in terms of the movement of the sun. The entire course of natural phenomena is thus seen to be an emanation or manifestation of the energy of time undirected by any other superintendent. Such a conception of time seems to be of an atheistic character, for even the highest gods, the *parameṣṭhin* and the *prajāpati*, are said to be produced from it.

In the first chapter of the *anuśāsana parvan* of the *Mahābhārata* there is a dialogue between Gautamī, whose son was bitten by a serpent, the hunter who was pressing for killing the serpent, the serpent, the *mṛtyu* or death and *kāla*. It appears from the dialogue that time is not only the propeller of all events by itself but all states of *sattva*, *rajas* and *tamas*, all that is moving and the unmoved in the heaven and in the earth, all our movements and cessation of movements, the sun, the moon, the waters, the fire, the sky, the earth, the rivers, the oceans and all that is being or not being are of the

[1] *Atharva-Veda*, XIX. 54. In the *Atharva-Veda* time is regarded as a generator of the sky and the earth and all beings exist through time. *Tapas* and Brahman exist in time and time is the god of all. Time produced all creatures. The universe has been set in motion by time, has been produced by it and is supported in it. Time becoming Brahman supports *parameṣṭhin*. In the *Śvetāśvatara Upaniṣad* time is regarded as being held by the sun as the ultimate cause. In the *Maitrī Upaniṣad*, VI. 14, it is said that from time all creatures spring, grow and decay. Time is a formless form (*kālāt sravanti bhūtāni, kālāt vṛddhiṃ prayānti ca.* | *kāle cā'staṃ niyacchanti kālo mūrtir amūrtimān*).

It is again stated in the same work that there are two forms of Brahman, Time and no-Time.

[2] That which is before the sun is no-Time and is devoid of parts, and that which is after the sun is Time with parts.

nature of time and brought into being by time and dissolved in time. Time is thus the original cause. Time, however, operates in accordance with the laws of *karma*; there is thus the beginningless relation between time and *karma* which determines the courses of all events. *Karma* in itself is also a product of time and as such determines the future modes of the operation of time. Here we have an instance of the second stage, the conception of time as the transcendental and immanent cause of all things. Here time is guided by *karma*. In the third stage of the conception of time, which is found in the *purāṇas* and also adopted by Bhikṣu, it is regarded as the eternal dynamic power inherent in Brahman and brought into operation by the will of God[1].

The word *puruṣa* is often used in the scriptural text in the singular number, but that signifies only that it is used in a generic sense, cf. *Sāṃkhya-sūtra*, I. 154 (*nā'dvaita-śruti-virodho jāti-paratvāt*)[2]. The difference between the superior *puruṣa* or God and the ordinary *puruṣas* is that while the latter are subject to experiences of pleasure and pain as a result of the actions or *karma*, the former has an eternal and continual experience of bliss through its reflection from its *sattvamaya* body to itself. The ordinary *puruṣas*, however, have not the experience of pleasure and pain as of constitutive definition, for in the stage of saintliness (*jīvanmukti*) they have no such experiences. God can, however, have an experience of the experiences of pleasure and pain of other *puruṣas* without having been affected by them. The ultimate principle or the Brahman is a principle of pure consciousness which underlies

[1] In the *Ahirbudhnya-saṃhitā*, the work of the *Pañcarātra* school, *niyati* (destiny) and *kāla* (time) are the two manifestations of the power of transcendent *kāla* as arising from *aniruddha*. From this *kāla* first arises the *sattva-guṇa* and from that the *rajo-guṇa* and thence the *tamo-guṇa*.

It is further said that it is time which connects and separates. The *kāla* of course in its own turn derives its power from the self-perceiving activity (*sudarśana*) of Viṣṇu. That the *prakṛti* transforms itself into its evolutes is also due to the dynamic function of *kāla*.

The *Māṭhara vṛtti* on the *Sāṃkhya-kārikā*, however, refers to the doctrine of *kāla* as the cause of the world (*kālaḥ sṛjati bhūtani, kālaḥ saṃharate prajāḥ | kālaḥ supteṣu jāgarti tasmāt kālas tu kāraṇam*) and refutes it by saying that there is no separate entity as *kāla* (*kālo nāma na kaś cit padārtho'sti*), there are only three categories, *vyakta, avyakta* and *puruṣa*, and *kāla* falls within them (*vyaktam avyaktam puruṣa iti trayaḥ eva padārthāḥ tatra kālo antarbhūtaḥ*).

[2] The *Ahirbudhnya-saṃhitā*, however, explains the singular number by the concept of a conglomeration of *puruṣa* or a colony of cells, as the honey-comb, which behaves as a totality and also in a multiple capacity as separate cells. *Ahirbudhnya-saṃhitā*, VI. 33.

the reality of both the *puruṣas*, *prakṛti* and its evolutes; and it is because they are emergent forms which have their essence in the Brahman that they can appear as connected together. The movement of the *prakṛti* is also ultimately due to the spontaneous movement of the pure consciousness, the basic reality.

The *viveka* and the *aviveka*, the distinction and the non-distinction, are all inherent in *buddhi*, and this explains why the *puruṣas* fail to distinguish themselves from the *buddhi* with which they are associated. The association of the *puruṣas* with the *buddhi* implies that it has in it both the characters of distinction and non-distinction. The difficulty is that the "revelation of the distinction" is so opposed by the force of non-distinction that the former cannot find scope for its manifestation. It is the purpose of *yoga* to weaken the force of the tendency towards non-distinction and ultimately uproot it so that revelation of distinction may manifest itself. Now it may be asked what is the nature of this obstruction. It may be replied that it is merely a negative condition consisting in the non-production of the cognition of the distinction through association with the products of *prakṛti*, such as attachment and antipathy, through which we are continually passing. The Sāṃkhya, however, says that the non-production of the distinction is due to the extreme subtleness of the nature of *buddhi* and *puruṣa* which so much resemble each other that it is difficult to distinguish their nature. But this view of the Sāṃkhya should not be interpreted as meaning that it is only the subtleness of the natures of these two entities that arrests our discriminating knowledge regarding them. For had it been so, then the process of yoga would be inefficacious in attaining such a knowledge. The real reason is that our association with attachment and antipathy with regard to gross objects obstructs our discriminating vision regarding these subtle entities. Our attachment to gross objects is also due to our long association with sense-objects. A philosopher, therefore, should try to dissociate himself from attachment with gross objects. The whole purpose of creation consists in furnishing materials for the experiences of *puruṣa* which seems to undergo all experiential changes of enjoyment and suffering, of pleasure and pain, in and through the medium of *buddhi*. With the dissociation of *buddhi*, therefore, all experience ceases. The God is essentially pure consciousness, and though the knowledge of Him as such brings about liberation, yet epithets of omnipotence, all-pervasiveness and other personal characteristics are attributed to Him because it is through an approach to God as a super-personal Being that devotion is possible, and it is through devotion and personal attachment that true knowledge can arise. It is said in the scriptures that God cannot be realized by *tapas*, gifts or sacrifices, but only by *bhakti*[1]. The highest devotion is of the nature of love (*attyuttamā bhaktiḥ prema-lakṣaṇā*).

God remains within all as the inner controller and everything is revealed to His super-consciousness without the mediation of sense-consciousness. God is called all-pervasive because He is the cause of all and also because He is the inner controller.

Bhakti consists in the whole process of listening to God's name, describing His virtues, adoration to Him, and meditation ultimately leading to true knowledge. These are all to be designated as the service of God. These processes of operations constituting *bhakti* are all to be performed with love. Bhikṣu quotes *Garuḍa purāṇa* to prove that the root "*bhaj*" is used in the sense of service. He also refers to the Bhāgavata to show that the true *bhakti* is associated with an emotion which brings tears to the eyes, melts the heart and raises the hairs of the body. Through the emotion of *bhakti* one dissolves oneself as it were and merges into God's existence, just as the river Ganges does into the ocean.

It will be seen from the above that Bhikṣu urges on the doctrine of *bhakti* as love, as a way to the highest realization. The metaphysical views that he propounded give but small scope for the indulgence of such an attitude towards divinity. For, if the Ultimate Reality be of the nature of pure consciousness, we cannot have any personal relations with such a Being. The ultimate state of realization is also the entrance into a state of non-difference with this Ultimate Being, who is not Himself a person, and therefore no personal relations ought to be possible with Him. In the *Vijñānāmṛta-bhāṣya*, IV. I. 3, Bhikṣu says that at the time of dissolution or emancipation the individuals are not associated with any content of knowledge, and are therefore devoid of any consciousness, and being of the nature of unconscious entities like wood or stone they

[1] *ahaṃ prakṛṣṭaḥ bhaktito'anyaiḥ sādhanaiḥ draṣṭuṃ na śakyaḥ, bhaktir eva kevalā mad-darśane sādhanam.*
Īśvara-gītā-ṭīkā (MS. borrowed from N. N. Gopīnātha Kavirāja, late Principal, Queen's College, Benares).

enter into the all-illuminating great Soul just as rivers enter into the ocean. Again, it is this great Soul that out of its own will sends them forth like sparks of fire and distinguishes them from one another and goads them to action[1]. This great Soul or *paramātman* is the inner-controller and mover of our selves. But it may be remembered that this great Soul is not also the Ultimate Principle, the pure consciousness, but is the manifestation of the pure consciousness in association with the *sattvamaya* body. Under the circumstances the metaphysical position does not allow of any personal relation between the human beings and the Ultimate Entity. But yet the personal relation with the divinity as the ultimate consciousness not being philosophically possible, that relation is ushered in more out of a theistic tendency of Bhikṣu than as a necessary natural conclusion. The theistic relation is also conceived in a mystical fashion in the indulgence of the emotions of love rising to a state of intoxication. Such a conception of Divine love is found in the *Bhāgavata-purāṇa*; and later on in the school of Vaiṣṇavism preached by Caitanya. It is different from the conception of devotion or *bhakti* as found in the system of Rāmānuja, where *bhakti* is conceived as incessant continual meditation. He seems to have been, therefore, one of the earliest, if not the earliest, exponent of emotionalism in theism, if we do not take into account the Purāṇic emotionalism of the *Bhāgavata-purāṇa*. There are instances in the writings of modern European philosophers also, where the difficult position does not justify an emotionalism that is preached merely out of the theistic experiences of a personal nature, and as an illustration one may refer to the idea of God of Pringle Pattison. In the conception of *jīva* or individuals also there seems to be an apparent contradiction. For while the *puruṣas* are sometimes described as pure consciousness, they are at other times described as inert and wholly under the domination of *paramātman* The contradiction is to be solved by the supposition that the inertness is only relative, i.e. the *puruṣas* are to be regarded as themselves inactive, being goaded to action by the inlying controller,

[1] *tasmāt pralaya-mokṣā-dau viṣaya-sambandhā-bhāvāt kāṣṭha-loṣṭrā-divat jaḍāḥ sānto jīvā madhyandinā-dityavat sadā sarvā-vabhāsake paramā-tmani vilīyante samudre nada-nadya iva punasca sa eva paramā-tmā sve-cchayā gni-vissphul iṅgavat tā-nupāyi-sambandhena svato vibhajyā'ntaryāmī sa na prerayati tathā coktaṃ cakṣuṣmatā'ndhā iva nīyamānā iti ataḥ sa eva mukhya ātmā-ntaryāmy amṛtaḥ. Vijñānā-mṛta-bhāṣya*, IV. I. 3.

paramātman. They are called "*jaḍa*," resembling stone or wood only in the sense that they are inactive in themselves. But this inactivity should not be associated with want of consciousness. Being sparks of the eternal consciousness they are always of the nature of consciousness. Their activity, however, is derived from the *paramātman*, so that, drawn by Him, they come out of the Eternal consciousness and play the role of a mundane individual and ultimately return to Brahman like rivers into the ocean at the time of emancipation. This activity of God is an eternal activity, an eternal creative impulse which is absolutely without any extraneous purpose (*carama-kāraṇasya kṛteḥ nityatvāt*)[1]. It proceeds from the spontaneous joy of God in a spontaneous manner like the process of breathing, and has no reference to the fulfilment of any purpose. In the *Vyāsa-bhāṣya* it is said that the creation of God is for the benefit of living beings. But Bhikṣu does not support any purpose at all. This activity is sometimes compared with the purposeless playful activity. But Bhikṣu says that even if there is any slight purpose in play that also is absent in the activity of God. The action also proceeds spontaneously with the creative desire of God, for which no body or senses are necessary. He is identical with the whole universe and as such His action has no objective outside of Himself, as in the case of ordinary actions. It is He who, depending upon the beginningless *karma* of human beings, makes them act for good or for evil. The *karma* itself, also being a part of His energy and a manifestation of His impulse, cannot be regarded as limiting His freedom[2]. The analogy of the doctrine of grace where the king bestows his grace or withholds it in accordance with the good or bad services of his servants is also regarded as helpful to conceive of the freedom of God in harmony with the deeds of the individual. If it is argued now, if the creative activity of God is eternal, it can depend on the *karma*, Bhikṣu's reply is that the *karmas* act as accessory causes determining the eternal creative impulse of God as producing pleasurable and painful experiences. Following the trend of the Purāṇic method Bhikṣu further suggests that it is the Hiraṇyagarbha created by God who appears as the law-giver of the law of *karma*, as manifested in the spontaneous activity of God. It is He, therefore, who is responsible for the suffering of humanity

[1] See *Vijñānā-mṛta-bhāṣya*, II. I. 32.
[2] *Ibid.* II. I. 33.

in accordance with their *karmas*. God helps the process only by letting it go on in an unobstructed manner[1]. In another passage he says that God perceives within Himself as parts of Him the *jīvas* and their conditioning factors (*upādhi*) as associated with merit and demerit (*dharma* and *adharma*); associating these conditions with the *jīvas* He brings them out of Himself. He is thus the maker of souls, just as the potter is the maker of pots[2].

The self is regarded as being itself untouchable and devoid of any kind of association (*a-saṅga*). The association between *prakṛti* and *puruṣa*, therefore, is not to be interpreted in the sense of a direct contact in the ordinary sense of the term, but the association is to be understood only as transcendental reflection through the conditioning factors which make the pure soul behave as a phenomenal self or *jīva*. The self has no knowledge as its quality or character, and is in itself pure consciousness, and there is at no time a cessation of this consciousness, which exists even during dreamless sleep. But in dreamless sleep there is no actual knowledge, as there is no content present at the time; and it is for that reason that the consciousness though present in the very nature of the self cannot be apperceived. The *vāsanās* or desires existing in the *antaḥkaraṇa* cannot affect the pure soul, for at that time the *antaḥkaraṇa* remains in a dissolved condition. Knowledge of contents or objects is possible only through reflections from the states of the *buddhi*. The pure consciousness being identical with the self, there cannot also be the self-consciousness involving the notion of a duality as subject and object during dreamless sleep. The pure consciousness remains the same and it is only in accordance with changes of mental state that knowledge of objects arises and passes away[3]. The *jīvas* are thus not to be regarded as themselves the products of the reflection of *paramātman* as the Śaṅkarites suppose; for in that case the *jīvas* would be absolutely unreal, and bondage and emancipation would also be unreal.

[1] *Vijñānā-mṛta-bhāṣya*, II. I. 33.

[2] *Īśvaro hi svā-ṃśa-sva-śarīrā-ṃśa-tulyau jīva-tad-upādhī svā-ntar-gatau dharmā-di-sahitau sākṣād eva paśyann a-para-tantraḥ sva-līlayā saṃyoga-viśeṣaṃ brahmā-dīnām api dur-vibhāvyaṃ kurvat kumbhakāra iva ghaṭam. Ibid.* II. I. 13.

[3] *Ibid.* II. 3. 5.

The Brahman and the World according to Vijñānā-mṛta-bhāṣya.

The production, existence, maintenance, modification, decay and destruction of the world are from Brahman as God. He holds within Himself all the energies constituting the *prakṛti* and *puruṣas*, and manifests Himself in other diverse forms; Brahman as pure consciousness is associated with the conditioning factor of His own being, the *māyā* as pure *sattva* quality in all this creative activity, so from that great Being who is devoid of all afflictions, *karmas* and their fruits are also produced. The fact that the *Brahma-sūtra*, II. 2, says that Brahman is that from which the world has come into being and is being maintained implies that the world as it is in its own reality is an eternal fact in the very being of the ultimately real and the unmanifested. The production, the transformation and the destruction of the world are only its phenomenal aspect[1]. Brahman is here regarded as the *adhiṣṭhāna-kāraṇa.* This means that Brahman is the basis, the ground, the *ādhāra* (container) as it were of the universe in which it exists as undivided and as indistinguishable from it and which also holds the universe together. Brahman is the cause which holds together the material cause of the universe so that it may transform itself into it[2]. Brahman is the principle of ultimate cause which renders all other kinds of causality possible. In the original Brahman, the *prakṛti* and the *puruṣas* exist in the eternal consciousness and as such are held together as being one with it. The Brahman is neither changeable nor identifiable with *prakṛti* and *puruṣa.* It is because of this that, though Brahman is of the nature of pure consciousness and unchangeable, yet it is regarded as being one with the universe and as the material cause. The material cause or *upādāna-kāraṇa* is the name which is given to changing material cause (the *vikāri-kāraṇa*) and to the ground cause or the *adhiṣṭhāna-kāraṇa.* The underlying principle of both the ground cause (*adhiṣṭhāna-kāraṇa*) and the material cause (*upādāna-kāraṇa*) is that the effect is held in it as merged in it or

[1] *atra cai'tad yata ity'anuktvā janmā-dyasya yata iti vacanād avyakta-rūpeṇa jagan nityam eva ity ācāryyā-śayaḥ. Vijñānā-mṛta-bhāṣya*, I. 1. 2.

[2] *kiṃ punar adhiṣṭhāna-kāraṇatvam ucyate tad evā' dhiṣṭhāna-kāraṇaṃ yatra' vibhaktaṃ yeno' paṣṭabdhaṃ ca sad upādānā-kāraṇaṃ kāryā-kāreṇa pāriṇamate. Ibid.*

indistinguishable from it[1]. The idea involved in *avibhāga* or oneness with the cause is not regarded as an ordinary relation of identity but as a sort of non-relational relation or a situation of uniqueness which cannot be decomposed into its constituents so that a relational bond may be affirmed of them. The upshot of the whole position is that the nature of the universe is so founded in Brahman which forms its ground that it cannot be regarded as a mere illusory appearance of it or as a modification or a product of it; but while these two possible ways of relation between the cause and the effect fail, the universe as such has no existence, significance or meaning without the ground in which it is sustained and which helps its evolutionary process. The ordinary relation of the sustainer and the sustained is inadequate here, for it implies a duality of independent existence; in the present case, however, where Brahman is regarded as the ground cause there is no such duality and the universe cannot be conceived as apart from Brahman which forms its ground and essence while remaining unchanged in its transcendent reality. Thus, though it may have to be acknowledged that there is a relation between the two, the relation has to be conceived as the transcendental one, of which no analogy is found elsewhere. The seeming pictorial analogy which falls far short of the situation is to be found in the case where water is mixed with milk[2]. Here the existence of the water is dependent upon the existence of the milk so long as the two exist in a mixed condition; and neither of them can be conceived without the other. The nature of the *prakṛti* and the *puruṣa* is also manifested from the essence of God's nature as pure consciousness. The causality of substance, qualities and actions is also due to the underlying essence of God which permeates all things. The difference between the relation of *samavāya* and this unique relation of indistinguishableness in the ground is that while the former applies to the case of the intimate relation of the effects in and through themselves, the latter refers only to the special fact of the indistinguishable character of the effect in the cause, and has no reference to the relation of the effect-parts among themselves with reference to the whole as an inseparable concatenation of effects. The ordinary organic relation such

[1] *Kāryā-vibhāgā-dhāratvasyai' vo' pādāna-sāmānya-lakṣaṇatvāt. Vijñānāmṛta-bhāṣya*, I. I. 2.

[2] *avibhāgaś cā' dhāratāvat svarūpa-sambandha-viśeṣo' tyanta-sammiśraṇa-rūpo dugdha-jalādy-ekatā-pratyaya-niyāmakaḥ. Ibid.*

as that which subsists between the parts of a living body is thus different from that which is referred to here as the indistinguishable character of the effects in the ground. The parts of the universe as comprising the living and the non-living may be regarded as inseparably united with one another in the whole, but such a relation is an intimate relation between the effects, and the whole is nothing but an assemblage of these. This is what may be called the special feature of *samavāya* relation. But in the unique relation of indistinguishableness in the ground the effect subsists in the ground in such a manner that the effect has no separate reality from the cause[1]. Brahman in this view is the basis or the substratum—the ground which supports the totality of the unity of *prakṛti* and the *puruṣas* to evolve itself into the universe with its varied forms[2]. It does not, therefore, in itself participate in the changing evolution and transformation of world-forms, but it always exists as one with it, and being in it and supported by it, it develops into the world.

Vijñāna Bhikṣu says that the Vaiśeṣikas believe that God is the dynamic or the instrumental agent, whereas he thinks that the causality of God cannot be regarded as being either of the *samavāyi*, *asamavāyi* or *nimitta* types, but is a fourth kind of conception—cause as ground or container[3]. He also describes this type of causation as being *adhiṣṭhāna*, a term with which we are familiar in Śaṅkara Vedānta. But the difference between the two kinds of conception of *adhiṣṭhāna kāraṇa* is indeed very great, for while Bhikṣu considers this to be the unchangeable ground which sustains the movements of the principle of change in it in an undivided unity, Śaṅkara regards *adhiṣṭhāna* as the basis of all changes which are unreal in themselves. According to Bhikṣu, however, the changing phenomena are not unreal, but they are only changes which are the modifications of a principle of change which subsists in an undivided unity with the ground cause. When they say that the world is both being and non-being (*sad-asadrūpa*), and is hence unreal and illusory, the Śaṅkarites suffer from a grave misconception. The

[1] *tatra samavāya-sambandhena yatrā' vibhāgas tad vikāri-kāraṇam; yatra ca kāryasya kāraṇā'vibhāgena avibhāgas tad adhiṣṭhāna-kāraṇam. Ibid.*

[2] *yadi hi paramā-tmā dehavat sarvaṃ kāraṇaṃ nā'dhitiṣṭheta tarhi dravya-guṇa-karmā-di-sādhāraṇā-khila-kārye itthaṃ mūla-kāraṇam na syāt. Īśvara-gītā-bhāṣya.* MS.

[3] *asmābhis tu samavāy-asamavāyibhyām udāsīnaṃ nimitta-kāraṇebhyaś ca vilakṣaṇatayā caturtham ādhāra-kāraṇatvam. Ibid.*

world is called *sat* and *asat* (being and non-being), because it represents the principle of becoming or change. It is affirmed as "this" and yet because it changes it is again not affirmed as "this." The future forms of the changing process are also non-existent as it were in the present form and the present form is also non-existent as it were in the future forms that are to be. Thus, any of its forms may be regarded as not existing and hence false when compared with an entity that always exists and in the same form[1]. All objects of the world so far as they are past and future are contradicted by their present states and are therefore regarded as false, but so far as they are perceived in their present state they are regarded as real[2].

The universe has, however, an eternal and immutable form as pure consciousness in the very nature of Brahman from which it is separated out as the world of matter and souls. The pure consciousness in itself is the only ultimate reality which is ever the same and is not subject to any change or process of becoming. Both the individual souls and the world of matter are ultimately dissolved and merged in Brahman, the pure and ultimate consciousness. These, therefore, are regarded as being names and forms when compared with the ultimate changeless Reality, Brahman[3]. But this does not mean that the universe of matter and souls is absolutely unreal and mere *māyā* or illusion. If all that appears were absolutely false, then all moral values would disappear and all notions of bondage and emancipation would become meaningless. If the falsity of all things except the pure consciousness can be proved by any means, that itself would prove that such proofs have validity and that therefore there are other things over and above pure consciousness which may be valid. If such proofs are invalid but can establish the validity of pure consciousness as against the validity of all other things, then such proofs may also prove the reality of all other things in the world. It may be held that what ordinary people consider as true can be proved to be invalid by what is regarded by them as valid means of proof; but on the Śaṅkarite view nothing is regarded as valid and therefore there are

[1] *eka-dharmeṇa sattva-daśāyāṃ pariṇāmi-vastūnām atītā-nāgata-dharmeṇa asattvāt. Vijñānā-mṛta-bhāṣya*, I. I. 3.

[2] *ghaṭā-dayo hi anāgatā-dy-avasthāṣu vyaktā-dy-avasthābhir bādhyante iti. ghaṭā-dayo mithyā-śabdena ucyante vidyamāna-dharmaiś ca tadānīṃ na bādhyante iti satyā ity api ucyante. Ibid.*

[3] *jñāna-svarūpaḥ paramā-tmā sa eva satyaḥ jīvāś cā'ṃśatayā amśiny ekībhūtāḥ athavā' vayavattvena paramā-tmā-pekṣayā te' py asantaḥ. Ibid.*

no proofs by which the validity of the world-process can be maintained. But the reply that naturally comes to such a view is that though the validity of the world may not be proved, yet that does not lead to the conclusion that the world-process is unreal; for even if its validity is not proved, its validity or reality may at least be doubtful. There is, therefore, nothing by which we may come to any conclusion about its invalidity and unreality. The reality of the universe is of a different order from that of Brahman, which is of the nature of pure consciousness, as the former consists of practical efficiency (*artha-kriyā-kāritva*). But even though in the state of a changing process the reality of the world is only its reality as becoming and as causal efficiency, yet it has also an ultimate reality in itself, since it has come into being from the ultimate reality, Brahman. The world of matter and souls exists in God as pure consciousness and therefore as one with Him. When from out of its state as pure consciousness it is manifested as the world of matter and souls, we mark it as the stage of creation. When again they retire back into God as being one with His consciousness, that is marked as the state of dissolution[1]. The universe of matter and souls is also ultimately to be regarded as being of the nature of consciousness, and is as such a constituent of the ultimate pure consciousness in which it remains as it were merged and lost. The world of visible forms and changes is also thus of the nature of thought, and only the ignorant regard them as mere objects[2]. When the scriptural texts speak of the identity of the world and Brahman they refer to this ultimate state in which the world exists in the pure consciousness—Brahman as one with it. But it is not only in the state of dissolution that the world exists in Brahman in undivided unity, but in the state of creation also the world exists in Brahman as one with it, for all the so-called mechanical and other kinds of forces that are to be found in matter and which constitute its reality are but the energy of God. And as the energy is always conceived as being one with that which possesses it, it is believed that the world with all its changes exists in God[3]. In the state of

[1] *pralayehi puṃ-prakṛtyā-dikaṃ jñāna-rūpeṇai'va rūpyate na tv artha-rūpeṇa arthato vyañjaka-vyāpārā-bhāvāt. Vijñānā-mṛta-bhāṣya*, I. I. 4.

[2] *jñāna-svarūpam akhilaṃ jagad etad abuddhayaḥ* I. *artha-svarūpaṃ paśyanto bhrāmyante moha-saṃplave. Ibid.*

[3] *śaktimat-kārya-kāraṇā-bhedenai'va brahmā-dvaitaṃ bodhayanti. . .ayaṃ ca sārva-kālo brahmaṇi prapañcā-bhedaḥ. Ibid.*

pralaya the world-energies exist in God as some form of consciousness or conscious energy which is later on manifested by Him as material energy or matter. The unity of the world-energies in God is such that though these retain some kind of independence yet it is so held up and mixed up as it were in the reality of God that it cannot be separated from Him. Their independence consists in the fact that they are of the nature of energy, but as God possesses them they can have no existence and they cannot be conceived as apart from Him. As thus described the world of matter has no permanent reality, and the consciousness of this fact may be called the *bādha* or contradiction (*pāramārthika-sattvā-bhāva-niścaya eva bādhaḥ*)[1]. But in spite of this *bādha* the universe has a relative or *vyavahārika* existence (*tādrśa-bādhe'pi ca sati jñāna-sādhanā-dīnāṃ vyavahārika-sattvāt*).

The causality of *prakṛti* and *paruṣa* is limited to their specific capacities which determine the nature of modifications. But God is the universal all-cause behind them which not only shows itself through these specific limitations but which regulates the inner harmony and order subsisting in them and in their mutual relations. Thus the visual organ is limited in its function to the operation of vision, and the tactile organ is limited in its function to the operation of touch, but the functions and activities of all these are organized by the individual self which operates and manifests itself through them. Thus Brahman in this sense may be regarded as being both the instrumental and the material cause[2]. According to Sāṃkhya and Yoga the *prakṛti* is supposed to be associated with the *puruṣas* through the inner and inherent teleology, but according to the Vedāntic view as interpreted by Bhikṣu their mutual association is due to the operation of God[3].

[1] *Vijñānā-mṛta-bhāṣya*, I. I. 4.

[2] *brahmaṇas tu sarva-śaktikatvāt tat-tad-upādhibhiḥ sarva-kāraṇatvaṃ yathā cakṣurā-dīnāṃ darśanā-di-kāraṇatvaṃ yat praty-ekam asti tat sarvaṃ sarvā-dhyakṣasya jīvasya bhavati, etena jagato' bhinna-nimitto-pādānattvaṃ vyākhyā-tam. Ibid.* I. I. 2.

[3] *sāṃkhya-yogibhyaṃ puruṣā-rtha-prayuktā pravṛttiḥ svayam eva puruṣeṇa ādya-jīvena saṃyuyyate...asmābhis tu prakṛti-puruṣa-saṃyoga īśvareṇa kriyate. Ibid.*

The Individual.

In his commentary on the *Īśvara-gītā*, Bhikṣu says that the more universal has a wider sphere than the less universal and therefore it is called Brahman in relation to it. The cause of an effect is wider and more universal than the effect and is therefore called Brahman in comparison with it. Thus there is a hierarchy of Brahmans. But that which is at the apex of the hierarchy is the highest universal and the ultimate cause, and is therefore called the highest Brahman. Brahman is thus the highest and the ultimate reality. The determinations that make the universe of matter exist in Brahman as merged in its nature as thought. Creation means that these determinations which exist there in a potential form and without any operation are manifested and made operative as the world of nature. God in His nature as pure consciousness has a full and complete acquaintance of all the possible developments and modifications of the pre-matter as evolving into the actual universe. The starting point in the evolution of the pre-matter or *prakṛti* is the moment of its association with the spirits. The scriptural text says that the Lord entered into the *prakṛti* and the *puruṣas*, disturbed the equilibrium and associated them with one another. The *puruṣas* are, however, like sparks of consciousness and it is not possible to produce any disturbance in them. The disturbance is thus produced in the *prakṛti* and the effect of such disturbance in the *prakṛti* on the *puruṣas* is interpreted as seeming disturbances in the *puruṣas* as well. The *puruṣas* are to be conceived as being parts of God and there cannot be a real identity between the *puruṣas* and the Brahman. The so-called identity between the *puruṣas* and the Brahman refers merely to the fact of the *puruṣas* being the constituent entities in the being of God such as that which exists between the parts and the whole. The assertion of the Śaṅkarites that the individual soul is the same as Brahman and that the difference is due to external limitations of nescience or on account of reflections through it is wrong. The kind of unity that exists between the individual souls and the Brahman lies in the fact that they are indistinguishable in character from it (*avibhāga*). If the reality of individual souls is denied, that would amount to a denial of religious and moral values and of bondage and emancipation.

In this connection it is also urged that the individual souls are derived from God just as sparks come out of fire or the son comes out of the father. The individual souls resemble God so far as they are of the nature of pure consciousness. But though they have come out of Him, yet they retain their individuality and thus preserves for them the sphere of their moral career. The individual souls are free and emancipated in their own nature, they are all-pervasive and they also hold the universe within them in their consciousness. In all these they share the nature of Brahman. But in association with the limiting conditions (*upādhi*) they appear as finite and limited. When the entire career of the individual souls is known as existing in Brahman as part of it, as being manifested out of it as separate entities, as leading a career of their own in association with the limiting conditions and ultimately dissociating themselves from them and realizing their own natures as one with Brahman and in a sense different from it, this is the true philosophic knowledge and realization of their own nature. When the individuals start their career and destiny in life they are different from Brahman; but there was a time when they remained in one undivided unity with Brahman. But in spite of this unity the Brahman is always felt as different and as the other of the individuals, and this difference is never sublated[1]. But the difference of this view from the Sāṃkhya is that the Sāṃkhya is satisfied only with considering the individuality and separateness of the *puruṣas*, but the Vedāntic view as interpreted herein cannot ignore the fact that in spite of their separateness they are one in essence with Brahman and have sprung out of it, and after the fulfilment of their career of individuality and destiny will again be merged in it, and even during their mundane career have an aspect of undividedness with Brahman inasmuch as they are the powers or energies of it[2]. The difference that exists between the individuals and Brahman is most apparent during the mundane career on account of the fact that the world of nature has a separate existence in the consciousness of the individual centres and each one of them is limited to his own experiences. But at the time of dissolution, when the world of nature merges in the Brahman as a potential level of its energies, the individuals are

[1] *bhedā-bhedau vibhāgā-vibhāga-rūpau kāla-bhedena aviruddhau anyonyā-bhāvaś ca jīva-brahmaṇor ātyantika eva. Vijñānā-mṛta-bhāṣya*, I. I. 2.

[2] *ata idaṃ brahmā-tma-jñānaṃ vivikta-jīva-jñānāt sāṃkhyo-ktād api śreṣṭham. Ibid.* I. I. 2.

also merged in it and have no separate spheres of experience for themselves and thus cease to have any descriptive definition of themselves.

The nature of the relation of part and whole that exists between the individuals and Brahman is regarded as that subsisting between the son and the father. The father is reborn in the son. Before birth the son lies in a state of undivided unity in the vital energy of the father and yet when he separates out of him it is the same vital energy of the father that repeats itself in its new career and has a sphere of activity which is definitely its own. Again, when it is said that the individuals are parts of Brahman, it should not be interpreted to mean that they have any share in the existence of Brahman as God or world-creator. God is not homogeneous in His nature, but the element of individuation and differentiation always exists in Him. Had He been a homogeneous being His parts would have no specific differentiation and they would be like the parts of space which are always indistinguishable from one another. But the fact that God has within Him the principle of differentiation explains the fact that the individuals resemble Brahman only in the aspect of their consciousness but have no share in His creative functions or omnipotence. The Sāṃkhyists hold that salvation is attained through dissociation of attachment as "mine" to one's experiences, mental faculties, senses, understanding and body, owing to one's knowledge of the fact that the self is the self-shining entity to which all experiences appear and within which they are held together as one with it though they are all different from it. But the Vedānta as herein interpreted holds that the attachment as "mine" vanishes with the knowledge of self as pure consciousness, with the knowledge of God as the being from which they come into being, by which they are maintained and into which they ultimately return, and with the knowledge that they all exist in the consciousness of God as parts of it; and that the self is not the real enjoyer of the experiences but is only the consciousness in which the universe and its experiences shine forth. Thus, though both in the Sāṃkhya and in the Vedānta as herein interpreted salvation is attained through the dissolution of the false attachment as "mine-ness," the dissolution of "mine-ness" is here due to an entirely different philosophic conception[1].

[1] *Vijñānā-mṛta-bhāṣya*, p. 56.

Consciousness is not a quality but it is the very substance of the self. Just as light is a substance which illuminates other things, so consciousness is also a substance which illuminates other things. When one says "I know it," knowledge appears to be a quality of "I" which is neither self nor a homogeneous entity. The "I" is a complex of sense-faculties, understanding, etc., to which a quality can be attributed; the self is not a complex entity, but a homogeneous simple substance—the consciousness. The complex entity, the "I," expresses all things by a manifestation of consciousness. Bliss or happiness, however, cannot be regarded as a self-revealing substance, but it is an independent substance like sorrow which is revealed by consciousness. Neither the Brahman nor the self can therefore be regarded as being of the nature of bliss or happiness as this is a modification of *prakṛti* and has therefore to be regarded as expressible (*dṛśya*) and not as expressing (*darśana*). The consciousness requires the intermediary of intellectual functions for the illumination of objects, but consciousness in itself does not require the intermediary of any other functions, as such a view would lead only to an infinite regressus without solving the point at issue. It is also wrong to suppose that the principle of consciousness exercises any operation in order to reveal itself, for an entity cannot operate on itself (*karma-kartṛ-virodhāt*). If for the above reasons the self cannot be regarded as being of the nature of bliss, then at the time of salvation also there cannot be any bliss in the self. There is only a cessation of sorrow at that time, or rather a cessation of both happiness and sorrow which is technically called a state of happiness or *sukha* (*sukhaṃ duḥkha-sukhā-tyayaḥ*)[1]. At the time of emancipation all conditioning factors such as the intellectual functions and the like are dissolved and as a consequence thereof all experiences of pleasure and pain also vanish, for these are substances belonging to objects which were presented to the self through these conditions. When the Upaniṣads say that the self is dearest to us, it need not necessarily be supposed that it is the pleasure that is dearest to us, for the self may be regarded as being valued for its own sake; it may also be supposed that pleasure here means the cessation of pain[2]. The desire for immortality or con-

[1] *Vijñānā-mṛtā-bhāṣya*, I. I. 2.

[2] *ātmatvasyā'pi prema-prayojakatvāt duḥkha-nivṛtti-rūpattvād vā bodhyam. Ibid.*

tinued existence of the self illustrates the feeling of fondness that we all have for ourselves. The other view, that the ultimate object of realization is extermination of all sorrow is also not open to any objection on the ground that pleasure and pain never belonged to the selves; for the association of pleasure and pain is only with reference to their enjoyment and suffering and not directly as a bond of attachment to the self. The term "*bhoga*," which may be translated only semi-accurately as "experience," has a twofold application as referring to *buddhi* or psychosis and to *puruṣa*. The *prakṛti* is composed of *sukha*, *duḥkha* and *moha* substances, and *buddhi* is an evolute of the *prakṛti*; therefore, when the *buddhi* is in association with *sukha* or *duḥkha*, such an association supplies the *buddhi* with the stuff of which it is made and thus sustains and maintains its nature and constitution. But when the word *bhoga* has a reference to *puruṣa*, it means that the pleasure or sorrow held in the *buddhi* is reflected on it and is thereby intuited. It is this intuition of pleasure and pain through their reflection in the *puruṣa* that is regarded as their *bhoga* or experience by *puruṣa*. The *buddhi* cannot have any *bhoga* or experience, even in a remote sense of the term, for the simple reason that it is unconscious. But it may well be argued that since the *puruṣa* is not in reality the ego, it cannot have any experience in any real sense of the term; and since it cannot in reality have any experience of sorrow, it cannot in reality regard its cessation as being of the utmost value to it. The reply to such an objection is that the realization of the fact that the cessation of sorrow is of ultimate value to the experiencer, the *puruṣa*, leads the *suddhi* on its onward path of progress. Had it not been so there would be no movement of the *buddhi* on lines of utility. So though pleasure and pain do not belong to *puruṣa*, they may yet be experienced by it and the *buddhi* may be guided by such experiences.

When the Upaniṣad says "that art thou," the idea at the back of it is that the self is not to be identified with any of the elements of the psychosis—the *buddhi*—or with any of the evolutes of the *prakṛti*. The self is part of the pure consciousness—the Brahman. When a man learns from the Upaniṣad text or one's teacher that he is a part of Brahman he tries to realize it through a process of meditation. The difference of the Vedāntic view from that of Sāṃkhya is that the latter rests with the individual selves as the ultimate entities whereas the former emphasizes the Brahman as the ultimate reality, and also the fact that the reality of all other things, the selves and the matter, depends ultimately on their participation in it.

Brahma-Experience and Experience.

Cause may be defined as the productivity due to direct and immediate perception of the material cause. The *buddhi* is regarded as an effect because, like jugs and other things, it is produced through some direct and immediate intuition of its causal material. This naturally implies that the *buddhi* has a causal material which is directly perceived by some Being and to which His creative activity is directed and this Being is God. It is said in the *Brahma-sūtras* that Brahman can be known by the testimony of the scriptures. But this cannot be true, for the Upaniṣads say that the Brahman cannot be expressed by words or known by intellect. The reply to this is that the denial contemplated in such passages refers only to the fact that Brahman cannot be known in entirety or in its uniqueness by the scriptural texts, but these passages do not mean that it is not possible to have a generic knowledge of the nature of Brahman. It is only when we have such a generic knowledge from the scriptures that we enter the sphere from which we may proceed further and further through the processes of Yoga and have ultimately a direct intuitive apperception of it. The specific nature of God as devoid of any quality or character only means that His nature is different from the nature of all other things, and though such a nature may not be realized by ordinary perception, inference or other sources of knowledge, there cannot be any objection to its being apprehended by the intuition of Yoga meditation. There are some Vedāntists who think that the Brahman cannot be felt or apprehended intuitively, but there is a mental state or function (*vṛtti*) which has the Brahman as its object. Such a mental state destroys the nescience and as a result of this the Brahman shines forth. But Bhikṣu objects to this and says that the *vṛtti* or mental function is admitted for relating the consciousness or the self with the objects, but once this connection is effected the objects are directly apprehended; so, in order to bring Brahman within the sphere of knowledge, the intuitive apperception is in itself sufficient for the purpose. It cannot be held that, since Brahman is itself of the nature of pure illumination, no special intuitive apprehension is necessary and that the existence of the mental function or *vṛtti* was admitted for explaining the dissolution of *ajñāna*; for Brahman, being of the nature of consciousness, can be realized only through intuitive apprehension which is itself of the nature of knowledge. Since all apprehension is direct and immediate, self-knowledge must also be of the same kind. There is also no necessity to assume a principle of obstruction which has to be overcome as a condition of the rise of knowledge. In the state of deep dreamless sleep a principle of obstruction in the shape of the function of *tamas* has to be admitted in order to explain the absence of knowledge which leads to the absence of all cognitive or practical behaviour. To the opponent's idea that since Brahman is self-luminous it cannot have any relation with anything else, and that since Brahman and the self are identical there cannot be any self-knowledge of Brahman, for the Brahman cannot be both the knower and the known, Bhikṣu's reply is that self-luminousness does not mean unrelatedness; and the absolute identity of the self and the Brahman cannot also be admitted, and even if it be admitted we can explain the method of Brahma-knowledge by the same manner in which our experiential knowledge or self-consciousness can be explained.

Bhikṣu thinks that since we do not find in the *Brahma-sūtras* any account of the origin and growth of knowledge, the Sāṃkhya-Yoga account of knowledge may well be accepted on account of the general affinity of the Sāṃkhya-Yoga ideas with the Vedānta. According to the Sāṃkhya-Yoga there is first a contact of the senses with their respective objects and as a result the *tamas* aspect of the *buddhi* is subordinated at the time; and the *buddhi* as pure *sattva* assumes the form of the object. This state of *buddhi* is called an objective state of the *buddhi* or a sensory idea or state (*sā buddhyavasthā viṣayā-kārā buddhi-vṛttir ity ucyate*). During dreams and contemplative states images of external objects arise in the mind and are directly perceived and therefore valid. The connection of the *puruṣa* with the external objects is thus effected through the intermediary of the *buddhi*. So long as the *buddhi* remains impure the *puruṣa* cannot get itself related to objects through it. It is for this reason that during deep sleep when the *buddhi* is dominated by *tamas* the *puruṣa*-consciousness cannot manifest itself or make itself related with other objects. As soon as the *buddhi* is modified into a sensory or image-state it is reflected in the *puruṣa*, which then reveals it as a flash of conscious state. It is in this manner that the pure infinite consciousness can manifest itself into finite forms of objects. As the *buddhi* is constantly transforming itself into various forms and reflecting them on the *puruṣa* from beginningless time there is a continuous flow of conscious states only occasionally punctuated by dreamless sleep. The *puruṣa* in its turn is also reflected in the *buddhi* and thereby gives rise to the notion of ego. In this connection Bhikṣu criticizes the view of Vācaspati that the reflection of the *puruṣa* in the *buddhi* is sufficient to explain the cognitive situation, and says that a reflection of consciousness cannot itself be conscious and hence cannot explain why the states of *buddhi* should appear as conscious. But the assumption that the states of *buddhi* are reflected in the consciousness explains their real connection with consciousness. It may be said that since it is only the reflections that are associated with consciousness, the things as they exist are not known. The reply to such an objection is that the *buddhi*-states are but copies of the external objects; and if the copies are intelligized, we have in the validity of such direct acquaintance of the copies the guarantee of their application to objects. It may be said again that when the reflections of the *buddhi*-states in the consciousness appear as one with it and therefore produce the phenomenon of knowledge we have in such phenomena an illusory unity of the consciousness with the states; our knowledge then becomes illusory. The reply to such an objection is that even if there is an element of illusion in knowledge, that does not touch the reality and validity of the objects to which such knowledge refers. Valid knowledge (*pramā*) thus consists of this reflection of the *buddhi*-states in the *puruṣa*. The fruit of the cognitive process (*pramāṇa-phala*) belongs to the pure consciousness or the *puruṣa* who thus behaves as the knower, though he is absolutely unattached to all experiences. The Vaiśeṣikas lay stress on the appearance of knowledge as produced and destroyed and therefore regard knowledge as being produced or destroyed by the collocation of causes. The reflection of the mental states to *puruṣa* is explained by them as if the knowledge belonged to the self. The Vedāntic epistemological process in which the *puruṣa* appears to be the knower and the enjoyer is explained by them as being due to a separate cognitive process called *anu-vyavasāya*.

The transcendental experience of God has also to be explained on the basis of the origin of ordinary experiential knowledge. Through the understanding of the meaning of the scriptural texts and by the processes of Yoga there arises in the *buddhi* a modification of the form "I am Brahman." This valid form of modification, being reflected in the *puruṣa*, is revealed as an intuitive apperception of the fact as true self-knowledge belonging to *puruṣa*. The difference between ordinary experiential knowledge and this knowledge is that it destroys egoism (*abhimāna*). In such a conception of self-knowledge the objection that the self cannot be both the knower and the known does not hold good; for the self that is known, being a mental state, is different in character from the transcendent self which knows it. The transcendent self as such is the knower, while its reflection in the *buddhi* as coming back to it is the self that is known[1]. The objection that the admission of the possibility of self-knowledge stands against the doctrine of the self-luminosity of the self is not valid. The self-luminosity of the self simply means that it shines by itself and does not require the aid of any conditions to manifest itself.

Self-Luminosity and Ignorance.

Citsukha has defined self-luminosity as that which not being knowable may yet be treated or felt as immediate (*avedyatve sati aparokṣa-vyavahāra-yogyatvam*). Bhikṣu argues that such a definition of self-luminosity (*svaprakaśatva*) is quite inadmissible. It is nowhere so defined in the Upaniṣads and it does not follow from the etymology of the word *svaprakaśatva*. The etymology only indicates the meaning "known by itself." Again, if a thing is not known or cognized, it cannot for that simple reason have any relation to us; and such a meaning would be directly against the scriptural testimony which affirms that the ultimate truth can be apprehended or intuited. It may be suggested that though the Brahma-state of the mind cannot be directly known yet it will have the effect of removing the *avidyā* in the *puruṣa*. But this is open to various objections. Firstly, the self-luminous is a valid means of knowledge—a *pramāṇa*; but the mere removal of the *avidyā* from

[1] *ātmā'pi bimba-rūpeṇa jñātā bhavati svagata-sva-pratibimba-rūpeṇa ca jñeyaḥ. Vijñānā-mṛta-bhāṣya*, I. I. 3.

the *puruṣa* cannot be regarded as valid knowledge or a *pramāṇa*. In this connection it is also relevant to ask the meaning of the term "*avidyā*." If it means an illusory mental state, it must be a state of the *buddhi*, and its destruction must also belong to the *buddhi* and not to the *puruṣa*. If it means the psychical instincts or root-inclinations which are the cause of errors, then also since such root-instincts belong to the *guṇas* of the *prakṛti* the destruction of such root-instincts must also qualify the *prakṛti*. If it is regarded as a *tamas*—substance which covers the self, the supposition would be inadmissible, for if the *tamas* inherent in the *buddhi* is not removed there cannot be any modification of the *buddhi* copying the object in it, and if the *tamas* in the *buddhi* is once so removed then there cannot be any reflection of it in the *puruṣa*. Thus the view that knowledge leads to the dissolution of the veil of ignorance cannot be supported. The veil is only related to the instruments of knowledge, such as the eye, and cannot therefore be regarded as having anything to do with the pure consciousness. The explanation of the rise of knowledge as being due to the removal of the veil in the pure consciousness cannot therefore be justified. There cannot be any veil in the self. If the self be of the nature of pure consciousness, there cannot be any veil of ignorance inherent in it as the two suppositions are self-contradictory. Again, if it is supposed that the world-appearance is due to the operation of the principle of ignorance or *avidyā* in the mind and if it is supposed that true knowledge dispels such ignorance, then we are led to the absolutely unwarrantable conclusion that the world may be destroyed by knowledge, or that when one self attains true knowledge the world-appearance as such ceases, or that when emancipation is attained during the lifetime of a saint he will have no experience of the world around him. If it is held that the emancipated saint has still an element of ignorance in him, then the theory that knowledge destroys ignorance has to be given up. Moreover, if the self be regarded as being absolutely unattached to anything (*a-saṅga*), it is wrong to suppose that it would be associated with *avidyā* or ignorance. The veil can have reference only to the mental states, but it cannot have any relation to pure and unchangeable consciousness; for we have no analogy for such a thing. Again, if it is held that there is natural association of ignorance with pure consciousness, such an association can never be broken off. If such an association be regarded as the consequence of some causal condition, it may well be said that such causality may be found in the mental states themselves. At least this would be a much simpler supposition than the primary assumption of a relationship of *avidyā* with pure consciousness and then to assume the operation of the mental states to dissolve it. The association of a veil with the mental states has to be admitted at least in the case of deep sleep, swoon or senility. Thus, if the veil has to be associated with the mental states, as the instrument of knowledge, it is quite unnecessary to assume it with reference to the self or pure consciousness. Patañjali, in his *Yoga-sūtra*, has defined *avidyā* as a mental state which apprehends the non-eternal as the eternal, the impure as the pure, the pleasure as sorrow. It is not, therefore, to be regarded as a separate substance inseparably associated with pure consciousness. In the same way it is wrong to define knowledge as the cessation of *avidyā*, which belongs to the *puruṣa* in this capacity. The proper way of representing it would be to say that knowledge arises in the *puruṣa* with the cessation of *avidyā* in the mental states. With the rise of the final knowledge as "I am Brahman" towards which the whole teleological movement of the *prakṛti* for the *puruṣa* was tending, the ultimate purpose of the *prakṛti* for the sake of the *puruṣa* is realized, and that being so the teleological bond which was uniting or associating the *buddhi* with the *puruṣa* is torn asunder and the mind or the *buddhi* ceases to have any function to discharge for the sake of the *puruṣa*. With the destruction of false knowledge all virtue and vice also cease and thus there is the final emancipation with the destruction of the integrity of the *buddhi*. *Avidyā* (false knowledge), *asmitā* (egoism), *rāga* (attachment), *dveṣa* (antipathy), *abhiniveśa* (self-love) may all be regarded as *avidyā* or false knowledge which is their cause, and *avidyā* may also be regarded as *tamas* which is its cause. This *tamas* obstructs the manifestation of *sattva* and it is for this reason that there is false knowledge. When the *tamas* is dominated by the *sattva*, the *sattva* manifests through its instrumentality the ultimate self. The words "knowledge" (*jñāna*) and "ignorance" (*ajñāna*) are used in the scriptures to denote *sattva* and *tamas*. The word *tamas* is used to denote *ajñāna* and there is no such *ajñāna* as indescribable or indefinite entity as is supposed by the Śaṅkarites. In ordinary experiential knowledge this *tamas* is only temporarily removed, but in the case of the rise of true and ultimate knowledge the power of the *guṇas* to undergo modification for the sake of the relevant *puruṣa* is destroyed. Before the *sattva* can show itself in its own *vṛtti* or state, it must dominate the *tamas* which would have resisted the *sattva* state. Thus the ontological opposition of the *sattva* and the *tamas* must settle their differences before a psychological state can make its appearance.

Relation of Sāṃkhya and Vedānta according to Bhikṣu.

Bhikṣu thinks that the Sāṃkhya and Yoga philosophies are intimately connected with the Vedānta and are referred to in the Upaniṣads. For this reason when certain topics, as for example the problem of experiential knowledge, are not described in the Vedānta, these are to be supplemented from the Sāṃkhya and Yoga. If there is any seeming antagonism between the two, these also have to be so explained that the opposition may be reconciled. Bhikṣu takes this attitude not only towards Sāṃkhya-yoga but also towards Nyāya-Vaiśeṣika, and the *Pañcarātra*. According to him all these systems have their basis in the Vedas and the Upaniṣads and have therefore an internal affinity which is not to be found in the Buddhists. The Buddhists are therefore the only real opponents. Thus he attempts to reconcile all the *āstika* systems of philosophy as more or less supplementary to one another or at least presenting differences which can be reconciled if they are looked at from the proper angles of vision. Bhikṣu collects his materials from the Upaniṣads, the Purāṇas and the *smṛtis* and tries to build his system of interpretation on that basis. It may, therefore, be regarded on the whole as a faithful interpretation of the theistic Vedānta which is the dominant view of the Purāṇas in general and which represents the general Hindu view of life and religion. Compared with this general current of Hindu thought, which flows through the Purāṇas and the *smṛtis* and has been the main source from which the Hindu life has drawn its inspiration, the extreme Sāṃkhya, the extreme Vedānta of Śaṅkara, the extreme Nyāya, and the extreme dualism of Madhva may be regarded as metaphysical formalisms of conventional philosophy. Bhikṣu's philosophy is a type of *bhedābheda* which has shown itself in various forms in Bhartṛ-prapañca,

Bhāskara, Rāmānuja, Nimbārka and others. The general viewpoint of this *bhedā-bheda* philosophy is that it believes in the reality of the universe as well as in its spirituality, the distinctness of the individual souls as well as in their being centres of the manifestation of God, moral freedom and responsibility as well as a spiritual determinism, a personal God as well as an impersonal reality, the ultimate spirit in which matter and pre-matter are dissoved into spirituality, an immanent teleology pervading through matter and souls both in their origin and mutual intercourse as well as in the holiness of the divine will, omnipotence and omniscience, in the superior value of knowledge as well as of love, in the compulsoriness of moral and social duties as well as in their abnegation.

The ordinary classical Sāṃkhya is well known to be atheistic and the problem arises as to how this may be reconciled with theism and the doctrine of incarnations. In interpreting *sūtra* I. I. 5, of the *Brahma-sūtra*, Bhikṣu says that since the scriptures say that "it perceived or desired," Brahman must be a Person, for desire or perception cannot be attributed to the inanimate pre-matter (*prakṛti*). Śaṅkara, in interpreting this *sūtra*, asserts that the purport of the *sūtra* is that *prakṛti* is not the cause of the world because the idea of a *prakṛti* or *pradhāna* is unvedic. Bhikṣu quotes a number of passages from the Upaniṣads to show that the idea of a *prakṛti* is not unvedic. *Prakṛti* is spoken of in the Upaniṣads as the cause of the world and as the energy of God. *Prakṛti* is also spoken of as *māyā* in the *Śvetāśvatara*, and God is spoken of as *māyāvī* or the magician who holds within Himself the magic power. The magician may withhold his magic, but the magic power lies all the same in him (*māyāyā vyāpāra-nivṛttir evā'vagamyate na nāśaḥ*)[1]. The ordinary *prakṛti* is always undergoing change and transformation and it is only the special *sattva*-stuff associated with God that is always regarded as unchanging.

A question that may naturally arise in this connection is, if God is Himself unchangeable and if the *sattva*-body with which He is always associated is also always unchangeable, how is it that God can have a desire to produce the world at any particular time? The only explanation of this is that the attribution of will to God at a particular creative moment is only a loose usage of language. It

[1] *Vijñānā-mṛta-bhāṣya*, I. I. 5.

means only that when the proper collocation of the causal conditions is ready for emergence into creative production at any particular point of time, it is designated as the manifestation of the creative will of God. God's knowledge and will cannot have a beginning in time[1]. But if God's creative will be regarded as the cause of the movement of the *prakṛti*, then the Sāṃkhya view that the movement of the *prakṛti* is solely due to its inherent teleology to be of service to the *puruṣas* becomes indefensible. The *sattva*, *rajas* and *tamas* in the *mahat* are indeed regarded in Sāṃkhya as the triad of three persons, Brahmā, Viṣṇu and Maheśvara—the three created gods as it were (*janye-śvara*). But the Sāṃkhya does not believe in any eternal God (*nitye-śvara*). According to Yoga the *sattva* part of *mahat* associated with eternal powers and existing eternally in the emancipated state is the person called *Īśvara*. His *sattva* body is, however, of the nature of an effect as it is derived from the *sattva* part of *mahat* and His knowledge is also not timeless.

In justification of Sāṃkhya, Bhikṣu maintains that the denial of God by the Sāṃkhya may be interpreted to mean that there is no necessity of admitting God for salvation. Salvation may be achieved by self-knowledge also. If this process is to be adopted, then it becomes quite unnecessary to prove the existence of God. It may, however, be remarked in this connection that this explanation of Bhikṣu can hardly be regarded as correct, for the *Sāṃkhya-sūtra* is not merely silent about God, but it makes a positive effort to prove the non-existence of God, and there is not one redeeming statement that can be interpreted to mean that Sāṃkhya was not antagonistic to theism. Bhikṣu, however, further reiterates that Sāṃkhya was not atheistic and refers to the statement in the *Śvetāśvatara* (VI. 16) that salvation can be obtained by knowing the ultimate cause as declared in the Sāṃkhya-yoga and to the statement of the *Gītā* where atheism is regarded as a demonic view.

In referring to Yoga, Bhikṣu says that it is curious that though the Yoga admitted the existence of God yet it did not make any effort to repudiate the idea that He might be partial or cruel; and instead of giving God His true cosmological place accepted a naturalistic view that *prakṛti* of itself passes through the transformatory changes, being determined by its own inherent teleology in relation to the *puruṣas*. *Īśvara*, in Patañjali's *Yoga-sūtra*, is an

[1] *Vijñānā-mṛta-bhāṣya*, I. 1. 5.

object of Yoga meditation and He shows His mercy to his devotees and other beings. Bhikṣu, however, thinks that unless God is made to serve a cosmological purpose the association of *prakṛti* with the *puruṣas* cannot be explained.

The *Īśvara* is not conditioned in His activities by any entities which are associated with *rajas* or *tamas* which are of a fluctuating nature but with an entity which is always the same and which is always associated with eternal knowledge, will and bliss[1]. The natural implication of this is that the will of God behaves like an eternal and unchangeable law. This law, however, is not a constituent of God but a constituent of *prakṛti* itself. It is through this part, an eternal unchangeable law which behaves as the eternal will and knowledge of God, that the phenomenal or the changeable part of *prakṛti* is determined.

In the *Gītā* Śrī Kṛṣṇa says that He is the highest *puruṣa* and that there is nothing higher than Him. Bhikṣu gives two explanations of such statements which seem to be in opposition to the concept of God explained above. One explanation is that the reference of Kṛṣṇa as God to Himself is only a relative statement, made in a popular manner which has no reference to the nature of absolute God who is unrelationable to ordinary experience. The other explanation is that Kṛṣṇa calls Himself God by feeling Himself as identified with God. There is thus a distinction between *para-brahma* and *kārya-brahma*; and Śrī Kṛṣṇa, being the *kārya-brahman*, popularly describes Himself as the *kāraṇa-brahma*. When other beings identify themselves with *brahma*, such identification is true only with reference to *kārya-brahma*, Śrī Kṛṣṇa or Nārāyaṇa. They therefore have no right to speak of themselves as the absolute God. Beginningless absolute Brahman is unknown and unknowable, even by the gods and the sages. It is only the Nārāyaṇa who can know Him in His absolute nature. Nārāyaṇa is therefore to be regarded as the wisest of all beings[2]. Those beings who in the previous creation became one with God by *sāyujya-mukti* exist in the *Vāsudeva-vyūha*. In the *Vāsudeva-vyūha* Vāsudeva alone is the

[1] *rajas-tamah-sambhinnatayā malinaṃ kārya-tattvaṃ parame-śvarasya no' pādhiḥ kintu kevalaṃ nitya-jñāne-cchā-nandā-dimat-sadai-ka-rūpaṃ kāraṇa-sattvam eva tasyo' pādhiḥ. Īśvara-gītā.* MS.

[2] *anādyam taṃ paraṃ brahma na devā*
narṣayo viduḥ
ekas tad veda bhagavān dhātā nārāyaṇaḥ
prabhuḥ. Vijñānā-mṛta-bhāṣya, I. I. 5.

eternal God; the other beings are but His parts. The other *vyūhas*, such as the Saṃkarṣaṇa, Pradyumna and Aniruddha, are but the manifestations of Vāsudeva (*vibhūti*) and they are to be regarded as partial creation of God or as Brahmā, Viṣṇu and Rudra. The power of the lesser gods, Viṣṇu or Śiva, is limited, since they cannot produce any change in the regulation of the cosmic affairs. When they speak of themselves as the Supreme God they do so only by a process of self-identification with the absolute God. The mahattatva, with its threefold aspect as *sattva*, *rajas* and *tamas*, forms the subtle body of Brahmā, Viṣṇu and Śiva or Saṃkarṣaṇa, Pradyumna and Aniruddha. These three gods, therefore, are supposed to have the one body, the "*mahat*," which forms the basic foundation and substratum of all cosmic evolution. It is for this reason that they are said to have the cosmos or the universe as their body. These three deities are regarded as mutually interdependent in their operations, like *vāta*, *pitta* and *kapha*. It is for this reason that they are said to be both different from one another and yet identical[1]. These three deities are identical with "*mahat*" which again is the unity of *puruṣa* and *prakṛti*. It is for this reason that Brahmā, Viṣṇu and Maheśvara are to be regarded as the partial manifestations (*aṃśāvatam*) of Gods and not direct incarnations[2].

The penetration of *Īśvara* into *pradhāna* and *puruṣa* is through His knowledge, will and effort by which He rouses the *guṇas* and helps the production of the *mahat*. Bhikṣu takes great pains to show that Bhagavān or absolute God is different from Nārāyaṇa or Viṣṇu who are direct manifestations of Him just as sons are of the father. Bhikṣu here differs from the opinion of the *Pañcarātra* school and of other thinkers such as Madhva, Vallabha and Gauḍīya Vaiṣṇavas who regard Nārāyaṇa, Viṣṇu and Kṛṣṇa as identical with God. The other *avatāras*, such as the Matsya, Kūrma, etc., are regarded by Bhikṣu as the *līlā-vatāra* of Viṣṇu and the *āveśā-vatāra* of God as *bhagavān* or *parame-śvara*.

[1] *Vijñānā-mṛta-bhāṣya*, I. I. 5.

[2] In this connection Bhikṣu quotes the famous verse of the *Bhāgavata*, *ete cā ṃśa-kalāḥ puṃsaḥ kṛṣṇas tu bhagavān svyam*. I. I. 5. He, however, paraphrases Kṛṣṇa as Viṣṇu and explains *svayaṃ bhagavān* as being the part of God just as the son is the part of the father: *atra kṛṣṇo viṣṇuḥ svayaṃ parame-śvaras tasya putravat sākṣād aṃśa ity arthaḥ*. *Ibid.* This, however, goes directly against the interpretation of the verse by the Gauḍīya school of Vaiṣṇavas who regard Kṛṣṇa as being the absolute God.

Māyā and Pradhāna.

Śaṅkara, in his commentary on the *Vedānta-sūtra*, I. I. 4, discusses the meaning of the term *avyakta* and holds that it has no technical meaning but is merely a negation of *vyakta* or manifested form. He says that the word *avyakta* is compounded of the negative particle *na* and *vyakta*. He points out that since the term *avyakta* has thus a mere etymological meaning and signifies merely the unmanifested, it cannot be regarded as having a technical application to the *Pradhāna* of Sāṃkhya. The *avyakta* according to Śaṅkara thus means the subtle cause, but he does not think that there is an independent subtle cause of the world corresponding to the *Pradhāna* of the Sāṃkhya[1]. He holds that this primal state of the existence of the universe is dependent upon God and is not an independent reality. Without the acceptance of such a subtle power abiding in God, God cannot be a creator. For without power God cannot move Himself towards creation; it is the seed power called *avidyā* which is denoted by the term *avyakta*. It is the great sleep of *māyā* (*māyāmayī mahā-supti*) depending upon God. In it all the *jīvas* lie without any self-awakening. The potency of the seed power is destroyed by knowledge in the case of emancipated beings and for that reason they are not born again[2]. Vācaspati, in commenting on it in his *Bhāmatī*, says that there are different *avidyās* with reference to different selves. Whenever an individual attempts to gain wisdom, the *avidyā* associated with him is destroyed, though the *avidyā* associated with other individuals remains the same. Thus, even though one *avidyā* is destroyed, the other *avidyās* may remain in an operative condition and may produce the world. In the case of the Sāṃkhyists, however, who admit one *pradhāna*, its destruction would mean the destruction of all. Vācaspati says further that if it is held that though the *pradhāna* remains the same yet the *avidyā* as non-distinction between *puruṣa* and the *buddhi* is responsible for bondage, then there is no necessity of admitting the *prakṛti* at all. The existence and the non-existence of *avidyā* would explain the problem of bondage and emancipation.

[1] *yadi vayaṃ sva-tantraṃ kāñcit prāg-avasthāṃ jagataḥ kāraṇatvenā' bhyupagacchema prasañjayema tadā pradhāna-kāraṇa-vādam. Vedānta-sūtra,* I. 4. 3.

[2] *muktānāṃ ca punar an utpattiḥ; kutaḥ vidyayā tasyā vīja-śakter dāhāt. Ibid.*

The objection that the distinction of selves depends upon *avidyā* and the distinction of *avidyā* upon the distinction of the selves is invalid, for the process is beginningless. The term *avyakta* refers to *avidyā* in a generic sense as including all *avidyās*. The *avidyā* rests in the individual but is yet dependent upon God as its agent and object. The *avidyā* cannot come into operation without having the Brahman as its support, though the real nature of the selves is Brahman; yet, so long as they are surrounded by *avidyā*, they cannot know their real nature.

In reply Bhikṣu says that since without power God alone is unable to create the manifold universe it has to be admitted that God does so by a power distinct from Him, and this power is the *prakṛti* and the *puruṣa*. If it is said that this power is *avidyā*, then also since it is a dual factor separate from Brahman that may as much nullify the monistic doctrine as the admission of *prakṛti* and *puruṣa*. It cannot also be said that in the time of *pralaya* the *avidyā* is non-existent, for in that case there being only Brahman the world would have to be admitted as coming into being from Brahman alone, and the selves that lie identified with Brahman and one with Him would, even though emancipated, undergo the world-process (*saṃsāra*). If it is held that bondage and emancipation are all imaginary, then there is no reason why people should undergo so much trouble in order to attain an imaginary emancipation. If it is held that *avidyā* may be said to have a secondary or *vyavahārika* existence at the time of *pralaya*, and if it is argued that under the circumstances bondage and emancipation may also be regarded as having a merely secondary existence, the view of monism would be unexceptional. But if such an *avidyā* be admitted which has mere *vyavahārika* or secondary existence, the same may be supposed with regard to *pradhāna*. If we inquire into the meaning and significance of the term *vyavahārika*, we find that its connotation is limited to the power of effectuation and service towards the fulfilment of the purpose. If that is so, then *prakṛti* may also be admitted to have a similar kind of existence[1]. It is true no doubt that the *pradhāna* is regarded as eternal, but this eternality is an eternality of ceaseless change. *Avidyā* is regarded by the Vedāntists as *apāramārthikā*, that is, *avidyā* is not true

[1] *pradhāne' pīdaṃ tulyaṃ pradhāne artha-kriyā-kāritva-rūpa-vyavahārika-sattvasyai'vā'smākam iṣṭattvāt. Vijñānā-mṛta-bhāṣya*, I. 4. 3.

absolutely. This negation of absolute truth may mean that it is not immediate and self-apparent or that it cannot manifest itself as being or that it has no existence in all times. But such limitations are true also of *pradhāna*. The *pradhāna* is eternal as changeful, but it is non-eternal in all its products. All the products of *prakṛti* are destructible; being unintelligent by nature they can never be self-apparent. Again, though *pradhāna* may be said to be existent in any particular form at any particular time, yet even at that time it is non-existent in all its past and future forms. Thus, since *vyavahārikatva* cannot mean absolute non-existence (like the hare's horn) and since it cannot also mean absolute existence it can only mean changefulness (*pariṇāmittva*); and such an existence is true of the *pradhāna*. Thus Śaṅkarites do not gain anything in criticizing the doctrine of *pradhāna*, as a substitute of the *avidyā* is supposed by them to be endowed with the same characteristics as those of the *prakṛti*.

It is thus evident that Śaṅkara's criticism against *prakṛti* may well apply to the *prakṛti* of Īśvara Kṛṣṇa, but it has hardly any application to the doctrine of *prakṛti* as conceived in the Purāṇas as interpreted by Bhikṣu, where *prakṛti* is regarded as a power of Brahman. If *avidyā* is also so regarded, it becomes similar to *prakṛti*. As it is believed to be existent in a potential form in God, even in the *pralaya*, most of the connotations of *avidyā* that distinguish it from the absolute reality in the Brahman are also the connotations of *prakṛti*.

According to the view propounded by Bhikṣu *pradhāna* is not regarded as having a separate and independent existence but only as a power of God[1].

In explaining *Brahma-sūtra* I. 4. 23, Bhikṣu points out that *Īśvara* has no other *upādhi* than *prakṛti*. All the qualities of *Īśvara* such as bliss, etc., proceed from *prakṛti* as is shown in *Patañjali-sūtra*. *Prakṛti* is to be regarded as the characteristic nature of Brahman, which is not directly the material cause of the world, but is only the abiding or the ground cause (*adhiṣṭhāna-kāraṇa*), and *prakṛti*, as it were, is its own character or part (*svīyo bhāvaḥ padārtha upādhir ity arthaḥ*). The relation between this *upādhi* and *prakṛti* is one of the controller and the controlled or the possessor

[1] *Prakṛ tasya tad-upapattaye pradhānaṃ kāraṇatva-śarīravac chaktividhayai'-vo'cyate na svātantryeṇe'ty a vadhāryata ity arthaḥ. Vijñānā-mṛta-bhāṣya*, I. 4. 4.

and the possessed. The fact that God can think or will also testifies to the fact that God must have as His instrument the *prakṛti* which can make such thinking possible for Him. For God is in Himself only pure consciousness. *Prakṛti*, however, behaves as the *upādhi* of God with its purer parts of the eternally pure *sattva*. *Kāla* and *adṛṣṭa* also form part of the *prakṛti* and as such are not regarded as the separate powers of God.

Bhikṣu's criticism of the Sāṃkhya and Yoga.

In commenting on the *Brahma-sūtra*, II. I. I, 2, 3, Bhikṣu says that Manu speaks of the original cause as being the *prakṛti*, and so also does the Sāṃkhya, and both of them are regarded as authoritative[1]. But since the Sāṃkhya doctrine of atheism is contradicted by the opinions of Patañjali and Parāśara, the view of the *Brahma-sūtras* cannot be interpreted merely on the atheistic suggestion of Sāṃkhya. It has also to be admitted that the atheistic portion of Sāṃkhya has no authoritative support either in the Vedas or in the Purāṇas and has therefore to be regarded as invalid[2].

It is wrong, however, to suppose that Kapila really intended to preach atheism. He quoted atheistic arguments from others and showed that even if God were not accepted emancipation could be obtained by differentiation of *prakṛti* from *puruṣa*. The Sāṃkhya also emphasizes the fact that emancipation can be obtained merely by knowledge. This, however, should not be interpreted as being in conflict with the Upaniṣadic texts which declare that emancipation can be obtained only by the true knowledge of God. For these signify only that there are two ways of obtaining emancipation, the inferior one being through knowledge of the distinction of *prakṛti* and *puruṣa*, and the superior one through the true knowledge of God. The Yoga also shows two ways of emancipation, the inferior one being through the ordinary Yoga processes, and the superior one through the renunciation to God of all actions and through devotion to Him. It is also wrong to suppose that the Sāṃkhya is traditionally atheistic, for in the *Mahābhārata* (*Śānti-parvan* 318. 73) and *Matsya Purāṇa* (4. 28) we hear of a twenty-sixth category,

[1] *sāṃkhyaṃ yogaṃ pañca-rātraṃ vedāḥ pāśupataṃ tathā* I. *paras-parāṇy aṅgāny etāni hetubhir na virodhayet. Vijñānā-mṛta-bhāṣya*, II. I. I.

[2] *itaś ce'śvara-pratiṣedhā-ṃśe kapila-smṛteḥ mūlānām anupalabdheḥ a-pratyakṣatvāt durvalatvam ity āha. Ibid.*

the God. So the difference between the theistic and the atheistic Sāṃkhya is due to the difference of representation as the true Sāṃkhya doctrine and the Sāṃkhya doctrine which proposes to ensure emancipation even for those who are not willing to believe in God. In this connection Bhikṣu admits the probability of two different schools of Sāṃkhya, one admitting *Īśvara* and the other not admitting it, and it is only the latter which he thinks to be invalid[1]. He also refers to the *Kūrma Purāṇa* in which the Sāṃkhyists and the Yogins are said to be atheistic. The chief defect of the Śaṅkara school is that instead of pointing out the invalidity of theistic Sāṃkhya, Śaṅkara denies all theistic speculations as non-vedic and misinterprets the *Brahma-sūtras* accordingly. Bhikṣu refers to *Praśna*, 4. 8, where the twenty-three categories of Sāṃkhya are mentioned and only *prakṛti* has been omitted. The *mahat-tattva* is not mentioned directly, but only as *buddhi* and *citta*. The fourfold division of the *buddhi-tattva* as *manas*, *buddhi ahaṃkāra* and *citta* is also admitted there. In the *Garbha Upaniṣad* eight *prakṛtis* and sixteen *vikāras* are mentioned. In the *Maitreyo-paniṣad* we hear of the three *guṇas* and their disturbance by which creation takes place. We hear also that the *puruṣas* are pure consciousness. In *Maitrī Upaniṣad*, v. 2, it is said that the *tamas*, being disturbed by the supreme being, gives rise to *rajas* and that to *sattva*[2]. In the *Cūlikā Upaniṣad* the categories of the Sāṃkhya doctrine are also mentioned in consonance with the monistic doctrine of the Vedānta. It also says that there are various schools of the Sāṃkhya, that there are some who admit twenty-six categories, others twenty-seven, and again others who admit only twenty-four categories. There is also said to be a monistic and also a dualistic Sāṃkhya and that they find expression in three or five different ways. Thus Vijñāna Bhikṣu says that the Sāṃkhya doctrine is definitely supported by the Upaniṣadic texts.

Concerning the Yoga also it can be said that only that part of it may be regarded as opposed by the Upaniṣads which holds a separate and independent existence of *prakṛti* as apart from *Īśvara*. In the *Sūtras* of Patañjali it is said that God helps the movement of the *prakṛti* only by removing the obstacles, just as a ploughman enables

[1] *athavā kapilai-ka-deśasya prāmāṇyam astu. Vijñānā-mṛta-bhāṣya*, II. I. 2.

[2] *tamo vā idm ekamagre āsīt vai rajasas tat pare syāt tat pareṇe'ritaṃ viṣamatvaṃ prayāty etad rūpaṃ tad rajaḥ khalv ī-ritaṃ viṣamatvaṃ prayāty etad vai sattvasya rūpaṃ tat sattvam eva. Maitrī Upaniṣad*, v. 2.

water to pass from one field to another. But the Upaniṣads definitely say that God is the generator of the movement and the disturbance of the *prakṛti*. The *sattva* body of God is thus there held to be a product of *prakṛti* as it comes into being from the *prakṛti* through desire in a previous creative cycle. The *sattva* body of God is thus derived from the *prakṛti*, through the will of God serving as the vehicle of the will of God for the removal of the obstructions in the course of the evolutionary process of the *prakṛti*. *Prakṛti* in itself therefore is not regarded by Patañjali as the *upādhi* of *Īśvara*[1]. Bhikṣu seeks to explain this part of the Yoga doctrine also in the same manner as he did with the Sāṃkhya by accepting the so-called *abhyūpagama-vāda*. He maintains that the Yoga holds that even if it is considered that the *prakṛti* is independent and runs into evolutionary activity by herself, undetermined by the eternal knowledge and will of God, and even if it be admitted that the eternal God has no eternal knowledge and will and that the movement of *prakṛti* is due to an inner teleology in accordance with *karma*, and that in the beginning of the creation *prakṛti* is transformed into the *sattvo'pādhi* of God, even then by self-abnegation to God *kaivalya* can be attained. Thus, in the Yoga view the *upādhi* of *Īśvara* is a product and not the material or the instrumental cause of the world, whereas in the Vedānta view as propounded by Bhikṣu the *upādhi* of *Īśvara* is both the material and the instrumental cause of the world, and this *upādhi* which forms the material stuff of the world is *prakṛti* herself and not her product. In the Yoga view God is eternal, but His thought and will are not eternal. This thought and will are associated with the *sattva* part of *prakṛti* which lies embedded in it at the time of *pralaya* which only shows itself at the beginning of a new creative cycle through the potency left in it by the will of God in the previous creative cycle. God, in the view of Yoga, is thus not both the material and the instrumental cause of the world as the Vedānta holds. According to the Vedānta as explained by Bhikṣu, the *prakṛti* plays her dual part; in one part she remains as the eternal vehicle of the eternal knowledge and will of God, and through the other part she runs through an evolutionary process by producing disturbances of *sattva*, *rajas* and

[1] *yogā hī'śvarasya jagan-nimittatvaṃ prakṛtitvenā'bhyupagacchanti Īśvaropādheh sattva-viśeṣasya purva-sargīya-tat-saṃkalpa-vaśāt sargā-dau sva-tantra-prakṛtita utpaty-aṇgīkārāt. Vijñānā-mṛta-bhāṣya*, II. I. 2.

tamas. This also explains the Purāṇic view of the gradual derivation of *sattva*, *rajas* and *tamas* as stages in the evolution of *prakṛti* through which at a later stage the cosmic evolution takes place. Thus the *prakṛti* which remains associated with God as the vehicle of His knowledge and will is unchangeable and eternal[1].

Īśvara-gītā, its Philosophy as expounded by Vijñāna Bhikṣu.

In the second part (*uttara-vibhāga*) of the *Kūrma Purāṇa* the first eleven chapters are called *Īśvara-gītā*. In the first chapter of this section Suta asks Vyāsa about the true knowledge leading to emancipation as originally instructed by Nārāyaṇa in his incarnation as a tortoise. It is reported by Vyāsa that in Vadarikāśrama in an assembly of the sages Sanat-kumāra, Sanandana, Sanaka, Aṅgirā, Bhṛgu, Kaṇāda, Kapila, Garga, Valadeva, Śukra, and Vaśiṣṭha Ṛṣi Nārāyaṇa appeared and later on Śiva also came there. Śiva then at the request of the sages gave a discourse regarding the ultimate nature of reality, the world and God. The real discourse begins with the second chapter. Vijñāna Bhikṣu wrote a commentary on the *Īśvara-gītā*; he thought that since the *Īśvara-gītā* contains the main purport of the *Bhagavad-gītā* it was unnecessary for him to write any commentary on the latter. Apart from the Sāṃkhya and Yoga works, Vijñāna Bhikṣu wrote a commentary on the *Brahma-sūtra*, a commentary on the Upaniṣads, and a commentary on the *Īśvara-gītā* of the *Kūrma Purāṇa*. In his commentary on the *Brahma-sūtra* he quotes a passage from Citsukhācārya of the thirteenth century. He himself probably flourished some time in the fourteenth century. Bhikṣu's other works are *Sāṃkhya-pravacana-bhāṣya*, *Yoga-vārtika*, *Yoga-sūtra*, *Sāṃkhya-sāra*, and the *Upadeśa-ratnamālā*. In his interpretation of the *Brahma-sūtra* and of the *Īśvara-gītā* he has followed the line of interpretation of Vedānta as adopted in the Purāṇas, where the Sāṃkhya-yoga and Vedānta appear to be wielded together into one indivisible harmonious system. The philosophy of the *Īśvara-gītā* as dealt with here is based upon Bhikṣu's commentary, called the *Īśvara-gītā-bhāṣya* which was available to the present writer as a manuscript by courtesy of M. M. Gopīnātha Kavirāja, of the Benares Sanskrit College.

[1] *Vijñānā-mṛta-bhāṣya*, pp. 271, 272.

The main questions that were asked by the sages which led to the discourse of Śiva are the following: (1) What is the cause of all? (2) Who suffers rebirth? (3) What is the soul? (4) What is emancipation? (5) What is the cause of rebirth? (6) What is the nature of rebirth? (7) Who can realize all? (8) What is the ultimate reality, the Brahman? The answers to these questions are not given serially, but the most important topics as they appeared to the instructor, Śiva, were handled by him in his own order of discourse. Thus the eighth question was taken up for answer before all other questions. This answer begins with a description of the nature of *Ātman* not as the individual soul, but as the highest self.

Vijñāna Bhikṣu seems to acknowledge the doctrine of absolute absorption or assimilation of the individual soul within the universal and infinite soul. And even during his existence in this world, the soul is said to be merely a witness.

He explains that in the answer to the eighth question in the *Kūrma Purāṇa*, II. l. 7, p. 453[1], the word *ātmā* refers to the Godhead, though in ordinary usage it stands only for the finite souls, and suggests the self-sameness of the finite and infinite souls. The reference here is thus to the *prākṛtā-tmā* and not to the *jīvā-tmā*[2]. God is called *sarvā-ntara* as He has already entered the hearts (*antaḥ*) of the diverse living beings and exists there in the capacity of being only a witness (*sarveṣāṃ sva-bhinnānām antaḥ-sākṣitvena' nugataḥ*)[3]. A *sākṣī* (witness) is he who illuminates (*sva-prati-vimbita-vastu-bhāsakaḥ*), without any efforts on his part (*vyāpāraṃ vinai' va*). He is called *antaryāmi* on account of his association with finite intelligences and through this association even the individual soul shares the greatness of the highest self.

Vijñāna Bhikṣu says that the line "*asmād vijāyate viśvam atrai' va pravilīyate*" occurs here by way of giving a reason for the *śakti-śaktimad-a-bhedatva* doctrine so ably put forth by calling the ultimate Reality or *paramā-tman*, *antaryāmin* and then explaining the doctrine a little by giving him a few adjectives more to bring out the significance of the esoteric doctrine or suggestion of *śakti-śaktimad-abhedatva*. Now it is said that as it is from Him that the inverse-effects are created, in Him they exist and in Him they are

[1] *Bibliotheca Indica* edition, 1890.
[2] See *Īśvara-gītā-bhāṣya*, MS.
[3] *evam antaryāmi-sattva-sambandhāt cin mātro'pi paramā-ntaryāmī bhavati sarvā-ntaratvena sarva-śaktiṣv' avibhāga-lakṣaṇā-bhedāt. Ibid.*

annihilated. He is non-different (or better, inseparable) from *puruṣa* and *prakṛti*, because of His being the support and the ground of the whole universe beginning from *puruṣa* and *prakṛti*; i.e. of the effects right down from *puruṣa* and *praktṛi* and inclusive of them. If like the body He had not superintended all the causal agencies, then the cause, like the *dravya*, *guṇa*, *karma*, etc., could not have effected any causal function (*yadi hi paramā-tmā dehavat sarvaṃ kāraṇaṃ nā'dhitiṣṭheta tarhi dravya-guṇa-karmā-di-sādhā-raṇā-khila-kriyā-rtha-mūla-kāraṇaṃ na syād iti*)[1]. If it is said that the sentence speaks of effectedness (or causality) as common to all tangible manifestations, then the idea of the previous sentence maintaining the identity between Brahman and the world would not be admissible[2].

Brahman is the *upādāna-kāraṇa* of the universe, but this universe is a *pariṇāmi-rūpa* of Brahman. His is not therefore the *pariṇāmi-rūpa*, because that will contradict the statements made by the scriptures declaring the Brahman to be unchangeable (*kūṭastha*). Then Vijñāna Bhikṣu defines that God being the ultimate substratum of all, the functioning of all types of causes is helped in its operation by Him and it is this that is called the *adhiṣṭhāna-kāraṇatā* of God.

Then he maintains his doctrine of *jīvātma-paramā-tmanor aṃśāṃśy-abheda* by the line "*sa māyī māyayā baddhaḥ karoti vividhās tanūḥ*" and says further that *Yājñavalkya-smṛti* and *Vedānta-sūtra* also preach the same doctrine. *Śrīmad-bhagavad-gītā* says the same thing. Then comes the elaboration of the same idea. A reference to Śaṅkara by way of criticizing him is made[3]. *Māyā-vāda* is called a sort of covert Buddhism and for support a passage from *Padma-purāṇa* has also been quoted.

Adhiṣṭhāna-kāraṇatva, or the underlying causality, is defined as that in which, essence remaining the same, new differences emerge just as a spark from the fire. This is also called the *aṃśāṃśi-bhāva*, for, though the *niravayava* Brahman cannot be regarded as having parts, yet it is on account of the emergence of different characters from a common basis that the characterized units are called the parts of the common basis. It should be noted that Vijñāna Bhikṣu is against the view that the Brahman undergoes any transformatory

[1] *Īśvara-gītā-bhāṣya*. MS. [2] *Ibid.*
[3] *Ibid.*

change. Though the Brahman does not undergo any transformatory change, yet new differences emerge out of it. In the sentence "*Sa māyī māyayā baddhaḥ*" the idea is that the *māyā* itself is an integral part of the Divine entity and not different from it. The *māyā* is like an *aṃśa* which is identical with the *aṃśin*.

Though in the scriptures both the distinction and the identity of the individual with the Brahman have often been mentioned, yet it is by the realization of the difference of the individual with the Brahman that ultimate emancipation can be attained[1].

The self is of the nature of pure consciousness and is not in any way bound by its experiences. The assertion of Śaṅkara that *ātmā* is of the nature of joy or bliss is also wrong; for no one can always be attached to himself, and the fact that everyone seeks to further his own interest in all his actions does not imply that the soul is of the nature of bliss. Moreover, if the soul is of the nature of pure consciousness, it cannot at the same time be of the nature of pure bliss; at the time of acquiring knowledge we do not always feel pleasure.[2]

Egoism (*abhimāna*) also does not belong to the soul but like *sukha* and *duḥkha* belongs to *prakṛti*, which are wrongly attributed to the self.[3] The soul is, however, regarded as an enjoyer of its experiences of pleasure and pain, a reflection of them on it through the *vṛtti*, and such a reflection of pleasure and pain, etc., through the *vṛtti* is regarded as the realization (*sākṣātkāra*) of the experiences. Such an enjoyment of experiences, therefore, is to be regarded as *anaupādhika* (or unconditional). This is also borne out by the testimony of the *Bhagavad-gītā* and Sāṃkhya. Such an enjoyment of the experiences does not belong to the *prakṛti* (*sākṣātkāra-rūpa-dharmasya dṛśya-dharmatva-sambhavāt*)[4]. The passages which say that the experiences do not belong to the *puruṣa* refer to the modifications of *vṛtti* in connection with the experiences. The assertion of Śaṅkara, therefore, that the *ātman* is as incapable of experiences (*bhoga*) as of the power of acting (*kartṛtva*) is therefore false.

Ajñāna, according to Vijñāna Bhikṣu, means *anyathā-jñāna*. *Pradhāna* is so called because it performs all the actions for the sake of the *puruṣa*; and it is through the fault of his association with *pradhāna* that the *puruṣa* is associated with false knowledge.

[1] *Īśvara-gītā-bhāṣya.* [2] *Ibid.* [3] *Ibid.*
[4] *Ibid.*

The *ātman* remains unchanged in itself and the differences are due to the emergence of the association of *buddhi* and other faculties which give rise to experience. At the time of emancipation *jīvas* remain undifferentiated with Brahman. *Prakṛti*, *puruṣa*, and *kāla* are ultimately supported in Brahman and yet are different from it.

There are indeed two kinds of scriptural texts, one emphasizing the monistic side, the other the dualistic. A right interpretation should, however, emphasize the duality-texts, for if everything were false then even such a falsity would be undemonstrable and self-contradictory. If it is argued that one may accept the validity of the scriptural texts until the Brahman is realized and when that is done it matters little if the scriptural texts are found invalid, the reply to such an objection is that, whenever a person discovers that the means through which he attained the conclusion was invalid, he naturally suspects the very conclusion arrived at. Thus the knowledge of Brahman would itself appear doubtful to a person who discovers that the instruments of such knowledge were themselves defective.

The individual soul exists in the *paramā-tman* in an undifferentiated state in the sense that the *paramā-tman* is the essence or ground-cause of the *jīvas*; and the texts which emphasize the monistic side indicate this nature of *paramā-tman* as the ground-cause. This does not imply that the individual souls are identical with Brahman.

Pleasure and pain do not belong to the self; they really belong to the *antaḥkaraṇa* and they are ascribed to the self only through the association of the *antaḥkaraṇa* with the self. In the state of emancipation the self is pure consciousness without any association of pleasure and pain. The ultimate end is the cessation of the suffering of sorrow (*duḥkha-bhoga-nivṛtti*) and not the cessation of sorrow (*na duḥkha-nivṛttiḥ*); for when one has ceased to suffer sorrow, sorrow may still be there and the avoidance of it would be the end of other persons. The assertion of Śaṅkara that there is bliss in the stage of emancipation is wrong. For during that stage there is no mental organ by which happiness could be enjoyed. If the self be regarded as of the nature of bliss, then also the self would be both the agent and the object of the enjoyment of bliss, which is impossible. The ascription of *ānanda* in the state of emancipation only refers to it in a technical sense, i.e., *ānanda* means the absence of pleasure and pain.

Bhikṣu admits a gradation of realities. He holds further that when one entity is stabler than another, the former is more real than the latter. Since *paramā-tman* is always the same and does not undergo any change or transformation or dissolution, He is more real than the *prakṛti* or *puruṣa* or the evolutes of *prakṛti*. This idea has also been expressed in the view of the Purāṇas that the ultimate essence of the world is of the nature of knowledge which is the form of the *paramā-tman*. It is in this essential form that the world is regarded as ultimately real and not as *prakṛti* and *puruṣa* which are changing forms.

The *prakṛti* or *māyā* has often been described as that which can be called neither existent nor non-existent. This has been interpreted by the Śaṅkarites as implying the falsity of *māyā*. But according to Vijñāna Bhikṣu it means that the original cause may be regarded as partly real and partly unreal in the sense that while it is unproductive it is regarded as unreal, and when it passes through the course of evolutionary changes it is regarded as real (*kiñcit sad-rūpā kiñcit asad-rūpā ca bhavati*).

Now coming to *sādhanā* he says that by *āgama*, *anumāna* and *dhyāna* one should attain self-knowledge. This self-realization leads to the *asamprajñāta-yoga* which uproots all the *vāsanās*. It is attained not only by the cessation of *ajñāna* but also by the destruction of the *karmas*. He also maintains that the emphasis of Śaṅkara on the understanding of the Upaniṣadic texts as a means to the attainment of self-realization is also wrong.

In the state of *mukti*, self having dissociated itself from the *liṅga-śarīra* becomes one with Brahman, just as the river becomes one with the sea. This is not a case of identity, but one of non-difference (*liṅga-śarīrā-tmaka-ṣoḍaśa-kala-śūnyena ekatām avi-bhāga-lakṣanā-bhedam atyantaṃ vrajet*). Here in the state of *mukti* the identity and difference of *jīva* and Brahman have been indicated on the analogy of the river and the sea.

Bhikṣu says that there is a difference between the Sāṃkhya and Yoga regarding the attainment of emancipation. The followers of the Sāṃkhya can attain emancipation only by the cessation of their *prārabdha karmas*. Since *avidyā* has been destroyed, the realization of emancipation has only to wait till the *prārabdhas* exhaust themselves. The followers of Yoga, however, who enter into a state of *asamprajñāta-samādhi* have not to suffer the fruits of the *prārabdha*, because being in a state of *asamprajñāta* meditation the *prārabdha* can no longer touch them. They can, therefore, immediately enter into a state of emancipation at their own sweet will.

According to Bhikṣu, though *Īśvara* transcends the *guṇas*, yet through his body as pure *sattva* he carries on the creative work and the work of superintending and controlling the affairs of the universe. Though his agency is manifested through his body as pure *sattva* as a directive activity, yet it is without any association of passions, antipathies, etc.

In the third chapter of the *Kūrma Purāṇa* it is said that *pradhāna*, *puruṣa* and *kāla* emerge from *avyakta*, and from them the whole world came into being. Bhikṣu says that the world did not emanate directly from Brahman but from *pradhāna*, *puruṣa* and *kāla*. There cannot be any direct emanation from Brahman; for that would mean that Brahman undergoes a change. A direct emanation would imply that evil and hell also sprang from Brahman. The emanation of *prakṛti*, *puruṣa* and *kāla* from Brahman is explained on the supposition that Brahman is a kind of ground-cause of *prakṛti*, *puruṣa*, and *kāla* (*abhivyakti-kāraṇa* or *ādhāra-kāraṇa*). But this emanation of *prakṛti*, *puruṣa* and *kāla* is not through modificatory processes in the manner in which curd is produced from milk. In the time of dissolution *prakṛti* and *puruṣa* are unproductive of any effects and may therefore be regarded as it were as non-existent. It is through the will of God that the *prakṛti* and *puruṣa* are drawn out and connected together, and the point of motivation is started for the processes of modification of the *prakṛti*. This point of motivation is called *kāla*. It is by such a course that all these three may be regarded as producing an effect and therefore as existent. It is in this sense that *prakṛti*, *puruṣa* and *kāla* are regarded as brought into being by God[1].

Avyakta as God is so called because it transcends human knowledge. It is also so called because it is a state of non-duality, where there is no difference between energy and its possessor, and where everything exists in an undifferentiated manner. *Avyakta* used in

[1] *na tu sākṣād eva brahmaṇaḥ...atra kālā-di-trayasya brahma-kāryatvam abhivyakti-rūpam eva vivakṣitam....prakṛti-puruṣayoś ca mahad-ādi-kāryo-nmukhatañ ca parame-śvara-kṛtād anyonya-saṃyogād eva bhavati, evaṃ kālasya prakṛti-puruṣa-samyogā-khya-kāryo-nmukhatvaṃ parame-śvare-cch ayai'va bhavati. Īśvara-gītā-bhāṣya.* MS.

the sense of *prakṛti* is the basis of change, or change as such; and *puruṣa* denotes the knower.

The *paramā-tman* is spoken of as the soul of all beings. This should not, however, be taken to mean that there is only the *paramātman* which exists and that all things are but false impositions on his nature. The *paramā-tman* or *Parame-śvara* is both different and identical with *kāla*, *pradhāna* and the *puruṣa*. The existence of the *prakṛti* and the *puruṣa* has to be regarded as less ultimate than the existence of God, because the existence of the former is relative as compared with the existence of God (*vikārā-pekṣayā sthiratvena apekṣakaṃ etayos tattvam*, p. 44). Time is regarded as an instrumental cause of the connection of *prakṛti* and *puruṣa*. Time is a superior instrumental agent to deeds, for the deeds are also produced by time (*karmā-dīnam api kāla-janyatvāt*). Though the time is beginningless, yet it has to be admitted that it has a special function with reference to each specific effect it produces. It is for that reason that at the point of dissolution time does not produce the evolutes of *mahat*, etc. *Mahat-tatva* is in itself a combination of the conscious centres and the material element.

When the word *puruṣa* is used in the singular number, such a use should not be interpreted to mean a denial of the individual *puruṣas*. It only means that in such instances of scriptural texts the word *puruṣa* has been used in a generic sense. *Puruṣas* are also of two kinds—the *apara* and the *para*. Both are in themselves devoid of any qualities and of the nature of pure consciousness. But there is this difference between the *para puruṣa* and the *apara puruṣa*, that while the former never has any kind of association with any experience of pleasure and pain, the latter may sometimes be associated with pleasure and pain which he at that time feels to be his own (*anye guṇā-bhimānāt saguṇā iva bhavanti paramātmā tu guṇā-bhimāna-śūnyaḥ*, p. 46). It must be understood, however, that the experiencing of pleasure and pain is not an indispensable part of the definition of *puruṣa*, for at the stage of *jīvan-mukti* the *puruṣas* do not identify themselves with the experiences of pleasure and pain, but they are still *puruṣas* all the same. God, however, who is called the superior *puruṣa*, does not associate Himself with the experiences that proceed as a fruit of *karma* and which are enjoyed in a spatial-temporal manner. But God continues to enjoy eternal bliss in association with His own special *upādhi* or conditions (*svo-pādhistha-nityā-nanda-bhoktṛtvaṃ tu paramā'tmano'pi asti*). When the scriptural texts deny the enjoyment of the experiences of pleasure and pain with regard to the Supreme *puruṣa*, the idea is that though the Supreme *puruṣa* underlies the ordinary *puruṣas* as their ground yet he is not in any way affected by their experiences (*ekasminn eva buddhāv avasthānena jīva-bhogataḥ prasaktasya paramā-tma-bhogasyai'va pratiṣedhaḥ*). So the Supreme *puruṣa* has in common with ordinary *puruṣas* certain experiences of his own. These experiences of pure eternal bliss are due to the direct and immediate reflection of the bliss in the *puruṣa* himself, by which this bliss is directly and immediately experienced by him. By such an experience the *puruṣas* cannot be admitted to suffer any change. He can, however, be aware of the mental states of ordinary persons as well as their experiences of pleasure and pain in a cognitive manner (such as that by which we know external objects) without being himself affected by those experiences. This enjoyment of experience is of course due to the action of God's mind through the process of reflection.

The monism of such a view becomes intelligible when we consider that the *puruṣa*, the *mahat*, the *ahaṃkāra* and all its products exist in an undifferentiated condition in the very essence of God. The ultimate *puruṣa* as the supreme cognitive principle underlies the very being of *puruṣas* and the faculties such as the *buddhi* and the *ahaṃkāra*, and also all in later material products. For this reason, by the underlying activity of this principle all our cognitions become possible, for it is the activity of this principle that operates as the faculties of the origins of knowledge. In the case of the experience of pleasure and pain also, though these cannot subsist outside the mind and may not apparently be regarded as requiring any separate organ for their illumination, yet in their case also it is the mind, the *buddhi*, that behaves as the internal organ. So though pleasures and pains cannot be regarded as having an unknown existence, yet their experiences are also interpreted as being due to their reflection in the mind.

When the *mahat* becomes associated with the *puruṣa* and no distinction is felt between it, the *puruṣas* and the original ground-cause, it is then that the cycle of world-existence appears. It is the super-consciousness of God that holds together the objective and the subjective principles. The objective principle, the *prakṛti*, and the subjective centres, the *puruṣas*, are held together in a state of non-distinction. It is this that gives rise to all experiences of sorrow and bondage with reference to the conscious centres. It may be asked how it is that the *buddhi* and the *puruṣa* are held in non-distinction instead of being distinguished from one another. The reply is that distinction and non-distinction are both possible elements in the *buddhi*, and the function of Yoga is to destroy the obstruction in the way of the realization of such a mutual distinction (*yogā-dinā tu pratibandha-mātram apākriyate*).

Love of God proceeds in two stages: first, from the notion of God as satisfying our highest needs; and, secondly, in the notion of Him as being one with the self of the devotee. These highest needs find their expression firstly in our notion of value as pleasure and satisfaction in our experiences; secondly, in our notion of value in our emancipation; thirdly, in our notion of value in the satisfaction that we achieve in our realization of the sublimity in experiencing the greatness of God (*Prema ca anurāga-viśeṣaḥ paramā-tmani iṣṭa-sādhanatā-jñānāt ātmatva-jñānāc ca bhavati. iṣṭam api dvi-vidhaṃ bhogā-pavargau tan-mahimā-darśano-ttha-sukhaṃ ca iti tad evaṃ māhātmya-pratipādanasya phalaṃ prema-lakṣaṇā bhaktiḥ*).

Māyā, as identified with *prakṛti*, should be regarded as substantive entity. The *prakṛti* has two elements in it, *sattva* and *tamas*. Through *sattva*, wisdom or true knowledge is produced; through *tamas* is produced delusion or false knowledge. It is this aspect of *prakṛti* as producing false knowledge that is called *māyā*. *Māyā* is described as being *triguṇā-tmikā prakṛti* or the *prakṛti* with three *guṇas*. But though the *māyā* is identified with *prakṛti*, yet this identification is due to the fact that the *tamas* side of *prakṛti* cannot be taken as apart from the *prakṛti* as a whole. When it is said in the scriptures that God destroys the *māyā* of Yogins, it does not mean that the *triguṇā-tmikā prakṛti* as a whole is destroyed, but only that the operation of the *tamas* side is suspended or destroyed or ceases only with reference to the Yogin. *Māyā* is also described as that which cannot produce an illusion in Him on whom it has to depend for its existence, i.e. God, but that it can produce illusion or false knowledge in others (*svā-śraya-vyāmohakatve sati para-vyāmohakatvam*).

It is further said that God creates the world by his *māyā-śakti* as composed of the three *guṇas*. The significance of the designation *māyā* in this connection implies that it is by the false identification of the *prakṛti* and the *puruṣa* that the latter evolutionary process of the formation of the world and world-experience becomes possible. The term *māyā* is generally restricted to *prakṛti* in its relation to God, whereas it is called *avidyā* as a delusive agent with reference to individuals.

True knowledge does not consist in a mere identification with Brahman as pure consciousness, but it means the knowledge of Brahman, his relationship with *pradhāna*, *puruṣa*, and *kāla*, and the manner in which the whole cosmic evolution comes into being, is maintained, and is ultimately dissolved in Brahman; and also in the personal relationship that he has with the individuals, and the manner in which he controls them and the ultimate ways of attaining the final realization. *Kāla* is, again, here referred to as the conditional *upādhi* through which God moves the *prakṛti* and *puruṣa* towards the evolution of the cosmic process.

The great difficulty is to explain how God who is regarded in essence of the nature of pure consciousness and therefore absolutely devoid of desire or will can be the cause of the great union of *prakṛti* with the *puruṣas*. The answer proposed by Bhikṣu is that in God's nature itself there is such a dynamization that through it He can continue the actualizing process and the combining activities of the *prakṛti* and *puruṣa* lying dormant in Him. Though *prakṛti* and *puruṣa* may also be regarded as the causes of the world, yet since the combination happens in time, time may be regarded primarily as a dynamic agent; the condition existing in God through which He renders the union is made possible (*mama svīyo bhāvaḥ padārthaḥ sva-bhāva upādhiḥ tatas tasya preraṇāt bhagavān a-pratihato mahā-yogasya prakṛti-puruṣā-di-saṃyogasya īśvaras tatra samarthaḥ . . .prakṛti-prati-kṣaṇa-pariṇāmānam eva kālo-pādhitvāt*). Since God moves both the *prakṛti* and the *puruṣa* through His own dynamic conditions, the whole universe of matter and spirits may be regarded as His body in the sense that they are the passive objects of the activity of God. God is thus conceived as dancing in his activity among his own energies as *prakṛti* and *puruṣas*. It may be argued that *puruṣa* being itself absolutely static, how can these be moved into activity consists of the fact that they are turned to the specific operations or that they are united with the *prakṛti*. Sometimes it is also suggested that the *prakṛti* is the condition of the *puruṣas* and that the movement of the *prakṛti* in association with the *puruṣas* is interpreted as being the movement of the *puruṣas*.

In the seventh chapter of *Īśvara-gītā* Brahman is defined as the Universal. Thus any cause may be regarded as Brahman in relation to its effect. So there may be a hierarchy of Brahmans as we proceed from a lesser universal to a higher universal. The definition of Brahman is: "*yad yasya kāraṇaṃ tat tasya brahma tad-apekṣayā vyāpakatvāt*." As God contains within Himself all the universals, He is called *brahma-māyā*. God is always associated with the *puruṣas*. But yet His dynamic activity in association with the *puruṣas* consists in bringing about such an association with *prakṛti* that the objects of the world may be manifested to them in the form of knowledge.

The *jīva* or individual is regarded as being a part of God, the relation being similar to that of a son and father. When the *jīvas* dedicate all their actions to God with the conviction that if it is God who works through them, then virtues and vices lose their force and become inefficacious to cause any bondage to them. As all *jīvas* are the parts of God, there is a great similarity between them in spite of their diversity. God exists in the *jīvas* just as the whole exists in the parts.

Vijñāna Bhikṣu conceives of the *adhiṣṭhāna-kāraṇa* as the ground cause, as one which in itself remains the same and yet new differences emerge out of it. This is also his doctrine of the part and the whole. The parts are thus supposed to be emergents from the whole which does not itself participate in any change. The relation is thus not organic in the sense that the dissolution of the parts would mean the dissolution of the whole. In the *pralaya* the parts are dissolved, yet pure Brahman remains just as it was in the stage of creation. So, again, when the parts are affected pleasures and pains are experienced, but the affection of the parts does not involve in the least the affection of the whole. But the whole is not affected by the sufferings that exist in the emergents. It is further stated that it is through the function of the ground-cause that the emergents, e.g. substance, quality and action, can express themselves or operate in their specific forms. The underlying whole, the ground-cause, has really no parts in itself. Yet from this common basis various emergents of appearances as characterized units show themselves, and since they are seen to emerge from it they are in this specific technical sense called the parts of the underlying ground cause.

It will thus be seen that the Brahman, the ground-cause, always remains unchangeable in itself, but it is said that the Brahman is associated with *māyā* and is united by it (*sa māyī māyayā baddhaḥ*). The idea is that the *māyā* is an integral part of the divine entity and not different from it. *Māyā* is like a part which is identical with the whole.

Though in the scriptures both the distinction and the identity of the individual with the Brahman have often been mentioned, yet it is by the realization of the difference of the individual from the Brahman that the ultimate emancipation can be attained[1].

In the *Bṛhad-āraṇyaka Upaniṣad*, II. 4. 5, it is stated that all other things are desired because we desire the self. Śaṅkara infers from it that we are primarily attached to the self, and since all attachments imply attachment to pleasure, it follows that the self is of the nature of pleasure or bliss. Other things are desired only when they are falsely regarded as ourselves or parts of ourselves. Bhikṣu denies this proposition. He says that firstly it is not true that we are always attached to our own selves; nor, therefore, is it true that seeking of happiness from other sources is always the seeking of the selves. It is, therefore, wrong to suppose that self is of the nature of bliss. If the soul is of the nature of pure consciousness, it cannot be the nature of pure bliss. If bliss and consciousness were the same, all knowledge would imply pleasure, but our knowledge is as much associated with pleasure as with pain. Pleasure and pain, as also egoism (*abhimāna*), belong to *prakṛti* or its product *buddhi* and are transferred through its function (*vṛtti*) to the self, which is the real enjoyer and sufferer of pleasure and pain. The self is thus the real experiencer and the experiences therefore do not belong to the *prakṛti* but to the self[2]. Through the operation of the sense-contact with the object and light the mental states are generated. These mental states are called *vṛtti* and belong to *buddhi* and therefore to *prakṛti*, but corresponding to each such mental state there is an intuition of them on the part of the *puruṣa* (*vṛtti-sākṣātkāra*)

[1] *yady api bhedā-bhedā-vubhāv eva śruti-smṛtyoruktau tathā'pi yathokta-bheda-jñāna-rūpa-vivekad eva sarvā-bhimāna-nivṛtyā sākṣāt mokṣaḥ. Īśvara-gītā.* MS.

[2] *sākṣāt-kāra-rūpa-dharmasya dṛśya-dharmatva-sambhavāt.* Bhikṣu's commentary on *Īśvara-gītā.* MS.

and it is this intuition that constitutes the real experience of the *puruṣa*. The word *bhoga* has an ambiguity in meaning. It sometimes refers to the mental states and at other times to their intuition and it is as the former state that the *bhoga* is denied of the *puruṣa*.

The *ajñāna* (ignorance) in this system means false knowledge. When the *puruṣa* intuits the *vṛttis* of the *buddhi* and thereby falsely regards those *vṛttis* as belonging to itself there is false knowledge which is the cause of the bondage. The intuition in itself is real, but the associations of the intuitive characters with the self are erroneous. When the self knows its own nature as different from the *vṛttis* and as a part of Brahman in which it has an undifferentiated reality, we have what is called emancipation. The existence of the self as undifferentiated with Brahman simply means that the Brahman is the ground-cause, and as such an unchangeable ground-cause Brahman is of the nature of pure consciousness. It is in its nature as pure consciousness that the whole world may be regarded as existing in the Brahman of which the *prakṛti* and the *puruṣa*, the one changing by real modifications and the other through the false ascription of the events of *prakṛti* to itself, may be regarded as emergents. The world is ultimately of the nature of pure consciousness, but matter and its changes, and the experience itself are only material and temporary forms bubbling out of it. But since these emergent forms are real emanations from Brahman an over-emphasis on monism would be wrong. The reality consists of both the ground-cause and the emergent forms. Śaṅkara had asserted that the duality was true only so long as the one reality was not reached. But Bhikṣu objecting to it says that since the monistic truth can be attained only by assuming the validity of the processes that imply duality, ultimate invalidation of the dualistic processes will also nullify the monistic conclusion.

CHAPTER XXIII

PHILOSOPHICAL SPECULATIONS OF SOME OF THE SELECTED PURĀṆAS

THE readers who have followed the philosophy of the Vedānta as interpreted by Vijñāna Bhikṣu in his commentary on the *Brahma-sūtra* and the *Īśvara-gītā* section of the *Kūrma Purāṇa* must have noticed that, according to him, the Vedānta was associated with the Sāṃkhya and Yoga, and in support of his view he referred to many of the Purāṇas, some of which are much earlier than Śaṅkara. Vijñāna Bhikṣu, therefore, quotes profusely from the Purāṇas and in the writings of Rāmānuja, Madhva, Vallabha, Jīva Goswamī and Baladeva we find profuse references to the Purāṇas in support of their views of the philosophy of the Vedānta.

It is highly probable that at least one important school of ideas regarding the philosophy of the Upaniṣads and the *Brahma-sūtra* was preserved in the Purāṇic tradition. Śaṅkara's interpretation of the Upaniṣads and the *Brahma-sūtra* seems to have diverged very greatly from the semi-realistic interpretation of them as found in the Purāṇas. It was, probably, for this reason that Śaṅkara seldom refers to the Purāṇas; but since Śaṅkara's line of interpretation is practically absent in the earlier Purāṇas, and since the extreme monism of some passages of the Upaniṣads is modified and softened by other considerations, it may be believed that the views of the Vedānta, as found in the Purāṇas and the *Bhagavad-gītā*, present, at least in a general manner, the oldest outlook of the philosophy of the Upaniṣads and the *Brahma-sūtra*.

It seems, therefore, desirable that the treatment of the philosophy of Rāmānuja and Vijñāna Bhikṣu should be supplemented by a short survey of the philosophy as found in some of the principal Purāṇas. All the Purāṇas are required to have a special section devoted to the treatment of creation and dissolution, and it is in this section that the philosophical speculations are largely found[1]. In the present section I shall make an effort to trace the philosophical speculations as contained in the *sarga-pratisarga* portions

[1] *sargaś ca pratisargaś ca vaṃśo manv-antarāṇi ca | vaṃśā-nucaritaṅ cai'va purāṇaṃ pañca-lakṣaṇaṃ.* || *Kūrma Purāṇa*, I. 12.

of some of the selected Purāṇas so as to enable readers to compare this Purāṇic philosophy with the philosophy of Bhāskara Rāmānuja, Vijñāna Bhikṣu, and Nimbārka.

The first manifestation of Brahman according to the *Viṣṇu Purāṇa* is *puruṣa*; then come the other manifestations as *vyaktā-vyakta* and *kāla*. The original cause of *pradhāna*, *puruṣa*, *vyakta* and *kāla* is regarded as the ultimate state of Viṣṇu. Here then we find Brahma-Viṣṇu[1].

In *Viṣṇu Purāṇa*, I. 2. 11, it is said that the Ultimate Reality is only pure existence, which can be described only as a position of an eternal existence. It exists everywhere, and it is all (this is Pantheism), and everything is in it (this is Panentheism) and therefore it is called Vāsudeva[2]. It is pure because there is no extraneous entity to be thrown away[3]. It exists in four forms: *vyakta*, *avyakta*, *puruṣa* and *kāla*. Out of His playful activity these four forms have come out[4]. *Prakṛti* is described here as *sadasad-ātmaka*[5] and as *triguṇa*[6]. In the beginning there are these four categories: Brahman, *pradhāna*, *puruṣa* and *kāla*[7], all these being different from the unconditional (*Trikālika*) Viṣṇu. The function of *kāla* is to hold together the *puruṣa* and the *pradhāna* during the creational period, and to hold them apart at the time of dissolution. As such it (*kāla*) is the cause of sensibles. Thus there is a reference to the ontological synthetic activity and the ontological analytical activity of *kāla*[8]. ("Ontological" in the sense that *kāla* appears here not as instrumental of the epistemological aspect of experience, but as something "being" or "existing," i.e. ontological.) As all manifested things had returned to the *prakṛti* at the time of the last dissolution, the *prakṛti* is called *pratisañcara*[9]. *Kāla* or time is beginningless

[1] Brahman is also regarded as *sraṣṭā*, Hari as *pātā* (Protector), and Maheśvara as *saṃhartā*.

āpo nārā iti proktā, āpo vai nara-sūnavaḥ
ayanaṃ tasya tāḥ pūrvaṃ tena nārāyaṇah smṛtaḥ. Manu. I. 10.

[2] *sarvatrā'sau samastaṃ ca vasaty atre'ti vai yataḥ.*
tataḥ sa vāsudeve'ti vidvadbhiḥ paripaṭhyate. Viṣṇu Purāṇa, I. 2. 12.

[3] *Heyā-bhāvāc-ca nirmalam. Ibid.* I. 2. 13.

[4] *vyaktaṃ viṣṇus tathā'vyaktaṃ puruṣaḥ kāla eva ca* I. *krīḍato bālakasye'va ceṣṭāṃ tasya niśāmaya. Ibid.* I. 2. 18.

[5] *Ibid.* I. 2. 19.

[6] *Ibid.* I. 2. 21.

[7] *Viṣṇu Purāṇa*, I. 2. 23.

[8] *Viṣṇoḥ svarūpāt parato hi tenye rūpe pradhānaṃ puruṣaśca vipra*
tasyai'va tenyena dhṛte viyukte rūpā-di yat tad dvija kāla-saṃjñām.
Ibid. I. 2. 24.

[9] *Ibid.* I. 2. 25.

and so exists even at the time of dissolution, synthesizing *prakṛti* or *puruṣa* together and also holding them out as different at the time of creation. At that time God enters by His will into *prakṛti* and *puruṣa* and produces a disturbance leading to creation[1]. When God enters into *prakṛti* and *puruṣa* His proximity alone is sufficient to produce the disturbance leading to creation; just as an odorous substance produces sensation of odour by its proximity without actually modifying the mind[2]. He (God) is both the disturber (*kṣobha*) or disturbed (*kṣobhya*), and that is why, through contradiction and dilation, creation is produced[3]. Here is once again the Pantheistic view of God, its first occurrence being manifested ultimately in four main categories, all of which are, so to speak, participating in the nature of God, all of which are His first manifestations, and also in which it is said that all is God, and so on. *Aṇu* means *jīvā-tman*[4]. Viṣṇu or *Īśvara* exists as the *vikāra*, i.e. the manifested forms, the *puruṣa* and also as Brahman[4]. This is clear Pantheism.

The commentator says that the word "*kṣetrajña*" in "*kṣetrajñā-dhiṣṭhānāt*" means *puruṣa*. But apparently neither the context nor the classical Sāṃkhya justifies it. The context distinctly shows that *kṣetrajña* means *Īśvara*; and the manner of his *adhiṣṭh-ātṛtva* by entering into *prakṛti* and by proximity has already been described[5]. From the *pradhāna* the *mahat-tattva* emerges and it is then covered by the *pradhāna*, and being so covered it differentiates itself as the *sāttvika*, *rājasa* and *tāmasa mahat*. The *pradhāna* covers the *mahat* just as a seed is covered by the skin[6]. Being so covered there spring from the threefold *mahat* the threefold *ahaṃkāra* called *vaikārika*, *taijasa* and *bhūtā-di* or *tāmasa*. From this *bhūtā-di* or *tāmasa ahaṃkāra* which is covered by the *mahat* (as the *mahat* itself was covered by *pradhāna*) there springs through its spontaneous self-modification the *śabda-tanmātra*, and by the same process there springs from that *śabda-tanmātra* the *ākāśa*—the gross element. Again, the *bhūtā-di* covers up the *śabda-tanmātra* and the *ākāśa* differentiated from it as the gross element. The *ākāśa*, being thus conditioned, produces spontaneously by self-modification the

[1] *Viṣṇu Purāṇa*, I. 2. 29. [2] *Ibid.* I. 2. 30.
[3] *Ibid.* I. 2. 31. [4] *Ibid.* I. 2. 32.
[5] *guṇa-sāmyāt tatas tasmāt kṣetrajñā-dhiṣṭhitan muṅe*
guṇa-vyañjana-saṃbhūtiḥ sarga-kāle dvijo-ttama. Ibid. I. 2. 33.
[6] *pradhāna-tattvena samaṃ tvacā bījam ivā'vrtam. Ibid.* I. 2. 34.

sparśa-tanmātra, which produces immediately and directly the gross *vāyu*. The *bhūtādi* again covers up the *ākāśa*, *śabda-tanmātra*, *sparśa-tanmātra* and the differentiated *vāyu* which later then produces the *rūpa-tanmātra* which immediately produces the gross light-heat (*jyoti*)[1]. The *sparśa-tanmātra* and the *vāyu* cover up the *rūpa-tanmātra*. Being thus conditioned, the differentiated gross *jyoti* produces the *rasa-tanmātra* from which again the gross water is produced. In a similar manner the *rasa-tanmātra* and the *rūpa-tanmātra*, being covered up, the differentiated gross water produces the *gandha-tanmātra*, from which again the gross earth is produced. The *tanmātras* are the potential conditions of qualities and hence the qualities are not manifested there. They are, therefore, traditionally called *aviśeṣa*. They do not manifest the threefold qualities of the *guṇas* as *śānta*, *ghora* and *mūḍha*. It is for this reason also that they are called *aviśeṣa*[2].

From the *taijasa-ahaṃkāra* the five conative and cognitive senses are produced. From the *vaikārika-ahaṃkāra* is produced the *manas*[3]. These elements acting together in harmony and unity, together with the *tanmātras*, *ahaṃkāra* and *mahat*, form the unity of the universe under the supreme control of God. As the universe grows up, they form into an egg which gradually expands from within like a water-bubble; and this is called the materialistic body of Viṣṇu as Brahman. This universe is encircled on the outer side by water, fire, air, the *ākāśa* and the *bhūtā-di* and then by the *mahat* and the *avyakta*, each of which is ten times as large as the earth. There are thus seven coverings. The universe is like a cocoanut fruit with various shell-coverings. In proper time, again by causing a preponderance of *tamas*, God eats up the universe in His form as Rudra, and again creates it in His form as Brahmā. He maintains the world in His form as Viṣṇu. Ultimately, however, as God holds the universe within Him, He is both the creator and the created, the protector and the destroyer.

Though the Brahman is qualityless, unknowable and pure, yet

[1] The commentator notes that when the *ākāśa* is said to produce *sparśa-tanmātra*, it is not the *ākāśa* that does so but the *bhūtā-di* manifesting itself as *ākāśa*, i.e. it is through some accretion from *bhūtā-di* that the *ākāśa* can produce the *sparśa-tanmātra*. *Ākāśaḥ ākāśamayo bhūtā-diḥ sparśa-tanmātraṃ sasarja.*

[2] See the commentary to *śloka*. *Viṣṇu Purāṇa*, I. 2. 44.

[3] The commentator notes that the word *manas* here means *antaḥkaraṇa*, including its four functions as *manas*, *buddhi*, *citta* and *ahaṃkāra*.

it can behave as a creative agent by virtue of its specific powers which are incomprehensible to us. As a matter of fact the relation between the powers or energies and the substance is unthinkable. We can never explain how or why fire is hot[1]. The earth, in adoring Hari, described Him as follows: "Whatever is perceived as having visible and tangible forms in this world is but your manifestation. The ordinary people only make a mistake in thinking this to be a naturalistic universe. The whole world is of the nature of knowledge, and the error of errors is to regard it as an object. Those who are wise know that this world is of the nature of thought and a manifestation of God, who is pure knowledge. Error consists in regarding the world as a mere naturalistic object and not as a manifestation of the structure of knowledge."[2]

In the *Viṣṇu Purāṇa*, I. 4. 50–52, it is said that God is only the dynamic agent (*nimitta-mātram*), the material cause being the energies of the objects of the universe which are to be created. These energies require only a dynamic agent to actualize them in the form of the universe. God is here represented to be only a formative agent, whereas the actual material cause of the world is to be found in the energies which constitute the objects of the world, through the influence and presence of God. The commentator notes that the formative agency of God consists merely in his presence (*sānnidhya-mātreinai'va*)[3].

In the *Viṣṇu Purāṇa*, I. 4, we find another account of creation. It is said that God in the beginning thought of creation, and an unintelligent creation appeared in the form of *tamas*, *moha*, *mahā-moha*, *tāmisra* and *andha-tāmisra*. These were the five kinds of *avidyā* which sprang from the Lord. From these there came a creation of the five kinds of plants as *vṛksa*, *gulma*, *latā*, *virūt* and

[1] *Viṣṇu Purāṇa*, I. 3. 1–2.

[2] *yad etad dṛśyate mūrtam, etad jñānā-tmanas tava.*
bhrānti-jñānena paśyanti jagad-rūpam ayoginaḥ. *Ibid.* I. 4. 39.
jñāna-svarūpam akhilaṃ jagad etad abuddhayaḥ
artha-svarūpaṃ paśyanto bhrāmyante moha-saṃplave.
Ibid. I. 4. 40.

[3] *nimitta-mātram evā'sīt sṛjyānāṃ sarga-karmaṇi*
pradhāna-kāraṇī-bhūtā yato vai sṛjya-śaktayaḥ. *Ibid.* I. 4. 51.
nimitta-mātraṃ muktvai'kaṃ nā'nyat kiñcid avekṣyate
nīyate tapatāṃ śreṣṭha sva-śaktyā vastu vastutām. *Ibid.* I. 4. 52.
sisṛkṣuḥ śakti-yukto'sau sṛjya-śakti-pracoditaḥ. *Ibid.* I. 5. 65.

In this passage it is hinted that the will of God and His power to create is helped by the energies of the objects to be created.

tṛṇa (to which are to be added the mountains and the hills) which have no inner or outer consciousness and may be described as having, as it were, closed souls (*saṃvṛtā-tman*). Not being satisfied with this He created the animals and birds, etc., called *tiryak-srota*. The animals, etc., are called *tiryag*, because their circulation is not upwards but runs circularly in all directions. They are full of *tamas*, and are described as *avedinaḥ*. The commentator notes that what is meant by the term *avedin* is that the animals have only appetitive knowledge, but no synthetic knowledge, i.e. cannot synthesise the experience of the past, the present and the future and cannot express what they know, and they have no knowledge about their destinies in this world and in the other, and are devoid of all moral and religious sense. They have no discrimination regarding cleanliness and eating; they are satisfied with their ignorance as true knowledge, i.e. they do not seek the acquirement of certain knowledge. They are associated with the twenty-eight kinds of *vādha*[1]. They are aware internally of pleasure and pain but they cannot communicate with one another[2]. Then, being dissatisfied with the animal creation, God created "the gods" who are always happy and can know both their inner feelings and ideas, and also the external objects, and communicate with one another. Being dissatisfied with that creation also He created "men," which creation is called *arvāk-srotas* as distinguished from the creation of gods which is called *ūrddhva-srotas*. These men have an abundance of *tamas* and *rajas*, and they have therefore a preponderance of

[1] In the *Sāṃkhya-kārikā*, 49, we hear of twenty-eight *vādhās*. The reference to *vādhās* here is clearly a reference to the technical *vādhās* of the Sāṃkhya philosophy, where it also seems certain that at the time of *Viṣṇu Purāṇa* the technical name of the Sāṃkhya *vādhās* must have been a very familiar thing. It also shows that the *Viṣṇu Purāṇa* was closely associated with the Sāṃkhya circles of thought, so that the mere allusion to the term *vādhā* was sufficient to refer to the Sāṃkhya *vādhās*. The *Viṣṇu Purāṇa* was probably a work of the third century A.D.; and the *Kārikā* of Īśvara Kṛṣṇa was composed more or less at the same time. In the *Mārkaṇḍeya Purāṇa* (Veṅkateśvara edition, ch. 44, v. 20) we have the reading *Aṣṭāviṃśad-vidhātmikā*. In the B. I. edition of *Mārkaṇḍeya* by K. M. Banerji we have also in ch. 47, v. 20, the same reading. The reading *vādhānvitā* occurs neither in the *Mārkaṇḍeya* nor in the *Padma Purāṇa* 13, 65. The supposition, therefore, is that the twenty-eight kinds in *Mārkaṇḍeya* were changed into twenty-eight kinds of *vādhā* through the Sāṃkhya influence in the third century. The *Mārkaṇḍeya* is supposed to have been written in the first half of the second century B.C. It is not easy to guess what twenty-eight kinds of animal creation were intended by Mārkaṇḍeya. But the identification of them with the twenty-eight kinds of Sāṃkhya *vādhā* seems to be quite inappropriate.

[2] *antaḥ prakāśās te sarva āvṛtās tu paras-paraṁ. Viṣṇu Purāṇa*, I. 5. 10.

suffering. There are thus nine creations. The first three, called the unintelligent creation (*avuddhi-pūrvaka*), is the naturalistic creation of (i) *mahat*, (ii) the *tanmātras*, and (iii) the *bhūtas*, the physiological senses. The fourth creation, called also the primary creation (*mūkhya-varga*), is the creation of plants; fifth is the creation of the *tiryag-srotas*; sixth the *ūrdha-srotas*; seventh the *arvāk-srotas* or men. The eighth creation seems to be the creation of a new kind. It probably means the distinctive characteristic of destiny of each of the four creations, plants, animals, gods and men. The plants have, for their destiny, ignorance; the animals have mere bodily energy; the gods have pure contentment; and the men have the realization of ends. This is called the *anugraha-sarga*[1]. Then comes the ninth *sarga*, called the *kaumāra-sarga*, which probably refers to the creation of the mental children of God such as *Sanatkumāra*, etc.

There are four kinds of *pralayas*: they are called the *naimittika* or *brāhma*, the *prākṛtika*, the *ātyantika* and the *nitya*. The *naimittika-pralaya* takes place when Brahmā sleeps; the *prākṛtika* occurs when the universe merges in *prakṛti*; the *ātyantika-pralaya* is the result of the knowledge of God, i.e. to say, when Yogins lose themselves in *paramā-tman*, then occurs the *ātyantika-pralaya*; and the fourth, viz. the *nitya-pralaya*, is the continual destruction that takes place daily.

In the *Vāyu Purāṇa* we hear of an ultimate principle which is associated with the first causal movement of God. This is regarded as the transcendental cause (*kāraṇam aprameyam*) and is said to be known by various names, such as Brahman, *pradhāna*, *prakṛti*, *prasūti* (*prakṛti-prasūti*), *ātman*, *guha*, *yoni*, *cakṣus*, *kṣetra*, *amṛta*,

[1] The *Vāyu Purāṇa*, VI. 68, describes it as follows:

sthāvareṣu viparyāsas tiryag-yoniṣu śaktitā
siddhā-tmāno manuṣyās tu tuṣṭir deveṣu kṛtsnaśaḥ.

The sixth *sarga* is there described as being of the ghosts.

bhūtā-dikānāṃ sattvānāṃ ṣaṣṭhaḥ sargaḥ sa ucyate.
Ibid. VI. 58–59.

te parigrahiṇaḥ sarve saṃvibhāga-ratāḥ punaḥ.
khādanāś cā'py aśīlāś ca jñeyā bhūtā-dikāś ca te. *Ibid.* VI. 30.

In the *Mārkaṇḍeya Purāṇa*, *anugraha-sarga* is described as the fifth *sarga*.

In the *Kūrma Purāṇa*, 7. 11, these *bhūtas* are regarded as being the fifth *sarga*. The *Kūrma Purāṇa* describes the first creation as the *mahat-sarga*, the second as *bhūta-sarga*, the third as *Vaikārike'-ndriya-sarga*, the fourth as the *mukhya-sarga*, and the fifth as *tiryak-sarga*. There is thus a contradiction, as the fifth *sarga* was described in the eleventh verse in the same chapter as the creation of ghosts. This implies the fact that probably two hands were at work at different times, at least in the seventh chapter of the *Kūrma Purāṇa*.

akṣara, *śukra*, *tapas*, *satyam*, *atiprakāśa*. It is said to cover round the second *puruṣa*. This second *puruṣa* is probably the *loka-pitāmaha*. Through the association of time and preponderance of *rajas* eight different stages of modification are produced which are associated with *kṣetrajña*[1]. In this connection the *Vāyu Purāṇa* speaks also of the *prākṛtika*, the *naimittika* and the *ātyantika-pralaya*[2]. It also says that the categories of evolution have been discovered both by the guidance of the *śāstras* and by rational argument[3], and that *prakṛti* is devoid of all sensible qualities. She is associated with three *guṇas*, and is timeless and unknowable in herself. In the original state, in the equilibrium of *guṇas*, everything was pervaded by her as *tamas*. At the time of creation, being associated with *kṣetrajña*, *mahat* emerges from her. This *mahat* is due to a preponderance of *sattva* and manifests only pure existence. This *mahat* is called by various names, such as *manas*, *mahat*, *mati*, *brahmā*, *pur*, *buddhi*, *khyāti*, *Īśvara*, *citi*, *prajñā*, *smṛti*, *saṃvit*, *vipura*[4]. This *mahat-prajñā*, being stirred by desire to create, begins the work of creation and produces *dharma*, *adharma* and other entities[5]. Since the cause of the gross efforts of all beings exists always as conceived in a subtle state in the *mahat*, it is called "*manas*." It is the first of all categories, and of infinite extent and is thus called *mahān*. Since it holds within itself all that is finite and measurable and since it conceives all differentiations from out of itself and appears as intelligent *puruṣa*, by its association with experience it is called *mati*. It is called *brahman* since it causes all growth. Further, as all the later categories derive their material from it, it is called *pur*. Since the *puruṣa* understands all things as beneficial and desirable and since it is also the stuff through which all understanding is possible, it is called *buddhi*. All experience and integration of experience and all suffering and enjoyment depending upon knowledge proceed from it; therefore it is called *khyāti*. Since it directly knows everything as the great Soul it is called *Īśvara*. Since all sense-perceptions are produced from it, it is called *prajñā*. Since all states of knowledge and all kinds of

[1] *Vāyu Purāṇa*, 3. 11, and compare the *Pañcarātra* doctrine as elaborated in *Ahirbudhnya*.

[2] *Vāyu Purāṇa*, 3. 23.

[3] *tac-chāstra-yuktyā sva-mati-prayatnāt*
samastam āviṣkṛta-dhī-dhṛtibhyaḥ. *Ibid.* 3. 24.

It speaks of five *pramāṇas*. *Ibid.* 4. 16.

[4] *Ibid.* 4. 25.

[5] *Ibid.* 4. 24.

karman and their fruits are collected in it for determining experience, it is called *citi*. Since it remembers the past, it is called *smṛti*. Since it is the storehouse of all knowledge, it is called *mahā-tman*. Since it is the knowledge of all knowledge, and since it exists everywhere and everything exists in it, it is *saṃvit*. Since it is of the nature of knowledge, it is called *jñāna*. Since it is the cause of all desideratum of conflicting entities, it is called *vipura*. Since it is the Lord of all beings in the world, it is called *Īśvara*. Since it is the knower in both the *kṣetra* and the *kṣetrajña*, and is one, it is called *ka*. Since it stays in the subtle body (*puryāṃ śete*) it is called *puruṣa*. It is called *svayambhu*, because it is uncaused and the beginning of creation. *Mahān* being stirred up by the creative desire manifests itself in creation through two of its movements, conception (*saṃkalpa*) and determination (*adhyavasāya*). It consists of three *guṇas*, *sattva*, *rajas*, and *tamas*. With the preponderance of *rajas*, *ahaṃkāra* emerged from *mahat*. With the preponderance of *tamas* there also emerges from *mahat*, *bhūtā-di*, from which the *bhūtas* and *tanmātras* are produced. From this comes the *ākāśa* as vacuity which is associated with sound. From the modification of the *bhūtā-di* the sound-potential (*śabda-tanmātra*) has been produced. When the *bhūtādi* covers up the sound-potential, then the touch-potential was produced. When the *ākāśa* covers up the sound-potential and the touch-potential, the *vāyu* is produced. Similarly the other *bhūtas* and qualities are produced. The *tanmātras* are also called *aviśeṣas*. From the *vaikārika* or *sāttvika-ahaṃkāra* are produced the five cognitive and the five conative senses and the *manas*[1].

These *guṇas* work in mutual co-operation, and thereby produce the cosmic egg like a water-bubble. From this cosmic egg, the *kṣetrajña* called *Brahmā*—also called *Hiranyagarbha* (the four-faced God)—is produced. This god loses His body at the time of each *pralaya* and gains a new body at the time of a new creation[2]. The cosmic egg is covered by water, light, heat, air, *ākāśa*, *bhūtādi*, *mahat*, and *avyakta*. The eight *prakṛtis* are also spoken of, and probably the cosmic egg is the eighth cover[3].

[1] This is different from other accounts. No function is ascribed to the *rājasa ahaṃkāra*, from which the conative senses are generally derived.

[2] *Vāyu Purāṇa*, 4. 68.

[3] The passage is obscure, as it is difficult to find out exactly what these eight *prakṛtis* are. *Ibid*. 4. 77–78.

In Chapter VIII it is said that *rajas* remains as the dynamic principle inherent in *sattva* and *tamas*, just as oil remains in seas *amum*. It is further said that Maheśvara entered the *pradhāna* and *puruṣa*, and with the help of the dynamic principle of *rajas* produced a disturbance in the equilibrium of the *prakṛti*[1]. By the disturbance of the *guṇas* three gods are produced, from *rajas* Brahmā, from *tamas* Agni, and from *sattva* Viṣṇu. The Agni is also identified with *kāla* or Time.

The *Vāyu Purāṇa* also describes the nature of *māheśvara-yoga*[2]. This is said to be constituted of five elements or *dharmas*, such as *prāṇāyāma*, *dhyāna*, *pratyāhāra*, *dhāraṇā*, and *smaraṇa*. *Prāṇāyāma* is of three kinds, *manda*, *madhyama*, and *uttama*. *Manda* is of twelve *mātrās*, *madhyama* of twenty-four, and *uttama* of thirty-six. When the *vāyu* is once controlled by gradual practice, then all sins are burnt and all bodily imperfections are removed. By *dhyāna* one should contemplate the qualities of God. Then *prāṇāyāma* is said to bring about four kinds of results: (i) *śānti*, (ii) *praśānti*, (iii) *dīpti*, and (iv) *prasāda*. *Śānti* means the washing away of sins derived from impurities from parents and from the association of one's relations. *Praśānti* means the destruction of personal sins, as greed, egotism, etc. *Dīpti* means the rise of a mystical vision by which one can see past, present and future and come in contact with the wise sages of the past and become like Buddha. *Prasāda* means the contentment and pacification of the senses, sense-objects, mind, and the five *vāyus*.

The process of *prāṇāyāma* beginning with *āsana* is also described. *Pratyāhāra* is regarded as the control of one's desires and *dharma* is regarded as the fixing of the mind on the tip of the nose, or the middle of the eyebrows, or at a point slightly higher than that. Through *pratyāhāra* the influence of external objects is negated. By *dhyāna* one perceives oneself like the sun or the moon, i.e. there is an unobstructed illumination. The various miraculous powers that the *yogī* attains are called the *upasargas* and it is urged that one should always try to keep oneself free from the callings of these miraculous powers. The various objects of *dhyāna*

[1] It has been noted before that the creation of the material world proceeded from the *tāmasa ahaṃkāra*, and that of the cognitive and conative senses from the *sāttvika ahaṃkāra*. The *rājasa ahaṃkāra* was not regarded as producing anything, but merely as a moment leading to disturbance of equilibrium. See also *Vāyu Purāṇa*, 5. 9.

[2] *Ibid.* chap. 11–15.

are regarded as being the elements originating from the earth, *manas* and *buddhi*. The Yogin has to take these objects one by one, and then to leave them off, so that he may not be attached to any one of them. When he does so and becomes unattached to any one of these seven and concentrates on Maheśvara associated with omniscience, contentment, beginningless knowledge, absolute freedom (*svātantrya*), unobstructed power, and infinite power, he attains Brahman. So the ultimate object of Yoga realization is[1] the attainment of Brahmahood as Maheśvara which is also called *apavarga*[2].

In the *Mārkaṇḍeya Purāṇa*, *yoga* is described as a cessation of *ajñāna* through knowledge, which is, on the one hand, emancipation and unity with Brahman, and, on the other, dissociation from the *guṇas* of *prakṛti*[3]. All sorrows are due to attachment. With the cessation of attachment there is also the cessation of the feeling of identifying all things with oneself (*mamatva*); and this leads to happiness. True knowledge is that which leads to emancipation, all else is *ajñāna*. By experiencing the fruits of virtues and vices through the performance of duties and other actions, through the accumulation of fruits of past *karman* (*apūrva*), and through the exhaustion of certain others, there is the bondage of *karma*. The emancipation from *karma*, therefore, can only result from an opposite procedure. The *prāṇāyāma* is supposed to destroy sins[4]. In the ultimate stage the *yogī* becomes one with Brahman, just as water thrown in water becomes one with it[5]. There is no reference here to *chitta-vṛtti-nirodha* as *yoga*.

Vāsudeva is described here as the ultimate Brahman, who by His creative desire has created everything through the power of time. Through this power He separated the two entities of *pra-*

[1] There is no reference in the chapters on *yoga* of the *Vāyu Purāṇa* to *vṛtti-nirodha* and *kaivalya*.

[2] There is a chapter both in the *Vāyu Purāṇa* and in the *Mārkaṇḍeya Purāṇa* on *ariṣṭa*, similar to what is found in the *Jayākhya-saṃhitā* where signs are described by which the *yogin* is to know the time of his death, though the description of his death is entirely different from that given in the other two works.

[3] *jñāna-pūrvo viyogo yo'jñānena saha yoginaḥ | sā muktir brahmaṇā cai'kyam anaikyaṃ prākṛtair guṇaiḥ. ||* *Mārkaṇḍeya Purāṇa*, 39. 1.

[4] The method of *prāṇāyama* and other processes of *yoga* is more or less the same as that found in the *Vāyu Purāṇa*.

[5] *Mārkaṇḍeya Purāṇa*, 40. 41.

The *Mārkaṇḍeya Purāṇa*, in this connection, says that the yogin should know the approach of his death by the signs described in ch. 40, so that he may anticipate it and may not get dispirited.

dhāna and *puruṣa* from within Himself and connected them both. The first entity that emerged from *prakṛti* in this creative process was *mahat*, from which emerged *ahaṃkāra*, and from which again emerged *sattva*, *rajas* and *tamas*. From *tamas* came the five *tanmātras* and the five *bhūtas*; from *rajas* came the ten senses and the *buddhi*. From *sattva* came the presiding gods of the senses and the *manas*[1]. It is further said that Vāsudeva exists in the *prakṛti* and the *puruṣas* and all the effects, both as pervading through them and also separate from them, that is, He is both immanent and transcendent. Even when He exists as pervading through them, He is not in any way touched by.their limitations and impurities. True knowledge is that which takes account of the nature of all those which have emanated from Vāsudeva in their specific forms as *prakṛti*, *puruṣa*, etc., and also of Vāsudeva in His pure and transcendent form[2].

It should be noted that in the *Padma Purāṇa* there is a mention of *brahma-bhakti*, which is either *kāyika*, *vācika* and *mānasika* or *laukikī*, *vaidikī* and *ādhyātmikī*. This *ādhyātmikī-bhakti* is further subdivided into the *sāṃkhya-bhakti* and *yoga-bhakti*[3]. The knowledge of twenty-four principles and of their distinction from the ultimate principle called *puruṣa*, as also of the relation among *puruṣa* and *prakṛti* and the individual soul, is known as *sāṃkhya-bhakti*[4]. Practice of *prāṇayāma* and meditation upon the Lord Brahma constitute the *yoga-bhakti*[5]. The term *bhakti* is here used in a very special sense.

In *Nāradīya Purāṇa* Nārāyaṇa is said to be the Ultimate Reality, that is, if seen in theological perspective it may be said to create from itself Brahmā the creator, Viṣṇu the protector and preserver, and Rudra the destroyer[6]. This Ultimate Reality has also been called *Mahā-viṣṇu*[7]. It is through his characteristic power that the universe is created. This *śakti* or power is said to be both of the type of existence and non-existence, both *vidyā* and *avidyā*[8]. When the universe is seen as dissociated from *Mahā-viṣṇu*, the vision is clearly due to *avidyā* ingrained in us; when, on the other hand, the consciousness of the distinction between the knower and the known disappears and only the consciousness of

1 *Skanda Purāṇa*, II. 9. 24, verses 1–10.
2 *Ibid.* verses 65–74.
3 *Padma Purāṇa*, I. 15, verses 164–177.
4 *Ibid.* verses 177–186.
5 *Ibid.* verses 187–190.
6 *Nāradīya Purāṇa*, I. 3. 4.
7 *Ibid.* verse 9.
8 *Ibid.* verse 7.

unity pervades, it is due to *vidyā* (it is *vidyā* itself)[1]. And just as Hari permeates or pervades through the universe, so also does His *śakti*[2]. Just as the quality of heat exists by pervading, i.e. as in and through Agni its support, even so the *śakti* of Hari can never be dissociated from Him[3]. This *śakti* exists in the form of *vyaktāvyakta*, pervading the whole universe. *prakṛti*, *puruṣa* and *kāla* are her first manifestations[4]. As this *śakti* is not separate from *Mahāviṣṇu*, it is said that at the time of first or original creation *Mahāviṣṇu*, being desirous of creating the universe, becomes, i.e. takes the forms of *prakṛti*, *puruṣa* and *kāla*. From *prakṛti*, disturbed by the presence of the *puruṣa*, comes out *mahat*, and from *mahat* comes into existence *buddhi*, and from *buddhi*, *ahaṃkāra*[5].

This Ultimate Principle has also been called Vāsudeva, who is said to be the ultimate knowledge and the ultimate goal[6].

Sorrow or misery of three kinds is necessarily experienced by all beings born in the universe—and the only remedy that sets them free from misery is the final obtaining of the Lord (or God)[7]. The ways to find God are two, the way of knowledge (*jñāna*) and that of action (*karma*). This *jñāna* springs up either from the learning of scriptural texts or from *viveka* (discriminative knowledge)[8].

1 *Nāradīya Purāṇa*, I. 3, verses 7–9.

2 *Ibid.* verse 12.

It should be distinctly noted here that the creation of the universe has been attributed to Hari through the *upādhi avidyā*, which is His own *śakti*. The whole account sounds the note of the Vedānta philosophy. The following line should be particularly noted:

avidyo-pādhi-yogena tathe'dam akhilaṃ jagat. *Ibid.* 3. 12.

And this line should be read with the previous verse—

viṣṇu-śakti-samudbhūtam etat sarvaṃ carā-caraṃ
yasmād bhinnam idam sarvaṃ yacce'gaṃ yacca teṅgati
upādhibhir yathā'kāśo bhinnatvena pratīyate.
Ibid. verses 10–11.

3 *Ibid.* verse 13.

4 *Ibid.* verse 17.

5 *Ibid.* verses 28, 31.

6 *Ibid.* verse 80.

7 For the concept of *antaryāmin* see verse 26 of *Adhyāya* 3 and also verse 48 of *Adhyāya* 33.

8 *Nāradīya Purāṇa*, verses 4, 5.

utpattiṃ pralayaṃ cai'va bhūtānām agatiṃ gatiṃ
vetti vidyām avidyāṃ ca sa vācyo bhagavān iti
jñāna-śakti-balai-śvarya-vīrya-tejāṃsy aśeṣataḥ
bhagavac-śabda-vācyo'yaṃ vinā heyair guṇā-dibhiḥ
sarvaṃ hi tatra bhūtāni vasanti paramā-tmani
bhuteṣu vasate sāntar vāsudevas tataḥ smṛtaḥ.
bhūteṣu vasate sāntar vasanty atra ca tāni yat
dhātā vidhātā jagatāṃ vāsudevas tatas smṛtaḥ.
Ibid. I. 46, verses 21–24.

The attributes of Vāsudeva are described in following four verses. It should also be noted that Bhagavān means Vāsudeva. (*Ibid.* verse 19.)

yoga is also defined in the next chapter. It is described as *Brahma-laya*. The *manas* is the cause of bondage and emancipation. Bondage means association with sense-objects, and emancipation means dissociation from them. When, like a magnet, the self draws the mind inside and directs its activities in an inward direction and ultimately unites with Brahman, that is called *yoga*[1].

Viṣṇu is described as having three kinds of *śakti* (power): *parā* or ultimate, the *aparā* (which is identical with individual efforts), and a third power which is called *vidyā* and *karma*[2]. All energies belong to Viṣṇu, and it is through His energies that all living beings are moved into activity[3].

The word *bhakti* has also been used in another chapter in the sense of *śraddhā*, and is held to be essential for all the various actions of life[4].

According to the *Kūrma Purāṇa* it seems that God exists firstly as the unmanifested, infinite, unknowable and ultimate director. But He is also called the unmanifested, eternal, cosmic cause which is both being and non-being and is identified with *prakṛti*. In this aspect He is regarded as *para-brahman*, the equilibrium of the three *guṇas*. In this state the *puruṣa* exists within Himself as it were, and this is also called the state of *prākṛta-pralaya*. From this state of unmanifestedness God begins to assert Himself as God and enters into *prakṛti* and *puruṣa* by His own inner intimate contact. This existence of God may be compared with the sex-impulse in man or woman which exists within them and manifests itself only as a creative impulse although remaining one and the same with them all the while. It is for this reason that God is regarded as both passive (*kṣobhya*) and dynamic (*kṣobhaka*). It is therefore said that God behaves as *prakṛti* by self-contraction and dilatation. From the disturbed *prakṛti* and the *puruṣa* sprang up the seed of *mahat*, which is of the nature of both *pradhāna* and *puruṣa* (*pradhāna*

1 *ātma-prayatna-sāpekṣā viśiṣṭā yā mano-gatiḥ*
tasyā brahmaṇi saṃyogo yoga ity abhidhīyate.
Nāradīya Purāṇa, 47. 7.

There is also a description of *prāṇāyāma*, *yama*, and *niyama*, etc., from v. 8 to v. 20.

2 *Ibid.* I. 47, verses 36–38. 3 *Ibid.* verses 47–49. 4 *Ibid.* I, verse 4.

5 *Kūrma Purāṇa* contains the following verse:
maheśvaraḥ paro'vyaktaś catur-vyūhaḥ sanātanaḥ
anantaś cā'prameyaś ca niyantā sarvato-mukhaḥ. (4. 5.)

Two points should be noted here. Firstly, that the Ultimate Reality has been called Maheśvara and not Viṣṇu. Secondly, *catur-vyūha* is one of the adjectives mentioned in this verse to explain the nature of that Ultimate Reality.

puruṣāt-makam). From this came into existence *mahat*, also called *ātman*, *mati*, *brahmā*, *prabuddhi*, *khyāti*, *Īśvara*, *prajñā*, *dhṛti*, *smṛti*, *samvit*. From this *mahat* came out the threefold *ahaṃkāra-vaikārika*, *taijasa* and *bhūtādi* (also called *tāmasa ahaṃkāra*). This *ahaṃkāra* is also called *abhimāna*, *kartā*, *mantā*, and *ātman*, for all our efforts spring from this.

It is said that there is a sort of cosmic mind called *manas* which springs directly from the *avyakta* and is regarded as the first product which superintends the evolution of the *tāmasa ahaṃkāra* into its products[1]. This *manas* is to be distinguished from the *manas* or the sense which is the product of both the *taijasa* and *vaikārika ahaṃkāra*.

Two kinds of views regarding the evolution, the *tanmātras* and the *bhūtas*, are given here in succession, which shows that the *Kūrma Purāṇa* must have been revised; and the second view, which is not compatible with the first, was incorporated at a later stage. These two views are as follows:

(1) *Bhūtādi* has, in its development, created the *śabda-mātra*, from which sprang into existence the *ākāśa*, which has sound as its quality. The *sparśa-mātra* was created from the *ākāśa*, developing itself; and from the *sparśa-tanmātra* came out *vāyu*, which, consequently has *sparśa* as its quality. *Vāyu*, in the state of development, created the *rūpa-mātra* from which came into existence *jyoti* (light-heat), which has colour (*rūpa*) as its quality. From this *jyoti*, in the condition of development, sprang up *rasa-mātra* (taste-potential), which created water, which has taste for its quality. The water, in the state of development, created the smell-potential (*gandha-mātra*), from which came into existence the conglomeration, which has smell as its quality.

(2) *Ākāśa* as the sound-potential covered up the touch-potential, and from this sprang up *vāyu*, which has therefore two qualities—the sound and touch. Both the qualities, *śabda* and *sparśa*, entered the colour-potential, whence sprang up the *vahni* (fire), with three qualities—the *śabda*, the *sparśa*, and the *rūpa*. These qualities, viz. *śabda*, *sparśa* and *rūpa*, entered the taste-potential, whence came into existence water having four qualities

1 *manas tv avyakta-jaṃ pro'ktaṃ vikārah prathamaḥ smṛtaḥ*
yenā'sau jāyate kartā bhūtā-dimś cā'nupaśyati.
Kūrma Purāṇa, 4. 21.

—*śabda*, *sparśa*, *rūpa* and *rasa*. These four qualities entered smell-potential, from which sprang into existence gross *bhūmi* (the earth), which has all the five qualities of *śabda*, *sparśa*, *rūpa*, *rasa*, and *gandha*.

Mahat, *ahaṃkāra* and the five *tanmātras* are in themselves unable to produce the orderly universe, which is effected through the superintendence of the *puruṣa* (*puruṣā-dhiṣṭhitatvāc ca*) and by the help of *avyakta* (*avyaktā-nugraheṇa*). The universe thus created has seven coverings. The production of the universe, and its maintenance and ultimate dissolution, are all effected through the playful activity (*sva-līlayā*) of God for the benefit of his devotees[1].

[1] The God is called Nārāyaṇa, because He is the ultimate support of all human beings:

narāṇām ayanaṃ yasmāt tena nārāyaṇas smṛtaḥ.

Kūrma Purāṇa, IV. 62.

APPENDIX TO VOLUME I

THE *LOKĀYATA*, *NĀSTIKA* AND *CĀRVĀKA*

THE materialistic philosophy known as the *Lokāyata*, the *Cārvāka* or the *Bārhaspatya* is probably a very old school of thought. In the *Śvetāśvatara Upaniṣad* a number of heretical views are referred to and among these we find the doctrine which regarded matter or the elements (*bhūtāni*) as the ultimate principle. The name *Lokāyata* is also fairly old. It is found in Kauṭilya's *Artha-śāstra*, where it is counted with Śaṃkhya and Yoga as a logical science (*ānvīkṣikī*)[1]. Rhys Davids has collected a number of Pāli passages in which the word *Lokāyata* occurs and these have been utilized in the discussion below[2]. Buddhaghoso speaks of *Lokāyata* as a *vitaṇḍā-vāda-satthaṃ*[3]. *Vitaṇḍā* means tricky disputation and it is defined in the *Nyāya-sūtra*, I. 2. 3, as that kind of tricky logical discussion (*jalpa*) which is intended only to criticize the opponent's thesis without establishing any other counter-thesis (*sā pratipakṣa-sthāpanā-hīnā vitaṇḍā*), and it is thus to be distinguished from *vāda* which means a logical discussion undertaken in all fairness for upholding a particular thesis. *Vitaṇḍā*, however, has no thesis to uphold, but is a kind of *jalpa* or tricky argument which seeks to impose a defeat on the opponent by wilfully giving a wrong interpretation of his words and arguments (*chala*), by adopting false and puzzling analogies (*jāti*), and thus to silence or drive him to self-contradiction and undesirable conclusions (*nigraha-sthāna*) by creating an atmosphere of confusion. But *vitaṇḍā* cannot then be a *vāda*, for *vāḍa* is a logical discussion for the ascertainment of truth, and thus the word *vitaṇḍā-vāda* would be self-contradictory. Jayanta, however, points out that the Buddhists did not make any distinction

[1] Kauṭilya, *Artha-śāstra*, I. I.

[2] *Dialogues of the Buddha*, vol. I, p. 166. In recent times two Italian scholars, Dr Piszzagalli and Prof. Tucci, have written two works called *Nāstika, Cārvāka Lokāyatika* and *Linee di una storia del Materialismo Indiano* respectively in which they attempt to discover the meaning of the terms *nāstika, cārvāka* and *lokāyata* and also the doctrines of the sects. Most of the Pāli passages which they consider are those already collected by Rhys Davids.

[3] *Abhidhāna-ppadīpikā*, v. 112, repeats Buddhaghoso's words "*vitaṇḍā-satthaṃ viññeyaṃ yaṃ taṃ lokāyatam.*"

between a pure logical argument and a tricky disputation and used the same word *vāda* to denote both these forms of argument[1]. This explains why *Lokāyata*, though consisting merely of *vitaṇḍā*, could also be designated as *vāda* in Buddhist literature. A few examples of this *vitaṇḍā* are given by Buddhaghoso in the same commentary in explaining the term "*loka-khāyikā*" (lit. "popular story," but "popular philosophy" according to P.T.S. Pāli Dictionary) —the crows are white because their bones are white, the geese are red because their blood is red[2]. Such arguments are there designated as being *vitaṇḍā-sallāpa-kathā*, where *sallāpa* and *kathā* together mean conversational talk, *sallāpa* being derived from *sam* and *lap*. According to the definitions of the *Nyāya-sūtra*, 2. 18, these would not be regarded as instances of *vitaṇḍā* but of *jāti*, i.e. inference from false analogies where there is no proper concomitance, and not *vitaṇḍā* as just explained. Rhys Davids quotes another passage from the *Sadda-nīti* of the *Aggavaṃsa* (early twelfth century) which, in his translation, runs as follows: "*Loka* means 'the common world' (*bāla-loka*). *Lokāyata* means '*āyatanti, ussāhanti vāyamanti vādassadenāti*'; that is, they exert themselves about it, strive about it, through the pleasure they take in discussion. Or perhaps it means 'the world does not make any effort (*yatati*) by it,' that it does not depend on it, move on by it (*na yatati na īhati vā*). For living beings (*sattā*) do not stir up their hearts (*cittaṃ na uppādenti*) by reason of that book (*taṃ hi gandhaṃ nissāya*)[3]." Now the *Lokāyata* is the book of the unbelievers (*titthia-satthaṃ yaṃ loke vitaṇḍā-sattham uccati*), full of such useless disputations as the following: "All is impure; all is not impure; the crow is white, the crane is black; and for this reason or for that"— the book which is known in the world as the *vitaṇḍā-sattha*, of which the Bodhisattva, the incomparable leader, Vidhura the Pundit, said: "Follow not the *Lokāyata*, that works not for the

[1] *ity udāhṛtam idaṃ kathā-trayaṃ yat paraspara-vivikta-lakṣaṇam*
sthūlam apy anavalokya kathyate vāda eka iti śākya-śiṣyakaiḥ.
Nyāya-mañjarī, p. 596.

[2] *Sumaṅgala-vilāsinī*, I. 90, 91.

[3] This translation is inexact. There is no reference to any book in the Pāli passage; in the previous sentence there was a word *vādassādana* which was translated as "through the pleasure they take in discussion," whereas the literal translation would be "by the taste (*assāda*) of the disputation," and here it means "pursuing that smell" people do not turn their minds to virtuous deeds.

progress in merit[1]." Thus, from the above and from many other passages from the Pāli texts it is certain that the *Lokāyata* means a kind of tricky disputation, sophistry or casuistry practised by the non-Buddhists which not only did not lead to any useful results but did not increase true wisdom and led us away from the path of Heaven and of release. The common people were fond of such tricky discourses and there was a systematic science (*śāstra* or *sattha*) dealing with this subject, despised by the Buddhists and called the *vitaṇḍā-sattha*[2]. *Lokāyata* is counted as a science along with other sciences in *Dīghanikāya*, III. I. 3, and also in *Aṅguttara*, I. 163, and in the *Divyāvadāna* it is regarded as a special branch of study which had a *bhāṣya* and a *pravacana* (commentaries and annotations on it)[3].

There seems to be a good deal of uncertainty regarding the meaning of the word *Lokāyata.* It consists of two words, *loka* and *āyata* or *ayata*; *āyata* may be derived as *ā+yaṃ+kta* or from *ā+yat* (to make effort)+*a* either in the accusative sense or in the sense of the verb itself, and *ayata* is formed with the negative particle *a* and *yat* (to make effort). On the passage in the *Aggavaṃsa* which has already been referred to, it is derived firstly as *a+yatanti* (makes great effort) and the synonyms given are *ussāhanti vāyamanti*, and secondly as *a+yatanti*, i.e. by which people cease to make efforts (*tena loko na yatati na īhati vā lokāyatam*). But Prof. Tucci quotes a passage from Buddhaghoso's *Sārattha-pakāsinī* where the word *āyata* is taken in the sense of

[1] See *Dialogues of the Buddha*, I. 168. The translation is inexact. The phrase "All is impure; all is not impure" seems to be absent in the Pāli text. The last passage quoted from *Vidhura-paṇḍita-jātaka* (Fausboll, VI, p. 286) which is one of the most ancient of the *jātakas* runs as follows: "*na seve lokāyatikaṃ na' etam paññāya vaddhanaṃ.*" The unknown commentator describes the *lokāyatika* as "*lokayātikan ti anattha-nissitam sagga-maggānāṃ adāyakaṃ aniyyānikam vitaṇḍa-sallāpam lokāyatika-vādaṃ na seveyya.*" The *Lokāyata* leads to mischievous things and cannot lead to the path of Heaven or that of release and is only a tricky disputation which does not increase true wisdom.

[2] Rhys Davids seems to make a mistake in supposing that the word *Vidaddha* in *Vidaddhavādi* is only the same word as *vitaṇḍā* wrongly spelt (*Dialogues of the Buddha*, I. 167) in the *Aṭthasālinī*, pp. 3, 90, 92, 241. The word *vidaddha* is not *vitaṇḍā* but *vidagdha* which is entirely different from *vitaṇḍā*.

[3] *lokāyataṃ bhāṣya-pravacanam, Divyāvadāna*, p. 630; also *chandasi vā vyākaraṇe vā lokāyate vā pramāṇa-mīmāṃsāyāṃ vā na cai-ṣām ūhā-pohaḥ prajñāyate. Ibid.* p. 633.

It is true, however, that *lokāyata* is not always used in the sense of a technical logical science, but sometimes in its etymological sense (i.e. what is prevalent among the people, *lokeṣu āyato lokā-yataḥ*) as in *Divyāvadāna*, p. 619, where we find the phrase "*lokāyata-yajña-mantreṣu niṣṇātaḥ.*"

āyatana (basis), and *lokāyata* according to this interpretation means "the basis of the foolish and profane world[1]." The other meaning of *lokāyata* would be *lokeṣu āyata*, i.e. that which is prevalent among the common people, and this meaning has been accepted by Cowell in his translation of *Sarva-darśana-saṃgraha* and here the derivation would be from *a+yam+kta* (spreading over)[2]. The *Amara-koṣa* only mentions the word and says that it is to be in the neuter gender as *lokāyatam*. It seems that there are two *lokāyata* words. One as adjective meaning "prevalent in the world or among the common people" and another as a technical word meaning "the science of disputation, sophistry and casuistry" (*vitaṇḍā-vāda-satthaṃ*); but there seems to be no evidence that the word was used to mean "nature-lore," as suggested by Rhys Davids and Franke, or "polity or political science" as suggested by other scholars. The *Śukra-nīti* gives a long enumeration of the science and arts that were studied and in this it counts the *nāstika-śāstra* as that which is very strong in logical arguments and regards all things as proceeding out of their own nature and considers that there are no Vedas and no god[3]. Medhātithi, in commenting upon *Manu*, VII. 43, also refers to the *tarka-vidyā* of the Cārvākas, and all the older references that have been discussed show that there was a technical science of logic and sophistry called the *Lokāyata*. Fortunately we have still further conclusive evidence that the *Lokāyata-śāstra* with its commentary existed as early as the time of Kātyāyana, i.e. about 300 B.C. There is a *Vārtika* rule associated with VII. 3. 45 "*varṇaka-tāntave upasaṃkhyānam*," that the word *varṇaka* becomes *varṇakā* in the feminine to mean a blanket or a wrapper (*prāvaraṇa*), and Patañjali (about 150 B.C.), in interpreting this *vārtika sutra*, says that the object of restricting the formation of the word *varṇaka* only to the sense of a cotton or woollen wrapper is that in other senses the feminine form would

[1] *Linee di una storia del Materialismo Indiano*, p. 17. *Sārattha-pakāsinī* (Bangkok), II. 96.

[2] Rhys Davids describes *lokāyata* as a branch of Brahmanic learning, probably Nature-lore, wise sayings, riddles, rhymes and theories, handed down by tradition, as to the cosmogony, the elements, the stars, the weather, scraps of astronomy, of elementary physics, even of anatomy, and knowledge of the nature of precious stones, and of birds and beasts and plants (*Dialogues of the Buddha*, I. 171). Franke translates it as "logische beweisende Naturerklärung," *Digha*, 19.

[3] *yuktir valīyasī yatra sarvaṃ svābhavikaṃ mataṃ-kasyā'pi ne'śvaraḥ kartā na vedo nāstikaṃ hi tat. Śukra-nīti-sāra*, IV. 3. 55.

be *varṇikā* or *varttikā* (e.g. meaning a commentary) as in the case of the *Bhāguri* commentary on the *Lokāyata*—*varṇikā bhāguri-lokāyatasya, vartikā bhāguri lokāyatasya*[1]. Thus it seems to be quite certain that there was a book called the *Lokāyata* on which there was at least one commentary earlier than 150 B.C. or even earlier than 300 B.C., the probable date of Kātyāyana, the author of the *vārttika-sūtra*. Probably this was the old logical work on disputation and sophistry, for no earlier text is known to us in which the *Lokāyata* is associated with materialistic doctrines as may be found in later literature, where *Cārvāka* and *Lokāyata* are identified[2]. Several *sūtras* are found quoted in the commentaries of Kamalaśīla, Jayanta, Prabhācandra, Guṇaratna, etc. from the seventh to the fourteenth century and these are attributed by some to *Cārvāka* by others to *Lokāyata* and by Guṇaratna (fourteenth century) to Bṛhaspati[3]. Kamalaśīla speaks of two different commentaries on these *sūtras* on two slightly divergent lines which correspond to the division of *dhūrta* Cārvāka and *suśikṣita* Cārvāka in the *Nyāya-mañjarī*. Thus it seems fairly certain that there was at least one commentary on the *Lokāyata* which was probably anterior to Patañjali and Kātyāyana; and by the seventh century the *lokāyata* or the *Cārvāka-sūtras* had at least two commentaries representing two divergent schools of interpretation. In addition to this there was a work in verse attributed to Bṛhaspati, quotations from which have been utilized for the exposition of the Cārvāka system in the *Sarva-darśana-saṃgraha*. It is difficult, however, to say how and when this older science of sophistical logic or of the art of disputation became associated with materialistic theories and revolutionary doctrines of morality, and came to be hated by Buddhism, Jainism and Hinduism alike. Formerly it was hated only by the Buddhists, whereas the Brahmins are said to have learnt this science as one of the various auxiliary branches of study[4].

It is well known that the cultivation of the art of disputation is very old in India. The earliest systematic treatise of this is to be found in the *Caraka-saṃhitā* (first century A.D.) which is only a

[1] Patañjali's *Mahā-bhāṣya* on *Pāṇini*, VII. 3. 45, and Kaiyaṭa's commentary on it.

[2] *tan-nāmāni cārvāka-lokāyate-ty-ādīni*. Guṇaratna's commentary on *Ṣaḍ-darśana-samuccaya*, p. 300. *Lokāyata* according to Guṇaratna means those who behave like the common undiscerning people—*lokā nirvicārāḥ sāmānyā lokās tadvād ācaranti sma iti lokāyatā lokāyatikā ity api*.

[3] *Ibid.* p. 307, *Tattva-saṃgraha*, p. 520.

[4] *Aṅguttara*, I. 163.

revision of an earlier text (*Agniveśa-saṃhitā*), which suggests the existence of such a discussion in the first or the second century B.C. if not earlier. The treatment of this art of disputation and sophistry in the *Nyāya-sūtras* is well known. Both in the Āyur-veda and in the Nyāya people made it a point to learn the sophistical modes of disputation to protect themselves from the attacks of their opponents. In the *Kathā-vatthu* also we find the practical use of this art of disputation. We hear it also spoken of as *hetu-vāda* and copious reference to it can be found in the *Mahābhārata*[1]. In the *Aśva-medha-parvan* of the *Mahābhārata* we hear of *hetu-vādins* (sophists or logicians) who were trying to defeat one another in logical disputes[2]. Perhaps the word *vākovākya* in the *Chāndogya Upaniṣad*, VII. 1. 2, VII. 2. 1, VII. 7. 1, also meant some art of disputation. Thus it seems almost certain that the practice of the art of disputation is very old. One other point suggested in this connection is that it is possible that the doctrine of the orthodox Hindu philosophy, that the ultimate truth can be ascertained only by an appeal to the scriptural texts, since no finality can be reached by arguments or inferences, because what may be proved by one logician may be controverted by another logician and that disproved by yet another logician, can be traced to the negative influence of the sophists or logicians who succeeded in proving theses which were disproved by others, whose findings were further contradicted by more expert logicians[3]. There were people who tried to refute by arguments the Vedic doctrines of the immortality of souls, the existence of a future world either as rebirth or as the *pitṛ-yāna* or the *deva-yāna*, the efficacy of the Vedic sacrifices and the like, and these logicians or sophists (*haituka*) who reviled the Vedas were called *nāstikas*. Thus, Manu says that the Brahmin who through a greater confidence in the science of logic (*hetu-śāstra*) disregards the authority of the Vedas and the *smṛti* are but *nāstikas* who should be driven out by good

[1] *Mahābhārata*, III. 13034, V. 1983; XIII. 789, etc.

[2] *Ibid.* XIV. 85. 27.

[3] Compare *Brahma-sūtra* "*tarkā-pratiṣṭhānād apy anyathā-numānam iti ced evam api avimokṣa-prasaṅgaḥ.*" II. 1. 11.

Śaṅkara also says: *yasmān nirāgamāḥ puruṣo-prekṣā-mātra-nibandhanāḥ tarkāḥ a pratiṣṭhitā bhavanti utprekṣāyāḥ nirankuśatvāt kair apy utprekṣitāḥ santaḥ tato'nyair ābhāsyante iti na pratiṣṭhitatvaṃ tarkānaṃ śakyam aśrayitum.*

Vācaspati, commenting on the commentary of Śaṅkara, quotes from *Vākya-padīya*: *yatnenā' numito' py arthaḥ kuśalair anumātṛbhiḥ abhiyuktatarair anyair anyathai'vo'papādyate.*

men[1]. The *Bhāgavata-purāṇa* again says that one should neither follow the Vedic cult, nor be a heretic (*pāṣaṇḍī*, by which the Buddhists and Jains were meant), nor a logician (*haituka*) and take the cause of one or the other party in dry logical disputations[2]. Again, in *Manu*, IV. 30, it is said that one should not even speak with the heretics (*pāṣaṇḍino*), transgressors of caste disciplines (*vikarmasthān*), hypocrites (*vaiḍāla-vratika*), double-dealers and sophists (*haituka*)[3]. These *haitukas*, sophists or logicians thus indulged in all kinds of free discussions and controverted the Vedic doctrines. They could not be the Naiyāyikas or the Mīmāṃsists who were also sometimes called *haituka* and *tarkī* because they employed their logical reasonings in accordance with the Vedic doctrines[4]. Thus we reach another stage in our discussion in which we discover that the *haitukas* used sophistical reasonings not only in their discussions, but also for repudiating the Vedic, and probably also the Buddhistic doctrines, for which they were hated both by the Vedic people and the Buddhists; and thus the sophistical or logical science of disputation and criticism of Vedic or Buddhistic doctrines grew among the Brahmanic people and was cultivated by the Brahmins. This is testified by *Manu*, II. 11, where Brahmins are said to take this *hetu-śāstra*, and this also agrees with *Aṅguttara*, I. 163, and other Buddhistic texts.

But who were these *nāstikas* and were they identical with the *haitukas*? The word is irregularly formed according to Paṇini's rule, IV. 460 (*asti-nāsti-diṣṭaṃ matiḥ*). Patañjali, in his commentary, explains the word *āstika* as meaning one who thinks "it exists" and *nāstika* as one who thinks "it does not exist." Jayāditya, in his *Kāśikā* commentary on the above *sūtra*, explains *āstika* as one who believes in the existence of the other world (*para-loka*), *nāstika* as one who does not believe in its existence, and *diṣṭika* as one who believes only what can be logically demonstrated[5]. But we have the

[1] *yo'vamanyeta te mūle hetu-śāstrā-śrayād dvijaḥ | sa sādhubhir vahiṣ-kāryo nāstiko veda-nindakaḥ. Manu*, II. 11.

[2] *veda-vāda-rato na syān na pāṣand īna haitukaḥ | śuṣka-vāda-vivāde na kañ cit pakṣaṃ samāśrayet. Bhāgavata*, XI. 18. 30.

[3] Medhātithi here describes the *haitukas* as *nāstikas*, or those who do not believe in the future world (*para-loka*) or in the sacrificial creed. Thus he says, *haitukā nāstikā nāsti paraloko, nāsti dattam, nāsti hutam ity evaṃ sthita-prajñāḥ*.

[4] *Manu*, XII. 111.

[5] *paralokaḥ astī'ti yasya matir asti sa āstikaḥ, tadviparīto nāstikaḥ; pramāṇā-nupātinī yasya matiḥ sa diṣṭikaḥ. Kāśikā* on Paṇini, IV. 4. 60. Jayāditya lived in the first half of the seventh century.

definition of *nāstika* in Manu's own words as one who controverts the Vedic doctrines (*veda-nindaka*[1]). Thus the word *nāstika* means, firstly, those who do not believe in the existence of the other world or life after death, and, secondly, those who repudiate the Vedic doctrines. These two views, however, seem to be related to each other, for a refusal to believe in the Vedic doctrines is equivalent to the denial of an after-life for the soul and also of the efficacy of the sacrifice. The *nāstika* view that there is no other life after the present one and that all consciousness ceases with death seems to be fairly well established in the Upaniṣadic period; and this view the Upaniṣads sought to refute. Thus, in the *Kaṭha Upaniṣad* Naciketa says that there are grave doubts among the people whether one does or does not exist after death, and he was extremely anxious to have a final and conclusive answer from Yama, the lord of death[2]. Further on Yama says that those who are blinded with greed think only of this life and do not believe in the other life and thus continually fall victims to death[3]. Again, in the *Bṛhad-āraṇyaka Upaniṣad* (II. 4. 12, IV. 5. 13) a view is referred to by Yājñavalkya that consciousness arises from the elements of matter and vanishes along with them and that there is no consciousness after death[4]. Jayanta says in his *Nyāya-mañjarī* that the *Lokāyata* system was based on views expressed in passages like the above which represent only the opponent's (*pūrva-pakṣa*) view[5]. Jayanta further states in the same passage that no duties are prescribed in the *lokāyata*; it is only a work of tricky disputation (*vaitaṇḍika-kathai'vā'sau*) and not an *āgama*[6].

References to the *nāstikas* are found also in the Buddhist litera-

[1] *Manu*, II. 11. Medhātithi in explaining *nāstikā'-krāntam* (*Manu*, VIII. 22) identifies *nāstikas* with *lokāyatas* who do not believe in the other world. Thus he says, *yathā nāstikaiḥ para-lokā-pavādibhir lokāyatikā-dyair ākrāntam*. But in *Manu*, IV. 163, *nāstikya* is explained by him as meaning the view that the Vedic doctrines are false: *veda-pramāṇakānām arthānāṃ mithyātvā-dhyavasāyasya nāstikya-śabdena pratipādanam.*

[2] *ye'yam prete vicikitsā manuṣye astī'ty eke nā'yam astī'ti cai'ke, etad-vidyām anuśiṣṭas tvayā'haṃ varāṇāṃ eṣa varas tṛtīyah. Kaṭha*, I. 20.

[3] *na sāmparāyaḥ pratibhāti bālaṃ pramādy-antaṃ vitta-mohena mūḍham; ayaṃ loko nāsti para iti mānī punah punar vaśam āpadyate me. Ibid.* II. 6.

[4] *vijñāna-ghana eva etebhyaḥ bhūtebhyo samutthāya tāny evā'nuvinaśyati, na pretya samjñā'sti ity are bravīmi. Bṛhad-āraṇyaka*, II. 4. 12.

[5] *tad evaṃ pūrva-pakṣa-vacana-mūlatvāt lokāyata-śāstram api na svatantram. Nyāya-mañjarī*, p. 271, V.S. Series, 1895.

[6] *nahi lokāyate kiñ cit kartavyam upadiśyate vaitaṇḍika-kathai'va'san na punaḥ kaś cid āgamaḥ. Ibid.* p. 270.

ture. The P.T.S. Pāli Dictionary explains the meaning of the word *natthika* as one who professes the motto of "*natthi*," a sceptic, nihilist, and *natthika-diṭṭhi* as scepticism or nihilistic view. It may, however, seem desirable here to give brief accounts of some of the heretics referred to in Buddhistic literature who could in some sense or other be regarded as sceptics or nihilists. Let us first take up the case of Pūraṇa Kassapa described in *Dīgha Nikāya*, II. 16, 17. Buddhaghoso, in commenting on the *Dīgha Nikāya*,I I. 2, in his *Sumaṅgala-vilāsinī*, says that, in a family which had ninety-nine servants, Kassapa was the hundredth servant and he having thus completed (*pūraṇa*) the hundredth number was called by his master *pūraṇa* (the completer), and Kassapa was his family name. He fled away from the family and on the way thieves robbed him of his cloth and he somehow covered himself with grass and entered a village. But the villagers finding him naked thought him to be a great ascetic and began to treat him with respect. From that time he became an ascetic and five hundred people turned ascetics and followed him. King Ajātaśatru once went to this Purāṇa Kassapa and asked him what was the visible reward that could be had in this life by becoming a recluse, and Pūraṇa Kassapa replied as follows: "To him who acts, O king, or causes another to act, to him who mutilates or causes another to mutilate, to him who punishes or causes another to punish, to him who causes grief or torment, to him who trembles or causes others to tremble, to him who kills a living creature, who takes what is not given, who breaks into houses, who commits dacoity, or robbery, or highway robbery, or adultery, or who speaks lies, to him thus acting there is no guilt. If with a discus with an edge sharp as a razor he should make all the living creatures on the earth one heap, one mass of flesh, there would be no guilt thence resulting, no increase of guilt would ensue. Were he to go along the south bank of the Ganges giving alms and ordering gifts to be given, offering sacrifices or causing them to be offered, there would be no merit thence resulting, no increase of merit. In generosity, in self-mastery, in control of the senses, in speaking truth, there is neither merit, nor increase of merit. Thus, Lord, did Pūraṇa Kassapa, when asked what was the immediate advantage in the life of a recluse, expound his theory of non-action (*akiriyam*)[1]." This theory definitely repudiates the doctrine of *karma* and holds

[1] *Dialogues of the Buddha*, I. 69–70.

that there is neither virtue nor vice and thus no action can lead to any fruit[1]. This is what is here called the doctrine of *akiriya* and it is in a way an answer to the question what may be the visible reward in this life of being a recluse. Since there is neither virtue nor vice, no action can produce any meritorious or evil effect—this is one kind of *nātthikavāda*. But it is wrong to confuse this *akiriya*[2] doctrine with the doctrine of inactivity (*akāraka-vāda*) attributed to Sāṃkhya by Śīlāṅka in his commentary on *Sūtra-kṛtāṅga-sūtra*, I. I. 13. That *akāraka* doctrine refers to the Sāṃkhya view that the souls do not participate in any kind of good or bad deeds[3].

Let us now turn to another nihilistic teacher, viz. Ajita Keśakambalī. His doctrines are briefly described in *Dīgha*, II. 22–24, where Ajita says: "There is no such thing as alms or sacrifice or offering. There is neither fruit nor result of good or evil deeds. There is no such thing as this world or the next (*n'atthi ayaṃ loko na paro loko*). There is neither father nor mother, nor beings springing into life without them. There are in the world no recluses or Brahmins who have reached the highest point, who walk perfectly and who, having understood and realized, by themselves alone, both this world and the next, make their wisdom known to others. A human being is built up of the four elements; when he dies the earth in him returns and relapses to the earth, the fluid to the water, the heat to the fire, his wind to the air, and his faculties pass into space. The four bearers, with the bier as the fifth, take the dead body away; till they reach the burning ground men utter eulogies, but there his bones are bleached and his offerings end in ashes. It is a doctrine of fools, this talk of gifts. It is an empty lie, mere idle talk, when men say there is profit therein. Fools and wise alike, on the dissolution of the body, are cut off, annihilated and after death they are not."[4] Ajita Keśakambalī was so called because he used to wear a garment made of human hair which was hot in summer and cold in winter and was thus a source of suffering.[4] It is easy to see that Ajita Keśakambalī's views were very similar to

[1] Buddhaghoso, in commenting on it says, *sabbathāpi pāpapunnānam kiriyam eva paṭikkhipati. Sumaṅgala-vilāsinī*, I. 160.

[2] This has been interpreted by Dr Barua as representing the doctrine of Pūraṇa Kassapa, which is evidently a blunder. *Prebuddhistic Indian Philosophy*, Calcutta, 1921, p. 279.

[3] *bāle ca paṇḍite kāyassa bhedā ucchijjanti vinassanti, na honti param maraṇā ti. Dīgha*, II. 23. *Dialogues of the Buddha*, pp. 73–74.

[4] *Sumaṅgala-vilāsinī*, I. 144.

the views of the Cārvākas as known to us from the fragments preserved as quotations and from accounts of them given by other people. Thus, Ajita did not believe in the other world, in virtue or vice, and denied that *karmas* produced any fruits. He, however, believed in the view that the body was made up of four elements, that there was no soul separate from the body, that with the destruction of the body everything of this life was finished, and that there was no good in the Vedic sacrifices.

Let us now turn to the doctrine of Makkhali Gosāla or Mankhaliputta Gosāla or Makkhali Gosāla who was a contemporary of the Buddha and Mahāvīra. Buddhaghoso says that he was born in a cow-shed (*go-sāla*). As he grew up he was employed as a servant; while going in the mud to bring oil he was cautioned by his master to take care not to let his feet slip (*mākhali*) in the mud; but in spite of the caution he slipped and ran away from his master, who, following him in a rage, pulled the ends of his *dhoti*, which was left in his hands, and Makkhali ran away naked. Thus left naked he afterwards became an ascetic like Pūraṇa Kassapa[1]. According to the *Bhagavatī-sūtra*, XV. 1, however, he was the son of Makkhali who was a *mankha* (a mendicant who makes his living by showing pictures from house to house) and his mother's name was Bhaddā. He was born in a cow-shed and himself adopted the profession of a *mankha* in his youth. At his thirtieth year he met Mahāvīra and after two years he became his disciple and lived with him for six years practising penances. Then they fell out, and Makkhali Gosāla, after practising penances for two years, obtained his Jina-hood while Mahāvīra became a Jina two years after the attainment of Jina-hood by Gosāla. After this Gosāla continued to be a Jina for sixteen years and Mahāvīra met him at the end of that period in Sāvatthi where there was a quarrel between the two and Gosāla died through fever by the curse of Mahāvīra Hoernlé shows in his edition of the text and translation of *Uvāsagadasāo*, pp. 110–111, that Mahāvīra died in 450–451 B.C. at the age of 56. Makkhali was the founder of the *Ājīvaka* sect. *Ājīvakas* are mentioned in the rock-hewn cave (which was given to them) on Barabar hills near Gaya, in the seventh Pillar Edict of Asoka in 236 B.C. and in the rock-hewn caves on Nāgārjuni hill in 227 B.C. in the reign of Asoka's successor Dāśaratha. They are also mentioned in the

[1] *Sumaṅgala-vilāsinī*, I. 143, 144.

Bṛhaj-jātaka (xv. 1) of Varāha Mihira in the middle of the sixth century A.D. Silāṅka (ninth century) also refers to them in his commentary on the *Sūtra-kṛtāṅga-sūtra* (I. 1. 3. 12 and I. 3. 3. 11), in which the *Ājīvakas* are mentioned along with *Trai-rāśikas* as being followers of Makkhali Gosāla[1]. Halāyudha also mentions the *ājīvas* as being the same as the Jains in general; but does not distinguish the *nirgranthas* from the *Digambaras* or identify the latter with the *Ājīvakas* as Hoernlé says in his article on the *Ājīvakas*. Hoernle further points out in the same article that in the thirteenth-century inscriptions on the walls of the Perumāl Temple at Poygai near Virinchipuram reference is made to the taxes imposed on the *Ājīvakas* by the Chola king Rājarāja in the years A.D. 1238, 1239, 1243 and 1259. Thus it is clear that the *Ājīvaka* school of Makkhali which was started by Makkhali in the fifth century B.C. continued to exist and spread not only in North India but also in South India, and other schools also have developed out of it such as the *Trai-rāsikas*. Pāṇini's grammar has a rule (IV. 1. 154), *maskara-maskariṇau veṇuparivrājakayoḥ*, which signifies that *maskara* means a bamboo and *maskarin* a travelling ascetic. Patañjali, however, in commenting on it, says that *maskarins* were those who advised the non-performance of actions and held that cessation (*śānti*) was much better (*māskṛta karmāṇi śāntir vah śreyasī ityāha ato maskarī parivrājakaḥ*). The word, therefore, does not necessarily mean *ekadaṇḍins* or those who bore one bamboo staff. The identification of Makkhali with *maskarins* is therefore doubtful[1]. It is also very doubtful whether the *Ājīvakas* can be regarded as the same as *Digambara* Jains, as Hoernlé supposes, for neither Varāha nor Bhoṭṭolpala identifies the *Ājīvakas* with the Jains, and Śīlāṅka treats them as different and not as identical[2]. Halāyudha also does not speak of the *Digambaras*

[1] The *Trai-rāśikas* are those who think that the self by good deeds becomes pure and free from *karma* and thus attains *mokṣa*, but seeing the success of its favourite doctrines it becomes joyous and seeing them neglected it becomes angry, and then being born again attains purity and freedom from *karma* by the performance of good deeds and is again born through joy and antipathy as before. Their canonical work is one containing twenty-one *sūtras*. In commenting on I. 3. 3. 11 Śīlāṅka mentions also the *Digambaras* along with the *Ājīvakas*, but it does not seem that he identifies them in the way Hoernlé states in his scholarly article on the *Ājīvakas* in the *Encyclopaedia of Religion and Ethics*. The exact phrase of Śīlāṅka is *ājīvakā-dīnāṃ para-tīrthikānāṃ digamvarāṇāṃ ca asad-ācaranair upaneyā*.

[2] Hoernlé, in his article on the *Ājīvakas* in the *Encyclopaedia of Religion and Ethics*, says: "From this fact that Gosāla is called Makkhaliputta or Mankhali (*Maskarin*), i.e. the man of the bamboo staff, it is clear that originally he belonged

as *Ājīvakas*[1]. It is, therefore, very doubtful whether the *Ājīvakas* could be identified with the *Digambara* Jains unless by a confusion in later times, probably on account of the fact that both the *Digambaras* and the *Ājīvakas* went about naked[2].

The fundamental tenet of Gośāla appears in more or less the same form in *Uvāsagadasāo*, I. 97, 115, II. 111, 132, *Saṃyutta Nikāya*, III. 210, *Aṅguttara Nikāya*, I. 286 and the *Dīgha Nikāya*, II. 20. In the last-mentioned work Gosāla is reported to say to king Ajātaśatru: "There is no cause for the sufferings of beings; they therefore all suffer without any cause; there is no cause for the purity (*viśuddhi*) of beings; they all become pure without any cause; there is no efficiency in one's own deeds or in the deeds of others (*n'atthi atta-kāre na'tthi parakāre*) or in one's free efforts (*puriṣa-kāre*); there is no power, no energy, no human strength or heroic endeavours (*parākkama*)[3]. All vertebrates (*sabbe sattā*), all animals with one or more senses (*sabbe pāṇā*), all lives emanating from eggs or ovaries (*sabbe bhūtā*), all vegetable lives, are without any power or efficiency. They become transformed in various forms by their inherent destiny, by their manifestation in various life-forms, and by their different natures (*niyati-saṅgati-bhava-pariṇati*), and it is in accordance with their six kinds of life-states that they suffer pains and enjoy pleasures." Again, in the *Sūtra-kṛtāṅga sūtra*, II. 6. 7, Gosāla is reported to say that there is no sin for ascetics in having intercourse with women[4]. These doctrines of Gosāla

to the class of *eka-daṇḍins* (or *daṇḍin*) ascetics; and, though he afterwards joined Mahāvīra and adopted his system, he held some distinguishing tenets of his own, and also retained his old distinguishing mark, the bamboo staff." This is all very doubtful, for firstly *mankha* and *maskarin* cannot be identified; secondly, *mankha* means a beggar who carried pictures in his hands—*mankhaś citra-phalaka-vyagra-karo bhikṣuka-viśeṣaḥ* (Abhayadeva Sūri's comment on the *Bhagavatī-sūtra*, p. 662. Nirnaya Sagara ed.). Gosāla's father was a *mankha* and his name was Mankhali from which Gosāla was called Makkhaliputta. Both Jacobi (*Jaina Sūtras*, II. 267 footnote) and Hoernlé (*Ājīvaka*, *Encyclopaedia of Religion and Ethics*, p. 266) are here wrong, for the passage referred to is Śīlāṅka's commentary on *Sūtra-kṛtāṅga-sūtra*, III. 3. 11 (*ājīvakā-dīnām para-tīrthikānāṃ digamvarāṇāṃ ca*), and the "*ca*" in the passage which is to be translated as "and" and not as "or" distinguishes the *Ājīvakas* from the *Digamvaras*.

[1] *nagnā ṭo dig-vāsāḥ kṣapaṇaḥ śramaṇaś ca jīvako jainaḥ, ājivo mala-dhārī nirgranthaḥ kathyate ṣaḍbhiḥ*. II. 190.

[2] *Divyāvadāna*, p. 427, refers to an episode where a Buddha image was dishonoured by a *nirgrantha* and in consequence of that 8000 *Ājīvakas* were killed in the city of Puṇḍravardhana. Dr Barua also refers to this passage in his small work, *The Ājīvakas*.

[3] As Buddhaghoso says, these are all merely specifications of *puriṣa-kāra* (*sarvaiva puriṣa-kāra-viv'ecanam eva*). *Sumaṅgala-vilāsinī*, II. 20.

[4] There is another passage in the *Sūtra-kṛtāṅga-sūtra*, III. 4. 9 (*evamege u asattha paṇṇavanti anāriyā; itthivāsam gayā bālā jinasāsana-parāmmuhā*), where

interest us only so far as they may be considered similar to the other *nāstika* teachings. But unlike other *nāstikas*, Gosāla believed not only in rebirths but also introduced a special doctrine of re-animation[1]. Several other doctrines which are not of philosophical, ethical or eschatological interest but which refer only to *Ājīvaka* dogmatics are related both in the *Dīgha Nikāya*, II. 20, and in the *Bhagavatī-sūtra*, XV, and have been elaborately dealt with by Hoernlé in his article on the *Ājīvaka* and his translation of the *Uvāsagadasāo*. The two important points that we need take note of here are that the *Ājīvakas* who were an important sect did not believe in the efficiency of our will or our *karma* and regarded sex-indulgence as unobjectionable to recluses. Other heretics are also alluded to in the *Sūtra-kṛtāṅga sūtra*, I. III. 4. 9–14, where they also are alluded to as having similar tendencies[2]. Thus it is said: "Some unworthy heretics, slaves of women, ignorant men who are averse to the Law of the Jainas, speak thus: 'As the squeezing of a blister or boil causes relief for some time, so it is with (the enjoyment of) charming women. How could there be any sin in it? As a ram

it is said that some wrongdoers and others who belong to the Jaina circle have turned their faces from the laws imposed upon them by Jina and are slaves of women. Hoernlé says (*Ājīvaka, Encyclopaedia of Religion and Ethics*, p. 261) that this passage refers to the followers of Gosāla. But there is no evidence that it is so, if at least we believe in Śīlāṅka's commentary. Śīlāṅka explains "*ege*" or "*eke*" as *bauddha-viśeṣā nīla-paṭādayaḥ nātha-vādika-maṇḍala-praviṣṭā vā śaiva-viśesāḥ* and *pasattha* as *sad-anuṣṭhānāt pārśve tiṣṭhanti iti parśvasthāḥ sva-yūthyā vā pārśvasthā-vasanna-kuśa-lā-dayaḥ strī-pariṣaha-parājitāḥ*. Thus, according to him, it refers to some Buddhists wearing blue garments, the *nātha-vādins*, the *Śaivas*, or some Jains with bad characters, or bad people in general.

[1] Gosāla thought that it was possible that one person's soul could reanimate other dead bodies. Thus, when he was challenged by Mahāvīra, who forbade his disciples to hold any intercourse with him, he is reported to have said that the Makkhaliputta Gosāla who was the disciple of Mahāvīra was long dead and born in the abode of the gods while he was in reality Udāyī-kuṇḍiyāyaṇīya, who in the seventh and the last change of body through reanimation had entered Gosāla's body. According to Gosāla, a soul must finish eighty-four thousand *mahā-kalpas* during which it must be born seven times in the abode of the gods and seven times as men, undergoing seven reanimations, exhausting all kinds of *karmas*. See *Bhagavati-sūtra*, XV. 673, Nirṇaya Sagaraed. See also Hoernlé's two Appendices to his translation of *Uvāsagadasāo* and the article on *Ājīvika, Encyclopaedia of Religion and Ethics*, p. 262. A *mahā-kalpa* is equal to 300,000 *saras* and one *sara* is the time required to exhaust the sands of the seven Ganges (each Ganges being 500 *yojanas* or 2250 miles in length, 2¼ miles in breadth, and 50 *dhanus* or 100 yards in depth), at the rate of putting 100 years for the removal of one grain of sand. See *ibid.*; also Rockhill's Appendix I to his *Life of the Buddha*.

[2] According to Śīlāṅka they were a sect of Buddhists wearing blue garments, Śaivas, the Nāthas, and some degraded Jains also.

drinks the quiet water, so it is with (the enjoyment of) charming women. How can there be any sin in it?' So say some unworthy heretics who entertain false doctrines and who long for pleasures as the ewe for her kid. Those who do not think of the future but only enjoy the present will repent of it afterwards when their life or their youth is gone[1]."

Again, some heretics (identified by Śīlāṅka with the *Lokāyata*) are reported in the *Sūtra-kṛtāṅga-sūtra*, II. I. 9–10, as instructing others as follows: Upwards from the sole of the feet up to the bottom of the tips of hair and in all transverse directions the soul is up to the skin; so long as there is the body there is the soul and there is no soul apart from this body, so the soul is identical with the body; when the body is dead there is no soul. When the body is burnt no soul is seen and all that is seen is but the white bones. When one draws a sword from a scabbard, one can say that the former lies within the latter, but one cannot say similarly of the soul that it exists in the body; there is in reality no way of distinguishing the soul from the body such that one may say that the former exists in the latter. One can draw the pith from a grass stalk, or bones from flesh or butter from curd, oil from sesamum and so forth, but it is not possible to find any such relation between the soul and the body. There is no separate soul which suffers pains and enjoys pleasures and migrates to the other world after the death of the body, for even if the body is cut into pieces no soul can be perceived, just as no soul can be perceived in a jug even when it is broken to pieces, whereas in the case of a sword it is found to be different from the scabbard within which it is put. The *Lokāyatas* thus think that there is no fault in killing living beings, since striking a living body with a weapon is like striking the ground. These *Lokāyatas*, therefore, cannot make any distinction between good and bad deeds as they do not know of any principle on which such a distinction can be made, and there is thus no morality according to them. Some slight distinction is made between the ordinary nihilists and the haughty nihilists (*pragalbha nāstika*) who say that if the soul was different from the body then it would have some specific kind of colour, taste or the like, but no such separate entity is discoverable, and therefore it cannot be believed that there is a separate soul. The *Sūtra-kṛtāṅga-sūtra*, II. I. 9 (p. 277), speaks

[1] See Jacobi's translation of *Sūtra-kṛtāṅga-sūtra*. *Jaina Sūtras*, II. 270.

of these *Pragalbha Nāstikas* as renouncing (*niṣkramya*) the world and instructing other people to accept their doctrines. But Śīlāṅka says that the *Lokāyata* system has no form of initiation and thus there cannot be any ascetics of that school; it is the ascetics of other schools such as the Buddhists who sometimes in their ascetic stage read the *Lokāyata*, became converted to *lokāyata* views, and preached them to others[1].

After the treatment of the views of the *lokāyata nāstikas* the *Sūtra-kṛtāṅga-sūtra* treats of the Sāṃkhyas. In this connection Śīlāṅka says that there is but little difference between the *lokāyata* and the Sāṃkhya, for though the Sāṃkhyas admit souls, these are absolutely incapable of doing any work, and all the work is done by *prakṛti* which is potentially the same as the gross elements. The body and the so-called mind is therefore nothing but the combination of the gross elements, and the admission of separate *puruṣas* is only nominal. Since such a soul cannot do anything and is of no use (*akiṃcitkara*), the *Lokāyatas* flatly deny them. Śīlāṅka further says that the Sāṃkhyists, like the *Lokāyatikas*, do not find anything wrong in injuring animal lives, for after all the living entities are but all material products, the so-called soul being absolutely incapable of taking interest or part in all kinds of activities[2]. Neither the *nāstikas* nor the Sāṃkhyists can, therefore, think of the distinction between good and bad deeds or between Heaven and Hell, and they therefore give themselves up to all kinds of enjoyments. Speaking of the *lokāyata nāstikas*, the *Sūtra-kṛtāṅga-sūtras* say as follows: "Thus some shameless men becoming monks propagate a law of their own. And others believe it, put their faith in it, adopt it (saying): 'Well you speak the truth, O Brahmaṇa (or) O Śramaṇa, we shall present you with food, drink, spices and sweetmeats, with a robe, a bowl, or a broom.' Some have been induced to honour them, some have made (their proselytes) to honour them. Before (entering an order) they were determined to become Śramaṇas,

[1] *yady api lokāyatikānāṃ nāsti dīkṣādikaṃ tathā'pi apareṇa śākyā-dinā pravrajyā-vidhānena pravrajyā paścāt lokāyatikam adhīyānasya tathāvidha-pariṇateḥ tad evā'bhirucitam.* Śīlāṅka's commentary on the *Sūtra-kṛtāṅga-sūtra*, p. 280 a (Nirṇaya Sagaraed).

In pp. 280–281 Śīlāṅka points out that the *Bhāgavatas* and other ascetics at the time of their renouncement of the world take the vow of all kinds of self-restraint, but as soon as they become converted to the *lokāyata* views they begin to live an unrestrained life. They then wear blue garments (*nīla-paṭa*).

[2] *Ibid.* pp. 281, 283.

houseless, poor monks, who would have neither sons nor cattle, to eat only what should be given them by others, and to commit no sins. After having entered their Order they do not cease (from sins), they themselves commit sins and they assent to another's committing sins. Then they are given to pleasures, amusements and sensual lust; they are greedy, fettered, passionate, covetous, the slaves of love and hate[1]."

But we find references to the *lokāyata* doctrines not only in the *Sūtra-kṛtāṅga-sūtra* but also in the *Bṛhad-āraṇyaka*, the *Kaṭha* as described above and in the *Chāndogya Upaniṣad*, VIII. 7, 8, where Virocana, the representative of the demons who came to Prajāpati for instruction regarding the nature of self, went away satisfied with the view that the self was identical with the body. Prajāpati asked both Indra and Virocana to stand before a cup of water and they saw their reflections, and Prajāpati told them that it was that well dressed and well adorned body that was the self and both Indra and Virocana were satisfied; but Indra was later on dissatisfied and returned for further instructions, whereas Virocana did not again come back. The *Chāndogya Upaniṣad* relates this as an old story and says that it is for this reason that those, who at the present time believe only in worldly pleasures and who have no faith (in the efficiency of deeds or in the doctrine of the immortality of the soul) and who do not perform sacrifices, are called demons (*asura*); and it is therefore their custom to adorn the dead body with fine clothes, good ornaments and provide food for it with which they probably thought that the dead would conquer the other world.

This passage of the *Chāndogya* seems to be of special importance. It shows that there was a race different from the Aryans, designated here as *asuras*, who dressed their dead bodies with fine clothes, adorned them with ornaments, provided them with food, so that when there was a resurrection of these dead bodies they might with that food, clothes and ornaments prosper in the other world and it is these people who believed that the body was the only self. The later *Lokāyatas* or *Cārvākas* also believed that this body was the self, but the difference between them and these *dehātmavādins* referred to in the *Chāndogya* is that they admitted "another world" where the bodies rose from the dead and prospered in the fine clothes, ornaments and food that were given to

[1] See Jacobi, *Jaina Sūtras*, II. 341–342.

the dead body. This custom is said to be an *asura* custom. It seems possible, therefore, that probably the *lokāyata* doctrines had their beginnings in the preceding Sumerian civilization in the then prevailing customs of adorning the dead and the doctrine of bodily survival after death. This later on became so far changed that it was argued that since the self and the body were identical and since the body was burnt after death, there could not be any survival after death and hence there could not be another world after death. Already in the *Kaṭha* and the *Bṛhad-āraṇyaka* we had proof of the existence of people who did not believe in the existence of any consciousness after death and thought that everything ended with death; and in the *Chāndogya* we find that Virocana believed in the doctrine that the body was the *ātman* and this doctrine is traced here to the custom of adorning the dead body among the *asuras*.

The tenets and doctrines of these *asuras* are described in the *Gītā*, XVI. 7–18, as follows: The *asuras* cannot distinguish between right and wrong conduct; they do not have any purity, truthfulness and proper behaviour. They do not think that the world is based on any truth and reality; they do not believe in God and consider all beings to have come out from the desires of the sexes and from nothing more than from mutual sex-relations. These foolish people with such views do harm to the world, engage themselves in ferocious deeds and destroy their own selves (as they have no faith in the other world or in the means thereto)[1]. Full of insatiable desire, egoism, vanity and pride, they take the wrong course through ignorance and live an impure life. They think that existence ends finally at death and that there is nothing beyond this world and its enjoyments, and they therefore give themselves up to earthly enjoyments. Bound with innumerable desires, anger, attachment, etc., they busy themselves in collecting materials of earthly enjoyments through wrong means. They always think of their riches, which they earn daily, and which they accumulate, with which they fulfil their desires in the present or wish to fulfil in the future; of the enemies whom they have destroyed, or whom they wish to destroy; of their powers, their success, their joys, their strength, and so forth.

A doctrine similar to that of the *Lokāyatikas* is preached by Jābāli in *Rāmāyaṇa*, II. 108, where he says that it is a pity that there

[1] Śrīdhara says that these refer to the *Lokāyatikas*. *Gītā*, XVI. 9.

should be some people who prefer virtue in the other world to earthly goods of this world; the performance of the different sacrifices for the satisfaction of the dead is but waste of food, for being dead no one can eat. If food eaten by people here should be of use to other bodies, then it is better to perform *śrāddhas* for people who make a sojourn to distant countries than to arrange for their meals. Though intelligent men wrote books praising the merit of gifts, sacrifices, initiation and asceticism, in reality there is nothing more than what is directly perceived by the senses.

In the *Viṣṇu Purāṇa* (I, 6. 29–31) certain people are alluded to who did not believe in the efficacy of the performance of sacrifices and spoke against the Vedas and the sacrifices; and in the *Mahābhārata*, XII. 186, it has been urged by Bharadvāja that life-functions can be explained by purely physical and physiological reasons and that the assumption of a soul is quite unnecessary. In the *Mahābhārata* references are made also to *haitukas* who did not believe in the other world; they were people with strong old convictions (*dṛḍha-pūrve*) who could hardly change their views; they were learned in the Vedas (*vahuśruta*), were well read in older *śāstras*, made gifts, performed sacrifices, hated falsehood, were great orators in assemblies, and went among the people explaining their views. This passage reveals a curious fact that even in the Vedic circles there were people who performed sacrifices, made gifts and were well read in the Vedas and in older literature, who despised falsehood, were great logicians and speakers and yet did not believe in anything except what exists in this world (*nai'tad astī'ti-vādinaḥ*). We know from the Buddhistic sources that the Brahmins were well versed in the *lokāyata* learning; we know also that in the Upaniṣadic circles the views of those who did not believe in life after death are referred to and reproached, and the *Chāndogya* refers to people among whom the doctrine that the self and the body were identical was current as a corollary underlying their custom of adorning the dead. In the *Rāmāyaṇa* we find that Jāvāli taught the doctrine that there was no life after death and that the ritualistic offerings for the satisfaction of the dead were unnecessary. In the *Gītā* we find also the holders of such views referred to, and they are there reported as performing sacrifices only in name, as they did not adhere to the proper ritualistic course[1]. But in the

[1] *yajante nāma-jajñais te dambhenā'vidhi-pūrvakam.* *Gītā*, XVI. 17.

Mahābhārata certain people are referred to who were well read in the Vedas and other older literature and yet did not believe in the other world and in the immortality of the soul. This shows that this heterodox view (that there was no life after death) was gradually spreading amongst certain sections of the Vedic people, and that though some of them were worthless people who utilized the doctrine only to indulge in sense-gratifications and to live in a lower plane of life, there were others who performed the Vedic practices, were well read in Vedic and other literature and yet did not believe in the doctrine of immortality or in a world beyond the present. Thus, even in those early times, on the one hand there were in the Vedic circle many moral and learned people who believed in these heretical views, whereas there were also immoral and bad people who lived a vicious life and held such heretical views either tacitly or openly[1].

We thus know that the *lokāyata* views were very old, probably as early as the Vedas, or still earlier, being current among the Sumerian people of pre-Aryan times. We know further that a commentary on the *Lokāyata-śāstra* by Bhāgurī was very well known in 200 or 300 B.C., but it is exceedingly difficult to say anything regarding the author of the *Lokāyata-śāstra*. It is attributed to Bṛhaspati or to Cārvāka[2]. But it is difficult to say who this Bṛhaspati may have been. One *Bṛhaspati-sūtra*, a work on polity, has been edited with translation by Dr F. W. Thomas and published from Lahore. In this work the *lokāyatas* have been mentioned in II. 5, 8, 12, 16, 29, and III. 15. Here they are very severely abused as thieves who regard religion as a mere means of advantage and who are destined to go to Hell. It is therefore absolutely certain

[1] The *Maitrāyaṇa Upaniṣad*, VII. 8, 9, says that there are many others who by adopting useless arguments, illustrations, false analogies and illusory demonstrations wish to oppose the Vedic ways of conduct; they do not believe in the self and are like thieves who would never go to Heaven and with whom no one should associate. One sometimes forgets that the doctrine of these people is nothing new but is only a different kind of Vedic science (*veda-vidyā'ntaran tu tat*). Bṛhaspati became Śukra and taught the *Asuras* this doctrine so that they might be inclined to despise the Vedic duties and consider bad to be good and good to be bad.

[2] The *Maitrāyaṇīya* attributes these doctrines to Bṛhaspati and Śukra; the *Prabodha-candro-daya* of Kṛṣṇa Miśra says that these were first formulated by Bṛhaspati and then handed over to Cārvāka who spread them among people through his pupils.

See also Mr D. Śāstrī's *Cārvāka-ṣaṣṭi*, pp. 11–13, where he refers to a number of authorities who attribute this to Bṛhaspati.

that the Bṛhaspati who was the author of these *sūtras* on polity could not have been the author of the *lokāyata* science. Nor could it have been the legal writer Bṛhaspati. In Kauṭilya's *Artha-śāstra* a Bṛhaspati is referred to as a writer on polity, but this must be a different one from the *Bārhaspatya-sūtra* published by Dr Thomas[1]. The Bṛhaspati of Kauṭilya's *Artha-śāstra* is reported there as admitting agriculture, trade and commerce (*vārtā*), law and statecraft (*daṇḍa-nīti*), as the only sciences; in the next passage of the same chapter (*Vidyā-samuddeśa*) *daṇḍa-nīti* is regarded as the one subject of study by Uśanas. In the *Prabodha-candro-daya* Kṛṣṇa Miśra makes Cārvāka hold the view that law and statecraft are the only sciences and that the science of *vārtā* (i.e. agriculture, commerce, trade, dairy, poultry, etc.) falls within them. According to this report the Cārvākas took only *daṇḍa-nīti* and *vārtā* into account, and thus their views agreed with those of Bṛhaspati and Uśanas, and more particularly with those of the latter. But we cannot from this assume that either Bṛhaspati or Uśanas mentioned by Kauṭilya could be regarded as the author of the original *lokāyata*. Bṛhaspati, the author of the *Lokāyata-śāstra*, is thus a mythical figure, and we have practically no information regarding the originator of the *lokāyata* system. It is probable that the original *lokāyata* work was written in the form of *sūtras* which had at least two commentaries, the earliest of which was probably as early as 300 or 400 B.C. There was at least one metrical version of the main contents of this system from which extracts are found quoted in Mādhava's *Sarva-darśana-saṃgraha* and in other places.

It is difficult to say whether Cārvāka was the name of a real person or not. The earliest mention of the name is probably to be found in the *Mahābhārata*, XII. 38 and 39, where Cārvāka is described as a Rākṣasa in the garb of an ascetic Brahmin with three staffs (*tridaṇḍī*), but nothing is said there about the doctrine that he professed. In most of the early texts the *lokāyata* doctrines are either mentioned as the *lokāyata* view or attributed to Bṛhaspati. Thus, in the *Padma Purāṇa* in the *Sṛṣṭ-khaṇḍa*, XII. 318–340, some of the *lokāyata* doctrines are described as being the instructions of Bṛhaspati. Kamalaśīla, of the eighth century, refers to the Cārvākas as being the adherents of the *lokāyata* doctrine; the *Prabodha-candro-daya* speaks of Cārvāka as being the great teacher who

[1] Kauṭilya's *Artha-śāstra*, pp. 6, 29, 63, 177, 192, Mysore ed. 1924.

propagated through a succession of pupils and pupils of pupils the *Lokāyata-śāstra* written by Vācaspati and handed over to him. Mādhava, in his *Sarva-darśana-saṃgraha*, describes him as one who follows the views of Bṛhaspati and the chief of the nihilists (*bṛhaspati-matā-nusāriṇā nāstika-śiromaṇinā*). Guṇaratna, however, in his commentary on the *Ṣaḍ-darśana-samuccaya*, speaks of the Cārvākas as being a nihilistic sect who only eat but do not regard the existence of virtue and vice and do not trust anything else but what can be directly perceived. They drank wines and ate meat and were given to unrestricted sex-indulgence. Each year they gathered together on a particular day and had unrestricted intercourse with women. They behaved like common people and for this reason they were called *lokāyata* and because they held views originally framed by Bṛhaspati they were also called *Bārhaspatya*. Thus it is difficult to say whether the word Cārvāka was the name of a real personage or a mere allusive term applied to the adherents of the *lokāyata* view.

Both Haribhadra and Mādhava have counted the Lokāyata or Cārvāka philosophy as a *darśana* or system of philosophy. It had a new logic, a destructive criticism of most of the cherished views of other systems of Indian philosophy, a materialistic philosophy, and it denied morality, moral responsibility and religion of every kind.

Let us, therefore, first take up the Cārvāka logic. The Cārvākas admitted the validity only of perception. There is nothing else but what can be perceived by the five senses. No inference can be regarded as a valid means of knowledge, for inference is possible only when the universal concomitance of the reason (*hetus*) with the probandum is known, and such a reason is known to be existing in the object of the minor term (*vyāpti-pakṣa-dharmatā-śāli hi liṅgaṃ gamakam*). Such a concomitance is possible when it is known not only to be unconditional but when there is no doubt in the mind that it could be conditional. Such a concomitance must first be known before an inference is possible; but how can it be known? Not by perception, for concomitance is not an objective entity with which the senses can come in contact. Moreover, the concomitance of one entity with another means that the entities are associated with each other in the past, present and future (*sarvo-pasaṃhārayatrī vyāptiḥ*), and the sense-organs can have no scope with regard to future associations or even with regard to all past time. If it is urged that the concomitance is between the class-character (*sāmānya-gocaram*) of the probandum (e.g. fire) and the class-character of the reason (e.g. smoke), then it is not necessary that the concomitance of the reason with the probandum should have actually to be perceived at all times by the sense-organs. But if the concomitance is between the class-character of smoke and fire, why should any individual fire be associated with every case of smoke? If the concomitance cannot be perceived by the sense-organs, it cannot be perceived by the mind either, for the mind cannot associate itself with the external objects except through the sense-organs. The concomitance cannot be known through inference, for all inference presupposes it. Thus, there being no way of perceiving concomitance, inference becomes impossible. Again, a concomitance which can lead to a valid inference must be devoid of all conditions; but the absence of such conditions in the past or in the future cannot be perceived at the time of making the inference. Moreover, a condition (*upādhi*) is defined as that which, having an unfailing concomitance with the probandum, has not the same concomitance with the reason (*sādhanā-vyāpakatve sati sādhya-sama-vyāptiḥ*)[1].

Again it is said that an inference is possible only when the reason (e.g. smoke) is perceived to be associated with the object denoted by the minor term (*pakṣa*, e.g. hill), but in reality there is no association of the smoke with the hill nor can it be a character of it, for it is a quality of fire. There is no universal agreement between smoke and hill so that one can say that wherever there is a hill there is smoke. Nor can it be said that wherever there is smoke there is both the hill and the fire. When the smoke is first seen it is not perceived as the quality of fire associated with a hill; therefore it is not enough to say that the reason (e.g. smoke) belongs to the minor term (*pakṣa*, e.g. hill) as its character (*pakṣa-dharma*), but that the reason belongs to the minor term associated with the probandum. The assertion that in an inference the reason must be known as a quality of the minor term (*pakṣa*) has therefore to be interpreted as being a quality of a part of the minor term as associated with the probandum.

A valid inference can be made when the two following con-

[1] *Sarva-darśana-saṃgraha*, I.

ditions are satisfied: (1) An invariable and unconditional concomitance is known between the reason and the probandum such that in every case when the reason is present the probandum must also be present in all places and in all times, without the association of any determining condition. (2) That a reason having such a concomitance with the probandum must be known to exist in the minor term (*pakṣa*) in which the probandum is asserted. Now the Cārvāka contention is that none of these conditions can be fulfilled and that therefore valid inference is impossible. Firstly, concomitance is ascertained through an experience of a very large number of cases (*bhūyo-darśana*) of agreement between the reason (*hetu*) and the probandum (*sādhya*). But according to the difference of circumstances, time and place, things differ in their power or capacity and thus since the nature and qualities of things are not constant it is not possible that any two entities should be found to agree with each other under all circumstances in all times and in all places[1]. Again, an experience of a large number of cases cannot eliminate the possibility of a future failure of agreement. It is not possible to witness all cases of fire and smoke and thus root out all chances of a failure of their agreement, and if that were possible there would be no need of any inference[2]. The Cārvākas do not admit "universals," and therefore they do not admit that the concomitance is not between smoke and fire but between smoke-ness (*dhūmatva*) and fire-ness (*vahnitva*)[3]. Again, it is impossible to assure oneself that there are no conditions (*upādhi*) which would vitiate the concomitance between the *hetu* and the *sādhya*, for though they may not now be perceivable they may still exist imperceivably[4]. Without a knowledge of agreement in absence (i.e. in a case where there is no fire there is no smoke), there cannot be any assurance of concomitance. It is impossible to exhaust in

1 *deśa-kāla-daśā-bheda-vicitrā-tmasu vastuṣu*
avinā-bhāva-niyamo na śakyo vastum āha ca.
Nyāya-mañjarī, p. 119.

2 *na pratyakṣī-kṛtā yāvad dhūmā-gni-vyaktayo'khilāḥ*
tāvat syād api dhūmo' sau yo' nagner iti śaṅkyate
ye tu pratyakṣato viśvaṃ paśyanti hi bhavādṛśaḥ
kiṃ divya-cakṣuṣām eṣām anumāna-prayojanam *Ibid.*

3 *sāmānya-dvārako' py asti nā'vinābhāva-niścayaḥ*
vāstavaṃ hi na sāmānyaṃ nāma kiñcana vidyate. *Ibid.*

4 Compare *Khaṇḍana-khaṇḍa-khādya*, p. 693:
vyāghāto yadi śaṅkā'sti na cec chaṅkā tatastarām
vyāghātā-vadhir āśaṅkā tarkaḥ śaṅkā-vadhiḥ kutaḥ.

experience all cases of absence of fire as being also the cases of the absence of smoke. Thus since without such a joint method of agreement in presence and absence the universal invariable concomitance cannot be determined, and since it is not possible to assure oneself of the universal agreement in presence or in absence, the concomitance itself cannot be determined[1].

Purandara, however, a follower of Cārvāka (probably of the seventh century), admits the usefulness of inference in determining the nature of all worldly things where perceptual experience is available; but inference cannot be employed for establishing any dogma regarding the transcendental world, or life after death or the laws of *Karma* which cannot be available to ordinary perceptual experience[2]. The main reason for upholding such a distinction between the validity of inference in our practical life of ordinary experience, and in ascertaining transcending truths beyond experience, lies in this, that an inductive generalization is made by observing a large number of cases of agreement in presence together with agreement in absence, and no cases of agreement in presence can be observed in the transcendent sphere; for even if such spheres existed they could not be perceived by the senses. Thus, since in the supposed supra-sensuous transcendent world no case of a *hetu* agreeing with the presence of its *sādhya* can be observed, no inductive generalization or law of concomitance can be made relating to this sphere[3]. In reply to this contention Vādideva says that such a change may be valid against the Mīmāṃsists who depend upon the joint method of agreement and difference for making any inductive generalization, but this cannot

[1]
niyamaś cā'numānā-ṅgaṃ gṛhītaḥ pratipadyate
grahaṇaṃ cā'sya nā'nyatra nāstitā-niścayaṃ vinā
darśanā-darśanābhyaṃ hi niyama-grahaṇaṃ yadi
tad apy asad anagnau hi dhūmasye'ṣṭam adarśanam
anagniś ca kiyān sarvaṃ jagaj-jvalana-varjitam
tatra dhūmasya nāstitvaṃ nai'va paśyanty ayoginaḥ.

Nyāya-mañjarī, p. 120.

[2] He is mentioned in Kamalaśīla's *Pañjikā*, p. 431, *Purandaras tv āha loka-prasiddham anumānaṃ cārvākair apī'ṣyate eva, yat tu kaiś cit laukikaṃ mārgam atikramya anumānam ucyate tan niṣidhyate.* Vādideva Sūri also quotes a *sūtra* of Purandara in his commentary *Syādvāda-ratnākara* on his *Pramāṇa-naya-tattva-lokā-laṅkāra*, II. 131: *pramāṇasya gauṇatvād anumānād artha-niścaya-durlabhāt.*

[3]
avyabhicārā-vagamo hi laukika-hetūnām
anumeyā'vagame nimittaṃ sa nāsti tantra-siddheṣu
iti na tebhyaḥ parokṣā-rthā'vagamo nyāyyo'ta idam
uktam anumānād artha-niścayo durlabhaḥ.

apply against the Jaina view of inference which is based on the principle of necessary implication (*anyathā-nupapattāv eva tat-svarūpatvena svīkārāt*).

Other objections also made against the possibility of a valid inference are as follows: (1) impressions made by inferential knowledge are dim and not so vivid (*aspaṣṭatvāt*) as those produced by perception; (2) inference has to depend on other things for the determination of its object (*svārtha-niścaye parā-pekṣatvāt*); (3) inference has to depend on perception (*pratyakṣa-pūrvakatvāt*); (4) inferential cognitions are not directly produced by the objects (*arthād anupajāyamānatvāt*); (5) inference is not concrete (*avastu-viṣayatvāt*); (6) it is often found contradicted (*bādhyamānatvāt*); (7) there is no proof which may establish the law that every case of the presence of the *hetu* should also be a case of the presence of the *sādhya* (*sādhya-sādhanayoḥ pratibandha-sādhaka-pramāṇā-bhāvād vā*)[1]. None of these can be regarded as a reason why inference should be regarded as invalid from the Jaina point of view. For in reply to the first objection it may be pointed out that vividness has never been accepted as a definition of *pramāṇa*, and therefore its absence cannot take away the validity of an inference; illusory perceptions of two moons are vivid, but are not on that account regarded as valid. Again, an inference does not always depend on perception, and even if it did, it utilized its materials only for its own use and nothing more. Perception also is produced from certain materials, but is not on that account regarded as invalid. The inference is also produced from objects and is as concrete as perception since like it it involves universals and particulars. Again, false inferences are indeed contradicted, but that is no charge against right inferences. The invariable relationship between a *hetu* and a *sādhya* can be established through mental reasoning (*tarka*)[2].

Jayanta points out in this connection that a law of universal agreement of the *sādhya* with the *hetu* has to be admitted. For an inference cannot be due to any mere instinctive flash of intelligence (*pratibhā*). If a knowledge of invariable and unconditional agreement was not regarded as indispensable for an inference, and if it was due to a mere instinctive flash, then the people of the Cocoanut

[1] Vādideva Sūri's *Syādvāda-ratnākāra*, pp. 131, 132. Nirṇaya Sagara Press, 1914.
[2] *Ibid.*

island who do not know how to make fire would have been able to infer fire from smoke. Some say that the invariable association of the *hetu* with the *sādhya* is perceived by mental perception (*mānasa-pratyakṣa*). They hold that in perceiving the association of smoke with fire and the absence of the former when the latter is absent, the mind understands the invariable association of smoke with fire. It is not necessary in order to come to such a generalization that one should perceive the agreement of smoke and fire in all the infinite number of cases in which they exist together, for the agreement observed in the mind is not between smoke and fire but between smoke-ness and fire-ness (*jvalanatvā-di-sāmānya-puraḥsaratayā vyāpti-grahaṇāt*). The objection against this view would be the denial of class-concepts as held by the Cārvākas, Buddhists, and others. There are others, again, who say that even if universals are admitted, it is impossible that there should be universals of all cases of absence of fire as associated with the absence of smoke, and under the circumstances unless all positive and negative instances could be perceived the inductive generalization would be impossible. They, therefore, hold that there is some kind of mystic intuition like that of a yogin (*yogi-pratyakṣa-kalpaṃ*) by which the invariable relation (*pratibandha*) is realized. Others hold that an experience of a large number of positive instances unaccompanied by any experience of any case of failure produces the notion of concomitance. But the Nyāya insists on the necessity of an experience of a large number of instances of agreement in presence and absence for arriving at any inductive generalization of concomitance[1]. The Çārvākas, of course, say to this that in determining the unconditional invariable agreement of every case of a *hetu* with its *sādhya* the absence of visible conditions may be realized by perception; but the possibility of the existence of invisible conditions cannot be eliminated even by the widest experience of agreement in presence, and thus there would always be the fear that the invariable concomitance of the *hetu* with the *sādhya* may be conditional, and thus all inference has the value of more or less probability but not of certainty, and it is only through perceptual corroboration that the inferences come to be regarded as valid[2]. The reply of Nyāya to this is that the assertion that in-

[1] *Nyāya-mañjarī*, p. 122.

[2] *athā-numānaṃ na pramāṇaṃ yogyo-pādhīnāṃ yogyā-nupalabdhyā'bhāva-niścaye' py' ayogyo-pādhi-śaṅkayā vyabhicāra-saṃśayāt śataśaḥ sahacaritayor api vyabhicāro-palabdheś ca loke dhūmā-di-darśanā-ntaraṃ vahnyā'di-vyavahāraś ca*

ference is not valid is itself an inference based on the similarity of inferential processes with other invalid mental processes. But this does not properly refute the Cārvāka position that inductive generalizations are only probable, and that therefore (as Purandara says) they acquire some amount of validity by being corroborated by experience and that they have no force in spheres where they cannot be corroborated by perceptual experience.

Since the Cārvākas do not attribute any more validity to inference than probability, other forms of *pramāṇas*, such as the testimony of trusty persons or the scriptures, analogy or implication, also were not regarded as valid. According to Udayana's statement, the Cārvākas denied the existence of anything that was not perceived, and Udayana points out that if this doctrine is consistently applied and people begin to disbelieve all that they do not perceive at any particular time, then all our practical life will be seriously disturbed and upset[1]. The school of *dhūrta Cārvākas*, in their *Sūtra* work, not only denied the validity of inference but criticized the Nyāya categories as enunciated in the *Nyāya-sūtra*, I. I. I, and tried to establish the view that no such enumeration of categories was possible[2]. It is no doubt true that the Cārvākas admitted perception as the only valid *pramāṇa*, but since illusions occurred in perception also, ultimately all *pramāṇas* were regarded as indeterminable by them.

The Cārvākas had to contend on the one hand with those who admitted a permanent soul, such as the Jains, the Naiyāyikas, the Sāṃkhya-yoga and the Mīmāṃsā, and on the other hand with the idealistic Buddhists who believed in a permanent series of conscious states; for the Cārvākas denied all kinds of existence after death. Thus they say that since there is no permanent entity that abides after death, there is no existence after death. As the body, understanding and sense-functions, are continually changing, there cannot be any existence after death, and hence no separate soul can be admitted. According to some, Cārvākas consciousness is pro-

sambhāvana-mātrāt saṃvādena ca prāmāṇyā-bhimānād. Tattva-cintāmaṇi Annumiti. For a similar view see Russel, "On the notion of Cause" in his *Mysticism and Logic.*

[1] Udayana's *Nyāya-kusumāñjali*, III. 5, 6.

[2] *cārvāka-dhūrtas tu athā'tas tattvaṃ vyākhyāsyāma iti pratijñāya pramāṇa-prameya-saṃkhyā-lakṣaṇa-niyamā-sakya-karaṇīyatvam eva tattvaṃ vyākhyātavān; pramāṇa-saṃkhyā-niyam-āśakya-karaṇīyatva-siddhaye ca pramiti-bhedān pratyakṣā-di-pramāṇān upajanyān īdṛśān upādarśayat. Nyāya-mañjarī*, p. 64.

duced (*utpadyate*) from the four elements, and according to others it is manifested (*abhivyajyate*) from them like fermenting intoxication (*surā*) or acids. It is on account of diverse kinds of arrangements and rearrangements of the atoms of air, water, fire and earth that consciousness is either produced or manifested and the bodies and senses are formed or produced. There is nothing else but these atomic arrangements, and there is also no further separate category[1].

The school of *Suśikṣita Cārvākas* holds that, so long as the body remains, there is an entity which remains as the constant perceiver and enjoyer of all experiences. But no such thing exists after the destruction of the body. If there was anything like a permanent self that migrated from one body to another, then it would have remembered the incidents of the past life just as a man remembers the experiences of his childhood or youth[2]. Arguing against the Buddhist view that the series of conscious states in any life cannot be due to the last conscious state before death in a previous life, or that no state of consciousness in any life can be the cause of the series of conscious states in another future life, the Cārvākas say that no consciousness that belongs to a different body and a different series can be regarded as the cause of a different series of conscious states belonging to a different body. Like cognitions belonging to a different series, no cognition can be caused by the ultimate state of consciousness of a past body[3]. Again, since the last mental state of a saint cannot produce other mental states in a separate birth, it is wrong to suppose that the last mental state of a dying man should be able to produce any series of mental states in a new birth. For this reason the Cārvāka teacher Kambalāśvatara says that consciousness is produced from the body through the operation of the vital functions of *prāṇa*, *apāna* and other bio-motor faculties. It is also wrong to suppose that there is any dormant consciousness in the early stages of the foetal life, for consciousness means the cognition of objects, and there cannot be any consciousness in the foetal state when no sense-organs are properly developed; so also there is no consciousness in a state of swoon, and

[1] *tat-samudāye viṣaye-ndriya-saṃjñā. Cārvāka-sūtra* quoted in Kamalaśīla's *Pañjikā*, p. 520.

[2] *Nyāya-mañjarī*, p. 467.

[3] *yadi jñānam na tad vivakṣitā-tīta-deha-varti-caram ajñāna-janyam. jñānatvāt yathā'nya-santāna-varti-jñānam.* Kamalaśīla's *Pañjikā*, p. 521.

it is wrong to suppose that even in these stages consciousness exists as a potential power, for power presupposes something in which it exists and there is no other support for consciousness excepting the body, and, therefore, when the body is destroyed, all consciousness ceases with it. It cannot also be admitted that at death consciousness is transferred to another intermediary body, for no such body is ever perceived and cannot therefore be accepted. There cannot also be the same series of consciousness in two different bodies; thus the mental states of an elephant cannot be in the body of a horse.

The Buddhist reply to this objection of the Cārvākas is that if by discarding after-life the Cārvākas wish to repudiate the existence of any permanent entity that is born and reborn, then that is no objection to the Buddhists, for they also do not admit any such permanent soul. The Buddhist view is that there is a beginningless and endless series of states of conscious states which, taken as a period of seventy, eighty or a hundred years, is called the present, past or future life. It is wrong on the part of the Cārvākas to deny the character of this series as beginningless and endless; for if it is so admitted, then a state of consciousness at birth has to be regarded as the first and that would mean that it had no cause and it would thus be eternal, for since it existed without any cause there is no reason why it should ever cease to exist. It could not also have been produced by some eternal consciousness or god, for no such eternal entities are admitted; it cannot be admitted as being eternal by itself; it cannot be produced by eternal atoms of earth, water, etc., for it may be shown that no eternal entities can produce anything. Thus, the last alternative is that it must have been produced by the previous states of consciousness. Even if the atoms are regarded as momentary it would be difficult to prove that consciousness was produced by them. The principle which determines causation is, firstly, that something is the cause which, being present, that which was worthy of being seen but was not seen before becomes seen[1]. Secondly, when two instances are such that though all the other conditions are present in them both, yet with the introduction of one element there happens a new phenomenon in the one which does not happen in the other, then that element is the cause of that

[1] *yeṣām upalambhe sati upalabdhi-lakṣaṇa-prāptaṃ pūrvam anupalabdhaṃ sad upalabhyate ity evam āśrayaṇīyam.* Kamalaśīla, *Pañjikā*, p. 525.

phenomenon[1]. The two instances, which differ from each other only in this that there is the effect in the one and not in the other, agree with each other in all other respects excepting that that in which there is the effect has also a new element which is not present in the other, and it is only in such a case that that element may be regarded as the cause of that effect. Otherwise, if the cause is defined as that which being absent the effect is also absent, then there is the alternative possibility of the presence of another element which was also absent, and it might be that it was on account of the absence of this element that the effect was absent. Thus, the two instances where an effect occurs and where it does not occur must be such that they are absolutely the same in every respect, except the fact that there is one element in the case where there is the effect which was absent in the other instance. The causal relation between body and mind cannot be established by such a rigorous application of the joint method of agreement and difference. It is not possible to employ the method of agreement to determine the nature of relation between one's own body and mind, for it is not possible to observe the body in the early foetal stage before the rise of mind, for without mind there cannot be any observation. In other bodies also the mind cannot be directly observed and so it is not possible to say that the body is prior to mind. The method of difference also cannot be employed, for no one can perceive whether with the cessation of the body his mind also ceases or not; and since the minds of other people cannot be directly perceived, such a negative observation cannot be made with reference to other people, and no assertion can therefore be made as to whether with the cessation of other people's bodies their minds also ceased or not. No inference can be drawn from the immobility of the body at death that it must be due to the destruction of mind, for it may still exist and yet remain inoperative in moving the body. Moreover, the fact that a particular body is not moved by it, is due to the fact that the desires and false notions which were operative with reference to that body were then absent.

Again, there are other reasons why the body cannot be regarded as the cause of mind; for if the body as a whole was the cause of

[1] *satṣu tad-anyeṣu samartheṣu ta-dhetuṣu yasyai'kasyā'bhāve na bhavatī'ty evam āśrayaṇīyam anyathā hi kevalaṃ tad-abhāve na bhavatī'ty upadarśane sandigdham atra tasya sāmarthyaṃ syāt anyasyā'pi tat-samarthasyā'bhāvāt.* Kamalaśīla, *Pañjikā*, p. 526.

mind, then slight deformities of the body would have changed the character of the mind, or minds associated with big bodies like those of elephants would be greater than those of men. If with the change of one there is no change in the other, the two cannot be said to be related as cause and effect. Nor can it be said that the body with the complete set of senses is the cause of mind, for in that case with the loss of any sense the nature and character of the mind would also be changed. But we know that this is not so, and when by paralysis all the motor organs are rendered inoperative, the mind may still continue to work with unabated vigour[1]. Again, though the body may remain the same, yet the mental temperament, character or tone might considerably change, or sudden emotions might easily unhinge the mind though the body might remain the same. Even if instances are found which prove that the conditions of the body affect the conditions of the mind, yet that is no reason why the mind or soul should cease to exist with the destruction of the body. If on account of co-existence (*saha-sthiti-niyama*) of body and mind they may be said to be connected with each other in bonds of causation, then since body is as much co-existent with mind as mind with body, the mind may as well be said to be the cause of body. Co-existence does not prove causation, for co-existence of two things may be due to a third cause. Heated copper melts, so through heat the foetal elements may be supposed to produce on the one hand the body and on the other hand to manifest mind or consciousness. So the co-existence of body and mind does not necessarily mean that the former is the material cause of the latter.

It is said that though the later mental states are perceived to be produced by the previous ones, yet the first manifested consciousness has a beginning and it is produced by the body, and thus the theory of the Buddhists that the series of conscious states is without beginning is false. But if the mental states are in the first instance produced by the body, then these could not in later cases be produced in other ways through the visual or other sense organs. If it is urged that the body is the cause of the first origin of knowledge, but not of the later mental states, then the later mental states ought to be able to raise themselves without being in any way dependent

[1] *prasuptikā-di-rogā-dinā kārye-ndriyā-dīnām upaghāte'pi mano-dhīr avikṛtaikā-vikalāṃ sva-sattām anubhavati*. Kamalaśīla, *Pañjikā*, p. 527.

on the body. If it is held that a mental state can produce a series of other mental states only with the help of the body, then each of them would produce an infinite series of such mental states, but such an infinite number of infinite series is never experienced. It cannot also be said that the body generates consciousness only at the first stage and that in all later stages the body remains only as an accessory cause, for that which once behaves as a generating cause cannot behave as an accessory cause. Thus, even if the physical elements be admitted to be impermanent, they cannot be regarded as the cause. If the mental states be regarded as having a beginning, it may be asked whether by mental states the sense-knowledge or the mental ideas are meant. It cannot be the former, for during sleep, swoon or inattentive conditions there is no sense-knowledge, even though the sense-organs are present, and it has therefore to be admitted that attention is the necessary pre-condition of knowledge, and the sense-organs or the sense-faculties cannot be regarded as the sole cause of sense-knowledge. The mind cannot also be regarded as the sole cause, for unless the sense-data or the sense-objects are perceived by the senses, the mind cannot work on them. If the mind could by itself know objects, then there would have been no blind or deaf people. Admitting for argument's sake that mind produces the cognitions, it may be asked whether this cognition is *savikalpa* or *nirvikalpa*; but there cannot be any *savikalpa* unless the association of names and objects (*saṅketa*) is previously learnt. It cannot be also *nirvikalpa* knowledge, for *nirvikalpa* represents the objects as they are in their unique character, which cannot be grasped by the mind alone without the help of the sense-organs. If it is held that even the sense-data are produced by the mind, then that would be the admission of extreme idealism and the giving up of the Cārvāka position. Thus, the conscious states are to be regarded as beginningless and without any origin. Their specific characters are determined by experiences of past lives, and it is as a reminiscence of these experiences that the instincts of sucking or fear show themselves even with the newly-born baby[1]. It has therefore to be admitted that the conscious states are produced neither by the body nor by the mind, but that they are beginningless and are generated by the previous

[1] *tasmāt pūrvā-bhyāsa-kṛta evā'yaṃ bālānām iṣṭā-niṣṭo-pādāna-parityāga-lakṣaṇo vyavahāra iti siddhā buddher anāditā.* Kamalaśīla, *Pañjikā*, p. 532.

states, and these by other previous states, and so on. The parental consciousness cannot be regarded as being the cause of the consciousness of the offspring, for the latter are not similar in nature, and there are many beings which are not of parental origin. It has, therefore, to be admitted that the conscious states of this life must be produced by the states of another life previous to it. Thus, the existence of a past life is proved. And since the mental states of this life are determined by the mental states of other lives, the mental states of this life also are bound to determine other mental states, and this establishes the existence of future lives; provided, however, that these mental states are associated with the emotions of attachment, anger, antipathy, etc. For the mental states can produce other mental states only when they are affected by the emotions of attachment, anger, etc., and these are inherited by the new-born baby from the mental states of his previous life which determined the series of experiences of his present life. Though the past experiences are transferred to the present life, yet owing to a severe shock due to the intervention of the foetal period these experiences do not at once show themselves in infancy, but reveal themselves gradually with age. One does not always remember what one experienced before; thus, in dreams and deliriums, though the elements of the past experience are present, yet they are reconstructed in a distorted form and do not present themselves in the form of memory. So the past experiences cannot ordinarily be remembered by the infant, though there are some gifted beings who can remember their past lives. It is wrong to suppose that the mind is supported by the body or inheres in it, for the mind is formless. Again, if the mind inhered in the body and was of the same stuff as the body, then the mental states should be as perceptible by the visual organ as the body itself. The mental states can be perceived only by the mind in which they occur, but the body can be perceived both by that mind as well as by others; therefore, these two are of entirely different character and are hence entirely different. The body is continually changing, and it is the unitary series of conscious states that produces the impression of the identity of the body. For though the individual consciousnesses are being destroyed every moment, yet the series remains one in its continuity in the past lives, the present life and the future. When the series is different, as in that of a cow and a horse or between two different persons, the states of the one series cannot affect those in the other. One conscious state is thus admitted to be determining another conscious state, and that another, and so on, within the series. Thus it has to be admitted that consciousness exists, even in the unconscious state; for had it not been so, then there would be a lapse of consciousness at that time and this would mean the breaking up of the series. States of consciousness are independent of the sense-organs and the sense-objects, as they are determined by the previous states; in dreams, when the sense-organs are not operating and when there is no sense-object contact, the conscious states continue to be produced; and in the case of the knowledge of past or future events, or the knowledge of chimerical things like the hare's horn, the independence of conscious states is clearly demonstrated. Thus it is proved that consciousness is neither produced by the body nor is in any way determined or conditioned by it, and it is determined only by its past states and itself determines the future states. Thus also the existence of the past and the future lives is proved.

The arguments of the Jains and of the Naiyāyikas against the Cārvākas are somewhat of a different nature from those of the idealistic Buddhists just described, as the former admitted permanent souls which the latter denied. Thus Vidyānandi, in his *Tattvārtha-śloka-vārtika*, says that the chief reason why the soul cannot be regarded as a product of matter is the fact of undisputed, unintermittent and universal self-consciousness unlimited by time or space. Such perceptions as "this is blue" or "I am white" depend upon external objects or the sense-organs, and cannot therefore be regarded as typical cases of self-consciousness. But such perceptions as "I am happy" which directly refer to the self-perception of the ego do not depend on the operation of any external instruments such as the sense-organs or the like. If this self-consciousness were not admitted to be established by itself, no other doctrine, not even the Cārvāka doctrine which seeks to demolish all attested convictions, could be asserted, for all assertions are made by virtue of this self-consciousness. If any consciousness required another consciousness to have itself attested, then that would involve a vicious infinite and the first consciousness would have to be admitted as unconscious. Thus, since the self manifests itself in self-consciousness (*sva-samvedana*), and since the body is perceived through the operation of the senses like all other physical things, the former is entirely different from the latter and cannot be produced by the latter, and because it is eternal it cannot also be manifested by the latter. Again, since consciousness exists even without the senses, and since it may not exist even when there is the body and the senses (as in a dead body), the consciousness cannot be regarded as depending on the body. Thus, the self is directly known as different from the body by the testimony of self-consciousness. The other arguments of Vidyānandi are directed against the idealistic Buddhists who do not believe in a permanent self but believe in the beginningless series of conscious states, and this discussion had better be omitted here[1].

Jayanta argues in the *Nyāya-mañjarī* that the body is continually changing from infancy to old age, and therefore the experiences of one body cannot belong to the new body that has been formed through growth or decay, and therefore the identity of the ego and recognition which form the essential constitutive elements of knowledge cannot belong to the body[2]. It is true no doubt that good diet and medicine which are helpful to the body are also helpful to the proper functioning of the intellect. It is also true that curds and vegetable products and damp places soon begin to germinate into insects. But this is no proof that matter is the cause of consciousness. The selves are all-pervading, and when there is appropriate modifications of physical elements they manifest themselves through them according to the conditions of their own *karmas*. Again, consciousness cannot also be admitted to belong to the senses, for apart from the diverse sense-cognitions there is the apperception of the ego or the self which co-ordinates these diverse sense-cognitions. Thus I feel that whatever I perceive by the eyes I touch by the hand, which shows distinctly that apart from the sense-cognitions there is the individual perceiver or the ego who co-ordinates these sensations, and without such a co-ordinator the unity of the different sensations could not be attained. The Suśikṣita Cārvākas, however, hold that there is one perceiver so long as the body exists, but that this perceiver (*pramātṛ-tattva*) does not transmigrate, but is destroyed with the destruction of the body; the soul is thus not immortal, and there is no after-world after the destruction of this body[3]. To this Jayanta's reply is that if

[1] *Tattvārtha-śloka-vārtika*, pp. 26–52. [2] *Nyāya-mañjarī*, pp. 439–441.
[3] *Ibid.* pp. 467, 468.

a self is admitted to exist during the lifetime of this body, then since this self is different from the body, and since it is partless and non-physical by nature, there cannot be anything which can destroy it. No one has ever perceived the self to be burnt or torn to pieces by birds or animals as a dead body can be. Thus, since it has never been found to be destroyed, and since it is not possible to infer any cause which can destroy it, it is to be regarded as immortal. Since the self is eternal, and since it has a present and past association with a body, it is not difficult to prove that it will have also a future association with a body. Thus, self does not reside either in any part of the body or throughout the body, but is all-pervading and behaves as the possessor of that body with which it becomes associated through the bonds of *karma*. *Para-loka* or after-life is defined by Jayanta as rebirth or the association of the soul with other bodies after death. The proofs that are adduced in favour of such rebirths are, firstly, from the instinctive behaviour of infants in sucking the mother's breast or from their unaccountable joys and miseries which are supposed to be due to the memory of their past experiences in another birth; and, secondly, from the inequalities of powers, intelligence, temper, character and habits, inequalities in the reaping of fruits from the same kind of efforts. These can be explained only on the supposition of the effects of *karma* performed in other births[1].

Śaṅkara, in interpreting the *Brahma-sūtra*, III. 3. 53, 54, tries to refute the *lokayatika* doctrine of soullessness. The main points in the *lokayatika* argument here described are that since consciousness exists only when there is a body, and does not exist when there is no body, this consciousness must be a product of the body. Life-movements, consciousness, memory and other intellectual functions also belong to the body, since they are experienced only in the body and not outside of it[2]. To this Śaṅkara's reply is that life-movements, memory, etc., do not sometimes exist even when the body exists (at death), therefore they cannot be the products of the body. The qualities of the body, such as colour, form, etc., can be

[1] *Nyāya-mañjarī*, pp. 470–473.

[2] *yad dhi yasmin sati bhavaty asati ca na bhavati tat tad-dharmatvena adhyavasīyate yathā'gni-dharmāv auṣṇya-prakāśau; prāṇa-ceṣṭā-caitaṇya-smṛtyādayaś cā'tma-dharmatvenā'bhimatā ātma-vā-dināṃ te' py antar eva deha upalabhyamānā bahiś cā'nupalabhyamanā asiddhe deha-vyat irikte dharmiṇi deha-dharmā eva bhavitum arhanti; tasmād avyatireko dehād ātmāna iti. Śaṅkara-bhāṣya* on *Brahma-sūtra*, III. 3. 53.

perceived by everyone, but there are some who cannot perceive consciousness, memory, etc. Again, though these are perceived so long as the living body exists, yet there is no proof that it does not exist when this body is destroyed. Further, if consciousness is a product of the body, it could not grasp the body; no fire can burn itself and no dancer can mount his own shoulders. Consciousness is always one and unchangeable and is therefore to be regarded as the immortal self. Though ordinarily the self is found to manifest itself in association with a body, that only shows that the body is its instrument, but it does not prove that the self is the product of the body, as is contended by the Cārvākas. The Cārvākas criticized the entire social, moral and religious programme of orthodox Hindus. Thus Śrīharṣa, in representing their views in his *Naiṣadhacarita*, says as follows: "The scriptural view that the performance of sacrifices produces wonderful results is directly contradicted by experience, and is as false as the Purāṇic story of the floating of stones. It is only those who are devoid of wisdom and capacity for work who earn a livelihood by the Vedic sacrifices, or the carrying of three sticks (*tridaṇḍa*), or the besmearing of the forehead with ashes. There is no certainty of the purity of castes, for, considering the irrepressible sex-emotions of men and women, it is impossible to say that any particular lineage has been kept pure throughout its history in the many families on its maternal and paternal sides. Men are not particular in keeping themselves pure, and the reason why they are so keen to keep the women in the harem is nothing but jealousy; it is unjustifiable to think that unbridled sex-indulgence brings any sin or that sins bring suffering and virtues happiness in another birth; for who knows what will happen in the other birth when in this life we often see that sinful men prosper and virtuous people suffer?" The Vedic and the *smṛti* texts are continually coming into conflict with one another, and are reconciled only by the trickery of the commentators; if that is so, why not accept a view in which one may act as one pleases? It is held that the sense of ego is associated with the body, but when this body is burnt, what remains there of virtue or vice, and even if there is anything that will be experienced by another ego and in another body and as such that cannot hurt me. It is ridiculous to suppose that any one should remember anything after death, or that after death the fruits of *karma* will be reaped, or that by feeding Brahmins after death the so-called departed soul will have any satisfaction. The image-worship, or the worship of stones with flowers, or of bathing in the Ganges as a religious practice is absolutely ridiculous. The practice of performing *śrāddha* ceremonies for the satisfaction of the departed is useless, for if the offering of food could satisfy the dead then the hunger of travellers could also be removed by their relations offering them food at home. In reality with death and destruction of the body everything ends, for nothing returns when the body is reduced to ashes. Since there is no soul, no rebirth, no god and no after-life, and since all the scriptures are but the instructions of priests interested in cheating the people, and the Purāṇas are but false mythical accounts and fanciful stories, the one ideal of our conduct is nothing but sense-pleasures. Sins and virtues have no meaning, they are only the words with which people are scared to behave in a particular manner advantageous to the priests. In the field of metaphysics the Cārvākas are materialists and believe in nothing beyond the purely sensible elements of the atoms of earth, water, air and fire and their combinations; in the field of logic they believe in nothing but what can be directly perceived; they deny *karma*, fruits of *karma*, rebirth or souls. The only thing that the Cārvākas cared for was the momentary sense-pleasures, unrestrained enjoyment of sensual joys. They did not believe in sacrificing present joys to obtain happiness in the future, they did not aim at increasing the total happiness and well-being of the whole life as we find in the ethical scheme of Caraka; with them a pigeon to-day was better than a peacock to-morrow, better to have a sure copper coin to-day than a doubtful gold coin in the future[1]. Thus, immediate sense-pleasures were all that they wanted and any display of prudence, restraint, or other considerations which might lead to the sacrifice of present pleasures was regarded by them as foolish and unwise. It does not seem that there was any element of pessimism in their doctrine. Their whole ethical position followed from their general metaphysical and logical doctrine that sense-objects or sense-pleasures were all that existed, that there was no supra-sensible or transcendent reality, and thus there was no gradation or qualitative difference between the pleasures and no reason why any restraint should be put upon our normal tendency to indulge in sense-pleasures.

[1] *varam adya kapotaḥ śvo mayūrāt*
varam saṃśayikān niṣkād asaṃśayikaḥ
kārṣāpaṇa iti lokāyatikāḥ. *Kāma-sūtra*, I. 2. 29, 30.

INDEX[1]

Abhayadeva Sūri, 524 *n.*
Abhaya-prada-rāja, 134
Abhaya-pradāna-sāra, 124
abhāva, 351, 428
abheda, 6, 194, 373
Abhidhāna-padīpikā, 512 *n.*
abhihitā-nvaya-vāda, 233
abhimāna, 48, 468, 485, 494, 510
abhimantā, 48
abhiniveśa, 470
abhinna, 32
Abhirāma Varācārya, 69, 134, 138
Abhirāma Varādhīśa, 111
Abhīti-stava, 121
abhivyakti, 387
Ablative case, 391
Ablutions, 22
Abnegation, 99
Abode, 52
Absence, 203; of cruelty, 29; of greed, 61; of obstruction, 280
Absolute, 41, 52, 398, 405, 474, 475; coincidence, 230; idealism, 358; immortality, 383; trustfulness, 91
Absolute surrender, 91
Absorption, 195
Abstract, 356
Absurd, 230 *n.*
Acceptance, 54
Accessory, 24, 37, 90, 124, 205, 259, 261, 273, 292, 310, 330, 331, 387, 444, 452; agent, 272, 275; cause, 544; collocations, 354; methods, 380 *n.*
Accordance, 54
acic-chakti, 416
acidaṃśa, 301
acit, 89, 160, 391, 396, 397; Veṅkaṭa's view of, 162 *et seq.*
acit-saṃsarga, 383
Acquaintance, 321, 460
Act, 205, 520
Actions, 7, 11, 16, 28, 31, 32, 41, 49, 50, 51, 52, 53, 55, 129, 186, 187, 198, 212 *n.*, 290, 294, 295, 300, 303, 304, 318, 349, 414, 441, 451, 452, 455, 485, 493, 506, 508, 521, 523
Active, 48; operation, 203; sense, 49; sympathy, 90
Activity, 27, 36, 42, 44, 47, 50, 51, 413, 446, 447, 448 *n.*, 452, 462, 465, 481, 492, 493, 497, 509
Actual perception, 185 *n.*, 313
Actual state, 37
Acyuta, 27, 29
adharma, 153, 349, 453, 503
adhigatārtha-gantṛ, 216
adhikaraṇa, 352
Adhikaraṇa-cintāmaṇi, 93 *n.*, 123, 125
Adhikaraṇa-darpaṇa, 123
Adhikaraṇa-sārārtha-dīpikā, 117, 118
Adhikaraṇa-sārāvalī, 118, 123, 125
Adhikaraṇa-sārāvalī-vyākhyā, 123
Adhikaraṇa-yukti-vilāsa, 118
Adhikāra-cintāmaṇi, 118
Adhikāra-saṃgraha-vyākhyā, 127
adhiṣṭhāna, 408, 422, 423, 439, 456
adhiṣṭhāna-kāraṇa, 47, 365, 454, 456, 478, 493
adhiṣṭhāna-kāraṇatā, 484
adhiṣṭhātṛtva, 498
adhīta-prabandhaḥ prapannaḥ, 91
Adhvaranāyikā, 114 *n.*, 125
adhyavasāya, 504
Adhyātma-cintā, 132
Adhyātma-cintāmaṇi, 135
Ad infinitum, 332, 417
Adjectival qualities, 254
Adjuncts, 303
Admission, 339
Admixture, 38
Adoration, 53, 54, 55, 70, 450
a-dravya, 225, 251
adṛṣṭa, 152, 164, 189, 292, 303, 444, 479; Veṅkaṭa's view of, 303–4
advaita, 4, 416
Advaita-kāmadhenu, 396 *n.*
Advaita-siddhi, 133
Advaita-vahiṣkāra, 132
Advaita-vana-kuṭhāra, 115 *n.*, 384
Advaita-vidyā-vijaya, 126
Advaita-vijaya, 361
Advaitic, 65
Advaitins, 129, 142, 295
Affection, 70, 292
Affinity, 466, 471
Affirmation, 193, 211, 419
Afflictions, 28, 44, 454

[1] The words are arranged in the order of the English alphabet. Sanskrit and Pāli technical terms and words are in small italics; names of books are in italics with a capital. English words and other names are in Roman with a capital. Letters with diacritical marks come after ordinary ones.

After-life, 541, 548
Agastya-saṃhitā, 23
Agency, 35, 172, 198, 412, 484, 488
Agent, 8, 11, 27, 31, 204, 290, 407, 412, 477, 486, 500
Aggavaṃsa, 513, 514
Agglutinative, 45
Aggregation, 287
Agni, 505, 508
Agni-purāṇa, 20
Agniveśa-saṃhitā, 517
Agreement, 296, 344, 372, 535, 536
aham-artha, 173, 425
ahaṃ anubhavāmi, 171
ahaṃkāra, 7, 25, 43, 47, 48, 49, 56, 91, 144, 145, 146, 156, 163, 172, 173, 256, 257, 258, 259, 260 *n.*, 280, 490, 499, 504, 507, 508, 510, 511; its nature, 171–3; Nimbārka's conception of, 411 *et seq.*
ahaṃkāra-vaikārika, 510
ahaṃ-pratyaya-vedya, 443
ahiṃsā, 61
Ahirbudhnya, 24, 34, 50, 57, 58, 60, 61, 62, 379, 503 *n.*
Ahirbudhnya-saṃhitā, 21, 24, 34, 36 *n.*, 37 *n.*, 39, 40 *n.*, 41, 42, 43 *n.*, 44 *n.*, 46 *n.*, 47 *n.*, 48 *n.*, 49 *n.*, 50 *n.*, 51 *n.*, 52 *n.*, 53 *n.*, 54, 55 *n.*, 56 *n.*, 57 *n.*, 58 *n.*, 59 *n.*, 60 *n.*, 62 *n.*, 379, 448 *n.*; accessories of Yoga in, 61; adoration in, 54; anatomy in, 59; *antaryāmin* doctrine of, 41; *avatāras* in, 38–9; *āsana* in, 60; Brahman, nature of, in, 35; Brahman, followers of, in, 35; developments of *ahaṃkāra* in, 48; *dharma* and *jñāna*, classification of, in, 62; emancipation in, 62; faith in, 54; God's grace in, 52; God, how to approach Him, in, 53; God's *līlā* in, 51; God, power of, different views of, in, 57; God, qualities of, in, 56; God, relation with *jīva*, in 50; *guṇas*, mutual partial similarity of, in, 46 *n.*; impure creations in, 42 *et seq.*; intermediate creation in, 42; *jīva* as *taṭastha-śakti*, 50 and 50 *n.*; *jīva*'s emancipation in, 52; *jīva*'s nature of, in, 51; *jīva*'s, relation of God with, in, 51; *kāla* and *niyati* in, 45; Lakṣmī as *māyā* in, 52; Lakṣmī as *śakti* in, 52; Lakṣmī, nature of, in, 52; *mahat*, development in, 47; *mahat* in, 47; man, fall of, in, 50; *manus* and *mānavas* in, 49; *mukti*, states of, in 56; nature of souls, in 61; *nyāsa* and *śaraṇāgati* in, 55; objects of *pramāṇas* in, 62; *pramā* and *pramāṇa*, definition of, in, 62; *prapatti* in, 54; *puruṣa* in, 43; *puruṣa* and *avidyā* in, 44; Saṃkarṣaṇa, Pradyumna and Anirudha in, 56; *sattva*, *rajas* and *tamas* in, 45; senses and personality, evolution of, in, 49; service of God in, 54; Sudarśana power, nature of, in, 53; Sudarśana power of, in, 57; *śabda-brahman*, evolution of, in, 58; *śabda*-energy and the *cakras* in, 58; *śakti* and creation in, 36–7; *śakti*, nature of, in, 36; *śakti* of God in, 44; time in, 46; time in relation with categories, in, 46; trinity of *prakṛti*, *puruṣa* and *kala*, in, 46–7; ultimate reality in, 34; ultimate reality, realization of, in, 34; *upāya-jñāna* in, 55; *vāsanā*, *karma* affecting the *jīvas*, in, 51; Viṣṇu-śakti as *bhāvaka* and *bhāvya* in, 50; *vyūhas* in, 38; *vyūha* doctrine in, 39; *yamas* and *niyamas*, enumeration of, in, 61; *yoga* in, 60
Ahobila, 123
Ahobila Raṅganātha Yati, 118, 131
Air, 60, 128, 499, 504, 540, 550
aiśvarya, 30, 35, 37, 47, 56
aitihya, 426
Aiyangar, Mr S. K., 64 *n.*, 66, 67 *n.*, 68, 81 *n.*, 104 *n.*
ajaḍa, 146, 171
ajaḍatva, 171
Ajātaśatru, 520, 524
Ajita, 521, 522
Ajita Keśakambalī, 521; his doctrines, 521
Ajmir, 103
Ajñāna, 144, 177, 178, 179, 195, 315, 317, 321, 327, 328, 329, 330, 338, 339, 362, 363, 364, 365, 366, 367, 368, 369, 370, 371, 372, 374, 393, 394, 407, 408, 409, 410, 411, 424, 426, 437, 439, 466, 470, 485, 487, 495, 506; characteristics, 365; constituents, 367; diverse supposition of it refuted by Rāmānuja, 177 *et seq.*; its assumption leads to vicious infinity, 177 *n.*; its criticism by Veṅkaṭa, 327 *et seq.*; Nimbārka's conception of, 407 *et seq.*; refuted by Rāmānuja, 177; stuff, 366; Saṅkara's view of it criticized by Mahācārya, 361 *et seq.*; Śaṅkarite view criticized by Mādhava Mukunda, 424 *et seq.*; unspeakable, 367; whole, 372

ajñātatayā jñātatayai'va, 249
akāla, 447
akāraka-vāda, 521
Akhaṇḍārthatva-bhaṅga, 126
akhyāti, 47, 180, 181, 182, 183, 184, 185, 186, 187, 237, 239, 241, 243, 245; view, 186 *n.*, 244, 245
akiṃcitkara, 527
akiriya, 521
akiriyam, 520
Akkaialvan, 97 *n.*
akṣara, 46, 503
alambuṣa, 59
alarka-śāka, 97 *n.*
alaukika, 426
'Alā-ud-dīn, 120
Allahabad, 101, 401 *n.*
All-complete, 303
All-illuminating, 451
All-merciful, 85, 99, 412
All-perceiving, 27
All-pervading, 393, 405, 413
All-pervasive, 23, 24, 262, 291, 292, 299, 426, 432; entities, 263
All-pervasiveness, 157, 450
Allegorical drama, 121
Alms, 102, 119
alpa, 292
Alternative, 180, 207, 209, 210, 312, 430
Aḷagārkoil, 103
Amalan-ādipirān, 69, 134 *n.*
Amara-koṣa, 515
Ambrosial sweetness, 84
Ammaṅgi, 105
Amorous, 73; longings, 83
amṛta, 502
amumtila, 505
aṃśa, 194, 485
aṃśā-ṃśibhāva, 484
aṃśāvatāra, 475
an-adhigatā-rtha-gantṛ, 215
an-adhyavasāya, 214
Analogy, 5, 128, 144, 192, 216, 219, 230, 269, 276, 298, 301, 315, 322, 341, 371, 410, 434, 452, 455, 469, 512, 513, 531 *n.*, 539
Analysis, 52, 180, 207, 297
Analytic, 31
Analytical, 497
Ananda Press, 94 *n.*
Ananta, 39 *n.*, 351
Ananta Bhaṭṭa, 98, 102
Ananta Dīkṣita, 98, 162 *n.*
Anantaguru, 112
Anantarāma, 408, 409, 410; his criticism of the *māyā* of Śaṅkara, 410 *et seq.*
Ananta-sūri, 94 *n.*, 98 *n.*, 110, 119
Anantācārya, 98, 105, 188, 241, 242 *n.*, 246, 247, 305; supports correspondence theory, 246–7; theory of illusion, 188
Anantārya, 102, 110, 112, 131, 133, 209, 297, 298, 395; his notion of class-concepts, 297; his view of relations of souls with God, 297
an-anubhāvyatva, 230, 231
an-anyathā-siddhatva, 390
an-anyathā-siddha-niyata-pūrva-vartitā, 397
Anatomy, 515 *n.*
anaupādhika, 485
anavadhāraṇa, 369
anavadhāraṇatvam eva āvaraṇam, 370
anavasthā, 9, 176
anavasthā-parihārāya, 249
anādy-ananta, 61
a-nāmaka, 25
andhatāmisra, 500
Andhrapūrṇa, 104, 105, 109
aneka-dharma, 212
anekānta, 210
Anger, 32, 48, 61, 545
Animals, 221, 441 *n.*
Animate, 116
Aniruddha, 13, 37, 38, 39, 42, 43, 44, 52, 56, 57, 157, 158, 443 *n.*, 448 *n.*, 475
Aniruddha-saṃhitā-mahopaniṣad, 23
anirvacanīya, 179, 238, 239, 243, 435
anirvacanīya-khyāti, 183, 188, 242, 245
anityatva, 199
aniyama, 227
Annihilation, 276, 324, 377
Antagonism, 437
Antagonistic, 374
antaḥ, 483
antaḥkaraṇa, 142, 152, 172, 173, 361, 364, 366, 368, 369, 370, 420, 434, 444, 453, 486, 499 *n.*
antaḥkaraṇa-vṛtti, 411
antaraṅga, 377
antaryāmi, 483
antaryāmy-avatāra, 39 *n.*
Antaryāmi-brahmaṇa, 390
antaryāmin, 40, 41, 200
Antecedent, 203, 342
Antipathy, 29, 30, 51, 87, 148, 449, 470, 488
Antiquity, 99
anubhava, 8, 9
anubhavā-numāna, 229
anubhāvya, 231
anubhūti, 143, 168, 170, 171, 177, 230 *n.*, 231, 318, 348

anugraha, 51, 52
anugrahasarga, 502
anumāna, 426, 427, 487
anumiti, 178 *n.*
anupalabdhi, 426, 428
anuśāsana parva, 447
anuvṛtti, 224
anuvṛtti-viṣayaka, 224
anuvṛtty-aviṣasayaka-jñāna, 224
anu-vyavasāya, 467
anvaya, 231
anvaya-vyatireki, 227, 228, 229, 427
Anvayārtha-prakāśikā, 197 *n.*
Anvayārya, 384
Anvayārya Dīkṣita, 384
anvitā-bhidhāna, 233; Veṅkaṭa, its upholder, 233
anvitā-bhidhāna-vāda, 233
anyathā-jñāna, 485
anyathā-khyāti, 179, 180, 181, 183, 184, 185, 186, 187, 210, 237, 239, 241, 242, 244, 245, 398
anyathāvabhāsaḥ, 179
anvyayi, 229
anyonyā-bhāva, 428
anyonyā-śraya, 329
anyūnānatirikta, 46
Aṅgirā, 482
Aṅguttara Nikāya, 516 *n*, 518, 524
Añjali-vaibhava, 127
Aṇṇa-guru, 115
Aṇṇavāyyaṅgācārya, 133
Aṇṇayācārya, 111, 137
Aṇṇayārya, 115, 130, 132, 133, 396
aṇu, 498
ap, 49 *n.*
apara, 489
aparā, 509
aparigraha, 61 *n.*
aparokṣa, 227, 367, 442
Aparyātmāmṛtācārya, 112
Apathy, 73
apavarga, 506
apāna, 59, 540
apāna vāyu, 59
apāramārthikā, 477
Aperture, 59
Apostolic, 66
Appayācārya, 122
Apyaya-dīkṣita, 114, 116, 121, 131, 133
Appeal, 56
Appearance, 52, 179, 180, 182, 187, 188, 193, 196, 199, 207, 218, 268, 290, 306, 325, 332, 333, 336, 337, 366, 367, 369, 407, 422, 471
Apperception, 80, 368, 465
Apprehension, 177, 183, 186, 215, 219, 239
apramāṇa, 247
aprameyatva, 230 *n.*
apravṛttimat, 46
aprākṛta-vapuḥ, 73
a-prāmāṇya, 202
apṛthak-siddha, 299
a-pṛthak-sthita, 35
apūrva, 303, 506
apūrvavidhi, 405 *n.*
arcāvatāra, 39 *n.*, 41
Arcir-ādi, 135 *n.*
Argument, 124, 184, 190, 289, 291, 313, 314, 503, 512, 513, 517, 546, 547; in a circle, 17
ariṣṭa, 506 *n.*
Arjuna, 39 158
artha, 62
artha-kriyā-kāritva, 436, 458
Artha-pañcaka, 135 *n.*
artha-paricchedaka, 240
artha-pariccheda-kāri, 240
arthāpatti, 128, 234, 235, 314, 426; upheld by Meghanādāri, 234-5
artha-prakāsá, 356
Artha-śāstra, 512, 532
Articles of worship, 70
Aruṇaghaṭī, 416
Aruṇādhikaraṇa-śaraṇa-vivaraṇī, 392
arvāksrotas, 501, 502
Aṛagiyas, 68, 85, 88, 89, 94, 105, 138
asamavāyi, 456
asamprajñāta, 488
asamprajñāta-samādhi, 446, 487
asamprajñāta yoga, 446
asaṃsargāgraha, 186
asaṅga, 453, 469
asat, 457
asatīva, 339
asādhāraṇa-kāraṇa, 224
Ascetic, 293, 305, 520, 523, 524, 527
Ash, 186
asmitā, 470
Asoka, 522
aspaṣṭatvāt, 537
Aspects, 311, 414, 419, 454
assāda, 513
Assembly, 482
Assertion, 313, 343, 344, 431, 432
Association, 26, 185 *n.*, 186, 187, 199, 224, 233, 284, 299, 300, 303, 308, 326, 327, 345, 389, 408, 412, 441, 469, 470, 474, 489, 493, 503, 509, 534, 535; of body, 389
Assumptions, 186 *n.*, 297, 298, 323, 338, 350, 424, 437, 439

asteya, 61
~~*asthira*, 292~~
Asti-brahmeti-śruty-artha-vicāra, 131
Astronomy, 515 *n.*
asura, 528, 529, 531 *n.*
Aṣṭādaśa-bheda-nirṇaya, 85, 86, 88, 89 *n.*, 90 *n.*, 91, 92 *n.*, 93 *n.*, 132, 138; its contents, 88 *et seq.*
Aṣṭādaśa-rahasyārtha-nirṇaya, 117
Aṣṭādaśa-rahasyārtha-vivaraṇa, 85, 86, 87 *n.*
aṣṭāṅga yoga, 24, 96, 98
Aṣṭāviṃśad-vidhātmikā, 501 *n.*
Aśvamedha-parvan, 517
a-tathā-bhūtā-rtha-jñānaṃ, 247
Atharva-Veda, 447
Atheism, 473, 479
Atheistic, 472, 480
atiprakāśa, 503
atiśaya, 203
atīndriya, 225, 354
Atomic, 7, 51, 89, 100 *n.*, 194, 281, 413, 432, 443, 444; individuals, 93; individual souis, 93; theory, 262
Atomists, 211, 264
Atoms, 128, 152, 155, 163, 183, 262, 264, 540, 541, 550
Attachment, 10, 29, 32, 34, 51, 71, 148, 287, 437, 441, 449, 450, 462, 464, 470, 506, 545
Attainment, 32, 60, 62, 70, 290, 429, 443, 445
Attention, 31, 310
Atthasālinī, 514 *n.*
Attitude, 344
Attribute, 80, 192, 193, 195, 222, 407, 413
Attribution, 325, 472
Attutayi, 98
Auditory, 308; knowledge, 5; perception, 281
Aufrecht, 127
aupādhika, 434
Author, 130
Authoritativeness, 20
Authority, 175, 517
Auto-intoxication, 82
avatāra, 38, 39, 40 *n.*, 129, 302, 401, 475
avayava, 227, 232, 263
avayavī, 263
avayavo-pacayā-pacayayor, 386
avācyatva, 230 *n.*
avāntara-vyāpāra, 203
avāstava, 436
avedinaḥ, 501
a-vedyatva, 231, 367
avibhāga, 455, 460
a-vidhi-gocaratva, 88 *n.*
avidyā, 4, 5, 29, 44, 46, 159, 160, 161, 163, 165, 169, 173, 174, 175, 176, 177, 178, 194, 196, 198 *n.*, 295, 296, 308, 316, 317, 319, 321, 322, 324, 326, 330, 331, 332, 333, 334, 335, 337, 338, 339, 343, 345, 364, 365, 366, 371, 372, 373, 374, 375, 393, 414, 421, 422, 423, 436, 441, 443, 444, 445, 468, 469, 470, 476, 477, 478, 487, 492, 500, 507, 508 *n.*; Brahman cannot assume diverse forms on account of, 176; Brahman cannot be *āśraya* of it, 176; conception of its cessation criticized, 338 *et seq.*; in relation to self-luminosity, as treated by Vijñana-Bhikṣu, 468 *et seq.*; it cannot veil Brahman, 176; its criticism by Veṅkaṭa, 330 *et seq.*; its opposition to *vidyā*, 176; Nimbārka's idea of, 411; Śaṅkara's conception refuted, 175 *et seq.*; the view of its difference from *māyā* criticized, 334 *et seq.*
avidyāyāṃ jīvaḥ jīvāda vidyā, 177 *n.*
a-visaṃvāditva, 216
a-viśada-svarūpa, 177
aviśeṣa, 499, 504
aviveka, 449
avuddhipūrvaka, 502
avyakta, 34, 36, 45, 257, 476, 477, 488, 497, 504, 510, 511
Avyakta-nṛsimhopaniṣad, 13
avyakti, 52
Avyaktopaniṣad, 13
a-vyavahita, 136
Awakened state, 178
Awareness, 184, 185 *n.*, 205, 217, 220, 248, 255, 319, 320, 321, 322, 340, 341, 344, 439
Ayodhyā, 103, 120
ayoni, 46
Ayyaṇṇa, 133
Ayyar, Sir Subrahmanya, Lectures, 64 *n.*, 65 *n.*
Ācāra-locana, 133
ācārya, 102
Ācārya-dīkṣita, 130
Ācārya-hṛdaya, 137, 138
Ācārya-pañcāśat, 117
Ācārya-viṃśati, 133
ādhāra, 454
ādhārā-kāro-pādhi, 333
ādheyatva, 298
ādhyāsika-sambandha, 423
ādhyātmikī, 507

Āditya, 20
Ādivarāhācārya, 132
Ādivarāha Vedāntācārya, 131
āgama, 14, 487, 519
Āgama-prāmāṇya, 14, 17, 98, 154, 155
āgantuka-dharmavattvam, 393
Āgaṅgā, 96
āgneya-maṇḍala, 59
Ājīvaka sect, 522
ājīvakas, 523, 524, 525
Ājīvakas, their views, 522
ājīvas, 523
ākāśa, 6, 48, 49 *n.*, 163, 164, 252, 260, 261, 263, 280, 282, 283, 284, 498, 499, 504, 510
Ākaśādhikaraṇa-vicāra, 133
Ālaya-vijñāna, 274, 275
Ālavandār, 67 *n.*, 97
Āḷvārtirunagari, 68
ānanda, 35, 154, 344, 444, 445, 486
Ānanda-dāyinī, 122, 123, 131
Ānandagiri, 105, 106, 107
Ānanda-tāratamya-khaṇḍana, 129, 133, 392
Ānanda-vallarī, 122
ānukūlyasya saṃkalpa, 92
ānvīkṣikī, 512
Āṅgirasa, 21
Āṇbillai, 105
Āṇbillai-Kaṇḍāḍai-yappan, 64
Āṇḍāl, 63, 64, 65, 66 *n.*, 67, 69, 77, 97, 109, 110, 134 *n.*
Āṇḍān lineage, 129
āparokṣya, 309
Ārādhana-krama, 122
Ārādhanā-saṃgraha, 125, 352
ārjava, 61
Ārtti-prabandha, 138
Āṟvār and Rāmānuja, difference of outlook, 112
Āṟvār Kula-śēkhara, 80 *n.*
Āṟvār literature, 91
Āṟvārs, 63, 64, 65, 66, 67, 68, 69, 74, 75, 78, 79, 83, 84, 85, 86, 88 *n.*, 89, 102, 105, 112, 124, 134, 138, 376; Āṇḍāl's filial love, 77; Aṇḍāl's love for God as Gopī, 77; the Aṟagiyas generally followed Āṟvārs, though there were differences in religious dogmas, 85; as Avatāras of, 64; castes of, 64; cessation of inclinations leads to God, 72; chronology of, 64–8; conception of bridegroom and bride, 79; difference of their devotion with that of the Śaivas, 83; difference between Āṟvārs and Aṟagiyas on religious dogmas, 85–6; distinguished from the Aṟagiyas, 68; episode of the King Kula-śēkhara, feeling oneself as wife of God, 73; fifth centum, 72–3; fourth centum, 72; God constantly wooing the devotee, 78; God fettered by His mercy, 78; God's grace, only means of salvation, 78; influence of the Purāṇic religion on the Āṟvārs, 81; lamentation for God, 73; lamentation illustrated, 74, 75, 76; love of God, ever growing, 79; meaning of, 68; Nāmm'-āṟvār's conception of soul, 79–80; Nāmm'-aṟvār's third centum, 71; ninth centum, 73; pangs for God, 71; pathological symptoms of love similar to those of the Vaiṣṇavas of the Gauḍiya school, 83; Periy-āṟvār's conception of himself as Yośodā, 77; philosophy of, 69 *et seq.*; Rādhā (Nappinäi) referred to as the consort of Kṛṣṇa, 81; reference to in Bhāgavata, 63; sources of, 64; stages of God's love, 79; summary of Śaṭhakopa's works, 70 *et seq.*; their auto-intoxication, 82; their controversy with the Vaiṣṇavas regarding religious dogmas, 84; their distinction from the Aṟagiyas, 94; their love ecstatic but not philosophic, 79; their love of God does not show signs of gross criticism, 83; their relation with the love of the Gauḍiya school, 81–2; their works divided into three rahasyas, 92; the Teṅgalai and Vaḍagalai schools represent the difference between the Āṟvārs and the Aṟagiyas, 86; they identify themselves as legendary personages associated with the life of Kṛṣṇa unlike Bhāgavata, 81; they reveal a knowledge of Purāṇic religion of Kṛṣṇa, 80; they reveal in the devotion all the principal types of emotion, 83; they visualized God everywhere through intoxication of love, 83; Tiru-maṅgaiy's filial love, 77; Tiru-maṅgaiy and Nāmm'āṟvār, difference of their love, 79; vision of God, 72; works of, 68–9
Āṟvār-Tirunagari, 103
Āṟvāric Teṅgalai school, 86
āsana, 30, 60, 61, 505
āstika, 471, 518
āstikya, 62
Āsuri Keśava, 98, 100

āśaya, 44
āśrama, 2, 11, 91, 293
āśraya, 176, 407
Aśvalāyana-smṛti, 20
ātma-caitanya, 8
ātma-khyāti, 238
ātma-nikṣepah, 92
ātma-samarpaṇa, 60
Ātma-siddhi, 207, 227
Ātman, 30, 34, 142, 173, 338, 483, 486, 502, 510, 529
ātmā, 80, 483, 485
ātmā-nubhava-lakṣaṇa-kaivalyā-khya-puruṣārthaḥ, 382
ātmāśraya, 255
ātmā vā are draṣṭavyaḥ, 8
Ātreya, 39, 106, 107, 119
Ātreya *gotra*, 109, 110, 118
Ātreyanātha, 114 *n.*, 125
Ātreyanātha sūri, 346
Ātreya Rāmānuja, 119
Ātreya varada, 132
Atri, 21; lineage, 352
ātyantika, 502, 503
āvaraṇa, 283, 369, 372
āvaraṇā-bhāva, 282
āveśāvatāra, 38, 39, 475
āyata, 514
āyatana, 515
Āyur-veda, 517

Bad, 80, 452, 521; actions, 414; deeds, 415, 444, 527
Badarī, 103
Badarī-nātha, 96
bala, 37, 56
Balabhadrācārya, 401
Baladeva, 496
Balarāma, 392, 429
bandha, 136
Bangkok, 515 *n.*
Baptism, 19
Barabar hills, 522
Barua, Dr, 521 *n.*, 524 *n.*
Basic, 475; cause, 365; consciousness, 362; reality, 449
Basis, 46, 182, 192, 332, 334, 422, 423, 439, 440, 454, 456, 468, 471, 489, 494, 515
Bath, 104
Bādarāyaṇa, 15, 17, 125, 235, 381; his so-called refutation of Pañcarātra is not correct, 17; refutes the Pañcarātras, 15
bādha, 459
bādhaka-saṃsarga-grahāṇam, 186
Bādhūla Śrīnivāsācārya, 361
bāla-loka, 513
Bāla-sarasvatī, 133
Bārhaspatya, 512, 533
Bārhaspatya-sūtra, 532
Beauty, 71, 98
Becoming, 457
Before and after, 284
Beginning, 343, 544
Beginningless, 5, 6, 26, 27, 34, 43, 51, 54, 177, 198 *n.*, 279, 284, 285, 330, 331, 339, 354, 367, 372, 373, 409, 413, 422, 423, 424, 425, 426, 444, 446, 448, 452, 467, 474, 477, 489, 497, 506, 544, 547; time, 316
Behaviour, 5, 179, 185, 187, 236, 240, 244, 246, 287
Behaviouristic action, 288
Beings, 30, 34, 42, 49, 54, 154, 190, 195, 239, 243, 312, 313, 314, 325, 339, 413, 421, 431, 436, 443 *n.*, 447, 448, 450, 452, 454, 456, 457, 465, 474, 477, 480, 483, 488, 489, 509, 524
Belief, 55, 187, 204, 290
Bell, 119 *n.*
Bellary, 399
Benares, 103
Benediction, 42
Beneficent, 52
Beneficial, 51, 62; effects, 335
Bengal, 94, 112
Bengal Asiatic Society, 401
Besnagar Column, 19
Bhadantabhāskara, 3 *n.*
Bhaddā, 522
bhadra, 30, 60
Bhagavad-ārādhana-krama, 113
Bhagavad-gītā, 97, 105, 379, 402, 482, 485
Bhagavad-guṇa-darpaṇa, 119 *n.*
Bhagavad-vishayam, 78 *n.*, 79, 79 *n.*
bhagavanmaya, 51
Bhagavat, 107
bhagavat-prīty-artham, 92
Bhagavat Senāpati Miśra, 117, 132
Bhagavatī-sūtra, 522, 524 *n.*, 525
bhagavān, 34, 107 *n.*, 475, 508 *n.*
Bhaktagrāmapūrṇa, 110
Bhaktāṅghrireṇu, 63
bhakti, 17, 19, 32, 33, 63, 63 *n.*, 93, 100, 139, 161, 292, 293, 378, 380, 382, 450, 451, 507, 509; as conjugal love, 70; as *dāsya*, 70; cult, 63; in Vijñāna Bhikṣu, 450 *et seq.*; Veṅkaṭa's views, 292 *et seq.*
bhakti-exultation, 78
Bhakti-sāra, 63, 96 *n.*

bhakti-yoga, 89, 91, 100
Bhandarkar, Sir R. G., 64 *n.*, 66, 67, 80 *n.*, 399, 402; *Report of the Search for Sanskrit Manuscripts 1882–1883*, 401
bhantikas, 182
Bharadvāja, 530
Bharadvāja *gotra*, 98
Bharadvāja lineage, 133, 440
Bharadvāja Saṃhitā, 379
Bhartṛhari, 108
Bhartṛmitra, 108
Bhartṛ-prapañca, 108, 471
Bharuchi, 139
Bhaṭṭa Bhāskara, 1, 2, 3 *n.*
Bhaṭṭanātha, 137, 138
Bhaṭṭārakaguru, 210, 214 *n.*, 226, 229, 234; his view of doubt, 210
Bhaṭṭārya, 134
Bhaṭṭojī Dīkṣita, 1, 19 *n.*; speaking of Bhāskara, 1
Bhāgavata cult, 19
Bhāgavata school, 3 n.
Bhāgavata-māhātmya, 63
Bhāgavata-purāṇa, 40 *n.*, 63, 63 *n.*, 66, 67, 80 *n.*, 81, 402, 451, 518
Bhāgavata-yoga, 24, 32
Bhāgavatas, 2, 15, 17, 19, 20, 71, 450, 475 *n.*, 518 *n.*, 527 *n.*; not low castes, 17
Bhāguri, 516, 531
Bhāmatī, 4, 196, 196 *n.*, 476
Bhāskara, 1, 2, 3, 3 *n.*, 4, 6, 8, 9, 10, 11, 106, 108, 113, 124, 155, 192, 193, 194, 195, 197, 200, 201, 301, 305, 413, 429, 433, 434, 472, 497; a tri-daṇḍin, 1; *bhakti*, nature of, 10; Brahman as transcendent, 10; Brahman not exhausted in transformation, 10; deeds, relation of, with knowledge, 7; difference between his view and that of Śaṅkara, 2; epistemology distinguished from Śaṅkara, 9; his *bhedābheda* concept, 6; his causality view of, 4–5; his date, 3; his difference with Kumārila, 8; his sea and wave illustration, 6; his view, God and soul relation of, 6; his view of Brahman, 301; his view of God, 155; his views contrasted with those of Rāmānuja, 192 *et seq.*; his views criticized from the Nimbārka point of view, 431 *et seq.*; *jīvan-mukti*, denial of, 10–11; *jñāna-samuccita-karma*, his view of, 8; knowledge, his view of, 8; liberation, nature of, 9; liberation of duties, 9; *mukti*, way to, 10; relation of *Brahma-sūtra* with *Mīmāṃsā-sūtra*, his concept of, 7; relation to Pañcarātras, p. 2; *sat cit* and *ananta*, identity of, 10; soul nature of, 7; soul relation with God, 7; substance and qualities, view of, 10; Śaṅkara, refutation of, 4–5; transcendent Brahman, nature of, 10; world as spiritual, 10
Bhāskara Bhaṭṭa, 3
Bhāskara-bhāṣya, 2 *n.*, 4, 6 *n.*, 7, 8 *n.*
Bhāskaradeva, 3 *n.*
Bhāskaradīkṣita, 3 *n.*
Bhāskaramiśra, 3 *n.*
Bhāskaranṛsiṃha, 3 *n.*
Bhāskarasena, 3 *n.*
Bhāskaraśāstrī, 3 *n.*
Bhāskarācārya, 3
Bhāskarācārya, Paṇḍita, 3 *n.*
Bhāskarānandanātha, 3 *n.*
Bhāskarāraṇya, 3 *n.*
Bhāskarites, 431
bhāṣya, 88 *n.*, 107 *n.*, 108, 109, 113, 114, 115, 116, 118, 138, 139, 181 *n.*, 196, 298, 352, 395, 400, 514
bhāṣya-kāra, 108
Bhāṣya-prakāśikā-dūṣaṇoddhāra, 114
Bhāṣya-vivaraṇa, 128
bhāṣyopodghāta, 106
Bhāṭṭa, 248
Bhāudājī, Dr 3
bhāva, 52
bhāva-jā, 29
bhāvaka, 50, 51, 53
Bhāva-prabodha, 114 *n.*, 125
Bhāva-pradīpikā, 116, 131
Bhāva-prakāśa, 122
Bhāva-prakāśikā, 114, 122, 131
Bhāva-prakāśikā-dūṣaṇoddhāra, 130
bhāva-rūpā'-jñāna, 361
bhāvya, 50, 51, 53
bheda, 6, 194, 223, 417
Bheda-darpaṇa, 115, 384, 388, 392
Bheda-maṇi, 115 *n.*, 384
Bheda-vāda, 133
bheda-vādī, 401
bhedābheda, 1, 28, 105, 107, 406, 413, 471, 472
Bhedā-bheda-vāda, 405
Bheda-dhikkāra-nyakkāra, 122
bhedāgraha, 186
Bhikṣu, 281 *n.*, 448, 450, 451, 452, 456, 460, 465, 466, 467, 468, 471, 472, 473, 474, 477, 478, 479, 487, 488

bhinnatve satyabhinna-sattākatvam, 373
bhoga, 300, 464, 485, 495
bhogya-śakti, 6
bhoktṛ, 6
Bhrānta-yogīndra, 63 *n.*
Bhṛgu, 482
Bhutan, 68 *n.*
Bhū-gola-nirṇaya, 122
Bhūmi, 41, 57, 511
Bhūri Bhaṭṭa, 402
Bhūri Śrīśailapūrṇa, 98, 109
bhūta-modifications, 183
Bhūtapurī, 100, 101
bhūtas, 163, 182, 260 *n.*, 261, 502, 504, 507, 510
bhūta-sarga, 502 *n.*
Bhūtatt'-āṟvār, 63, 64, 65, 68, 66 *n.*, 68 *n.*, 134 *n.*
Bhūtayogīndra, 63 *n.*
bhūta-yoni, 25
bhūtādi, 48, 163, 259, 260, 261, 498, 499, 504, 510
bhūtāni, 512
bhūtātmā, 25
bhūti, 44
bhūti-bhedāḥ, 44
bhūti-śakti, 42
bhūty-aṃśaḥ, 44
bhūyo-darśana-gamya, 228
Bibliotheca Indica, 483 *n.*
Bile, 182
bindu, 58
Bio-motor, 59, 258; faculties, 540
Birth, 33, 51, 287, 290, 294, 370, 382, 431, 462, 549
Bison, 234
Bittideva, 104, 113
bījāṅkura, 177
Black Rati, 38
Blind, 367; man, 390
Bliss, 16, 34, 35, 41, 50, 51, 52, 71, 144, 154, 175, 295, 302, 304, 311, 365, 366, 404, 408, 413, 414, 441, 442, 443, 445, 448, 463, 474, 485, 486, 489, 494
Blissful, 62; emotion, 71; nature, 383
Blissfulness, 325
Blue colour, 153
Boar, 38
boddhā, 48
bodha-lakṣaṇa, 10
Bodhāyana, 105, 108, 109, 139, 180, 181 *n.*, 192, 350
Bodhāyana-vṛtti, 102, 103 *n.*
Bodhisattva, 513
Bodily charms, 83
Body, 7, 31, 33, 41, 55, 58, 59, 60, 80, 139, 191, 192, 194, 195, 199, 201, 288, 289, 291, 295, 297, 298, 300, 301, 302, 308, 325, 327, 352, 365, 369, 391, 412, 414, 444, 448, 450, 451, 456, 462, 475, 504, 522, 526, 528, 529, 540, 541, 542, 543, 544, 546, 548, 549, 550; of God, 71
Bombay, 200 *n.*
Bond 26; of sympathy, 71
Bondage, 5, 7, 24, 27, 44, 51, 57, 136, 201, 292, 295, 334, 364, 365, 370, 407, 410, 412, 414, 421, 432, 433, 437, 453, 457, 460, 476, 477, 491, 495, 506, 509
Brahmā, 306, 473, 474
brahma-bhakti 507
brahma-carya, 61
Brahma-causality, 116, 388, 396
brahma-cārin, 124
Brahma-character, 366
Brahmadatta, 108, 291; his view of Brahman, 291
Brahma-experience, 465; treatment by Vijñāna Bhikṣu, 465
Brahmahood, 17, 405 *n.*, 506
Brahma-jñāna-nirāsa, 130
Brahma-knowledge, 2, 4, 89, 305, 308, 326, 336, 337, 435, 466
Brahma-lakṣaṇa-vāda, 133
Brahma-lakṣaṇa-vākyārtha, 130
Brahma-lakṣaṇa-vākyārtha-saṃgraha, 130
brahma-laya, 509
Brahma-manifestation, 373
Brahman, 1, 2, 5, 6, 7, 8, 9, 10, 12, 20, 26, 28, 30, 31, 33, 34, 35, 37, 39, 68, 89, 93, 106, 116, 126, 136 *n.*, 153, 154, 155, 156, 165, 166, 174, 175, 176, 177, 178, 192, 193, 194, 195, 196, 197, 198, 199, 200, 201, 208, 211, 224, 239, 291, 295, 299, 300 *n.*, 301, 302, 303, 307, 309, 312, 313, 314, 315, 316, 317, 319, 320, 322, 323, 325, 326, 328, 329, 330, 331, 332, 333, 334, 335, 336, 337, 338, 340, 343, 345, 350, 351, 352, 365, 366, 367, 369 371, 372, 373, 374, 381, 383, 384, 385, 386, 387, 388, 389, 391, 392, 394, 395, 396, 397, 398, 404, 405, 406, 407, 408, 409, 412, 415, 416, 417, 418, 419, 420, 421, 422, 423, 424, 429, 430, 432, 433, 434, 435, 436, 437, 438, 439, 440, 445, 446, 447, 448, 452, 454, 455, 456, 457, 458, 460, 461, 462, 464, 465, 466, 477, 483, 484,

Brahman (*cont.*)
485, 486, 487, 492, 493, 494, 495, 497, 506, 509; material and efficient cause, 301
Brahmanandin, 106, 107
Brahman-consciousness, 317
Brahmanhood, 383 *n.*
Brahmanic, 515 *n.*
Brahman of Śaṅkara, 396
Brahman's nature, 397
Brahmaṇa, 527
brahma-randhra, 31, 59
Brahma-rātra, 23
brahma-samasattāka-vikārā-ṅgīkārāt, 396
Brahma-saṃhitā, 40 *n.*; *avatāras* in, 40 *n.*
Brahma-sarga, 25
Brahma-state, 468
Brahma-sūtra, 1, 3, 4, 7 *n.*, 15, 17, 102, 105, 107, 108, 113, 116, 117, 118, 124, 125, 126, 133, 139, 195, 196, 305, 349, 350, 381, 402, 404, 405 *n.*, 406 *n.*, 440, 454, 465, 466, 472, 478, 479, 480, 482, 496, 517 *n.*, 548
Brahma-sūtra-bhāṣya-pūrva-pakṣa-saṃgraha-kārikā, 117
Brahma-sūtra-bhāṣyā-rambha-prayoyana-samarthana, 118
Brahma-sūtra-bhāṣya-saṃgraha-vivaraṇa, 118
Brahma-sūtra-bhāṣya-vyākhyā, 117, 130
Brahma-sūtra-bhāṣyopa-nyāsa, 117, 125
Brahma-sūtra-dīpikā, 118, 133
Brahma-sūtrārtha-saṃgraha, 108, 116, 130
Brahma-śabdārtha-vicāra, 130, 131
Brahma-śakti-vāda, 133
Brahmatantra-jiyar, 111
Brahma-vidyā-kaumudī, 115
Brahma-vidyā-vijaya, 117, 126
Brahma-viṣṇu, 497
Brahmā, 12, 13, 25, 38, 40 *n.*, 43, 45, 52, 232, 475, 499, 503, 504, 505, 507, 510
Brahmā-jñāna-vādī, 177 *n.*
brahmāṇḍa, 38
Brahmāṇḍa-purāṇa, 20
brahmātmatva, 431
Brahminic, 2, 19
Brahmins, 14, 17, 1 *n.*, 97, 441 *n.*, 516, 517, 518, 521, 549
brahmī, 47
brahmopāsanam, 382
brāhma, 502
Breath, 60
Breath-control, 23
Bṛhad-āraṇyaka Upaniṣad, 494, 519, 519 *n.*, 528, 529
Bṛhad-āraṇyako-paniṣat-prakāśikā, 126
Bṛhaj-jātaka, 523
Bṛhaspati, 12, 140 *n.*, 516, 531, 532, 533
Bṛhaspati-sūtra, 531
Bridegroom, 79, 378
Brindaban, 63, 120, 440
Buddha, 39, 505, 522
Buddhaghoso, 512, 513, 520, 521 *n.*, 522, 524 *n.*
buddhi, 7, 43, 47, 49, 56, 80, 144, 147, 148, 163, 449, 453, 464, 465, 466, 467, 468, 469, 470, 476, 480, 486, 490, 491, 494, 495, 499 *n.*, 503, 506, 507, 508; in relation to *sukha-duḥkha* in Vijñāna Bhiksu, 464
Buddhism, 143, 516
buddhi-states, 467
Buddhist doctrine of momentariness, refutation by Veṅkaṭa, 268 *et seq.*
Buddhist theory, 262
Buddhist view, 251–2, 541
Buddhistic doctrines, 518
Buddhistic literature, 520
Buddhistic texts, 518
Buddhists, 1, 129, 205, 216, 236, 238, 254, 255, 268, 269, 270, 271, 275, 276, 282, 398, 424, 443, 471, 512, 513, 518, 519, 525, 527, 538, 539, 540, 541, 543, 546; view of invalidity inadmissible, 236
buddhi-tattva, 25
Bukka I, King, 121
Bukka's son Kampana, 121
Burning capacity, 249
Burning object, 249

Caitanya, 403
caitanya, 8, 81, 141, 451
Caitanya-caritāmṛta, 403 *n.*
Cakāra-samarthana, 123
cakra, 58, 60, 64
cakṣus, 502
Calmness, 52
Campakeśa, 115, 117, 131
Caṇḍa-māruta, 117, 123, 126, 129
Capacity, 149, 349, 354; of fire, 249
Caraka-saṃhitā, 516
carama, 135 *n.*
Carama-guru-nirṇaya, 125
Carama-śloka-churukku, 94
Caramopāya-tātparya, 122
Cardinal faith, 86

Cardinal points, 85, 86
Carnatica, 104 *n.*
Carnatik, 63
Case, 288
Case-ending, 239
Case-relation, 233
Caste, 17, 42, 43, 49, 293, 416, 441 *n.*, 518, 549
Caste-distinction, 44
Caste-duties, 33, 414
Casuistry, 514, 515
Catalogue, 400
Catalogue of Sanskrit Manuscripts in the Private Libraries of the North-Western Provinces, 379, 400 *n.*, 401 *n.*
Catalogus Catalogorum, 127
Category, 2, 30, 36, 37, 45, 46, 47, 48, 49, 80, 89, 98, 128, 129, 150, 223, 224, 239, 257, 258, 297, 328, 339, 340, 350, 351, 353, 354, 355, 417, 428, 429, 435, 480, 503, 540; of difference, 417; of time, 284
Catholic, 104
Catuḥ-ślokī, 94 *n.*, 98, 99, 123
Catuḥ-ślokī-vyākhyā, 131
Catur-vyūha, 509 *n*
Causal, 46, 265, 341, 344, 470, 473, 484; agents, 267; constituent, 267; doctrine, 199; efficiency, 268, 271, 276, 436, 458; entity, 371; instruments, 203; material, 465; moment, 273; movement, 502; nature, 395; operation, 205, 263, 265, 266, 267, 270, 272, 276, 343; principle, 192; qualities, 256; relations, 279, 342; state, 42, 200, 344; substance, 344, 391
Causality, 53, 128, 205, 206, 276, 278, 299, 300, 389, 396, 455, 456, 459, 470
Causation, 354, 397, 456, 541, 543
Cause, 4, 8, 9, 24, 42, 46, 58, 174, 179, 181, 184, 186, 187, 189, 190, 192, 193, 194, 195, 197, 198, 199, 204, 206, 232, 256, 257, 260 *n.*, 266, 267, 270, 271, 276, 277, 278, 279, 293, 295, 299, 306, 310, 330, 333, 339, 341, 342, 343, 350, 354, 365, 366, 385, 388, 389, 396, 406, 410, 413, 433, 441, 447 *n.*, 448, 452, 454, 455, 456, 460, 465, 469, 470, 472, 473, 479, 483, 493, 495, 503, 509, 520, 524, 539 *n.*, 541, 542, 543, 545, 547; and effect, 258; qualities, 257
Causeless, 46, 354
Cause-moment, 273
Cause-space, 273
Cause-time, 273
Cārvāka, 139, 140, 276, 280, 282, 286, 288, 289, 432, 512, 515, 516, 522, 528, 531, 533, 536, 538, 539, 541, 544, 546, 549, 550; contention, 535; criticisms against by Jains and Naiyāyikas, 546; criticisms of the Buddhists, against, 541 *et seq.*; doctrine, 546; his logic, 533 *et seq.*; his logic criticized by Jayanta, Udayana, etc., 537 *et seq.*; logic, 533; other criticisms against, 548 *et seq.*; reference to, 531 *et seq.*; their arguments for denying soul, 289 *n.*; types of, 539
Cārvārka-ṣaṣti, 531 *n.*
Cārvākism, 139
Cease, 310
Central question, 50
Centum, 72
Ceremonial duties, 160
Ceremonials, 41
Cessation, 27, 28, 52, 61, 136, 177, 287, 292, 293, 295, 310, 321, 338, 339, 365, 366, 369, 371, 372, 374, 393, 445, 453, 463, 470, 486, 506, 523, 572; of bondage, 364; of rebirth, 70
ceṣṭā, 300
chala, 512
Chalāri-smṛti, 103
Change, 196, 313, 314, 321, 325, 338, 344, 443 *n.*, 445, 447, 456, 457, 458, 485, 488, 489, 490, 493, 495
Changeable, 313, 323
Changeless, 34, 61, 195, 389, 396, 457
Character, 46, 180, 181, 193, 194, 195, 209, 210, 297, 311, 312, 315, 319, 323, 324, 331, 332, 333, 334, 336, 351, 407, 408, 411, 430, 465, 534, 548
Characteristic, 185, 207, 209, 212, 300, 317, 325, 350, 426, 450; quality, 317
Characterless, 166, 195, 356
Charity, 86, 87
Charm of God, 83
Chāndoagyopaniṣad-bhāṣya, 117
Chāndogya, 101, 106, 528, 529, 530
Chāndogya Upaniṣad, 3, 106, 107, 126, 517, 528; heretics referred to, in, 528
Chāndogyo-paniṣad-prakāśikā, 126
Chemical change, 141
Chimerical, 179, 191, 241, 271, 312, 314, 319, 331, 339, 406, 435; entities, 239, 243, 271, 333, 344, 440; objects, 274; theory, 266

Choice, 304
Chowkhamba, 202 *n.*, 209 *n.*
Chronological, 68
cic-chakti, 32, 416
cidaṃśa, 301
cin-mātram, 165
cintanātmakam indriyam, 48
Circular, 255
Circulation, 59
Circumstances, 182, 320, 323, 349, 430
cit, 154, 391, 396, 397, 444
citi, 503, 504
Cit-prakaraṇa, 160 *n.*
Citsukha, 111, 468
citsukhācārya, 318, 482
citta, 281 *n.*, 480, 499 *n.*
citta-vṛtti-nirodha, 62, 506
Class-characters, 167, 232, 534
Class-concept, 224, 226 *n.*, 297, 436
Class-notions, 61
Classification, 30, 129, 212
Clay, 3, 4 *n.*, 199; materials, 3
Clearness, 217
Clinging to God, 87
Closed souls, 501
Cloth, 190, 193, 256, 265
Clouds, 50
Code of duties, 88
Coeval, 183
Co-existence, 273, 543
Co-existent, 286, 423
Co-extensive, 291, 292
Cognate, 43
Cognition, 8, 9, 217, 218, 248, 289, 310, 311, 315, 318, 320, 323, 325, 335, 347, 360, 368, 410, 411, 428
Cognitive, 31, 49, 61, 318, 466; experiences, 300; characters, 241; operation, 359; process, 467; relation, 358; sense, 25, 48, 280; situation, 467
Coherence, 300; of qualities, 254
Coimbatore, 121
Cola, 65, 67, 94, 98, 103, 113, 523; kings, 104
Collocating entities, 275
Collocation, 141, 152, 204, 206, 264, 292, 354, 360, 473; of accessories, 354; of causes, 203
Collocative agents, 342
Collocative causes, 248
Colony, 42, 43
Colophon of Mitra, 403
Colour, 61, 141, 167, 182, 251, 389; perception, 280
Colour-data, 253
Colour-datum, 253
Combinations, 326
Commands, 303
Commentary, 1 *n.*, 3, 99, 102 *n.*, 106, 107, 108, 114, 115, 116, 117, 120, 122, 123, 125, 126, 127, 130, 131, 132, 134, 138, 214, 260 *n.*, 305, 349, 402, 403, 440, 460, 476, 482, 516, 517 *n.*, 518, 523, 532; literature, 86
Commentator, 107 *n.*, 196, 444
Commission, 398
Common, 207
Communication, 309, 428
Communion, 70, 99, 376
Companions, 83
Compendium, 135
Complete, 36, 296
Complex, 188, 193; feeling, 90
Comprehension, 419
Computation, 96
Conative, 49; organs, 412; senses, 31, 61, 280, 504
Conceit, 173
Concentration, 30
Concept, 42, 53, 185, 186, 195, 254, 264, 297, 340, 344, 390, 406, 434, 435
Conception, 45, 192, 195, 295, 297, 301, 321, 328, 333, 335, 341, 351, 389, 397, 398, 447, 448, 451, 456, 462, 468, 504
Conceptual cognitions, 341
Conceptual forms, 311
Conch-shell, 179, 180, 181, 182, 183, 184, 185, 186, 187, 188, 208, 210, 211, 241, 244, 247, 253, 254, 270, 337, 346, 368, 371, 408; silver, 179, 184, 237, 246, 312, 314, 335, 336, 340, 343, 344, 398; silver illusion, 185 *n.*, 186, 188
Conciliatory, 20
Conclusions, 211, 319, 409, 451, 458, 469, 486, 495
Concomitance, 225, 226, 228, 229, 230, 263, 273, 319, 427, 438, 513, 533, 534, 535, 536, 538
Concrete, 49, 187
Condition, 51, 180, 181, 193, 211, 301, 306, 310, 312, 318, 323, 333, 344, 346, 412, 413, 416, 420, 421, 422, 428, 432, 433, 434, 461, 463, 468, 473, 476, 489, 492, 493, 534, 535; of reality, 243
Conditional, 289, 390, 533, 538; qualities, 285, 286
Conditioned, 193, 446, 474
Conduct, 16, 550

Conflict of knowledge, 212 *n.*
Confusion, 25, 140
Conglomeration, 37, 163, 252, 262, 275, 278, 288
Conjeevaram, 68
Connection, 43 *n.*
Connotation, 299
Conscious, 27, 31, 41, 290, 416, 467, 491; energy, 459; entities, 89; principle, 29; state, 540, 543, 546
Consciousness, 368, 369, 373, 377, 406, 407, 413, 420, 429, 438, 439, 440, 452, 454, 459, 460, 462, 463, 467, 469, 479, 486, 507, 519, 529, 540, 541, 543, 545, 546, 547, 548, 549; its character, 141, 142
Considerations, 420
Consonance, 44, 58
Consort, 70, 81
Constancy, 29
Constituent conscious-entities, 287
Constituents, 188, 256, 310, 323, 335, 414, 415, 419, 424, 430, 455, 458
Constituted entity, 256
Construction, 191, 195
Contact, 263, 270, 281 *n.*, 316, 453, 466
Container, 456
Contemplation, 68
Contemporary, 131 *n.*, 135
Content, 250 *n.*, 310, 329, 336, 439; of awareness, 185 *n.*; of knowledge, 242, 247, 314
Contentions, 211, 311, 315, 348
Contentless, 250, 310, 311
Contentment, 61, 506
Contents of thoughts, 198
Contiguity, 46, 296, 316, 324, 325, 421; of consciousness, 240, 420
Contraction, 393
Contradiction, 9, 186, 192, 210, 239, 269, 314, 318, 321, 327, 336, 337, 342, 374, 386, 398, 435, 436, 451, 459, 470, 498, 502 *n.*; of knowledge, 179
Contradictory, 17, 207, 211, 269, 310, 319, 337, 421
Contrary, 322; conclusion, 230
Contributions, 346
Control, 30, 32, 58, 303, 430, 443 *n.*, 444, 499; of mind, 29
Controller, 99, 200, 386, 415, 429, 430, 451, 478
Controversialist, 406
Controversy, 68, 128, 130, 328, 416
Conviction, 54, 55
Co-operation, 409
Corporeal structure, 431
Correct, 180
Correction, 179
Correspondence, 247, 348, 357; theory, 246
Corroboration, 340, 341, 357
Cosmic, 443 *n.*, 475, 482, 492, 509, 510; affairs, 475; egg, 504; matter, 163
Cosmogony, 515 *n.*
Cosmological, 474
Cotton-seed, 273
Counterpart, 58
Couples, 38
Course, 31, 34, 51, 52, 56, 57
Cow, 234
Cowell, 515
Creation, 25, 27, 36, 38, 42, 45, 50, 51, 52, 56, 58, 116, 158, 182, 188, 192, 195, 196, 302, 443 *n.*, 444, 449, 452, 458, 460, 476, 498, 500, 501, 502, 504, 508
Creative, 50, 465, 473; activity, 452, 454; desire, 48; moment, 472
Creator, 16, 412, 476, 507
Creatures, 447 *n.*
Creed, 433
Criterion, 314
Criticism, 76, 112, 116, 179, 215, 217, 304, 339, 342, 429, 433, 478, 479, 518, 533
Crooked, 158
Cults, 81
Currency, 95
Customs, 2
Cūlikopaniṣad, 480
Cycle, 41, 51, 446, 481, 490
Cymbals, 80

dakṣiṇa, 381 *n.*
Dakṣiṇa-kalārya, 381, 382, 383, 384
Dancer, 85
Dantivarman, 67
daṇḍa-nīti, 532
daṇḍin, 524 *n.*
Darkness, 178
darśana, 463, 533
Daśaratha, 429, 522
Daśa-ślokī, 399, 400, 403
daśāvat, 251
Data, 210, 428
Dattātreya, 40 *n.*
Dattātreyopaniṣad, 13
Date-juice, 226
Datum, 287
Davids, 515

dayā, 57, 61
Dayārāmadeva, 402
Dāmodara, 39
Dāmodara Gosvāmī, 399
dāna, 33, 61
Dāśarathi, 98, 102, 104, 109, 110, 113
Dāsārya, 63 *n.*
dāsya, 70
Dead, 550
Death, 69, 291, 431, 447, 519, 530, 531, 536, 539, 548, 550
Death-coma, 79
Decay, 447 *n.*, 454, 547
Decision, 210
Deduction, 314
Deeds, 7, 15, 33, 54, 61, 290, 292, 299, 301, 303, 349, 388, 415, 429, 444, 452, 489, 513 *n.*, 521, 524, 528
Deep concentration, 22
Deep emotion, 378
Deep sleep, 142, 151, 178
Defect, 175, 177, 179, 182, 184, 185 *n.*, 203, 230, 238, 331, 332, 334, 336, 338, 356, 430, 437, 439, 442
Defectlessness, 250
Defects of organs, 181
Defence, 300
Definable, 230
Definite effects, 279
Definition, 128, 217 *n.*, 221, 232, 295, 298, 299, 300, 318, 345, 348, 373, 390, 424, 448, 462, 519, 537; of error, 247; of validity, 248
dehātmavādins, 528
Deity, 31, 38, 39, 41, 58, 60, 126, 295, 303
Delirious, 79
Deliverance, 376
Delusion, 325
Delusive, 45
Demerit, 15, 153, 453
Demons, 25
Demonstrable, 230
Denial, 186
Dependence, 55, 272, 299
Descartes, 202 *n.*
Description, 52, 436
Desires, 7, 33, 34, 44, 45, 48, 61, 92, 146, 160, 191, 296, 298, 303, 350, 416, 429, 441, 463, 472, 503, 504, 505, 506, 529
Destiny, 43, 45, 444, 461, 501, 502
Destroyer, 499, 507
Destructible, 199, 373, 425
Destruction, 26, 33, 38, 51, 52, 58, 178, 239, 271, 272, 308, 314, 344, 353, 365, 407, 410, 428, 442, 443 *n.*, 454, 469, 476, 550
Destructive agents, 266
Deśikācārya, 116, 131
Detachment, 442
Determinate, 166, 220, 311, 466; knowledge, 216, 217, 221, 224, 340; object, 177
Determinateness, 218
Determination of validity, 357
Determinations, 42, 113, 504
Deussen, 108 *n.*
devadatta, 59, 60
Devakī Śrī, 95
Devamannātha, 102 *n.*, 110
Devanātha, 133
Deva-nāyaka-pañcāśat, 122
Devarāja, 110, 111, 114, 138
Devarājaguru, 137, 138
Devarāja Sūri, 122
Devarājācārya, 123, 127
Devarāṭ, 102 *n.*, 110
deva-yāna, 517
Devācārya, 401, 404
Devācārya, Paṇḍita Anantarāma, 399
Devādevī, 69
Development, 42, 49
Deviprasad Paṇḍita, 400 *n.*
Devī, 57
Devotee, 28, 38, 39 *n.*, 55, 70, 82, 89, 90, 99, 129, 337, 378, 379, 405, 442, 491
Devotion, 10, 13, 32, 61, 70, 78, 82, 84, 88, 89, 100, 129, 134, 161, 442, 450, 451; to God, 89
Devotional, 69, 293; development, 81; faiths, 81; Devotional songs, 83
dhanañjaya, 59
Dhanurdāsa, 104
Dhanvantari, 40 *n.*
Dharma, 40 *n.*, 47, 62, 124, 125, 153, 254, 294, 349, 394, 405, 453, 503, 505
Dharmadevācārya, 404
Dharmakureśa, 133
Dharmarājādhvarīndra, 9, 204, 216
dharma-sādṛśya, 224
Dharma-śāstras, 21
dharmatva, 254
Dharmarāja, 228
dhāraṇa, 61
dhāraṇā, 30, 505
Dhenu, 52
dhī-sphuṭatā, 217
dhoti, 522
Dhruva, 39 *n.*
dhruvā-nusmṛti, 293
dhṛti, 57, 61, 510
dhūma-dhūmatva, 226 *n.*
dhūmatva, 535
dhūrta cārvāka, 516, 539

dhvaṃśā-bhāva, 428
dhyāna, 10, 30, 61, 388, 487, 505
dhyānādinā paricaryā, 10
Dialectic, 239, 426
Dialectical, 111, 194, 304, 437; analysis, 112; criticism, 277
Dialogues of the Buddha, 512 *n.*, 514 *n.*, 515 *n.*, 520 *n.*, 521 *n.*
Dictum, 320
Didactic poem, 121
Difference, 6, 28, 30, 180, 181, 182, 184, 185, 186, 187, 188, 192, 193, 194, 195, 204, 220 *n.*, 228, 266, 303, 312, 322, 330, 331, 342, 343, 350, 351, 353, 354, 355, 356, 359, 383, 405, 411, 413, 417, 418, 419, 422, 433, 434, 435, 436, 443, 448, 455, 456, 471, 480, 485, 486, 489, 536, 542, 550; conception of the Nimbārkas school of, 417 *et seq.*
Difference-in-identity, 432, 433
Differenceless, 406, 420
Differencelessness, 167
Different, 42, 302, 330, 336, 339, 397, 406, 413, 416, 441; order, 419
Different-from-existent-and-non-existent, 339
Differentia, 212, 429
Differentiating characteristic, 185 *n.*
Differentiation, 200, 462, 479
Difficulty, 192
Digamvara Jains, 523, 524
Digamvaras, 523
dik, 163, 283, 284
Dilation, 444
Dina-caryā, 137
Direct, 309, 465; intuition, 363; knowledge, 217, 312; perception, 308
Disappearance, 309
Disciple, 98, 102, 110, 114, 122, 123, 126, 138, 522
Discipline, 28, 29, 33, 442
Disciplined, 32
Discrimination, 292
Discriminative, 49; knowledge, 52
Discussions, 123, 352, 418
Disfavour, 51, 52, 159, 160, 164
Disinclination, 33, 47, 52, 292, 442; of mind, 29
Displeasure, 291, 303, 304
Disposition, 54
Disputation, 515, 517, 518, 519
Dissipation, 287
Dissociation, 393
Dissolution, 36, 45, 49, 50, 158, 196, 301, 314, 450, 458, 461, 466, 469, 493, 498, 521; of doubt, 390
Distant perception, 254
Distinct perception, 254
Distinction, 47, 181, 185 *n.*, 186 *n.*, 288, 307, 331, 411, 419, 434, 449, 485, 491, 494
Distinctive differences, 167
Distinctness, 254
diṣṭika, 518
Diverse forms, 36
Diversity, 196
Divine, 41, 472; beauty, 136; entity, 485; functions, 38; grace, 84, 378; love, 451
Divine Wisdom, 80 *n.*
Divine Wisdom of the Drâviḍa Saints, 78, 79 *n.*
Divinity, 450
Division, 208
divya, 214 *n.*
Divya-prabandha, 64, 130, 134, 135, 137, 138
Divya-prabandha-vyākhyā, 131
Divya-sūri-carita, 64, 94, 95, 105, 113 *n.*
Divya-sūri-prabhāva-dīpikā, 118, 132
Divyāvadāna, 514, 524 *n.*
Dīghà, 515 *n.*, 521
Dīgha Nikāya, 514, 520, 524, 525
Dīkṣita, 19 *n.*
Dīpa-prakāśa, 135
Dīpa-sāra, 128 *n.*
dīpti, 505
Docility, 54
Doctrinal, 305
Doctrine, 28, 43, 50, 55, 86, 192, 195, 196, 297, 330, 334, 338, 340, 346, 349, 406, 422, 427, 430, 434, 472, 483, 484, 512 *n.*, 516, 517, 518, 519, 521, 522, 523, 525, 526, 527, 528, 529, 530, 539, 546, 548, 550; of *bhakti*, 450; of causality, 276; of *kāla*, 448 *n.*; of *prakṛti*, 478
Doḍḍyācārya, 121 *n.*
Dogmas, 303
Domestic life, 62
Dormant, 56
doṣa, 165, 175, 184, 188, 238
Doubt, 207, 208, 209, 210, 211, 212, 213, 215, 236, 241, 251; its analysis, 211; its classification, 213; itself indubitable, 236; Nyāya view of it, 207 *n.*; Veṅkaṭa's conclusive remarks on, 208 *et seq.*; Veṅkaṭa's criticism of Nyāya view, 207–8; Veṅkaṭa's special treatment of it, 207 *et seq.*; Veṅkaṭa's treatment similar to that of Descartes, 202

Doubtful property, 213
Dramatic action, 82
Dramiḍa, 108, 139
Dramiḍācārya, 105, 106, 107, 108
Dramiḍopaniṣad-bhāṣya, 126
Dramiḍopaniṣat-tātparya, 69, 70 *n.*, 71 *n.*, 72 *n.*, 73 *n.*
Draviḍa - śruti - tattvārtha - prakāśikā, 127
Dravidian, 132, 383 *n.*
Draviḍopaniṣat-sāra, 124
Draviḍoponiṣat - sāra - ratnāvalī - vyākhyā, 127
Draviḍopaniṣat-tātparyāvalī, 124
dravya, 212 *n.*, 251, 343, 484
dravyatva, 431
Drāviḍa, 63
Drāviḍa-bhāṣya, 106
Drāviḍa texts, 383
Drāviḍa-vedānta, 137
Drāviḍācārya, 106
Dream, 4, 5, 182, 258, 325, 415, 440; experiences, 5
Dreamless sleep, 258, 310, 311, 321, 324, 325, 326, 327, 344, 362, 363, 364, 411, 412, 420, 443, 453, 467
Drunkenness, 169
dṛḍha-pūrve, 530
dṛśya, 438, 463
Dṛśyatvā-numāna-nirāsa, 133
Dualism, 330, 332, 337, 338, 339, 347, 407
Dualistic, 352, 406, 486; texts, 422
Duality, 4, 37, 154, 218, 344, 375, 417, 419, 420, 422, 431, 432, 455, 495
Duality-texts, 486
Dubrenil, Professor, 65
duḥkha, 464, 485
duḥkha-nivṛttiḥ, 486
Dulling, 256
Dullness, 328
Durupadeśa-dhikkāra, 127
Duties, 8, 11, 19, 293, 294, 307, 379, 441, 519
Dūrārtha-dūrīkaraṇa, 131
Dvaitā-dvaita, 413
Dvaya-churukku, 94
Dvayam, 135 *n.*
dveṣa, 470
Dvivedin Paṇḍita Vindhyeśvarī Prasāda, 1 *n.*
dvyaṇuka, 263
Dvāpara-yuga, 401
Dvārakā, 96
dvārāntara-nirapekṣa, 277
Dvārasamudra, 120
Dynamic, 29, 44, 456, 500; agency, 446; function, 448 *n.*; operation, 261; power, 448
Dynasty, 67
Dyutimatī, 98, 100
Ear, 167
Earliest devotees, 82
Early History of Vaiṣṇavism in South India, 64 *n.*, 67 *n.*, 81 *n.*
Earth, 41, 46, 128, 181, 208, 212, 349, 393, 447, 500, 506, 521, 540, 541, 550
Earth-matter, 342
Earth-particles, 188
Earth-substances, 188
Earthiness, 258
Ecstasy, 63 *n.*; of joy, 376
Ecstatic delight, 83
Ecstatic experiences, 79
Ecstatic joy, 376
Eddies, 83
Effect, 4, 15, 35, 49, 56, 153, 184, 189, 190, 191, 192, 193, 194, 195, 199, 229, 256, 257, 265, 266, 267, 276, 277, 291, 293, 294, 299, 303, 306, 332, 339, 341, 342, 343, 344, 359, 365, 434, 435, 443, 446, 455, 456, 460, 465, 488, 489, 493, 521, 542, 543; moment, 272, 273; state, 200, 344
Effectness, 300
Effect-stage, 299
Effect-thing, 199
Effectuation, 54
Efficacious, 28, 29
Efficiency, 203, 268, 341, 458, 524, 528
Efficient, 203; causes, 301, 386
Efforts, 56, 58, 190, 249, 290, 298, 300, 304, 333, 374, 475, 503
Ego, 13, 42, 56, 144, 208, 211, 257, 290, 345, 366, 367, 408, 409, 411, 412, 443, 547, 549
Ego-consciousness, 362, 367
Ego-entity, 325, 362, 408
Ego-experience, 334, 366, 368, 370
Ego-intuition, 409, 410, 411, 412
Ego-notion, 324, 325
Ego-substratum, 425
Egohood, 325
Egoism, 31, 51, 90, 91, 317, 375, 378, 379, 408, 468, 470, 485, 494, 505, 529
Egoistic desire, 378
ekadaṇḍins, 523, 524 *n.*
Ekaśṛṅgatanu, 40 *n.*
ekāntins, 21, 87
ekāntitva, 87
Ekārṇavaśāyin, 40 *n.*

ekātma-rūpa, 40 *n.*
Ekāyana, 21
Ekāyana veda, 21
Element, 25, 30, 42, 45, 46, 49, 181, 182, 196, 205, 337, 462, 467, 505, 506, 512, 515 *n.*, 519, 521, 522, 527, 541, 542, 544, 545, 547, 550
Elementary, 127
Emanated, 37
Emanation, 37, 198 *n.*, 447, 488, 495
Emancipated, 296, 300, 476; souls, 177 *n.*; stage, 301
Emancipation, 29, 32, 50, 52, 57, 61, 62, 71, 88, 136, 143, 145, 146, 159, 161, 177, 292, 293, 294, 295, 304, 314, 316, 324, 326, 327, 336, 364, 365, 366, 371, 374, 382, 383, 384, 388, 408, 412, 414, 420, 421, 429, 433, 442, 445, 446, 450, 453, 457, 460, 463, 476, 477, 479, 483, 485, 486, 487, 488, 491, 494, 495, 506, 509; attainable by God's grace, 304; view of the Nimbārka school of, 420 *et seq.*
Embrace, 72, 73
Emergence, 45, 48, 196
Emergents, 45, 494, 495
Emerges, 47
Emotion, 29, 82, 83, 377, 450, 451; of love, 79
Emotional analysis, 82
Emotional stage, 82
Emotional transformation, 82
Emphasis, 311, 348, 413, 434
Encyclopaedia of Religion and Ethics, 523 *n.*, 524 *n.*, 525
End, 41, 42, 51, 54, 298, 343, 352, 420, 441, 443, 486, 502
Endearment, 90
Enemy, 70
Energy, 30, 31, 37, 42, 44, 45, 48, 49, 53, 56, 57, 79, 414, 416, 418, 424, 447, 454, 458, 489, 500, 502, 524; of God, 404
Enjoyable, 6
Enjoyed, 37
Enjoyer, 6, 32, 37
Enjoyment, 291, 292, 412, 464, 485, 486, 490, 503, 529
Enlightened, 80
Enlightenment, 53
Enquiry, 197
Entirely, 194
Entirety, 432, 434
Entity, 5, 8, 9, 26, 27, 41, 42, 44, 163, 178, 179, 186, 193, 206, 210, 211, 235, 243, 253, 274, 275, 289, 299, 306, 311, 312, 313, 314, 315, 316, 317, 319, 321, 324, 325, 327, 328, 330, 332, 333, 335, 337, 339, 341, 342, 343, 344, 345, 351, 352, 353, 389, 408, 410, 416, 421, 423, 425, 430, 436, 439, 440, 448, 451, 457, 463, 464, 474, 487, 497, 503, 504, 506, 507, 539, 541
Environments, 30
Epigraphia Carnatica, 104 *n.*
Epigraphica Indica, 121 *n.*
Epigraphical, 64, 105
Epigraphists, 67
Epistemological, 9, 80, 467
Epithets, 450
Epitome, 53
Equilibrium, 29, 36, 46, 259, 460, 503, 505, 509
Equinox, 295
Erroneous, 335; manifestation, 360
Error, 179, 180, 182, 185, 186, 187, 210, 240, 241, 253, 307, 330, 334, 337, 346, 383 *n.*, 441, 469, 300; of conception, 398
Eschatological, 295, 525
Esoteric, 57, 583; doctrine, 134
Essence, 28, 31, 35, 329, 345, 393, 413, 415, 424, 426, 431, 433, 434, 436, 442, 445, 449, 455, 461, 490; of intuition, 177
Essential characteristic, 151
Essential qualities, 70
Eternal, 5, 9, 34, 35, 36, 52, 128, 161, 169, 172, 177, 192, 195, 204, 208, 209, 212, 213, 267, 279, 284, 285, 286, 291, 299, 321, 325, 330, 336, 337, 339, 345, 347, 354, 365, 373, 386, 387, 393, 394, 404, 409, 426, 433, 447, 448, 452, 454, 457, 470, 473, 481, 482, 489, 497; bliss, 404; power, 198; world, 80
Eternity, 314, 345, 393; of souls, 177 *n.*
Ethical, 525; position, 550
Ēlōrembāvāy, 77
Events, 448
Evidence, 181, 390
Evil, 5, 26, 34, 293, 294, 302, 446, 521
Evolutes, 26, 487
Evolution, 25, 26, 30, 31, 36, 49, 58, 196, 280, 299, 317, 456, 475, 482, 492, 503, 510
Evolutionary, 37, 45, 46, 445, 447, 455, 481; cause, 47; changes, 24
Excitement, 61
Excommunicated, 20
Exercises, 293

Existence, 31, 33, 41, 42, 50, 51, 182 *n.*, 184, 189, 190, 191, 192, 195, 196, 199, 297, 311, 312, 314, 315, 316, 317, 319, 323, 327, 332, 339, 345, 346, 347, 350, 352, 353, 358, 359, 406, 410, 412, 413, 415, 416, 419, 427, 430, 431, 433, 434, 435, 436, 437, 442, 443, 445, 454, 455, 459, 464, 476, 477, 489, 497, 507, 509, 518, 533
Existent, 47, 182 *n.*, 313, 339, 343, 445, 486; entity, 358
Existent-and-non-existence, 339
Expansion, 393, 444
Experience, 8, 9, 29, 34, 41, 45, 79, 83, 87, 142, 152, 166, 170, 178, 182, 185 *n.*, 186, 187, 188, 235, 236, 238, 243, 251, 253, 254, 255, 258, 262, 269, 274, 277, 287, 288, 290, 292, 301, 302, 307, 312, 315, 316, 317, 323, 324, 325, 326, 327, 328, 334, 344, 347, 360, 363, 364, 370, 383, 398, 413, 414, 415, 420, 421, 437, 441, 443, 444, 445, 448, 461, 462, 463, 464, 465, 468, 469, 474, 485, 486, 490, 495, 497, 503, 535, 538, 539, 540, 544, 545; treatment of by Vijñāna Bhikṣu, 466 *et seq.*
Experienced, 37
Experiencer, 37
Experiency, 168
Experiential, 185 *n.*; knowledge, 468, 470, 471
Expiation, 22, 23
Explanation, 212, 235, 301
Exposition, 387
Expressions, 3, 4, 34, 53, 443
Extension, 85
External, 44, 53, 341, 426; data, 253; objects, 189, 204, 205; perception, 426; world, 154, 423
Extra-mental, 204, 205
Eye, 167, 182

Fact, 189, 195, 201, 309
Factor, 204, 205, 209, 322, 453, 454, 463, 477
Faculty, 28, 462
Failure, 535
Faith, 54, 98, 304, 380 *n.*
Fallacies, 128
False, 4, 153, 155, 157, 173, 174, 180, 181, 188, 194, 198, 208, 210, 235, 252, 254, 291, 293, 296, 306, 307, 312, 313, 314, 315, 317, 324, 325, 326, 327, 329, 332, 333, 337, 340, 341, 343, 350, 351, 364, 371, 397, 406, 407, 408, 418, 424, 433, 437, 438, 440, 457, 470, 485, 486, 543, 549; appearance, 283, 325, 431, 435, 437; association, 186; *avidyā*, 332; effect, 365; imposition, 320, 325; individuality, 376; knowledge, 5, 310, 378, 408, 423, 441, 485, 491, 495; means, 326; notion, 370, 420, 437; perception, 244, 310; things, 371
Falsehood, 5, 165, 174, 186, 199, 314, 317, 326, 332, 337, 341, 357, 398, 410, 530
Falsity, 186, 309, 310, 312, 313, 314, 315, 316, 326, 350, 398, 410, 437, 436, 438, 457, 486; of the world, 199, 239
Fasting, 33
Fathomless, 79
Fault, 70
Faultless character, 248
Faulty reason, 178
Fausboll, 514 *n.*
Favour, 51, 159, 160, 164, 303
Favourable, 292
Fear, 5, 56
Features, 46 *n.*, 209
Feeling, 52, 289, 464; of dullness, 256
Female lover, 83
Females, 42
Filial affection, 83, 89, 90
Finger-ring, 186
Finite, 44, 263, 461, 483; forms, 467
Finiteness, 194
Fire, 6, 42, 181, 184, 186, 193, 208, 211, 226 *n.*, 295, 447, 451, 461, 484, 499, 500, 534, 536, 538, 540, 549, 550
Fish, 38
Fitness, 429
Five elements, 183
Flames, 276
Flow, 442
Foetus, 44, 287
Food, 80
Force, 50, 59
Forehead, 120
Forgiveness, 29
Form, 5, 34, 41, 49, 52, 56, 193, 299, 310, 322, 339, 343, 389, 445, 447 *n.*, 454, 456, 457, 458, 459, 466, 468, 476, 477, 486, 493, 495, 499, 500; of activity, 158
Formal, 364
Formless, 10, 193, 197, 310, 332, 447 *n.*
Foundation, 475; of *prapatti*, 380 *n.*; stone, 12
Fragrance, 27, 221, 222

Franke, 515
Free, 317, 461, 523 *n.*
Freedom, 78, 441, 452, 506; of will, 160
Free-will, 45, 292
Friendliness, 70
Friends, 83
Friendship, 87, 375
Fructification, 414
Fructify, 415
Fruition, 32, 33, 265, 291, 303, 443
Fruits, 26, 28, 33, 55, 290, 294, 349, 441 *n.*, 444, 445, 454, 488, 489, 504, 506, 521, 522, 548, 550
Fulfilment, 29
Fullness, 406
Function, 36, 37, 38, 49, 56 *n.*, 60, 188, 196, 312, 326, 459, 463, 465, 484, 489, 499 *n.*, 504 *n.*, 530, 548; of *Lakṣmī*, 379
Fundamental, 47, 524; tenets, 21
Funeral sacrifices, 23
Future, 446, 447, 457, 533; lives, 545

Gadā, 64
Gadya-trayam, 86 *n.*, 102, 113, 118, 123
Gaekwad, 26 *n.*
gandha, 49 *n.*, 511
Gandhamādana, 25
gandha-mātra, 510
gandha-tanmātra, 163, 260, 499
gandhavattva, 227
Ganges, 520, 525, 550
Gaṅgaikoṇḍaṣodapuram, 96
Gaṅgaikoṇḍasola, 96
Gaṅgala Bhaṭṭa, 402
Garbhopaniṣad, 480
Garga, 482
Garuḍa, 364
Garuḍavāha, 105
Garuḍa-vāhana, 64, 94
Garuḍa purāṇa, 450
Garuḍopaniṣad, 13
Gauḍa-brahmānandī, 133
Gauḍīya, 13, 50 *n.*
Gauḍīya school, 51, 81, 82, 83; pathological symptoms of love similar to that of the Āṛvārs, 83
Gauḍīya vaiṣṇavas, 82, 475; their analysis of love follows the analysis of the rhetorical school, 82; their relation with the Āṛvārs, 82
gauḥ, 47
Gaurī, 52
Gautama, 96 *n.*, 119
Gautamī, 447
Gaya, 522
Gāndhārī, 59
Gāruḍa, 20
Gāyatrī-śata-dūṣaṇī, 133
General character, 185 *n.*
General idea, 445
General opposition, 226
Generalization, 536, 538
Generator, 481
Generosity, 520
Genesis, 128, 163
Genus, 193
Germs, 44
ghaṭatva-prakārakam, 224
ghaṭatvāt, 230
ghora, 499
Ghoṣa, 102 *n.*
Gifts, 33, 54, 55, 450
Gītā, 20, 33, 40, 51, 91, 100, 118, 138, 214, 379, 380, 383, 473, 474, 529, 530; heretics referred to, in, 529
Gītā-bhāṣya, 123, 137, 214 *n.*
Gītārtha-saṃgraha, 98, 99, 100, 123, 131
Gītārtha-saṃgraha-rakṣā, 98 *n.*, 99 *n.*, 123
Gītā-saṃgraha-vibhāga, 131
Gītā-sāra-rakṣā, 131
Gītā-tātparya-dīpa, 138
Glittering, 181
Goal, 50, 445, 508
God, 5, 6, 7, 10, 11, 13, 14, 16, 26, 27, 28, 29, 30, 32, 41, 42, 44, 45, 46, 47, 48, 50, 51, 52, 53, 54, 55, 56, 57, 62, 69, 70, 71, 72, 73, 74, 78, 79, 83, 84, 85, 86 *n.*, 87, 88, 89, 90, 91, 92, 93, 95, 100, 106, 112, 119 *n.*, 125, 128, 129, 132, 135, 136, 182, 189, 190, 192, 196, 200, 203, 225, 232, 261, 286, 291, 292, 294, 295, 296, 297, 298, 299, 301, 302, 303, 307, 335, 349, 351, 352, 364, 374, 375, 376, 377, 378, 379, 380, 382, 383, 384, 385, 387, 388, 389, 391, 392, 394, 395, 398, 404, 412, 413, 414, 415, 416, 420, 422, 424, 426, 428, 429, 430, 431, 434, 437, 440, 441, 442, 443, 444, 445, 446, 447, 448, 450, 451, 452, 453, 454, 455, 456, 458, 459, 460, 462, 465, 468, 472, 473, 474, 475, 476, 478, 479, 480, 481, 482, 483, 484, 488, 489, 491, 492, 493, 498, 499, 500, 502, 505, 508, 509, 511 *n.*, 515; Bhāskāra's view, 155; His nature in Vijñāna Bhikṣu, 474 *et seq.*; in Rāmānuja's school, 296 *et seq.*; in *Vāyu Purāṇa*, 502 *et seq.*; in

God (*cont.*)
Viṣṇu Purāṇa, 498 *et seq.*; Īśvaragītā, 490 *et seq.*; proof of His existence available only from scriptural testimony, 189; Rāmānuja's view, 155 *et seq.*; refutation of Śaṅkara's view of, 153, 154; refutation of the Nyāya and Yoga view of, 157; theistic proofs, failure of, 189 *et seq.*; Veṅkata's view of, 157 *et seq.*; Yādavaprākśa's view of, 156; Yāmuna's view of it, 152 *et seq.*; Yāmuna's ultimate conclusion about, 154, 155
God Kṛṣṇa, 73
God, Nimbārka's idea of, 472 *et seq.*
God Raṅgahātha, 121
God's grace, 380
God's manifestation, 392
God's mercy, 376
God's relation with man, 70
Godhood, 50
Gods, 27, 58, 293, 474, 501, 502, 505, 525; dispute regarding the relative superiority of, 304
Goḍa, 63
Gold, 343
Gomaṭham Siṭiyāṛvān, 104
Gomathattut-tiruvinnagar-appan, 97 *n.*
gomukha, 60
Good, 5, 26, 29, 34, 62, 80, 158, 293, 304, 414, 415, 444, 452, 521, 527; deeds, 523 *n.*
Gopalacariyar, 109 *n.*
Gopana, 121
Gopāla Bhaṭṭa, 402
Gopālasūri, 18
Gopālatāpanī Upaniṣad, 13
Gopālatāta, 133
Gopālācārya, 401
Gopālottaratāpanī Upaniṣad, 13
Gopikā, 378
Gopī, 69, 74, 77, 81, 82
Gopī-nātha, 96
Goppaṇārya, 121 *n.*, 135
goptṛtva-varaṇam, 92
Goṣṭhīpūrṇa, 95, 98, 102, 109
Gosāla, 522, 523, 524, 525
Gotama, 235; logic, 234
gotra, 3
Government Oriental Manuscripts, 203
Government Oriental Manuscript Library, 69 *n.*
Govinda, 39, 101, 102 *n.*, 109
Govinda Bhaṭṭa, 100
Govinda Bhattācārya, 402
Govindadāsa, 102 *n.*
Govindācārya, 102 *n.*, 111 *n.*, 113 *n.*, 133
Govindācārya's *Life of Rāmānuja*, 110 *n.*
Govindānanda, 107
Govindārya, 127
Govindeśa, 109
Gōvindāchāryar, 78, 94, 97 *n.*, 105 *n.*
Grace, 28, 32, 52, 55, 68, 70, 72, 86, 99, 161, 413, 442, 452; of God, 70, 214 *n.*, 380
Gradation, 486
Grandson, 130, 131
Grantha, 81 *n.*
Gratitude, 109
Grāma-pūrṇa, 102
Greatness, 99, 195
Greed, 48, 87, 505
Greeks, 19
Grief, 71
Gross, 24, 31, 46, 47, 48; dimension, 264; elements, 25, 43, 498; objects, 449
Grossness, 264
Ground, 190, 192, 196, 334, 338, 420, 423, 431, 454, 456, 464, 490; cause, 197, 456, 486, 488, 493, 494, 495
Ground-*ajñāna*, 367
Groundless, 366
Grow, 447 *n.*
Growth, 547
guḍa, 226
guha, 502
Guhadeva, 1 *n.*
gulma, 500
guṇa, 25, 26, 27, 28, 29, 31, 34, 36, 37, 42, 43, 45, 46, 56, 147, 148, 156, 157, 212 *n.*, 259, 469, 471, 475, 480, 484, 488, 491, 491, 499, 504, 505, 506, 509
Guṇa-darpaṇa, 115 *n.*, 384
guṇa-guhya, 25
guṇa-potential, 45
Guṇaratna, 516, 533
guṇa reals, 156
guṇa-sāmya, 46
guṇa-yoni, 46
guṇāvatāras, 40 *n.*
Guru, 28, 45
Guru-bhakti-mandākinī, 403
Guru-bhāva-prakāśikā, 115, 127, 131 *n.*
Guru-bhāva-prakāśikā-vyākhyā, 115
Guru-paramparā, 64, 65, 66, 94, 95, 112, 121, 399, 400, 401

Guru-paramparā-prabhāvaṃ, 64, 94 *n.*, 105
Guru-sāmānādhikaraṇya-vāda, 133
Guru-tattva-prakāśikā, 115, 131
Gurūpasatti-vijaya, 126
Guzerat, 63

Habit, 29, 32, 548
Hagiologists, 94, 96
haituka, 517, 518 *n.*, 530
haitukān, 518
Halabhūti, 105 *n.*
Halāyudha, 523
Hall, 69
Haṃsa, 40 *n.*, 401
Haṃsa-saṃdeśa, 121, 122
Happiness, 9, 16, 164, 365, 441, 463, 494, 506, 549, 550
Hare's horn, 5, 312, 407, 435, 478
Hari, 40 *n.*, 497 *n.*, 500, 508
Haribhadra, 533
Haribhāskara, 3 *n.*
Harideva, 402
Hari-dina-tilaka, 122
Haridvāra, 94
Hari-guṇa-maṇimālā, 130
Hari-guru-stava-mālā, 401
Harivaṃśa, 20, 81
Harivyāsadeva, 399, 402
Harivyāsa muni, 403
Harmful, 294, 335; results, 51, 52
Harmony, 452, 459
Hastigiri-māhātmya, 124
Hasti-jihvā, 59
Hastiśaila, 101
Hastyadrinātha, 114 *n.*, 125
Hatred, 87
Haya-grīva-stotra, 122
Hayaśīrṣa, 39 *n.*
Hayaśīrṣa-saṃhītā, 22; its contents, 22
Hārda-sañcaya, 416
Hārīta, 20, 130
He, 498
Head, 239, 295
Heart, 7, 58, 59, 71, 158
Heat, 128, 198
Heaven, 13, 24, 40, 43 *n.*, 294, 349, 441 *n.*, 447, 514 *n.*, 527
Hell, 40, 349, 441 *n.*, 527, 531
Helpless surrender, 379, 380
Helplessness, 99
Hemādri, 20
Heretics, 103, 518, 520, 526
Heretical views, 531
Heterodox view, 531
hetu, 152, 217, 225, 227, 228, 230, 231, 427, 533, 535, 536, 537, 538
hetu-śāstra, 517
hetu-vāda, 517
heya-guṇān pratiṣidhya, 175
High faith, 380 *n.*
Higher form, 37
Highest soul, 61
Hill, 208, 211, 534
Hindu life, 471; thought, 471; view, 471
Hinduism, 516
Hindus, 549
Hiraṇyagarbha, 296, 381, 452, 504
Hiraṇya-garbha-saṃhitā, 24
hita, 62
Hoernlé, 522, 523, 524 *n.*, 525
Holiness, 22
Holy Lives of the Âzhvârs, 78, 94
Homogeneous, 307, 332, 396, 397, 432, 462, 463
Homoiomeriae, theory of, 246
Honeycomb, 43
Hooper, 68 *n.*, 77 *n.*, 78 *n.*
Horse, 167
Householder, 103
Hoysala, 103, 104, 113
hṛd-yāga, 60
hṛī, 62
Hṛṣīkeśa, 39
Human, 444; beings, 191; body, 189; lover, 73; soul, 87, 89, 122, 413
Humanity, 70, 71
Humbleness, 376
Husband, 90
Hymns, 69, 99
Hymns of the Āḷvars, by J. S. M. Hooper, 74 *n.*
Hyper-logical, 255
Hypocrites, 518
Hypothesis, 332

icchā, 41, 57
icchā-śakti, 42 *n.*
idaṃ vācyaṃ, 230
idaṃ vācyaṃ prameyatvāt, 230 *n.*
Idea, 34, 42, 51, 54, 180, 182, 185 *n.*, 205, 206, 210, 300, 317, 352, 353, 412, 439, 440, 441, 451, 455, 466, 472, 473, 490, 494, 496, 544
Ideal, 53, 420, 550
Idealistic, 205, 253, 546; Buddhist, 238
Ideality, 288
Ideational, 438
Identical, 28, 302, 309, 313, 336, 341, 345, 351, 406, 416, 418, 419, 420, 432, 433, 434, 466
Identification, 53, 66, 180, 374, 417, 420

Identity, 6, 37, 58, 193, 194, 195, 198, 256, 269, 290, 303, 308, 312, 330, 336, 337, 345, 346, 406, 411, 417, 418, 419, 420, 444, 445, 455, 458, 460, 466, 485, 495; of consciousness, 141; texts, 403
Identity-in-difference, 445
Idol, 31
Iḍā, 59, 60
Iḍu, 138
Ignorance, 4, 6, 7, 44, 46, 51, 160, 173, 177, 178, 194, 317, 318, 324, 327, 328, 331, 334, 361, 362, 363, 365, 368, 369, 371, 376, 377, 378, 386, 409, 414, 420, 421, 422, 425, 436, 437, 439, 441, 445, 468, 469, 470, 495, 502, 529
Ignorant, 51
Ilaya Perumal, 100
Illness, 396
Illumination, 149, 217, 316, 320, 331, 373, 374, 416, 463, 466
Illusion, 30, 142, 147, 171, 175, 177 *n.*, 179, 180, 181, 184, 185, 186, 187, 188, 195, 196, 210, 211, 237, 240, 241, 242, 243, 244, 246, 264, 270, 307, 308, 310, 314, 325, 330, 331, 334, 335, 336, 338, 341, 374, 388, 398, 407, 408, 409, 410, 411, 418, 422, 423, 425, 426, 438, 439, 440, 441, 457, 467, 491, 539; *akhyāti* and *yathārtha-khyāti* contrasted, 182; Anantācārya's treatment of it, 188; as *akhyāti*, 237; as *akhyāti* refuted by Meghanādāri, 243–4; as *a-nirvacanīya-khyāti*, 238–9; as *a-nirvacanīya-khyāti* refuted by Meghanādāri, 242–3; as *anyathā-khyāti*, 237; as *anyathā-khyāti* and *akhyāti* compared, 244–5; as *anyathā-khyāti* and *yathārtha-khyāti*, 241; as *anyathā-khyāti* refuted by Meghanādāri, 241–2; as dreams, 182; as *nirviṣaya-khyāti* refuted, 239; as *yathārtha-khyāti*, 237; as *yathārtha-khyāti* and *trivṛt-karaṇa*, 182–3; as *yathārtha-khyāti* supported, 245–6; Buddhist theory of *ātma-khyāti* refuted, 238; condition of, 237; different interpretation—*khyātis*, 237; its relation with maxim of *pratinidhi-nyāya*, 183; its relation with *trivṛt-karaṇa*, 240–1; Prabhākara's view, 185 *n.*; Rāmānuja's *sat-khyāti* supported by Vādihaṃsāmbuvāha, 183; Sudarśana's comment on the *akhyāti* view, 186 *n.*; Śaṅkarite view criticized by Mādhavamukunda, 422 *et seq.*; theory of *akhyāti* refuted, 180; theory of *anyathā-khyāti*, 179; theory of *anyathā-khyāti* favoured by Rāmānuja and Veṅkaṭa, 180; theory of *yathārtha-khyāti*, 180; theory of *yathārtha-khyāti* advocated by Bodhāyana, etc., 180; theory of *yathārtha-khyāti* also accepted by Rāmānuja, 180–1; treatment by Vādihaṃsāmbuvāha, 184 *et seq.*; Vādihaṃsāmbuvāha's criticism of *anirvacanīya-khyāti*, 188; Vādihaṃsāmbuvāha's wavering between *akhyāti* and *anyathā-khyāti*, 187
Illusoriness, 418
Illusory, 176, 182, 184, 187, 208, 211, 239, 344, 365, 367, 374, 388, 395, 410, 422, 423, 424, 439, 456, 467, 469, 531 *n.*, 537; appearance, 154, 246, 331, 343, 422, 455; Brahman, 422; cognition, 246; construction, 331, 370; entity, 246; experiences, 371; imposition, 320, 331, 333, 423, 438, 440; knowledge, 185; notion, 242; object, 398; percept, 246; perception, 237, 242, 244, 246, 321; relations, 424; series, 177 *n.*; silver, 185 *n.*, 341, 368; world-creation, 339
Illustration, 209, 311, 326, 334
Image, 18, 28, 39 *n.*, 41, 182, 185 *n.*, 186 *n.*, 211, 234, 336
Image-building, 17
Image-incarnations, 41
Image-worship, 17, 19, 22, 23, 550; its antiquity, 19
Imaginary, 419, 423, 446, 477; identification, 81; imposition, 423
Imagination, 49, 163
Immanent, 195, 448, 472, 507
Immaterial, 281
Immediacy, 367, 439; of succession of, 273
Immediate, 203, 266, 308, 309, 319, 369; emancipation, 378; intuition, 230, 231, 318, 319; perception, 185 *n.*, 308, 318, 465; realization, 309; reference, 369; succession, 273
Immortal, 198, 547, 548, 549
Immortality, 381, 382, 384, 463, 517, 528, 531
Immutable, 457
Imparting agents, 357
Imperfect souls, 430
Imperfection, 194, 415

Impermanent, 292
Implication, 128, 183, 216, 234, 310, 314, 347, 353, 365, 366, 426, 474, 537, 539
Imposed, 182
Imposition, 185, 186, 333, 406, 422, 423, 432, 439, 440
Impressions, 8, 209, 227, 287, 290, 410, 423, 437, 537
Improbable, 404 *n.*
Impulse, 44, 452
Impulsion, 40
Impure, 42, 44, 50, 56, 438, 470; nature, 338
Impurity, 46, 51, 54, 80, 156, 505
Inactivity, 451
Inanimate, 57, 429; creation, 194
Incantations, 23
Incarnation, 39, 64, 69, 70, 119 *n.*, 302, 472, 475, 482
Inclination, 32, 61
Incompatible, 325
Incomprehensible, 218, 238
Incongruity, 269
Indefinability, 410, 435, 436
Indefinable, 177, 218, 230 *n.*, 239, 243, 316, 340, 410, 436; silver, 242
Indefinite, 2
Indefiniteness, 370
Independence, 51, 54, 55, 455
Independent, 443
Indescribability, 340
Indescribable, 179
Indeterminate, 270; cognition, 128; knowledge, 311; matter, 164; perception, 166
India, 401
Indian Antiquary, 66 *n.*
Indian philosophy, 96 *n.*
Indians, 19
Indispensable, 180, 201; condition, 180
Indistinctness, 254
Individual, 30, 190, 193, 206, 211, 232, 287, 289, 291, 303, 323, 370, 377, 403, 413, 414, 416, 417, 429, 431, 433, 434, 441, 443, 444, 451, 452, 459, 462, 485, 492, 493, 494; capacity, 288; cognition, 318, 319, 358; experiences, 82; limitations, 82; self, 79, 170; selves, 335, 370, 413, 426, 464; souls, 2, 6, 7, 26, 38, 56, 158, 159, 176, 190, 191, 194, 198 *n.*, 199, 200, 297, 298, 299, 301, 377, 385, 387, 395, 396, 413, 420, 423, 429, 432, 434, 460, 461, 472, 483; units, 287
Individuality, 90, 461
Individuation, 462
Indra, 295, 528
Indra-rātra, 23
indriya, 300
Indubitable, 370
Inductive generalization, 536
Inert, 408
Inexpressible, 179
Infatuation, 76
Inference, 14, 16, 128, 146, 152, 168, 169, 179, 185 *n.*, 190, 192, 211, 214, 215, 216, 217, 225, 226, 227, 229, 230, 231, 232, 233, 235, 256, 296, 309, 313, 315, 327, 328, 329, 340, 353, 360, 361, 364, 406, 426, 427, 428, 465, 517, 534, 535, 536, 537, 539; Veṅkaṭa's treatment of it, 225 *et seq.*
Inferential, 62, 310, 411; process, 427
Inferior, 53, 54
Inferred, 341
Infinite, 10, 27, 34, 51, 149, 161, 165, 176, 196, 200, 255, 296, 306, 320, 340, 351, 353, 413, 431, 467, 503, 506, 509, 544; individuals, 421; joy, 161; knowledge, 153; nature, 304; regress, 248, 249, 250, 255, 256, 259, 262, 267, 277, 329, 330, 463; series, 177 *n.*; universe, 191
Infiniteness, 194
Infinitude, 51, 71
Influence, 47, 56, 61, 205, 293, 304, 366, 437, 500; of love, 378
Influx, 38
Inherence, 128, 308, 423
Inherent, 261
Initiation, 19, 22, 23, 87, 104, 139
Injunctions, 14, 123, 124
Injury, 61
Inner Controller, 27, 39 *n.*, 40, 41, 159, 200, 450, 451
Inner dynamic, 47
Inner microcosm, 29
Inner organ, 172
Inquiry, 28, 209, 212, 306, 307
Inscriptions, 64, 523
Inseparable, 423; characteristic, 150; quality, 150; relation, 222
Insignia, 2
Insignificance, 54
Insincerity, 379
Inspiration, 80, 111, 130, 471
Inspired persons, 39
Installation, 22, 23
Instinctive, 287; root-desire, 253
Instructions, 25, 38, 413, 550

Instrumental, 266, 303, 388, 389, 459; agencies, 396; agent, 397, 456; cause, 2, 204, 266, 301, 388, 389, 391, 481, 489
Instrumentality, 247, 308, 391
Instruments, 191, 204, 205, 336, 470, 479; of knowledge, 203
Insult, 173
Integrity, 405
Intellect, 295, 304, 465, 547
Intellectual, 32, 45, 548; operation, 8, 9; powers, 288; state, 387, 438
Intelligence, 10, 26, 154, 166, 175, 178, 192, 193, 483, 537, 548
Intelligent, 26, 29; being, 191, 192
Intelligibility, 438
Intelligible, 419
Intelligizing, 47
Intense self-surrender, 89
Intention, 124
Interest, 89, 441
Intermediary, 203, 257
Intermediate causes, 397
Intermingling, 181
Intermixture, 182
Internal, 426; action, 8; situation, 377; structure, 389
Interpretation, 40, 108, 195, 196, 306, 351, 471, 475 *n.*, 486, 496, 512, 515, 516
Intimate knowledge, 80
Intoxicated, 79
Intoxicating, 141; emotion, 377
Intoxication, 63 *n.*; 377; by love, 378
Introspection, 141
Intuited, 442
Intuition, 27, 34, 62, 167, 168, 170, 176, 227, 318, 319, 348, 364, 372, 409, 412, 442, 464, 465, 538
Intuitional experience, 175
Intuitive, 168, 369, 466; experience, 361; knowledge, 68, 214 *n.*, 216; wisdom, 61
Invalid, 236, 278, 326, 411, 417, 440, 477, 479, 537; inference, 208; knowledge, 247; propositions, 202
Invalidity, 201, 202, 248, 347, 348, 356, 458
Invariable, 203, 251, 266, 278, 535, 536, 539; antecedence, 279; antecedent, 277; association, 226, 538; concomitance, 538; priority, 278
Inverse, 37
Involution, 37
Iraṇḍam-tiru-vantādi, 134 *n.*
Irrational, 177 *n.*
Irrationality, 177 *n.*
Itihāsasamuccaya, 20
ittham-bhāva, 254
iyad-guṇaka, 157
īkṣaṇa, 413
Īkṣaty-adhikaraṇa-vicāra, 133
Īśopaniṣat, 123
īśvara, 47, 128, 129, 152, 153, 154, 155, 156, 157, 158, 160, 161, 163, 225, 335, 443, 446, 473, 474, 475, 480, 481, 488, 498, 503, 504, 510
Īśvara Bhaṭṭa, 94
Īśvara's body, 157
Īśvara-gītā, 460, 474 *n.*, 482, 494 *n.*, 496; its philosophy, 460 *et seq.*, 482 *et seq.*
Īśvara-gītā-bhāṣya, 285 *n.*, 456 *n.*, 482, 483 *n.*, 484 *n.*
Īśvara-gītā-ṭīkā, 450 *n.*
Īśvara-kṛṣṇa, 30, 478, 501 *n.*
Īśvara-mīmāṃsā, 124 *n.*
Īśvaramuni, 94, 97
īśvara-praṇidhāna, 62 *n.*
īśvara-pūjana, 61
Īśvara-saṃhitā, 21, 22; its contents, 22
Īśvara's will, 159

Jacobi, 524 *n.*, 526 *n.*, 528 *n.*
jaḍa, 452
Jagannātha, 103, 399
Jagannātha Yati, 118, 133
Jaimini, 124, 125, 381
Jain king, 104
Jaina, 304, 525, 537; objection, 393; view, 537
Jaina sūtras, 524 *n.*, 526 *n.*
Jainism, 516
Jains, 104, 206, 302, 393, 518, 523, 525 *n.*, 539, 546
jalpa, 512
janye-śvara, 473
japa, 13, 62
Jaundiced, 182
Jayanta, 203, 206, 512, 516, 519, 537, 547, 548
Jayatīrtha, 111
Jayāditya, 518
Jayākhya, 21, 22
Jayākhya-saṃhitā, 24, 25, 26 *n.*, 27 *n.*, 28, 29, 30, 31 *n.*, 506 *n.*; consciousness how possible, 26; creation as Sāṃkhya evolution, 25; emanations of Vasudeva in, 29; God-function of, 29; God, nature of, 27; *guṇa* and *avidyā*, 29; knowledge as static and dynamic, 29; liberation only possible through knowledge of ultimate reality, 24; *prakṛti* appears as in-

Jayākhya-saṃhitā (*cont.*)
telligent, how, 26; *Samādhi*, nature, of, 29; *Sāṃkhya*, difference with, 30; soul, progress of, 28; soul, ultimate realization of, 28; *śuddha-sarga* in, 27; theory of *vāsanā*, 26; two kinds of creation in, 25; ultimate reality can be known only through teacher, 25; ultimate reality is beyond the *guṇas*, 25; *yama* and *niyama* in, 29; *yoga*, different ways of, 30; *yoga* leading to final emancipation, 31
Jābāli, 529
jātakas, 514 *n.*
jāti, 297, 354, 355, 512
jāti-rūpa, 216
Jāti-Vādihamsa's conception of it, 354
Jāti-Veṅkaṭa's conception of it, 355
Jāvāli, 530
Jealousy, 87
Jewish Christian, 50 *n.*
jijñāsā, 307
Jijñāsā-darpaṇa, 115, 392
Jina-hood, 522
jīva, 26, 44, 49, 50, 51, 52, 128, 129, 158, 177 *n.*, 187, 193, 194, 208, 301, 329, 330, 336, 346, 407, 418, 443, 444, 451, 453, 476, 486, 493
Jīva Goswamī, 496
jīva-brahmai-kya, 417
jīvanmukta, 295, 442
jīvan-mukti, 10, 327, 437, 441, 448
jīvā-jñāna-vādī, 177 *n.*
jīvātman, 498
jīvātmā, 483
jīveśvaraikya-bhaṅga, 126
jñāna, 8, 37, 41, 47, 56, 62, 63, 80, 160, 206, 351, 357, 371, 470, 504, 508
jñāna-daśā, 379
jñāna-guṇāśraya, 172
jñāna-janya, 371
jñāna-karma-samuccaya, 307
jñāna-kriyā, 148
jñanaṃ, 178 *n.*
Jñāna-ratna-darpaṇa, 115 *n.*, 384
jñāna-rūpa, 61
jñāna-samuccita-karma, 8
jñānasādhyatvāt, 371
jñāna-sāmānya-virodhī, 362
Jñāna-sāra, 102, 110, 138
jñāna-svabhāva, 216
jñāna-svarūpa, 172
jñāna-vyāpāra, 205
jñāna-viśeṣa, 161
Jñāna-yāthārthya-vāda, 133, 209 *n.*, 210, 241 *n.*, 246 *n.*, 247 *n.*
jñāna-yoga, 22, 33, 34, 89, 91; its meaning, 22
jñānā-bhāva, 178 *n.*, 425
jñānā-karaṇaka-jñānatvam, 220
jñātatā, 148
jñātā, 411
jñātṛtva, 172
jñeya, 28
Joint causality, 197
Joint method of agreement, 536
Joint method of agreement and difference, 542
Joy, 485, 550
Judgment, 210
Judgmental form, 250 *n.*
Jug, 168, 190, 199, 220, 221, 224, 230, 243, 258, 362, 363, 397
Just will, 78
Justice, 195, 374
Jyāyan, 53
jyoti, 499, 510

Kadanmallai, 64
kaiṅkarya, 136
Kaiṭabha, 25
Kaivalya, 93, 136, 161, 382, 383, 384, 506 *n.*
Kaivalya-śata-dūṣaṇī, 127
Kaiyaṭa, 516 *n.*
kalana, 45
kalana-kāraṇa, 47
Kali, 65
Kalijit, 110, 111, 122, 134
Kali-santaraṇopaniṣad, 13
Kalivairī, 110
Kalki, 39 *n.*
Kalkin, 40 *n.*
kamala, 30
Kamalaśīla, 516, 532
Kamalaśīla's *Pañjikā*, 536 *n.*, 540 *n.*, 541 *n.*, 542 *n.*, 543 *n.*
Kamalā, 114
Kamalākṣa Bhaṭṭa, 100
Kamaṭheśvara, 40 *n.*
Kambalāśvatara, 540
Kampana, 121
Kanikṛṣṇa, 96 *n.*
Kanjivaram, 119
Kannaḍa, 81 *n.*
Kaṇāda, 482
Kaṇḍaḍanātha, 98
Kaṇḍādaiyappan, 105
Kaṇṇan, 74 *n.*
Kaṇṇiṇṇu-śirattāmbu-vyākhyāna, 127
Kaṇṇinuṇ-śiruttāmbu, 134 *n.*
kapha, 475
Kapila, 21, 40 *n.*, 479, 482

Kapyāsa text, 352
Kapyāsam puṇḍarīkam, 101
karaṇa, 280
Karimāra, 95
Karimāran, 94
karma, 8, 11, 26, 49, 51, 52, 61, 152, 153, 157, 159, 161, 172, 201, 212 *n.*, 258, 291, 292, 293, 295, 301, 349, 366, 375, 383, 385, 386, 393, 409, 411, 412, 413, 443, 444, 445, 446, 448, 452, 453, 454, 481, 484, 487, 489, 508, 509, 520, 522, 523 *n.*, 525, 536, 547, 548, 549, 550; Vijñāna Bhikṣu, 452; Nimbārka's conception of, 411 *et seq.*; Nimbārka's idea of, 414 *et seq.*
Karmaharadeva, 402
Karman, 303, 504
Karma-yoga, 22, 33, 34, 89, 91; its meaning, 22
kartā, 387, 411, 510
kartṛtva, 35, 485
Karukānātha, 96
Kasturī Raṅgācarya, 381, 383; his general view, 381 *et seq.*; his treatment of the sectarian differences of Baḍgolāi and Teṅgalai, 381 *et seq.*
Kaṭha, 519 *n.*, 528, 529
Kaṭha Upaniṣad, 519
Kaṭhavally-upaniṣat-pakāśikā, 127
kathā, 201, 513
Kathā-sarit-sāgara, 108 *n.*
Kathā-vatthu, 517
Kaṭhopaniṣad, 379
Kattur-āṟgiya-vanavalapillai, 110
kaumāra-sarga, 502
Kauṇḍinya Śrīnivāsa Dīkṣita, 384
Kauśika-Śrībhāṣya-Śrīnivāsa, 122
Kauśitakopaniṣat-prakāśikā, 127
Kautilya, 512, 532
Kautilya, *Artha-śāṣtra*, 512 *n.*
Kavicakravartī Trivikrama, 3
Kavilologu, 121
Kavirāja Gopīnātha, 482
Kavitārkikasiṃha, 119
Kāla, 36, 42, 43, 45, 46, 47, 52, 389, 446, 447, 448, 479, 486, 488, 489, 492, 497, 505, 508; different conceptions of, 447; in relation to *Karma*, 448; in Vijñāna Bhikṣu, 446
kāla-ghaṭa-saṃyogā-dikaṃ, 389
Kālamukhas, 16
Kālanemighna, 40 *n.*
kāla-śakti, 45
kālatraye'pi, 428
Kāma, 40 *n.*, 62
kāma, as *nitya* and *naimittika*, 293–4
Kāma-sūtra, 550 *n.*
kāmya, 294
Kāntātman, 40 *n.*
kānti, 57
Kāntimatī, 98, 100
Kāñcī, 63 *n.*, 65, 66, 78, 101, 102, 120
Kāñcīpūrṇa, 98, 101, 102, 109
kāṇḍa, 59
Kāpālika, 3 *n.*, 16
kāraka-cakra, 206
kāraṇa, 156, 204
kāraṇa-brahma, 474
kāraṇam aprameyam, 502
kāraṇānumāna, 229
kāraṇāvasthā, 200
Kārikā, 440, 501 *n.*
Kāṟi, 65
Kāṟimāṟan, 65
kārpaṇya, 54, 92
kārya, 4, 189, 265
kārya-brahma, 474
kārya-kāraṇā-dhikaraṇa-vāda, 381 *n.*
kārya-prāga-bhāva-samanvita, 275
kāryādhikaraṇa-tattva, 132, 381, 384
kāryādhikaraṇa-vāda, 132, 381, 383, 384
kāryā-numāna, 229
kāryāvasthā, 200
Kāsārayogin, 63 *n.*
kāśikā, 518, 518 *n.*
Kāśmīrāgama-prāmāṇya, 17
Kāśyapa, 20
Kāśyapa-saṃhitā, 23
Kātyāyana, 302, 515, 516; his view of God, 302
Kāṭhaka-siddhāntin, 3 *n.*
Kāverī, 63
kāyika, 507
Kerala, 67
Kernel, 2
Kesara-bhūṣaṇa, 133
Keśava, 39, 402
Keśava Kāśmīrī, 402
Keśava Kāśmīrī Bhaṭṭa, 402, 403 *n.*
Keśava Yajvan, 98, 100
Keṭṭi ammais, 104
kevalā-nvayi, 228, 229, 230, 427; inference, 230
kevala-vyatireki, 226, 227, 229, 230, 231, 232, 427
Khaṇḍana-khaṇḍa-khādya, 201, 535 *n.*
khyātis, 184, 410, 503, 510
khyāty-ayogāt, 243
Kidambi Rāmānuja Pillan, 110
Kidambi-Tirumalai-Nayinār, 137
Kilaiyagaṭṭāṟvār, 95

kiñcit-kara, 277
Kiśoradāsa Pandit, 399, 404
kīrti, 57
kleśa, 44
Knots, 437
Knower, 172, 315, 325, 326, 333, 411, 423, 466, 467, 468, 489, 507
Knowing relation, 250 *n.*
Knowledge, 4, 7, 8, 9, 28, 29, 32, 33, 34, 35, 37, 41, 47, 49, 51, 54, 91, 129, 146, 176, 178, 179, 181, 184, 185 *n.*, 187, 188, 193, 204, 205, 206, 210, 238, 250 *n.*, 292, 293, 295, 300, 307, 308, 309, 310, 312, 317, 318, 321, 323, 324, 325, 327, 328, 329, 335, 336, 340, 346, 347, 348, 352, 357, 361, 369, 371, 386, 409, 410, 411, 412, 418, 423, 424, 425, 426, 427, 430, 436, 437, 440, 443, 445, 449, 453, 461, 462, 465, 466, 467, 469, 470, 471, 472, 473, 474, 475, 479, 481, 482, 485, 486, 488, 490, 491, 492, 493, 500, 501, 502, 503, 504, 506, 507, 508, 533, 537, 547; and the known, 423; its self-validity, 247 *et seq.*
Known, 466
Kolli, 67
Kollikavaladasar, 137
Koluttuṅga I, 103, 104
Koluttuṅga II, 104
Koṇḍinna, 115
Koṅgu, 67
Koyilkaṇḍādaiaṇṇan, 111
Krama-dīpikā, 403
Kratu, 21
kraurya, 376, 379
kriyamāṇa karma, 443
kriyā, 36, 37, 41, 51, 57
kriyākhya, 29, 44
kriyākhya-jñāna, 29
kriyā-śakti, 42
Kroḍātman, 40 *n.*
kṛkara, 59
Kṛmikaṇṭha, 104, 105
Kṛpācārya, 401
Kṛṣṇa, 38, 39 *n.*, 40 *n.*, 69, 70, 71, 72, 74 *n.*, 77, 80, 81, 82, 83, 121, 304; 378, 401, 405, 442 *n.*, 474, 475; his life, 83
Kṛṣṇa Bhaṭṭa, 401
Kṛṣṇadeśika, 18, 137
Kṛṣṇamaṅgala, 96
Kṛṣṇa Miśra, 531 *n.*, 532
Kṛṣṇapāda, 110, 111, 118, 134, 135
Kṛṣṇapāda-lokaguru, 131
Kṛṣṇa-samāhbhaya, 110
Kṛṣṇa-stava-rāja, 400
Kṛṣṇasūri, 111, 112
Kṛṣṇatātācārya, 123, 131
Kṛṣṇopaniṣad, 13
Kṛtakoṭi, 105 *n.*
Kṛtamālā, 63
kṛtsnā-jñāna-pratītis tāvad asiddhā, 361
Kṛttikā, 279; constellation, 229
kṣamā, 57, 61
Kṣamā-ṣoḍaśī-stava, 111
kṣaṇa, 274
kṣaṇa-dvaya-sambandha-śūnyatva, 273
kṣaṇa-kāla-sambandhatvaṃ, 273
kṣaṇa-kālatvaṃ, 273
kṣaṇa-mātra-vartitva, 273
kṣaṇa-sambandhitva, 269
kṣaṇa-pādhitvaṃ, 274
Kṣattriya, 64
Kṣetra, 31, 32, 502, 504
Kṣetrajña, 31, 498, 503
Kṣetrajña-śakti, 51
kṣobha, 498
kṣobhaka, 509
kṣobhya, 498, 509
Ku-dṛṣṭi-dhvānta-mārtaṇḍa, 396, 397 *n.*
kuhu, 59
kukkuṭa, 60
Kula-sēkhara, 64, 66 *n.*, 67, 68, 69, 76, 82, 134
Kula-śēkhara Peru-māl, 63, 65, 66, 96 *n.*
Kula-śekharāṅka, 66, 67
Kulārka, 229
Kumāra, 401
Kumāra-Vēdānta-deśika, 111, 122
Kumāra Vedāntācārya, son of Veṅkaṭa, 123, 126; his works, 125
Kumārila, 8, 148, 205, 347, 348, 357
Kumbakonam, 68, 73, 95, 103, 116 *n.*
Kumbha-koṇa Tātayārya, 126, 127
kuṇḍala, 67, 416, 434
Kuṇḍalinī, 36
Kuṇḍalī, 58
Kuṇḍalī-śakti, 58
Kurakā, 95
Kuranātha, 102
Kureśa, 98, 102, 103, 104, 109, 110, 111, 113, 114, 134; his contribution in writing *Śrībhāṣya*, 103; his eyes put out, 103
Kureśa-vijaya, 113 *n.*
Kurugai-kkaval-appan, 98
Kurukā, 98
Kurukānātha, 98
Kurukeśvara, 109
Kurukur, 68
Kuruttalvan, 66, 102

Kuruttama, 66
Kuvera, 39
Kuyil, 77
Kūrma, 39 *n.*, 40 *n.*, 59, 60, 475
Kūrmapurāṇa, 19, 20, 480, 482, 483, 488, 496, 502 *n.*, 509, 510, 511 *n.*; philosophical elements in, 509 *et seq.*
kūṭastha, 49, 484
kūṭastha puruṣa, 50

Laghu-bhāgavatāmṛta, 40 *n.*; *avatāras* in, 40 *n.*
Laghu-bhāva-prakāśikā, 129
Laghu-māñjuṣā, 403
Laghu-prakāśikā, 116
Laghu-sāmānādhikaraṇya-vāda, 133
Laghustava-rāja-stotra, 403
lakṣaṇā, 306
Lakṣmaṇārya-siddhānta-saṃgraha, 130
Lakṣmī, 36, 41, 45, 52, 53, 56, 57, 70, 99, 100 *n.*, 157, 375, 379
Lakṣmī Dāśarathi, 98
Lakṣmī-devī, 115
Lakṣmīnātha, 96
Lakṣmī-tantra, 39 *n.*, 56 *n.*, 57, 379
Lakṣmītantra, *avatāras* in, 39–40 *n.*
lakṣya, 340
Lamentation, 72, 73
Lamp, 25, 444
Laṅkā, 82
latā, 500
Laugākṣibhāskara, 3 *n.*
laukika, 426
laukikī, 507
Law, 412, 448, 474; of Excluded Middle, 242; of Contradiction, 242
lāghava, 180
Legendary account, 83
Legendary life, 81, 83
Legendary lovers, 81
Legendary personages, 81, 82
Lesser gods, 475
Letters, 4
Liberation, 5, 7, 8, 9, 10, 24, 39, 170, 173, 257, 450; during lifetime, 10
Life, 41, 293, 327, 420, 443, 461, 471, 509, 519, 521, 522, 526, 530, 531, 536, 545
Life-force, 59
Life-functions, 7
Life-history, 82
Life-movements, 548
Life of Rāmānuja, 113 *n.*
Light, 46, 178, 198, 280; and heat, 163
Light-heat-potential, 48, 260
Light-potential, 163
Limitation, 194, 195, 432
Limited, 292; sense, 43; time, 285
Lineage, 3, 129, 132
Linee di una storia del Materialismo Indiano, 512 *n.*
Linguistic, 218; usage, 239, 282
Liṅga, 16, 22
Liṅga-purāṇa, 20
liṅga-śarīra, 487
Literary, 69
Literature, 43, 56, 58, 112, 531
Living, 456
līlā, 51, 158
līlā-vatāra, 40 *n.*, 475
Location, 41
Locus, 58, 283, 290, 328, 351, 417, 435, 437; its negation, 255; of subsistence, 397; of the negation, 283
Logic, 119, 235, 236, 533; depends on admission of objective realities, 236; in Bengal, 133
Logical, 80, 111, 183, 194, 442, 513; apparatus, 256; argument, 113; categories, 236; criticism, 154; doctrine, 550; implications, 184; proof, 313; situation, 341
Logically valid, 236, 253
Logicians, 517, 518
Loka, 513, 514
Lokabhāskara, 3 *n.*
loka-khāyikā, 513
Lokanātha, 40 *n.*
loka-pitāmaha, 503
loka-saṃgraha, 92
Lokācārya, 110, 122, 134, 136, 137, 155, 157, 160, 163, 260, 374, 380, 381; his views, 136
lokācārya-tad-anubandhināṃ, 381 *n.*
Lokācārya I, 134, 135
Lokāyata, 512, 513, 514, 515, 516, 519, 526, 530, 532, 533; its significance, 512 *et seq.*
lokāyata doctrines, 528, 529, 532
lokāyata view, 532
Lokāyata-śāstra, 515, 531, 533
Lokāyatika, 512 *n.*, 527, 529, 548
lokeṣu āyata, 515
Loneliness, 79
Longings, 70
Lord, 22, 27, 31, 33, 41, 42, 44, 50, 51, 53, 54, 56, 83, 87, 88, 307, 412, 430, 508
Lord (*Bhagavān*), 21
Lord Kṛṣṇa, 99
Lost objects, 89
Lost soul, 88
Lotus, 58, 153, 271

Love, 136, 294, 376, 377, 414, 450, 451, 472, 491; stricken, 378
Love-sickness, 83
Lover, 70, 83, 84, 377
Loving embraces, 73
Lower caste, 93
Lower form, 37
Lower order, 88
Lowliness, 54
Lucidity, 79
Lump of clay, 46, 259, 332; of salt, 10
Lunar, 295

Madan Mohan Library, Benares, 399
Madhu, 25, 47
Madhura-kavihṛdaya, 124
Madhura-kavi, 69
Madhura-kaviy-āṛvār, 63, 64, 65, 66*n.*, 67, 94, 95, 134 *n.*
Madhurantakam, 103
Madhusūdana, 39, 40 *n.*
Madhva, 111, 112, 113, 125, 304, 305, 387, 399, 400, 401, 403, 475, 496
Madhva-mukha-mardana, 399, 400
madhya, 58
madhyama, 505
Madhya Pratoli Bhaṭṭārya, 109
madhyastha, 201
Madhya-vīthi Bhaṭṭārya, 109
Madras, 69 *n.*, 94 *n.*, 104 *n.*, 106 *n.*
Madras Govt. Oriental MS., 239 *n.*
Madras Presidency, 64
Madura, 65, 67, 120
Magical creation, 394
Magician, 335
Mahadyogin, 63
mahat, 46, 47, 63 *n.*, 163, 256, 257, 258, 259, 260 *n.*, 446, 473, 475, 489, 490, 499, 502, 504, 507, 509, 510, 511
mahātman, 504
mahat prajñā, 503
mahattattva, 475, 480, 489, 498
Mahābhārata, 12, 17, 19, 20, 21, 40 *n.*, 260 *n.*, 379, 443 *n.*, 447, 479, 517, 530, 531, 532; Nara and Nārāyaṇa in, 12; reference to heretics in, 530
Mahācārya, 117, 125, 127, 130, 131, 135, 305, 361, 364, 365, 366, 367, 368, 370, 371, 373; his works, 125, 126
Mahādevī, 98
mahā-kalpas, 525
Mahālakṣmī, 41, 67 *n.*
mahāmoha, 500
mahān, 503, 504
Mahānada, 63
Mahānadī, 63
Mahāpūrṇa, 98, 100, 101, 102, 103, 109, 139
Mahā-puruṣa-nirṇaya, 98, 99 *n.*
mahā-pūrva-pakṣa, 175 *n.*
Mahārāṣṭra, 63
Mahārya, 63 *n.*, 96
Mahā-sanatkumāra-saṃhitā, 23, 37
mahā-siddhānta, 175 *n.*
Mahā-vidyā doctrines, 229
mahā-viśvāsa, 54
Mahā-viṣṇu, 56, 507, 508
Mahāvīra, 522, 524 *n.*, 525 *n.*
Mahāyāna, 1 *n.*
Maheśvara, 39 *n.*, 473, 497 *n.*, 506, 509 *n.*
Mahomedans, 121, 135
Maintenance, 38, 51, 52, 56, 195, 196, 454
Maitrāyaṇīya Upaniṣad, 531 *n.*
Maitreyo-paniṣad, 480
Maitrī Upaniṣad, 447
Majesty, 35, 136
Makkhali, 522
Makkhali Gosāla, 522; his views, 522
Makkhaliputta Gosāla, 525 *n.*
Males, 42
Malik Kafūr, 120
Mallipura, 63 *n.*
Mal-observation, 279
Mamallai, 65
mamatva, 506
mamātmā, 140
Manakkal, 67 *n.*
Manakkal-lambej, 97
manana, 405, 422
manas, 8, 9, 13, 25, 38, 48, 49, 56, 57, 80, 139, 142, 144, 148, 151, 153, 158, 163, 191, 257, 258, 280, 281, 499, 503, 504, 506, 507, 509, 510
Manavalamahāmuni, 110
manda, 505
Mandangudi, 69
Mandates, 441
Manhood, 70
Manifest, 36
Manifestation, 4, 17, 26, 32, 35, 36, 37, 38, 39 *n.*, 40 *n.*, 42, 44, 45, 47, 51, 53, 57, 150, 163, 198, 215, 218, 247, 250, 265, 267, 311, 336, 338, 355, 356, 359, 360, 361, 365, 367, 373, 387, 412, 447, 449, 451, 473, 487, 497, 498, 500, 508, 524
Manifested condition, 156
Manifesting, 39; power, 41
Manifold, 32, 197
Maṇi-sāra-dhikkāra, 122
Manīṣideva, 402

mankha, 522, 524 *n.*
Mankhali, 523
Mankhaliputta Gosāla, 522
Man-lion, 38
Manner, 60
mano-doṣāt, 185 *n.*
manomaya, 57
mantā, 510
mantras, 13, 22, 23, 25, 28, 29, 30, 31, 57, 58, 60, 69, 102, 403
Manu, 1 *n.*, 14, 17, 21, 146, 479, 515, 518, 519; denies the *Pañcarātrīns*, 14
manus, 44, 45, 46, 47, 48, 49, 50, 56, 57
Manu-saṃhitā, 16
Manuscripts, 119, 126, 135, 138, 305, 346, 399
Manu Vaivasvaṭa, 40 *n.*
Maṅgala-dīpikā, 126
Maṅgācārya, 127 *n.*
Maṅgācārya Śrīnivāsa, 118
Maṇavāla, 94 *n.*
Maṇavāla Mā-muni, 64, 65, 137
maṇi-pravāla, 64, 105, 123, 137, 138
Maraner, 98
Maraner Nambi, 98
Marici, 21
Mark 17, 20, 524 *n.*
Marriage, 69
Marudha-grāma-pūrṇa, 102, 110
Maskarin, 523, 524 *n.*
Masters, 83
Material, 10, 25, 26, 29, 49, 181, 189, 190, 208, 288, 388, 389, 418, 449, 481, 495; cause, 2, 37, 46, 55, 188, 196, 197, 266, 286, 301, 302, 341, 342, 365, 385, 388, 389, 397, 404, 454, 459, 465, 500, 543; changes, 301; element, 489; energy, 459; forms, 37; identity, 252; impurities, 384; part, 301; products, 527; stuff, 329
Material world, 181, 194, 199, 200, 291, 297, 384, 385, 416
Materialistic, 512
Materialists, 550
Materiality, 195, 256, 383
Maternal grandfather, 122
Maternal uncle, 109, 183
Mathuradeva, 402
Mathurā, 94, 96, 103, 120
mati, 47, 57, 61, 503, 510
Matsya, 39 *n.*, 40 *n.*, 475
Matsya Purāṇa, 16, 479
Matter, 26, 49, 125, 157, 193, 200, 211, 299, 406, 430, 431, 434, 435, 457, 458, 459, 465, 492, 495, 501, 519; Veṅkaṭa's view of it, 162 *et seq.*
Matter-stuff, 385
maṭha, 103, 104, 111
Maxim of determining similarity by real representation, 183
mayāra, 60
Mayilai, 64
Mādhava, 39, 103, 110, 127, 400, 532, 533, 632
Mādhavadāsa, 109, 110
Mādhava Mukunda, 416, 420, 426, 437; controversy with the monist, 416 *et seq.*; his criticism of *jīva-brahmai-kya*, 417; his criticism of Rāmānuja and Bhāskara, 429 *et seq.*; his criticism of Śaṅkarite *ajñāna*, 424 *et seq.*; his criticism of Śaṅkarite emancipation, 420 *et seq.*; his criticism of the category of "difference", 417 *et seq.*; his criticism of the theory of illusion of Śaṅkara, 422 *et seq.*; his refutation of the falsity of the world, 435 *et seq.*; his treatment of *pramāṇas*, 426 *et seq.*
Mādhavācārya, 2
mādhyamika, 201, 238, 340
Mādhyamika Buddhists, 238
Mādhyamika-pakṣa, 177
Māheśvara, 3 *n.*, 505
māheśvara yoga, 505
mākhali, 522
Mālādhara, 98, 109
mānasa-pratyakṣa, 220, 359, 361, 538
mānasika, 507
mānavas, 49
Māna-yathātmya-nirṇaya, 119, 128 *n.*, 216, 229, 234
Māṇḍūkyopaniṣat-prakāśikā, 127
Māṇikka-vāchakar, 84
Mārāṭhā, 3
Mārkaṇḍeya Purāṇa, 501 *n.*, 502 *n.* 506; philosophical treatment in, 506
Mārkaṇḍeya-saṃhitā, 24
Māṛa, 65
Māṛaṅkāri, 65
Māṛañ-jadaiyan, 65
Māṭhara vṛtti, 448
māyā, 1, 2, 4, 5, 26, 29, 42, 52, 100 *n.*, 129, 132, 165, 196, 197, 198, 334, 335, 336, 383, 393, 396, 410, 412, 424, 434, 440, 454, 457, 472, 476, 485, 486, 491, 492, 494; in *Īśvara-gītā*, 497; in relation to *pradhāna* as treated by Vijñāna Bhikṣu, 476 *et seq.*
Māyā-kośa, 38
Māyāvāda, 484
māyāvādin, 4, 443

māyāvī, 472
Meals, 105
Meaning, 195, 233
Meaningless, 99
Means, 55, 298, 310
Measure, 264
medhā, 57
Medhātithi, 515, 518 *n*., 519 *n*.
Mediate knowledge, 425
Mediate process, 247
Meditation, 10, 11, 22, 23, 30, 31, 32, 39, 40 *n*., 41, 42, 58, 60, 69, 80, 137, 219, 292, 293, 295, 364, 388, 405, 414, 415, 437, 442, 446, 450, 451, 465, 474
Medium, 449
Meghanādāri, 111, 114, 115, 125, 214, 215, 216, 217, 229, 234, 239, 240, 241, 242, 243; adopts only *yathārtha-khyāti*, 241, 245, 246, 247 *n*., 248, 249, 346, 348, 349; arguments in favour of validity of knowledge, 247; his admission of five *pramāṇas*, 216; his admission of *upamāna*, 234; his arguments in favour of *yathārtha-khyāti*, 245-6; his conception of various categories connected with conception, 218 *et seq.*; his definition of perception, 217; his refutation of *akhyāti*, 243; his refutation of *anirvacanīya-khyāti*, 242-3; his refutation of *anyathā-khyāti*, 241-2; his refutation of *nirviṣaya-khyāti*, 246; his refutation of objections against self-validity, 248-50; his refutation of the Nyāya view of *parataḥ prāmāṇya*, 347; his treatment of memory, 214 *et seq.*; his treatment of nature validity, 215-16; his treatment of object, 217; his treatment of perception in relation to validity, 215-16; his view of *karma* and fruits, 349; his view of perception contrasted with that of Rāmānuja, 218; his view of *svataḥ-prāmāṇya-vāda*, 346; his view that intuition is self-valid, 348; his view of time, 348; his works, 125; *pramāṇa* and *artha-paricchedа-katva*, 240; supports *arthā-patti*, 234-5
Melody, 80
Melukot, 104, 113
Meḷaiyagaṭṭāṛvār, 95
Memory, 5, 8, 128, 150, 151, 167, 168, 178, 180, 181, 184, 185 *n*., 186 *n*., 209, 210, 214, 215, 216, 220 *n*., 223, 234, 239, 245, 249, 250, 268, 287, 348, 360, 363, 364, 376, 410, 420, 545, 548, 549; its treatment by Veṅkaṭa and Meghanādāri, 214-15; its validity, 237
Memory-image, 244, 245, 247
Memory-knowledge, 248
Mental, 204, 205; intuition, 359, 361; modes, 364; organs, 445; perception, 426, 538; powers, 47; process, 185 *n*., 539; state, 310, 334, 339, 372, 373, 439, 465, 469, 470, 495, 540, 541, 543, 544, 545; temperament, 543
Merciful, 54, 374
Mercy, 78, 85, 99, 292, 375, 413, 474; of God, 374, 375
Merit, 15, 153, 191, 453, 520
Meritorious, 521; actions, 294
Messengers, 83
Metals, 41
Metaphysical, 237; position, 451; views, 450
Metaphysico-cosmological theory, 246
Metaphysics, 550
Method, 55, 183, 195; of agreement, 228, 356
Microcosm, 26
Microscopic, 390
Mind, 28, 30, 31, 32, 33, 34, 38, 48, 54, 60, 152, 172, 182, 189, 191, 192, 207, 209, 291, 294, 295, 308, 420, 423, 427, 434, 440, 442, 444, 490, 498, 505, 527, 542, 543; contact, 202; substance, 194
Minimum assumption, 186 *n*.
Minor, 427; gods, 22; term, 533, 534, 535
Minor Religions, 81 *n*.
Minor Religious Systems, 64 *n*., 399
Minority sect, 20
Miraculous, 505; power, 30, 60
Mirage, 282, 369
Mirror, 27, 144, 208, 211, 334
Misapprehension, 182, 183, 185, 251
Mis-association, 245
Misconception, 456
Mis-correspondence, 357
Mis-perception, 418
Misery, 28, 87, 164, 295, 302, 303, 308
Mistake, 5
Mistress, 75, 377
Miśra, 139
miśra-varga, 57
miśra-varga-sṛṣṭiṃ ca karoti, 38
Mita-prakāśikā, 115
mitāhāra, 61
Mithilā, 112

Mithyātva-khaṇḍana, 133
Mitra, Dr Rajendra Lal, 400
Mīmāṃsā, 107, 108 *n.*, 124, 247, 357, 350, 358, 539
Mīmāṃsakas, 15, 347
Mīmāṃsaka school, 205
Mīmāṃsā-pādukā, 124
Mīmāṃsā theory of error as non-discriminating memory-image and perception refuted, 247
Mīmāṃsā-sūtra, 7 *n.*, 107 *n.*, 108 *n.*, 124, 125
Mīmāṃsists, 152, 429, 518, 536
mleccha, 93, 441 *n.*
Mode, 42, 53, 194, 419; of syllogism, 364
Modification, 2, 3, 4, 6, 80, 183, 260 *n.*, 299, 323, 367, 423, 435, 454, 455, 459, 463, 468, 471, 495, 503
moha, 464, 500
mohana, 46
mohātmaka, 256
mokṣa, 62, 71, 523 *n.*
Mokṣa-dharma, 260 *n.*
Mokṣa-kāraṇatā-vāda, 133
Mokṣa-siddhi, 118, 352
Molecular, 206
Molecule, 183, 262
Moment, 47, 273, 277, 285, 286
Momentariness, 252, 268, 269, 272, 274
Momentarists, 271
Momentary, 268, 270, 275, 284; entities, 270; unit, 268, 269
Monetarist, 273
Monetary, 273
Monism, 4, 176, 308, 316, 320, 340, 371, 391, 477, 490, 495
Monist, 100, 106, 129, 416, 419
Monistic, 101, 196, 422, 486, 495; doctrine, 197, 477, 480; identity, 336; interpretation, 351, 417; texts, 5, 352, 406, 431; view, 406
Monotheistic, 13; God, 43 *n.*
Moon, 42, 59, 210, 228, 295, 310, 340, 447, 537
Moral, 29, 32, 33, 472, 501, 549; apprehension, 32; freedom, 472; heroes, 88; responsibility, 291, 533; sphere, 273; values, 457, 460
Morality, 303, 516, 533
Mother's breast, 77
Motion, 206
Motivation, 44
Motive, 54, 293, 294
Motor organs, 543
Mouth, 59
Movement, 44, 45, 53, 56, 189, 210, 446, 449, 481, 493, 504
mṛd-dravya, 258
mṛttva, 258
mṛtyu, 447
Much, 494
Mud, 397
Mudal-āṛvārs, 68 *n.*
Muḍal-tiru-vantādi, 134 *n.*
mugdha, 328
mukta, 60
mukti, 11, 50, 51, 89, 487
Mukti-darpaṇa, 115 *n.*, 384
Mukti-śabda-vicāra, 127
Mukunda, 425, 426
Mukunda-mālā, 66, 67, 80 *n.*
Mumukṣu-ppaḍi, 135 *n.*
Mumukṣū-pāya-saṃgraha, 114 *n.*, 125
Mundane, 16, 34, 41, 295, 452; bondage, 414; forms, 40; gods, 38; life, 43 *n.*, 292
Muni-vāhana-bhoga, 124
Munṛām-tiru-vantādi, 134 *n.*
Muṇḍakopaniṣat-prakāśikā, 127
Muttering, 23; of mantras, 62
Mutual agreement, 201
mūḍha, 499
mūla, 46
Mūla-bhāva-prakāśikā, 115, 117 ,126
mūla-doṣāpekṣā, 177 *n.*
mūlā-dhāra, 58
mūrdhaṇya-nāḍī, 295
Mysore, 113, 121, 124 *n.*
Mysore Gazetteer, 104 *n.*
Mystic, 53; cognition, 168
Mysticism and Logic, 539 *n.*
Mythical, 364, 550
Mythological, 25

na, 476
na cai'kyaṃ nāśa-bādhayoḥ, 239
Nacchiyār, 69
Naciketa, 519
Naḍāḍur Ammal, 110
Naḍāḍur Āṛvān, 104
naimittika, 293, 294, 502, 503
naimittika pralaya, 502
Naināräcārya, 111
Naiṣadhacarita, 549
Naiyāyikas, 146, 152, 155, 211, 219, 221, 225, 230, 233, 262, 263, 264, 265, 280, 291, 300, 347, 355, 358, 359, 393, 518, 539, 546
Nakṣatra-mālikā, 138
namaḥ, 53
Nambi, 67 *n.*, 100
Nambilla, 110

Namburi Varada, 110
Namburi Varadārya, 110, 111
Namburi Varadarāja, 134, 135
Names, 3, 4, 34, 47, 48, 209, 457, 544
Nāmm'-āṛvār, 63, 64, 65, 66, 68, 69, 74, 78, 79, 83, 94, 95, 98, 110, 134
Nandagōpāl, 77
Nandivarman, 67
Nanjiar, 110, 134, 135
Nan-mukham Tiru-vantādi, 68
Nappinnāi, 77, 81
Nara, 12, 40 *n.*
Naraharideva, 402
Narasiṃha, 40 *n.*
Narasiṃha-sūri, 122
Narasiṃhavarman I, 65, 67
Narasimhiengar, Mr M. T., 134 *n.*, 138
Narcotic, 79
Nasik, 3
Natesan and Co., 104 *n.*
natthi, 520
natthika, 520
natthika-diṭṭhi, 520
nātthikavāda, 521
Natural, 51; omniscience, 214 *n.*
Nature, 35, 42, 44, 45, 46, 50, 52, 53, 54, 56, 57, 100 *n.*, 128, 146, 166, 180, 193, 195, 197, 206, 253, 256, 306, 310, 315, 317, 325, 331, 334, 344, 350, 389, 407, 408, 411, 413, 414, 415, 420, 428, 431, 439, 442, 448, 499, 450, 461, 466, 483, 485, 545; of Lakṣmī, 375; of soul, 79
Navaratna-mālā, 135 *n.*
Nava-vidha-sambandha, 135 *n.*
Navel, 58
Navel-wheel, 59
Navyaraṅgeśa, 122
Naya-dyu-maṇi, 114 *n.*, 115, 116, 125, 215 *n.*, 216 *n.*, 217 *n.*, 219 *n.*, 220 *n.*, 234 *n.*, 239 *n.*, 242 *n.*, 243 *n.*, 245 *n.*, 247 *n.*, 346, 347 *n.*, 348 *n.*, 349 *n.*, 392
Naya-dyu-maṇi-dīpikā, 115, 116, 392
Naya-dyu-maṇi of *Naya-dyu-maṇi-dīpikā*, 115
Naya-dyu-maṇi-saṃgraha, 115, 116, 392
Naya-kuliśa, 118
Naya-mālikā, 116 *n.*
Naya-maṇi-kalikā, 130
Naya-mukha-mālikā, 114, 116, 133
Naya-prakāśikā, 114, 346
Naya-vīthi, 186 *n.*
nābhi-cakra, 59
Nācchiyār-tirumoḻi, 134 *n.*
nāda, 58
nāḍīs, 59, 60
nāga, 59
Nāgārjuna, 307, 522
nāga-vāyu, 60
Nāl-āyira-divya-prabandham, 64, 66, 69, 77
Nāl-āyira-prabandham, 69
nāmadheya, 4
nāma-dheyam, 3
nāma-saṅkīrtana-rataḥ, 96
Nām-mukam, 134 *n.*
Nārada, 13, 25, 40 *n.*, 401; his journey to Śveta-dvīpa, 13
Nāradīya, 20
Nāradīya-purāṇa, 507, 508 *n.*; philosophical elements in, 507
Nārāyaṇa, 12, 13, 16, 17, 19, 21, 39, 40 *n.*, 42 *n.*, 68 *n.*, 86, 89 *n.*, 100 *n.*, 101, 126, 128, 129, 132, 136, 157, 304, 352 *n.*, 375, 379, 401, 474, 475, 482, 507, 511 *n.*; alone, 126; as highest God, 12; associated with Pañcarātra, 12; his worship in the Śvetadvīpa, 13
Nārāyaṇadeva, 402
Nārāyaṇa muni, 116, 131
Nārāyaṇa Śarmā, 404
Nārāyaṇīya, 40 *n.*, 443 *n.*
Nārāyaṇopaniṣad, 13
Nāstika, 512, 517, 518, 519, 525, 527; its significance, 517 *et seq.*
Nāstika cārvāka, 512 *n.*
nāstikaśāstra, 515
Nāthamuni, 66, 67 *n.*, 85, 94, 95, 96, 97, 98, 119, 180, 181 *n.*, 233, 235; he practised *aṣṭāṅga yoga*, 96 *n.*; his life, 94 *et seq.*
Nāthas, 525 *n.*
nātha-vādins, 525
Negation, 5, 169, 186, 202, 214, 230, 232, 243, 255, 271, 272, 283, 312, 314, 327, 330, 331, 332, 339, 342, 344, 351, 352, 353, 354, 412, 420, 424, 428, 431, 445, 467, 476; antecedent to being, 279; of occupation, 282; of *vācyatva*, 230 *n.*
Negation-precedent-to, 328, 330, 351; production, 338, 341, 344, 345, 353, 369
Negative, 181, 183, 186, 187, 252, 343; causes, 354; characters, 170; concept, 282; concomitance, 229; entity, 341; instance, 228, 229; means, 376; pain, 364; qualifications, 323; relation, 231
Nerve, 59, 295
Nervous system, 58

Nescience, 177, 311, 316, 361, 362, 441, 442, 460, 465
neti, 431
Neutral datum, 253
New knowledge, 184
New measure, 264
nididhyāsana, 405, 442
nidrā, 57
Nigamaparimala, 124
nigraha, 51
nigrahasthāna, 512
Nihilism, 177, 269, 307, 320, 332, 334, 419
Nihilist, 350, 520, 533
Nihilistic, 520, 521; Buddhists, 201; philosophy, 177 *n.*; sect, 533
niḥsambandhaḥ, 11
niḥsvabhāva, 356
Nikāśa, 123
Nikāya, 524
Nikṣepa-rakṣā, 122
Nimba, 399
Nimbapura, 399
Nimbāditya, 399, 400, 401
Nimbārka, 399, 400, 402, 403, 404, 405, 409, 420, 422, 424, 426, 427, 428, 433, 434, 440, 472, 497, 506; his *bhāṣya*, 400; his conception of *ahaṅkāra*, 411 *et seq.*; his conception of *ajñāna*, 404 *et seq.*; his conception of *karma*, 411; his criticism of Śaṅkara, 409 *et seq.*; his idea of *avidyā*, 414; his idea of God, 412 *et seq.*; his idea of *karma*, 414 *et seq.*; his philosophy, 400, 404 *et seq.*; his works, 400–2; Nature of self, 411 *et seq.*; school, 401, 408, 440; system, 413; teachers and pupils of the school, 379 *et seq.*; view, 430
Nimbārka-matam, 401
Nimbārkists, 410, 411, 434, 440
nimitta, 2, 388, 456
nimitta-kāraṇa, 157, 191, 398
nimitta-kāraṇatā, 396
nimittamātram, 500
Nineteenth century, 188
Niṇru kumiṛume, 78
nir-adhiṣṭhāna-bhramā-nupapattiḥ, 238
niranvaya-vināśa, 274, 276
nirapekṣatayānanda, 36
niravayava, 201
nirbharatva, 86
nirgranthas, 523
nirguṇa, 25
nirhetuka, 85
Nirvāṇa, 28
nirvikalpa, 217, 219, 220, 221, 224, 270, 311, 544; knowledge, 544
nirvikalpa jñāna, 221
nirvikalpa-pratyakṣa, 166, 223
nirviśeṣa, 165, 195
nirviśeṣa caitanya, 420
Nirviśeṣa-pramāṇa-vyudāsa, 133
nir-viṣaya-khyāti, 239, 246
niṣkala, 31
niṣkramya, 527
niṣprapañca brahman, 10
nitya, 36, 293, 294, 502
nitya-raṅgitva, 87 *n.*
nitya-śūratva, 88 *n.*
nivartaka, 61
nivṛtta, 165
niyama, 29, 33, 61, 62 *n.*, 509 *n.*
Niyamānanda, 399, 403
niyati, 42, 43, 45, 57, 448 *n.*
Nīlameghatātācārya, 133
nīla-paṭa, 527 *n.*
Nīlā, 41, 42, 57
nīrūpa, 238 *n.*
Nīti, 235
Noble qualities, 70, 71
Non-appearance, 365
Non-apprehension, 180, 181, 182, 183, 184, 185, 186, 187, 188, 237, 284
Non-being, 239, 312, 314, 456, 457, 509
Non-Buddhists, 514
Non-dependence, 37
Non-difference, 487
Non-different, 484
Non-discrimination, 247
Non-distinction, 449, 491
Non-duality, 488
Non-earthiness, 227
Non-eternal, 199, 208, 209, 212, 213, 386, 446, 470, 478
Non-eternality, 386
Non-eternity, 394
Non-existence, 27, 177, 211, 229, 235, 344, 410, 428, 435, 436, 473, 476, 478, 507
Non-existent, 5, 47, 177, 266, 284, 327, 339, 344, 407, 423, 433, 436, 440, 445, 457, 477, 486
Non-existing, 184
Non-illumination, 314
Non-illusory, 246
Non-living, 456
Non-material, 146, 171
Non-materiality, 171
Non-mundane, 39
Non-observation, 279, 334
Non-occupiedness, 164

Non-perception, 128, 182, 207, 241, 342, 351, 426
Non-performance, 523
Non-physical, 548
Non-production, 449
Non-relational, 455
Non-sensible, 354
Non-sentient, 54
Non-spiritual characteristics, 172
Non-substance, 251
Non-vedic, 15, 16, 17, 19
Normal caste, 379
Normal duties, 92, 380
North India, 63, 523
Northern India, 103
Nothingness, 36
Notices, 400 *n.*; of *Sanskrit Manuscripts*, 403
Notion, 297, 298, 300, 310, 324, 337, 341, 343, 349, 351, 353, 418, 443, 538, 542; of validity, 248
Not-self, 409
Not-silver, 183
Nṛsiṃha, 39 *n.*, 40 *n.*
Nṛsiṃhadeva, 122, 123
Nṛsiṃharāja, 123, 131
Nṛsiṃha-rājīya, 122
Nṛsiṃhasūri, 131
Nṛsiṃha-tāpinī Upaniṣad, 13
Nṛsiṃhārya, 109, 110
Nṛsiṃhottara-tāpinī Upaniṣad, 13
Nuns, 104
nūkhya varga, 502
N.W. Provinces Catalogue, 400
Nyagrodhaśāyin, 40 *n.*
nyāsa, 55, 90, 131
Nyāsa-kārikā, 380
Nyāsa-tilaka, 122, 125, 131, 380
Nyāsa-tilaka-vyākhyā, 122, 125, 380
Nyāsa-vidyā-bhūṣaṇa, 132
Nyāsa-vidyārtha-vicāra, 133
Nyāsa-vidyā-vijaya, 127
Nyāsa-viṃśati, 122, 380
Nyāsavivṛti, 131
Nyāya, 9, 128, 131, 153, 154, 157, 203, 204, 206, 207 *n.*, 208, 212 *n.*, 234, 235, 262, 263, 300, 358, 471, 517, 538; categories, 539; logic, 226; objection, 249; refutation of the doctrine of whole and parts by Veṅkaṭa, 263 *et seq.*; Veṅkaṭa's refutation of atomic theory, 262 *et seq.*
Nyāya-bhāskara, 133
Nyāya-kuliśa, 118, 128 *n.*, 184, 186 *n.*, 250 *n.*, 251 *n.*, 352, 353 *n.*, 354 *n.*, 355 *n.*, 356 *n.*, 357 *n.*, 358 *n.*, 360 *n.*
Nyāya-kusumāñjali, 1, 539 *n.*
Nyāya-mañjarī, 203, 204 *n.*, 205 *n.*, 206 *n.*, 513 *n.*, 516, 519, 535 *n.*, 536 *n.*, 538 *n.*, 539, 540 *n.*, 547, 548
Nyāya-pariśuddhi, 96 *n.*, 119, 123, 125, 127, 128 *n.*, 131, 180, 202 *n.*, 208 *n.*, 209 *n.*, 210, 213 *n.*, 216 *n.*, 219 *n.*, 220 *n.*, 222 *n.*, 223 *n.*, 225 *n.*, 226, 227 *n.*, 228 *n.*, 232 *n.*, 233 *n.*, 234 *n.*, 235, 236 *n.*, 237 *n.*, 239 *n.*
Nyāya-pariśuddhi-vyākhyā, 131
Nyāya-ratnāvalī, 131
Nyāya-sāra, 123, 127, 128 *n.*, 202 *n.*, 203 *n.*, 222 *n.*, 223 *n.*, 237 *n.*, 238 *n.*
Nyāya-siddhāñjana, 117, 123, 126, 128 *n.*, 157 *n.*, 251, 259 *n.*, 261 *n.*, 280 *n.*, 297, 382, 383 *n.*
Nyāya-siddhāñjana-vyākhyā, 117, 126
Nyāya-sudarśana, 119 *n.*, 128 *n.*
Nyāya-sūtra, 76 *n.*, 208, 211–12, 300 *n.*, 512, 513, 517, 539
Nyāya-tattva, 96, 119, 128 *n.*, 233, 235
Nyāya-Vaiśeṣika, 162, 471
Nyāyāmṛta-taraṅgiṇī, 138
Ṇattva-tattva-vibhūṣaṇa, 133
Ṇattvopapatti-bhaṅga, 133
Ṇatva-candrikā, 131
Ṇatva-darpaṇa, 115
Ṇatva-tattva-paritrāṇa, 129

Object(s), 30, 33, 41, 47, 49, 50, 178, 179, 181, 182, 184, 185 *n.*, 189, 190, 205, 206, 210, 244, 280, 289, 297 *n.*, 298, 307, 309, 311, 312, 315, 316, 317, 318, 319, 320, 343, 347, 348, 351, 415, 419, 423, 426, 427, 439, 442, 444, 457, 458, 466, 467, 474, 477, 500, 506, 544; its matter according to Veṅkaṭa and Meghanādāri, 217; of awareness, 231, 318, 319; of knowledge, 241, 243; of perception, 246, 346
Objection, 298, 299, 303, 308, 315, 316, 317, 320, 321, 333, 343, 392, 408, 409, 417, 418, 422, 437, 477, 537
Objective, 53, 58, 179, 182, 490; awarenesses, 238; cognition, 9; entities, 188, 247, 360, 362; factors, 236; world, 246
Objectively, 182 *n.*
Objectivity, 315, 325
Obligatory, 441; duty, 124, 137, 293
Observation, 209, 257
Obstacles, 33
Obstruction, 183, 282, 449, 466, 481
Obstructive attitude, 376
Occasion, 47, 60
Occasionalism, 159

Occupation, 282
Occurrence, 205
Ocean, 52, 301, 302, 304, 445, 447, 450, 451, 452
Odorousness, 212 *n.*
Odour-potential, 48
Offering, 23, 550
Older school, 91, 92
Omnipotence, 24, 51, 200, 450, 462, 472
Omnipotent, 10, 11, 15, 34, 303, 443; being, 336
Omniscience, 24, 50, 51, 158, 195, 198, 200, 432, 433, 472, 506
Omniscient, 9, 11, 27, 44, 152, 303, 318, 335, 405, 430, 443
Oṃkāra-vādārtha, 392
Ontological, 118, 180, 185 *n.*, 195, 497; argument, 231
Ontologically, 180
Openings, 59
Operation, 45, 46, 56, 185, 204, 205, 206, 267, 297, 312, 318, 329, 331, 411, 412, 413, 423, 427, 433, 446, 448, 459, 460, 470, 475, 547
Opinion, 93, 210
Opponent, 116 *n.*, 230, 249
Opportunity, 292
Opposites, 230
Opposition, 208
Order, 49, 58, 195
Ordinary, 43; methods, 58; personality, 82
Organ, 48, 490
Organic, 151, 455
Organs of sight, 182
Origin, 212, 466, 468, 490; of *Bhakti* in *Bhāgavata-māhātya*, 63; of knowledge, 543
Original, 42, 58; course, 396
Origination, 321
Oscillation, 264
Otherness, 351
Oudh Catalogue, 400 *n.*

Padma, 20, 60
Padmalocana Bhaṭṭa, 98
Padmanābha, 39, 110, 118
Padmanābhācārya, 401
Padmanābhārya, 352, 361
Padma Purāṇa, 484, 507, 532
Padmapurāṇa, reference to Bhakti in, 507
Padma Saṃhitā, 23
Padma-tantra, 39 *n.*, 42 *n.*; *avatāras* in, 39 *n.*
Padmācārya, 401
Padmākara Bhaṭṭa, 401
Pain, 146, 148, 171, 189, 256, 259, 290, 301, 302, 344, 349, 412, 427, 442, 449, 463, 464, 485, 486, 489, 490, 493, 494
Painful, 256, 289, 415, 416, 452
Pairs, 42
pakṣa, 231, 427, 534, 535
pakṣadharma, 534
Palar, 63
Pallava king, 67
Pallavamalla, 65
Pallava-maṭha, 137
Pallavas, 65, 67
Pamphlet, 123, 124
Panar, 64, 69
Panentheism, 497
Pangs, of love, 72; of separation, 73; of sorrow, 70
Pantheism, 497, 498
Pantheistic, 498
pañcama, 15, 17
Pañca-pādikā-vivaraṇa, 196, 197 *n.*, 198 *n.*
Pañcarātra(s), 2, 12, 14, 15, 16, 17, 18, 19, 20, 22, 38 *n.*, 40 *n.*, 42 *n.*, 50, 56, 57, 58, 62, 103, 105, 122, 125, 132, 157, 303, 379, 448 *n.*, 471, 475; antiquity of, 12; conflict between Brahminic authorities about, 19; contents of, 18–19; doctrine, 503; instructed by God, 14; its antiquity, 19; its ideal different from the Vedas, 17; its relation with the Vedas, 18; its validity attested in *Puruṣa-nirṇaya* of Yāmuna, 16; not polytheistic, 17; originated how, 21; *Purāṇas* that are favourable and unfavourable to it, 20; *puruṣa-sūkta*, associated with, 12; regarded as *tantra*, 18 *n.*; relation with the Vedas, 12; religion, 20; rituals not non-Vedic, 17; sacrifice, 12; texts, 13; valid as the injunction of God, 14; worship, 19
Pañcarātra literature, 18, 21, 24; its validity attested by Yāmuna, 10; works enumerated, 21 *et seq.*
Pañcarātra-rakṣā, 18, 122
Pañcarātra-rakṣā-saṃgraha, 18
Pañcarātra-saṃhitā, 12 *n.*, 155
Pañcarātra-śāstra, 21
Pañcarātrins, 14, 19, 20; denounced in *smṛti* and *Purāṇa*, 19–20; identical with *Bhāgavatas* and *Sātvatas*, 15; possess a lower stage, 15
pañca-saṃskāra, 102

Pañcādhyāyi-śāstra, 3 *n.*
Pañcāgni-vidyā, 382, 384
Pañcī-karaṇa, 182, 237, 240
Pañjikā, 131
Paṇḍita, 94, 130, 177 *n.*
para, 41, 42, 489
para-brahma, 474, 509
Parakāla, 63
Parakāladāsa, 111
Parakāla Yati, 115, 117, 126, 127, 305
para-loka, 518, 548
Parama, 32
Parama-pāda-sopāna, 124
Parama-saṃhitā, 22, 24, 32, 33; Bhakti, rise of, in, 33–4; its contents, 22; *karma* and *jñāna-yoga* in, 33; *karma-yoga* and *jñāna-yoga* in, 22; *vairāgya*, nature of, in, 33; *yoga* in, 32
Para-mata-bhaṅga, 123, 124, 128 *n.*
Parama-tattva-nirṇaya, 23
paramārtha, 165, 378
paramātman, 7, 34, 445, 451, 452, 453, 487, 489, 502
parameśvara, 89, 475, 489
Parameśvara-saṃhitā, 23
Parameśvarvarman II, 65
parameṣṭhin, 447
Paranda-paḍi, 135 *n.*
Para-pakṣa-giri-vajra, 403, 414 *n.*, 416, 417 *n.*, 418 *n.*, 425 *n.*, 428 *n.*, 429 *n.*, 430 *n.*, 431 *n.*, 432 *n.*, 433 *n.*, 434 *n.*, 435 *n.*, 437 *n.*, 440 *n*
Paraśurāma, 38, 40 *n.*, 429
Paraśurāmadeva, 402
parataḥ pramāṇa, 9
parataḥ-prāmāṇya, 248, 249
para-tantra-sattvā, 430
Para-tattva, 24
Para-tattva-dīpikā, 122
Para-tattva-nirṇaya, 138
Para-tattva-prakāśa, 23
Para-tattva-prakāśikā, 127
Paravastu Prativādibhayaṅkara Aṇṇayācārya, 111
Paravādibhayaṅkara, 112
parā, 509
parā-kāśatva, 88 *n.*
parāmarśa, 225, 427
Parāṅkuśa, 65, 78
Parāṅkuśa-pūrṇārya, 102 *n.*
Parāntaka, 67
Parāntaka Cola I, 96
Parāntaka, King, 65
Parāntaka Pāṇḍya, 65
parārthānumāna, 427
Parāśara, 134, 260 *n.*, 479
Parāśara Bhaṭṭa, 235
Parāśara Bhaṭṭāraka, 119
Parāśara Bhaṭṭārya, 102 *n.*, 104, 109, 110, 134, 135
Parāśara purāṇa, 19
Parāśara saṃhitā, 22; its contents, 22–3
parātman, 486
Parents, 70
Parikara-vijaya, 131, 361
parimāṇa, 254, 264, 397
parimita-gambhīra-bhāṣiṛā, 108
pariṇāma, 6, 106, 197
pariṇāma kāraṇa, 365
pariṇāmi kāraṇa, 365, 366
pariṇāmi-rūpa, 484
paritrāṇa, 40
parokṣa, 62
parokṣa-vṛtti, 425
Part, 30, 49, 178, 189, 191, 192, 194, 195, 262, 286, 291, 295, 300, 301, 307, 308, 312, 408, 409, 411, 422, 430, 432, 433, 434, 444, 447 *n.*, 453, 456, 462, 464, 475, 493, 494
Particles, 263, 264; of consciousness, 141
Particular, 193, 299, 537; proposition, 202
Partless, 201, 263, 306, 358, 365, 422, 432, 548; atoms, 263; real, 372
Paryaṃka, 30
Passionate lover, 82
Passionate yearning, 83
Passions, 32, 51, 54, 317, 318, 488
Past, 182, 446, 447, 457, 533; experience, 184, 185 *n.*
paśyantī, 58
Patañjali, 61 *n.*, 62, 239, 444, 470, 473, 479, 480, 515, 516, 518, 523; his *Mahā-bhāṣya*, 516 *n.*
Patañjali-sūtra, 478
Paternal affection, 158
Path, of *bhakti*, 380 *n.*; of knowledge, 89; of right, 61; of virtue, 158
Pathological symptoms, 83
Paths of duties, 91
Paṭṭars, 104
paurāṇic, 482
Paurāṇic emotionalism, 451
pauruṣa, 30
Pauṣkara, 21, 22
Pauṣkara-saṃhitā, 23, 24
Payasvinī, 59, 63
Pazhanadai-vilakkan, 94 *n.*
Pādukā-sahasra-nāma, 122
Pāli, 512, 513 *n.*; texts, 514
Pāli Dictionary, 520

Pāli-English Dictionary, 513
Pañcarātrikas, 3 *n.*
Pāṇḍya, 65, 67, 98
Pāṇini, 108 *n.*, 516 *n.*, 518, 523
pāramārthika, 313
pāramārthikī, 371
pāratantrya, 87
Pārāśara, 20
Pārāśarya, 125
Pārāśarya-vijaya, 117, 305
Pārāśaryya-vijayā'di-pūrvā'cārya-prabandhā-nusāreṇa, 128 *n.*
Pārijātahara, 40 *n.*
Pārijāta-saurabha, 406 *n.*
pāṣaṇḍī, 518
pāṣaṇḍino, 518
Pāśupata, 3 *n.*, 16
Pāśupata-tantra, 155
Pātālaśayana, 40 *n.*
Pāvaka, 39
Pela Puradeśika, 132
Penance, 13, 24, 29, 34, 160
People, 43 *n.*
Perceivability, 438, 439
Perceived qualities, 252
Perceiver, 284, 315, 321, 398, 547
Percept, 185 n.
Perception, 14, 80, 128, 141, 151, 152, 166, 168, 174, 177, 179, 181, 182, 184, 185, 187, 188, 199, 202, 208, 210, 211, 212, 214, 215, 216, 217, 218, 220, 221, 222, 224, 237, 241, 242, 252, 254, 268, 269, 270, 280, 284, 306, 307, 310, 311, 312, 313, 315, 324, 326, 327, 328, 334, 343, 351, 353, 356, 368, 390, 398, 406, 412, 426, 427, 465, 472, 533, 537; its definition, 216–17; *savikalpa* and *nirvikalpa*, 220–4; treatment by Veṅkaṭanātha and Meghanādāri, 216 *et seq.*; view on, by later members of the Rāmānuja school, 220 *et seq.*
Perceptual, 79, 309, 411; cognition, 250 *n.*; evidence, 298; experience, 320, 326, 327, 328, 390, 536; knowledge, 212, 326; form, 246
Perfect, 295; knowledge, 50
Perfection, 31, 122, 194
Performance, 33, 293, 530
Periya-jīyar, 94 *n.*, 110, 111, 137
Periyalnāmbi, 103
Periya Nambi, 67 *n.*
Periyar, 63
Periya-tiru-maḍal, 69, 134 *n.*
Periya-tirumoḻi, 134 *n.*
Periya-tiru-moṟi, 69
Periya-tiru-muḍiy-aḍaivu, 64, 105
Periya tiru-vantādi, 69, 134 *n.*
Periy-āṟvār, 63, 64, 65, 66 *n.*, 68, 69, 77
Periy-āṟvār-tirumoṟi, 134 *n.*
Periy-āṟvār-tiruppalāṇḍu, 134 *n.*
Permanent, 144, 198, 291, 343, 541, 546; world, 198 *n.*
Permāḍi, 66
per se, 431
Person, 49, 189, 191, 401, 472
Personal continuity, 143
Personal effort, 378
Personal God, 472
Personal identity, 142
Personal service, 104
Personality, 49, 100 *n.*
Peru-māl, 64, 134 *n.*
Peru-māl Jīyar, 64
Perumāl Temple, 523
Perumāl-tirumoḻi, 134 *n.*
Peru-māl-tiru-moṟi, 69
Pervasive entities, 263
Pessimism, 550
Pēy, 68
Pēy-āṟvār, 63, 64, 65, 66 *n.*, 68 *n.*, 134 *n.*
Phala-bheda-khaṇḍana, 125
Phenomena, 205, 238, 340, 365, 407, 456
Phenomenal, 454; world, 155, 164
Phenomenalism, 238, 285
Phenomenon, 142, 180, 266, 272, 302, 467, 542
Philosopher, 202, 449
Philosophical, 120, 126, 181, 305, 307, 364, 395, 525; doctrines, 22; elements, 24; importance, 21; reality, 377; speculation, 79; topics, 23; wisdom, 89
Philosophy, 34, 107, 112, 119, 195, 235, 305, 319, 413, 445, 471, 472, 482, 496, 508 *n.*, 512, 513
Phraseology, 196
Phrases, 309
Physical, 205, 310, 530; elements, 547; practices, 60
Physico-biological, 298
Physics, 515 *n.*
Physiological, 530; change, 140
Pictorial, 455
Piece of iron, A, 26
Pilgrimage, 55, 120
Pillai Lokācārya, 110, 111, 120, 134, 135, 137, 138
Piḷḷai Lokamjīyar, 105
Piḷḷai Lokācāryar, 64
Pillar edict, 522
Pillān, 66

Pinb'-aṟagiya, 64
Pinb'-aṟagiya Perū-māl Jīyar, 94 *n.*, 105
Piṅgalā, 59, 60
Pioneers, 84
Pirān, 63
Piszzagalli, Dr, 512 *n.*
pitṛ-yāna, 517
pitta, 475
Pity, 52
Piyaruli-ceyalare-rahasya, 135
Pīyūṣaharaṇa, 40 *n.*
Place, 185 *n.*
Playful, 51
Pleasurable, 46, 256, 289, 415, 416, 452; ends, 294
Pleasure, 71, 146, 148, 154, 171, 189, 256, 259, 282, 290, 291, 292, 301, 302, 303, 304, 326, 349, 365, 412, 427, 442, 444, 449, 463, 464, 470, 485, 486, 489, 490, 493, 494, 513, 528, 550
Plurality, 165, 174, 194, 264, 398
Poetry, 68, 121
Point, 192, 195, 209, 416
Poison, 364
Polemic, 403
Polemical discussions, 305
Polemical work, 123
Political science, 515
Polity, 515, 532
Pollution, 303
Pontifical, 111; chair, 134
Pope, 84 *n.*
Position, 194, 195, 331, 339, 349, 352
Positive, 178, 183, 186, 187, 252, 323, 343, 351, 362, 441; *ajñāna*, 364, 365; bliss, 136; category, 243; defects, 331; entity, 164, 177, 271, 272, 282, 317, 327, 339, 341, 345, 353, 354, 424; experience, 238, 282; ignorance, 330, 332, 336; inference, 329; instances, 230; means, 376; moment, 272; nescience, 361, 362; perception, 363; pleasure, 294; proposition, 229; state, 344; stuff, 332, 364
Positivity, 282
Possibilities, 207
Posture, 30, 60
Potency, 347
Potential, 35, 37, 266, 445, 461; effect, 266; form, 50, 56; power, 541
Pots, 453
Potter, 453
Potter's wheel, 342
Power, 35, 41, 42, 43, 44, 46, 50, 51, 52, 53, 56, 57, 60, 136, 153, 155, 184, 190, 193, 197, 301, 441, 445, 471, 473, 475, 477, 500, 505, 506, 509, 524, 540, 548
Poygaiy, 64, 68, 523
Poygaiy-āṟvār, 63, 65, 66 *n.*, 68 *n.*, 134 *n.*
Prabandham, 67
prabandhas, 91
Prabandha-sāra, 94 *n.*
Prabandha-sāram, 66
Prabhācandra, 206, 516
Prabhākara, 181, 185 *n.*; his view, 185 *n.*
prabhā-tadvatoriva 416
Prabodha-candro-daya, 122, 531 *n.*, 532
prabuddhi, 510
Practical, 265, 458; behaviour, 4, 466; conduct, 5; experiences, 341, 371; philosophy, 22
Practice, 29, 30, 31, 33, 293
Pradhāna, 25, 34, 472, 475, 476, 477, 478, 485, 489, 492, 497, 498, 502, 505, 506, 509
Pradhānā-śataka, 124
pradhvaṃsā-bhāva, 353
Pradyumna, 13, 37, 39, 42, 43, 52, 56, 57, 157, 158, 443 *n.*, 475; stage, 57
pragalbha nāstika, 526, 527
Pragmatic value, 335
prajāpati, 48, 295, 447, 528
prajñā, 47, 503, 510
Prajñānidhi, 126
Prajñā-paritrāṇa, 119, 128 *n.*, 208, 212, 214 *n.*, 234
Prakaraṇa-pañcikā, 185 *n.*, 186 *n.*
prakāra, 156
prakāśa, 358, 373, 416
Prakāśa-saṃhitā, 23
Prakāśātman, 196, 197, 198 *n.*; criticized by Rāmānuja, 197; his view of relation between *māyā* and Brahman, 198 *n.*
Prakāśātmā, 25
prakṛti, 24, 25, 26, 28, 30, 31, 32, 34, 36, 38, 43, 45, 46, 47, 49, 56, 57, 61, 144, 147, 156, 158, 163, 164, 172, 173, 239, 256, 257, 258, 259, 260 *n.*, 261, 266, 280, 296, 301, 381, 384, 444, 445, 446, 449, 453, 454, 455, 456, 459, 460, 463, 464, 469, 472, 473, 474, 476, 477, 479, 480, 481, 482, 484, 485, 486, 487, 489, 491, 492, 493, 494, 495, 498, 502, 503, 504, 505, 506, 507, 508, 509
prakṛti-prasūti, 502

pralaya, 13, 36, 56, 156, 169, 446, 459, 477, 481, 493, 502, 503
pramā, 62, 203, 467
pramāṇa, 62, 125, 201, 202, 203, 204, 205, 206, 214, 215, 216, 234, 235, 236, 239, 240, 247, 248, 249, 346, 351, 361, 390, 423, 426, 427, 428, 468, 469, 503 *n.*, 537, 539; as *artha-paricchedakatva*, 240; Buddhist view of it, 205; difference between Rāmānuja Nyāya and Śaṅkara, 204; difference of view regarding it between Veṅkaṭa and Meghanādāri, 240; Jaina view, 205; Jayanta's view, 203; Kumārila's view, 205; Meghanādāri's definition of, 239; refutation of it by Śrīharṣa, 201; Vātsya-Śrīnivāsa's treatment of it, 203; Veṅkaṭa's definition, 236; Veṅkaṭa's treatment of it, 201 *et seq.*
pramāṇa-phala, 205, 467
Pramāṇa-saṃgraha, 20
Pramāṇa-sāra, 133, 138
Pramāṇas, treatment by Mādhava Mukunda, 426 *et seq.*
pramāṇārtha, 62
pramātā, 368
pramātṛ-tattva, 547
prameya, 248
Prameya-kamala-mārtaṇḍa, 206
Prameya-mālā, 349, 351 *n.*
Prameya-saṃgraha, 128 *n.*, 214 *n.*, 216 *n.*, 234
Prameya-sāra, 110
Prameya-śekhara, 135 *n.*
prameyatva, 230 *n.*
prameyatvāt, 230
Praṇatārtihara, 109
Praṇatārtihara Pillan, 110
Prapanna, meanings of, 91
Prapanna-paritrāṇa, 135 *n.*
Prapanna-pārijāta, 352, 380
Prapanna-sāvitrī, 137
Prapannā-mṛta, 63 *n.*, 94, 97 *n.*, 98, 100, 102 *n.*, 105, 108, 109 *n.*, 110 *n.*, 138 *n.*
Prapannāmṛta relates, 97 *n.*
Prapañca-mithyātva-bhaṅga, 126
prapatti, 54, 55, 68, 86, 89, 90, 91, 92, 96, 99, 101, 120, 122, 136, 137, 375, 376, 377, 378, 379, 380; according to Saumyajāmātṛ Muni, 374 *et seq.*; its accessories, 92; its *aṅgas*, 91 *n.*; its history, 379; its meaning, 90; its schools, 92 *et seq.*; its stages, 379
Prapatti-kārikā, 125
Prapatti-naiṣṭhikam, 86 *n.*
Prapatti-prayoga, 380
prapāṭhaka, 106
Prasaṅga-ratnākara, 396 *n.*
prasāda, 505
praśānti, 505
Praśna, 480
Praṣnopaniṣat-prakāśikā, 127
prasūti, 502
pratibandha, 538
pratibhā, 537
pratijñā, 427
Pratijñā-vāda, 133
pratinidhi-nyāya, 183
pratisañcara, 497
Pratiṣṭhā-kāṇḍa, 22
Prativādībhakeśarī, 117
Prativādibhayaṅkara, 112, 138
pratīter apahnava eva syāt, 238
pratyakṣa, 220, 224, 426
Pratyāhāra, 30, 61, 505
pravacana, 514
pravartaka, 61
pravāhā-nāditva, 177 *n.*
Prayoga-ratna-mālā, 116, 131
prayojana, 420
Prābhākara view, 248
prāga-bhāva, 169, 177, 279, 328, 338, 353, 428
Prājāpatya-smṛti, 20
prākaṭya, 148
prākṛta, 30
prākṛta-maṇḍala, 415
prākṛta-pralaya, 509
prākṛtā-tmā, 483
prākṛtika, 502, 503
prāmāṇika, 313
prāmāṇya, 202, 346, 347
prāṇa, 7, 47, 49, 59, 80, 405, 540
prāṇa vāyu, 59
prāṇāyāma, 22, 23, 30, 32, 60, 61, 505, 506, 509 *n.*
Prāpti-daśā, 379
Prāpyā-nubhava-daśā, 379
prārabdha, 445, 487, 488
prārabdha karma, 378, 389, 414, 443, 487
prātikūlyasya varjanam, 92
prāvaraṇa, 515
prāyaścitta, 92, 294; Veṅkaṭa's view, 294
Pre-Aryan, 531
Pre-Buddhistic Indian Philosophy, 521 *n.*
Preceptor, 28, 87, 89, 139, 156
Pre-condition, 253
Predicate, 80, 193, 271, 283, 438
Prediction, 345
Pre-existent effect, 265

Preferences, 34
Prejudices, 317
prema-bhakti, 401
Prema-sāra, 102
Premises, 178
Prerogative grace, 85
Presence, 54
Present, 181, 284, 285, 446, 533
Presentation, 180, 182
Pride, 529
Priest, 104, 550
Primary, 41; cause, 179 *n.*; entities, 440; forms, 39; sense, 306
Primeval, 42 *n.*
Primordial, 44, 45, 447; elements, 128
Principle, 31, 32, 47, 57, 201, 502, 505, 507, 508, 512; of agreement, 226; of consciousness, 322, 463
Pringle Pattison, 451
priori, 205
Priority, 419
Prior moment, 278
Priyālvar-tiru-moṛi, 138
prīti, 161
Prīti-kārita, 136
prīti-rūpo-paśāntatva-lakṣaṇam, 382
Probability, 214
Probandum, 225, 228, 229, 231 *n.*, 427, 534, 535
Proceedings and Transactions of the Third Oriental Conference, 106 *n.*
Process, 30, 32, 42, 49, 50, 52, 54, 55, 56, 205, 292, 442, 453, 455, 458, 475, 495
Procession, 69
Product, 26, 29, 34, 36, 208, 331, 409, 423, 448, 449, 455, 477, 510, 548
Production, 184, 199, 204, 206, 265, 267, 268, 277, 278, 284, 292, 300, 328, 330, 331, 341, 342, 344, 411, 416, 428, 447, 454, 473, 481
Productive capacity, 354
Productivity, 465
Progress, 464, 514
Progressive, 37
Prohibited actions, 62
Proofs, 189, 406, 407, 457, 458
Proportion, 46, 54
Propositions, 190, 193, 201, 202, 223, 225, 227, 319
Protection, 54
Protector, 499, 507
Proximity, 316, 498
Prudence, 550
pṛthivī, 49 *n.*
Psychical, 469; elements, 29
Psychological, 180, 185 *n.*, 210, 237; state, 380 *n.*; transformations, 395
Psychologically, 180
Psychosis, 29, 30, 151, 412, 464
Publicity, 120
Pulaha, 21
Pulastya, 21
Puṃ-śakti, 51
Punamalī, 98
Punishment, 51, 92, 415
Puṇḍarīkākṣa, 95, 96, 97, 98, 102 *n.*, 109, 118
Puṇḍravardhana, 524 *n.*
puṇya, 294
Pupil, 117, 127, 130, 131
pur, 503
Purandara, 536, 539
Purāṇa, 16, 19, 20, 71, 72, 99, 105, 125, 445, 448, 471, 479, 486, 496. 497, 520, 550
Purāṇa Kassapa, 520, 522; his views, 520
Purāṇic, 452, 497, 549; legends, 80
Purāṇika, 122
Pure, 32, 34, 42, 44, 50, 311, 413, 420, 423, 430, 454, 467, 469, 470, 479, 490, 499, 500; action, 56; being, 10, 167, 175, 192, 193, 200, 291, 302, 311; bliss, 27, 344, 444, 494; brahman, 333, 432, 440; consciousness, 24, 26, 28, 29, 35, 51, 57, 143, 145, 166, 170, 171, 309, 311, 319, 320, 322, 323, 324, 325, 345, 362, 363, 367, 368, 369, 370, 372, 373, 374, 408, 409, 419, 421, 423, 445, 446, 448, 449, 450, 451, 453, 455, 457, 458, 460, 461, 462, 485, 492, 494; creation, 27; energy, 447; existence, 497; experience, 169; form, 438; illumination, 195, 407; impure-creation, 57; indeterminate, 344; intelligence, 26, 147, 148, 154; knowledge, 176, 408, 439, 441; nature, 302, 306, 338; revelation, 169; self, 408; soul, 453; space, 283
Purest qualities, 430
Purification, 60, 442
Purificatory rites, 22
Purity, 6, 29, 160, 406, 438, 441, 524
Purī, 94, 96, 103, 120
purovarti vastu, 241
Purpose, 452, 474
Puruṣa, 23, 27, 29, 30, 31, 32, 36, 42, 43, 44, 45, 46, 47, 49, 52, 57, 147, 148, 259, 266, 296, 445, 446, 448, 449, 451, 453, 454, 455, 456, 459, 460, 461, 464, 466, 467, 468, 469,

Puruṣa (*cont.*)
470, 471, 473, 474, 475, 477, 479, 480, 484, 485, 486, 487, 488, 489, 490, 491, 492, 493, 495, 497, 498, 503, 504, 505, 507, 508, 509, 511, 527; conception of in Vijñāna Bhikṣu, 448; consciousness of, 464
puruṣakāra, 378
Puruṣa-ninnaya, 16, 96, 139, 352
puruṣa-sūkta, 12, 44, 105, 155
puruṣārtha, 136
Puruṣārtha-ratnākara, 132
puruṣāvatāra, 40 *n.*
"*puruṣo ha nārāyaṇaḥ*", 12
Puruṣottama, 38, 70, 116, 132, 403
Puruṣottama prasāda, 403
Puruṣottamānya, 112, 411
puryāṃ śete, 504
pūrṇa, 36
puṣṭi, 57
Pūrṇadeva, 402
Purva-mīmāṃsā, 350
pūrva-pakṣa, 519
pūrvā-nubhūta-rajata-saṃskāra-dvārā, 246
Pūṣā, 58
Pūtayogin, 63

Qualifications, 28, 305, 308, 323
Qualified, 165, 193, 430; concept, 244; entity, 255, 279; monism, 430
Qualifying relation, 252
Qualitative, 550
Quality, 10, 25, 30, 34, 35, 36, 48, 53, 54, 56, 61, 156, 181, 197, 207, 208, 209, 212 *n.*, 254, 255, 256, 284, 288, 306, 311, 317, 324, 336, 340, 343, 348, 351, 356, 357, 361, 411, 426, 429, 430, 433, 435, 441, 442, 455, 463, 465, 489, 493, 503, 505, 508, 510, 548
Qualityless, 31, 306, 406, 407, 408, 423, 430, 435, 499
Queen, 98
Question, 195

Raghunāthācārya, 133
Raghunāthārya, 117
Raghūttama, 137, 138
Rahasya-mātṛkā, 124
Rahasya-navanītam, 123
Rahasya-padavī, 123
Rahasya-rakṣā, 99 *n.*, 123, 380 *n.*
Rahasya-ratnāvalī, 126
Rahasya-ratnāvali-hṛdaya, 124
rahasyas, 94
Rahasya-sandeśa, 124
Rahasya-sandeśa-vivaraṇa, 124
Rahasya-śikhā-maṇi, 124
Rahasya-traya, 110 *n.*, 138
Rahasya-traya-culuka, 124, 125
Rahasya-traya-jīvātu, 131
Rahasya-traya-kārikā, 132
Rahasya-traya-mīmāṃsā, 117
Rahasya-traya-mīmāṃsā-bhāṣya, 126, 131
Rahasya-traya-sāra, 18, 63 *n.*, 124, 125 132
Rahasya-traya-sāra-saṃgraha, 133
Rahasya-traya-sāra-vyākhyā, 132
Rahasya-traya-sārārtha-saṃgraha, 125
rajas, 25, 43, 45, 46, 47, 48, 129, 156, 163, 259, 447, 473, 474, 475, 480, 481, 482, 501, 503, 504, 505, 507
Rajendracola, 96, 104
rajoguṇa, 448
rakṣiṣyatīti viśvāsaḥ, 92
Rallying, 79
Ramyajāmātṛ-mahā-muni, 94 *n.*, 98 *n.*
Ramya-jāmātṛ muni, 89, 110, 111, 112, 137; his works and relation to Rāmānuja, 137, 138
Raṅgadāsa, 130
Raṅganātha, 69, 98, 121, 135
Raṅganāthācārya, 132
Raṅgarāja, 132, 138
Raṅga Rāmānuja, 115, 116, 127; his works, 126, 127
Raṅga Rāmānuja Muni, 126
Raṅgācārya, 110, 116, 130, 133, 382, 384, 395, 396, 398 *n.*
Raṅgeśa, 102
Rapturous, 73, 79; passions, 83
rasa, 49 *n.*, 226, 510, 511
Rasa-bhaumāmṛta, 122
rasa-mātra, 510
rasa-tan-mātra, 163, 260, 261, 499
rati, 57
Rational, 177 *n.*
Ratna-prabhā, 107 *n.*
Ratna-sāriṇī, 114, 116, 132, 352
Raurava hell, 20
Ravishing joy, 83
Ravishing love, 79
Ravishment of soul, 79
Ray of lamp, 384
Rays, 182, 444
Rādhā, 81, 82, 401
Rādhā-kṛṣṇaśaraṇadeva, 402
rāga, 10, 470
rāga-prāpta-prapatti, 377
Rāghavācārya, 94, 133
Rāhoḥ śiraḥ, 4
Rāhu, 4, 239

Rāhujit, 40 *n.*
Rājagopāla, 95
Rājarāja, 523
rājasa, 31, 163, 498
rājasa ahaṃkāra, 31, 259, 504 *n.*
Rājasa-śāstra, 21, 22
Rākṣasa, 532
Rāma, 38, 39, 40 *n.*, 82, 429
Rāmacandra Bhaṭṭa, 401
Rāmadeśika, 102 *n.*
Rāmakṛṣṇa, 204
Rāma Miśra, 95, 97, 98, 114, 125, 181 *n.*, 395 *n.*
Rāma-miśra-deśika, 114
Rāmanātha Yogī, 133
Rāma-rahasya Upaniṣad, 13
Rāma Subrahmaṇyasāśtrī, 132
Rāmatāpinī Upaniṣad, 13
Rāmatīrtha, 106, 107, 197 *n.*
Rāmānuja, 1 *n.*, 3, 24, 64, 66, 67, 80, 85, 86, 88 *n.*, 89, 94, 99, 101, 102, 103, 104, 105, 106, 107, 108, 109, 110, 111, 112, 113, 114, 115 *n.*, 116, 117, 119, 123, 125, 130, 132, 133, 134, 137, 138, 139, 155, 156, 157, 159, 161, 165, 168, 171, 172, 173, 176, 177, 179, 180, 181, 182, 185 *n.*, 186 *n.*, 187, 192, 193, 194, 195, 196, 198, 200, 201, 203, 204, 206, 210, 214, 218, 219, 220, 225, 226, 227, 229 *n.*, 233, 237, 239, 240, 251, 261, 264, 274, 277, 281, 285, 295, 290, 297, 298, 305, 313, 315, 317, 321, 348, 352, 354, 379, 380, 381, 385, 386, 387, 388, 395, 396, 399, 400, 404, 429, 430, 451, 472, 496, 497; *avidyā* of Śaṅkara refuted, 175 *et seq.*; criticism of Śaṅkara's ontological views, 196; his conception of individual volitions, 298–9; his controversy with Śaṅkara on the nature of reality, 165 *et seq.*; his criticism of *māyā*, 197; his criticism of Prakāśātman, 197; his criticism of theistic proofs, 189 *et seq.*; his life, 100 *et seq.*; his ontological views, 195 *et seq.*; his principal disciples, 109 *et seq.*; his refutation of Śaṅkara's theory of illusion, 179; his *sat-kārya-vāda*, 199–200; his theory of illusion, 179 *et seq.*; his view criticized from the Nimbārka point of view, 429 *et seq.*; his view of God, 155 *et seq.*; his view of God in relation to self, 159 *et seq.*; his view that all knowledge is real, 179 *et seq.*; his view of perception contrasted with that of Meghanādāri, 218; his views of *pramāṇa* contrasted with those of Śaṅkara and Nyāya, 204; his view of relation of cause and effect, 198–9; his views contrasted with those of Bhāskara, 192 *et seq.*; literature of the school, 114; logic, 226, 229; philosophy, 346; principal episodes of his life, 113; theory, 346; view, 270; view of self-validity of knowledge, 247 *et seq.*
Rāmānuja, Life of, 97 *n.*, 105 *n.*
Rāmānuja school, 202, 209, 281, 317, 318, 340, 346, 352, 364; refutation by the Śaṅkarites, 113
Rāmānuja-bhāṣya, 157, 180, 298, 380 *n.*
Rāmānuja-carita-culuka, 117, 126
Rāmānujadāsa, 98, 110, 117, 123, 125, 305, 361; his works, 125, 126
Rāmānujadāsa (Mahācārya), his refutation of *ajñāna* being Bhāvarūpa, 361 *et seq.*
Rāmānujadāśabhikṣu, 132
Rāmānujaguru, 138
Rāmānuja-muṛandādi, 66 *n.*, 137
Rāmānuja-nava-ratna-mālikā, 133
Rāmānuja-siddhānta-saṃgraha, 129, 204 *n.*, 224 *n.*, 226, 227, 297
Rāmānuja-siddhānta-śara, 117, 126
Rāmānujācārya, 111, 117, 131, 183, 250, 251, 354, 355, 356, 358; his refutation of the objections against self-validity, 250 *n.*, 251
Rāmānujācārya II, 352, 361
Rāmānujārya, 137
Rāmānujārya-divya-charitai, 103, 104, 105
Rāmānujists, 86, 239, 265, 291, 301, 322, 325, 327, 388, 435
Rāmāyaṇa, 82, 379, 396 *n.*, 530; reference to heretics in, 530
Rāmāyaṇa, 529
Rāmottarottara-tāpinī Upaniṣad, 13
rāśis, 39
Rāu, Mr T. A. Gopī-nātha, 65, 66, 68, 96, 103, 104; Lectures, 103
Rāvaṇa, 82
Real, 4, 166, 179, 181, 182, 183, 193, 194, 195, 196, 208, 306, 309, 313, 314, 315, 316, 325, 330, 332, 333, 337, 338, 339, 343, 353, 364, 373, 388, 417, 419, 423, 435, 437, 441, 454, 457, 486, 495; agent, 411; basis, 182, 210; fact, 365; knower, 411; knowledge, 237, 371; nature, 337; object, 181, 240; silver, 244; world, 350
Realism, 184, 210

Reality, 10, 16, 27, 28, 34, 42, 60, 173, 179, 194, 198, 201, 210, 211, 300, 310, 313, 322, 325, 326, 332, 386, 417, 435, 445, 449, 454, 455, 456, 457, 458, 460, 465, 472, 476, 482, 483, 487, 525 *n.*, 526, 529, 550; as qualified or unqualified—Śaṅkara and Rāmānuja's controversy on, 115 *et seq.*
Realization, 70, 106, 295, 304, 306, 308, 310, 311, 339, 382, 383, 414, 415, 437, 441, 442, 443, 464, 485, 492, 502
Reason, 53, 178, 189, 212, 231 *n.*, 264, 326, 427, 438, 533, 534, 535
Reasoning, 255, 437; in a circle, 409
Rebirths, 7, 28, 51, 299, 329, 370, 382, 407, 441, 483, 517, 525, 548, 550
Receptacle, 333
Reception, 359
Receptive, 48
Recluse, 520, 521
Recognition, 128, 142, 143, 221, 269, 437
Recollection, 79, 290
Red goddess, 37
Reference, 30, 344, 351, 447, 454, 489, 519, 523
Reflections, 29, 31, 147, 211, 411, 421, 422, 440, 448, 453, 460, 464, 467, 485, 490, 528
Refutation of the Buddhist view of soul, 142
Refutation of the Śaṅkara view of soul, 142 *et seq.*
Refutations, 133, 177 *n.*, 252, 305, 422, 424
Regression, 330
Relata, 218, 315, 424
Relation, 50, 53, 54, 193, 206, 218, 299, 301, 314, 315, 316, 335, 416, 423, 424, 426, 444, 448, 451, 455, 456, 459, 460, 462, 471, 500, 539, 542; of contact, 129; of inherence, 55
Relationless, 11
Relative existence, 198
Relative pluralism, 302
Relative positions, 349
Relatively real, 197
Relativistic, 210
Release, 514
Religion, 81, 86, 303, 471, 531, 533
Religious, 120, 501, 549; duties, 91; faith, 86; festivities, 23; marks, 19; performances, 38; practices, 19; stages, 2; value, 305
Reminiscence, 79, 105
Remoteness, 316
Representation, 180, 480
Repression, 62
Reproduction, 245
Researches, 64
Resolve, 54
Respiration, 59
Responsibility, 472
Restraint, 550
Resultant, 37
Results, 294, 442
Retention, 60
Revelation, 171, 215, 250 *n.*, 270, 307, 309, 323, 326, 347, 411, 412, 449; of knowledge, 169
Reverence, 404
Reward, 51, 415
Rhetorical school, 82; their analysis of art communication as influenced in the Gauḍīya Vaiṣṇavas, 82
Rhys Davids, 512, 513, 514 *n.*, 515 *n.*
Rice, Mr, 104 *n.*
Right actions, 327
Right apprehension, 183
Right conditions, 246
Right feelings, 327
Right knowledge, 5, 203, 204, 245, 309, 326, 327, 411, 423
Rites, 16, 19, 39 *n.*, 103
Ritual, 2, 18, 19, 22, 23, 70; ceremonies, 17
Ritualistic, 8, 16, 24, 120, 132; differences, 381; worship, 22, 23
Rival sects, 120
Rohiṇī, 229, 279
Root, 34, 46, 59
Root-*ajñāna*, 369
Root-cause, 187, 244
Root-elements, 45
Root-ignorance, 369
Root-impressions, 43, 44, 54, 258, 281, 287, 308, 372
Root-instincts, 29, 30, 33, 34, 51, 469
Rudra, 16, 475, 507
Rules, 128
Russel, 539 *n.*
Rūpa, 40 *n.*, 49 *n.*, 510, 511
Rūpa Gosvāmī, 82
rūpa-mātra, 510
rūpa-tan-mātra, 163, 260, 261, 499
Ṛg-veda, 12
ṛju-vivaraṇa, 106
Ṛṣi Nārāyaṇa, 482
Ṛṣi-rātra, 23
ṛṣis, 21

sabbe bhūtā, 524
sabbe pāṇā, 524

sabbe sattā, 524
Sac-caritra-rakṣā, 122
Sacrifice, 23, 29, 55, 293, 350, 384, 450, 519, 520, 530; of Nārāyaṇa, in *Śata-patha*, 12
Sad-artha-saṃkṣepa, 128 *n.*
sad-asad-anirvacanīyā, 165
sad-asad-ātmaka, 497
sad-asadrūpa, 456
sad-asad-vilakṣaṇa, 177
sad-asad-vyatirekaḥ, 239 *n.*
Sadā-cārabodha, 133
Sadda-nīti, 513
Sad-vidyā-vijaya, 126, 361, 365 *n.*, 366 *n.*, 370 *n.*, 372 *n.*
ṣaḍ-darśana-samuccaya, 516 *n.*, 533
Sages, 13, 21, 25, 45, 220, 474, 483
Sahasra-gīti, 102 *n.*, 104, 109 *n.*, 134
Sahasra-gīti-bhāṣya, 113 *n.*
Sahasra-gīti-vyākhyā, 110
Sahasra-kiraṇī, 123
sahetuka, 85
sahopalambha, 146
Saint, 13, 40, 71, 189
Sainthood, 414, 441
Saintliness, 448
sajātīya-guṇavattvam, 257
sakala, 30, 31
sal-lakṣaṇa, 10
sallāpa, 513
sallāpa-kathā, 513
Salvation, 24, 32, 44, 55, 56, 78, 89, 129, 292, 307, 421, 432, 444, 463, 473
Samara-puṅgavācārya, 127 *n.*
samavāya, 219, 222, 256, 301, 455, 456; relation, 256
samavāya-samavāyi-bhinnam, 388
samavāyi, 456
samādhi, 22, 29, 33, 60, 61
samāna, 59, 60
samāna-dharma, 211, 212, 213
samārādhana, 10
Samāsa-vāda, 133
sambandha-jñānitvam, 87 *n.*
sambhava, 426, 428
Saṃeness, 142; of quality, 161
sampradāya, 400
Sampradāya-pariśuddhi, 123
samuccaya, 8
saṃghāta, 252, 262
Saṃgīta-mālā, 128 *n.*
Saṃgraha, 119
Saṃhitās, 21, 24, 39
saṃkalpa, 34, 36, 45, 191, 504
saṃkalpa-sūryodaya, 120, 121, 122
saṃkalpamayī mūrti, 42
Saṃkarṣaṇa, 13, 21, 22, 34, 37, 39, 52, 56, 57, 157, 158, 443 *n.*, 475
Saṃkṣepa-śārīraka, 106, 107, 197 *n.*
saṃsarga, 187
saṃsarga-vyāpāra, 185
saṃsāra, 43 *n.*, 477
Saṃsāra-sāmrājyam, 135 *n.*
saṃskāra, 8, 63 *n.*, 98, 209, 223, 372, 423
saṃsthāna, 356
saṃśaya-dvaya-samāhāra, 213
Saṃvat 1112, 399
Saṃvat 1806, 399
saṃvin-nānātva-samarthana, 133
saṃvit, 168, 170, 503, 504, 510
saṃvṛtā-tman, 501
saṃyoga, 225
saṃyuktāsraya, 225
Saṃyutta, 524
Sana, 21
Sanaka, 21, 40 *n.*, 400, 482
Sanandana, 21, 482
Sanatkumāra, 21, 482, 502
Sanatsujāti, 21
Sanātana, 21
Sandal, 221; paste, 7
Sandhyā-vandana-bhāṣya, 118, 130
San-mārga-dīpa, 395 *n.*, 398 *n.*
san-mātra, 200
san-mātra-grāhī, 167
sannyāsin, 102, 137
Sanskrit, 1 *n.*, 9, 64, 107, 123, 125, 134, 135, 137, 138; literature, 3 *n.*; texts, 132
Sanskrit Manuscripts, 401 *n.*
Sanskritic, 383 *n.*
santoṣa, 61, 62 *n.*
Saṅgati-mālā, 119, 234, 383 *n.*
Saṅgati-sāra, 133
saṅketa, 544
saṅkucita-svarūpam, 172
sañcita, 443
saṇkocavikāśārham, 172
sa-pakṣa, 230, 231
saprakāśatva, 358
Sapta-gāthā, 138
Saptati-ratna-mālikā, 133
Sarasvatī, 52, 57, 59, 399
sarga, 502
sarga-pratisarga, 496
Saroyogin, 63
sarvabhṛt, 61
Sarva-darśana-saṃgraha, 120, 400, 515, 516, 532, 533, 534 *n.*
Sarva-darśana-śiromaṇi, 118, 132
sarva-dharma-vahiṣkṛta, 20
sarva-ga, 61

Sarvajñātma muni, 106, 107, 197
sarva-svabhāva-viraha, 271
sarva-vittva, 231
sarvā-ntara, 483
Sarvārtha-siddhi, 122, 128 *n.*, 209, 251 *n.*, 252 *n.*, 255 *n.*, 256 *n.*, 257 *n.*, 264 *n.*, 265 *n.*, 266 *n.*, 267 *n.*, 268 *n.*, 269 *n.*, 270 *n.*, 272 *n.*, 274 *n.*, 276 *n.*, 277 *n.*, 278 *n.*, 279 *n.*, 281 *n.*, 282 *n.*, 283 *n.*, 286 *n.*, 288 *n.*, 289 *n.*, 290 *n.*, 291 *n.*, 292 *n.*, 293 *n.*, 294 *n.*, 295 *n.*, 296 *n.*, 302 *n.*, 346, 352, 353 *n.*, 354 *n.*, 355 *n.*
sat, 154, 444, 457
satataṃ kurvato jagat, 36
Satisfaction, 92
sat-kārya-vāda, 43, 200, 265, 267; other views contrasted with those of Rāmānuja, 200
sat-kārya-vādin, 200
sat-khyāti, 128, 183, 184, 410
sattā, 243
sattākhya, 29
sattākhya-jñāna, 29
sattha, 513, 514
sattva, 25, 30, 42, 43, 45, 46, 47, 48, 57, 128, 129, 156, 163, 259, 446, 447, 470, 471, 473, 475, 479, 480, 481, 482, 488, 491, 504, 505, 507; part, 473; quality, 454; body, 472, 481
sattva-guṇa, 45, 448
sattvamaya, 448, 451
sattva-stuff, 472
sattvo-pādhi, 481
sattvā, 358, 513
Satya, 27, 29, 61, 351
satyam, 503
satyaṃ jñānam anantam brahma, 165
Saugandhakulya, 97
Saumya Jāmātṛ muni, 24, 110, 111, 115, 120, 131 *n.*, 132, 134, 135, 137, 138, 374, 380, 381; his conception of Lakṣmī, 375; his conception of *prapatti*, *bhakti* and *prema*, 377; his doctrine of *prapatti*, 376 *et seq.*
Saura-kāṇḍa, 22
Sauri-rāja-caraṇāra-vinda-śaraṇāgati-sāra, 132
sausādṛśya, 297, 355
sa-vigraha, 31
savikalpa, 217, 220, 221, 222, 223, 224, 311, 544; knowledge, 219
sa-vikalpa-pratyakṣa, 166
Saviour, 86 *n.*
sādhana, 62
sādhanā, 487
sādhya, 62, 228, 230, 231, 427, 535, 536, 537, 538
sādṛśya, 355, 427; Vādihaṃsa's conception of it as *saṃsthāna*, 356; Veṅkaṭa's conception of it, 355
sākṣād-avatāra, 38, 39
sākṣātkāra, 62, 485
sākṣātkāri-pramā, 216
sākṣāt-śakti, 41, 42 *n.*, 57
sākṣāttva, 217
sākṣi-consciousness, 325, 326, 337, 363, 367
sākṣin, 325, 326
sākṣī, 144, 173, 483
sālokya, 443 *n.*
sālokya-mukti, 50
sāmagrī, 204, 220
sāmānya-gocaram, 534
sāmīpya, 443 *n.*
sāmpra dāyika. 181 *n.*
Sāṃkhya, 18, 23, 30, 43, 52, 62, 144, 148, 156, 200, 256, 258, 259, 261, 265, 266, 296, 440, 445, 449, 459, 461, 462, 464, 471, 472, 473, 476, 479, 480, 481, 482, 485, 496, 498, 512, 521, 527; categories, 25; doctrine, 479, 480; inference, 256; in relation to Vedānta according to Vijñāna Bhikṣu, 471 *et seq.*; mode, 157; philosophy, 501 *n.*; theory, 265; theory of *sat-kārya-vāda*, refutation by Veṅkaṭa, 365 *et seq.*; view, 281 *n.*
Sāṃkhya-kārikā, 448, 501 *n.*
Sāṃkhya-Pātañjala, 45
Sāṃkhya-pravacana-bhāṣya, 482
Sāṃkhya-sāra, 482
Sāṃkhya-sūtra, 448, 473
Sāṃkhya-yoga, 466, 539; Vijñāna Bhikṣu's criticism of, 479 *et seq.*
Sāṃkhyist, 46, 147, 163, 256, 257, 259, 261, 265, 266, 343, 386, 462, 476, 527
Sāra-darpaṇa, 115, 384, 389 *n.*, 392
Sāra-dīpa, 124
Sāra-niṣkarṣa-ṭippanī, 127
Sāra-saṃgraha, 124, 135 *n.*
Sāra-sāra, 124
Sārattha-pakāsinī, 514, 515 *n.*
Sārā-rtha-catuṣṭaya, 352
Sārā-rtha-saṃgraha, 110 *n.*
sārūpya, 442 *n.*
sāttvika, 31, 163, 498
sāttvika ahaṃkāra, 259, 504
Sāttvika purāṇas, 20
sātvata, 12, 15, 17, 19, 22

Sātvata-saṃhitā, 12 *n.*, 21, 40 *n.*, 42 *n.*, 57
sātvata-śāsana, 62
Sātvika-śāstra, 21
Sāvatthi, 522
sāyujya, 161, 443 *n.*
sāyujya-mukti, 474
Scepticism, 244, 520
Sceptics, 520
Scholars, 86, 104
Scholarship, 94
Scholastic, 133, 373; criticism, 364
School, 111; of logic, 112
Schrader, 37, 38, 40 *n.*, 41, 42 *n.*, 50
Science, 34, 512, 514, 516, 518
Scientific, 181
Scope, 328, 422
Scriptural, 33, 180, 223; criticism, 388; duties, 61, 89, 90, 91, 92, 100, 293, 307; injunctions, 303; interpretation, 326; knowledge, 307, 326; testimony, 136, 211, 214, 296, 306, 326, 327, 352, 406, 426, 468; texts, 5, 15, 16, 17, 181, 192, 199, 208, 280, 302, 329, 338, 340, 383, 385, 387, 388, 392, 396, 397, 407, 426, 429, 431, 438, 448, 458, 465, 468, 486, 490, 508, 517; view, 549
Scriptures, 4, 7, 8, 9, 25, 50, 52, 54, 146, 166, 168, 174, 189, 203, 216, 256, 259, 281, 289, 294, 296, 302, 303, 306, 319, 326, 340, 350, 361, 371, 380 *n.*, 406, 407, 428, 437, 442, 452, 465, 472, 494, 539
Sea, 6, 487
Secondary, 38, 41; sense, 306
Sectarian, 305; authors, 18; difference, 381; quarrels, 120
Section, 305
Sect of Brahmins, 2
Sects, 512 *n.*
Seed, 184, 330, 429, 509
Self, 12, 26, 129, 140, 143, 146, 148, 149, 150, 151, 172, 208, 287, 288, 289, 290, 292, 306, 308, 315, 323, 324, 327, 330, 345, 346, 361, 365, 369, 408, 409, 411, 412, 426, 428, 439, 441, 442, 443, 444, 445, 453, 459, 463, 464, 469, 470, 483, 485, 486, 487, 494, 495, 509, 523 *n.*, 528, 529, 547, 548, 549; how its knowledge rises according to Rāmānuja, 159; in relation to God according to Rāmānuja, 159 *et seq.*; Nimbārka's conception of, 411 *et seq.*; Veṅkaṭa's view of self in relation to God, 161 *et seq.*; according to Yāmuna, its nature, 140 *et seq.*; and the problem of consciousness, 149 *et seq.*; refutation of Kumārila's view, 148; refutation of the Sāṃkhya view, 147
Self-abnegation, 55, 60, 62, 414
Self-apperception, 93
Self-conscious, 27, 412; entities, 159
Self-consciousness, 9, 140, 146, 151, 154, 155, 173, 216, 274, 315, 324, 369, 466, 546, 547
Self-contradiction, 90, 239, 269
Self-contradictory, 193, 202, 230, 231, 239, 256, 266, 272, 334, 342, 398, 469, 486, 512
Self-control, 22, 33, 160
Self-criticism, 32
Self-dependent, 36
Self-destruction, 324
Self-discriminative, 382
Self-dynamism, 433
Self-ejected idea, 244
Self-evident, 315
Self-existent, 297
Self-fulfilment, 382
Self-identification, 475
Self-identity, 269
Self-illuminating, 35, 358
Self-illumination, 176, 358
Self-introspection, 141
Self-invalidity, 249
Self-knowledge, 290, 383, 384, 466, 467, 468, 487
Self-love, 443, 470
Self-luminosity, 317, 325, 345, 358, 359, 367, 407, 438, 468; its treatment by Vijñāna Bhikṣu, 468 *et seq.*
Self-luminous, 61, 171, 176, 178, 243, 290, 310, 315, 316, 319, 325, 340, 347, 360, 361, 370, 407, 408, 438, 439, 466, 468
Self-luminousness, 439
Self-manifestation, 214, 248
Self-manifesting, 142, 149, 150
Self-mastery, 520
Self-offering, 60, 62
Self-perceiving, 413
Self-realized, 24
Self-realization, 28, 29, 302, 382, 383, 487
Self-revealed, 315
Self-revealing, 160, 166, 168, 171, 230, 240, 249, 306, 315, 358
Self-revelation, 170, 306, 318
Self-shining, 332

Self-sufficiency, 35
Self-surrender, 86, 87, 89, 112, 120, 136, 379
Self-surrendering, 78; association, 91
Self-valid, 9, 247, 250, 348, 357
Self-validity, 240, 249, 250 *n.*, 251, 289, 347, 348, 356, 357, 428; of cognition, 240; of knowledge, Bhaṭṭa and Prabhākara view, 249
Selves, 44, 345, 346, 411, 451, 465, 476, 477; as inseparable from God, 298–300
Semi-conscious, 83
Senai Nathan, 67 *n.*
Senānātha, 117
Seṇḍa, 66
Seniors, 185 *n.*, 186 *n.*
Sensations, 253, 386
Sense, 7, 8, 9, 27, 30, 32, 33, 43, 47, 48, 49, 80, 181, 182, 189, 196, 280, 281 *n.*, 289, 300, 306, 311, 317, 325, 414, 427, 435, 462, 466, 502, 505, 540, 543, 545, 547
Sense-appearances, 290
Sense-character, 254, 284, 285
Sense-cognitions, 289, 547
Sense-consciousness, 450
Sense-contact, 189, 203, 204, 206, 270, 280, 311
Sense-data, 251, 291, 544
Sense-faculty, 280, 463
Sense-function, 281, 539
Sense-gratifications, 531
Sense-impressions, 223
Sense-inclinations, 22
Sense-knowledge, 206, 217, 544
Sense-objects, 32, 152, 411, 449, 546, 550
Sense-organ, 8, 9, 13, 28, 172, 179, 184, 185 *n.*, 189, 204, 205, 206, 222, 223, 270, 280, 290, 295, 347, 411, 533, 534, 540, 543, 544, 546
Sense-perception, 31, 151, 217, 223, 503
Sense-pleasures, 550
Sense-qualities, 251, 252, 253
Sense of possession, 71
Sensible, 288, 290; qualities, 27, 31
Sensory, 467
Sensual joys, 550
Sensuous, 325
Sentient, 54
Separate *ajñānas*, 369
Separate wholes, 263, 264
Separateness, 264
Separation, 71, 72, 327
Sequence, 184, 273
Series, 310, 353, 540, 543, 544, 545, 546, 547
Servants, 83, 84, 87; of God, 89
Service, 54, 88
Servitude, 136, 161, 377; of God, 89
Seśvara-mīmāṃsā, 18 *n*, 124
Sevadeva, 402
Sex-emotions, 549
Sex-indulgence, 549
Shapes, 5
Shining, 336; character, 232, 243, 244; entity, 242
Shop, 181
siddha-prema, 378
siddha-vastu-virodhī, 354 *n.*
Siddhānta-cintāmaṇi, 115, 116, 388, 389 *n.*, 390 *n.*, 391 *n.*, 392
Siddhānta-jāhnavī, 404
Siddhānta-nirṇaya, 122
Siddhānta-ratna, 403
Siddhānta-ratnāvalī, 12, 18, 132
Siddhānta-saṃgraha, 130, 203 *n.*
Siddhānta-setukā, 404
Siddhānta-siddhāñjana, 133
Siddhānta-śiromaṇi, 3
Siddhānta-śravaṇa, 61
Siddhānta-vaijayantī, 18
Siddhi-traya, 98, 105, 108, 109, 128 *n.*, 154, 155, 229 *n.*
Siddhy-upāya-sudarśana, 127
Significance, 53, 293, 297
Silver, 179, 180, 181, 182, 183, 184, 185, 186, 187, 188, 241, 242, 244, 245, 310, 336, 337, 346, 408; elements, 241; image, 245
Similar, 298
Similarity, 142, 179, 182, 183, 234, 297, 298, 351, 355, 423, 426, 427, 428
Simplicity, 180, 186 *n.*
Simultaneity, 142, 254
Simultaneous, 276; perception, 281
siṃha, 60
Sin, 34, 295, 303, 388, 441, 446, 505, 524, 526, 528, 550
Sincerity, 158
Sinful, 294, 304, 549
Sinner, 99
Sirup-pullur-udaya-Pillai, 97 *n.*
Situation, 332, 434, 455
Six qualities, 37
Sītā-upaniṣad, 41, 42 *n.*, 57
skanda, 402
Skanda-purāṇa, 19 *n.*, 507 *n.*
Skill, 194
Sky, 128, 447
Sleep, 169, 240, 257

smaraṇa, 505
smaraṇam, 178 *n.*
Smell, 251
Smell-potential, 163, 510
Smoke, 211, 226 *n.*, 534, 536, 538
smṛti, 14, 15, 16, 20, 57, 125, 471, 503, 504, 510, 517, 549; literature, 19
Sneha-pūrti, 395 *n.*
Social, 472, 549
Sophistry, 514, 515, 516, 517
Sophists, 518
Sorrow, 52, 441, 443 *n.*, 444, 445, 463, 464, 470, 486, 491, 506, 508
Sorrowful, 46
Sottanambi, 109 *n.*
Souls, 6, 7, 10, 35, 57, 59, 60, 61, 62, 80, 83, 125, 139, 140, 147, 151, 154, 155, 157, 177 *n.*, 189, 194, 200, 286, 291, 295, 298, 299, 300, 301, 302, 381, 385, 393, 395, 412, 413, 422, 430, 431, 434, 435, 441, 443, 444, 451, 453, 457, 458, 483, 485, 489, 503, 517, 519, 525, 526, 527, 530, 531, 539, 543, 546, 547, 549, 550
Sound, 5, 33, 48, 58, 167
Sound-potential, 504, 510
Source, 292, 295, 303, 348, 494, 521, 530; of knowledge, 185 *n.*, 465
South, 18
South India, 19, 80, 138, 523
South Indian, 81 *n.*
Southern India, 63
Space, 6, 27, 34, 48, 82, 163, 195, 199, 228, 252, 264, 273, 277, 282, 301, 521; relations, 284
Spaceless, 72
Sparks, 6
sparśa, 49 *n.*, 261, 510, 511
sparśa-tan-mātra, 163, 260, 261, 499, 510
Spatial, 313, 324, 343, 353; character, 353; contiguity, 316; difference, 245; qualification, 238; quality, 245; units, 264
Spatial-temporal, 489
Spatio-temporal, 226
Special, 43, 208; powers, 38; quality, 393
Species, 173
Specific cause, 279
Specific characters, 46 *n.*
Specific effect, 279
Specific modes, 364
Specific nature, 356
Specific qualities, 263
Spectator, 82
Speculations, 496
Speech, 3, 4, 34, 48, 53, 168
sphoṭa, 107 *n.*, 108 *n.*
Spider, 59, 406
Spirit, 32, 55, 298, 299, 302, 350, 406, 460, 472, 492; part, 301, 302; of service, 70
Spiritual, 10, 28, 35, 41, 44, 47, 48, 60, 373, 385, 386; emancipation, 378; energy, 51; entities, 36; fact, 377; form, 37, 38; love, 81; nature, 406; transformation, 10; zeal, 72
Spirituality, 472
Spontaneity, 56, 85, 442
Spontaneous, 27, 34, 35, 36, 85, 214, 215, 292, 452; agency, 37; grace, 88; production, 277
Sportive, 444
Sṛṣṭi-khaṇḍa, 532
Staffs, 532
Stage, 44, 46 *n.*, 47, 48, 50, 56, 58, 60, 79, 292, 311, 422, 458, 486, 491, 503, 541, 544; of life, 11, 416; of love, 82
Stars, 515 *n.*
State, 35, 41, 50, 52, 56, 290, 295, 339, 344, 414, 438, 439, 441, 443, 444, 445, 446, 457, 458, 469, 471, 476, 486, 488, 494, 495, 503, 545, 546
Static, 29, 446, 492; entities, 36
Statical, 46
Status, 437
Stick, 1 *n.*, 2, 342, 549
Stone, 41
Stotra-ratnam, 98, 99, 101
Stotra-ratnākara, 123
Stotra-trayī, 403
Strength, 35, 404
Structural Brahman, 434
Structural cause, 47
Structure, 500
Study of the Vedas, 29
Sub-commentary, 137, 138
Sub-conscious image, 237; impressions, 228, 268
Sub-consciousness, 8, 222, 227, 258, 270, 281, 437
Subhāṣita-nīvi, 121
Subject, 178, 193, 194, 204, 280, 283, 297 *n.*, 368
Subjective, 170, 179, 238, 268, 490
Subjectivity, 325
Submission, 54
Subodhinī, 116, 132
Subserviency, 299
Subsidiary, 27, 39, 58, 90
Subsistence, 256

Substance, 10, 34, 35, 80, 129, 147, 183, 193, 195, 199, 208, 209, 211, 212, 222, 224, 245, 251, 252, 253, 254, 256, 258, 288, 299, 303, 334, 343, 344, 361, 425, 430, 431, 455, 463, 464, 493, 500
Substantiality, 431
Substantive, 385
Substitution, 210
Substratum, 142, 188, 238, 408, 456, 475, 484
Subtle, 35, 42, 45, 58, 61, 298, 415, 445, 475, 504; aspects, 194; body, 24; cause, 476; constituents, 299; essence, 80; form, 29, 301; matter, 414; state, 396, 397
Succession, 142, 207, 310, 353
Sudarśana, 34, 35, 41, 51, 53, 57, 126, 130, 132, 401, 448 *n.*
Sudarśana Bhaṭṭa, 111
Sudarśanaguru, 126, 130
Sudarśana-saṃhitā, 23
Sudarśana-sura-druma, 133
Sudarśana Sūri, 109 *n.*, 113, 114, 115, 118, 120, 130, 135, 176 *n.*, 177 *n.*, 181 *n.*, 182, 186 *n.*; his refutation of *ajñāna*, 177 *n.*; his works, 130
Sudarśana śakti, 50
Sudarśanācārya, 118, 126, 298; his view of relation of souls to God, 297
Suffering, 52, 291, 292, 303, 304, 412, 464, 521, 524
Suffix, 166, 233
Suggestion, 343, 344
sukha, 463, 464, 485
Sumaṅgala-vilāsinī, 513 *n.*, 520, 521 *n.*, 522 *n.*, 524 *n.*
Sumerian, 531; civilization, 529
summum bonum, 136, 379, 420
Sun, 6, 42, 59, 153, 228, 295, 349, 447
Sundara Bhaṭṭa, 404
Sundaradeśika, 112
Sundararāja-deśika, 117, 130
Super-consciousness, 450, 490
Superintendence, 31, 152, 189
Superintendent 56, 58, 104
Superintending, 38
Superior, 53, 54; devotees, 380
Superiority, 53
Supplementary, 123
Support, 34, 56, 300, 330, 333, 334, 338, 350, 422, 477
Supposition, 322, 330, 332, 406, 408, 410, 423, 439
Supra-sensible, 550
Supreme, 28, 33, 42, 49, 54, 55, 475; bliss, 136; cause, 191; energy, 45; excellence, 136; intoxication, 83; person, 189, 190, 191; power, 36, 52; resignation, 86
surā, 540
susadṛśa-saṃsthāna, 355
susadṛśatvam, 224
Sustained, 455
Sustainer, 455
suśikṣita cārvāka, 516, 540, 547
suṣumnā, 59, 415
suṣumnā nāḍī, 58
suṣupti, 144, 178
Suta, 482
Sutākhya, 138
sūkṣma, 61, 281
sūkṣma-kāla-guṇā-vasthā, 42
Sūta-saṃhitā, 19
sūtra, 1, 108 *n.*, 109, 116, 125, 140, 195, 196, 472, 480, 516, 518, 523 *n.*, 532, 539; of Jaimini, 124
Sūtra-kṛtāṅga, 524, 527, 528
Sūtra-kṛtāṅga-sūtra, 521, 523, 524, 525, 526, 527; heretics referred to, in, 526
svabhāva, 46
Svabhū, 402
Sva-dharmā-dhva-bodha, 400 *n.*, 401
svajanyatvam, 372
svalakṣaṇa, 255, 271
sva-līlayā, 511
sva-mūrtāv api svayam eva hetuḥ, 240
sva-prakāśa, 230
svaprakāśatva, 468
svarūpa, 217 *n.*, 347
svarūpa-dhī, 217
svarūpa-sādṛśya, 224
Svarūpācārya, 401
svarūpāveśa, 38
svastika, 30, 60
svataḥ-pramāṇa, 9; upheld by the Rāmānuja school, 247 *et seq.*
svataḥ-prāmāṇya, 240, 347, 348, 356, 428
svataḥ-prāmāṇya-vāda, 346; Meghanādāri's view, 346
svatastva, 428
sva-vilāsa, 40 *n.*
svavilāsa-avatāra, 40 *n.*
svayambhū, 504
Svayambhuva, 21
svayaṃ-prakāśa, 167
svayaṃ-rūpa, 40 *n.*
svayaṃ-siddha, 214 *n.*
svābhāvika, 434
svābhāvika bhedā-bheda-vāda, 406
svādhyāya, 62 *n.*
svālakṣaṇya, 255

svāmi-kṛpā, 85
svāmī, 86
svāṃśa, 40 *n.*
svāṃśa-avatāra, 40 *n.*
svārasika-bādhā-dṛṣṭer ananyathā-siddheśca, 251
svārthā-numāna, 427
svātantrya, 506
svātantrya-mūla icchātmā, 45
Sweetness, 226
Swoon, 169, 240
syādvāda-ratnākāra, 536 *n.*, 537 *n.*
Syllogism, 321
Symbol, 53, 326
Sympathy, 73, 120
Synonymous, 277
Synthesis, 187
Synthetic, 31, 47, 185, 501; association, 187
System, 32, 192, 297, 304, 347, 422, 451, 471, 482, 495, 516 *n.*, 524 *n.*, 527; of philosophy, 533
Systematic doctrine, 68
Śabara, 124
Śabara Bhāṣya, 349
Śabara Svāmin, 107
śabda, 31, 49 *n.*, 129, 233, 260 *n.*, 426, 510, 511
Śabda-brahman, 58
śabda-mātra, 510
śabda-pramāṇa, 233
śabda-tan-mātra, 48, 163, 259, 260, 261, 499, 504
Śaila-raṅgeśa, 94
Śaila-raṅgeśa-guru, 98 *n.*
Śaila Śrīnivāsa, 384, 385, 386, 388; his conception of causality, 385 *et seq.*; his criticism of Umā-Maheśvara, 396 *et seq.*; his refutation of Śaṅkarite attacks on Rāmānuja doctrine, 385 *et seq.*; his refutation of the objections to Rāmānuja's doctrine by various opponents, 392 *et seq.*
Śaiva, 3 *n.*, 18, 19, 105, 113, 155, 304, 525; hymns, 84; king, 104
Śaivism, 18, 64, 81 *n.*, 102 *n.*, 399; its love of God distinguished from Āṛvārs, 84; Māṇikka-vāchakar's love of God, 84; of South India, 84
śakti, 35, 36, 37, 38, 41, 43, 44, 45, 51, 52, 53, 56, 57, 155, 156, 197, 354, 507, 508, 509
Śaktyātman, 40 *n.*
śakty-āveśa, 38
Śālikanatha, 185 *n.*
śauca, 61, 62 *n.*
Śaṅkara, 1, 2, 3, 7, 8, 65, 105, 107, 108, 111, 112, 124, 125, 130, 165, 166, 173, 174, 195, 196, 198, 200, 204, 304, 305, 306, 307, 308, 309, 317, 320, 322, 350, 381, 395, 417, 456, 471, 472, 476, 480, 484, 486, 487, 494, 496, 548; a crypto-Buddhist, 1; his *avidyā* refuted, 175 *et seq.*; his controversy with Rāmānuja on the nature of reality, 165 *et seq.*; his interpretation of causality, 3; his theory of illusion refuted, 179; literature, 405; philosophy 198, 316; school, 123, 142, 304, 312; system, 422; *Theory*, 422; view, 396
Śaṅkara-bhāṣya, 198 *n.*, 548 *n.*
Śaṅkara Vedānta, 228, 403, 456
Śaṅkara-vijaya, 2
Śaṅkarism, 143
Śaṅkarite epistemology, 9
Śaṅkarite view, 293, 387, 424
Śaṅkarites, 102, 113, 143, 144, 145, 153, 154, 155, 169, 173, 177, 178, 179, 188, 201, 204, 210, 223, 238, 239, 311, 313, 315, 318, 319, 321, 322, 323, 324, 325, 326, 327, 328, 329, 330, 334, 336, 337, 340, 341, 343, 345, 346, 347, 350, 361, 363, 364, 365, 366, 367, 374, 385, 388, 394, 398, 409, 417, 418, 419, 420, 421, 428, 430, 434, 435, 456, 470, 478, 486
Śaṅkhinī, 59
Śaraṇā-gati, 55
Śaraṇā-gati-gadya, 379, 380 *n.*
Śaraṇā-gati-gadyam, 86 *n.*
śarīra, 297, 298, 300, 389; its definition, 297 *et seq.*
Śarīra-bhāvādhikaraṇa-vicāra, 131
Śāntadāsa Vāvājī, 402
Śārīraka-mīmāṃsā-vṛtti, 117
Śārīraka-nyāya-kalāpa, 117, 132
Śārīraka-śāstrārtha-dīpikā, 117, 127
Śārīraka-śāstra-saṃgati-sāra, 117
Śarīra-vāda, 133, 297 *n.*, 298 *n.*, 299 *n.*, 300 *n.*
śaṣtra, 21, 25, 56, 102, 161, 413, 503, 514, 530
Śāstraikya-vāda, 133
śāstra-sampradāya-pravartaka, 7 *n.*
Śāstrārambha-samarthana, 133
Śāstrī, Mr D., 531 *n.*
Śāstrī, M. M. S. Kuppasvāmī, 106 *n.*
Śata-dūṣaṇī, 117, 122, 123, 126, 130, 131, 305, 319 *n.*, 396
Śata-dūṣaṇī-vyākhyā, 131

Śata-dūṣaṇī-vyākhyā-sahasra-kiraṇī, 127
śataka, 70
Śatakoṭi-dūṣaṇa-parihāra, 133
Śatakoṭi-khaṇḍana, 133
Śata-patha Brāhmaṇa, 12
Śaṭhakopa, 63, 65, 67 *n.*, 69, 70, 71, 78, 94, 102 *n.*, 108, 116, 138
Śaṭhakopa muni, 130
Śaṭhakopa Yati, 112, 123, 130
Śaṭhakopācārya, 114, 139
Śaṭha-marṣaṇa, 94 *n.*, 129, 132
Śaṭhāri Sūri, 130
Śavara, 107, 108 *n.*
śākhā-candra-darśana, 340
Śāktas, 19
Sāmba-purāṇa, 19
śānta, 499
Śāntātman, 40 *n.*
Śānti, 37, 505, 523
Śānti-parvan, 12, 260 *n.*, 479
Śāṇḍilya, 3, 17, 21, 25
Śāṇḍilyabhāskara, 3 *n.*
Śāṇḍilya-smṛti, 20
Śāradā-maṭha, 102
Śātātapa, 20
śeṣa-śeṣitā, 53
śeṣa-vṛtti-paratva, 87 *n.*
Śeṣāryā, 297
śeṣī, 160
Śilpārtha-sāra, 122
Śiṛiya-tiru-maḍal, 69, 134 *n.*
Śiva, 12, 16, 37, 38, 39, 40 *n.*, 52, 84, 132, 232, 304, 475, 482, 483
Śiva-rātṛa, 23
Śilāṅka, 521, 523, 525, 526, 527
Śloka-vārttika, 206 *n.*
Śoṭṭha-pūrṇa, 97
śraddhā, 57, 382, 509, 550
Śramaṇa, 527
śravaṇa, 405, 442
Śravaṇa Bhaṭṭa, 402
śrāddhas, 530, 550
Śrāntabhāskara, 3 *n.*
Śrimadhurā, 98
Śriyaḥ-pati-ppaḍi, 135 *n.*
Śrī, 37, 41, 57, 89, 99; its meaning, 89
Śrī-bhāṣya, 103, 113, 114, 115, 116, 117, 118, 120, 123, 125, 126, 128 *n.*, 131, 132, 137, 175 *n.*, 195 *n.*, 200 *n.*, 383
Śrī-bhāṣya-bhāvāṅkura, 133
Śrī-bhāṣyopanyāsa, 117
Śrī-bhāṣyā-ratha, 138
Śrī-bhāṣya-sāra, 117
Śrī-bhāṣya-sārārtha-saṃgraha, 116, 117, 129
Śrī-bhāṣya-siddhānta-sāra, 117
Śrī-bhāṣya-vārttika, 117
Śrī-bhāṣya-vivṛti, 114
Śrī-bhāṣya-vyākhyā, 117
Śrībittiputtūr, 69
Śrī Brahma, 400
Śrīdhara, 39, 529 *n.*
Śrīharṣa, 111, 201, 549
Śrīkṛṣṇa, 96, 430, 474
Śrīkṛṣṇa-deśika, 112
Śrī-kṛṣṇastava, 403
Śrīmad-bhagavad-gītā, 113
Śrī-nātha, 96
Śrīnivāsa, 109, 115, 116, 118, 127, 129, 130, 236 *n.*, 297, 386, 387, 392, 393, 399, 401, 402, 403, 406 *n.*; pupil of Mahācārya, his works, 127, 128
Śrīnivāsadāsa, 123, 127, 129; his works, 127
Śrīnivāsa-dīkṣita, 115, 130, 396
Śrīnivāsa Rāghavadāsa, 129
Śrīnivāsa Sūri, 121
Śrīnivāsa Tātācārya, 116, 384
Śrīnivāsa-tāyārya, 396
Śrīnivāsa-yati, 138
Śrīnivāsācārya, 114, 117, 123
Śrī-pañca-rātra-rakṣā, 122
Śrīpati, 40 *n.*
Śrīraṅgam, 69, 97, 98, 101, 102, 103, 104, 110, 113, 120, 121, 135, 137
Śrī-raṅga-nātha, 94 *n.*, 121 *n.*
Śrīraṅganātha-gāyaka, 109
Śrīraṅganāyakī, 110
Śrī Raṅgasūri, 381
Śrīraṅgācārya, 111, 117
Śrīrāma, 39 *n.*
Śrī Rāma Pillai, 109 *n.*, 111
Śrī Rāmānuja Pillan, 110
Śrī-rāmānuja-yogi-pāda, 395 *n.*
Śrī Rāmānujācārya, 104 *n.*
Śrīśailadāsa, 130
Śrīśaila lineage, 109, 115, 122, 131
Śrīśailanātha, 110, 111
Śrīśailapūrṇa, 98, 102 *n.*, 109
Śrīśaila Rāghavārya, 130
Śrīśaila Śrīnivāsa, 18, 111, 115, 127, 133, 388, 389 *n.*, 392
Śrīśaila Tātayārya, 18, 130, 131
Śrīśaila Yogendra, 129
Śrīśaileśa, 137
Śrīsudarśana Press, 305
Śrī-tattva-darpaṇa, 133
Śrīvacana-bhūṣaṇa-vyākhyā, 135, 375 *n.*, 376 *n.*, 377 *n.*, 378 *n.*, 379 *n.*
Śrīvacana-bhūṣaṇa, 90 *n.*, 135, 137, 138, 374, 375 *n.*, 380 *n.*
Śrīvaiṣṇava, 18, 19, 24, 95, 99, 102,

Śrīvaiṣṇava (*cont.*)
107, 108, 112, 120, 125, 135, 138, 304, 305, 379; many works written in defence against the Śaivas, 18; philosophy, 22; school, 134; system, 136; their quarrel with the Śaivas, 18
Śrī-vaiṣṇavism, 89, 102 *n.*, 105, 127
Śrīvallabhadeva, 65
Śrīvatsa, 57
Śrīvatsa-siddhānta-sāra, 113, 116
Śrīvatsāṅka, 139
Śrīvatsāṅka Miśra, 102, 105, 108, 109, 129
Śrīvatsāṅka Śrīnivāsa, 116
Śrīvatsāṅka Śrīnivāsācārya, 117
Śrīvānācala Yogīndra, 138
Śrīvāsaguru, 112
Śrīveṅkaṭaguru, 112
Śrīveṅkaṭācārya, 112
Śrīveṅkaṭeśa, 112
Śrīviṣṇucitta, 114
Śruta-bhāva-prakāśikā, 127
Śruta-pradīpikā, 130
Śruta-prakāśikā, 109 *n.*, 111, 113, 114, 115, 120, 126, 127, 128 *n.*, 130, 131, 136, 137, 157, 176 *n.*, 177 *n.*, 179 *n.*, 180, 181 *n.*, 186 *n.*, 188, 298
Śruta-prakāśikācārya, 135
Śruta-prakāśikā of Sudarśana Sūri, 392
Śruta-prakāśikā-sāra-saṃgraha, 114
Śruti, 352 *n.*, 371; texts, 390
Śruti-dīpikā, 115
Śruti-siddhānta-mañjarī, 403 *n.*
Śruti-siddhānta-saṃgraha, 240, 441 *n.*, 442 *n.*, 443 *n.*
Śruty-anta-sura-druma, 403, 404
śuddha-brahma, 197
śuddha-sarga, 27
Śuddhasattva Lakṣmaṇācārya, 115
Śuddhasattvalakṣaṇārya, 131 *n.*
Śuddhasattva Yogīndra, 115
Śuddhasattvācārya, 131 *n.*
śuddhetarā-sṛṣṭi, 42
śuddhi, 464
śuddhy-aśuddhimaya, 44
Śukra, 482, 503, 531 *n.*
Śukranīti, 515
Śukra-nītī-sāra, 515 *n.*
Śuktyaṃśa, 183
Śūdra, 20, 64, 68, 98, 104
śūnyatvarūpiṇī, 36
Śūnya-vāda, 177, 206 *n.*
śūnya-vādī, 201
Śveta-dvīpa, 13, 19, 443 *n.*
Śvetāśvatara, 379, 472, 473, 512
Śvetāśvatara Upaniṣad, 447 *n.*
Śvetāśvataropaniṣat-prakāśikā, 127
Śyāma Bhaṭṭa, 402
Śyāmadeva, 402
Śyāmācārya, 401
ṣaḍ-aṅga-yoga, 24
ṣaḍ-guṇa, 37

Tactile, 253, 254; organ, 459; sensation, 253
tad-āyatta-sthiti-pūrvikā, 406
tad-bhāvā-patti, 420
tadvikāratva, 266
tad-vyāpyatva, 431
taijasa, 25, 48, 498, 510
Taittirīya-prakāśikā, 402
Taittirīya Upaniṣad, 402
Taittirīyo-paniṣat, 131, 379
Taittirīyo-paniṣat-bhāṣya, 138
Taittirīyo-paniṣat-prakāśikā, 127
Taivattuk-k-arasu-Nambi, 97 *n.*
tajjanyatva, 266
tamas, 25, 43, 45, 46, 47, 48, 129, 163, 259, 447, 466, 469, 471, 473, 474, 475, 480, 482, 491, 500, 501, 513, 504, 505, 507
tamasa mahat, 498
Tamil, 63 *n.*, 64, 66, 95, 96, 102, 105, 107, 110, 111 *n.*, 121, 124, 125, 131, 134, 137
Tamil Veda, 95
tamoguṇo, 448 *n.*
tamomaya, 46
Tangible, 5, 500
Tani-praṇava, 135 *n.*
Tanjore, 67
tanmātra, 25, 43, 156, 163, 256, 259, 260 *n.*, 445, 499, 502, 504, 507, 510, 511
tantra, 107
tantu-samavetatvāt, 256
tapaḥ, 62 *n.*
tapas, 55, 450, 503
Tapta-mudrā-vidrāvaṇa, 396 *n.*
tarka, 227, 537
tarkavidyā, 515
tarkī, 518
Taste, 251
Taste-potential, 48, 163, 510
Tatar-āṇṇar, 137
tathā-bhūta, 348
tathātva, 357
Tat-kratu-nyāya-vicāra, 131, 133
Tattva-bhāskara, 132
Tattva-candrikā, 396 *n.*
Tattva-dīpa, 89, 132
Tattva-dīpana, 128 *n.*
Tattva-dīpa-saṃgraha-kārikā, 132

tattva-jñāna, 143
Tattva-kaustubha, 19 *n.*, 20
Tattva-mārtaṇḍa, 115
Tattva-mātṛkā, 123, 124
Tattva-muktā-kalāpa, 119, 120, 122, 124, 131, 251, 256 *n.*, 257 *n.*, 303 *n.*, 304 *n.*, 346
Tattva-navanītam, 123
Tattva-nirṇaya, 128 *n.*, 133, 352, 352 *n.*
Tattva-nirūpaṇa, 261
Tattva-padavī, 123
Tattva-pradīpikā, 318
Tattva-prakāśikā, 402
Tattva-prakāśikā-veda-stuti-ṭīkā, 402
Tattva-ratnākara, 119, 128 *n.*, 210, 214 *n.*, 216 *n.*, 226, 227, 228, 229, 232 *n.*, 234
Tattva-ratnāvalī, 124
Tattva-ratnāvalī-saṃgraha, 124
Tattva-saṃgraha, 516 *n.*, 544 *n.*
Tattva-saṃkhyāna, 23
Tattva-sandeśa, 124
Tattva-sāra, 114, 116, 132, 352
Tattva-śekhara, 135, 136, 137
Tattva-śikhā-maṇi, 124
Tattva-ṭīkā, 105 *n.*, 114, 120, 123
Tattva-traya, 39, 40 *n.*, 41, 43 *n.*, 56, 57, 125 *n.*, 135, 137, 138, 157, 159 *n.*, 160 *n.*, 260 *n.*, 261 *n.*; *vyūha* doctrine in, 39 *n.*
Tattva-traya-bhāṣya, 135
Tattva-traya-culuka, 124, 125, 128 *n.*
Tattva-traya-culuka-saṃgraha, 125
Tattva-traya-nirūpaṇa, 128 *n.*
Tattva-traya-pracaṇḍa-māruta, 128 *n.*
Tattva-viveka-ṭīkā-vivaraṇa, 1
Tattvārtha-sāra, 96 *n.*
Tattvārtha-śloka-vārtika, 546, 547 *n.*
taṭastha, 51, 377
tādātmyā-dhyāsa, 334
tāmasa, 31, 163, 510
tāmasa ahaṃkāra, 259, 260
tāmasa śāstra, 22
tāmisra, 500
Tāmraparṇī, 63, 95
Tāntric system, 57
Tāntric works, 58
Tārāsāropaniṣad, 13
Tātācārya, 98, 109, 131, 132
Tātācārya-dina-caryā, 131
Tātārya, 129
Tātāyārya, 115, 126
Tātparya-candrikā, 123
Tātparya-dīpikā, 114, 116, 118, 123, 132, 380 *n.*
Tautology, 372
Teacher, 62, 102, 122, 124, 182, 235, 400, 405
tejas, 35, 37, 40 *n.*, 49 *n.*, 56, 163, 181, 260, 261; substance, 188
Teleological, 470
Teleology, 30, 261, 459, 472, 473
Telugu Brahmin, 399
Temper, 548
Temple, 17, 18, 58, 69, 96, 104, 111, 121
Temple-building, 17
Temple-gods, 18
Temple-keepers, 121
Temporal, 42, 313, 314, 324, 353; character, 284, 285, 331, 353; conditions, 343; contiguity, 316; identity, 252; relations, 321; succession, 274
Temporary, 495
Tendency, 30, 34, 45, 51, 210, 288, 349, 449, 550
Tender equality, 84
Tenets, 524 *n.*
Teṅgalai, 120, 380, 381, 382; school, 120; their difference with the Vadagalai is based on the greater or less emphasis on *prapatti*, 86–7
Terms of reference, 419
Test, 341
Testimony, 192, 196, 203, 211, 247, 289, 296, 303, 310, 326, 390, 426, 465, 485, 547
"*Tettarumtiral*," 67
Text, 340, 350, 398, 438, 446
Textual criticism, 388
Theism, 451, 472
Theistic, 189, 196, 480; tendency, 451
Theological, 303; dogma, 395
Theory, 28, 30, 179, 180, 181, 183, 184, 187, 210, 291, 296, 308, 331, 348, 351, 352, 413, 421, 426, 515 *n.*, 516, 520, 543; illusion, 237, 238, 239, 241; of knowledge, 238
Thesis, 315, 322, 416, 419, 420, 427, 512
Thief, 213
Thing itself, 186
Things, 34, 45 *n.*, 48, 190, 192, 193, 195
"This," 180, 184, 185 *n.*
Thomas, Dr F. W., 531, 532
Thought, 32, 46, 47, 53, 61, 304, 460
Thought-activity, 44, 50, 51, 53
Thought-experiences, 385
Thought-movement, 44

Threads, 197
Tides, 228
Tikalakkiḍandān-tirunāvīruḍaiyāpiṟān-Tātar-aṇṇar, 137
tilakālaka, 56
Time, 27, 34, 35, 42, 43, 45, 46, 47, 51, 56, 82, 185 *n*., 195, 199, 228, 252, 273, 277, 278, 279, 284, 285, 286, 287, 309, 348, 349, 389, 447, 448, 472, 473, 489, 504, 515
Time-conception, 285
Time-energy, 45
Timeless, 72, 447, 473
Time-moments, 274
Time-units, 286
Tinnevelly, 68, 137
Tiru-chaṇḍa-vruttam, 68, 134 *n*.
Tirukkovalur, 103
Tirukkurgur, 65
Tirukkurukaippiran Pillai, 134
Tirukkurun-dāṇḍakam, 69, 134 *n*.
Tirukkurungudi, 103
Tirukurugaipiran Pillai, 109 *n*., 110
Tirumalācārya, 133
Tirumal-Tiru-moṟi, 76
Tiru-mantra-churukku, 94
Tiru-maṅgaiy, 66, 69, 77
Tiru-maṅgaiy-āṟvār, 63, 64, 65, 66 *n*., 67, 68, 79, 83, 134 *n*., 137
Tiru-maṟiṣai, 63
Tiru-maṟiṣai Pirān, 63, 64, 65, 66 *n*., 68, 96 *n*., 106 *n*., 134 *n*.
Tiru-mālai, 69, 134 *n*.
Tiru-moṟi, 69
Tirunarayanapperumāl, 104
Tiru-neḍum-dāṇḍakam, 69, 134 *n*.
Tirunirmalai, 103
Tiru-pall'-āṇḍu, 69
Tiru-paḷḷiy-eṟuchi, 69, 134 *n*.
Tirupati, 103
Tiru-pān-āṟvār, 63, 64, 65, 66, 68, 69, 134 *n*.
Tiru-pāvai, 69, 77
Tiruppalavai-vyākhyāna, 127
Tiruppāvai, 134 *n*.
Tiruppullani, 103
Tirupputkuḷi, 103
Tiruvaigundipuram, 103
Tiruvallikeṇi, 103
Tiruvanandapuram, 103
Tiru-vantādi, 68, 134 *n*.
Tiruvaṇpariśāram, 103
Tiruvarangattamudanār, 137
Tiruvaṭṭar, 103
Tiru-vācha kam, 84
Tiruvārādhana-krama, 138
Tiru-vāṣiṅyam, 69, 134
Tiruvāymoṟi-nuṟundādi, 138
Tiru-vāy-moṟi, 66, 69, 79, 80 *n*., 105, 109 *n*., 110, 134 *n*., 137
Tiruveḷukūr-tirukkai, 134 *n*.
Tiru-veṟugūtt-irukkai, 69
Tiru-vṛuttam, 69, 74, 134 *n*.
tiryag, 501
tiryak-srotas, 501, 502
Ṭoḍappā, 110
Toṇḍar-aḍi-poḍiy-āṟvār, 63, 64, 65, 66 *n*., 68, 69, 134 *n*.
Toṇḍāṇūr, 104
Totality, 264
Totārambā, 110, 119, 122
Touch, 251
Touch-potential, 48, 260, 504
Toy, 167
Tradition, 57, 63, 104 *n*., 496, 515 *n*.
Traditional, 64, 65
traiguṇya, 46
Trai-rāśikas, 523
Traits, 195, 212
Trance, 30, 79
Transcendent, 39, 41, 44, 47, 99, 156, 175, 195, 197, 391, 426, 455, 507, 536; beauty, 83; Brahman, 10; nature, 413; reality, 550; self, 468; world, 536
Transcendental, 24, 30, 38, 448, 453, 468; cause, 502; form, 73
Transformation, 2, 6, 10, 36, 37, 47, 156, 182, 196, 197, 199, 281, 286, 298, 302, 332, 341, 368, 371, 385, 386, 393, 395, 396, 397, 416, 440, 454, 456, 487
Transformer, 45 *n*.
Transforming entities, 385
Transition, 349
Transitoriness, 28
Transmigrations, 291
Transmission, 287
Transparent, 46
trasareṇu, 155, 163, 263
Travancore, 66, 67
Treaties, 86
Treatment, 207, 297, 426
Tricky, 513
tridaṇḍa, 1, 549; its meaning, 1 *n*.
Tridaṇḍī Brahmins, their views, 2
tridaṇḍī, 2, 532
triguṇa, 259, 497
triguṇā-tmikā prakṛti, 491
Trikālika, 497
Trikāṇḍamaṇḍana, 3 *n*.
Trinity, 46, 47
Tripartite, 29, 47 200; union, 46

Tripād-vibhūti-mahānārāyaṇa Upaniṣad, 13
Triplicane, 68
Trivikrama, 39, 40 *n.*
trivṛt-karaṇa, 182, 183, 188, 240
Triyaga, 440
True, 194, 208, 316, 331, 424, 437, 457, 471, 482, 507; adoration, 54; cause, 338; knowledge, 160, 178, 330, 331, 347, 429, 450, 491, 492, 506; wisdom, 416
Trustworthy, 357
Truth, 5, 8, 202, 308, 313, 326, 335, 413, 478, 517, 529
Truthfulness, 29
Tryambaka, 130
Tṛṃśa-praśno-ttara, 133
tṛṇa, 501
tṛṣā, 48
tuccha, 239, 241
Tucci, Dr G., 512 *n.*
Tuppu, 118
tuṣṭi, 57
Tuvaḷil, 78
Tūlikā, 126, 114, 131 *n.*
Twinkle, 378
Tyāga-śabdārtha-ṭippanī, 130
Types, 51; of soul, 61
Ṭaṅka, 1 *n.*, 108, 139

Udak-pratoḷi-kṛṣṇa, 110
Udayana, 1, 2, 539
udāharaṇa, 427
udāna, 59, 60
Udāyī-kuṇḍiyāyaṇīya, 525 *n.*
Uddyotakara, 212 *n.*
Ujjvala, 52
Ujjvala-nīla-maṇi, 82
Ukkalammal, 105
Ukkal Āṛvān, 105
Ultimate, 42, 52, 509; antecedent, 397; attainment, 38; consciousness, 420, 457; destiny, 383; emancipation, 38; end, 136, 416; goal, 100, 136; ideal, 414; object, 464; principle, 451; state, 445; truth, 196, 327, 426, 468; union, 429
Ultimate reality, 24, 25, 27, 31, 37, 165, 197, 406, 450, 457, 460, 497, 507, 509 *n.*; as *nirviśeṣa* and *sariśeṣa*, 165 *et seq.*; as unqualified, refuted, 173–5
Ultimately real, 197, 200, 371
Ultra-sensual, 225
Umā-Maheśvara, 395, 396; his criticism of Rāmānuja, 396
Unaffectedness, 37
Unassociated Brahman, 430
Unborn, 291
Uncaused, 299
Uncertainty, 370, 398
Unchangeable, 34, 46, 196, 301, 323, 469, 549; unity, 287
Unconditional, 203, 226, 272, 390, 485, 497, 533, 535
Unconditioned, 272
Unconscious, 26, 27, 29, 41, 79, 408, 416, 546; power, 43; world, 429
Unconsciousness, 150
Uncontradicted, 251, 314, 358; experience, 246
Uncontradictory, 236
Understanding, 462, 463, 539
Undifferentiated, 35, 200, 372, 495; consciousness, 238
Unfavourable effects, 292
Uniformity, 278
Unintelligent, 25, 26
Unintelligible, 144
Union, 33, 38, 53
Unique, 189, 193, 316, 424, 454
Uniqueness, 255, 455
Unit of time, 273
Unitary, 545
Units, 420
Unity, 25, 26, 31, 42, 46, 53, 192, 193, 194, 413, 414, 418, 419, 434, 456, 459, 460, 461, 462, 506, 508; of a flame, 343; of being, 175; of consciousness, 345; texts, 307, 308, 309, 310
Unity-in-difference, 28, 30, 405
Universal, 45, 86, 193, 217, 218, 224, 243, 254, 279, 312, 323, 341, 355, 356, 387, 460, 493, 535, 536, 537, 538; agreement, 229; cognition, 358; concomitance, 228, 230, 533; consciousness, 198; destruction, 169; existence, 345; experience, 219, 319; illumination, 198; negation, 272, 328; proposition, 225
Universality, 298
Universe, 32, 35, 41, 45 *n.*, 53, 56, 87, 190, 191, 195, 197, 239, 315, 412, 434, 454, 455, 456, 457, 459, 460, 472, 475, 484, 492, 499, 500, 507, 508, 511
Unknowable, 230 *n.*, 499
Unlimited, 10; servitude, 88
Unproduced, 204
Unprohibited food, 61
Unqualified, 165, 430
Unreal, 2, 179, 181, 194, 314, 330, 332, 338, 339, 346, 433, 436, 456, 458, 487

Unreality, 5, 201, 210, 332, 458
Unreasonableness, 177 *n.*
Unrelatedness, 466
Unseen merit, 292
Unspeakable, 35
Untouchables, 104
Unvedic, 472
uñcha-vṛtti, 119
Upadeśa-ratna-mālai, 64, 94 *n.*
Upadeśa-ratna-mālā, 134, 135, 138, 482
upahitasvarūpa, 306
Upakāra-saṃgraha, 124
upamāna, 234, 426, 427; upheld by Meghanādāri, 234
upamiti, 128
Upaniṣad(s), 5, 12, 13, 16, 101, 105, 126, 146, 148, 153, 154, 182, 196, 211, 291, 293, 296, 387, 394, 398, 442, 446, 447, 463, 464, 465, 468, 471, 480, 481, 496, 512, 519
Upaniṣad-bhāṣya, 127
Upaniṣad-brahmayogin, 13
Upaniṣadic, 112, 113, 126, 208, 240, 392, 519; texts, 201, 394, 405, 479, 480, 487
Upaniṣadists, 211
Upaniṣad-maṅgala-dīpikā, 126
Upaniṣad texts, 381, 464
Upaniṣad-vākya-vivaraṇa, 127
Upaniṣat-prakāśikā, 127
upasargas, 505
Upavarṣa, 7 *n.*, 105, 107, 108
Upavarṣācārya, 7 *n.*
upavāsa, 33
upādāna, 2, 191, 196, 388, 391
upādāna-kārnaṇa, 157, 454, 484
upādhi, 269, 278, 301, 386, 413, 422, 432, 453, 478, 479, 481, 489, 492, 508 *n.*, 534, 535, 561
upādhi-rūpa, 216
upāsaka, 89
upāsanā, 293, 381
upāya, 376
upāya-jñāna, 55
upāya stage, 377 *n.*, 378
upāya-svarūpa-jñāna, 88 *n.*
upāya-śūnyatā, 87
Upendra Bhaṭṭa, 401
upeya, 377
Upper India, 19
Uraipūr, 67
Usage, 334
Uśanas, 532
utpatti, 199
uttama, 505
Uttara-kalārya, 381, 382, 383
uttara-mantrin, 65
Uttara-mīmāṃsā, 350
Uttara-nārāyaṇa, 57
uttara-vibhāga, 482
Uvāsagadasāo, 522, 524
Uyyakkoṇḍār, 67 *n.*, 97
ūha, 214
ūrddhva-srotas, 501

Vacuity, 36, 353
Vadari, 77
Vadarikāśrama, 482
vadhū, 47
Vaḍagalai, their difference with the Teṅgalai is based on the greater or less emphasis on *prapatti*, 86–7
Vaḍakalai, 67, 120, 121, 381
Vaḍavāvaktra, 40 *n.*
vahni, 510
vahnitva, 535
vahuśruta, 530
Vaibhava-prakāśikā, 121 *n.*
Vaibhāṣika Buddhists, 251
vaidhī, 378
vaidikī, 507
vaiḍāla-vratika, 518
Vaigai, 63
Vaijayantī, 105 *n.*
vaikārika, 48, 498, 499, 504, 510
vaikārika-indriya-sarga, 502 *n.*
Vaikhānasa, 22, 57
Vaikuṇṭha, 50, 93
Vairamegha, 67
Vairamegha Pallava, 66
vairāgya, 33, 47, 63
Vaiśeṣika, 208, 456, 467; supposed, 163
Vaiśvadeva-kārikā, 122
Vaiṣṇava, 12, 39 *n.*, 63, 65, 83, 87, 98, 104, 105, 293, 379; commentators, 1 *n.*; literature, 10; marks, 22; rites, 102; systems, 139; temple, 65, 138; tradition, 99 *n.*; writers, 192
Vaiṣṇava Upaniṣads, 13; division of, 13
Vaiṣṇavism, 13, 63 *n.*, 64, 81 *n.*, 96 *n.*, 105, 110, 139, 399, 451
Vaiṣṇavite Reformers of India, 119 *n.*
Vakulā-bharaṇa, 139
Valadeva, 482
Valid, 185 *n.*, 202, 203, 208, 468, 533, 537, 539; inference, 537; knowledge, 236, 248, 467, 469; memory, 237; perception, 215
Validity, 16, 190, 201, 202, 203, 213, 216, 229, 230, 238, 247, 248, 250, 321, 326, 346, 347, 348, 356, 357, 428, 457, 458, 495, 534, 536, 537, 539; its nature as treated by Meghanādāri, 215–16; of cognition, 249

Vallabha, 400, 475, 496
Value, 464, 472
Vanamamalai-jiyar, 111
Vanamālī Miśra, 440, 441 *n.*; his interpretation of Nimbārka philosophy, 440 *et seq.*
Vangi-puratt-acchi, 97 *n.*
Vanity, 529
Vañjikulam, 67
Varada, 98, 157, 159, 352
Varadadāsa, 132
Varada Deśikācārya, 125
Varadaguru, 111, 125
Varadakṛṣṇa, his definition of perception, 216
Varadanārāyaṇa, 208; his view of doubt, 208
Varada Nārāyaṇa Bhaṭṭāraka, 119
Varadanātha, 111, 118, 123, 125, 380
Varadanāyaka Sūri, 125
Varadarāja, 78
Varadarāja Sūri, 125
Varadarāt, 114 *n.*, 125
Varadaviṣṇu, 109, 111, 216
Varadaviṣṇu Miśra, 109, 111, 119, 180, 212 *n.*, 214 *n.*, 217, 226, 229, 234, 383 *n.*
Varada Viṣṇu Sūri, 131
Varadācārya, 93 *n.*, 102, 119
Varadārya, 112, 118, 119, 125
Varagalai, 381
varaṇadaśā, 379
Varavara, 39, 41, 94 *n.*, 157, 159 *n.*, 160, 163, 260, 261; his view of time, 163
Varavara muni, 110, 135, 136, 137
Varavara-muni-campu, 138
Varavara-muni-dinacaryā, 138
Varavara-muni-kāvya, 138
Varavara-muni-śataka, 138
Varāha, 16, 20, 39 *n.*, 40 *n.*, 523
Varāha Mihira, 523
Vararaṅga, 97, 109 *n.*
Variable, 243
Variability, 243
varṇa, 293
varṇaka, 515
varṇikā, 516
varttikā, 516
Varuṇa, 59, 295
vastu, 250 *n.*
Vaśiṣṭha, 21, 23, 482
Vaśiṣṭha-saṃhitā, 19
Vatsabhāskara, 3 *n.*
Vaṭapūrṇa, 104, 109
Vācaspati, 3, 196, 467, 476, 517 *n.*, 533
vācārambhaṇam, 3
vācika, 507
vāda, 381, 512, 513
Vādādri-kuliśa, 127
vādassādana, 513 *n.*
vādha, 314, 501
Vādhūla, 109
Vādhūla *gotra*, 98, 110, 114 *n.*
Vādhūla-kula-tilaka, 127 *n.*
Vādhūla Narasiṃgha-guru, 114
Vādhūla Narasiṃha, 132
Vādhūla Śrīnivāsa, 114, 117, 123, 126, 131 *n.*, 135, 305
Vādhūla Varadaguru, 114
Vādhūla varada Nārāyaṇaguru, 138
Vādhūla Veṅkaṭācārya, 114
Vādideva, 536
Vādideva Sūri, 536 *n.*, 537 *n.*
Vādihaṃsa, 111; his conception of *jāti*, 354; his view of *svataḥ-prāmāṇya-vāda*, 356 *et seq.*; his view of *svaprakāśatva*, 358 *et seq.*
Vādi-haṃsa-navāmvuda, 352, 361; his notion of negation, 352
Vādihaṃsāmbuvāha, 117, 184, 185, 187; his treatment of illusion, 184 *et seq.*
Vādihaṃsāmbuvāha Rāmānujācārya, 186 *n.*
Vādihaṃsāmbuvāhācārya, 118, 119, 183, 187
Vādikesarī, 135, 138
Vādikeśarī Miśra, 132
Vādi-traya-khaṇḍana, 124, 193 *n.*, 305
Vādivijaya, 111
vādi-vipratipattiḥ, 212 *n.*
Vāgīśvara, 40 *n.*
Vāgvijaya, 118, 130
vākovākya, 517
vākya-kara, 106, 107
Vākya-padīya, 517 *n.*
Vākyārtha-saṃgraha, 130
Vāmana, 39, 40 *n.*
Vāmanadeva, 40 *n.*, 146
Vāṇīvilāsa Press 1910, 380 *n.*
Vāraṇādrīśa, 110, 114 *n.*
vārtā, 532
vārttika, 515
vārttikasutra, 515, 516
vāsanā, 26, 27, 33, 34, 43, 51, 54, 253, 273, 308, 453, 487
Vāsudeva, 2, 13, 16, 17, 21, 27, 29, 31, 34, 37, 38, 39, 42 *n.*, 57, 155, 157, 158, 443 *n.*, 474, 475, 497, 506, 508
Vāsudeva-vyūha, 474
Vāsudevendra, 13
Vāsudevopaniṣad, 13
Vāśiṣṭha, 20

vāta, 475
vātsalya, 89
Vātsīputriya, 251
Vātsya, 119, 297
Vātsya Anantārya, 126
Vātsya *gotra*, 111, 112
Vātsya Nṛsiṃhadeva, 122
Vātsya Śrīnivāsa, 112, 203; his notion of class-concepts, 297; his treatment of *pramāṇa*, 203
Vātsya Varada, 110, 111, 114, 116, 118, 119, 130, 132, 349, 350, 351, 380; his analysis of the concept of difference, 351; his notion of God, 351; his refutation of Śrīharṣa's view of the falsity of the world, 350; his refutation of the denial of the category of difference, 350; his view of *bidhi*, 349–50
Vātsya Varadaguru, 109
Vātsyāyana, 208, 212 *n.*, 235
Vātsyāyana-bhāṣya, 207 *n.*
vāyu, 7, 48, 49 *n.*, 59, 60, 163, 253, 261, 499, 504, 505, 510
Vāyu purāṇa, 20, 502, 503, 505, 506 *n.*; its philosophy, 502 *et seq.*
Veda, 2, 14, 15, 16, 18, 21, 24, 25, 62, 88, 124, 165, 198 *n.*, 203, 347, 349, 357, 401, 429, 441, 471, 515, 517, 530, 531
veda-nindaka, 519
Vedas instructed by God, 15
Vedavid, 40 *n.*
veda-vidāṃ matam, 181
Vedavyāsa Bhaṭṭa, 111, 130
Vedānta, 1, 8, 96, 97, 100, 115, 117, 125, 130, 138, 197, 200, 305, 307, 352, 401, 403, 406, 416, 462, 466, 471, 480, 481, 482, 496, 508 *n.*; in relation to Sāṃkhya according to Vijñāna Bhikṣu, 471 *et seq.*; its *bhedābheda* interpretation, 105 *et seq.*; dialectic, 153; view, 235
Vedānta-deśika, 119, 361
Vedānta-deśika-vaibhava-prakāśikā, 121 *n.*, 131
Vedānta-līpa, 103, 113, 118, 159, 201, 349
Vedāntaguru, 112
Vedānta-kaṇṭako-ddhāra, 131
Vedānta-kaustubha, 130, 132, 402
Vedānta-kaustubha-prabhā, 402, 415 *n.*, 416
Vedāntakārikāvali, 132
Vedāntamañjuṣā, 404 *n.*
Vedānta-paribhāṣā, 9, 204, 216
Vedānta-pārijāta-sauraleha, 400, 402
Vedānta-ratna-mañjuṣā, 403, 411, 412
Vedānta Rāmānuja, 18, 132, 380
Vedānta-saṃgraha, 113
Vedānta-saṃgraha-tātparya-dīpikā, 130
Vedānta-sāra, 103, 113, 118, 349
Vedānta-siddhānta-pradīpa, 400, 403
Vedānta-siddhānta-saṃgraha, 440
Vedānta-sūtra, 2, 56 *n.*, 476, 484
Vedānta-tattva-vodha, 400, 408, 409 *n.*, 410 *n.*, 411 *n.*
Vedānta-vijaya, 117, 126, 128 *n.*, 130
Vedāntācārya, 119, 132
Vedāntic, 111, 438, 461, 467; instructions, 308; schools, 385; texts, 61, 337; view, 464; writers, 385
Vedāntin, 109
Vedāntists, 139, 156, 465, 477
Vedāntī Mādhava, 134, 135
Vedāntī Mādhavadāsa, 110 *n.*
Vedārtha-saṃgraha, 101, 103, 106, 107, 118, 128*n.*, 130, 160, 201, 218, 305
Vedic, 16, 17, 18, 43 *n.*, 57, 293, 518, 549; circles, 530; cult, 518; doctrines, 517, 519; duties, 15, 165, 404, 416, 429; injunctions, 165, 349, 350, 441; people, 19, 20, 531; religion, 40, 95; rites, 14, 20; sacrifices, 517, 522, 549; school, 181; science, 531 *n.*; scriptures, 366; sects, 20; texts, 17, 112, 390, 391, 394
Vegetables, 97 *n.*
Veil, 366, 371, 372, 374
Veiling, 369; agent, 369
Veṅkaṭa, 18, 63 *n.*, 66 *n.*, 67, 94, 96 *n.*, 98 *n.*, 99, 105 *n.*, 107, 110, 111, 114, 115, 117, 118, 119, 120, 121 *n.*, 122, 123, 124, 125, 126, 127, 130, 131, 132, 135, 155, 157, 159, 161, 163, 183, 201, 203, 207, 208, 209, 210, 211, 212 *n.*, 213, 214, 216, 217, 219 *n.*, 220, 221, 223, 225, 226, 227, 228, 229, 232, 233, 234, 235, 236 *n.*, 238, 240, 241, 250 *n.*, 251, 254, 255, 256, 257, 261, 262, 263, 265, 268 *n.*, 269, 270, 277, 280, 281, 282, 286, 288, 289, 290, 291, 292, 295, 296, 297, 301, 302, 303, 305, 306, 307, 308, 311, 313, 314, 316, 317, 318, 319, 323, 324, 325, 326, 327, 340, 342, 344, 346, 352, 353, 355, 356, 380, 381, 382, 383, 426; analysis of momentariness, 273 *et seq.*; an upholder of *anvita-bhidhāna-vāda*, 233; a constructor of Rāmānuja logic, 235; conclusive remarks on

Veṅkaṭa (*cont.*)
doubt, 208 *et seq.*, decision, nature of, 210; definition of *pramāṇa*, 236; doubt and *ūha*, 214; error, definition of, 210; error and doubt, relation, 208 *et seq.*; his agreement with the *Pañcarātra* view of God, 303; his admission of three *pramāṇas*, 214; his admission of three types of illusion from three points of view, 241; his analysis of doubt, 211; his classification of doubt, 212–13; his conception of *jāti*, 355; his conception of *sādṛśya*, 355; his criticism of Bhāskara, 301; his criticism of Brahmadatta, 291; his criticism of *Nyāya-sūtra* and *Prajñā-paritrāṇa* regarding doubt, 211; his criticism of Nyāya theory of doubt, 207; his criticism of Sāṃkhya argument in favour of *prakṛti*, 256 *et seq.*; his criticism of the *avidyā*, 330 *et seq.*; his criticism of the Sāṃkhya view of God, 296; his criticism of the Śaṅkara conception of the unity of self, 345; his criticism of the view that *ajñāna* is a positive entity, 327 *et seq.*; his criticism of the view that *ajñāna* rests in the individual *jīvas*, 329; his criticism of the view that all effects are false owing to their contradiction, 341 *et seq.*; his criticism of the view that *avidyā* and *māyā* are different, 334 *et seq.*; his criticism of the view that Brahman is pure bliss, 344; his criticism of the view that consciousness cannot be produced, 321; his criticism of the view that consciousness is identical with self, 323 *et seq.*; his criticism of the view that consciousness is one, 322; his criticism of the view that emancipation is attained by right knowledge, 326; his criticism of the view that indeterminate Brahman could be eternal, 345; his criticism of the view that pure consciousness is *sākṣin*, 325; his criticism of the view that pure consciousness is unqualified, 323; his criticism of the view that realization of monistic identity produces emancipation, 336 *et seq.*; his criticism of the view that scriptural testimony is superior to perception, 326; his criticism of the view that the notion of the self as knower is false, 325; his criticism of the Yoga view of God, 296; his criticism of Yādava Prakaśa, 302; his definition of perception, 216; his doctrine of emancipation, 292; his eschatological conception, 295; his life and literature, 119–25; his Nyāya theory, refutation of, 262 *et seq.*; his relation of the view that consciousness is identical with self, 290; his refutation of Buddhist and Cārvāka theory of *ākāśa*, 282; his refutation of Buddhist doctrines of momentariness, 268 *et seq.*; his refutation of Cārvāka causality, 276; his refutation of contentless consciousness, 310–11; his refutation of different views of God, 302; his refutation of Kātyāyana's views of God, 302; his refutation of Sāṃkhya-satkārya-vāda, 265 *et seq.*; his refutation of *nirvikalpajñāna*, 311; his refutation of Śaṅkara, 304 *et seq.*; his refutation of Śaṅkara's theory of *anubhūti*, 318–19; his refutation of Śrīharṣa's refutation of *pramāṇa*, 202; his refutation of the denial of production of individual cognitions, 319 *et seq.*; his refutation of the Buddhist denial of substance, 251 *et seq.*; his refutation of the denial of the category of difference, 312; his refutation of the doctrine of the all-pervasiveness of souls, 291; his refutation of the falsity of the world on the ground of validity, 313–14; his refutation of the falsity of the world on the ground of absence of relation between the perceiver and the perceived, 314 *et seq.*; his refutation of the Nyāya doctrine of the formation of whole from parts, 263 *et seq.*; his refutation of the possibility of *jijñāsā* according to Śaṅkara's interpretation, 306; his refutation of the view of the reflection of Brahman under *avidyā*, 291; his refutation of the view that *avidyā* rests in Brahman, 317–18; his refutation of the view that perception refers to pure Being, 311; his refutation of the view that Brahman is qualityless, 306; his refutation of the view that the self-luminosity of Brahman is contentless, 316–17; his refutation of the view that the utterance of unity texts can lead to immediate perception, 308–10; his re-

futation of the view that the world is illusory, 312–13; his special treatment of doubt, 207 *et seq.*; his support to the theory of *jñāna-karma-samuccaya*, 307; his support of the Vedic testimony, 203; his theory of consciousness, a quality of self, 288; his treatment of *avayava*, 232; his treatment of doubt, 202; his treatment of doubt compared with that of Varada Nārāyaṇa, 208; his treatment of inference, 225 *et seq.*; his treatment of *kevala-vyatirekin*, 226–7; his treatment of memory as *pramāṇa*, 214; his treatment of object, 217; his treatment of *parāmarśa*, 229; his treatment of *pramāṇa*, 201 *et seq.*; his treatment of *śabda-pramāṇa*, 233; his treatment of substance, 251 *et seq.*; his treatment of *tarka*, 227; his treatment of types of inference, 229 *et seq.*; his treatment of *vyāptigraha*, 228; his treatment of *vyāpti*, 225–6; his view of *apūrva* or *adṛṣṭa*, 303; his view of *bhakti*, 292 *et seq.*; his views of emancipation attainable by God's grace, 304; his view of God, 157 *et seq.*; his view of incarnation, 302–3; his view of *karma* and *mukti*, 295; his view of *karma* and *prāyaścitta*, 293–4; his view of matter, 162 *et seq.*; his view of *prakṛti*, *mahat*, *tanmātra*, etc., 163 *et seq.*; his view of self in relation to God, 161 *et seq.*; his view of the relation of the souls with God, 297; his view of validity of memory, 237; his view of virtue and vice, 291; his view that errors cannot vanish by Brahma-knowledge, 307; his view that world appearance continues even after the destruction of *avidyā*, 308; nature of *ākāśa*, 282; nature of the senses, 280 *et seq.*; nature of time, 284; nature of soul, 286 *et seq.*; offered a critic of Gotama's logic, 235; refutation of Cārvāka theory of soul, 286 *et seq.*; refutation of the view that consciousness belongs to the senses, 289; refutation of the view that scriptural texts cannot signify Brahman, 340; Śaṅkara's conception of cessation of *avidyā* criticized, 338 *et seq.*
Veṅkaṭadāsa, 132
Veṅkaṭa-deśika, 112
Veṅkaṭanāthārya, 117
Veṅkaṭa Sudhī, 12, 18, 132
Veṅkaṭācārya, 112, 117
Veṅkaṭādhvarī, 131, 132
Veṅkaṭārya, 112
Verbal knowledge, 216, 217, 308, 310
Verbal testimony, 128
Vernal, 295
Verse, 117, 181
vibhava, 39, 42, 129, 158
vibhava-avatāras, 40 *n.*
vibhava-devatā, 21
vibhavāvatāra, 41
vibhu, 262, 386
vibhūti, 475
Vibration, 206; potential, 163
Vice, 291, 304, 349, 441, 493, 506, 521, 522, 533
Vicious, 255, 267, 304, 349; circle, 419, 433; infinite, 9, 253, 267, 277, 286, 316, 320, 334, 341, 353, 355, 359, 417, 421, 424, 433; infinitude, 177 *n.*
Victor, 78
Vidaddha, 514 *n.*
Vidaddhavādi, 514 *n.*
vidagdha, 514 *n.*
videhī muktas, 441
vidhi, 8, 350
Vidhisudhākara, 133
Vidhura, 513
Vidhura-paṇḍita-jātaka, 514 *n.*
vidyā, 47, 49, 507, 508, 509
Vidyādhideva, 40 *n.*
Vidyānandi, 546, 547
Vidyāpati, 3
Vidyāpati Bhāskara Bhaṭṭa, 3
Vidyāraṇya, 120
vidyā-yoni-śarīra, 415
View, 50, 56, 181, 182, 184, 185, 187, 192, 196, 204, 206, 289, 291, 297, 302, 303, 305, 307, 318, 330, 335, 349, 350, 409, 410, 429, 433, 435, 456, 458, 461, 469, 473, 477, 496, 498, 510, 512, 519, 520, 521, 522, 532, 533, 538
Vihagendra saṃhita, 23, 24, 41, 57
Vihaṅgama, 40 *n.*
Vijayanagara, 120, 121
vijayā, 57
Vijayīndra, 127
Vijayīndra Bhikṣu, 117
Vijayīndra-parājaya, 127, 305
Vijayollāsa, 126
Vijñāna Bhikṣu, 445, 456, 480, 482, 483, 484, 485, 486, 493, 496, 497; his conception of the individual, 460 *et seq.*; his conception of the relation of the world with God, 454 *et seq.*;

Vijñāna Bhikṣu (*cont.*)
his criticism of Sāṃkhya and Yoga, 479 *et seq.*; his notion of God, 461; his philosophy, 445 *et seq.*; his treatment of *avidyā*, 468 *et seq.*; his treatment of *bhakti*, 450 *et seq.*; his treatment of Brahma experience, 465 *et seq.*; his treatment of experience, 467; his treatment of *karma*, 452 *et seq.*; his treatment of the nature of God, 474 *et seq.*; his treatment of the relation of Sāṃkhya to Vedānta, 471 *et seq.*; his view of gradation of realities, 445; his view of *karma*, 445; *kāla* in, 446; *māyā* and *pradhāna* in, 476 *et seq.*; relation of self and *ānanda* in, 445; world and Brahman in, 446 *et seq.*
vijñānam, 185 *n.*
vijñāna-vādin, 142, 205
Vijñānā-mṛta-bhāṣya, 450, 451 *n.*, 453 *n.*, 454 *n.*, 455 *n.*, 457 *n.*, 458 *n.*, 459 *n.*, 461, 462 *n.*, 463 *n.*, 468 *n.*, 472 *n.*, 473 *n.*, 477 *n.*, 478 *n.*, 480 *n.*, 481 *n.*, 482 *n.*
Vikalpa, 4
vikāra, 3, 260 *n.*, 386, 480
Vikāra-veda, 21
vikāri kāraṇa, 454
vikārin, 61
vikarmasthān, 518
Vikrama Cola, 104
vikriyātmaka, 172
vikṛta, 342
vikṛty-ātmā, 25
vilakṣaṇa-mahatvā-dy-adhikaraṇatvād, 257
Vimba-tattva-prakāśikā, 122
vināśa, 314
Vindhyeśvarī Prasāda, referring to Vaiṣṇava commentators, 1 *n.*
Vindhyeśvarī Prasāda Paṇḍita, 1 n., 2, 3 *n.*
Violation, 128
vipratipattiḥ, 212 *n.*, 213
vipura, 503, 504
Virinchipuram, 523
Virocana, 528
Virodha-bhañjanī, 384
Virodha-nirodha, 115, 130, 384, 385, 386 *n.*, 387, 392, 393 *n.*, 394 *n.*, 395
Virodha-parihāra, 124
Virodha-varūthinī, 395, 396
Virodha-varūthinī-pramāthinī, 130, 396
Virtues, 29, 33, 34, 47, 291, 294, 295, 303, 304, 349, 388, 441, 450, 493, 506, 521, 522, 530, 533, 549, 550
Virtuous, 51, 295, 304, 349, 437, 549
viruddha-dharmā-dhyāsavān, 268
vīrut, 500
Virāṃśolaippillai, 138
Visible, 5, 500
Vision, 71, 459, 471, 505
Visual, 543; organ, 222, 240, 241, 243, 459, 545; perception, 219, 310; sense, 217
viśadā-vabhāsa, 217
viśeṣaṇa, 429
viśiṣṭa-jñāna, 221
Viśiṣṭā-dvaita, 111, 116 *n.*, 118, 119, 120, 123, 125, 159, 234, 235, 351, 389, 392, 393, 395
Viśiṣṭā-dvaita logic, 234
Viśiṣṭā-dvaita-siddhānta, 127
Viśiṣṭā-dvaitavāda, 119
Viśiṣṭā-dvaitins, 393
viśiṣṭārtha, 233
viśiṣṭatva, 218
viśuddhi, 524
Viśva-guṇādarśa, 131
Viśvajaya, 118
Viśvarūpa, 40 *n.*
Viśvācārya, 401
Viśvāmitra, 23
Viśvāmitra *gotra*, 119
Viśvodarā, 59
Viṣayatā-vāda, 133
Viṣaya-vākya-dīpikā, 117, 126
Viṣṇu, 12, 19, 20, 24, 25, 31, 33, 37, 38, 39, 40 *n.*, 44, 45, 50, 52, 57, 58, 61, 63, 64, 66, 67 *n.*, 68, 69, 87, 89, 96, 155, 304, 415, 448 *n.*, 473, 475, 498, 499, 505, 507, 509
Viṣṇucitta, 69, 111, 119, 137, 214 *n.*, 220 *n.*, 234, 235, 383 *n.*; a predecessor of Veṅkaṭa in the construction of Rāmānuja logic, 235
Viṣṇucittan, 63
Viṣṇudharmottara, 20
Viṣṇu Miśra, 159
Viṣṇu Purāṇa, 20, 81, 260 *n.*, 497, 498 *n.*, 499 *n.*, 500, 501 *n.*, 530; its philosophy, 497 *et seq.*
Viṣṇu-saṃhitā, 23, 24, 31, 32; *ahaṃkāra* in, 31; *Bhāgavata-yoga* in, 32; *bhakti* and *yoga*, 32; God, nature of, 31; philosophy of, 23–4; *prakṛti*, theory of, 31; Sāṃkhya in, 23–4; *ṣaḍ-aṅga-yoga* in, 24; view of all-pervasive soul different from the Śrīvaiṣṇavas, 24
Viṣṇu-śakti, 36
Viṣṇu-tattva-rahasya, 132

Viṣṇu-tattva-saṃhitā, 22; its contents, 22
Viṣṇu-vardhana, 104 *n*.
Viṣvaksena, 63 *n*., 64, 67 *n*.
Viṣvaksena-saṃhitā, 24, 30, 41 *n*., 43, 56, 57; *vyūha* doctrine in, 39 *n*.
Vital energy, 462
Vital functions, 540
Vital spirit, 80
vitaṇḍā, 512, 513, 514 *n*.
vitaṇḍā-sattha, 514
vitaṇḍā-vāda-sattham, 512
vivarta-paramparā, 332
Vivādārtha-saṃgraha, 132
viveka, 449, 508
Vivid impression, 217
Vividness, 217
vīra, 60
Vīranārāyaṇa, 94
Vīra-rāghava-dāsa, 114, 116, 132, 352
vīrya, 35, 37, 56
Void, 56
Volition, 298, 299
Volitional activity, 47
Vrajabhūṣaṇasaraṇadeva, 402
vrata, 33, 62
Vṛddha-manu, 20
vṛddhi, 47
Vṛhan-nāradīya-purāṇa, 20
vṛksa, 500
Vṛkṣa-bhaumāmṛta, 122
Vṛndāvana, 94
Vṛndāvanadeva, 402
vṛtti, 105, 281, 372, 373, 374, 411, 423, 439, 465, 466, 471, 485, 494, 495
vṛtti-jñāṇa, 204
vṛtti-kāra, 105, 107, 108
vṛtti-kārasya, 105 *n*.
vṛtti-nirodha, 506 *n*.
vṛtti-prativimbitam, 373
vṛtti stage, 363
Vucci Veṅkaṭācārya, 132
vyakta, 476, 497
vyaktā-vyakta, 497, 508
vyakti, 52
vyaṅga, 265
vyāpya, 225
vyatireki, 230; inference, 230 *n*., 232; type, 231
vyatireki anumāna, 231, 234
Vyavahāraika-satyatva-khaṇḍana, 125
vyavahārika, 459, 477
vyavahārikatva, 478
Vyavahārikatva-khaṇḍana-sāra, 133
vyavahārikī, 371
vyavahita, 136
vyāhata-sādhya-viparyayāt, 229
vyākhyāna-maṇḍapa, 137
vyāna, 59, 60
vyāpaka, 225
vyāpāra, 204
vyāpti, 225, 228, 427
Vyāsa, 18 *n*., 20, 39, 482
Vyāsa Bhaṭṭār, 109 *n*.
Vyāsa-bhāṣya, 452
Vyāsadeva, 402
Vyāsa-tātparya-nirṇaya, 133
Vyāsatīrtha, 111, 426
vyoma, 31
vyūha, 17, 37, 38, 39, 41, 42, 56, 157, 475; doctrine, 19; manifestations, 22

Waking consciousness, 363
Warangal, 120
Water, 42, 46, 128, 181, 369, 540, 541, 550
Waves, 6, 106, 302
Way of knowledge, 184
Ways, 60
Wedding, 377, 378
Western, 95
Wheel, 58, 60
Whirlpool, 83
White, 182, 256; goddess, 37
Whiteness, 193, 254
Whole, 189, 262, 263, 264, 298, 408, 413, 432, 433, 455, 456, 493, 494, 542
Will, 41, 45, 46, 48, 49, 191, 295, 298, 375, 412, 415, 441, 446, 448, 451, 472, 473, 474, 475, 481, 482, 488, 498, 500 *n*., 525
Will-activity, 45
Wisdom, 33, 38, 54, 307, 384, 414, 416, 446, 476, 491, 514, 521
Wise, 53
Wish, 54, 192, 295
Women, 20
Wonderful entity, 79
Words, 5, 29, 53, 61, 194, 309, 318
Work, 42, 46, 53, 56, 60, 303, 350
World, 6, 27, 34, 35, 41, 42, 53, 54, 55, 56, 57, 153, 174, 190, 191, 192, 193, 195, 196, 198 *n*., 200, 205, 293, 299, 301, 302, 312, 313, 314, 320, 321, 350, 365, 366, 388, 390, 391, 397, 413, 415, 416, 435, 438, 440, 442, 443 *n*., 445, 446, 456, 457, 458, 472, 476, 482, 488, 515, 517, 518, 531; of effects, 256; of matter, 200; view of its falsity refuted from the Nimbārka point of view, 435 *et seq.*

World-appearance, 155, 175, 177, 178, 196, 197, 210, 239, 307, 308, 309, 310, 312, 313, 331, 335, 337, 345, 367, 409, 423, 436, 439
World-creation, 296, 302, 330, 331, 365, 370
World-creator, 462
World-energy, 58, 459
World-existence, 490
World-experience, 374
World-force, 24
World-forms, 37, 456
World-illusion, 333, 337, 338
Worldly bonds, 22
Worldly objects, 258
World-materials, 152
World-objects, 367, 371
World-order, 197
World-phenomena, 155, 196, 340
World-process, 292, 458, 477
World-reality, 157
Worship, 10, 22, 32, 39, 40 *n*., 58, 61, 104, 193; of God, 382
Wretchedness, 99
Writers, 111, 196
Wrongful, 180

yad-artha-vyavahārā-nuguṇā, 244
Yajñamūrti, 102, 104, 109, 110
Yajña Varāha, 40 *n*.
Yajñeśa, 102, 110
Yajñopavīta-pratiṣṭhā, 122
yama, 29, 33, 61, 509 *n*., 519
Yama saṃhitās, 20
Yamunācārya, his life and works, 97 *et seq*.
Yaśasvinī, 59
Yaśodā, 77, 81 *n*.
yathārtha, 180, 188
yathārtha-khyāti, 180, 181, 182, 186 *n*., 237, 240, 243, 245, 246 *n*.
yathārthaṃ, 185 *n*.
yathārthā-vadhāraṇam, 62
yathā - vasthita - vyavahārā - nuguṇam, 236, 240
Yati-dharma-samuccaya, 102 *n*.
Yati-liṅga-samarthana, 352
Yati-pati-mala-dīpikā, 127
Yati-prativandana-khaṇḍana, 133
Yati-rāja-viṃśati, 137, 138
Yatiśekhara-bhārata, 109
Yatīndra-mata-dīpikā, 117, 127, 128; analysis of, 128, 129
Yatīndrapravaṇa, 110, 121 *n*., 137
Yatīndra-pravaṇa-bhadra-campu, 138
Yatīndra-pravaṇa-prabhāva, 138
Yatīndra-pravaṇa-prabhāvam, 64
Yatīndrapravaṇācārya, 135
yaugapadya, 228
Yavanas, 441 *n*.
yavanī, 47
Yādava, 100 *n*., 101
Yādava hill, 22
Yādavaprakāśa, 100, 101, 102, 109, 113, 124, 156, 201, 280, 285, 301, 305; his view of Brahman, 301; his view of God, 156; his view of time, 285
Yādavābhyudaya, 120, 121
Yādavādri, 104, 137
Yādṛcchika-ppaḍi, 135 *n*.
Yājñavalkya, 519
Yājñavalkya-smṛti, 484
Yāmuna, 14, 16, 17, 18, 79, 85, 95, 98, 99, 100, 101, 102, 105, 108, 109, 113, 114, 123, 139, 140, 142, 152, 153, 154, 155, 157, 159, 227, 235; Cārvāka's criticism of soul, 139; his disciples, 109; his general position, 139; his theory of self, 140; his view of God, p. 152 *et seq*.
Yāmuna's philosophy, 140
Yāmunācārya, 97, 139, 229 *n*.
Yellow, 182, 254
Yoga, 18, 22, 24, 30, 31, 32, 33, 52, 60, 61, 62, 80, 96, 97, 100, 157, 220, 281 *n*., 446, 449, 459, 465, 468, 471, 473, 474, 479, 480, 481, 482, 487, 491, 496, 506, 509, 512
yoga-bhakti, 507
Yoga processes, 479
Yoga-rahasya, 96
Yoga-sūtra, 61 *n*., 62 *n*., 470, 473, 482
Yoga-vārttika, 482
Yoga-view, 296
yogānuśāsana, 62
Yogic knowledge, 214
Yogic practice, 28
Yogin, 27, 30, 31, 42, 58, 60, 62, 96, 152, 446, 491, 506, 538
yogi-pratyakṣa, 168, 189
Yogivāha, 63
yogī, 505
yoni, 46, 502